Roman Honor

Roman Honor

The Fire in the Bones

Carlin A. Barton

UNIVERSITY OF CALIFORNIA PRESS

Berkeley   Los Angeles   London

University of California Press
Berkeley and Los Angeles, California

University of California Press, Ltd.
London, England

Library of Congress Cataloging-in-Publication Data
Barton, Carlin A.
Roman honor: the fire in the bones / Carlin A. Barton.
    p.   cm.
Includes bibliographical references and index.
ISBN 0-520-22525-2 (cloth: alk. paper).
    1. Latin literature—History and criticism.   2. Honor in literature.
3. National characteristics, Roman.   4. Honor—Rome—History.
5. Rome—Historiography.   I. Title.
PA6029.H62 B37   2001
870.9'353—dc21   00-037409
                                                    CIP

Manufactured in the United States of America

    10   09   08   07   06   05   04   03   02   01

        10   9   8   7   6   5   4   3   2   1

The paper used in this publication is both acid-free and totally chlorine-free. It meets the minimum
requirements of ANSI/NISO Z39.48-1992 (R 1997) *(Permanence of Paper).* ♻

For my father,
Roger Webster Barton

The hallowing of Pain
Like hallowing of Heaven
Obtains at a corporeal cost—
—All is the Price of All—
EMILY DICKINSON (1863)

CONTENTS

PREFACE

The realm of ideas and symbols will have to be lived closer to the bone.
TERRENCE DES PRES[1]

This book is an attempt to coax Roman history closer to the bone, to the breath and matter of the living being, to what the young Marx called "immediate sensuous consciousness."[2] It deals with what, for the Romans, was the life that mattered, the life of matter—and the life of matter was honor.

If my previous work concerned the icy mineral opacity of Roman violence and cruelty, this is a book about the airy white flame that was always, as it were, in the marrow. And so, in this book, I attempt to give as much attention to the radiant as to the frost-hardened aspects of Roman emotional life.

This book addresses Roman emotional life through its volatile equilibrations, its daring homeopathic and homeostatic adjustments, its points of stress and dizziness and collapse, its radical realignments. It deals with a set of patterns of sentiment and the ways these patterns are inflected or inverted in the course of Roman history.

With this book, finally, I offer to the broadest audience I can reach the most complex understanding of the spiritual and emotional life of the ancient Romans I can articulate. I hope that it will convey to the reader some small part of the joy and yearning that went into its writing and the love that its author feels for a dead race.

---

1. *The Survivor: An Anatomy of Life in the Death Camps,* Oxford, 1976, p. 209. "Words, as it were, must return to base" (Godfrey Lienhardt, "Self: Public, Private: Some African Representations," in *The Category of the Person: Anthropology, Philosophy, History,* ed. Michael Carrithers, Steven Collins, and Steven Lukes, Cambridge, 1985, pp. 141–155.

2. "All history is the preparation for 'man' to become the object of sensuous consciousness...immediate sensuous consciousness" (*Economic and Philosophic Manuscripts of 1844,* in *The Marx-Engels Reader,* 2d ed., ed. Robert C. Tucker, New York, 1978, p. 90).

ACKNOWLEDGMENTS

I extend my warmest thanks to Abel Alves, Joyce Berkman, Mark Bond-Webster, Daniel Boyarin, Daniel Bridgman, John Higginson, Barbara Kellum, Robert Knapp, Jim O'Hara, Larry Owens, Gareth Schmeling, Russell Skelton, Patricia Wright, my department, my reader Kate Cooper, my editors Mary Lamprech and Kate Toll, and my copyeditor Erika Büky.

I am very greatly indebted to Doris Bargen, Sandra Joshel, Carole Straw, and Robert Paul Wolff for having read and commented on the whole manuscript—in Professor Joshel's case more than once.

Finally, I wish to express the endless gratitude and appreciation I feel for the man who has been and continues to be for me the greatest model of scholar and human being whom I know, Erich S. Gruen.

CHAPTER ONE

Introduction

The Tarquinii took Brutus with them to Delphi—more as an object of sport than as a companion. And it is said that Brutus carried with him, as a gift for Apollo, a rod of gold enclosed within a hollow stick of cornel wood—an image, obliquely, of his own spirit.
LIVY 1.56.9[1]

Roman culture was without inwardness.
FLORENCE DUPONT, *DAILY LIFE IN ANCIENT ROME*[2]

My need to understand the Roman emotions of honor arose from my previous study of *homo in extremis*, of humans faced with the inordinate and the impossible. In studying the ways in which the Romans accommodated themselves to the horrors of civil war, the collapse of the Republic, and the establishment of the autocracy, I was led to the study of what it was that the Romans fought hardest to preserve. What did the Romans think was the core and definition of being? When everything solid melted into air, what would they cling to? When they fought on the nakedest possible plane, what did they fight for? What was the spirit that Livy's Brutus hid from the tyrannical Tarquins lest it be destroyed?

Even those who are well-disposed toward the ancient Romans, scholars who have devoted their lives to them, hesitate to grant them a rich and complex inner emotional life. They have ever been the model men of action flat-footing it on the stage of world history, strong but seldom soulful. I hope that this book will go at least part of the way toward creating a sense of the resonant inwardness of Roman life partially hidden from us by the obscurities and obliquities of that life.

WHAT MOVED THE ROMANS

Impulses and emotions explain nothing: they are always results, either of the power of the body or the impotence of the mind. In both cases they are consequences, never causes.
CLAUDE LÉVI-STRAUSS, *TOTEMISM*[3]

Many Roman historians would, perhaps, agree with Lévi-Strauss. But the Romans understood themselves above all as emotional beings. When the Romans

---

1. *Is tum ab Tarquiniis ductus Delphos, ludibrium verius quam comes, aureum baculum inclusum corneo cavato ad id baculo tulisse donum Apollini dicitur, per ambages effigiem ingenii sui.*
2. *Daily Life in Ancient Rome*, Oxford, 1993, p. 240.
3. *Totemism*, trans. Rodney Needham, Boston, 1962, p. 71.

1

mapped chains of cause and effect, they located the source of movement and action in the passions. How, you might ask, is it possible that the robust and practical Romans built their roads and their empire on the vague and shifting sands of the emotions? In our world, as the Roman historian Miriam Griffin points out, "passionate" and "practical" are opposites.[4] But it was exactly the Roman love of action, their *libido vivendi*, that attuned them to the emotions as the greatest levers, the *motores*, of action.[5] It was the Romans' commitment to, their immersion in the world, that gave the emotions motive and explanatory force. What we, with our ideal of freedom from the befuddling fumes of passion, might ascribe to politics or economics, class or gender, the Romans would attribute to fear, desire, shame, arrogance, ambition, envy, greed, love, or lust. Latin words for emotion *(motus, commotio, affectus, perturbatio)* emphasize their dynamic, disturbing force. (Our English "emotion" comes from Latin *emotus*, the past participle of *emoveo*, to move out or away.) It is as moving forces, motives, the sources of energy and action, that I treat emotions in this book.

The Romans did not conceive of the emotions as repugnant to reason or calculation, but rather as a way of understanding their engagement in thought. Here I can do no better than to quote the modern anthropologist Michelle Rosaldo:

> It will make sense to see emotions not as things opposed to thought but as cognitions implicating the immediate, carnal "me." ... Feeling is forever being given shape through thought and that thought is laden with emotional meaning. ... What distinguishes a "cold" cognition from a "hot" is fundamentally a sense of the engagement of the actor's self. Emotions are thoughts somehow "felt" in flushes, pulses, "movements" of our livers, minds, hearts, stomachs, skin. They are embodied thoughts, thoughts steeped with the apprehension "I am involved." Thought/affect thus bespeaks the difference between mere hearing of a child's cry and a hearing *felt*—as when one realizes that danger is involved or that the child is one's own. ... Emotions are about the ways in which the social world is one in which *we* are involved.[6]

Characteristic structures and categories of status and gender functioned, of course, in ancient Rome, but it was the particular emotional constellations in

---

4. "Cynicism and the Romans: Attraction and Repulsion," in *The Cynics*, ed. R. Bracht-Branham and Marie-Odile Goulet-Cazé, Berkeley, 1996, p. 198.

5. The Romans would have agreed with Silvan Tomkins and Carroll Izard that "affects are the primary motives of man" ("Introduction," in *Affect, Cognition, and Personality*, ed. Silvan Tomkins and Carroll Izard, London, 1965, p. vii). Cf. John Blacking, "Towards an Anthropology of the Body," in *The Anthropology of the Body*, ed. John Blacking, London, 1977, p. 5.

6. "Towards an Anthropology of Self and Feeling," in *Culture Theory: Essays on Mind, Self and Emotion*, ed. Richard A. Schweder and Robert A. LeVine, Cambridge, 1984, pp. 138, 143.

which these ideas moved that gave them meaning and that constitute the subject of this book.[7] (As for "politics" and "economics," the Romans simply did not recognize these as distinct or autonomous spheres of thought or action.)[8]

We may think that our patterns of constructing cause and effect are the "real," "underlying," or "deeper" ones—or at least the controllable ones—and that if the Romans did not have a political or gender discourse as we have, they were deluded or obscurantist. Perhaps they could not distinguish the material basis of life from the vain superstructures of ideology. Or perhaps they were unaware of or cynically hiding the stark truths of their power relationships behind a sophistic and gaseous rhetoric. Or perhaps, in their raw simplicity, they lacked self-conscious introspection, an adequate vocabulary or a fine understanding. But the categories of explanation that we find most stable and satisfying, most "concrete," had, for that very reason, little motive power for the Romans. We like to isolate and fix our motives; the Romans liked them to move. Our motives can be dominated and engineered; those of the Romans were elusive and unstable. Europeans, and perhaps even more Americans, believe that human be-

---

7. I use the word "Romans" advisedly. I do not intend it, as a category, to be essentializing or totalizing but rather a collective and composite term for a group of people who shared an array of ways of understanding the world, of making associations and connections, of putting together cause and effect. It is a way of designating a people with a common mythology and repertoire of stories, images, words, and metaphors. I use "Romans" without limiting qualifications when I am deliberately emphasizing these common elements. When I want to emphasize divisions of the Romans by other classifications, such as status and gender, I qualify the term "Romans." As I have created composite "Romans," so I have created a convenient and composite "we," which is based, more than anything, on the ideas and opinions of myself and all the students I have known and taught over the last thirty years.

8. Following the lead of scholars such as Marcel Mauss, Karl Polanyi, Jan Heesterman, Georges Gusdorf, Moses Finley, Donald Earl, and Catherine Edwards, I do not separate an "economics" or a "politics" from the total of social and psychological relationships that formed Roman culture. For models of treating "the total social phenomenon," see Marcel Mauss, *The Gift: Forms and Functions of Exchange in Archaic Societies,* trans. Ian Cunnison, New York, 1967; Georges Gusdorf, *L'expérience humaine du sacrifice,* Paris, 1948; Jan Heesterman, *The Broken World of Sacrifice: An Essay on Ancient Indian Ritual,* Chicago, 1993. For the treatment of "economics" as "embedded" or "submerged" in social relationships, see Karl Polanyi, "The Place of Economies in Societies" and "The Economy as Instituted Process," in *Trade and Market in the Early Empires,* ed. K. Polanyi et al., Glencoe, Illinois, 1957, pp. 239-70, and his essays in *Primitive, Archaic, and Modern Economies: Essays of Karl Polanyi,* ed. George Dalton, Garden City, New Jersey, 1968. For the inextricability of "politics" or "economics" from the social and moral life of the Romans, see Donald Earl, *The Moral and Political Tradition of Rome,* London, 1967: "The Romans, on the whole, lacked either interest in or capacity for abstract political theorizing. To the Republican politician politics was a personal and social matter. He therefore thought and expressed his thought in personal terms and social terms"(p. 20); and "The Romans did not distinguish morality sharply from politics or economics but looked at affairs from a point of view which may be termed 'social' " (p. 17).

ings and human societies can be operated on—but only if they hold still long enough! Only from a stationary point can we move the world. (We are always looking to "nail down" that point.) Only if our worlds have been fixed can we fix them. Only if our worlds are constructed can they be deconstructed—or reconstructed. Concomitantly, because neither the emotions, nor the soul, nor our selves as public objects or intersubjective formulations are clear and controllable, we reject them as ultimate sources of value and explanation. But the restless Romans, on account of their elaborate systems of reciprocities, thought less in terms of synchronic structures than in terms of motion, tension, torsion. The spirit *(animus)* and the existence of one's self as a social object *(fama)* were the airy stuff of the really real for the Romans precisely because they were—like all great forces of the universe—volatile and fugitive, impossible, finally, to domesticate.[9]

The result of our lack of attention to, suspicion of, and even contempt for the fatuous emotions has been that some of the most pervasive aspects of Roman life, in particular the sentiments of honor, have received only partial and peripheral treatment from Roman historians. One of my goals, in the following chapters, is to synthesize many of the existing fine and detailed studies of particular elements of Roman honor in order to begin to describe a dynamic Roman "physics" of the emotions.

THE BODY OF EMOTIONS

"O dark, dark, dark, dark, dark, amid the blaze of noon!"
MILTON, *SAMSON AGONISTES*

At the beginning of his introduction to *The Nazi Doctors,* the social psychologist Robert Jay Lifton describes an interview he conducted with a dentist who had survived Auschwitz to settle in Israel. When asked about his experiences in the death camp, "He looked about the comfortable room of his home with its beautiful view of Haifa, sighed deeply, and said 'This world is not this world.' "[10]

This world is not this world. We have only the same words to talk about the ineffable and unspeakable as we do about the mundane. Sometimes the most real, if it can be expressed at all, can only be expressed through a kind of nonsense. "The earth seemed unearthly," declares Conrad's Marlowe.[11]

As a historian looking back two thousand years, I have no choice but to study the Roman emotions of honor through the particular gestures, codes, and

---

9. The Romans, forced to think in our metaphors, would have found themselves not "fixed" but *destitutus,* "in a fix."

10. *The Nazi Doctors: Medical Killing and the Psychology of Genocide,* New York, 1986, p. 3.

11. *Heart of Darkness,* New York, [1899] 1963, p. 36.

categories that reveal those emotions to us. But it is important to me that the reader know that I know that these emotions were not exhausted by, nor necessarily even contained in, these symbols and symbolic acts. Words and symbols are like the torches carried by the servants of Seneca through the long prison of the Naples tunnel. "Nothing could be dimmer," Seneca declares, "than those torches, which allow us not to pierce the darkness, but to see it" (*Epistulae* 57.2).[12] By the light of these signs we see the darkness. Without them we see nothing at all.

The Romans, like the dentist of Haifa, believed that they experienced more than could be put into words. Virgil speaks of *infandi labores*, "unspeakable trials" (*Aeneis* 1.597), *infandus dolor*, "unspeakable sorrow" (2.3), and *infandus amor*, "love too deep for words" (4.85).[13] "Light troubles speak," Seneca tells us, "the weighty are struck dumb" (*Phaedra* 607).[14] "Incredible events," Pseudo-Quintilian informs us, "cannot be expressed in words; some things are too enormous for the limitations of human speech" (*Declamationes maiores* 19.12).[15] Livy asserts that words could not describe the misery of the Romans when they received news of the disaster at Cannae (22.54.8). Pliny fails to find words for the disgrace of the senate in effusively and slavishly honoring Claudius's freedman Pallas (*Epistulae* 8.6.5).[16] Words do not, of course, quite fail if one can say that they fail, but the authors hope to evoke in their audience the sensation of feeling overwhelmed. "The fullness of my voice," Apuleius's Lucius proclaims, "is inadequate to express what I feel about your majesty; a thousand mouths and as many tongues would not be enough, nor even an endless flow of inexhaustible speech" (*Metamorphoses* 11.25).[17] The Romans believed, like the anthropologist John Blacking, that "many things happen to us for which our society has no labels."[18]

There are a number of thinkers who, since Freud, have thought of human cultures as great icebergs, with only the smallest fraction of what is experienced be-

---

12. *Nihil illo carcere longius, nihil illis facibus obscurius, quae nobis praestant, non ut per tenebras videamus, sed ut ipsas.*

13. Cf. *Aeneis* 1.251.

14. *Curae leves loquuntur, ingentes stupent.*

15. *non habent incredibilia vocem; quaedam maiora sunt, quam ut capiat modus sermonis humani.*

16. The scope and magnitude of Caesar's conquests are such that "it is almost beyond the powers of the mind or thought of anyone to grasp" (*vix cuiusquam mens aut cogitatio capere possit* [Cicero, *Pro Marcello* 2.6]).

17. *nec mihi vocis ubertas ad dicenda quae de tua maiestate sentio sufficit, nec ora mille linguaeque totidem vel indefessi sermonis aeterna series.* "I'm struck with pity and my tongue is stupefied with sorrow" (*miseret me, lacrimis lingua debiliter stupet* [Pacuvius 228, Warmington ed.].) "Deep in her breast burns the silent wound" (*tacitum vivit sub pectore vulnus* [Virgil, *Aeneis* 4.67]).

18. "Towards an Anthropology of the Body," p. 21.

ing articulated.[19] For those acutely aware of the insufficiency of our vocabulary, the body becomes, as it was for Freud, a great book of the spirit.[20]

Primo Levi, in his spare and moving *Survival at Auschwitz,* described the fate of people wrenched from their web of affiliations, institutions, and systems on which they relied. When the etiquette and traditions of daily life fell away, when the belief systems, the philosophies and religions of a people collapsed, what *could* remain? What then distinguished the living from the living dead, those with a vital spirit and those whose eyes no longer held the light, the "Musselmen"? One of the men who did not sink like a stone in the sewer of Auschwitz was Levi's Steinlauf, who continued to wash his hands in its dirty water, who sewed the buttons on his tattered shirt, who stood upright.[21] Similarly, Nathan McCall, in his powerful autobiography *Makes Me Wanna Holler,* describes the humiliations of a black teenager growing up in America. For McCall, as for many of his peers, it was the posture, the "attitude," the walk, the way he wore his hat or sneakers that sus-

19. For a brief but concise review of the history of the notion of the cultural "unconscious" that the anthropologists borrowed from the psychologists, see Edward Hall, *The Silent Language,* New York, 1959, pp. 63–65. "One of the most significant of these...theories was that culture existed on two levels: overt culture, which is visible and easily described, and covert culture, which is not visible and presents difficulties even to the trained observer. The iceberg analogy was commonly used when teaching this theory to students and laymen alike.... Anthropologists like Kluckhohn started speaking of explicit and implicit culture. Explicit culture, such things as law, was what people talk about and can be specific about. Implicit culture, such as feelings about success, was what they took for granted or what existed on the fringes of awareness" (ibid., pp. 64–65). See Ralph Linton, *The Study of Man,* New York, 1936, and *The Cultural Background of Personality,* New York, 1945, pp. 38–42, 123. Marx thought of the social world as allowing only the smallest part of the fullness of being of a human (his or her "species being") to be realized.

20. Conversely, spoken language can be understood as embodied action. As Ernest Gellner remarks, "Most uses of speech are closer in principle to the raising of one's hat in greeting than to the mailing of an informative report" (*Plough, Sword and Book: The Structure of Human History,* Chicago, 1988, p. 51). William Allman points out that most verbal communication between humans is the equivalent of "verbal grooming," a sort of crooning or stroking, in which very little information is imparted. Humans, like dogs and cats, often understand more from the tone and accompanying facial expressions than from the words being said. They have to interpret the verbal through the nonverbal (*The Stone Age Present,* New York, 1944, pp. 170–172). The anthropologist James F. Weiner remarks, "A lot of jaw-flapping takes place without achieving any real exchange of information at all, especially given the extraordinary vagueness and polyvocality possessed by even the simplest and most unremarkable terms, leading one commentator [Pierre Bourdieu] to remark that 'the commonplaces which make communication possible are the same ones that make it practically ineffective'" (*Key Debates in Anthropology,* ed. Tim Ingold, New York, 1966, p. 174); cf. Pierre Bourdieu, "The Historical Genesis of the Pure Aesthetic," in *Analytic Aesthetics,* ed. R. Shusterman, Oxford, 1989, p. 154.

21. "So we must certainly wash our faces without soap in dirty water and dry ourselves on our jackets. We must polish our shoes, not because the regulation states it, but for dignity and propriety. We must walk erect, without dragging our feet, not in homage to Prussian discipline but to remain alive, not to begin to die" (*Survival at Auschwitz,* New York, 1961, p. 36). Billy A., an inmate of an American high-security prison, explains: "The way I keep my self-respect is by keeping my body clean" (James Gilligan, *Violence: Reflections on a National Epidemic,* New York, 1997, p. 100).

tained him.[22] The "point of honour" of the Berber Kabyle of Algeria was, according to Pierre Bourdieu, "embedded in the agents' very bodies . . . in the form of bodily postures and stances, ways of standing, sitting, looking, speaking or walking."[23] The body I speak of in this book, then, is not as "material" as our modern Western body; it is more like our body plus music. The delivery (the posture and gesture) of an orator, Cicero tells us, "is, as it were, the speech of the body" (*actio quasi sermo corporis* [*De oratore* 3.222]).[24] "Every motion of the soul," he explains, "has its appearance, voice and gesture; and the entire body of a man, all his facial and verbal expressions, like the string of a harp, sound just as the soul's motion strikes them" (3.216).[25]

Inevitably, in my attempt to coax Roman history closer to the bone, the body became one of the compelling foci of my understanding of Roman emotional experience. Roman honor was, at its best, a homeostatic system, but it was *always* a homeopathic system, and the body was the axis of the balancing systems that invested every aspect of Roman emotional life.[26] When more fragile symbolic circuitry failed, when the expressive and defensive codes by which one lived deserted one or were simply inadequate (as is so often the case), it was the body itself, and its postures and attitudes, that emerged as both the chief target of those who would break one's spirit *and* the chief weapon against the loss of one's spirit, one's being, one's honor. For these reasons I have attended to the bent back, the lowered eye, the covered head, the blush, the extended hand; not to the exclusion of the symbol, but as its supplement and check.

Another reason for attending to the body is that although our symbolic universes may have evolved drastically, the physical experience of our bodies may have evolved less so. And so we can use our own bodies, the sensations of our own bodies to help feel our way back into the Romans' emotional life and to bridge the modern bifurcation between feeling and thought. In the words of Blacking, "My knowledge is both generated and restricted by the perceptions and cognitive processes of my society, but through my body I can sometimes understand more

---

22. *Makes Me Wanna Holler*, New York, 1994.

23. *Outline of a Theory of Practice*, trans. Richard Nice, Cambridge, 1979, p. 15.

24. Cf. *Orator* 55; Quintilian, *Institutio oratoria* 11.3.1.

25. *corpusque totum hominis et eius voltus omnesque voces, et nervi in fidibus, itas sonant, ut a motu animi quaeque sunt pulsae.*

26. For that reason, the mutilation and humiliation of one's own body could be the final act of self-redemption. See Carlin Barton, "Savage Miracles: The Redemption of Lost Honor in Roman Society and the Sacrament of the Gladiator and the Martyr," *Representations* 45 (Winter 1994): 41–71. See also M. P. Baumgartner, "Social Control from Below," in *Towards a General Theory of Social Control*, ed. Donald Black, vol. 1, Orlando, 1984, pp. 328–331; Gilligan, *Violence*, pp. 49–52. In an attempt to redeem their honor, imprisoned young Irishmen turned on themselves what Terrence Des Pres calls "the excremental attack," the humiliation that reduces a human to filth, during the so-called "dirty protest" that led up to the hunger strike of 1980 (Pedraig O'Malley, *Biting at the Grave: The Irish Hunger Strikers and the Politics of Despair*, Boston, 1990, pp. 22–24, cf. 110–11).

than I know through my own or another's society because I have more experience than society labels."[27] By giving the body a privileged place in our perceptions, we can also learn to feel more, to perceive more. We can know through our own flesh things about the Romans that we cannot know through their words. We might divide the world into spiritual and physical, psychic and somatic, intellectual and instinctual; but the Romans did not. Their universe was psychosomatic. What moved the *animus (caput, pectus)* moved the universe. The movements of the universe were geared to the motives of the body. What C. J. Herington says of Seneca could be applied to all of Roman life: "His discourse slips, without warning or break, from the vastness of the soul to the vastness of the starry sky. The stormy wanderings of Ulysses are equated with the daily experience of the soul."[28]

There was, for the Romans, a kind of shared body in the universe, a kind of "panvitalism" like that of Max Scheler. Embodied things were not stolid and low-charged, nor were they opposed to highly charged and disembodied spiritual essences. Nothing was solid or material in the Roman world. Nothing was inert. Nothing was anything by itself.

MISTAKING THE SYMBOL FOR THE SENTIMENT

It is because we tend to think of cultural codes as either totally embracing or totally obfuscating all that can be known about honor that we have so few words to speak about honor.

In the United States, in the nineteenth century, the vocabulary of honor became identified, above all, with particular and discredited codes. On the one hand, "honor" became associated with, and the justification for, the patriarchal slaveholding society of the American South, with its social and racial obduracies and its violence. The historian Edward Ayers quotes the Savannah *Sunday Morning News* of April 14, 1894: "Is there danger of a revival of that old and false code of

---

27. Blacking, "Towards an Anthropology of the Body," pp. 5–6. "My concern for an anthropology of the body rests on a conviction that feeling, and particularly fellow-feeling, expressed as movements of bodies in space and time and often without verbal connotations, are the basis of mental life" (p. 4). I think of Montaigne's aphorism from "On Experience": "I know it when I feel it."

28. "Senecan Tragedy," *Arion* 5 (1966): 433. For the sympathy between the microcosm of embodied human emotions and the embodied macrocosm, see especially the works of Charles Segal, "Boundary Violation and the Landscape of the Self in Senecan Tragedy," *Antike und Abendland* 29 (1983): 172–187, and "Ovid's Metamorphic Bodies: Art, Gender, and Violence in the Metamorphoses," *Arion* 5 (1998): 9–41. Cf. Donald Mastronarde, "Seneca's *Oedipus:* The Drama in the Word," *Transactions and Proceedings of the American Philological Society* 101 (1970): 291–315, esp. p. 297; B. Walker, review of Giancotti, *Octavia, Classical Philology* 52 (1957): 163–173. Compare the approach taken by David Bakan in *Disease, Pain and Sacrifice: Toward a Psychology of Suffering*, Chicago, 1968. The absence of a divide between human events and cosmic events is manifested in Roman augury, astrology, haruspication, and the interpretation of omens.

social ethics that prompted its holders to resort to the duel and to go 'heeled' for an emergency?"[29] In another context, honor became associated with organized crime and so a euphemism for posturing lawless arrogance, the absence of self-restraint by the powerful, and a façade for contemptible and dishonest acts.[30] In these cases, honor appeared as a medieval sentiment irrelevant or opposed to a modern democratic or egalitarian society.[31]

This is not the first time the vocabulary of honor has been discredited. Bartolomé Bennassar, speaking of early modern Spain, remarks that "a distorted ideal of honor long sterilized Spanish energies. For Lazarillo de Tormes [1554], honor was but 'a thirst in vainglory and a lie,' 'a priesthood without virtue.' For Guzmán de Alfarache [1599], it was 'a mask under which one may steal and lie, and a useless burden to boot.'"[32] Instead of representing effectiveness and activity, "honor" masked and justified sloth and inertia. If there was ever a false consciousness, it was honor.[33]

The following remarks are from John Lendon's recent excellent discussion of the status codes of Roman honor: "One of honour's main functions was to conceal sterner realities. It was a fanciful and grandiose icing on a predictably bitter cake.... Honour... acts as a cloak or lubricant to other forms of power.... Honour was useful as a rhetoric of concealment."[34]

29. *Vengeance and Justice: Crime and Punishment in the Nineteenth-Century American South*, Oxford, 1984, p. 272.

30. In a brilliant discussion, Michael McCartney shows how the seemingly incompatible American ideal of the "honest" citizen and the Mafia notion of *omertà* have operated and continue to operate in a complementary and dialectical relationship, one that Americans, with their love of simple dichotomies, generally lack the vocabulary and understanding to articulate ("Democracy and the Dangerous Man: Mafia Justice and Citizen Virtue," Ph.D. diss., Univ. of Massachusetts, 1997).

31. See Irving Babbitt, "Lights and Shades of Spanish Character," in *Spanish Character and Other Essays*, Boston, 1940, p. 19.

32. Bartolomé Bennassar, *The Spanish Character: Attitudes and Mentalities from the Sixteenth to the Nineteenth Century*, trans. Benjamin Keen, Berkeley, 1979, p. 236. See esp. pp. 223–236.

33. Marx decries the "false consciousness" that allowed the vicious and dishonorable exploiters of their fellow men the title to honor. "Law, morality, religion are... so many bourgeois prejudices, behind which lurk in ambush just as many bourgeois interests" (*Manifesto of the Communist Party*, in *The Marx-Engels Reader*, ed. Robert C. Tucker, New York, 1978, p. 482). For Peter Berger, the association of honor with an ethos of violence constitutes an argument for ridding ourselves of the notion of honor—and substituting for it a self-contained and independent "dignity" ("On the Obsolescence of the Concept of Honor," in *The Homeless Mind*, New York, 1973, pp. 83–96). Fox Butterfield argues similarly: "What is needed... is a shift in thinking that begins at home, that teaches that respect comes from within, not from worrying about the opinions of others" (*All God's Children: The Bosket Family and the American Tradition of Violence*, New York, 1995, p. 329).

34. *Empire of Honour*, Oxford, 1977, pp. 24–25. In a recent discussion, Thomas Habinek brands the Roman notion of the *mos maiorum* ("the traditions of the ancestors") as a constricting ideal of honor invented around the time of the Second Punic War and cynically foisted on the Roman people by the dominant Roman male elite: "There is no reason to think that the *mos maiorum* had a real, historical force independent of that ascribed to it by its contemporary promoters." To honor that "tradition"

One of the themes of this book is the history of a similar discrediting of the vocabulary of honor in ancient Rome during the last century of the Republic and the discarding or radical alteration of the meanings of the highly charged words and symbols used to express related notions and emotions during the civil wars and early Empire.

In all these cases the vocabulary of honor was rejected along with the gestures and ideas with which it was associated. In discarding the symbolic codes, however, the society lost the words and formalized behaviors for expressing feelings that were already hard to talk about: certain elemental and powerful emotions that crossed (and continue to cross) all lines of status and gender, that belonged to women and slaves, children, horses, and dogs as fully as to Roman senators, Spanish hidalgos, Southern gentlemen, and Mafia dons; the deep well of emotions that have as much to do with silence as with speech, with defecating as with dressing up, with poverty as with wealth, with equality as with hierarchy. Another aim of this book is to show that the emotions of honor, set adrift from the social and linguistic codes by which they were articulated, were never more powerful than when they could no longer be expressed.

The depletion of our own stock of words and metaphors capable of articulating these emotions has made it difficult to talk about or even perceive the Romans' rich thicket of symbols and metaphors. Sadly, when we speak about Roman notions of honor in English, the profusion of Roman ideas and emotions is reduced to our depleted vocabulary. We who speak and write in English are compelled to use the word "honor" as a sort of umbrella term, occasionally substituting "pride" or "self-esteem" and adding or subtracting "guilt" and "shame."[35] English "honor" is a word used indiscriminately for both the code and the emotions; it confuses or conflates the code of behavior and the emotions expressed (or suppressed) by the code. And so it is important to point out that, although our English word "honor" is a direct descendant of the Latin *honor*, the latter played a relatively modest part in the Romans' vocabulary of emotions; it rarely subsumed, as it does in English, the tangle of ideas and emotions of which it formed

was to honor the Roman aristocracy, who controlled it to their own advantage (*The Politics of Latin Literature*, Princeton, 1998, p. 53, cf. pp. 35–36, 39). Cf. R.E. Smith, "The Aristocratic Epoch in Latin Literature," *Essays on Roman Culture*, 1976, pp. 187–223. Elvin Hatch observes the general assumption, in modern social thought, of a deeply cynical self-interest on the part of men and women who talk about honor. He remarks, wisely I believe, that if a large percentage of the members of any society shared these scholars' attitude toward honor, that society would very soon collapse into a Hobbesian war of all against all ("Theories of Social Honor," *American Anthropologist* 91 [1989]: 341–353, esp. p. 351). One could argue that the development of similar cynical assumptions about honor among Romans in the last century of the Roman Republic both symptomized and facilitated the collapse of Roman culture into civil war.

35. McCartney explains the American fascination for stories of the Mafia in part by reference to our yearning for a vocabulary to express the emotions of honor: "It is as if we no longer have a language capable of conveying the sentiment of honor" ("Democracy and the Dangerous Man," p. 72).

a part. *Honores*, in Latin, were the prizes, the tokens of the esteem and recognition that one received from others and that gave one status. These *honores* might include offices, crowns, statues, and panegyrics. With a few notable exceptions, the word did not refer to the emotions. Simply for lack of an alternative, however, I use English "honor," and frequently. But my efforts are directed not to defining the English term "honor," but to the harder task of describing the dynamics of an array of emotions that the English word "honor" can only point in the direction of, an array of emotions working with and in counterpoint to the articulate codes and statuses of ancient Roman society.

HONOR AND STATUS

With what earnestness they pursue their rivalries! How fierce their contests! What exultation
they feel when they win, and what shame when they are beaten! How they dislike reproach!
How they yearn for praise! What labors will they not undertake to stand first among their peers!
How well they remember those who have shown them kindness and how eager to repay it!
CICERO, *DE FINIBUS* 5.22.61[36]

Cicero is speaking of little boys.

Because current thought tends to emphasize the code and the discourse to the detriment or exclusion of embodied emotional life, we tend to think of honor as defining or belonging to those who are explicitly "honored" within a particular code or discourse. Lendon talks of "the honourless low."[37] Richard Saller writes: "Propertied Romans lived in their houses in relations marked by a fundamental distinction between family members whose bodies were protected by their honor and those of lower status who had no honor to protect them from above."[38] He writes of "the elite—the men most preoccupied with honor."[39] But emotionally the slave was every bit as sensitive to insult as his or her master. The plebeian was as preoccupied with honor as the patrician, the client as the patron, the woman as the man, the child as the adult.[40]

According to Ayers, "Poverty and degradation often raise the stakes of

---

36. *Quanta studia decertantium sunt! Quanta ipsa certamina! ut illi efferuntur laetitia cum vicerunt! ut pudet victos! ut se accusari nolunt! quam cupiunt laudari! quos illi labores non perferunt ut aequalium principes sint! quae memoria est in iis bene merentium, quae referendae gratiae cupiditas!*

37. *Empire of Honour*, p. 27. But see below for his cogent remarks on the honor of those with little status.

38. *Patriarchy, Property, and Death in the Roman Family*, Cambridge, Mass., 1994, p. 152. Similar statements appear on pp. 101, 143, 145.

39. *Patriarchy, Property, and Death*, p. 72.

40. Anyone who believes that the sentiments of honor and the codes of tradition are a matter for elites would do well to read Milovan Djilas on Montenegro, J.K. Campbell on Greece, Michael Herzfeld on Crete, Julian Pitt-Rivers, David Gilmore, and Stanley H. Brandes on Spain, Pierre Bourdieu on Algeria, and Ruth Horowitz on Chicago.

honor."[41] According to the journalist Fox Butterfield, "Whites believed that slaves had no honor, but the bondsmen did not see it that way. They had been stripped of all their earthly possessions, even their families and their humanity. For many of the slaves, all that was left was personal honor."[42]

Sandra Joshel's close study of the inscriptions reveals the insistence with which Roman slaves and freedmen (male and female) claimed and bestowed honor, in the form of status, heritage, community, and family ties.[43] "As long as he lived, he was a man. . . . As long as he lived, he lived honorably," reads the epitaph of Iucundus, slave and litter-bearer (*Corpus Inscriptionum Latinarum*, vol. 6.2, no. 6308).[44] "Here are laid the bones of an auctioneer, a man of honor and good faith," reads the epitaph of Aulus Granius (ibid., vol. 1.2, no. 1210).[45] "Glory," laments Horace, the son of a freedman, "drags along the lowly no less than the highly-born, bound in chains to her resplendent chariot" (*Satirae* 1.6.23–24).[46] The slaves of a farm or household, Lendon points out, constituted their own community of honor, and while slaves might have no honor in aristocratic eyes, even aristocratic authors realized that slaves granted each other (in Lendon's words) "slavish honour in slavish eyes."[47] It was not only in the Never-Never Land of Roman comedy that slave boys dreamt of *gloria, laus, decus*.[48]

41. *Vengeance and Justice*, p. 235.

42. *All God's Children*: p. 32. Cf. pp. 63, 329. For the profound concern of slaves for their honor see also Orlando Patterson, *Slavery and Social Death*, 1982, Cambridge, Mass., pp. 337–338. Issues of honor dominate the literature of African-Americans as well as feminist and gay literature. In Louis Dumont's classic study of the caste system of India, there is no more status-conscious group than the Untouchables (*Homo Hierarchicus: The Caste System and Its Implications*, Chicago, 1966). For the importance of honor to contemporary prostitutes, see Gail Pheterson, "The Whore Stigma: Female Dishonor and Male Unworthiness," *Social Text* 37 (1993): 39–64.

43. *Work, Identity and Legal Status at Rome: A Study of the Occupational Inscriptions*, Norman, Oklahoma, 1992, esp. pp. 46, 56, 90–91, 117–118, 120–121.

44. *Iucundus Tauri*
lecticarius quandi
us vixit vir fuit . . . quan
dius vixit honeste vixit.
See Joshel, *Work, Identity and Legal Status at Rome*, p. 90.

45. *Pudentis hominis frugi c[u]m magna fide / praeconis Oli Grani sunt [o]ssa heic sita.* Compare the epitaph for the cattle merchant Quintus Brutius (*Corpus Inscriptionum Latinarum*, vol. 1.2, no. 1259) or that of the pantomimist Lucius Aurelius Pylades (*Inscriptiones Latinae Selectae*, vol. 2.1, no. 5186; Lendon, *Empire of Honour*, p. 101). Claims to *fides* and *castitas* were made by and for men and women of every status. See, for example, *Corpus Inscriptionum Latinarum*, vol. 6.2, no. 11357; vol. 6.4, no. 26192; and vol. 1.2, nos. 1221 and 1836.

46. *sed fulgente trahit constrictos gloria curru / non minus ignotos generosis.*

47. *Empire of Honour*, p. 97. For the hierarchies of slave status within a household, see Cicero, *Paradoxa Stoicorum* 36–37; cf. the late-fourth-century invective of Claudian, *In Eutropium* (*Carmina* 1.29–31, J. Koch ed.). Plautus's Sceledrus resents the preferment of his fellow slave: "He gets the first call to dinner and the most appetizing tidbits go to him. He's only been with us three years perhaps—and now he's got the best position in the household" (*primus ad cibum vocatur, primo pulmentum datur; / nam illic noster est fortasse circiter triennium, / neque cuiquam quam illi in nostra meliust famulo familia* [*Miles Gloriosus* 349–351]).

48. See the dreams of Plautus's slave boy Pinacium (*Stichus* 279–280). Freedmen might take great

Those with low status might feel keenly the contempt of the elite. Cato the Elder, in a fragment preserved by Gellius, asserts that "[Even] slaves bitterly resent *iniuria* (insult, injury, injustice)."[49] "You will find," Seneca declares, "slaves who would prefer to be whipped than to be slapped, and who believe death and beatings more tolerable than scornful words" (Seneca, *De constantia* 5.1).[50] And there were none so poor or so despised that they could not repay aristocratic abuse with gossip, slander, lampoons, or verses. The humblest could hiss you at the games or piss on your statue.[51] They could kill you.

The values of the ancient Romans, especially during the Republic, were overwhelmingly those of a warrior culture. Soldiers of every status competed feverishly for the commendations, the *coronae, hastae,* and *armillae* that recognized their courage and industry. Valerius Maximus observes the Roman soldier yearning for glory: "There is no status so low that it cannot be touched with the sweetness of glory" (*Nulla est tanta humilitas, quae dulcedine gloriae non tangatur* [8.14.5]).[52] And every Roman soldier, especially when abroad, aspired to the status of prince, strutting through a peaceful town or rampaging through a defeated one.

In ways and for reasons I hope to show, the strategies of Roman aristocrats for preserving or redeeming their spirits were never divorced from and often—and increasingly, in the early Empire—very like those of the dependent and the enslaved.[53] The honor of the poor moved in delicate counterpoint to that of the aristocracy, the honor of the women to that of the men. Sometimes their strategies were mirrors, sometimes complements, sometimes alternatives, sometimes opposites, sometimes mockeries, but they were always in relation.[54] They worked within various codes, between them, and against them. It was an intricate dance

---

pride in their place within a burial club, a religious sodality, a trade guild—or a band of brigands. Cf. Lendon, *Empire of Honour,* pp. 97–98. As Lendon remarks, "The despised of the empire...were willing to spend freely to gain honours which publicized their stigma: ornaments, since they could not hold offices, or membership in the Augustales, a priesthood of the emperor much sought by rich freedmen who could not become members of the town senate" (pp. 101–102). For the honor of Roman freedmen and women, see especially the recent work by Barbara Kellum, "The Play of Meaning" (forthcoming).

49. *Servi iniurias nimis aegre ferunt* (*Noctes Atticae* 10.3.7).

50. *Sic invenies servum qui flagellis quam colaphis caedi malit et qui mortem ac verbera tolerabiliora credat quam contumeliosa verba.*

51. "The shouted abuse of the base, anonymous lampoons and verses, anonymous gossip, and anonymous slander all excited acute concern" (Lendon, *Empire of Honour,* p. 51, with the sources cited there).

52. *Nulla est tanta humilitas, quae dulcedine gloriae non tangatur* (8.14.5). See esp. Polybius 6.39.

53. Barbara Kellum makes the point that by the early Empire, the "elite" is not all that elite anymore ("The Play of Meaning," ms. p. 4). Indeed, if the backgrounds of the literary figures of the Republic are taken into account, the "elite" never was.

54. Horace's *Satirae* 1.6 is an excellent example of the strategies of the son of a freedman for relating to the aristocratic Roman codes of honor.

in time, often dictated by tradition but also filled with improvisations, miscues, and hopeless mistakes.[55]

UNSCIENTIFIC STRATEGIES
FOR ORCHESTRATING DISORDER[56]

I hold with the statement of Ronald Laing: "Our view of the other depends on our willingness to enlist all the powers of every aspect of ourselves in the act of comprehension."[57] I hold, as well, with Nietzsche's statement: "All seeing is essentially perspective, and so is all knowing. The more emotions we can allow to speak in a given matter, the more different eyes we can put on in order to view a given spectacle, the more complete will be our conception of it, the greater our 'objectivity.'"[58]

I hope that the more varied my perspectives, the more things I will see in that field where a cow looks for grass, a dog for a hare, a stork for a lizard. And so I have tried, while researching this book, to listen to the Roman testimony as Freud might have listened to the speech and gestures of his patients in the "talking cure." With no hope of a cure, I have given my attention, as freely and fiercely as I could, to every relevant expression of affect that I could detect. It does not matter, for my purposes, whether the actors and speakers are historical persons or fictional *personae*, whether their words are willful obfuscations or naked confessions. I have attempted to discern the depths of the Roman soul in the moving configurations of their thought: the symmetries and syncopations, rhythms and reciprocities, the obliquities, torsions, discords, ruptures, reversals, broken contours, and collapses. (It was ambiguity, after all, that defined and protected Brutus's soul.) I listened for as many and as varied voices and gestures as I could, keeping in mind that my goal was, in the end, to create a sort of composite psychological portrait of the Romans, a case history of a sort.

I have tried to devise a strategy that would allow me, in interpreting Roman thought for a modern audience, to hint at what may have lain outside (or hidden within) the scope and capacity of these symbolic expressions: the spirit confined in the rod of cornel wood. It often happened that, in the Roman world, paradoxes and ambiguities were used to point beyond the compass of words, past the confines of a limited vocabulary.[59] Many highly charged Latin words *(fides, pudor,*

---

55. Pierre Bourdieu discusses the complex strategizing, with its uncertainties and behavioral variations, that could be played out in Kabylia on the simple theme of reciprocating a gift. If one looked just at the provisions of the "honor code," the behaviors would seem regimented and determined. The code, Bourdieu argues, gives hardly a hint of the complexities, uncertainties, high tensions, risks, and timing involved *(Outline of a Theory of Practice,* pp. 5–9; cf. 10–30). In other words, the script is simple compared to the play.

56. See the "Philosophical Coda," p. 289.

57. *The Divided Self,* Harmondsworth, 1965, p. 32.

58. Nietzsche, *The Genealogy of Morals,* trans. F. Golffing, Garden City, New York, 1956, 3.14, p. 256.

59. For the attempts of the Gnostics to attain to the core of existence by uttering nonsense, see Pa-

sanctitas, gratia, religio, fama)[60] had built-in complexes of antitheses that help the hearer, once aware of them, to grasp something untranslatable, indeed, ineffable, in the Roman psyche. (Latin is not a "literal" language. The longer one studies it, the more ambiguous it becomes; the very words of the language point at the impossibility of fixing their meanings.)

I have tried, wherever possible, to let the Romans speak for themselves. Ironically, *because* of my desire to quote as much as possible, I have had to impose a rather elaborate and artificial organization on the material I am presenting. I have used some of the strategies employed by the Romans themselves: contradiction, paradox, ambiguity. But to avoid totally obfuscating the Roman world for a modern audience, I have relied, as well, on another tactic: "To know a people's character," Erik Erikson remarked, "one has to know their laws of conduct and the way they circumvent them."[61] And so I sketch, in this book, some of the most persistent of the formalized or normative "codes" (games, scripts, scores) of the Romans in their most idealized forms, and then show the ways in which they were skirted, diverted, undermined, or destroyed—as well as redirected, reinvented, and reorganized, as one might describe the Romans' laws of nature together with their monsters and omens. My heuristic strategy is to divide my analyses into a general synchronic or "functionalist" overview—to serve as a sort of basso continuo—and then to juxtapose and complement this rather static line with a more historical and dynamic counterpoint. It is far from a neat or a perfect system, but it was the best I could devise to deal with both the enduring and the changing aspects of the Roman "physics" of the emotions.

I recognize that the order that I bring to this material (especially my attempts to disentangle the synchronic and diachronic aspects of Roman emotional life) is not the order that the Romans would have brought to it: they would have found such deliberate ordering unnecessary. But to sketch the compensatory systems, their points of collapse, and the remedies the Romans devised for these breaks, I have brought to the material the minimum of simplification and systemization that I felt necessary to begin to translate, into English, the Roman symbolic world that, left in its wild state, is too complex to grasp. It is a heuristic order violating the disarray of my subjects' own experience. My goal in patterning the Roman material has been to articulate for myself and my reader complex emotions for which we have few and inadequate words in English.

Modern historians and their readers are accustomed to the freight-train model of causal construction, whereby A pushes B pushes C. But, to be truer to the way

tricia Cox Miller's "In Praise of Nonsense," in *Classical Mediterranean Spirituality,* ed. A. H. Armstrong, New York, 1986, pp. 481–505.

60. Cf. *mactare, hostis.*

61. "Childhood and Tradition in Two American Indian Tribes," *The Psychoanalytic Study of the Child* 1 (1945): 340.

the Romans thought and felt, I have written this book as a series of interlocking patterns in which ideas and themes appear and reappear in different contexts (more like a car winding through the unmarked back roads of western Massachusetts than whizzing across the Bonneville salt flats). Rather than being interwoven in a neat and systematic grid, the ideas I discuss often overlap, contradict one another, or have paradoxical valances. Sometimes the reader will have to wait quite a while before the complements or antitheses (and so the full importance of a statement) appear. In that way, my book reads more like a novel or a musical score than most historians are accustomed to. But I want to reassure the reader that while much in this book may be whimsical—and more simply wrong—little is serendipitous.

I hope that this contrapuntal approach will seem appropriate when dealing with the Romans, for whom dichotomies were not the fundamental way of organizing experience. To be sure, the Romans insistently paired and contrasted ideas, but they tended to link them less as antinomies than as ambiguous and reversible paradoxes or complementarities. Their thinking was layered and sedimented, reticular and analogical rather than linear. For these reasons I am cautious when it comes to splitting the world into two.[62] In this book the "articulate" oppressors and the "inarticulate" or "erased" oppressed do not stare blankly at one another across an abyss.[63]

The Romans' ways of thinking and acting—often incompatible with those of a modern thinker—make more sense when they are relocated in their own thought world (like the poetry of Emily Dickinson read on the common in Amherst, or the paintings of Tiepolo viewed in the Church of the Jesuits in Venice). I have, nevertheless, read rather wantonly outside the boundaries of my field—not with the goal of applying any theory or set of theories to the Roman material but with the goal of perceiving and explaining more in that material, of becoming conscious of as many possible ways of organizing and associating the ideas and phenomena I have observed in Roman life. And so when, in the

---

62. I have been inspired by Paul Richards, who was in turn inspired by an article of J. Guyer in which, developing an extended musical metaphor based on notions of polyrhythm and polymetre, she discusses the ways in which lives within the same household can be highly differentiated and at the same time not necessarily in open conflict or disarray. Men and women can, so to speak, dance to different drumbeats (Ingold, *Key Debates,* p. 126). See J. Guyer, "The Multiplication of Labor: Gender and Agricultural Change in Modern Africa," *Current Anthropology* 29 (1988): 247–272. I have been influenced as well by Judith Hallett, "Women as Same and Other in Classical Roman Elite," *Helios* 16 (1989): 59–78.

63. For the complementary inversions that problematize the sometimes excessively facile distinctions between oppressed and oppressors in modern Western thought, see Paulo Friere, *Pedagogy of the Oppressed,* New York, 1970, pp. 29–31; Thomas Szasz, *The Myth of Mental Illness: Foundations of a Theory of Personal Conduct,* New York, 1974, pp. 171–172; Baumgartner, "Social Control From Below," p. 336; Hatch, "Theories of Social Honor," pp. 344, 350.

midrashim that fill up my footnotes—and occasionally spill over into the text—I use an illustration from a modern source or another culture, it is not because I think the Romans are interchangeable with us—or with any other culture—but because I hope that the ideas expressed in the modern examples or anecdotes can help to translate or mediate, to "shine a light on" the ideas and behaviors of the ancient Romans for a modern audience.

LETTING THE ROMANS BE

Finally, I believe that we can perform a feat of the imagination with regard to the Romans that our grandparents could not. So long as Greek and Roman literature constituted the core of education in Europe and America, the Romans could not be left to "speak for themselves." When they were not horrible warnings, they were allegories of empire, glorified *exempla,* other selves for British, French, Spanish, Italian, English, German, or American imperial dreams and aspirations. Now that the Romans are increasingly peripheral, increasingly irrelevant to modern life, now that, for us, so little hangs on what they say, the Romans are no longer required to serve as projections of our Euro-American selves. They do not have to be heroes or models, ego ideals or superegos. If we no longer imagine them at the center of our world, we can, at last, imagine them at the center of their own. We can imagine their inner lives to be as complex and layered, as rich and composted with emotion as we feel our own to be. Now that the Romans no longer have to serve us, we can serve them—by imagining them richly.

Admittedly, it would require a six-fingered violinist—or Apollo himself—to play all the notes I have sketched for this work. But if I must fall and fail (and mutilate my metaphors), I prefer to go careening off the roof rather than trip on a flat sidewalk.

So here I am, in the middle way...
Trying to learn to use words, and every attempt
Is a wholly new start, and a different kind of failure...
And so each venture
Is a new beginning, a raid on the inarticulate
With shabby equipment always deteriorating
In the general mess of imprecision of feeling,
Undisciplined squads of emotion. And what there is to conquer
By strength and submission, has already been discovered
Once or twice, or several times,...
—but there is no competition—
There is only the fight to recover what has been lost
And found and lost again and again: and now, under conditions
That seem unpropitious. But perhaps neither gain nor loss.
For us there is only the trying....
                              T. S. Eliot, "East Coker"

CHAPTER TWO

A Sort of Prelude

The Tao of the Romans

The judgment of the censor imposed on the condemned scarcely any penalty save the blush.
CICERO, *DE REPUBLICA* 4.6.6[1]

The implication of Cicero's remark is that the blush was, in itself, penalty enough. "If we can cause the man who murdered Cicero to blush, we will have succeeded," declares the Elder Seneca's Porcius Latro (*Controversiae* 7.2.1).[2] As Wilfried Nippel reminds us, like most premodern cities, Rome had no central peacekeeping force.[3] The suppression of the vendetta depended above all on the self-mastery *(decorum, disciplina, modestia, temperantia)* and the sense of honor *(pudor, fides)* of the inhabitants, quickened by a fear of losing face and a dizzy horror of disgrace.[4] Rome was like the Republic described by Cicero in which the citizens

---

1. *Censoris iudicium nihil fere damnato nisi ruborem obfert.* Cicero continues: "Since, therefore, his decision affects only the name, such censure is called 'ignominy'" *(Itaque ut omnis ea iudicatio versatur tantummodo in nomine, animadversio illa ignominia dicta est* [= Nonius p. 25, W. Lindsay ed.]).

2. *id solum proficiemus, ut qui Ciceronem occidit tantum erubescat.* "If this causes him shame, I will consider him to have atoned; I will be satisfied" *(Si hoc pudet, fecisse sumptum, supplici habeo satis* [Plautus, *Mostellaria* 1165]).

3. "Policing Rome," *Journal of Roman Studies* 74 (1984): 20–29; *Public Order in Ancient Rome*, Cambridge, 1995, pp. 2–46.

4. For the Romans' fear of *infamia*, a notion that takes for granted a generalized and shared sense of honor, see Michèle Ducos, "La crainte de l'infamie et l'obéissance à la loi," *Revue des études latines* 57 (1979): 146–165; Freyburger, *Fides*, Paris, 1986, p. 49. For various aspects of the "government" of shame in ancient Rome, particularly the *flagitatio*, the *occentatio*, and the *carmen famosum*, see Hermann Usener, "Italische Volksjustiz," *Kleine Schriften* vol. 4, Osnabrück [1906] 1965, pp. 356–382; G. L. Hendrickson, "Verbal Injury, Magic or Erotic Comus? (*Occentare ostium* and Its Greek Counterpart)," *Classical Philology* 20 (1925): 289–308; Léon Pommeray, *Études sur l'infamie en droit romain*, Paris, 1937, pp. 5, 19–23, 63–67; Eduard Fraenkel, "Two Poems of Catullus," *Journal of Roman Studies* 51 (1961): 46–51; Paul Veyne, "Le folklore à Rome et les droits de la conscience publique sur la conduite individuelle," *Latomus* 42 (1983): 3–30. More generally: J. M. Kelly, *Roman Litigation*, Oxford, 1966, esp. pp. 21–24; "'Loss of Face' as a Factor Inhibiting Litigation," *Studies in the Civil Judicature of the Roman Republic*, Oxford, 1976, 93–111; A. W. Lintott, *Violence in Republican Rome*, Oxford, 1968, pp. 6–21; Amy Richlin, *The Garden*

seek approbation and avoid opprobrium. "They are inhibited not so much by fear of the penalties ordained by law as by the sense of shame with which nature has endowed man as a certain dread of just censure.... Shame, no less effectively than fear, restrains the citizens. The same applies, indeed, to the love of praise" (*De republica* 5.4).[5] *Verecundia*, Cicero asserts elsewhere, is the custodian of all the virtues, fleeing dishonor and strenuously pursuing praise (*De partitione oratoria* 23.79).[6] "There is no one so wild as not to be greatly moved—if not by the desire for those things honorable in themselves—then by the fear of reproach and dishonor" (ibid. 26.91–92).[7]

No study of Roman laws and institutions can tell us as much about how the Romans governed themselves as can a study of their mechanisms of shame and honor. Our modern Romes have been built, at their best, on a scaffold of laws erected according to an ideological blueprint, buttressed by well-armed police, and cemented by tenacious bureaucrats. But the Roman body politic was regulated by the warm physical glow of the blush. In the words of the historian of Roman law A. H. J. Greenidge, "We find the most important obligations almost un-

of Priapus: Sexuality and Aggression in Roman Humor, 2nd ed., New Haven, 1992; Catherine Edwards, *The Politics of Immorality,* Cambridge, 1993; Anthony Corbeill, *Controlling Laughter: Political Humor in the Late Roman Republic,* Princeton, 1996, esp. pp. 19, 24. For the importance of shame even in modern countries with central peacekeeping forces, see John Braithwaite, *Crime, Shame, and Reintegration,* Cambridge, 1989; F. Adler, *Nations Not Obsessed with Crime,* Littleton, Colorado, 1983. For skillful analyses of the government of shame in other cultures, see Max Gluckman, "Gossip and Scandal," *Current Anthropology* 4 (1963): 307–315; Jean Briggs, *Never in Anger,* Cambridge, Mass., 1970; Lila Abu-Lughod, *Veiled Sentiments: Honor and Poetry in a Bedouin Society,* Berkeley, 1986; William J. Goode, *The Celebration of Heroes: Prestige as a Control System,* Berkeley, 1978.

5. *nec vero tam metu poenaque terrentur, quae est constituta legibus, quam verecundia, quam natura homini dedit quasi quendam vituperationis non iniustae timorem . . . ut pudor civis non minus a delictis arceret quam metus. Atque haec quidem ad laudem pertinent.* The reforms of the ancient king Numa resulted, according to Livy's account, in the city being governed by a sense of self-restraint and obligations of the oath rather than by fear of the laws or of punishments (*fides et ius iurandum pro legum ac poenarum metu civitatem regerent* [1.21.1].) Compare Ovid's "Golden Age": "It was *pudor* itself, rather than fear, and without the exercise of violence, that governed the people" (*Proque metu populum sine vi pudor ipse regebat* [*Fasti* 1.251]). "Know that the Latins are the people of Saturn; they need no restraints or laws to make them righteous *(aequam);* they hold themselves in check by their own wills and by the way, the tradition (or the will, *more*) of their ancient god" (*ne ignorate Latinos / Saturni gentem, haud vinclo nec legibus aequam / sponte sua veterisque dei se more tenentem* [Virgil, *Aeneis* 7.202–204]). Cf. Tacitus, *Annales* 3.26.1–2, 3.54.10. What Ronald Syme says of the idealized state of Cicero's *De republica* can be applied as well to the "Golden Ages" of Ovid and Virgil: these states governed by shame were inspired not by theory but by history; they were visions of Rome in a past age ("A Roman Post-Mortem: An Inquest on the Fall of the Roman Republic," in *Essays on Roman Culture: The Todd Memorial Lectures,* ed. A. J. Dunston, Toronto, 1976, p. 148).

6. *Custos vero virtutum omnium, dedecus fugiens, laudemque maxime consequens, verecundia est.*

7. *Nemo est enim tam agrestis, quem non, si ipsa honesta minus, contumelia tamen et dedecus magnopere moveat.* In these passages Cicero asserts that the fear of ignominy is even stronger than the desire for praise—for the rustic no less than for the educated man influenced by the abstract demands of a philosophical notion of the good.

defended by legal sanctions in the early Roman law; they were a matter of simple honour."[8] The only punishment backing up the *lex Valeria de provocatione* of 300 B.C.E. was that the violator would be declared to have acted dishonorably *(improbe factum)*. "I believe," Livy says, "that this seemed a sufficiently strong sanctioning of the law *(vinculum satis validum legis)*—such was the shame *(pudor)* of men in those days" (10.9.6). Tacitus informs us that prior to the *senatus consultum* of the reign of Tiberius, the only punishment suffered by the prostitute was the shame of having to profess her name before the aediles. That was, he asserts, punishment enough *(Annales* 2.85).[9]

Romans expected of one another a high degree of behavioral finesse, a sort of social *Fingerspitzengefühl*. Lapses were noted.[10] Plautus's elderly gentleman Demipho imagines the unwanted attention, the infamy that would accrue to his wife and family if his son should give a beautiful attendant to his mother: "If she followed a *materfamilias,* her beauty would be a scandal. Whenever she walked through the streets everyone would watch and observe her. Everyone would nod and wink and whistle and pinch and call aloud. People would harass us; they would serenade us; they would cover my door with verses scribbled in charcoal" *(Mercator* 405–409).[11]

Catullus engages figuratively in just such a public shaming, a *flagitatio*. The poet marshals his hendecasyllables, like a gang of rowdy adolescents, to pursue in the street a woman who refused to return some tablets of his poetry: "Since nothing else works, let's force a blush from the face of the brazen bitch. Let's all chant in a loud voice: 'Rotten whore—Give me back my tablets. Give them back, you rotten whore!' " (42.16–20).[12]

---

8. *Infamia: Its Place in Roman Public and Private Law,* Oxford, [1894]1977, p. 67.

9. *more inter veteres recepto, qui satis poenarum adversum impudicas in ipsa professione flagitii credebant.* Tacitus believed that in the early days of Rome there were few laws; rather, *modestia* and *pudor* governed. Law replaced shame as the city declined in morality. "Then, when the state was most corrupt, laws were most abundant" *(corruptissima re publica plurimae leges [Annales* 3.27]).

10. See Pommeray, *Études sur l'infamie,* pp. 41–42; Wilfried Nippel, *Public Order in Ancient Rome,* Cambridge, 1995, p. 8. For the indulgence of irregular behavior, see the chapters on the blush.

11. *illa forma matrem familias*
   flagitium sit si sequatur; quando incedat per vias,
   contemplent, conspiciant omnes, nutent, nictent, sibilent,
   vellicent, vocent, molesti sint:
   occentent ostium:
   impleantur elegeorum meae fores carbonibus.

12. 42.16–20:

   quod si non aliud potest, ruborem
   ferreo canis exprimamus ore
   conclamate iterum altiore voce
   "moecha putida, redde codicillos,
   redde, putida moecha, codicillos."

Long years before Virgil or Statius created their personifications, *fama* and *rumor publicus* acted as the custodians of the *mores* of the citizens.[13] And because of the critical social functions of shame, the Romans could not afford the degree of privacy that we highly value.[14] Plutarch, speaking of the censorship, remarks, "The Romans did not think it proper that anyone should be left free to follow his personal preference and appetites, whether in marriage, the begetting of children, the regulation of his daily life, or the entertainment of his friends, without a large measure of surveillance and review." The Roman censor, a sort of chief shamer, was given "the right to inquire into the lives and manners of the citizens,...to watch, regulate, and punish any tendency to licentiousness or voluptuous habits and departures from the customary way of living" (Plutarch, *Cato maior* 16.1–2).[15] Dionysius of Halicarnassus contrasts the Roman with the Athenian, for whom the house door marked the boundary "within which he was free to live as he pleased":

> The Romans, throwing open every house and extending the authority of the censors even to the bedchamber, made that office the overseer and guardian of everything that took place in the homes, for they thought that a master should not be cruel in the punishment of his slaves, nor a father unduly harsh or lenient in the training of his children, nor a husband unjust in his partnership with his lawful wife, nor children disobedient to their elderly parents; nor should brothers strive for more than their equal shares; and they thought there should be no banquets or revels lasting all night long, no wantonness and corrupting of youthful comrades, no neglect of the ancestral honors of sacrifices and funerals, nor any other of the things that are done contrary to propriety *(to kathekon)* and the advantages of the state *(to sumpheron tei polei)*. (20.13.2–3)

Men and women were surveyed from every point of the social compass. Beryl Rawson reminds us that the intimate proximity of slaves and servants to their

---

On these lines see Fraenkel, "Two Poems of Catullus," pp. 46–51. Crito, should he try to take the property of the dead Chrysis away from her designated heir, expects just such a *flagitatio* (Terence, *Andria* 814–816). For other examples see the scenes in Plautus, *Mostellaria,* lines 532ff., esp. 603–605, *Pseudolus* 555–556, and Apuleius, *Apologia* 75.

13. Plautus, *Miles gloriosus* 1368–1372; *Trinummus* 738–740; Terence, *Phormio* 911; Virgil, *Aeneis* 4.181–88; Statius, *Silvae* 1.2.26–30. For *existimatio* playing the role of public judge, see fragment 31 of Varro's *Eumenides* (*Menippearum Reliquae,* Heraeus ed., in Petronius, *Saturae* 6th ed., ed. F. Beucheler, Berlin, 1922).

14. On the absence of privacy in ancient Rome, see Greenidge, *Infamia,* pp. 61–67; Beryl Rawson, "Adult-Child Relationships in Roman Society," in *Marriage, Divorce and Children in Ancient Rome,* ed. Beryl Rawson, Oxford, 1991, p. 11. For the early "privative" aspects of Latin *privatus,* see Yan Thomas, "*Vitae necisque potestas,*" in *Du châtiment dans la Cité: Supplices corporels et peine de mort dans le monde antique,* Rome, 1984, p. 526; John Scheid, "La Spartizione à Roma," *Studi storici* 4 (1984): 952 and n. 24.

15. As Nippel points out, the censors' power to mark the Roman with ignominy was not exercised in a systematic or consistent fashion; it was, rather, aimed at the highest classes, those who should serve as examples for the whole of society (*Public Order,* pp. 8–9).

masters in every class of Roman society would have resulted in masters being subject to, and aware of, close and constant observation.[16] Lucian imagines his poor philosopher, having spent a lifetime in the service of a wealthy Roman family, being dismissed, finally, because he, like the other servants, knew the mysteries of his masters and "had looked on them unveiled" (*De mercede* 41).

The Romans believed that the person allowed excessive privacy would lose all self-control and become shameless, like the old emperor Tiberius on Capri: "Having at last obtained the license granted by secrecy, and being, as it were, no longer in the eyes of the public, Tiberius rapidly succumbed to the vices that he had tried for a long time, without great success, to disguise" (Suetonius, *Tiberius* 42.1).[17] When, according to Dionysius, many prominent citizens of Rome left the city in protest against the outrages of the *decemviri* and their gangs of wanton youths in 450 B.C.E., "it greatly increased the arrogance of the licentious youth not to have before their eyes those persons in whose presence they would have been ashamed to commit any wanton act" (11.2.4). Pliny the Younger asserts that youth, the "slippery" age, needs "not only a teacher but a custodian and monitor" (*Epistulae* 3.3.4).[18] "We must," Cicero avows, "take great care that the reputations of the women are guarded by the clear light of day when they are subject to the eyes of many" (*De legibus* 2.15.37).[19]

In Rome (as in all cultures structured by the reciprocities of the vendetta) a sense of shame functioned, above all, as a deterrent. And so Roman punishments, when they did occur, tended to be theatrical, designed to mortify the transgressor. A man's statue might be torn down and broken into pieces. He might be publicly displayed or forced to perambulate carrying the conspicuous weight of odd and ugly bonds and impediments. He might be stripped naked and flogged *in conspectu populi Romani*.[20] He might be torn to bits by a crowd. His body might be hurled down the Gemonian steps or precipitated from the Tarpeian rock. His corpse might be dragged by a hook to the Tiber.[21] The debtor in default might find his

---

16. "Adult-Child Relationships," pp. 21–22.

17. *ceterum secreti licentiam nanctus et quasi civitatis oculis remotis, cuncta simul vitia male diu dissimulata tandem profudit.* It was easy to despise divine witnesses when there were no human ones (Juvenal, *Satirae* 13.75–76). The soldier in civil war, his face hidden behind a helmet, was shameless (Lucan, *Bellum civile* 4.706).

18. *in hoc lubrico aetatis non praeceptor modo sed custos etiam rectorque quaerendus est.* Cf. Persius, *Satirae* 5.30–40.

19. *diligentissime sanciendum est, ut mulierum famam multorum oculis lux clara custodiat.*

20. Cf. Livy 8.33.2.

21. For punishments as deterrents and/or humiliations, see Frederic D. Allen, "On '*os columnatum*' (Plautus *M.G.* 211) and Ancient Instruments of Confinement," *Harvard Studies in Classical Philology* 7 (1896): 37–69; Ramsay MacMullen, *Roman Social Relations 50 b.c. to a.d. 184*, New Haven, 1974, p. 112; François Hinard, "La male mort," in *Du châtiment dans la cité*, esp. pp. 298ff; Dominique Briquel, "Formes de mise à mort dans la Rome primitive," in *Du châtiment dans la cité*, pp. 225–240; T. P. Wise-

name posted to the Columna Maenia. The errant servant might be whipped under the yoke by his *pater.* The thieving soldier might have his right hand cut off in the sight of his comrades.[22] The insolvent senator might be compelled to sit in a part of the theater conspicuously set apart for bankrupts.[23]

The Romans understood, however, that limits and restraints must apply even to the shaming that punished shamelessness. There was a fine line between scolding and abuse, between loud and clamorous reproach (or witty insult) and false and malicious calumny. Among the earliest provisions of Roman law (*Twelve Tables* 8.1b = Cicero, *De republica* 4.10.12) was a law making it a capital offense to chant abuse *(occentare)* or chant curses *(carmina)* that would destroy the social existence, the *fama* of another. While, as Erich Gruen points out, no evidence exists to show that anyone was ever convicted under that clause,[24] later law gave the victim of public insult, insult that was *adversus bonos mores*, some redress through the praetor's edict.[25] The "government of shame" was a balancing system difficult to adjudicate; it remained overwhelmingly a matter of a shared public sense.

That the Republic survived and flourished for so many centuries without a central peacekeeping force was due, above all, to the Roman "way," the *disciplina Romana,* the *decorum,* the formalized and ritualized behaviors of the culture.[26] The Roman way demanded a degree of mutual surveillance and inhibition that modern Americans might find only in an Orwellian nightmare or a maximum-security prison. But to understand Roman culture, one must understand that the strictures of Roman tradition were also the necessary preconditions for the creation and existence of the Roman soul.

---

man, *Catullus and His World*, Cambridge, 1985, pp. 6–7; Aline Rouselle, "Personal Status and Sexual Practice in the Roman Empire," in *Fragments for a History of the Human Body, Part Three*, ed. Michel Feher, Ramona Naddaff, and Nadia Tazi, New York, 1989, esp. p. 330 n. 64; K. M. Coleman, "Fatal Charades: Roman Executions Staged as Mythological Enactments," *Journal of Roman Studies* 80 (1990): 44–73.

   22. Frontinus, *Strategemata* 1.4.16; cf. all of 4.1.

   23. Livy 2.36.1; Cicero, *Philippicae* 2.18.44; Richard Saller, *Patriarchy, Property, and Death in the Roman Family,* Cambridge, 1994, p. 137.

   24. *Studies in Greek Culture and Roman Policy,* Berkeley, 1990, p. 103. Gruen dismisses the doubtful case of Naevius.

   25. See Nippel, *Public Order,* pp. 41–42. "Only two cases [of prosecution for defamation] are known from the late 2nd c., both involving defamatory statements from the stage, leveled against literary figures, Lucilius and Accius. But they fell under the rubric of *iniuria,* evidently governed by the Praetor's Edict, not the Twelve Tables" (Gruen, *Studies in Greek Culture and Roman Policy,* p. 103 n. 108).

   26. For the *disciplina Romana,* see Livy 22.3.4; Josephus, *Bellum Iudaicum* 3.70–109. Plutarch declares that there were no parricides at Rome for six hundred years, until after the Hannibalic war (*Romulus* 22.4).

THE MIDDLE WAY

The Roman way was the way of the ancestors, the *mos maiorum*. It was like "the refining fire" described by T. S. Eliot, "where you must move in measure, like a dancer."[27] It was the script of tradition that framed the performance of the Roman spirit, the acting, the action, the *agon*, the work that proved the soul, the *animus*, the effective energy at the core of one's being.[28]

Roman tradition was the score of a concerto, and the Roman a pianist performing before a full house. To the extent that they shared the tradition, the audience—the spectators and witnesses—would be aware of the difficulty of the performance and could appreciate its finesse. As the philosopher Herbert Fingarette remarks in connection with Confucian ritual: "We distinguish sensitive and intelligent performances from dull and unperceptive ones; and we detect in the performance confidence and integrity, or perhaps hesitation, conflict, 'faking,' or 'sentimentalizing.' "[29] However long the practice, however oft-repeated the move, the performance could transcend the regimentation. The performance could be beautiful and wild and free. Indeed, exactly in proportion to the work and discipline, exactly in proportion to the self-overcoming, formalized behavior might feel like the fullness of self, the summit of self-expression. For the Romans, like the Confucians, to submit to ancestral customs and rituals was a form of honing, polishing, measuring, self-overcoming. It was the meticulous cutting of a diamond. "As physical beauty, by the apt arrangement of the limbs, stirs the eyes and delights them for the very reason that all the parts of the body combine in harmony and grace, so this decorum, shining out of the conduct of our lives, inspires the approval of our fellow man by the order, constancy, and self-control it imposes on every word and deed" (Cicero, *De officiis* 1.28.98).[30] *Decorum* was, for Cicero, moderation and temperance "with a certain polish" (*moderatio et temperantia ... cum specie quadam liberali* [*De officiis* 1.27.96].)[31]

Roland Barthes asks: "Why, in the West is politeness regarded with suspicion? Why does courtesy pass for a distance (if not an erasure, in fact) or a hypocrisy? Why is an 'informal' relation...more desirable than a coded one?" He explains:

---

27. "Little Gidding," in *The Complete Poems and Plays,* New York, 1952, p. 142.

28. Victor Turner correctly points out that action is 'agonistic.' "Act, agon, agony, and agitate all come from the same Indo-European base *ag-, 'to drive,' from which came Latin *agere*, to do, and the Greek *agein*, to lead" (*From Ritual to Theatre: The Human Seriousness of Play,* New York, 1982, p. 103).

29. *Confucius: The Secular as Sacred,* New York, 1972, p. 53.

30. *Ut enim pulchritudo corporis apta compositione membrorum movet et delectat hoc ipso, quod inter se omnes partes cum quodam lepore consentiunt, sic enim decorum, quod elucet in vita, movet approbationem eorum, quibuscum vivitur, ordine, constantia et moderatione dictorum omnium atque factorum.*

31. For the relationships between beauty and ritualized behaviors, between the appropriate and the effective in Roman thought, see Mario Perniola, "Decorum and Ceremony," trans. Barbara Spackman, in *Recoding Metaphysics: The New Italian Philosophy,* ed. Giovanna Borradori, Evanston, Illinois, 1988, p. 111.

In the West each person is ideally an "autarchy," "a personal empire" ruled over by its ego.[32] For us, codes are weighty impositions from the outside. As Pasi Falk says, "All are (in principle) 'others' in relations to the code."[33] Ellen Oliensis remarks, "The concept of decorum is never innocent. Decorum is always an expression of power. In any sphere—aesthetic, sexual, political, moral—decorum enforces subordination: of parts to whole, woman to man, slave to master, desire to reason, individual to state."[34] At their worst, formalized behaviors are, for Westerners, deadening and oppressive; at best, they are frivolous and lacking depth. As Michelle Rosaldo writes: "For us, the *attributes* of individuals describe the core of what we *really* are. Ritual actions, things we do 'because of' roles and norms, become *mere* artifice and play."[35]

But to grasp the infrangible bond between form and effectiveness implicit in Roman concepts of ritualized behavior, as Mario Perniola suggests, "we must first free ourselves of the prejudice that considers ceremony as stereotyped, superfluous, residual, idolatrous, maniacal, desperate behavior, seeing it as formalism and sclerosis, lacking in depth and substance."[36]

The Roman was radically present in a role or game where life or reputation was at risk. Rather than "mere" ritual, Roman self-conscious and formalized behavior was more like our English "propriety" (from *proprietas,* the word from

---

32. *Empire of Signs,* trans. Richard Howard, New York, 1982, p. 68.

Occidental impoliteness is based on a certain mythology of the "person." ... Western man is reputed to be double, composed of a social, factitious, false "outside" and of a personal authentic "inside" (the site of divine communication). According to this scheme, the human "person" is that site filled by nature (or by divinity, or by guilt), girdled, closed by a social envelope which is anything but highly regarded: the polite gesture ... is the sign of respect exchanged ... in spite of and by the intermediary of this limit. However, as soon as the "inside" of the person is judged respectable, it is logical to recognize this person more suitably by denying all interest in his worldly envelope: hence it is the supposedly frank, brutal, naked relation, stripped (it is thought) of all signalectics, indifferent to any intermediary codes, which will best respect the other's individual value: to be impolite is to be true—so speaks (logically enough) our Western morality.... [The Western person thinks:] "I shall reduce my salute, I shall pretend to make it natural, spontaneous, disencumbered, purified of any code." (pp. 63, 65)

For Westerners' criticisms of the formalized behaviors of the Chinese as lacking in sincerity, frankness, truthfulness, and objectivity, see Huston Smith, "Western and Comparative Perspectives on Truth," *Philosophy East and West* 30 (1980): 428–29.

33. "Corporeality and Its Fates in History," *Acta Sociologica* 28 (1985): 118.

34. "Canidia, Canicula, and the Decorum of Horace's Epodes," *Arethusa* 24 (1991): 107. Oliensis's thoughtful analysis of Horace goes on to reveal, however, a much more subtle functioning of decorum than her initial statements would suggest (statements that arise, I would venture, from the modern nostalgia for a lost "genuine" and "transparent" being). By her own account, Roman decorum does much more than silence and oppress; it forms the basis for a delicate and complex counterpoint.

35. Emphases mine. "Toward an Anthropology of Self and Feeling," *Culture Theory: Essays on Mind, Self and Emotion,* ed. Richard Schweder and Robert A. LeVine, Cambridge, 1984, p. 147.

36. "Decorum and Ceremony," p. 112.

which we also derive our word "property"): the nature or quality proper to someone or something. Roman *decorum, quod decet* (what befit, what was appropriate
and becoming to one),[37] with its elaboration of roles and masks, was *proprius*, one's
own, appropriate to oneself, one's way of defining, of realizing, of creating a self.
The goal of formalized action, for the Roman, as for the Confucian, was an enhanced state of being: a state of grace.[38] In a long fragment of Ennius preserved
in Gellius, the poet describes the charming behavior and eloquence of the "good
companion" (i.e., the client) who, even with the handicap of inferior status, man-
ages a stylized but most delicate and self-satisfying performance. Deft and suave,
he knows exactly the measure of his stature and the weight of his words. He
knows when to remain silent and when to speak. Speaking, he knows the right
word for the right time. He knows the ancient manners and the laws of god and
men, and he knows the new ones as well. He is as proud as he is modest (*Noctes Atticae* 12.4.4 = Ennius p. 234, Vahlen ed.).

In this delicate balancing act, the point of greatest stress and drama was the
middle.[39] The Roman way succeeded for centuries because, like the Confucian, it endowed compromise and balance with an emotional glamor.[40] One
approached the Roman way, like the *tao*, "in fear and trembling, with caution
and care, as though on the brink of a chasm, as though treading thin ice"
(*Analects* 8.3).[41]

For us in the West, far from glamor, the word "moderation" sounds a note of
gentle inadequacy. None of us want to act *mediocriter*. For us "mediocrity" is shapeless frustration. There is no romance in Middle America, middle management, or
middle age. People with great force of character, in our culture, are extremists.
They go "ultra-running"; they wield bazookas. But for the Romans the extremist,

---

37. Cicero defines *decorum: quid conveniat et quid deceat* (*De officiis* 1.28.98).

38. As Pierre Bourdieu points out, "The inculcation of the arbitrary abolishes the arbitrariness of
both the inculcation and the significations inculcated" (*Outline of a Theory of Practice*, trans. Richard
Nice, Cambridge, 1979, p. 76). We can, as Bourdieu notes (p. 77), make the strictures into a pleasure
and a challenge. Think of the challenge of learning to play with facility the flat straight keyboard of a
piano with splayed fingers of uneven lengths and a body with limbs that bend at angles and rotate in
directions comically at odds with the unforgiving structure of the instrument. It is the ability to more
than adapt, more than fit, more than manage that is deeply satisfying.

39. The notion of balance was fundamental to all Roman notions of justice and morality. The
just man was *aequus*, not only equitable but measured and balanced. The evil man was *iniquus* or
nequam, unfair, unbalanced, worthless, vile. "Virtue," Horace asserts, "is a mean between vices, removed from both extremes" (*virtus est medium vitiorum et utrimque reductum* [*Epistulae* 1. 18.9]).

40. "The success of Confucianism, its triumph over 'all the hundred schools' from the second
century B.C. onwards, was due in large measure to the fact that it contrived to endow compromise (unlike nineteenth century English Liberalism) with an emotional glamour" (Arthur Waley, *The Analects of
Confucius*, New York, [1938] 1989, p. 37).

41. "The Master said, 'How transcendent is the moral power of the Middle Use!'" (*Analects* 6.27).

the man who would not compromise, was the tyrant, and one was enough to disrupt or destroy the whole social system.[42] And so, for the ancient Romans, honor pivoted on the Heroic Middle; it was a tense and dramatic high-wire act on a line at once taut and perilous. *Aurea mediocritas* was not the timid restraint, the joyless surrender to conventionality of the modern bourgeois, nor was it an excuse for complacency or inactivity. On the contrary, in the Roman mind, moderation was a sort of firebreak against the conflagration of ambition and passion that threatened at all times to engulf the commonwealth. Poise, equanimity, came hard and unnaturally. To be modest, to be "measured," showed the determination, the will of men and women to take their fates in their hands, to direct their own behavior in face of endless temptations to self-indulgence or self-pity.[43] Cicero equates Roman decorum with "what is done with a great and 'virile' spirit" (*quod enim viriliter animoque magno fit, id...decorum videtur* [*De officiis* 1.27.94]). Roman decorum demanded Elgin-watch movements, but offered, in return, exhilaration and a vivid sense of immediacy.

Those who were able to go beyond the script and appear to act spontaneously were intensely admired. For this reason Hannibal's military tactics and Cicero's jokes were highly esteemed. *Sprezzatura* was as important to the Roman, armed with culled and practiced witticisms, as it was to Castiglione's courtier. As the *Auctor ad Herennium* points out, "a good performance has the result that the matter appears to arise from the *animus*" (3.15.27).[44] The highest expression of the orator's artistry, for Quintilian, was its invisibility (*Institutio oratoria* 1.11.3).[45]

Roman life was highly scripted, even regimented, in comparison to our own. But what made the strictures bearable were the spaces, the interstices, the loopholes that kept the script, the score, from being a trap. It was *fortuna*—the wobble,

---

42. Our idealized "man of principle" or "man of conscience" in public life, as well as the politician with a "platform," would have been perceived in the Republic not only as rigid but as dangerously asocial and fundamentally self-serving. Such a man was idealized beginning in the civil war period, particularly in the form of Cato Uticensis and the Stoic *sapiens*, for reasons that I hope will become clear.

43. The best understanding of the Roman ideal of moderation I have come across is that of Erich Burck, "Drei Grundwerte der römishen Lebensordnung (*labor, moderatio, pietas*)," *Gymnasium* 58 (1951): 167–174.

44. 3.15.27: *pronuntiationem bonam id perficere, ut res ex animo agi videatur.*

45. The Romans cultivated a studied casualness, a *negligentia diligens.* Artistry should conceal itself (*ars est celare artem*). Rosalind Thomas points out that in earlier Roman oratory, the appearance of spontaneity was carefully cultivated, and the orator either memorized his text or actually improvised; and that even in the show declamations of the Second Sophistic, improvisation was very important (*Literacy and Orality in Ancient Greece,* Cambridge, 1992, p. 160). See Fritz Graf, "The Gestures of Roman Actors and Orators," in *A Cultural History of Gesture,* ed. Jan Bremmer and Herman Roodenburg, Ithaca, 1991, p. 51; Maud Gleason, *Making Men: Sophists and Self-Presentation in Ancient Rome,* Princeton, 1994, esp. pp. 116–118; Corbeill, *Controlling Laughter,* pp. 28–29 and nn. 31–32.

the improvisation, the possibility and temptation to transgress, and the possibility, as well, of death and defeat—that made self-control bearable, that made it beautiful.[46] What made one's speech and gestures more than "chains" of signification were wordplay, irony, poetry, silliness, nonsense. It was a discipline, ultimately, without safety.

46. Compare Bourdieu's Kabyle: "Only a virtuoso with a perfect command of his 'art of living' can play on all the resources inherent in the ambiguities and uncertainties of behaviour and situation in order to produce situations appropriate to do that of which people will say, 'There was nothing else to be done'" (*Outline of a Theory of Practice*, p. 8; cf. pp. 5–7). "Even the most strictly ritualized exchanges, in which all the moments of action, and their unfolding, are rigorously foreseen, have room for strategies" (p. 15). Compare the "social sense," the '*agl*, of Lila Abu-Lughod's Bedouins.

PART ONE

The Moment of Truth in Ancient Rome

Honor and Embodiment in a Contest Culture

I like a look of Agony
Because I know it's true.
EMILY DICKINSON (CA. 1861)

On the morning of June 6, 1989, a riveting series of photographs appeared on the front page of the *Union News* in Springfield, Massachusetts; it showed a young Chinese man in a white shirt casually blocking with his body the advance of a line of tanks into Tiananmen Square. These were photographs that appeared on the front page of nearly every newspaper in America.

It was a playful, almost whimsical gesture for this man to make: to saunter out in front of the lead tank, to move a little left, to move a little right—to gamble everything in one heart-stopping and almost frivolously theatrical moment. Perhaps it was that juxtaposition of terror and whimsy that transfixed us: terror and grief for the stark fragility of that one human life and a thrilling admiration for the person who would spite its frailty.

This was the Roman *discrimen*, the "moment of truth," the equivocal and ardent moment when, before the eyes of others, you gambled what you were. This was the *agon*, the contest, when truth was not so much revealed as created, realized, *willed* in the most intense and visceral way, the truth of one's being, the truth of being.[1]

When, before the eyes of the enemy Etruscans and their king and commander Porsena, Livy's would-be assassin Mucius was threatened with torture by fire, the

---

1. Charles Segal has remarked that "in Seneca the ultimate truth of human character is revealed in moments of tremendous violence" ("Boundary Violation and the Landscape of the Self in Senecan Tragedy," *Antike und Abendland* 24 [1983]: 175). I believe that Professor Segal's statement can be applied to Roman culture in general and to the Republic in particular with only the following qualifications: the truth of the extreme situation was not ultimate but provisional, and this truth was not so much revealed as realized.

unarmed youth confounded the enemy by thrusting his right hand into the flames of the altar and standing, unflinching, while it burned. He said to the king, "See how cheaply men hold their bodies when they set their sights on glory" (2.12.13).[2] With those words and that gesture he responded to the threat of torture. It was a terrifying scene, but insofar as generations of Romans were the audience for this act, it brought down the house.

As the art historian Bettina Bergmann points out, the Romans had a taste for moments of high tension, frozen instants of "explosive emotions," "excruciating suspended animation," "moments of decision": Medea contemplating her children with a dagger on her lap; the sacrificial bull poised to receive the blow of the ax; the wounded gladiator anticipating the death blow; Phaedra clasping her letter to Hippolytus; Helen resisting the blandishments of Paris.[3] Because of their desire to find and express the "truth" of their being in action, the Romans were eager to interpret any and every confrontation as an ordeal, an opportunity for the exercise of will. But there were, in the Roman mind, good contests and bad ones. A good contest obeyed restrictions: it needed to be a) framed and circumscribed within implicit or explicit boundaries accepted by the competitors, b) between relative equals, c) witnessed, and d) strenuous.[4] The contest between Mucius and Porsena was a hard but good one. Porsena was the enemy, but, in Livy's mind, he and Mucius were playing by the same rules. The Etruscan chieftain could recognize Mucius's gesture and appreciate the courage that it took. Overwhelmed with admiration for Mucius's act, and for what it told of the Roman spirit, King Porsena freed his mutilated captive, raised the siege, and sought an alliance with the Romans.

Ultimately Porsena, by not exploiting his overwhelming physical advantage, allowed the contest to be one of will and not of violence; he allowed his opponent a handicap and equalized the competition. But Deng Xiaoping was no Porsena. The premier of China, if he was playing by any rules at all, was not playing by

---

2. *"En tibi," inquit, "ut sentias quam vile corpus sit iis qui magnam gloriam vident."* The burning hand that Mucius could bear to watch, declares Martial, Porsena could not (1.21).

3. Bergmann describes each such scene as "an intensely theatrical situation" ("The Pregnant Moment: Tragic Wives in the Roman Interior," in *Sexuality in Ancient Art: Near East, Egypt, Greece and Italy*, ed. Natalie Kampen et al., Cambridge, Mass., 1996, p. 9). For the "moment of truth" in representations of the gladiatorial games, see Georges Ville, *La gladiature en Occident des origines à la mort de Domitien*, Rome, 1981, pp. 410, 423–424. For the moment of greatest tension depicted in sacrificial rites, see Paul Zanker, *The Power of Images in the Age of Augustus*, trans. Alan Shapiro, Ann Arbor, 1988, p. 114.

4. For some of the strictures placed on aristocratic competition in the Roman Republic by the aristocrats themselves, see Nathan Rosenstein, *Imperatores Victi: Military Defeat and Aristocratic Competition in the Middle and Late Republic*, Berkeley, 1990, esp. pp. 114–115, 153–156. As Georg Simmel points out, it is not in cooperative but in agonistic and competitive relationships that "the norms of the game often are rigorous and impersonal and are observed on both sides with the severity of a code of honor" (*Conflict*, trans. Kurt H. Wolff, in *Conflict and the Web of Group Affiliations*, Glencoe, Illinois, 1955, p. 35).

the same rules as the man in the white shirt. And that, as I hope to show, makes all the difference.

In chapter 3 I map—synchronically and panoptically—the ways in which the ideal of the good contest affected Roman notions of reality, of embodiment, of social and psychological being. I discuss patterns that endured over the whole of the temporal span covered by my researches (the Republic and early Empire). I emphasize the ways in which the Romans wanted and needed to see themselves.

In chapter 4 I trace the ways in which the bad contest affected Roman notions of reality and their experience of the body, and the remedies they devised for the devastating social and psychological imbalances created by the bad contest. This chapter employs a more diachronic approach: it addresses the ways the patterns outlined in chapter 3 (crossing status and gender divisions or defined by them) were modified or inverted by historical circumstances.

In both chapters I sketch the persistent counterpoint between the principal metaphors expressing honor (light and fire) and those expressing dishonor (stone and ice), and the ways and reasons that the metaphors for dishonor inverted and usurped those for honor.

CHAPTER THREE

Light and Fire

Fire is the test of gold; adversity of the strong man.
SENECA, *DE PROVIDENTIA* 5.10[1]

As gold is proven by fire, so are we by ordeals.
MINUCIUS FELIX, *OCTAVIUS* 36.9[2]

Virtus and the *honores* won in the crucible of the contest were shining and volatile; the refining fire of the ordeal produced a heightened sense of vividness, a brilliant, gleaming, resplendent existence.[3] The man of honor was *speciosus, illustris, clarus, nobilis, splendidus:* the woman of honor was, in addition, *candida, casta, pura.* Valerius Maximus describes brave Cloelia as a *lumen virtutis* (3.2.2).[4] Cicero declares that Julius Caesar was "the fairest light of all nations and all history" (*omnium gentium atque omnis memoriae clarissimum lumen* [*Pro rege Deiotaro* 5.15]). Ovid's Cyclops praises Galatea as "shining brighter than glass" (*splendidior vitro* [*Metamorphoses* 13.791]).

---

1. *Ignis aurum probat, miseria fortes viros.*

2. *itaque ut aurum ignibus, sic nos discriminibus arguimus.* "Just as gold is tested in the flames, so *fides* must be tried in duress." (*scilicet ut fulvum spectatur in ignibus aurum, / tempore sic duro est inspicienda fides* [Ovid, *Tristia* 1.5.25].) "Devouring fire purges all things and melts the dross from out of the metals; therefore it purges the shepherd and the sheep" (*omnia purgat edax ignis vitiumque metallis / excoquit: idcirco cum duce pergat ovis* [Ovid, *Fasti* 4.785–786]). For the annealing, purifying force of fire, see also Virgil, *Georgica* 1.84–93. For the fire in the Mucius Scaevola legend as a form of ordeal, a test of wills, see Walter Otto, "Fides," in Pauly-Wissowa, *Paulys Realencyclopädie der classischen Altertumswissenschaft,* vol. 6.2, Stuttgart, 1909, 2281–2282, col. 2283; Rudolf Hirzel, *Der Eid,* Leipzig, 1902, p. 199 n. 1.

3. Honor shone: "The glory of one's ancestors acts as a kind of light" (*maiorum gloria posteris quasi lumen est* [Sallust, *Bellum Iugurthinum* 85.23]). "Caesar yearned for a high command, an army, and a new war where his virtue could shine forth" (*sibi magnum imperium, exercitum, bellum novum exoptabat, ubi virtus enitescere posset* [Sallust, *Catilina* 54.4]). "Would that there were some commonwealth where honor could shine forth" (*sit modo aliqua res publica, in qua honos elucere possit* [Cicero, *Ad familiares* 10.10.2]). Cf. Cicero, *Pro Marcello* 6.19, *Pro rege Deiotaro* 11.30.

4. Cf. 3.8.7, 5.8.4; Ennius apud Cicero, *De senectute* 4.10; Plautus, *Trinummus* 664; Cicero, *De lege agraria* 2.1.1; Horace, *Carmina* 3.2.17–18; Hans Drexler, "*Honos,*" in *Römische Wertbegriffe,* ed. Hans Oppermann, Darmstadt, 1967, pp. 459–460.

The Romans of the early and middle Republic lived in a face-to-face culture with an acute sensitivity to the bonds *(religiones, obligationes, moenia,* and *munera)* that defined them. Society and community were conceived of and expressed as a product of the bond. At the same time, boundaries were not stable: all Roman boundaries were highly charged but also restless, irritable, and permeable membranes, more like rings of fire than walls of adamant. Every wall was a wager, every bond a risk. The Romans' most sacred forms of contract, the vow and the oath, were bets in which one staked one's name, one's head, one's eyes.[5]

Undergoing the ordeal *(labor, periculum, discrimen, certamen, contentio, agon)* was the act of defining one's boundaries, of determining one's share or portion. It was necessary for one's sense of being.[6] And because in a contest culture no one's part was fixed, the *discrimen* established, momentarily, one's position. It located one in a field, in a pecking order. One gambled what one *was.*[7]

To have a glowing spirit, one needed to expend one's energy in a continuous series of ordeals. *Labor, industria, disciplina, diligentia, studium, vigilentia* were, for the Romans, the strenuous exertions that one made in undergoing the trial and in shouldering the heavy burden.[8] It was Aeneas carrying his father and the house-

5. "Le serment consistait en une ordalie: c'est l'absorption du soufre qui devait vérifier la sincérité du jurant" (Émile Benveniste, *Le vocabulaire des institutions indo-européennes,* vol. 2, Paris, 1969, p. 115). For the ancient Romans, verbal definition was both the most powerful and the most fragile bond.

6. Of the voluntary risk-taker, Erving Goffman remarks: "His activity is defined as an end in itself, sought out, embraced, and utterly his own. His record during performance can be claimed as the reason for participation, hence an unqualified, direct expression of his true make-up and just basis for reputation" ("Where the Action Is," in *Interaction Ritual: Essays on Face-to-Face Behavior,* New York, 1967, p. 185).

7. The Pythian Apollo's dictate "Know thyself!" is interpreted by Cicero as an admonition to learn the strength of one's body and spirit *(nostri vim corporis animique)* and to follow the way of life that enabled one to make fullest use of that force *(De finibus* 5.16.44). One learned through the contest the strength of one's body and spirit. "No man," Seneca declares, "is more unhappy than he who never faces adversity. For he is not permitted to prove himself" *(nihil umquam mihi videtur infelicius eo, cui nihil umquam evenit adversi. non licuit enim illi se experiri* [*De providentia* 3.3]).

8. A few characteristic examples: "The reputation that I have gained by sweat, by labor, and by going without sleep" *(existimationem multo sudore labore vigiliisque collectam* [Cicero, *Divinatio in Caecilium* 22.72]); "to strive through great labors and great perils to achieve the highest praise and glory" *(maximis laboribus et periculis ad summa laudem gloriamque contendere* [*Philippicae* 14.12.32]). Cf. Cato the Elder, *Oratorum Romanorum Fragmenta,* ed. H. Malcovati, vol. 1, frag. 69; Terence, *Eunuchus* 399; Publilius Syrus 617, Friedrich ed.; Cicero, *Pro Plancio* 20.50, *De oratore* 3.4.14, *Pro Murena* 16, *Pro Sulla* 5, *Ad Quintum fratrem* 1.1.43; Sallust, *Catilina* 7.4-5, 8.5, 10.1, 54.4, *Bellum Iugurthinum* 1, 6-7 (esp. 7.4), 85.7, 18, 29-30, 33-34, 40-41, 93.1, 100; Virgil, *Aeneis* 1.628-29, 2.283-285, 9.607-608, *Georgica* 2.472; Horace, *Carmina* 3.2.1-2; Pliny, *Epistulae* 3.5; Tacitus, *Historia* 3.2-3. For the centrality of energetic activity to Romans' notions of honor, see Helmut Wegehaupt, *Die Bedeutung und Anwendung von "dignitas" in den Schriften der republikanischen Zeit,* Breslau, 1932, pp. 15-16; Lily Ross Taylor, *Party Politics in the Age of Caesar,* Berkeley, 1949, pp. 28-29; Erich Burck, "Drei Grundwerte der römischen Lebensordnung *(labor, moderatio, pietas),*" *Gymnasium* 58 (1951): 162-167; Jean-Marie André, *L'otium dans la vie morale et intellectuelle romaine,* Paris, 1966, esp. chapters 1 and 2; Ulriche Knoche, "Der römische Ruhmesgedanke," in *Römische Wert-*

hold gods on his back (Virgil, *Aeneis* 8.731);[9] Cato holding up the collapsing Republic (Seneca, *De constantia sapientis* 2.2);[10] Claudius or Trajan shouldering the weight of the world (Tacitus, *Annales* 12.5; Pliny, *Panegyricus* 57.5).[11]

In *labores* and *pericula* one demonstrated effective energy, *virtus*. *Virtus* was, in the words of Georges Dumézil, "la qualité d'homme au maximum."[12] There was no *virtus* in the Republic without the demonstration of will.[13] "The whole glory of virtue," Cicero declares, "resides in activity" (*De officiis* 1.6.19).[14] Seneca spoke of the "man of exalted spirit" *(homo excelsi ingenii):* "Just as the flame leaps straight

---

begriffe, pp. 430–431; Dieter Lau's exhaustive study *Der lateinische Begriff Labor,* Munich, 1975, esp. pp. 7–10, 18, 22, 63, 70, 294 n. 120; N.M. Horsfall, "Virgil, History and the Roman Tradition," *Prudentia* 8 (1976): 80; Francesca Santoro L'Hoir, "Heroic Epithets and Recurrent Themes in *Ab Urbe Condita, Transactions and Proceedings of the American Philological Association* 120 (1990): 221–241. Roman heroes of *labor* included Hercules, Curius, Fabricius, Regulus, and Cato the Elder.

9. "The piety of Aeneas was proven when, through the fire, he carried on his shoulders both the sacred things of his city and the sacred charge of his father" (*Aeneas, pietas spectata per ignes / sacra patremque umeris, altera sacra, tulit* [Ovid, *Fasti* 4.37–38]).

10. Cf. Seneca, *Ad Polybium* 7.1–2.

11. *gravissimos principis labores quis orbem terrae capessat. Gravitas,* "heaviness," qualified the person able to sustain the weight of arduous labor and obligations. See Cicero, *Pro Roscio Amerino* 112. On *gravitas* in general, see Moses Hadas, "*Gravitas quousque,*" *Classical Journal* 31 (1935): 17–24; H. Wagenvoort, *Roman Dynamism,* Oxford, 1947, pp. 104–127, "*Gravitas et Maiestas,*" *Mnemosyne* 5 (1952): 287–306; Otto Hiltbrunner, "*Vir gravis,*" *Sprachgeschichte und Wortbedeutung: Festschrift Albert Debrunner,* Bern, 1954, pp. 195–207; Georges Dumézil, "*Maiestas et Gravitas:* De quelques différences entre les romains et les austronésiens," *Revue de Philologie* 3e s. 25 (1951): 7–21, *Idées romaines,* Paris, 1969, pp. 125–152; Levi Robert Lind, "The Tradition of Roman Moral Conservatism," *Studies in Latin Literature and Roman History* 1, Brussels, 1979, pp. 34–38. The notion of *honor* could also be connected, in the Roman mind, with the ability to support a heavy burden. While modern linguists such as J.B. Hofmann, A. Ernout, and A. Meillet decline to offer an etymology for the Latin *honos/ honor,* the Roman Varro connected it with the notion of *onus,* the burden: "*Honos* is from *onus.* Therefore the 'honorable' *(honestum)* is said of what is charged with a burden *(oneratum).* As it is said: 'Onerous is the honor which maintains the state'" (*Honor ab onere: itaque honestum dicitur quod oneratum, et dictum: onus est honos qui sustinet rem publicam* [5.73]). See Carl Blümlein, "Zum Wortspiele *onus-honor,*" *Archiv für lateinische Lexikographie,* vol. 8, Leipzig, 1893, p. 586.

12. *Horace et les Curiaces,* Paris, 1942. For the range of meanings and the history of the Latin word *virtus,* see J. Hellegouarc'h, *Le vocabulaire latin des relations et des partis politiques sous la République,* Paris, 1963, pp. 242–246; Karl Büchner, "Altrömische und Horazische *virtus,*" in *Römische Wertbegriffe,* pp. 376–401; Knoche, "Der römische Ruhmesgedanke," p. 430; Werner Eisenhut, *Virtus Romana: Ihre Stellung im römischen Wertsystem,* Munich, 1973; Timothy J. Moore, *Artistry and Ideology: Livy's Vocabulary of Virtue,* Frankfurt am Main, 1989, pp. 5–17; Wendy J. Raschke, "The Virtue of Lucilius," *Latomus* 49 (1990): 352–369.

13. "Virtue is full of activity, and your god, doing nothing, has no share in virtue" (*virtus autem actuosa est et deus vester nihil agens expers virtutis* [Cicero, *De natura deorum* 1.40.110]).For the importance of effective energy, see Lau, *Der lateinische Begriff Labor,* pp. 69, 355 n. 34. For the Romans, as for the philosopher F.H. Bradley, the end of volition was positive self-realization: "It finds opposition, is forced to expand" ("On Pleasure, Pain, Desire and Volition," *Mind* 49 [1888]: 34).

14. *Virtutis enim laus omnis in actione consistit.*

into the air and cannot be prostrated or repressed any more than it can be made to keep quiet, so our spirit is always in motion, and the more ardent the spirit, the greater its motion and activity" (*Epistulae* 39.3).[15] Cicero speaks of "that elation of spirit that is discerned in perils and labors" (*De officiis* 1.19.62).[16] The absence of energy *(inertia, desidia, ignavia, socordia)* was nonbeing.[17] Inactivity froze the spirit.[18]

The desire for honor and glory set men on fire (Cicero, *Tusculanae disputationes* 1.2.4).[19] "By nature we yearn and hunger for honor, and once we have glimpsed, as it were, some part of its radiance, there is nothing we are not prepared to bear and suffer in order to secure it" (2.24.58).[20] Sallust describes the challenge presented by their ancestors' wax images: "I have often been told that Quintus Fabius Maximus and Publius Scipio Africanus and other illustrious men were wont to say: 'When they beheld the images of their ancestors, their spirits were violently inflamed to virtue'" (*Bellum Iugurthinum* 4.5).[21]

Roman honor required will, determination, and effective energy, of women as surely as of men. Purity and chastity were not as dull and passive sounding for a Roman as they are for a modern American. For the Romans, to be *pura* and *casta*

---

15. *quemadmodum flamma surgit in rectum, iacere and deprimi non potest, non magis quam quiescere, ita noster animus in motu est, eo mobilior et actuosior, quo vehementior fuerit.*

16. *ea animi elatio, quae cernitur in periculis et laboribus.*

17. The Romans opposed *industria, duritia, exercitio,* and *officium* to notions such as *luxuria, avaritia, inertia, segnitia, pigritudo,* and *torpedo.*

18. In peace and inactivity, the Roman spirit slept (Valerius Maximus 7.2.3, cf. 7.2.1). Cf. Sallust, *Catilina* 16.3; *Bellum Iugurthinum* 1.4, 31.2; Livy 1.31.5; Columella 11.1.26; Gellius, *Noctes Atticae* 11.2.6. A Roman, according to Cicero, might quote these lines of Ennius's *Ajax* in reproach: "You, son of Salmacis, win spoils that have cost you neither sweat nor blood" (*Salmacida, spolia sine sudore et sanguine* [*De officiis* 1.18.61]).

19. *honos alit artes omnesque incenduntur ad studia gloria.*

20. *sumus enim natura . . . studiosissimi appetentissimique honestatis, cuius si quasi lumen aliquod aspeximus, nihil est quod, ut eo potiamur, non parati sumus et ferre et perpeti.* Valerius Maximus, following Cato the Elder, imagines that Roman youths were incited, long ago, to a *certamen virtutis* by banquet songs that praised the valor of famous men (2.1.10). See Cato, *Origines,* frag. 118, Peter ed.; Cicero, *Tusculanae disputationes* 1.2.3, 4.2.3; *Brutus* 19.75; Nevio Zorzetti, "The *Carmina Convivalia*," trans. Judy Moss, in *Sympotica: A Symposium on the Symposion,* ed. Oswyn Murray, Oxford, 1990, pp. 289–307, and "Poetry and the Ancient City: The Case of Rome," trans. John Van Sickle, *Classical Journal* 86 (1991): 377–82, esp. pp. 313–14. Compare Polybius's remarks on the enthusiasm engendered in Roman youths by the aristocratic funeral: "The young men are inspired to endure everything, for the common good, and in order to obtain the glory that attends the valor of the brave man" (6.54.3; cf. 6.53–54). *Virtus* was costly.

21. *saepe ego audivi Q. Maximum, P. Scipionem, praeterea civitatis nostrae praeclaros viros solitos ita dicere, quom maiorum imagines intuerentur, vehementissume sibi animum ad virtutem adcendi.* The dead Anchises, offering his son Aeneas underworld glimpses of unborn heroes, "fired his spirit with the love of fame to come" (*incenditque animum famae venientis amore* [Virgil, *Aeneis* 6.889]). Valerius Flaccus's Jason describes the eternal freshness of glory, "standing on the shores of Phasis, calling to the young men": "You alone, glory," he declares, "fire hearts and minds!" (*tu sola animos mentesque peruris, / gloria!* [*Argonautica* 1.76–77]). The *exempla virtutis* were expected to move, to stimulate the beholder. See Knoche, "Der römische Ruhmesgedanke," p. 424; Seneca, *De providentia* 6.3.

required an ardent will. Livy tells the story of a certain Virginia, who, after engaging in a stormy quarrel with other patrician women, was booted by them from the shrine of Patrician Chastity for having married a plebeian. Fiercely proud of herself for being *pudica* and *univira* (married to the same man whom she first wed as a maiden), she created her own shrine to Plebeian Chastity and exhorted the plebeian matrons to compete in the contest of chastity just as strenuously as the men competed in the contest of virtue (10.23.8). Valerius Maximus's *sanctissima* Sulpicia won, by the vote of other Roman women, the "contest of chastity" (8.15.12).[22] Pliny the Younger attributes a strong and stalwart spirit to the sexually pure, holy, grave, brave, constant, chaste, and doomed Fannia (*Epistulae* 7.19.4). Purity in and of itself could win a woman glory (Terence, *Hecyra* 796–798). It is possible, as the etymologist T. G. Tucker suggests, that Latin *purus* shares its root with Greek *pur*, fire. Latin "purity" shimmered and burned like the purifying fire.[23]

CONSUMING THE SPIRIT

It is not what I eat that is
my natural meat,
the hero says.
MARIANNE MOORE[24]

Here it is important to point out that in Roman culture, as in very many cultures, a male was not necessarily a man. One was ontologically a male but existentially a man. Born a male *(mas)* or a human *(homo)*, one made oneself a man *(vir)*.[25] A *vir* was not a natural being.[26] In the words of David Gilmore, "manhood... is a precarious or artificial state that boys must win against powerful odds.... Manhood is problematic, a critical threshold that boys must pass through testing."[27] Cicero

---

22. On a different occasion, Claudia won this same title (Pliny, *Historia naturalis* 7.35.120).

23. *Etymological Dictionary of Latin*, Chicago, 1985, s.v. "purus."

24. "The Hero," *The Complete Poems of Marianne Moore*, New York, 1967, pp. 8–9.

25. For an overview of the various meanings of the word *vir*, see Pierre Hamblenne, "*Cura ut vir sis!*...ou une *vir(tus)* peu morale," *Latomus* 43 (1984): 370–372.

26. Because our fundamental assumptions are so different, it is often difficult to translate Latin into English without fitting it into those assumptions. Because we tend to have an ontological, a "natural" manhood, the unqualified *vir* in Latin is often translated into English, with very misleading consequences, as the "real" man. The logic in the Latin is reversed in the English; we make the existential, "unnatural," Latin *vir* into the ontological or essential "real" man.

27. *Manhood in the Making: Cultural Concepts of Masculinity*, New Haven, 1990, p. 11. "There is [in many cultures] a constantly occurring notion that real manhood is different from simple anatomical maleness, that it is not a natural condition that comes about through biological maturation" (loc. cit. See also all of chapter 1). Walter Burkert stresses the "denaturalizing" function of initiation rituals (*Creation of the Sacred*, Cambridge, Mass., 1996, pp. 74–75). For the continued importance of the contest in the construction of "manliness" in the Roman Empire, see especially Maud W. Gleason, *Making Men: Sophists and Self-Presentation in Ancient Rome*, Princeton, 1994.

tells the story of the warlord Gaius Marius, "a rustic man, but a man indeed" (*rusticanus vir, sed plane vir*), who refused to be placed in restraints when operated on for varicose veins...in one leg. After this act of unprecedented fortitude (one frequently emulated thereafter), Marius nevertheless refused to have the operation performed on his other leg. Cicero explains: "Being a *vir* he bore the pain. Being a *homo* he did not want to bear any more pain than necessary" (*Tusculanae disputationes* 2.22.53).[28] The "natural" man, the *homo*, in Marius rejected any pain that was not necessary to endure; the "unnatural" man, the heroic *vir*, prided himself in his ability to endure much more pain than necessary. In encouraging Publius Sittius to bear physical suffering bravely and to battle fortune with a stout heart, Cicero urges him to remember that he is a *vir* even while being a *homo* (*Ad familiares* 5.17.3).

It is with the words "if you are men" that Lucretia challenges Brutus and Collatinus to avenge her violation (Livy 1.58.8).[29] "The kingdom is yours, Servius," declares Tanaquil, "if you are a man" (Livy 1.41.3).[30] Compare the words of Apuleius's Fotis to Lucius: "Fight," she said, "and fight vigorously, for I will not retreat before you nor turn my back on you. Stiffen up and close in for a vigorous frontal assault—if you are a man! Slay, for you are about to die. There's no leaving alive from today's battle" (*Metamorphoses* 2.17).[31]

Tullius incites the Volsci by saying, "Rome has declared war on you, and she will be sorry for it...if you are men" (Livy 2.38.5).[32] It is with the words "if you wish to be men" that Publius Umbrenus incites the Allobroges to join the rebellion of Catiline and Lentulus (Sallust, *Catilina* 40.3).[33] Lentulus, in turn, charges Catiline: "Consider well the predicament that you are in and remember that you are a man" (44.5).[34] The survivors of Cannae, relegated to Sicily in disgrace and inactivity (*resides ac segnes*), demand the very toughest of perils and dangers (*asperrima quaeque ad laborem periculumque*). "It is neither an end to our disgrace nor a re-

---

28. *tulit dolorem ut vir, et ut homo maiorem ferre sine causa necessaria noluit.*

29. *"Sextus est Tarquinius, qui hostis pro hospite priore nocte vi armatus mihi sibique, si vos viri estis, pestiferum hinc abstulit gaudium."*

30. *"tuum est, Servi, si vir es, regnum."*

31. *"Proeliare," inquit, "et fortiter proeliare, nec enim tibi cedam nec terga vertam; comminus in aspectum, si vir es, derige et grassare naviter et occide moriturus. Hodierna pugna non habet missionem."* Compare the raw challenge to Octavian made by Martial's Fulvia: either fuck me or fight me (*aut futue aut pugnemus* [Martial 11.20]).

32. *"bellum vobis indictum est, magno eorum malo qui indixere si viri estis."* In 216 B.C.E. Titus Manlius Torquatus expected the soldiers to respond with enthusiasm to the words "Let us die, and by our death set free the beleaguered legions." He goes on: "I would consider you not to be men, to say nothing of being Romans, if no one had come forward to have a share in such virtue" (*"nec viros equidem nec Romanos vos ducerem, si nemo tantae virtutis exstitit comes"* [Livy 22.60.12]). Cf. Horace, *Epodi* 16.39.

33. *"at ego," inquit, "vobis, si modo viri esse voltis, rationem ostendam, qua tanta ista mala effugiatis."*

34. *"fac cogites, in quanta calamitate sis, et memineris te virum esse."* Cicero's version is very similar and contains the same challenge: "Take care to be a man and consider the point to which you have come" (*"Cura ut vir sis et cogita quem in locum sis progressus"* [*In Catilinam* 3.12]).

ward for our valor that we ask; only let us prove our spirit *(experiri animum)* and exercise our courage *(virtutem exercere)*. We ask for hardship and danger that we might fulfill the office of soldiers and of men" *(ut virorum... officio fungamur* [Livy 25.6.19–22]). Seneca's Achilles, warned to run away from war and told to sit at home and live to ripe old age, "chose the sword and professed himself a man" *(fassus est armis virum* [Troades 214]). "Who," Seneca asks, "only let him be a man and intent upon honor—is not eager for the honorable ordeal and prompt to assume perilous duties? To what energetic person is not idleness a punishment?" *(De providentia* 2.2).[35]

A male was transformed into a man by the willful expenditure of energy. Above all, a man willed himself to be expendable.[36] Like the sun, a man fed the fire of his honor on his own substance. The *magnus animus,* the *animus virilis,* squan-

---

35. *quis autem, vir modo, et erectus ad honesta, non est laboris adpetens iusti et ad officia cum periculo promptus? Cui non industrio otium poena est?* Cf. Cicero, *Pro Milone* 30.82. Pierre Hamblenne summarizes the objective and subjective conditions for being a *vir* in ancient Rome:

> Le recours au dénominatif *vir* semble dépendre de *conditions extérieures* ou *objectives:* le *vir* prend conscience de sa personnalité ou des exigences de sa nature quand une situation de *crise* a percé ou est vécue dans son amplitude....Il est plus rare que la *crise* reste *latente:* on espère d'autrui qu'il démontrera qu'il est un *vir....*L'application du vocable postulerait également l'existence d'une *condition subjective:* l'*attitude* adoptée par l'individu: celle-ci peut être *spécifique:* 1) ...la *prise de conscience immédiate* de la "crise"...2) le fait *d'être* quand survient le pire, *prêt à tout,* moralement et matériellement....3) la *volonté,* devant l'obstacle d'aller jusqu'au bout." *("Cura ut vir sis!"* p. 385, emphases in original.)

It is possible that the contest, in so far as it defined the *vir,* may reflect a more primitive type of initiation described by Pliny the Elder: Tarquinius Priscus first presented his son with a golden amulet when, while still of an age to wear the bordered robe, he had killed an enemy in battle *(Historia naturalis* 33.4.10). Cf. Plutarch, *Quaestiones romanae* 101 *(Moralia* 287F–288A). For possible traces of earlier initiation rites, see Augusto Fraschetti, "Roman Youth," trans. Camille Naish, in *A History of Young People in the West,* ed. Giovanni Levi and Jean-Claude Schmitt, pp. 57–61; J. N. Bremmer, "Romulus, Remus, and the Foundation of Rome," in *Roman Myth and Mythography,* ed. J. N. Bremmer and N. M. Horsfall, London, 1987, pp. 33–34, 38–43. During the Republic, the assumption of the *toga virilis* at the age of sixteen or seventeen began rather than ended the period of testing of a Roman male in field and forum. See Florence Dupont, *Daily Life in Ancient Rome,* trans. Christopher Woodall, Oxford, 1989, p. 229. As the initiatory function of warfare and public speaking that had provided a sharp clear test of manhood in the Republic became attenuated (especially for the elite) in the Empire, manhood came to require of males a more violent and constant psychological and emotional rejection of femininity. Without a strenuous and decisive initiatory ordeal, women would have to be more other than same.

36. "To be men, most of all, they must accept the fact that they are expendable" (Gilmore, *Manhood in the Making,* p. 223). For the evolutionary and biological aspects of male expendability, see the brief but excellent summary in Walter J. Ong, *Fighting for Life: Contest, Sexuality, and Consciousness,* Amherst, Mass., 1981, pp. 52–56. To come to grips with his biological nature, a male must overcome his instinct for survival *as a creature*—that part of himself that he shares with females. A female, being less expendable biologically, is not required to suffer such a sharp division in her psyche; she does not need so violent a denaturing to become a woman.

dered itself in contempt of its own dear life.[37] Virgil's Euryalus declares to Nisus: "Here, here is a soul that scorns the light of life and holds that honor you are aiming at as cheaply bought if all its price is life" (*Aeneis* 9.205–206).[38] Livy's Torquatus argues against redeeming the Roman soldiers captured at Cannae with the following words: "Fifty thousand citizens and allies lay dead around you on that day. If so many *exempla virtutis* did not move you, nothing will ever move you; if such a great disaster did not make you hold your lives cheaply, nothing will ever make you do so" (Livy 22.60.14].)[39] It was the unnaturalness, the artifice of his actions that, for the Romans, told the will of a *vir.*[40] Being a man was a mannerism.

As an aside, the absence of a "feminine" version of *virtus* is not as puzzling or insulting as it might seem. Because it did not come naturally for a male to have *virtus*, it was no less natural for the Romans to attribute *virtus* to a female, who, equally unnaturally, showed exceptional will and energy. The *virtus* on which Plautus's feisty Alcmena prides herself is the energy she has shown both in preserving her chastity and in defending it (*Amphitruo* 925). When, in 80 B.C.E., Cicero praised the *virtus* of Caecilia, he was admiring the diligence, the energy, the courage, and the resolve with which she protected his client Roscius from Sulla and his favorite Chrysagonus. (Simultaneously, Cicero used Caecilia's bravery and energy as a reproach and challenge to the cowardly and subservient aristocrats who backed down from confrontation with the dictator and his minions [*Pro Roscio Amerino* 10.27].)[41] The Romans associated *virtus* with *vis, vires* (physical power,

37. "The *virtus* proper to a man is fortitude, for which there are two main tasks: scorn of death and scorn of pain. We must practice these if we wish to possess *virtus*—or rather—if we wish to be *viri*" (*viri... propria maxime est fortitudo, cuius munera duo sunt maxima mortis dolorisque contemptio. Utendum est igitur his, si virtutis compotes vel potius, si viri volumus esse* [*Tusculanae disputationes* 2.18.43]).

38. *est hic, est animus lucis contemptor et istum / qui vita bene credat emi, quo tendis, honorem.*

39. *quinquaginta milia civium sociorumque circa vos eo ipso die caesa iacent. si tot exempla virtutis non movent, nihil umquam movebit; si tanta clades vilem vitam non fecit, nulla faciat.* For stiffening the courage of others by disdaining one's own life, see Velleius 2.7.2; Seneca, *Epistulae* 77.14–15; Pliny, *Epistulae* 3.16.6; Dio 46.53.3; Paul Plass, *The Game of Death in Ancient Rome*, Madison, 1995, p. 86.

40. According to Nathan Rosenstein, "It was precisely this readiness to face extreme danger when no necessity compelled that was acknowledged as the supreme manifestation of personal courage at Rome and that won decorations for valor." For this reason, he explains, the generals who deliberately placed themselves in danger, or who refused to surrender or even survive when all was lost, were admired more than the soldiers on the line, "for theirs was the product of an individual decision, not something expected of them because they were part of a group" (*Imperatores Victi: Military Defeat and Aristocratic Competition in the Middle and Late Republic*, Berkeley, 1990, pp. 130–131).

41. The challenge or *exemplum* of a brave and active woman, even more than that of another man, provoked a man to action. Quintilian suggests that those who want to inflame the courage of a man should forget about Horatius and Torquatus and tell him the story of the woman who slew Pyrrhus. And those who want to give a man the courage to die should not tell him about Cato or Scipio, but should tell him instead the story of Lucretia (*admirabilior in femina quam in viro virtus* [*Institutio oratoria* 5.11.10]). The courage of Arria was taken as an example and a challenge by her husband, Paetus (Pliny, *Epistulae* 3.16.1,6), as Portia's was by Brutus (Plutarch, *Brutus* 13.11) and Cleopatra's by Antony

vigor, vitality, energy, violent or forceful action).⁴² Accordingly, they also associated *vir* with *vis* and with *viriditas*, the flourishing vigor and potency of youth.⁴³ But it is important to note that they also associated the female *virgo* (or *vira*) with the same notions.⁴⁴ The *vir* and the *virgo* had in common youthful vigor, growth, fertility, freshness, and energy.⁴⁵

The deliberate wasting of oneself and one's forces was a form of generosity, of liberality. Horace describes Aemilius Paulus, the conqueror of Macedonia, as "prodigal of his great spirit" (*animae magnae prodigum Paulum* [*Carmina* 1.12.37–38]).⁴⁶ When, in the early fourth century B.C.E., a crevice mysteriously opened in the Forum, the soothsayers declared that if the Romans wished the Republic to endure forever (*si rem publicam Romanam perpetuam esse vellent*), they must sacrifice the greatest source of their strength. The valiant young warrior Marcus Curtius stepped forth. After admonishing his fellows that the strength of Rome lay in *arma virtusque*, devoted himself to a sacrificial death. Fully armed and riding a horse splendidly ca-

---

(Plutarch, *Antony* 76.3). Pliny the Younger cites Fannia, the daughter of Arria and Paetus, as an example of courage *(fortitudinis exempla)* for both men and women (*Epistulae* 7.19.7). The equestrian statue of the ancient Roman heroine Cloelia still taunted indolent youths, according to Seneca (*Ad Marciam* 16.2). The courage of Epicharis was taken as a direct challenge by her male torturers (Tacitus, *Annales* 15.57). For the challenge to a *vir* created by the lover's unfaithfulness, see Horace, *Epodi* 15.11–16. Cf. Cicero, *De officiis* 1.18.61; Plass, *Game of Death*, pp. 86, 226 n. 6.

42. Some examples drawn from Livy: *vis virtusque* (21.41.17), *vi ac virtute* (22.5.2), *vim virtutemque* (23.45.10), *vi ac virtute* (15.23.1), *vis atque virtus* (25.38.10), *vi atque virtute* (26.39.11), *virtute ac viribus* (34.14.11). Cf. Livy 4.58.4, 24.5.14, 31.33.9, 42.47.7–8. *vir enim vocatur a viribus* (Cassiodorus, *Expositio Psalmorum, Corpus Christianorum*, Series Latina, vol. 97 [1958]: 1.1.1.108–109). "He is called a *vir* because the *vis* in him is greater than in the female, and from this *virtus* gets its name" (*vir nuncupatus est, quia maior in eo vis est quam in femina; unde et virtus nomen accepit* [Lactantius, *De opificio dei* 12.16]; Isidore, *Etymologiae* 11.2.17, Lindsay ed.). Cf. Eisenhut, *Virtus Romana*, p. 121; Moore, *Artistry and Ideology*, p. 11.

43. For the conjunction of *virtus, vis*, and *viriditas*, see Isidore, *Etymologiae* 17.6.8., Lindsay ed.

44. "The *Querquetulanae virae* are thought to have been the nymphs who presided over the oak trees at the time of year when they came into bloom *(virescenti)*.... The ancient Romans called women *viras* whence we still have *virgines* et *viragines*" (Festus-Paulus p. 314, Lindsay ed.). For *vira* as an ancient word for woman, see also Isidore, *Etymologiae* 11.2.23, Lindsay ed. The Roman "virgin" *(virgo)* was not our "virgin" at all, but a "ripe" young woman ready for a man. "She is said to be a *virgo* on account of her youthful bloom and vigor *(viridiori aetate)* (ibid. 11.2.21). "Young cows and bulls are called *vituli et vitulae* on account of their *viriditas*, that is, their youthful vigor and fertility—just so the virgin, *virgo*, gets her name" (*Vitulus et vitula a viriditate vocati sunt, id est aetate viridi, sicut virgo* [ibid. 12.1.32. Isidore is quoting, almost verbatim, Servius, *In Bucolica* 3.30.]) See also the entries for *virgo* in P. Pierrugues, *Glossarium Eroticum Linguae Latinae*, Berlin, 1908; the *Oxford Latin Dictionary*, Oxford, 1982; Robert Malby, *A Lexicon of Ancient Latin Etymologies*, Leeds, 1991.

45. In the Empire, as "manliness" becomes increasingly unearned, innate, and ontological, it becomes increasingly paradoxical for a woman to possess *virtus*.

46. "The great soul belongs not to the man who is generous with what belongs to others, but the man who extracts from himself what he gives to another" (*Non est magni animi qui de alieno liberalis est, sed ille qui, quod alteri donat, sibi detrahit* [Seneca, *De clementia* 1.20.3]).

parisoned, he leapt into the chasm (Livy 7.6.1–6).[47] For the Romans, the voluntary death of a Curtius or a Decius Mus was, to use the words of Bakhtin, "a pregnant and birth-giving death."[48] And so Roman *virtus*, the aggressive and self-aggrandizing will of the strutting warrior (with its potential to disrupt all bonds and balance within Roman society) was controlled by its expiatory, sacrificial aspects; a man atoned for expanding by expending his being, by wasting the breath of his life. "Manhood," as Gilmore explains, "is the defeat of childhood narcissism."[49]

In the Roman contest culture, then, to will death was not to deny life but to carve its contour.[50] The contest drew its profile on the moment between exhilaration and annihilation, the electric and terrifying moment of the sacred.[51] "Who, with the prospect of envy, death, and punishment staring him in the face, does not hesitate to defend the Republic, he truly can be reckoned a *vir*" (Cicero, *Pro Milone* 30.82).[52]

47. "When, in an ominous portent, the foundations of the Empire were collapsing, Curtius filled up the gulf with the greatest of treasures, that is, virtue and piety and a splendid death" (*sidentia imperii fundamenta ostento fatali Curtius maximis bonis, hoc est virtute ac pietate ac morte praeclara, expleverat* [Pliny, *Naturalis historia* 15.20.78]). Cf. Varro, *De lingua latina* 5.148; Dionysius 14.11 1–5; Valerius Maximus 5.6.2.

48. "Who dies by *virtus* nevertheless does not perish" (*Qui per virtutem periit at non interiit* [Plautus, *Captivi* 690, cf. 683–89]). Mikhail Bakhtin, *Rabelais and His World*, trans. Helene Iswolsky, Cambridge, Mass., 1968 [1929], pp. 394-395.

49. *Manhood in the Making*, p. 224.

50. For Yolande Grisé, a voluntary death could express the intensity of the Roman love of life and of action: "Ultime stratégie de survie en quelque sorte, engendrée par rien d'autre que cet extraordinaire amour de l'homme romain pour l'*agi*. À cet égard, l'assertion de Schopenhauer énonce fort lucidement l'aspect le plus romain d'un acte comme le suicide: 'loin d'être la négation du vouloir-vivre (le suicide) en est une affirmation passionnée.'. . . il est donc permis de dire qu'il fut l'approbation de la vie jusque la mort, une sorte d'incommensurable *libido vivendi*" (*Le suicide dans la Rome antique*, Paris, 1982, p. 92). "À Rome, peut-être plus qu'ailleurs, loin de nier tout désir de vivre, le suicide fut vécu comme l'affirmation même d'un goût de vivre tel qu'on plaçait la qualité de la vie au-dessus d'une quantité de jours vécu trop médiocrement: on ne refusait pas la vie, mais une condition de vie" (p. 284). "He never wished to live who did not wish to die" (*vivere noluit qui mori non vult* [Aufidius Bassus, quoted by Seneca, *Epistulae* 30.10]). Of another culture, Bartolomé Bennassar remarks, "This [Spanish] interest in death is only love of life carried to its most logical conclusion. Unamuno has expressed it perfectly: 'To forget death is to forget life itself' " (*The Spanish Character, Attitudes, and Mentalities from the Sixteenth to the Nineteenth Century*, Berkeley, 1979, p. 237). Compare the "Confession" of Dostoevsky's Ippolit in *The Idiot*: "Perhaps suicide is the only action I still have time to begin and end by my own will. And perhaps I want to take advantage of the last possibility of action."

51. For voluntary death as the "moment of truth" in Roman culture, see Peter Schunck, "Studien zur Darstellung des Endes von Galba, Otho, und Vitellius in den Historien des Tacitus," *Symbolae Osloenses* 39 (1964): 38–82. For the ancient Romans, the border between life and death was at the center of existence. For us, life is at the center and death is at the periphery.

52. *proposita invidia, morte, poena qui nihilo segnius rem publicam defendit, is vir vere putandus est.* "It is not the part of a *vir*, and least of all a Roman, to hesitate to surrender that breath of life to the fatherland that he owes to nature." (*non est viri minimeque Romani dubitare eum spiritum, quem naturae debeat, patriae reddere* [Cicero, *Philippicae* 10.10.20]).

At least until the age of Augustus, as Paul Zanker points out, Latin had no vo-cabulary to speak of "salvation" as an ultimate value in the Christian sense.[53] In Cicero's day, Roman history was still filled with examples of Romans putting the dangerous and honorable before the salutary and expedient, "led by the splendor of honor and without any thought for their own interest" (*De finibus* 5.22.64).[54] "That which appears most splendid," he asserts, "is that done with a great and exalted spirit and in disregard of the concerns of mortal life" (*De officiis* 1.18.61).[55]

The willingness to expend everything—up to and including the state—was, para-doxically, the final insurance of the continued existence of both the state and the spirit. Sulla, anticipating a fight with the enemy Iugurtha, admonishes his small force: "You will be the safer the less you spare yourself" (*Bellum Iugurthinum* 107.1).[56] When the slave Libanus, anticipating torture, offers his hide without reserve to Leonida's dangerous plot, the latter exclaims: "Hold on to this firmness of spirit and we will be safe" (Plautus, *Asinaria* 317–320).[57] When someone inquired of Scipio, preparing to cross from Sicily to Africa to fight the Carthaginians, on what he dared to place his faith, Scipio pointed to three hundred soldiers being drilled in a field and then to a tower overlooking the sea. "There is not one of those men," he said, "who would not, at my command, climb to the top and throw himself down head first" (Plutarch, *Regum et imperatorum apophthegmata*, Scipio Maior 4 [*Moralia* 196C]). As Seneca succinctly put it, "Who scorns his own life is lord of yours" (*Epistulae* 4.8).[58]

53. *The Power of Images in the Age of Augustus*, trans. Alan Shapiro, Ann Arbor, 1988, p. 44. Andreas Alföldi traces the gradual transformation of the Roman notion of the "savior" from the hero who risked his life in battle to the powerful politician and thence to the emperor/father/god, the *salvator mundi* (Propertius 4.6.37) in *Der Vater des Vaterlandes im römischen Denken*, Darmstadt, 1971. For the impor-tant implications of this evolution, see part 2.

54. *dignitatis splendore ductos immemores fuisse utilitatum suarum.* "All, without exception, approve and applaud that disposition of the spirit that not only seeks no advantage for itself, but contrary to its own advantage preserves its faith" (*Nemo est igitur quin hanc affectionem animi probet atque laudet quo non modo utili-tas nulla quaeritur sed contra utilitatem etiam conservatur fides* [*De finibus* 5.22.63]). So much power has "the honorable" that it can render "the useful" all but invisible (*Tanta vis est honesti, ut speciem utilitatis obscuret* [*De officiis* 3.11.47]). Honor entailed danger—inevitably. See the potted arguments in the *Auctor ad Herennium* 3.5.9. Cf. Cicero, *Partitiones oratoriae* 90; *De finibus* 2.17.56–57; *De officiis* 3.32.114–116; Anthony A. Long, "Cicero's Politics in *De Officiis*" in *Justice and Generosity: Studies in Hellenistic Social and Political Philosophy*, ed. André Laks and Malcolm Schofield, Cambridge, 1994, p. 218 n. 13.

55. *splendidissimum videri, quod animo magno elatoque humanasque res despiciente factum sit.* For the *rerum hu-manarum despicientia* of the *vir*, see also *Tusculanae disputationes* 2.13.32, *De officiis* 1.20.66.

56. *quanto sibi in proelio minus pepercissent, tanto tutiores fore.* The *Auctor ad Herennium* offers the following paradoxical argument to the person who prefers honor to safety: "Not he who is safe in the present, but he who lives honorably, lives safely—whereas he who lives shamefully cannot be secure for ever" (*eum tute vivere qui honeste vivat, non qui in praesentia incolumnis, et eum qui turpiter vivat incolumem in perpetuum esse non posse* [3.5.9].)

57. *si istam firmitudinem animi optines, salvi sumus.*

58. *quisquis vitam suam contempsit, tuae dominus est.* The Romans delighted in the story of the person whose spirit could not be defeated because he or she held nothing in reserve, from Lucretia to

Verginius wins the contest of wills between himself and the vastly more powerful Appius Claudius by slaughtering his beloved daughter. In the Romans' potlatch mentality, Verginius's willingness to sacrifice what he loved most in the world was his trump card.[59] The Roman military was made invincible by men like the consul Titus Manlius Torquatus, who executed his own son for military disobedience, preferring "the claims of majesty and *imperium* to his natural instincts and paternal affections" (*De finibus* 7.23).[60] Cicero's Regulus rejects the supplications of his family for the same reason that Livy's Brutus rejects the prayers of his sons and the Christian Perpetua repeatedly dismisses her father's tearful entreaties:[61] no act could so clearly prove the will of a man or woman as one that went against the promptings of one's nature as a human being (and no urge was as natural for a human as to love one's child).[62] We are appalled to hear Lucan's Vulteius, addressing his troops on the eve of their mass and mutual suicide, declare that their honor would be the greater if their children and old folks were there to die with them (*Bellum civile* 4.503–504).[63] But, like Seneca's and Euripides's Medea, like the Jepthah of Judges, or the mother of

---

Seneca's convict who strangled himself with the outhouse sponge (*Epistulae* 70.20–21). A Roman could redeem even lost honor by self-destruction. Lucretia, Cicero tells us, washed from herself the stain of her rape by her voluntary death (*per vim oblatum stuprum voluntaria morte lueret* [*De finibus* 5.22.64]). "Let me arm the hand that will vindicate my honor," Seneca's suicidal Phaedra exclaims (*proin castitatis vindicem armemus manum* [*Phaedra* 261, cf. 250–254, 258–260]). See Valerius Maximus 5.8.4; Lucan, *Bellum civile* 4.465–581. For self-vindication by self-destruction, see Carlin Barton, "Savage Miracles: The Redemption of Lost Honor in Roman Society and the Sacrament of the Gladiator and the Martyr," *Representations* 45 (winter 1994): 41–71.

59. Cicero admires the Spartan mother who, when she heard the news of her son's death in battle, remarked, "To that end I bore him, to be someone who would not hesitate to meet death for his country" (*Idcirco, inquit, genueram, ut esset qui pro patria mortem non dubitaret occumbere* [*Tusculanae disputationes* 1.42.102]). Cornelia was as proud of her two murdered sons as of her conquering father (cf. Plutarch, *Gaius Gracchus* 19).

60. *Quod vero securi percussit filium, privavisse se etiam videtur multis voluptatibus, cum ipsi naturae patrioque amori praetulit ius maiestatis atque imperi.*

61. Regulus: *De officiis* 1.13.39. For the conviction of the Romans of the Republic that, however great the personal cost, fatherland came before family, see Lucilius 1353–1354, W. Krenkel ed.; Cicero, *Ad familiares* 4.5.2, 12.14.7; Plutarch, *Fabius Maximus* 24.2; W. Kroll, *Die Kultur der ciceronischen Zeit*, vol. 1, Leipzig, 1933, p. 6.

62. For the "natural" and particular love of parents for children, see Cicero, *De officiis* 1.4.12, Polybius 6.54.5. Enduring the death of one's child took tremendous fortitude, the kind demonstrated by Cornelia (Seneca, *Ad Marciam* 16.3; Plutarch, *Gaius Gracchus* 19), Arria (Pliny, *Epistulae* 3.16.3–6), or the Elder Cato (Cicero, *De senectute* 4.12). Cf. Tacitus, *Annales* 3.6; Yan Thomas, *"Vitae necisque potestas," Du châtiment dans la Cité: Supplices corporels et peine de mort dans le monde antique*, Rome, 1984, pp. 516–517 n. 39.

63. "In not holding us captive together with our old folks and children, envious Fortune has subtracted much from our honor" (*Abscidit nostrae multum fors invida laudi, / quod non cum senibus capti natisque tenemur*).

Second and Fourth Maccabees, men and women of honor made very unnatural parents.[64] The Romans' refusal to ransom their own soldiers after Cannae reflects this competitive wasting: according to Polybius, Hannibal felt less joy at having crushed the Romans than shock at the greatness of spirit *(megalopsychia)* shown by the Romans and by the Roman captives themselves, who, rejected by their countrymen, voluntarily surrendered themselves to the power of the Punic general and to their doom in fulfillment of their oaths (6.58.13). The Romans, Polybius explains, recognized the sinister intention behind Hannibal's merciful offer to ransom back the survivors of Cannae: Hannibal needed the money, to be sure, but more to the point, he knew that he could undermine the ferocity of the Romans in battle if he could cause them to hope for life (6.58.9).[65]

Cicero follows Polybius in asserting that Hannibal's will was broken, his *animus fractus*, when he received news that the Romans were "discarding" their soldiers at the moment when they were most in need of them (*De officiis* 3.32.114).[66] The defeated Romans not only refused to ransom their own men but ordained by law that soldiers must either vanquish or die, so that, according to Polybius, there might be no hope of survival in case of defeat (6.58.11).[67] And so, Manlius, walled up in the citadel during the Gallic occupation, though suffering the extremities of

---

64. Compare the father of Pseudo-Quintilian, *Declamationes maiores* 19, esp. 19.4 (Hakanson ed.); the wife of Hasdrubal in Valerius Maximus 3.2, *externa* 8; Florus 1.31.17; Appian, *Punica* 19.131; Josephus's brigand of Galilee (*Bellum Iudaicum* 1.312–313), Simon of Scythopolis (ibid. 2.469–476), the Spartan Damatria (Plutarch, *Lacaenarum apophthegmata* [*Moralia* 240F]), and the mother, Sethe, in Toni Morrison's novel *Beloved* (New York, 1987). Parents who valued their honor and that of their children, John Crook explains, sometimes disinherited the latter. "It was an overturning of nature," he says (*"Patria Potestas," Classical Quarterly* n.s. 17 [1967]: 120).

65. Cf. Ernst Bux, *"Clementia Romana:* Ihr Wesen und ihre Bedeutung für die Politik des römishen Reiches," *Würzburger Jahrbucher für die Altertumswissenschaft* 3 (1948): 208. Augustus used the same strategy as Hannibal, and for the same purposes, but (for reasons that will become clear) with more success. Horace's Regulus foresaw the ruin that would come to Rome *(perniciem veniens in aevum)* should their captive youths *not* perish without pity *(si non periret immiserabilis captiva pubes* [*Carmina* 3.5.13–18]).

66. The Etruscan enemy was stupefied by Horatius's seemingly suicidal stand at the bridge (Polybius 6.55.2; Livy 2.10.9; Valerius Maximus 3.2.1). The Gallic invaders were shocked into immobility by the defenseless audacity of the Roman *seniores*, as well as by the apparently foolhardy bravery of men like Fabius Dorsuo (Livy 5.41.8–9, 5.46.3). The Samnites were amazed at the superhumanity of the Roman general Decius who, before galloping alone into their ranks, devoted himself to death (Livy 8.9.10).

67. *aut vincere aut emori* (Cicero, *De officiis* 3.32.114). Suetonius's Mallonia stabbed herself, like Lucretia, rather than be dishonored by the emperor Tiberius, "that foul-mouthed, hairy, stinking old man" (*Tiberius* 45). For other examples of the Roman ideal of "death before dishonor," see Naevius, *Bellum Punicum*, frags. 59–62, Warmington ed.; Cicero, *Tusculanae disputationes* 2.24.58, *De Officiis* 1.23.81; Caesar, *De bello Gallico* 5.37; Sallust, *Catilina* 20.9; Livy 3.45.11, 22.50.6–7, 23.29.7; Horace, *Carmina* 3.2.1–24; Seneca Rhetor, *Controversiae* 10.3.3; Seneca, *Phaedra* 259–261; Juvenal, *Satirae* 8.83; Tacitus, *Historia* 4.58.2; Appian, *Bellum Hannibalicum* 5.28; Josephus, *Bellum Iudaicum* 6.362.

hunger, cast down loaves of bread from the citadel. "He did this," according to Florus, "to deprive the enemy of their hopes" (1.7.15).[68] All was the price of all.

THE ELIXIR OF DESPERATION

Even the smallest challenge was important in Roman life. The Roman, Horace tells us, will fight over anything: whether the hair of goats can be called wool; whether Castor or Dolichos is more cunning; whether the road built by Appius or that built by Minucius is better for a journey to Brundisium (*Epistulae* 1.18.15, 19–20).[69] The litigious and casuistic Romans loved to wrangle over their own relative merits and those of the Attic or Asiatic styles.[70] But the more extreme the ordeal, the greater its annealing, its defining power. "The greater the difficulty, the greater the splendor" (Cicero, *De officiis* 1.19.64).[71] "The greater the torment the greater the glory" (Seneca, *De providentia* 3.9).[72] "He has won without glory who has won without peril" (ibid. 3.4).[73] Fortune, Seneca believed, sought out the great soul to be challenged. "Mucius was tested by fire, Fabricius by poverty, Rutilius by exile, Regulus by torture, Socrates by poison, Cato by death. One cannot

---

68. *Manlius... ut spem hostibus demeret, quamquam in summa fame,... panes ab arce iaculatus est.* Cf. Livy 4.48.4.

69. A Roman was implicated not only in the endless chain of his or her own contests, but also in the competitions of everyone with whom he or she identified. On the candidacy of his friend whom he has recommended to the Emperor, the Younger Pliny declares, "My sense of honor, my reputation, my dignity is at stake" (*meus pudor, mea existimatio, mea dignitas in discrimen adducitur* [*Epistulae* 2.9.1]).

70. A Roman had to be the best, the greatest, the first, the *unus vir.* I can give only a small sampling of similarly expressed claims: Quintus Metellus, in the funeral oration for his father Lucius Caecilius Metellus, who died in 221 B.C.E., said that his father wished to be "first among warriors, the best of orators, the bravest of commanders, to perform great deeds under his own auspices, to enjoy the greatest honor, to be the smartest and to be considered the most eminent of senators" (*voluisse enim primarium bellatorem, optimum oratorem, fortissimum imperatorem, auspicio suo maximas res geri, maximo honore uti, summa sapientia esse, summum senatorem haberi* [Pliny, *Naturalis historia* 7.43.140]). The inscription on the sarcophagus of Lucius Cornelius Scipio (who died circa 240–230 B.C.E.) reads: "This one most Romans agree was the best of all good men" (*honc oino ploirume cosentiont Romane / duonoro optimo fuise viro* [*Corpus Inscriptionum Latinarum*, vol. 1.2, no. 9 = *Inscriptiones Latinae Selectae*, vol. 1, no. 3].). Cicero took as his own the Homeric slogan "Ever to excel" *(aien aristeuein)* (Cicero, *Ad Quintum fratrem* 3.5.4; 1.1.43). Who was the most courageous Roman of all time, according to Pliny the Elder, was ever a matter of debate in Rome (*Historia naturalis* 7.28.101). Plautus's parasite Saturio brags that no one could ever beat him or his ancestors in eating (*Persa* 53–59). Cf. Cicero, *De senectute* 61; Caesar, *De bello civili* 1.4; Livy 39.40; Valerius Maximus 8.15.12; Florus 2.13.14; Pliny, *Historia naturalis* 7.34–35.120, 7.43.140; T. P. Wiseman, "Competition and Co-operation," in *Roman Political Life 90 B.C.—A.D. 69*, Exeter, 1985, pp. 3–19; l'Hoir, "Heroic Epithets," pp. 230–233; John Lendon, *Empire of Honour*, Oxford, 1997, pp. 34–35.

71. *quo difficilius, hoc praeclarius.* "Virtue aims at what is hard" (*tendit in ardua virtus* [Ovid, *Epistulae ex Ponto* 2.2.111]). Cf. Sallust, *Bellum Iugurthinum* 89.6.

72. *quanto plus tormenti, tanto plus erit gloriae.*

73. *eum sine gloria vinci, qui sine periculo vincitur.*

find a great *exemplum* except in misfortune."[74] The second-century Christian Minucius Felix admonished the Romans: "Your men of power, whom you commend as moral examples, flourished through their tribulations."[75] As for us, he asserts, "God tries and examines each one through adversity; he weighs the spirits of individuals through perils, exploring the will of a man up to the extreme moment of death" (*Octavius* 36.8–9).[76] "Without an adversary," Seneca asserts, "*virtus* shrivels.[77] We see how great and how viable *virtus* is when, by endurance, it shows what it is capable of" (*De providentia* 2.4).[78] "Adversity does not defeat the spirit of a brave man. Rather, the spirit holds its ground and imprints its own complexion onto everything that happens" (ibid. 2.1–2).[79]

Sallust notes with pride how often a small band of Romans routed a larger force of enemies or stormed a fortified town: "To men like these no ordeal was

74. *ignem experitur in Mucio, paupertatem in Fabricio, exilium in Rutilio, tormenta in Regulo, venenum in Socrate, mortem in Catone. magnum exemplum nisi mala fortuna non invenit.* Cf. Seneca, *Epistulae* 98.12. For Syrus the slave, "No great or memorable deed is accomplished without peril" (*non fit sine periclo facinus magnum nec memorabile* [Terence, *Heautontimorumenos* 314]). "That was a manly act: to bear adverse fortune easily" (*erat istuc virile, ferre advorsam fortunam facul* [Accius 440, Warmington ed.]).

75. *omnes... vestri viri fortes, quos in exemplum praedicatis, aerumnis suis inclyti floruerunt.* For Livy's Torquatus, the dead on the field of Cannae were the *exempla virtutis* (22.60.14). Why, Seneca asks, are good men subject to pain and suffering and death? The answer: "So that they might teach others to endure them; they were born to serve as a pattern" (*Ut alios pati doceant: nati sunt in exemplar* [*De providentia* 6.3]).

76. *[deus] in adversis unumquemque explorat et examinat, ingenium singulorum periculis pensitat, usque ad extreman mortem voluntatem hominis sciscitatur.*

77. The Romans appreciated the worthy foe. There were still three statues of Hannibal in the Rome of Pliny the Elder, more than two and a half centuries after the end of the Hannibalic War (*Historia naturalis* 34.15.32). Timothy Moore points out that no man in Livy is credited as often with the quality of *virtus* as Hannibal. His Roman conqueror Scipio comes second (*Artistry and Ideology*, p. 13). Livy has Scipio praise Hannibal's generalship at Zama (Livy 30.35.5) as Tacitus extols the German general Arminius (*Annales* 2.88.3–4). For other characteristic examples of admiration expressed by Romans toward their personal adversaries, see Pliny, *Historia naturalis* 7.44.144; Plutarch, *Regum et imperatorum apophthegmata;* Cicero 20 (*Moralia* 205E); Suetonius, *Julius* 75.4.

78. *marcet sine adversario virtus; tunc apparet quanta sit quantumque polleat, cum quid possit patientia ostendit.* "Mars loves a fair field" (*Aequum Mars amat* [Petronius, *Satyricon* 34]). The Romans liked to imagine themselves as so wanting a fair and strenuous contest, a contest that followed rules, that they would disown—or at least be embarrassed by—any unfair advantage or dirty trick. And so Camillus sent back home in bonds the traitorous Faliscan schoolmaster who would have surrendered his pupils as hostages to the Romans, and Fabricius refused to poison the enemy Pyrrhus when given the chance. Cf. esp. Livy 42.47.5–8; Ennius, *Annales* 194–207, Vahlen ed.; Cicero, *De officiis* 1.13.40, 3.22.86; Livy 5.27, 26.39.11; Frontinus, *Strategemata* 4.4.1–2; Valerius Maximus 6.5.1; Petronius, *Satyricon* 15.19; Gellius, *Noctes Atticae* 3.8; Plutarch, *Pyrrhus* 21, *Regum et imperatorum apophthegmata*, Fabricius 4–5 (*Moralia* 195B); Pseudo-Sallust, *Epistulae ad Caesarem* 2.7.1; Tacitus, *Annales* 2.88.

79. *adversarium impetus rerum viri fortis non vertit animum. Manet in statu et quicquid evenit in suum colorem trahit.* "Every represented torment of the human body implies a reflection on what it means to be a human being; and the more radical the former, the more urgent the latter" (Glenn W. Most, "*Disiecti membra poetae:* The Rhetoric of Dismemberment in Neronian Poetry," in *Innovations of Antiquity*, ed. Ralph Hexter and Daniel Selden, New York, 1992, pp. 409–410).

unfamiliar, no position rough or difficult, no armed foe formidable; their courage conquered all obstacles. But the greatest competition for glory was amongst themselves; each rushed to be the first to strike an enemy, to climb a wall, to be conspicuous in action" (*Catilina* 7.5–6).[80]

Statesmen like Cato the Elder, Marius, and Cicero liked to think of themselves as struggling to the top against all odds and opposition. In the same way, writers like Livy, Sallust, Virgil, and Florus conceived of Roman history as a succession of trials, from the expulsion of the monarchy and the Gallic invasions to the wars against Carthage and the Catilinarian conspiracy. The triumph of Rome was the end and fruit of a long series of often disastrous bouts with enemies, rebels, and diseases.[81]

At perhaps the shining moment of all Livy's Roman history, the messengers arrived at the city with news of Hannibal's defeat of the Romans at Cannae in 216 B.C.E. Fifty thousand dead on the field. "No other nation in the world," according to Livy, "could have suffered so tremendous a series of disasters and not been overwhelmed" (22.54.10).[82] And the great soul, the *magnus animus,* of the Romans was revealed in their unwillingness to so much as mention peace after Cannae.[83] For the imperial historian Florus, at the crucial moment the Gallic horde, having smashed the Romans at the battle of the Alia, approached the walls of the defenseless city. "Then, as on no other occasion, true Roman *virtus* was revealed" (1.7.8).[84] What you were, finally, was what you could live without. It was the honed, stripped-down soul that shone with the greatest splendor.

---

80. *talibus viris non labor insolitus, non locus ullus asper aut arduus erat, non armatus hostis formidulosus; virtus omnia domuerat. sed gloriae maxumum certamen inter ipsos erat: se quisque hostem ferire, murum ascendere conspici dum tale facinus faceret, properabat.* There was lively competition amongst the soldiers, according to Polybius, for public recognition of their courage—courage shown in giving or risking their own lives for the Republic or one another (6.39, 6.54.4).

81. "The whole of [Livy's] Roman history is...represented as a period of trial, in which the military and civil virtues of the Roman people are thoroughly tested and hardened so that they become physically and morally capable of world-leadership" (P. G. Walsh, "Livy and Stoicism," *American Journal of Philology* 79 [1958]: 359; cf. 360–61). "Roman History [in Virgil] is...presented as in part a series of perils and trials overcome....In Sallust, Roman *virtus* was symbolized by survival against all odds" (Horsfall, "Virgil, History and the Roman Tradition," pp. 79–80. See Polybius 6.10.13–14, 1.63.9; Sallust, *Catilina* 53.2–4; Livy 6.21.2; Florus 1.7.2 ff.; Moses Hadas, "Livy as Scripture," *American Journal of Philology* 61 (1940): 445; Donald Earl, *The Political Thought of Sallust,* Cambridge, 1961, p. 98; G. Maslakov, "Valerius Maximus and Roman Historiography: A Study of the *exempla* Tradition," *Aufstieg und Niedergang der römischen Welt,* 2.32.1, Berlin, 1984, p. 452.

82. *nulla profecto alia gens tanta mole cladis non obruta esset.*

83. *Nec tamen eae clades defectionesque sociorum moverunt ut pacis usquam mentio apud Romanos fieret....quo in tempore ipso adeo magno animo civitas fuit* (Livy 22.61.13–14). Cf. Livy 22.53–61.

84. *Fuso exercitu iam moenibus urbis propinquabant. Erant nulla praesidia. Tum igitur sic, ut numquam alias, apparuit vera illa Romana virtus.* He immediately recounts the story of the Roman *seniores* devoting themselves to death and awaiting "each in his dignity" *(in sua quisque dignitate)* certain annihilation at the hands of the Gauls (1.7.9–10).

"The Romans had a greater spirit after the terrible disaster of Cannae than they would ever have in success," Cicero declares (*De officiis* 3.11.47).[85] "The Romans, both singly and as a group, are most to be feared when they stand in real danger" (Polybius 3.75.8).[86] Mucius, according to Livy, was more to be feared than fearing at the very moment when, destitute of help, he stood before the tribunal of king Porsena (2.12.8).[87] As Nathan Rosenstein's work shows, the Romans did not stigmatize defeat; rather they, like the mother of the murdered Gracchi, prided themselves on their ability to bear it with equanimity *(ferre aequo animo)*.[88] Livy quotes Publius Scipio Africanus: "We Romans have kept and continue to keep the same spirit irrespective of any changes in our fortunes. Our souls are neither inflated by success nor diminished by failure" (37.45.12).[89] The victory of the Roman Horatii over the Alban Curiatii was intensified, for Livy, by the narrowness of Horatius's escape from death (1.25.13).[90] Indeed, in the minds of the Romans, their willingness to die and ability to endure defeat *justified* their aggressiveness and ensured their ultimate victory. Florus says of the invasion of the Gauls: "I do not know if this period should be considered mournful for the Roman people on account of its disasters, or glorious owing to the test which it offered for their valor. But certainly, the force of the calamity was such that I can only think that it was inflicted on them by heaven as a trial, because the immortal

85. *Cannensi calamitate accepta maiores animos habuit quam umquam rebus secundis: nulla timoris significatio, nulla mentio pacis.*
86. "It being in all cases the traditional Roman custom to show themselves most imperious and severe *(authadestatous kai barutatous)* in the season of defeat" (Polybius 27.8.8; cf. Livy 30.7.6). For the notion that Rome had far greater strength and spirit in adversity than in peace, see Sallust, *Catilina* 10.1–4, 11.8, *Bellum Iugurthinum* 31.20, 41.4–9; Livy 23.14.1. Caesar (like Antony or Captain Bligh) had a greater spirit in adversity than in success. *(semper tibi maiorem in adversis quam in secundis rebus animum esse* [Pseudo-Sallust, *Epistulae ad Caesarem* 2.1.5].) Livy compares the sufferings of the Romans at the hands of the Carthaginians with those that the Carthaginians had suffered at the hands of the Romans, from the battle of the Aegates Islands in the First Punic War to Zama in the Second. The Carthaginians' woes could not compare to the Romans—except that the former bore their woes with less spirit *(nulla ex parte comparandae sunt nisi quod minore animo latae sunt* [22.54.11]).
87. *ante tribunal regis destitutus tum quoque inter tantas fortunae minas metuendus magis quam metuens.*
88. *Imperatores Victi,* esp. p. 40; Plutarch, *Gaius Gracchus* 19.
89. *animos... eosdem in omni fortuna gessimus gerimusque, neque eos secundae res extulerunt nec adversae minuerunt.* As Ennius wrote of the day of battle, "On this day—whether we live or whether we die—the greatest glory will show herself to us" *(nunc est ille dies cum gloria maxima sese / nobis ostendat si vivimus sive morimur* [*Annales* 391–392, Vahlen ed.]). "It is never disgraceful to be overcome in a contest for honorable ends, provided that you do not throw down your arms and that, even when conquered, you still wish to conquer" *(Numquam enim in rerum honestarum certamine superari turpe est, dummodo arma non proicias et victus quoque velis vincere* [Seneca, *De beneficiis* 5.2.1, cf. 5.2.3–4]). For Roman indifference to defeat, see also Polybius 21.17.1; Livy 2.12.9, 42.62.7, 11, *periochae* 67; Tacitus, *Annales* 3.6.4; Zonaras 8.18; D. C. Earl, "Political Terminology in Plautus," *Historia* 9 (1960): 238 and *The Moral and Political Tradition of Rome,* London, 1967, p. 32; Rosenstein, *Imperatores Victi,* pp. 121–122, 133–140.
90. *Romani ovantes ac gratulantes Horatium accipiunt, eo maiore cum gaudio, quo prope metum res fuerat.*

gods wished to know whether Roman valor deserved to rule the world" (1.7.2).[91] Lucilius remarks, "The Roman people have frequently been defeated by force and overcome in many battles—but they have never lost the war—and that is all that matters" (frags. 683–684, W. Krenkel ed.).[92] "That lot," Livy declares, "has been given to us by some fate that in all great wars, having been defeated, we prevail" (26.41.9).[93]

It is difficult for a modern postcolonialist to interpret the defensive postures of ruthless Roman imperialism as anything save cynicism. But it was, I would argue, the strength of the Roman agonistic ideal that allowed the Romans both to be ferociously aggressive and simultaneously to see themselves as strenuously defending themselves and their allies or righteously retaliating for wrongs done.[94] "Up

91. *Quod tempus populo Romano nescio utrum clade funestius fuerit, an virtutis experimentis speciosius. Ea certe fuit vis calamitatis ut in experimentum inlatam putem divinitus, scire volentibus immortalibus dis, an Romana virtus imperium orbis mereretur.* "In Sallust, Roman *virtus* was symbolized by survival against odds.... In Livy—and far more in explicitly in Florus—the Romans are confronted by enemies, discord and disease for a purpose" (Horsfall, "Virgil, History and the Roman Tradition," p. 79).

92. *ut Romanus populus victus vi et superatus proeliis / saepe est multis, bello vero numquam, in quo sunt omnia.*

93. *Ea fato quodam data nobis sors est, ut magnis omnibus bellis victi viceremus.* "The Germans proclaimed that the Romans were invincible; no disaster could overcome them! When they had wrecked their fleet and lost their arms, when the shore was littered with the bodies of their horses and their men, they had broken in again with the same courage and ferocity—as if their numbers had been increased!" (*Quippe invictos et nullis casibus superabilis Romanos praedicabant, qui perdita classe, amissis armis, post constrata equorum virorumque corporibus litora eadem virtute, pari ferocia et velut aucto numero inrupissent* [Tacitus, *Annales* 2.26].) As has frequently been observed, the positive function of the enemy was to provide the strenuous ordeal that enabled the Romans to manifest the quality of their spirits. For the notion of the *metus hostilis*, the annealing "counterweight of fear" galvanizing the Roman spirit, see Polybius 6.18.1–4; Sallust, *Bellum Iugurthinum*, 41.1–3, 87.4, *Catilina* 10.1–2; Valerius Maximus 7.2.1–3; Livy 1.19.4, 2.35.145; Velleius 2.1.1; Plutarch, *Cato Maior* 27.1–3; Florus 1.47.1–3, 1.34.19; Augustine, *De civitate dei* 1.30–31; Orosius, *Historiae adversus paganos* 5.8; C. O. Brink and F. W. Walbank, "The Construction of the Sixth Book of Polybius," *Classical Quarterly* n.s. 4 (1954): 97–122, esp. pp. 103–104; *Commentary on Polybius*, vol. 1, Oxford, 1957, p. 697; Earl, *The Political Thought of Sallust*, pp. 13, 15, 41–49, 98, 104; Ulrich Knoche, "Der Beginn des römischen Sittenverfalls," *Vom Selbstverstandnis der Römer*, Heidelberg, 1962, pp. 111ff.; Hermann Strassburger, "Poseidonios on Problems of the Roman Empire," *Journal of Roman Studies* 55 (1965): 41–42; A. E. Astin, *Scipio Aemilianus*, Oxford, 1967, pp. 276–280; Lind, "Tradition of Roman Moral Conservatism," pp. 8–9, 54.

94. "Our people were by this time masters of the world because they defended their allies" (*noster autem populus sociis defendendis terrarum iam omnium potitus est* [Cicero, *De republica* 3.24.35]). For the retributive and defensive aspects of war that loomed so large in the Roman mind, see Livy 1.32.6–14, 30.31.4, 39.36.12; Matthias Gelzer, "Römische Politik bei Fabius Pictor," *Hermes* 68 (1933): 129–166, esp. p. 165; J. Rufus Fears, "The Cult of Virtues," *Aufstieg und Niedergang der römischen Welt*, 2.17.2, Berlin, 1981, p. 865; Susan Mattern, *Rome and the Enemy: Imperial Strategy in the Principate* (Berkeley, 1999, pp. 119–121, 183-194). Mattern describes the Romans as reacting very aggressively to seemingly minor breaches of treaty, as exaggerating the threat posed by rivals, and responding to crises with conquest or even attempted genocide while insisting that their concerns were for their own security. The Romans were particularly fond of the preemptive strike because it could always be interpreted as defensive.

against the wall" was, for the Romans, the most stimulating and indeed the strongest position. Like the valiant anadromic fish that fight their way up the Connecticut River, the Romans seemed to have a tropism for the swiftest current against them. To feel that they had won in warfare, as in the law court, Romans needed to see themselves as on the defensive.[95] In Roman stories of single combat (always the most prestigious form of combat), it was the big, blustering barbarian who made the aggressive move, the staunch little Roman who prevailed. To extrapolate from a fragment of a speech of Tiberius Gracchus preserved by Plutarch, the fighting words of the Roman soldiers were all defensive: "the ancestral lands," "the tombs of our ancestors," "the altars of our gods" (*Tiberius Gracchus* 9.5). The Romans needed to see themselves as fighting for *patria, domus, di penates.*[96]

And so, strangely to our modern preconceptions, when the great imperialists of the ancient Mediterranean recreated themselves as Homeric heroes, it was as defeated Trojans rather than victorious Achaeans. Silius's general Varro, his army smashed at Cannae, was thanked for not abandoning in despair the city of the Trojan "sons of Laomedon" (*Punica* 10.629). It is not the story of the victorious Achaeans but that of the defeated Trojans that thrilled the heart of Virgil's Dido, as it did the hearts of Virgil's Roman audience ("We were Trojans. There was a Troy").[97] Erich Gruen points out that this identification allowed the Romans to associate themselves with and simultaneously to distinguish themselves from the Greeks.[98] I agree with Gruen, but I would add that the Roman identification with the Trojans was also an emotional one: they romanticized the challenge of desperation. Pliny the Elder points out that of all the rewards given by the Romans for glorious deeds—the jeweled crown, the golden crown, the crown for scaling enemy ramparts, the crown for boarding men-of-war, the triumphal crown, the civic crown for saving the life of a citizen—none was as ancient or as respected as the crown of grass *(corona graminea),* the crown conferred upon the leader of a forlorn hope (*graminea numquam nisi in desperatione suprema contigit [Naturalis historia*

95. For Roman aggressive self-defense, see Terence, *Eunuchus* 4–6; Polybius, *Historiae* vol. 4, frag. 99, Buttner-Wobst ed.; Augustus, *Res gestae* 26. "For the Romans, although they were fighting far from their country, had been easily persuaded by their generals that they were fighting in defense of Italy and the city of Rome" (*Romanis enim, quamquam procul a patria pugnarent, facile persuaserant duces pro Italia atque urbe Romana eos pugnare* [Livy 19.29.7]).

96. Richard Saller, *Patriarchy, Property, and Death in the Roman Family,* Cambridge, 1994, p. 90. Camillus's fighting words were temples, wives, children, the soil of our native land (Livy 5.49.3); cf. Cicero, *De officiis* 1.17.53–55, 57.

97. The Romans were as preoccupied as the Japanese or the Irish with the image of the failed or doomed hero, as proud of the Fabii who fell at Cremera as the Spartans were of the men who fell at Thermopylae. See Barton, "Savage Miracles."

98. "The Advent of the Magna Mater," *Studies in Greek Culture and Roman Policy,* Leiden, 1990, pp. 5–33.

22.4.6–7]). For Pliny this was the highest honor a human being could attain (22.4.10).

Indeed, the edge that desperation gave to valor is a theme appearing throughout Roman literature. The consul Cato, in his first major battle near Emporiae in Spain in 195 B.C.E., deliberately chose his position in order to cut off his troops from any possibility of escape, so that there would be no hope for them except in their courage (*nusquam nisi in virtute spes est* [Livy 34.14.3 and 16.1]).[99] Lucan's Vulteius encourages his men:

> Let the enemy understand that our men are unconquered, and let them fear those spirits that rage while ready for death. They will try to tempt us with an offer of terms; they wish to destroy our resolve with the hope of living a dishonorable life.... Let them promise to pardon us; let them urge us to hope for salvation—so that when we plunge the hot steel into our vitals, they will not think that it is because we have given in to despair. (*Bellum civile* 4.505–512)[100]

"Nothing is more formidable than despair," the Roman general Vespasian declares (Josephus, *Bellum Iudaicum* 3.209).[101] In warfare, in the gladiatorial arena, in all the perils of human existence, it was not victory that mattered so much as that the struggle be "from the marrow" *(summis medullitas viribus)*, to borrow an expression from Apuleius (*Florida* 18.32). Seneca's virgin Polyxena, marching to her death, "took no step backward" *(audax virago non tulit retro gradum* [*Troades* 1151]).[102] Livy tells the story of the dying Roman soldier at Cannae, who, unable any longer to grasp a weapon with his hand, attacked the enemy with his teeth (22.51.9).

If every wall of one's defenses was breached but one preserved one's *animus*, one's *voluntas*, one still had being. Indeed, the breaching of all boundaries—provided the will endured—enhanced the power of that will. In considering various candidates for "bravest of all Romans," Pliny passes over such legendary figures

---

99. Cf. Appian, *Iberica* 40. For other stories of desperate Roman courage in warfare and determined resistence in defeat, see Livy 25.37.17–38.23, 30.7.6, 42.62.11.

100. *indomitos sciat esse viros timeatque furentes*
    et morti faciles animos.... Temptare parabunt
    foederibus turpique volent corrumpere vita.
    O utinam... /promittant veniam, iubeant sperare salutem,
    ne nos, cum calido fodiemus viscera ferro,
    desperasse putent.

Cf. 531–81. Consider Virgil's beautiful and famous line: "One salvation alone remains to the defeated: to hope for none" *(una salus victis nullam sperare salutem* [*Aeneis* 2.354]). Cf. Seneca, *Naturales questiones* 6.2.2.

101. *ouden gar alkimoteron einai tes apognoseos.* Cf. 3.141–154, 5.494.

102. According to Inga Clendinnen, "no step backward" was also the motto of the greatest warriors of the Aztec "Flowery Wars" ("The Cost of Courage in Aztec Society," *Past and Present* 107 [1985]: 61).

as Lucius Siccius Dentatus or Marcus Manlius Capitolinus, dismisses the great warlords of the late Republic, and crowns Marcus Sergius, grandfather of Catiline. "Sergius in his second campaign lost his right hand; in two campaigns he was wounded twenty-three times, with the result that he was crippled in both hands and both feet. Only his spirit was unimpaired" (*neutra manu, neutro pede satis utilis, animo tantum salvo* [*Historia naturalis* 7.28.104–106]). Pliny is thrilled not by victory or by daring exploits, but by the unbowed spirit. Seneca remarks,

> The Spartans take care that their citizens remain unconquerable, and it is *virtus* and a strong will that render them invincible, since even in insuperable odds their spirit is not defeated. For this reason no one says that the Fabii were "conquered," but that they were "killed," and Regulus was "captured" by the Carthaginians, not "defeated," and whoever else does not submit his *animus* even while oppressed by the violence and weight of raging fortune likewise cannot be overcome. (*De beneficiis* 5.3.2)[103]

Plutarch paraphrases the words that the younger Cato, driven into a corner, addressed to the Italians of Utica on the eve of their surrender to the enemy Caesar: "For his part, he had not only been unvanquished all his life but was indeed a victor now as far as he chose to be" (*Cato Minor* 64.5).[104] The last words directed by the doomed Scaurus to his captors, the ferocious Cimbri, about to cross the Alps and invade Italy, were: "The Romans cannot be defeated" (*Romanos vinci non posse* [Livy, *periochae* 67]).

The Romans of the Republic, to be sure, savored their victories and celebrated their victors—but they did so cautiously and sparingly. Victory was deliriously festive but also momentary, conditional, and dangerous. They could absorb victory only in small doses, however delicious, because of its perilous social and spiritual side-effects.[105] Victory was proof of the superhuman character of the victorious general, proof of his exceptional vigor and potency; but it also threatened to inebriate the already powerful man and tempt him to rise above the restraints and limitations necessary to the fragile balances of civic life. The Romans understood that the too-successful warrior threatened to become the arrogant and hubristic rogue male,[106] a danger to his own people and, simultaneously, in danger from

---

103. *Hoc, quod illi* [*Lacedaemonii*] *in suis civibus custodiunt, virtus ac bona voluntas omnibus praestat, ne umquam vincantur, quoniam quidem etiam inter superantia animus invictus est. Ideo nemo trecentos Fabios victos dicit, sed occisos; et Regulus captus est a Poenis, non victus, et quisquis alius saevientis fortunae vi ac pondere oppressus non submittit animum.*

104. Romans were loath to be victims; they were *invicti*. For us, being a victim clears the conscience and allows us to seek revenge without guilt. For the Romans, confessing defeat signaled a broken spirit and the abandonment of all claims to honor. See part 2.

105. Fears emphasizes the limited nature of the Roman Republican triumph. "[The *triumphator*] was for the moment transported into the divine" ("The Theology of Victory at Rome," *Aufstieg und Niedergang der römischen Welt* 2.17.2, Berlin, 1981, p. 781).

106. Consider the story of Camillus's excessively splendid triumph over Veii:

them. Moreover, his apotheosis was an open invitation to the gods to direct their envy and malice toward the Roman people and their champions. Elaborate and unceasing precautions were taken by the Romans against these emotions, which (being ever in excess) threatened to disrupt every balancing system in Roman culture, most of all at moments of great good fortune.[107] The acclamation of the general as *imperator* ("victorious general") by his soldiers (i.e., as a free gift from his soldiers) helped to deflect the charge of arrogance from the head of the general, as did the ritual ridicule aimed at the general by his soldiers during the triumphal procession, the apotropaic *bulla* hung around his neck, the phallus hung on his chariot, and the admonitions "to look behind him and to remember that he was mortal" droned in his ear by the slave who stood beside him in his chariot.[108] The

Whether it was due to the magnitude of his exploit in taking the city...or to the congratulations showered upon him, Camillus was lifted up to vanity, cherished thoughts far from becoming to a civil magistrate subject to the law, and celebrated a triumph with great pomp: he actually had four white horses harnessed to a chariot on which he mounted and drove through Rome, a thing which no commander had ever done before or afterwards did. (Plutarch, *Camillus* 7.1 [Perrin trans.])

Cf. Livy 5.23.

107. See Carlin Barton, *The Sorrows of the Ancient Romans,* Princeton, 1993, chapters 3–6.

108. The victory must, at least in part, be attributed to the gods: "D'une part la Victoire atteste le caractère surhumain de l'âme, son exceptionelle puissance. D'autre part, les dieux peuvent faire aux hommes la grâce de descendre en eux pour un temps plus ou moins long leur âme chétive, et cette incarnation devient alors le cause immédiate de la Victoire" (André Piganiol, *Recherches sur les jeux romains,* Strasbourg, 1923, p. 125). Wilhelm Kroll, J. Rufus Fears, and H. S. Versnel, among others, interpret the triumphal garb (the dress and insignia of Jupiter Optimus Maximus, borrowed for the occasion from the Capitoline temple), as allowing the *triumphator* to represent Jupiter—and the ancient Etruscan king—on earth for a day. In other words, the Roman general assumed the excess of glory not in his own *persona* but in that of the god/king whom he was playing for a short time, as an honor, like playing Jesus in a passion play (Kroll, *Die Kultur der ciceronischen Zeit,* vol. 1, pp. 42–43; Fears, "Theology of Victory at Rome," p. 781). The divinization of the victorious general was, simultaneously, the epiphany of Jupiter (Versnel, *Triumphus,* Leiden, 1970, pp. 35–37, 42–48, 66–93). Fears emphasizes that in the Greek world since Alexander, victory was a monarchical concept focused on the charismatic individual. Although Rome increasingly absorbed these monarchical ideas into their notion of victory beginning in the early third century B.C.E., it was not until the time of the great warlords of the civil war that the system of inhibitions, which prevented any human from becoming too powerful, broke down in Rome. "In the Hellenistic world the numinous quality of victory adhered to the personality of the charismatic individual king and general.... Roman victories were rather a cooperative effort, the joint achievement of the commonwealth. Hence the mystique of victory must be attached to the personification of the *res publica*...; the magical victory-bearing epithet adheres to the person of Jupiter and Roma: *Jupiter Victor, Roma Victrix* ("Theology of Victory at Rome," p. 777, cf. 774–782). For the inseparability, in the Republic, of the victory of a Roman general from the collective honor and prosperity of the Roman people, see Cicero, *Pro Archia* 22; Erich Gruen, *Studies in Greek Culture and Roman Policy,* Berkeley, 1990, 110, 117–118, 121–123. Versnel points out that *felicitas* was not only "fortune" and "fertility" but also "bringing good fortune," "bestowing fertility." The ceremonies that elevated the victorious general were designed in part to capture, intensify, and channel the exceptional fortune of the *triumphator* to the benefit of the whole people (*Triumphus,* pp. 363–372).

supplicationes, the humble thank-offerings to the gods from the Roman people that preceded the Triumph; the victorious general's acts of liberality to gods and men on behalf of himself, his soldiers, and the state; and the attribution of the victory to the favor and inspiration of the gods were all designed to implicate the powers that be in the victory and forestall their resentment.[109] (The Romans praised a man's victories and accomplishments to the skies once he was safely dead, but to do so during his lifetime was an act of malice.)[110] The best hero, as in every warrior culture, was the dead hero. There were practical, if paradoxical, reasons of state for the Romans' romance with despair.

MAKING FACES

It was then the custom, in bad times, for a Roman to wear, on his face, the look of success.
LIVY 42.62.11[111]

As a mortal, what one risked in the contest was one's "face." Latin *facies* (from *facere,* to be effective, to pose, place, make) was not, like our "face," something one was born with; it was something that one made, that one willed into existence. It was the manifestation of one's being, the thing presented to view, the spectacle, form, or aspect. "Some think that the *facies* of a man refers only to the face, eyes, and cheeks, what the Greeks call *prosopon:* whereas *facies* refers to the whole form, the dimensions and, as it were, the construction *(factura)* of the entire body, being formed from *facio* as *species* is from *aspectus* and *figura* from *fingere*" (Gellius, *Noctes Atticae* 13.30.2).[112] "In its proper sense *facere,* 'to make,' is from *facies* 'appearance'; he is said to *facere,* 'to make,' a thing, who puts a *facies* on the thing which he makes. As the *fictor,* when he says *fingo,* 'I shape,' puts a *figura,* 'shape,' on the object" (Varro, *De lingua latina* 6.78).[113]

---

109. For the *supplicationes* after a victory, see Léon Halkin, *La supplication d'action de graces chez les romains,*" Paris, 1953. On the triumph see also R. Laqueur, "Über das Wesen des römischen Triumphs," *Hermes* 44 (1909): 215–236; Moore, *Artistry and Ideology,* pp. 10, 16. There were expiatory and purifying as well as celebratory aspects of the Roman triumph. See Burck, "Drei Grundwerte," p. 167.

110. Plutarch says of Caecilius Metellus, "he was forever warring with Scipio Aemilianus while Scipio lived, but felt very sad when he died and commanded his sons to take part in carrying out the bier. He said that he felt grateful to the gods, for Rome's sake, that Scipio had not been born to another nation" (Plutarch, *Regum et imperatorum apophthegmata,* Metellus 3, *Moralia* 202A). The elder Cato, in the *Origines,* would not name a Roman commander except by his rank—although he might name a military tribune or an elephant distinguished by an extraordinary act of valor.

111. *Ita tum mos erat in adversis rebus voltum secundae fortunae gerere....*

112. *quidam "faciem" esse hominis putant os tantum et oculos et genas, quod Graeci prosopon dicunt, quando "facies" sit forma omnis et modus et factura quaedam corporis totius, a "faciendo" dicta, ut ab "aspectu" "species" et a "fingendo" "figura."*

113. *proprio nomine dicitur facere a facie, qui rei quam facit imponit faciem. Ut fictor cum dicit "fingo" figuram imponit,... sic cum dicit "facio" faciem imponit.* For the evolution of *facies* from the face to the façade, see chapter 4.

One's face was one's *persona*, one's mask.[114] The *persona* was composed of the reputation *(existimatio, fama,* and *nomen)*, supported by effective energy *(virtus)*, and enforced by a sensitivity to shame *(pudor)*. The *persona* guaranteed the existence of the will, the driving vitality at the core: the *animus*. Accius's captive Andromache showed by her face that her spirit had not been broken *(Astyanax,* frags. 151–152, Warmington ed.).[115] Valentinus showed by his face that although he had been captured, he had not been defeated in spirit (Tacitus, *Historia* 4.85).[116] Young Hippolytus would not alter the ferocious expression on his face when the bull from the sea rose up to dismember him, but thundered that the vain terror could not break his spirit (Seneca, *Phaedra* 1064–1066).[117] The *persona* and the role expressed by it were the very boundary and definition of one's being, the *sine qua non* of existence. For the Romans there was no depth without surface.[118]

The face was also a provocation; whatever *persona* you publicly professed was a line drawn in the sand.[119] "I am a Roman. My name is Mucius," Livy's captive hero proclaims (2.12.9).[120] Marcus, the son of Cato Uticensis, fell at the battle of

---

114. For the *persona*, see F. Max Muller, *Biographies of Words*, London, 1888, pp. 32–47; Adolf Trendelenburg, "A Contribution to the History of the Word Person," trans. Carl H. Haessler, *Monist* 20 (1910): 336–363; Hans Rheinfelder, *Das Wort "Persona"*; *Geschichte seiner Bedeutungen mit besonderer Berücksichtigung des französischen und italienischen Mittelalters*, Halle, 1928; Marcel Mauss, "L'âme, le nom, et la personne," *Oeuvres*, vol. 2, Paris, 1969, pp. 131–135; Mauss, "A Category of the Human Mind: The Notion of Person, the Notion of 'Self,'" in *Sociology and Psychology: Essays*, trans. Ben Brewster, London, 1979; Robert C. Elliott, *The Literary Persona*, Chicago, 1982, pp. 19–32; Christopher Gill, "Personhood and Personality: The Four-*Personae* Theory of Cicero, *De Officiis* I," *Oxford Studies in Ancient Philosophy* 6 (1988): 169–199. See also the articles by Louis Dumont, Arnaldo Momigliano, and Godfrey Lienhardt in *The Category of the Person*, ed. Michael Carrithers, Steven Collins, and Steven Lukes, Cambridge, 1985.

115. *abducite intro, nam mihi miseritudine / commovit animum excelsa aspecti dignitas.*

116. *dux hostium Valentinus nequaquam abiecto animo quos spiritus gessisset, vultu ferebat.*

117. *feroci natus insurgens minax / vultu nec ora mutat et magnum intonat / haud frangit animum vanus hic terror meum.* Cf. Seneca, *Controversiae* 10.3.13.

118. Richard Majors and Janet Mancini Billson remark on the "masking" behavior of Black youths that "the cool, expressive life-style is not only a way of getting around dispiriting blocks to legitimate means of creative expression, it also acts as a way for the black male to accentuate or display his interior, deeper, self" *(Cool Pose: The Dilemmas of Black Manhood in America,* New York, 1992, p. 70). To quote a famous phrase of Nietzsche's, "Every profound spirit needs a mask" *(Beyond Good and Evil,* trans. R.J. Hollingdale, London, 1973, p. 40).

119. One looked for the contest when one professed one's *nomen* or identity. The Romans, for instance, assumed that the man or woman who proclaimed *Christianus sum* or *Joudaios eimi* were doing so as challenges. One can think of Cassius Clay or Lou Alcindor presenting to the public their new names. Would their audiences respect them? It was a wager. Britannicus refused to call his newly adopted brother by his adoptive name "Nero" and continued to call him "Ahenobarbus," to the latter's fury (Suetonius, *Nero* 7.1). When Vipsanius Agrippa became Marcus Agrippa, dropping the name that signaled his humble origin, his detractors continued spitefully to refer to it (Seneca Rhetor, *Controversiae* 2.4.13). Cf. Terence, *Eunuchus, prologus* 1–3.

120. *"Romanus sum,"* inquit, *"civis; C. Mucium vocant. hostis hostem occidere volui."*

Philippi. While the army fled, he stood his ground, and, as a final act, shouted out his name and that of his father (Plutarch, *Brutus* 49.9). The bleeding, shivering, pain-wracked Porcia says to Brutus: "I am Cato's daughter" (Plutarch, *Brutus* 13.7).[121]

VISIBILITY

I am a man among men; I stroll about with my head uncovered.
TRIMALCHIO IN PETRONIUS, *SATYRICON* 57.5[122]

For the Romans, being was being seen. Cicero regretted serving in Cilicia (as he had regretted serving in Sicily) because it meant acting in squalid obscurity, far from the urban limelight (*Ad familiares* 2.12.2). He wanted to be, in Horace's scornful words, "the good man whom the forum and every tribunal sees" (*vir bonus, omne forum quem spectat, et omne tribunal* [*Epistulae* 1.16.57]). One made oneself as conspicuous, as tender a target as possible. As Richard Brilliant points out, the full frontal posture with arm extended was the stance of honor in Roman art.[123]

Conversely, seeing was the privileged source of knowledge. In the words of Plautus, "Look, and then you'll know" (*em specta, tum scies* [*Bacchides* 1023]). "Those who see, they know distinctly" (*qui vident, plane sciunt* [*Truculentus* 490]). "They believe because they see" (*credunt quod vident* [*Asinaria* 202]).[124]

Being visible was a basic biological risk, to borrow a phrase from R. D. Laing. The proven person had weathered that risk. The proven person was *probatus, spectatus, expertus, argutus*.[125] It is with a test in mind that Terence's Syrus and Dromo,

---

121. Those who submitted might lose their names. "We are aware that the defeated take the name of their conquerors; therefore the *nomen Latinum* might have perished with the victory of Aeneas" (*novimus quod victi victorum nomen accipiunt: potuit ergo victore Aenea perire nomen Latinum* [Servius, *In Aeneida* 1.6; cf. 4.618; Virgil, *Aeneis* 12.820 ff.]). The victorious general might "take" the name of the people whom he conquered (Germanicus, Parthicus, Britannicus, etc.). Plautus's Sosia, having been defeated by Mercury, abandoned his name, as well as his voice, to the victor (*Amphitruo* 379–384). One's name, like one's *virtus* or *fama*, needed to be won again and again and was easily lost.

122. *Homo inter homines sum, capite aperto ambulo.*

123. *Gesture and Rank in Roman Art*, New Haven, 1963. For the full frontal position as the "sincere" position, see John Spiegel and Pavel Machotka, *Messages of the Body*, New York, 1974. The honorable man of Kabylia was, according to Pierre Bourdieu, "the man who faces, outfaces, stands up to others, looks them in the eye" (*Outline of a Theory of Practice*, trans. Richard Nice, Cambridge, 1977, p. 15).

124. Here figuratively, of touching, of seeing with the *oculatae manus*. Cf. Terence, *Heautontimorumenos* 1023: *rem quom videas, censeas.*

125. "It was manifest, however, that he was an unwaveringly good man, of known and tested integrity and an utterly blameless life, and many and shining examples of his probity and sincerity were produced" (*sed eum constabat virum esse firme bonum notaeque et expertae fidei et vitae inculpatissimaeque, multaque et inlustria exempla probitatis sinceritatisque eius expromebantur* [Gellius, *Noctes Atticae* 14.2.5]). "He was a vigorous man of proven courage in the cause of the plebs" (*vir acer et pro causa plebis expertae virtutis* [Livy 3.44.3]). Cf. Virgil, *Aeneis* 10.173. *Argutus* was bright, glancing, lively as well as clarified, proved, shown.

the slaves of Chremes and his son Clitiphon, arrive suddenly at the home of Antiphila, the young woman loved by Clitiphon. They barge in with the intention of
surprising and exposing Antiphila. "By breaking in on a woman unexpectedly
one can find out how she's been spending her life in your absence; it gives one a
way of judging the everyday conduct of her life, and it's that everyday conduct
that shows, finally, what a person's *ingenium* is" (*Heautontimorumenos* 274–290).[126] To
his comrades intending to test their wives by returning unexpectedly from the
front, Livy's Collatinus declares: "Let every man regard as the surest test *(spectatissimum sit)* what meets his eyes when the woman's husband enters unexpectedly"
(Livy 1.57.7).[127] Antiphila and Lucretia are "proven" by their testing. Cicero's
brave Caecilia was a *spectatissima femina* (*Pro Sexto Roscio* 50.147). Tacitus's Octavia
was a woman of *probitas spectata* (*Annales* 13.12.2). The wife of Quintus Metellus
was *pudicitia conspicua* (Valerius Maximus 7.1.1). Proven men were *spectati viri* (Plautus, *Mercator* 319).[128] When Simo discovers that his son has frequented the house
of the prostitute Chrysis but has not slept with her, he declares, "I consider him to
be sufficiently tested *(spectatum satis)* and a great example of self-control *(magnum
exemplum continentiae*" [Terence, *Andria* 91–92; cf. 93–95]).[129]

---

126. *hoc studio vitam suam te absente exegerit,*
     ubi de improvisost interventum mulieri
     nam ea res dedit tum existimandi copiam
     cottidianae vitae consuetudinem,
     quae quiousque ingenium ut sit declarat maxume.

They find her, alone with one old maidservant, carelessly dressed, without makeup or ornament,
diligently laboring at the loom. See also the scene in the *Bacchides* beginning lines 829–831. Antiphila
was like Postumia Matronilla described on her stone epitaph as *pudica religiosa laboriosa frugi efficaxs vigi-
lans sollicita / univira unicuba [t]otius industriae et fidei / matrona* (*Inscriptiones Latinae Selectae*, vol. 2.2, no.
8444).

127. *id cuique spectatissimum sit quod necopinato viri adventu occurrerit oculis.* When Plautus's Alcmena is
shocked to discover on her doorstep the husband who had only just left her, her first assumption is that
Amphitryon has devised a trial for her. "Why has he returned so soon after saying he had to rush off?
Is he deliberately trying me? Does he want to test how much I miss him when he goes away?" *Nam
quid ille revortitur, / qui dudum properare se aibat? an ille me temptat sciens / atque id se volt experiri, suom abitum ut
desiderem?* (Plautus, *Amphitruo* 660–662).

128. "And people especially admire the man who is not moved by the desire for money. If a man
has proved himself in this direction, they consider him to have been tried by fire" (*qui pecunia non movetur... hunc igni spectatum arbitrantur* [Cicero, *De officiis* 2.11.38]). The fidelity of Claudius's freedman Pallas
was *spectatissima* (Pliny, *Epistulae* 8.6.13).

129. For example, "Our hearts are strong in battle and our spirits and our youthful vigor tried in
action" (*sunt nobis fortia bello / pectora, sunt animi et rebus spectata iuventus* [Virgil, *Aeneis* 8.150–151]). "I
thought you had sufficiently tested me and my way of life by now" (*me quidem iam satis tibi spectatam
censebam esse et meos mores* [Plautus, *Persa* 171]). *tuam probatam mi et spectatam maxume adulescentiam* (Lucilius
apud Nonius vol. 3, p. 703, Lindsay ed). *fidem... spectatam iam et diu cognitam* (*Divinatio in Caecilium* 4.11);
homo in rebus iudicandis spectatus et cognitus (Cicero, *In Verrem* 1.10.29); *homines... spectati et probati* (*De oratore*
1.27.124); *spectata ac nobilitata virtus* (Cicero, *Pro Flacco* 63); *spectata multis magnisque rebus singularis integritas*
(*Philippicae* 3.10.26); *ni virtus fidesque vostra spectata mihi foret* (Sallust, *Catilina* 20.2). *spectatae integritatis vir*

It is important to understand that, in ancient Rome, looking was not passive but active. To look was a challenge. The *spectator* was inspector, judge, and connoisseur.[130] In the prologue of the *Heautontimorumenos,* Terence presents his comedy as a case being tried in court, with the actor as the orator and the *spectatores* as judges. Plautus's goddess is judge and mistress (*spectatrix atque era* [*Mercator* 842]). "You know what a refined judge of beauty I am," declares Terence's Chaerea (*quom ipsus me noris quam elegans formarum spectator siem* [*Eunuchus* 566]). "None of the generals... was a keener observer and judge of bravery" (*neminem omnium imperatorum... acriorem virtutis spectatorem ac iudicem fuisse* [Livy 42.34.7]).[131]

Who failed the test of being seen was *improbus,* "unsound," not satisfying a standard, improper, incorrect, morally defective.[132] The *improbus* claimed more than his or her due; he or she was shameless, greedy, presumptuous, immoderate in size or extent. The word of the *improbus* was worth nothing.[133] When Sallust's Turpilius, commander of Vaga, alone survived the slaughter of his garrison by the inhabitants, he lost credibility. Because, in this critical moment, he preferred his miserable life to an inviolate reputation, he was considered *improbus* and *intestabilis:* his word no longer counted (*Bellum Iugurthinum* 67.3]).[134]

(Livy 26.49.16); *spectata est per mala nostra fides* (Ovid, *Epistulae ex Ponto* 2.7.82); *Tiberium... spectatum bello* (Tacitus, *Annales* 1.4.3).

130. See Kellum, "The Play of Meaning: The Visual Culture of Ancient Roman Freedmen and Freedwomen" (forthcoming), mss. pp. 13, 15.

131. *acrior virtutis spectator ac iudex* (Livy 42.34.7). (*argentum) dem spectandum* (Plautus, *Persa* 440, cf. *Miles gloriosus* 158). *ut fulvum spectatur in ignibus aurum* (Ovid, *Tristia* 1.5.25). One can compare the Latin notion of the *arbiter. Arbitrari* meant to hear, behold, observe, or see as well as think, and the *arbiter* was a judge as well as spectator and witness. See Plautus, *Amphitruo prologus* 15; *Captivi* 220; *Mercator* 1005; *Miles gloriosus* 1137. The *testis,* witness, was also a judge. When one called on the gods or other men as "witnesses," one also called on them as "judges." See, for example, Tacitus, *Annales* 3.16. For the Romans of the early and middle Republic, justice was immanent, based on the contest, the oath, the ordeal. For the *legis actiones* as forms of the ordeal, see Pierre Noailles, *Du droit sacré au droit civil,* Paris, 1949; H. Lévy-Bruhl, *Recherches sur les actions de la loi,* Paris, 1960; Alan Watson, *Rome of the Twelve Tables,* Princeton, 1975, pp. 125–133. For the judicial or semijudicial *sponsio* as a trial of one's honor, see Cicero, *Pro Quinctio* 8.30; *De officiis* 3.19.77. For the agonistic aspects of Roman judicial proceedings, see especially John Crook, *Law and Life of Rome 90 B.C.–A.D. 212,* Ithaca, 1967, p. 255; "*Sponsione Provocare:* Its Place in Roman Litigation," *Journal of Roman Studies* 66 (1976): 132–138; J. M. Kelly, "Loss of Face as a Factor Inhibiting Litigation," *Studies in the Civil Judicature of the Roman Republic,* Oxford, 1976, pp. 93–111, esp. p. 101. See also J. Huizinga, *Homo Ludens: A Study of the Play Element in Culture,* Boston, 1950, chapter 4, "Play and Law," pp. 76–88. For the notion of immanent justice in medieval Europe, see Edward Peters, *Torture,* New York, 1985, pp. 42–43.

132. Cicero quotes a fragment from Ennius's *Medea:* "Many who stayed at home for that reason remained unproven" (*multi qui domi aetatem agerent propterea sunt improbati* [*Epistulae ad familiares* 7.6 = Ennius, *Tragoediae* 261, Vahlen ed.]). Cf. Virgil, *Aeneis* 5.397.

133. The reader of Virgil knows the worth of the words of Dares, *improbus iste / exsultat fidens* (*Aeneis* 5.397–398).

134. *quia illi in tanto malo turpis vita integra fama potior fuit, improbus intestabilisque videtur.* The failure of a witness or a *libripens* (the holder of the scales) to perform his duty when called on resulted in his being

The relationship between the viability of one's word and the viability of one's body, between losing all credit and being castrated, is illustrated by the funny scene in Plautus's *Curculio*, where, playing on the two meanings of *testis* (witness and testicle), the slave Palinurus warns his young master Phaedromus to be careful in loving, "so that it will not disgrace you if the people should come to know what you love; take care you do not become *intestabilis*" (*ne id quod ames populus si sciat, tibi sit probro / semper curato ne sis intestabilis* [29–30]). "Love, but with your 'witnesses' present" (*quod amas amato testibus praesentibus* [31]).[135]

AUDIBILITY

The Romans judged the weight of a person's word not against an abstract standard of truth but by how much was risked in speaking; they considered the stakes (the *sacramentum*, the "deposit" or "forfeit" that backed up one's words). Words had weight when the speaker's reputation, *persona, fama, nomen*, life were risked in speaking.[136] When Vitellius refused to believe the intelligence reports given him by the centurion Julius Agrestis, the latter declared, "Since you require some decisive proof... I will give you a proof that you can believe." He slew himself on the spot, thereby, according to Tacitus, confirming his words (*Historia* 3.54).[137] When a common soldier arrived at the camp of Otho bringing news of defeat, he was called a liar, a coward, and a runaway by the other soldiers. To certify his words, he fell on his sword at the emperor's feet (Suetonius, *Otho* 10.1). (Suetonius tells us that it was this act by a common soldier that challenged the emperor Otho to hold his own life cheaply.) How does Porcia demonstrate her credibility, her trustworthiness, to herself and to her husband, Brutus? She stabs herself in the thigh with a knife. "She showed Brutus the wound and explained the test" (*deiknusin autoi to trauma kai diegeitai ten peiran* [Plutarch, *Brutus* 13]). Livy's Lucretia declares that though her body has been violated, her spirit is without guilt.

---

declared *improbus intestabilisque* (*Lex XII tabularum* 8.22 = Gellius, *Noctes Atticae* 15.13.11). Having failed those who depended on him at a critical moment, his word was henceforward worth nothing. On this provision of the Twelve Tables, see Michèle Ducos, "La crainte de l'infamie et l'obéissance de la loi," *Revue des études latines* 57 (1979): 158–160.

135. Cf. *Curculio* 621–23; *Miles gloriosus* 1417. On these passages see David Daube, *Roman Law*, Edinburgh, 1969, p. 74.

136. The Romans believed that having nothing to lose made one shameless (Sallust, *Catilina* 37.3). The poor and the enslaved did not necessarily see it that way. Demaenetus says of the slave Libanus, "He would rather die a horrible death than not scrupulously fulfill what he had promised" (*moriri sese misere mavolet, / quam non perfectum reddat quod promiserit* [Plautus, *Asinaria* 121–122]). "If you discover that I have lied in anything I have said," declares Terence's slave Davos, "slay me!" (*si quicquam invenies me mentitum, occidito* [*Andria* 864]).

137. "*quando quidem*," inquit, "*magno documento opus est, ... dabo cui credas.*" *atque ita digressus voluntaria morte dicta firmavit.*

"Death, she says, will be my witness *(mors testis erit)*" (1.58.7). To the modern ear, Lucretia's words are counterintuitive and all but incomprehensible. But a Roman would understand that Lucretia's willingness to give up everything, to expend herself completely, substantiated her words. It made them powerful. It made them true.[138] It is important to notice that just as a common soldier could challenge a king, a woman could challenge a man, and a slave could challenge a master. (The brave suicide of his slave Eros, for instance, was a challenge to Antony [Plutarch, *Antony* 76.4].) Social and sexual hierarchies could be mitigated as well as reinforced by the Roman's agonistic mentality, because, within a contest culture, whatever one's claims to honor, they were perpetually open to testing. The honor, the fullness of one's being in ancient Rome was never safely or permanently earned.[139] It was a general rule of the Roman emotional economy that honor should not rest too long with any living person.[140]

A person who had demonstrated his or her expendability had weighty words. When a natural grotto collapsed while the emperor Tiberius was dining within, Sejanus shielded the emperor from falling stones with his own body. "As a result of this act he was held in still greater esteem, and though his counsels were ruinous, he was listened to with confidence, as a man who had no care for himself" (Tacitus, *Annales* 4.59).[141] The words of Virgil's great man carry the weight he has earned for them in trials, in service, in acts of piety (*Aeneis* 1.151).[142] "Because they were not poor or inconsequential men," Cicero asserts, "who said that they had seen two suns shining in the sky, we would do better to seek an explanation for the phenomenon than to withhold credence from their words" (*De republica* 1.10.15).[143]

The actor and the orator might say similar things in similar ways, but because what they risked was so different, their words were given altogether different

---

138. No logic was so convincing. Nothing else could give so much power to one's words. This is what the philosopher Socrates knew when he drank the cup of hemlock. In Plutarch's preserved fragment of a public speech by Tiberius Gracchus, the latter urges his listeners to give no credence to the "fighting words" of the senators. The drift of his argument is that these words are empty because there is nothing behind them; the aristocrats who spoke them risked nothing (*Tiberius Gracchus* 9.4–5).

139. See Knoche, "Der römische Ruhmesgedanke," p. 431; Alvin Gouldner, *Enter Plato*, New York, 1965, p. 53.

140. "It is the way of men to prefer not to see the same person excel in too many enterprises" (*est mos hominum, ut nolint eundem pluribus rebus excellere* [Cicero, *Brutus* 21.84]). Through excessive success in competition, men like Spurius Cassius, Spurius Maelius, Marcus Manlius, Sextus and Appius Claudius, Scipio Africanus, Scipio Aemilianus, Tiberius Gracchus, Gaius Gracchus, and Julius Caesar erected themselves into targets of envy and the vendetta. Success became a legitimate cause for a hatred in the Roman compensatory physics of the emotions. All extremes were wont to invert.

141. *maior ex eo, et quamquam exitiosa suaderet, ut non sui anxius, cum fide audiebatur.*

142. *pietate gravem ac meritis virum.*

143. *neque enim pauci neque leves sunt, qui se duos soles vidisse dicant, ut non tam fides non habenda quam ratio quaerenda.* Even if Gaius Fannius Chaerea should attempt to introduce what is in his account books, Cicero declares, more weight would be given to his character than to the written evidence (*Pro Roscio Commoedo* 1.1ff.).

valances. The word of actors, slaves, or the poor was worth nothing because they were seen as having nothing to lose. "Let him swear by the altars of Samothrace and of Rome, the poor man is believed to have no respect for the gods and their thunderbolts" (Juvenal, *Satirae* 3.144–146).[144] When Mnesilochus finds himself penniless, he exclaims "*inanis sum*" (Plautus, *Bacchides* 531). He and his words were, henceforth, empty.[145]

In the *Pro Quinctio* Cicero attempts to discredit the plaintiff Naevius by accusing him of being: a) poor, b) a *scurra* (a word that by Cicero's day had come to mean a parasite who earned his dinners by being a "scurrilous" wit), and c) a *praeco*, an auctioneer, a voice for sale (3.11).[146] Like the impoverished, like Juvenal's bankrupt Damasippus, his voice belonged to whoever would pay for it. Nothing was at stake when he spoke.[147] The poor man, the parasite, and the auctioneer had no inhibition, no shame in speaking, and therefore no modesty or measure (*Pro Quinctio* 3.13).[148]

Likewise, the *persona* that met no resistance, the face that went without challenge, like that of Plautus's Pyrgopolynices or Terence's Thraso—braggart warriors both—was not confirmed; on the contrary, the face that went without challenge was rendered transparent (as the flatterer Palaestrio and his devilish companions knew) and everyone could see through it to the void within. If a speaker's face could not be confirmed, neither could his speech. The untested was *vaniloquus*.[149] He was, to borrow a line from J. P. Sullivan's Petronius, a "balloon on legs, a walking bladder," an *uter inflatus* (*Satyricon*, 42).[150] The being of the untested was a vanity.[151]

The danger to one's spirit from praise that came too easily was like the danger to one's spirit from too easy success and good fortune. "Fortune turns her spoiled

---

144. *iures licet et Samothracum / et nostrorum aras, contemnere fulmina pauper / creditur atque deos.* The dispossessed Numidian prince Adherbal, reduced to repeatedly supplicating the Roman senate for aid against Iugurtha, experienced how little faith was put in the words of those who had nothing left to lose (*et iam antea expertus sum parum fidei miseris esse* [Sallust, *Bellum Iugurthinum* 24.4]).

145. As someone who, in defeat, had chosen to preserve his life, the slave could not expect to be trusted. See Pliny, *Historia naturalis* 33.6.26; Seneca, *De tranquillitate* 8.8; Pliny, *Epistulae* 1.21. For a slave praised for honesty, see *Corpus Inscriptionum Latinarum*, vol. 6.2, no. 9222; Sandra Joshel, *Work, Identity, and Legal Status at Rome*, Norman, Oklahoma, 1992, p. 58.

146. Cf. 31.95.

147. See *Satirae* 8.185–186.

148. *Nec mirum si is, qui vocem venalem habuerat, ea, quae voce quaesiverat, magno sibi quaestui fore putabat.* For more on the voice see part 2.

149. Cf. Silius Italicus, *Punica* 8.17, 14.280–281; Cicero, *De officiis* 1.38.137.

150. One could be "inflated by compliance" (*inflatus assentationibus* [Livy 24.6.8]). Plautus's Argyrippus, like Purgopolynices, was first puffed up and then destroyed by affirmation and flattery (*Asinaria*, esp. 204–226). For Julius Caesar puffed up by flattery to his own destruction, see Dio 44.3.1–3.

151. Concomitantly, "The man who praises himself soon finds a mocker" (*Qui se ipse laudat cito derisorem invenit* [Publilius Syrus 545, Friedrich ed.]). Compare the Greek notion of *kenodoxia*, vainglory (Polybius 3.81.9). The man who would not, or could not, submit his *persona* to challenges was weightless.

darlings into dolts," asserts Publilius Syrus (173, Friedrich ed.).[152] As a result, one's spirit and life, like a balloon, could be burst with the slightest prick. "Unimpaired good fortune cannot withstand a single blow" (Seneca, *De providentia* 2.6).[153]

We have the notion that you can save your soul even if you have lost your face. But the Romans lost their souls when they lost their faces. The penetrable, false, or broken *persona* enclosed only emptiness; the exposed Roman was *vanus, inanis, cassus*. The *discrimen* disclosed, for instance, that there was nothing but cowardice beneath the Helvetii's reputation for great valor (Tacitus, *Historia* 1.68).[154] Metellus, the general dispatched by the Romans against the defiant Numidian Jugurtha, was, according to Marius, a man of regal arrogance but, as the course of the war had shown, an *homo inanis* (Sallust, *Bellum Iugurthinum* 64.5).[155] Relieved of the burden or mask, removed from the endless challenges of the contest, freed from the oppressive demands of decorum and modesty, a Roman was not the authentic, genuine, original self as we imagine it, but a void.

At the same time, the proven person, the person with the *praeclarus facies*, the radiant visage, presented a heightened challenge, even an insult, to others. It was the industry and proven chastity *(spectata castitas)* of Livy's Lucretia, toiling at the loom late into the night, that won her the "Contest of Wives." Having proved her self-control, her boundaries, and so her inviolate spirit, she became the target of the tyrannical Tarquin (Livy 1.57.10).[156] Just so, successfully enduring the tests of Appius Claudius's bribes and promises, the hard-to-get Verginia, "hedged about, guarded against all shamelessness" *(omnia pudore saepta),* incited the arrogant Claudius with the desire to violate her and the honor of her family (Livy 3.44.4). "It was not beauty alone and a comely body that incited Tiberius's lust, but the youthful modesty of some and the noble ancestry of others" (Tacitus, *Annales* 6.7.3 [= 6.1.3]).[157] According to the *Auctor ad Herennium,* "the industry of Scipio Africanus brought him virtue, his virtue brought him glory, his glory brought him rivals" (4.25.34 = Quintilian, *Institutio oratoria* 9.3.56).[158]

152. *Fortuna nimium quem fovet stultum facit.* Successful persons, according to Cicero, can becomes so *inflati opinionibus,* so accustomed to flattery, that they cease to test themselves and begin to take admiration as their due—and so expose themselves to ridicule (Cicero, *De officiis* 1.26.91).

153. *Non fert ullum ictum inlaesa felicitas.*

154. *illi ante discrimen feroces, in periculo pavidi.*

155. Flamininus did not take seriously the words of the ambassadors of Antiochus and the Aetolians—nor, he believed, should the Achaeans—because "all the fierceness of the Aetolians consisted in words and not in actions and was seen in councils and assemblies more than in battle" (Livy 35.49.2). The unproven Aetolians were *vaniloquii* (cf. 35.48.2).

156. "Both her form and her proven chastity incited Sextus Tarquinius. An evil desire to take her by force seized him" (*Ibi Sex. Tarquinium mala libido Lucretiae per vim stuprandae capit; cum forma tum spectata castitas incitat*).

157. *nec formam tantum et decora corpora, sed in his modestam pueritiam, in aliis imagines maiorum incitamentum cupidinis habebat.*

158. *Africano virtutem industria, virtus gloriam, gloria aemulos comparavit.* The example of the *spectatissima*

THE VERY INSTANT OF TRUTH

A Roman's hyperconsciousness of his or her "face" produced a keen sense of embodiment. The person who underwent surveillance in a contest, who risked death or humiliation, lived critically in the moment, like a deer trapped in the headlights of an oncoming car.[159] For the Roman on the spot, up against the wall, the world was sharp, immediate, visceral. As in archaic Greek thought and much of Japanese thought—and for similar reasons—the Romans tended to physicalize everything, to make everything present. Reality was immanent; it was *spectatus, expertus, probatus, perspicuus, argutus, manufestus*. It hit you in the face; you could smack it with your hand. The following scene from Plautus's *Amphitruo* illustrates how "realized" reality could be in Roman culture. The slave Sosia confronts on the street his mirror image, the god Mercury. The god challenges the mortal:

Mercury: Where do you think you're going?
Sosia: What's it to you?
Mercury: Are you free or slave?
Sosia: I'm whatever I want to be.
Mercury: Oh yeah?
Sosia: Yeah!
Mercury: You're a whipped slave!
Sosia: You lie!
Mercury: Now I'll make you say I'm telling the truth. (341–345)[160]

---

fides atque innocentia of Claudius's freedman Pallas, along with the wealth and honor offered to him by the senate and emperor, would spur other men to rival and emulate him (*et Pallantis spectatissima fides atque innocentia exemplo provocare studium tam honestae aemulationis posset* [Pliny *Epistulae* 8.6.13]). Pliny, on the contrary, despises this upstart.

159. For examples of being put on the spot, see Plautus, *Amphitruo* 335ff.; Seneca, *Epistulae* 11.1; Quintus Curtius Rufus, *Historiae Alexandri Magni* 6.11.36–37. The physical effects of such a challenge were similar to those produced by the face-to-face confrontation with a god. See, for example, Livy 1.16.6; Virgil, *Aeneis* 4.280–282; Seneca, *Epistulae* 115.4; H. Wagenvoort, *"Fas sit vidisse," Studies in Roman Literature, Culture and Religion*, London, 1956, esp. pp. 184–188. They were also similar to those produced by horror. In Virgil's epic, Sinon tells the Trojans that the oracle of Apollo has demanded a human sacrifice to enable the Achaeans to return home: "Then their spirits were confounded, a cold tremor cursed through the marrow of their bones" (*obstipuere animi, gelidusque per ima cucurrit / ossa tremor* [Virgil, *Aeneis* 2.119–121]).

160. M: *quo ambulas tu…?*
S: *quid id exquiris tu…?*
M: *servosne es an liber?*
S: *utcumque animo conlibitum est meo.*
M: *ain vero?*
S: *aio enim vero.*
M: *verbero!*
S: *mentiris nunc.*
M: *at iam faciam ut verum dicas dicere.*

The god proceeds to whip Sosia not only into affirming Mercury's words but even into surrendering to the god his name and his identity.[161] In this little Roman *agon*, the type that occurs every day in the sixth-grade schoolyard, reality is established by contest.[162] The plays of Plautus are filled with wonderful examples of the insistent inflation of the contest. Every tiff is a tumult, every wrangle a war. Whatever other roles a Roman might play, he was always a warrior. "Our oratory, finally, must be led forth from this sheltered and domestic training camp into the fray, into the dust and clamor of battle, into the front line of forensics! Every aspect of our speaking should be put to the test; her strength of spirit must be proven; her sheltered preparation must be brought forth into the light of truth" (Cicero, *De oratore* 1.34.157).[163]

The necessity of establishing the truth of one's being by contest was apparent to the Roman even when alone. Plautus's Mnesilochus feels that his very being is challenged by the favors done to him by his friend Pistoclerus.[164] It represents, for Mnesilochus, a little "moment of truth," but as great in its import for his self-esteem as the greatest battle. He speaks to himself: "Now, Mnesilochus, what you are is made manifest; now the contest is joined. Are you or are you not what you should be? Are you a bad man or a good man? . . . Are you just or unjust? stingy or generous? companionable or disagreeable? Beware lest you allow your own slave to surpass you in doing well! But I warn you, whatever it is that you turn out to be, you won't be able to hide!" (*Bacchides* 399–403).[165] Notice, first, that the slave has challenged the master, and, second, that the truth of Mnesilochus's character is not ontological but existential; it can be discovered only in action. Roman reality was, then, for much of its history, immanent, relative, and contingent, achieved rather than recognized, authored by speech and deed. Like Mne-

161. In the *Bacchides*, the slave Chrysalus confesses to his old master Nicobulus that his young master has exposed Chrysalus's outrageous lies: "He's accused me? Great! I'm the bad one! I'm the cursed criminal! Just you watch! I'll make his words into nothing!" (*men crimanatust? optimest! ego sum malus, / ego sum sacer, scelestus. specta rem modo. / ego verbum faciam nullum* [783–785].)

162. The contest that establishes the truth of one's speech may be as simple and direct as eye contact. When Amphitryon wants to know if Sosia is speaking truly, he challenges the latter to look him in the eye (*Amphitruo* 750–751).

163. *educenda deinde dictio est ex hac domestica exercitatione et umbratili medium in agmen, in pulverem, in clamorem, in castra, atque in aciem forensem; subeundus usus omnium, et periclitandae vires ingenii; et illa commentatio inclusa in veritatis lucem proferenda est.*

164. For the notion that a person was *beneficio provocati*, challenged by the kindness or benefits of others, see Cicero, *De officiis* 1.15.48. Notice that the forces moving and adjusting the scales of Roman justice were the emotions of honor.

165. *nunc, Mnesiloche, specimen specitur, nunc certamen cernitur,*
    sisne necne ut esse oportet, malus, bonus quoivis modi,
    iustus iniustus, malignus largus, comis incommodus.
    cave sis te superare servom siris faciundo bene. Utut eris, moneo, haud celabis.

silochus, one staked one's claim to the truth of one's existence and had to be prepared to defend that truth in an unending series of trials.

DOING TRUTH

As a result of living in a contest culture, Roman ideas of truth (like Roman notions of the sacred) were more active, palpable, and embodied than our own. How much more active and embodied they were can be gleaned from a comparison of a few of our English words with their Latin cognates. Our "fact" is passive; for us a fact just "is." The Roman's *factum* was something made or done. To our idealizing and compartmentalizing thought, some essential quality is captured and expressed in a category like "species." But for the Romans (especially of the Republic), the *species* was the thing presented to view, the spectacle, sight, or visual appearance.[166] Something *manifestus* was something that one could catch in the hand; it was palpable, evident.[167] "Existence" for us is ontological. But Latin *existere* was to come into view, to appear, come forward, show oneself, come into being; *exstare* was not only to exist, it was to project, protrude, stand out, be conspicuous, to catch attention.

For us, "to experience" is primarily passive. But in Latin *experiri* meant to try, to test, to find or know by experience, to make a trial of, to contend with, to measure strength with. In Plautus's *Mercator,* the cook, angry at old Lysimachus for claiming he does not know him and did not hire him, challenges the old man: "Do you want to try me?" (*vin me experiri?* [768]). "Let us decide the matter of life and death by the sword; let us test our *virtus* in battle" (*ferro...vitam cernamus,...virtute experiamur* [Ennius apud Cicero, *De officiis* 1.12.38]). The Roman soldiers who survived Cannae, banished to Sicily, longed to "try their spirit" (*experiri animum* [Livy 25.6.19]).[168]

166. Cf. Cicero, *Pro Marcello* 6.20; *Ad familiares* 4.4.3. Beginning in the Ciceronian period, for reasons that I discuss in chapter 4, *species* began to take on the meaning of "illusion," like *facies,* which increasingly became "façade."

167. "Never have I seen a man more manifestly caught" (*nec magis manufestum ego hominem umquam ullum teneri vidi* [Plautus, *Menaechmi* 594]). *manifestus ex opere labor* (Quintilian, *Institutio oratoria* 10.3.8); cf. Plautus, *Trinummus* 895; *Mostellaria* 511. As Richard Onians points out, Latin *sapere,* to know, was to have sap, blood, juice, because consciousness was in the chest with the lungs, heart, breath, and blood (*The Origins of European Thought about the Body, the Mind, the Soul, the World, Time, and Fate,* Cambridge, 1954, pp. 61–63). Many Latin words for knowledge express the physical aspects of what are, for us, principally metaphysical notions. *Comprehendere, deprehendere, capere,* and their relatives all stress the notion of grasping, seizing; *cognoscere,* like "to know" in archaic English usage, was to have sexual intercourse with as well as to know.

168. Terence's desperate Charinus will try anything before submitting (*omnia experiri certumst prius quam pereo* [Andria 311]). *dicam enim tibi, Catule, non tam doctus quam, id quod est maius, expertus* (Cicero, *De oratore* 2.17.72). *experiendo tamen magis quam discendo cognovi* (Cicero, *Ad familiares* 1.7.10). Cf. Plautus, *Amphitruo* 662; Cicero, *Pro Quinctio* 2.9; Livy 25.38.11; Virgil, *Aeneis* 7.434; Quintilian, *Institutio oratoria* 12.11.16; Nepos, *Alcibiades* 1.1. *Experiens* as an adjective meant not only "experienced" in our sense, but

Verus as an adjective was a very old Latin word that had several meanings. It could be used as a simple explicative or affirmative *(verum!)*. Most often, in Plautus and Republican literature, it meant "true" in the sense of firm, capable of withstanding a test or trial. For example: "Farewell,...continue conquering with true [*vera*, stalwart] courage as you have done so far" *(Casina* 87–88).[169] In this sense the Romans seem to have related *verus* to words with similar sounds and meanings: *assevere, persevere, severus*.[170] Cicero's Laelius affirms that "a public meeting, though composed of very ignorant men, can, nevertheless, usually see the difference between a 'demagogue' *(popularis)*, that is, a shallow, flattering citizen, and one who is *constans, verus,* and *gravis*" *(De amicitia* 95).[171]

Veritas seems to have begun its Latin life as the abstraction of a quality of human behavior, like *gravitas* or *simplicitas*. It appears in a few instances as early as Terence and has a meaning not far from *severitas* (rigor, sternness, austerity, integrity of judgment), as opposed to compliance or levity: "There was stern *veritas* in his face, *fides* in his words" *(Tristis veritas inest in voltu atque in verbis fides* [*Andria* 858]). "*Obsequium* secures friends, *veritas* only enemies" *(Obsequium amicos, veritas odium paret* [*Andria* 68–69]).[172] Livy's Capitolinus declares, "I know that I could say other things that you would be happier to hear, but necessity compels me, even if my *ingenium* did not admonish me, to speak *vera pro gratis*, the *vera* rather than the *gratis*. It is not that I do not wish to please you, Quirites, but I wish, much more, for you to be safe" (Livy 3. 68.9).[173] Cicero, the first to make frequent use of the word *veritas* to translate the abstract truth, the *aletheia* of Greek philosophers, still, on occasion, employed it with its ancient associations with selflessness, severity, and constancy. "Friendships are nurtured by *veritas*, alliances by *fides*, close relationships by *pietas*" *(veritate amicitia, fide societas, pietate propinquitas colitur* [*Pro Quinctio* 6.26]).[174]

Generally, in earlier Roman thought, the "truth" of what one said was intimately linked with the ability of the speaker to endure a test or trial of some sort.[175] How might the women accused of poisoning their husbands prove their innocence? They swallowed the alleged poison (Livy 8.18).[176] How might the

---

also "active," "industrious," "enterprising": *homo gnavus et industrius, experientissimus ac diligentissimus arator* (Cicero, *In Verrem* 2.3.21.53). *promptus homo et experiens* (ibid. 2.4.17.37). *vir acer et experiens* (Livy 6.34.4). *ingenii est experientis amor* (Ovid, *Amores* 1.9.32).

169. *valete, bene rem gerite et vincite / virtute vera, quod fecistis antidhac.*

170. For the ways in which Romans made word associations not based on our concepts of "scientific" etymology, see below, n. 192.

171. *Contio, quae ex imperitissimis constat, tamen iudicare solet, quid intersit inter popularem, id est assentatorem et levem civem et inter constantem et verum et gravem.*

172. See chapter 4.

173. *His ego gratiora dictu alia esse scio: sed me vera pro gratis loqui etsi meum ingenium non moneret, necessitas cogit. Vellem equidem vobis placere, Quirites: sed multo malo vos salvos esse.*

174. Cf. *De officiis* 1.19.63: *veritatis amicos.*

175. This is especially true in Plautus and Terence.

176. Unfortunately, they failed the test.

Vestal Tuccia prove her purity in the face of slanderous accusations? She carried water in a sieve (Valerius Maximus 8.1, *absoluti* 5).[177] How, when a *rumor iniquus* accused her of unchastity, might the Roman matron Claudia Quinta prove that she was "really" chaste? She took hold of the rope and, with one tug, freed a boat that had run aground at the mouth of the Tiber (Livy 29.14; Ovid, *Fasti* 4.305–444).[178] We would want and assume the truth of our words to correspond with "what is," but according to the logic of the ancient Romans, the truth of a Roman's words corresponded to the truth of his or her being, and that truth was enacted—most forcefully, as in these instances, by the very unnatural act.

The provisional and contested nature of reality (including the reality of one's being) and the immediacy and particularity of experience infused all Roman ways of thinking.[179] The Romans did not have an "integrated psychic whole," and they tended not to synthesize or carefully correlate parts to a whole.[180] Boundaries and obligations tended to accumulate and to overlap without being

177. See Amy Richlin, "Carrying Water in a Sieve: Class and Body in Roman Women's Religion," in *Women and Goddess Traditions in Antiquity and Today*, ed. Karen L. King, Minneapolis, 1997, pp. 330–374.

178. Cf. Pliny, *Historia naturalis* 7.35.120; Suetonius, *Tiberius* 2.3. It was a boat carrying the goddess Cybele, who was being conveyed from Pessinus to Rome in 204 B.C.E. The soothsayers had announced that only a chaste woman could move it.

179. Pliny the Elder speaks disapprovingly of the practice of drinking gladiator's blood as a curative. The consumers imagine that they are drinking the hot, breathing, living, potent *efficacissimus animus* of the gladiator (*sanguinem quoque gladiatorum bibunt....illi ex homine ipso sorbere efficacissimum putant calidum spirantemque et vivam ipsam animam* [*Historia naturalis* 28.2.4]). The Romans taking of heads and keeping of relics also bespeak the physicality of the spirit of the person.

180. Our notions of "law" and "constitution" are radically different from those of the Romans of the Republic. The following paragraphs are heavily dependent on the work of Fritz Schulz. (It is not necessary to share Schulz's uncritical enthusiasm for Roman imperialism to admire his generalizations concerning the basic tendencies of Republican law, tendencies manifested in other aspects of Roman life.) For Schulz, the Roman juristic talent was to isolate and analyze, not to synthesize or to view comprehensively (*Principles of Roman Law*, Oxford, 1936, p. 19). The "classical" jurists were disinclined to abstractions (p. 41), deductions (p. 51), or definitions—at least until the late Republic (pp. 43, 152). "Romans are basically opposed to codification" (p. 7. Cf. pp. 8, 13). "The question of legal systems interested them very little" (p. 53). Even while the Romans prided themselves on their adherence to traditional forms, they had little sense of the historical development of their laws or the evolution of the *mos maiorum*. As a result, while tending to orthopraxy, they often made radical innovations in those forms (p. 28). As Thomas Habinek remarks, "It tends to be the very texts and concepts that are most embedded in the social and cultural *realia* of the Roman world that have the greatest potential for reinterpretation and redeployment on the part of succeeding generations" ("Towards a History of Friendly Advice: The Politics of Candor in Cicero's *De Amicitia*," in *The Poetics of Therapy*, ed. R. C. Nussbaum, p. 183). Roman law was not unlike the customary law of Kabylia described by Pierre Bourdieu, which "always seems to pass from particular to particular case, from the specific misdeed to the specific sanction, never expressly formulating the fundamental principles which 'rational' law

codified or systematized.[181] The Romans were slow to deduce principles or create Utopias.[182] There is a reason that modern philosophers and political theorists ignore the Romans: though rich and complex, the thought of the Romans is not easily translated into the categories or linearities of modern Western thought, with its rigid dichotomies and principle of noncontradiction.[183]

Rather than idealize, the Romans reified and dramatized.[184] The *exemplum* of the Romans, according to the *Auctor ad Herennium,* "places its subjects before the eyes since it describes everything so vividly that I would say it can almost be touched with the hand" (4.49.62).[185] "This is the aspect of the study of history that is especially salutary and profitable: you are able to gaze at examples of every

spells out explicitly" (*Outline,* p. 199 n. 15). For this same flexibility and suppleness applied to Roman imperial policy, see Bux, "*Clementia Romana,*" pp. 204, 207, 209, 212, 226–27, 230. Lind discusses the way Roman commitment to the *mos maiorum* allowed for adaptive and often radical innovation. He uses as a typical example the arguments that Cicero, firm defender of the *mos maiorum,* offerred for giving Pompey an extraordinary command in the *Pro lege Manilia* ("Tradition of Roman Moral Conservatism," p. 5). For David Daube, the systematization of earlier Roman law is largely the product of modern scholarship; he points to the nonexistence or late coinage of many of the abstract terms used by scholars to organize and systematize that law (*Roman Law,* pp. 11–63, esp. 14, 17, 19, 35, 44, 48, 51).

181. "There was a disinclination to abolish any valid law, rather was it allowed to lapse through disuse; a new rule was often set up side by side with one antiquated or moribund, to be used at choice" (Shultz, *Principles,* p. 85; cf. pp. 86–89, 92–95). For both stability and homeostasis in Roman law, see Mario Perniola, "Decorum and Ceremony," trans. Barbara Spackman, in *Recoding Metaphysics,* Evanston, 1988, p. 115. For stability and homeostasis in the traditions of other oral or oligoliterate societies, see John Vansina, *Oral Tradition as History,* Madison, 1985, pp. 120–123, cf. xii, 190–191.

182. "With very few exceptions there is no question at all of giving reasons for legal institutions and fundamental legal rules" (Shultz, *Principles,* p. 98).

Critical observations in regard to Roman constitutional law, discussions as to the best form of government, may well have taken place under Greek influence, but they took literary shape in Rome only in books by Polybius [esp. 6] and by Cicero [*De legibus, De republica*], who, although a Roman, was all too dependent on Greek models. Comparative constitutional law, as studied by Aristoteles, was not undertaken by the Romans either; they were complete strangers also to constitutional Utopias such as Plato's *Politeia.* (pp. 97–98)

183. For a good description of a tradition that was, like that of the Romans, a continuous process of creation, see Jack Goody's description of the poetic recitations of the Bagre society of the LoDagaa of northern Ghana (*The Domestication of the Savage Mind,* Cambridge, 1977, pp. 28–29).

184. For the way in which this aspect of Roman life was expressed in the wall-paintings of a Pompeian house, see Bettina Bergmann, "The Roman House a Memory Theatre: The House of the Tragic Muse," *Art Bulletin* 76.2 (1994): 225–256.

185. *exemplum . . . ante oculos ponit, cum exprimit omnia perspicue ut res prope dicam manu temptari possit.* Pliny speaks of the *manifestissimum exemplum* (*Historia naturalis* 37.60.165). The *exemplum* (from *eximere,* to take out, extract) is the person "sacralized" in the Roman sense of "set apart." The *exemplum* served as a standard by which others could be evaluated. See Thomas Habinek, *The Politics of Latin Literature,* Princeton, 1998, p. 46. For a father teaching his son by pointing out negative and positive *exempla,* see Horace, *Satirae* 1.4.105–129. See also H. Marrou, *A History of Education in Antiquity,* trans. G. Lamb, London, 1956, pp. 234–236, 252–253; Lind, "Tradition of Roman Moral Conservatism," pp. 11–13, 19.

kind displayed on a conspicuous monument,... some to imitate for the benefit of yourself and the Republic, and others—thoroughly shameful—to avoid."[186] To quote Miriam Griffin, "Real *exempla* not only showed what it was right to do but *proved that it could be done.*"[187]

Roman proverbs and maxims, the *praecepta paterna*, according to Seneca, derive their power from the immediacy of their effects on the sensibilities of the Romans. "Precepts touch our emotions" (*adfectos ipsos tangunt* [*Epistulae* 94.28]).[188]

For the Romans, as for many cultures only lately and incompletely literate, the most common and effective way of unifying was not by synthesis or abstraction but through formulaic repetition, and the most common and effective way of expressing relation was through variations on the repeated story or theme.[189] Bettina Bergmann's remarks on Pompeian wall-painting could be applied to many aspect of Roman life and thought:

186. *Hoc illud est praecipue in cognitione rerum salubre ac frugiferum, omnis te exempli documenta in inlustri posita monumento intueri; inde tibi tuaeque rei publicae quod imitere capias, inde foedum inceptu foedum exitu quod vites.* Cf. Quintilian, *Institutio oratoria* 12.2.30; Festus-Paulus, vol. 1, p. 72, Lindsay ed.

187. Emphasis mine. "Cynicism and the Romans: Attraction and Repulsion," in *The Cynics*, ed. R. Bracht Branham and Marie-Odile Goulet-Cazé, Berkeley, 1996, p. 199.

188. Maxims and proverbs approached in their brevity our notion of abstract thought, but it was the power of the formulaic reiteration and the echoing effect over time that made them powerful words for the Romans. Their "staying power" lay in the ease with which they stayed in the mind. Cf. Seneca, *Epistulae* 94, esp. 27–29, 40. Here Seneca argues against those Greek philosophers who saw value only in the generalized and universal philosophical principle.

189. Rome was, rather than a literate society, a conditionally literate or "oligoliterate" society in which the dominant patterns of thought, related to the spoken word, were gradually influenced and modified by literate patterns of thought. For the limitations of Roman literacy, see especially William V. Harris, *Ancient Literacy*, Cambridge, Mass., 1989. As Rosalind Thomas points out, even with considerable literacy in Rome, the stress was on oral performance (*Literacy and Orality in Ancient Greece*, Cambridge, 1992, p. 159). As Jack Goody and Ian Watt remark, "Even within a literate culture, the oral tradition—the transmission of values and attitudes in face-to-face contact—nevertheless remains the primary mode of cultural orientation, and, to varying degrees, it is out of step with various literate traditions" ("The Consequences of Literacy," *Comparative Studies in Society and History* 5 [1963]: 335). In Rome, as in many preliterate or partially literate societies, knowledge was transmitted, above all, in what Goody and Watt describe as "a long chain of interlocking conversations between members of the group" (ibid., pp. 306, 325–327, 344). These interlocking conversations were also, simultaneously, an interlocking series of challenges and responses. Without the fixity and stability of the written word, orally transmitted knowledge depended a great deal on memorization and stabilization through repetition, pattern, and narration. "The Romans traditionally perpetuated their moral values through retelling such *exempla* (rather than through systematic moral philosophy or sacred texts)" (Saller, *Patriarchy, Property, and Death*, p. 109; cf. p. 110). For the role of redundancy and repitition and the use of *exempla* and prototypes in the communication of oral traditions, see Vansina, *Oral Tradition as History*, pp. 69–70, 105–6. For the privileged place of the dramatic tale in preliterate societies, see Burkert, *Creation of the Sacred*, pp. 57–58, 62.

The repetition of a general, unifying scheme, the insertion of variations, and the contiguous relations of multiple corollaries in proximity and alternation produce a narrative continuum. To be sure, the creative processes of elite poets like Propertius and Ovid cannot be equated with those of a local artisan executing an assigned task. But similar habits of order and perception produced quite related effects. Because the Campanian wall painter freely compiled motifs and schemes, the walls of Pompeian houses, like the Augustan poems, often seem to be endless versions of a few basic themes.[190]

François Baratte remarks, on the chasened silver drinking cups from the Boscoreale treasure, that "the decoration on one face of a cup was often designed to reflect that on the next face, one cup on the next, the designs developing into a veritable narrative, on which the drinkers might comment to one another."[191] These characteristics of Roman visual arts are closely related to Anthony Boyle's discussion of the deft and highly self-conscious ways that Roman poets imitated and echoed their predecessors to create a layered and resounding depth of association.[192] "As difficult as it may be for us to believe," asserts Barbara Kellum, "in the world of ancient Rome, repetition was not only a key rhetorical strategy, it was a source of visual and intellectual pleasure."[193] Roman thought had a certain rhythmic return, like waves with an undertow.

Rather than abstract, the Romans reify, contextualize. The spoken word (like a statue or a painting) was not so much a way to symbolize, in our sense, as a way to realize; through speech the *animus* was affirmed and concretized in the world. I believe that J. Rufus Fears and Andrew Wallace-Hadrill are right to overturn the way in which coin-types such as *Fides* and *Clementia* have been interpreted. The making of *fides* and *clementia* into gods was not an abstraction (in the sense of a decontextualization, an essentialization) but a hypostatization, a giving of a particular form to a vaguely categorized and conceptualized power.[194] As Cicero ex-

---

190. "The Pregnant Moment: Tragic Wives in the Roman Interior," p. 210. John R. Clarke describes a series of related erotic paintings in "Look Who's Laughing at Sex: Men and Women Viewers in the Apodyterium of the Suburban Baths of Pompeii," in *The Roman Gaze: Vision, Power and the Body in Roman Society*, ed. David Fredrick (forthcoming).

191. *Le trésor d'orfèvrerie romaine de Boscoreale*, Paris, 1986, p. 56. Notice, first, that all these series lack a fixed center; they are, potentially, perpetual motion machines. Second, they lack any absence of nostalgia for the "original"; the "absent" original is not necessarily privileged over the present and manifest.

192. "Introduction: The Roman Song," in *Roman Epic*, ed. A.J. Boyle, London, 1993, pp. 1–18. In Roman etymologies, the association of ideas often takes the place of a systematic history of words. Barbara Kellum gives the following wonderful—and typical—example from Varro: "Now *adagio* is only *ambagio* with a letter changes, which is said because it *ambit* 'goes around' the discourse and does not stop at one thing" (*De lingua latina* 7.31; "Play of Meaning," ms. p. 18.) Kellum speaks of "the Roman sense of relational meaning" (ms. pp. 18–21), and their "rich network of visual and conceptual interconnections" (ms. p. 21).

193. Ibid., ms. p. 2.

194. "[*Pax, fides, victoria*, etc.] were not abstractions. Quite the opposite: *Pax* was a concrete condition brought about by the concrete manifestation of a concrete divine power. 'Abstraction' is the an-

plains, the Romans designated as *deus* those things that manifested some extraordinary force or potency (*vis maior aliqua* [De *natura deorum* 2.23.61]).[195] Indeed, Arnobius offers a wonderfully extended description of the myriad Roman gods that gained their names, their forms, and their identities *consequent* to the manifestations of their effectiveness. Needless to say, for the Christian Arnobius, the failure of the Roman gods to precede their "incarnations" argued against the reality of their divinity (*Adversus nationes* 4.1–13). But for the Romans, it was exactly the manifestation of their energy, their *vires*, that proclaimed the reality of the gods' existence, which was then captured and channeled, re-cognized and re-presented in a particular form with a particular name.[196]

Even those Romans most influenced by later Greek thought, an Ovid or a Virgil, remain storytellers, embodying, actualizing, all that they can articulate.[197] For that reason the greatest Roman thinkers were not philosophers but historians and poets; they have profound and complex things to say about social and emotional life, but they say them through stories.[198]

We are accustomed in the West to think of a culture—and especially the culture of the Romans—as a matter of relatively stable orders of laws and institutions, schematic programs, codes, and belief systems. But, I would like to suggest, following Michelle Rosaldo, that a culture can be studied through its associative chains and the images that suggest what, within a culture, can reasonably be linked with what. "We come to know it [another's culture] through collective stories that suggest the nature of coherence, probability and sense within the actor's world."[199]

tithesis of the Roman conception of divinity; for the Romans in cult matters, the divine is by definition concrete and each godhead is an object exercising will and bound by temporal spatial and functional specifices" (Fears, "Cult of Virtues," p. 831, cf. 833, 837–838); cf. Wallace-Hadrill, "The Emperor and His Virtues," *Historia* 30 (1981): 298–323.

195. In the way that they designated a male with force of will a *vir*.

196. Fears, "Cult of Virtues," pp. 924–28, "Theology of Victory at Rome," pp. 740–42.

197. For the Romans, the more concrete, the more expressive—hence their exceptional interest and ability in architecture and building. R. L. Gordon's "The Real and the Imaginary Production and Religion in the Graeco-Roman World" (*Art History* 2 [1979]: 5–34) has helped me to formulate the notions contained in this section. Gordon discusses statues not as figures of transcendence but as realizations, not as representations of a fixed truth but as reifications of the wondrous, the inarticulate and impossible. (While Gordon includes the Greeks in his generalizations, the main source from which he is working is the Roman Pliny.) See also Charles Segal, "Ovid's Metaphoric Bodies: Art, Gender, and Violence in the Metamorphoses," *Arion* 5 (1998): 10–41, esp. pp. 16–17. I have found other helpful ideas in the discussion of the notion of actualization by play in Huizinga's *Homo Ludens*, pp. 14–15.

198. For the privileged place of the dramatic tale in preliterate societies, see Burkert, *Creation of the Sacred*, pp. 57–58, 62. The lack of interest of Western philosophers and political theorists in Roman thought can be traced to their inherited ideal of disinterested and decontextualized thought, their desire to pin down and fix meanings. Few philosophers would be genuinely happy as brigands or burglars or Romans.

199. "Towards an Anthropology of Self and Feeling," *Culture Theory: Essays on Mind, Self and Emotions*, ed. Richard A. Schweder and Robert A. LeVine, Cambridge, 1984, p. 140.

FRIABLE FACES

As a result of living in a contest society, the Romans, like the Homeric Greeks, the Japanese, and the Bedouin, were sensitive to their "face"; they were *delicatus*, "thin-skinned," liable to blush.[200] The *os durum*, the *os ferreum*, the hard, stony, brazen face, belonged to the stupid and shameless. With our love of dichotomies, we have a tendency to see in the Romans a "hard" and inviolable manliness and a "soft" and vulnerable womanliness.[201] But this opposition does not begin to cover the complex Roman dialectic between hardness and softness. The adjective *callidus* meant callused and shameless as well as wily. "Consider the terms used for a fool: blockhead, woodenpate, dolt, leadenwit" (*quae sunt dicta in stulto: caudex, stipes, asinus, plumbeus* [Terence, *Heautontimorumenos* 877–878]).[202] "My master," Palaestrio declares in the *Miles gloriosus*, "has the hide of an elephant and the stupidity of a stone" (235).[203] "No stone is more stolid."[204]

The stories of Roman sensitivity to insult are legion. Like characters out of Dostoevsky, the Romans were subject to violent attacks of self-esteem. A few examples must suffice. Seneca imagines the irritations of the "touchy" aristocrat: "He greeted me with too little courtesy; he failed to cling to my kiss; he abruptly cut off a conversation barely begun with me; he did not invite me to dinner; he appeared to avert his face" (*De ira* 2.24.1).[205] The younger Fabia was stung by her sister's casual laugh (Livy 6.34.6–7). Julius Caesar opened a civil war to "repel insult from himself" (*contumeliam propulsare* [Cicero, *Pro Ligario*

---

200. Seneca, *De constantia sapientis* 5.1. For the *os molle*, see Seneca, *Epistulae* 11.4: "Nothing was more sensitive than the face of Pompey; he always blushed in the presence of a group" (*nihil erat mollius ore Pompeii: numquam non coram pluribus rubuit*).

201. See, for example, William Fitzgerald, "Power and Impotence in Horace's *Epodes*," *Ramus* 17 (1988): 176–191, esp. p. 191 n. 8; Jonathan Walters, "Invading the Roman Body: Manliness and Impenetrability in Roman Thought," in *Roman Sexualities*, ed. Judith P. Hallet and Marilyn B. Skinner, Princeton 1997, pp. 29–43. Walters notices, however, that the antinomy does not seem to work for the soldier or the schoolboy whose bodies *were* violable. Cf. Seneca, *De clementia* 1.16.3; Gleason, "Truth Contests," pp. 23–26.

202. *Stultus* (stupid) was cognate with *stolidus* (inert, unmovable, dull, senseless). Cf. A. Ernout and A. Meillet, *Dictionnaire étymologique de la langue latine*, Paris, 1985, p. 655. The *caudex* was a "blockhead"; the *ferreus* (steely) was insensible and characterized by *asperitas* (roughness) and *immanitas* (savageness).

203. *erus meus elephanti corio circumtentust, non suo, / neque habet plus sapientiae quam lapis.*

204. *nullumst hoc stolidius saxum.* Hardness was associated with impudence, stupidity, cruelty, numbness, and stupor: *os durum!* (Terence, *Eunuchus* 806); *ore improbus duro* (Lucilius apud Gellius, *Noctes Atticae* 11.7.9); *os tuum ferreum senatus convicio verberari noluisti* (Cicero, *In Pisonem* 26.63); *duri puer oris et audax / constitit ante diem risitque* (Ovid, *Metamorphoses* 5.451–452); *sunt quidem praeduri in hoc oris* (Quintilian, *Institutio oratoria* 6.4.11). Cf. Plautus, *Mercator* 629–632; *Truculentus* 916; Cicero, *In Catilinam* 4.3, *Ad familiares* 15.21.3, *De amicitia* 87; Ovid, *Amores* 1.6.27–28, *Heroides* 10.131–132; Tibullus 1.2.66; Pliny, *Historia naturalis* 11.92.226; Pliny, *Epistulae* 2.3.7; Statius, *Thebais* 4.340; Plutarch, *Antonius* 53.4; Robert Kaster, "The Shame of the Romans," *Transactions and Proceedings of the American Philological Association* 127 (1997): 14 and n. 34.

205. *ille me parum humane salutavit; ille osculo meo non adhaesit; ille inchoatum sermonem cito abrupit; ille ad cenam non vocavit; illius vultus aversior visus est.*

18]).[206] Sejanus destroyed Drusus because the latter had once slapped him on the face (Tacitus, *Annales* 4.3). As the psychologist Leon Wurmser remarks, "The more competitive the person, the more sensitive he is to relative shortcomings and slights and the more indefatigable in comparing himself with his rival."[207]

As I stressed in the introduction, this touchiness was not confined to the ruling class in Rome any more than in the American South. It was felt in the kitchens and stables as keenly as in the inner-city schoolyard or the battlefield. In Livy's account, it was the wounds on the chest of a decorated plebeian soldier—and the tracks of the whip on his back—that set off the riots that launched the "Struggle of the Orders," the great contest between the patricians and the plebs that wracked the early centuries of the Republic (2.23.3–15). Sensitivity to ridicule made the plebs contentious. They demanded a public prosecution of the patrician Claudia when she verbally insulted them in 246 B.C.E.[208] The poor man, according to Juvenal, finds nothing harder to bear than the ridicule directed at the rents and patches on his clothing, the leather splitting on his sandals (*Satirae* 152–153).[209] Horace's poor man, fearful that he might seem a servile flatterer, speaks with pugnacious candor (*Epistulae* 1.18.5–8, 16–19).

THE SPECTER OF SOLIDITIES

Fortune is glass; just when it shines it shatters.
PUBLILIUS SYRUS 189, FRIEDRICH ED.[210]

The Romans' sense of embodiment was not only keen but brittle. The Romans, like the Homeric Greeks or the Heian Japanese, had a keen sense of their own

206. Cf. Caesar, *De bello civile* 1.9; Cicero, *Ad Atticum* 7.11.1. For more examples of Roman touchiness, see Plautus, *Casina* 874–877, *Cistellaria* 500–501, *Curculio* 325, 392; Terence, *Hecyra* 306–313; Cicero, *Ad Brutum* 25 (1.16); Livy 22.61.8–9, 39.4.13; Horace, *Satirae* 2.1, esp. lines 21–23, 44–46; Seneca, *De constantia sapientis* 5.1–2, 18.1–5; *De ira* 3.30; Tacitus, *Annales* 3.31.4–6, 15.49; Rosenstein, *Imperatores Victi*, p. 134 n. 75.

207. *The Masks of Shame*, Baltimore, 1981, pp. 78–79.

208. Livy, *periochae* 19; Suetonius, *Tiberius* 2.3; Gellius, *Noctes Atticae* 10.6; Valerius Maximus 8.1, *damnati* 4. For the sensitivity to insult of the plebs, see Zvi Yavetz, "The Urban Plebs in the Days of the Flavians, Nerva and Trajan," in *Opposition et résistance à l'empire d'Auguste à Trajan*, ed. Adalberto Giovannini, Geneva, 1986, pp. 169–170, and the remarks by Barbara Levick appended to that article (p. 185).

209. *nil habet infelix paupertas durius in se / quam quod ridiculos homines facit.* On the other hand, sensitivity to shame could make a plebeian shy. It conquered the resolve of Livy's humble Titus Latinius to report his portentous dream. "Though his spirit was not free from a sense of obligation *(religio)*, nevertheless shame and fear before the majesty of the magistrates—lest he depart an object of mirth in the mouths of men" paralyzed him *(quamquam haud sane liber erat religione animus, verecundia tamen maiestatis magistratuum timorque vicit, ne in ora hominum pro ludibrio abiret* [2.36.3]). Livy's peasant is only one of many for whom the desire to preserve their being and fear of exposure created an enervating sensibility.

210. *fortuna vitrea est; tum cum splendet frangitur.* In another place: "Whatever is adorned by fortune is soon despised" *(Quidquid fortuna exornat, cito contemnitur* [Publilius Syrus 550, Friedrich ed]). Compare Tacitus's description of the anxiety felt by the spectators at Germanicus's triumph (*Annales* 2.41).

frailty. "Praise is offered to virtue, but it melts away far more quickly than ice in spring."[211] "Everything human is fragile and fleeting" (Cicero, *De amicitia* 27.102).[212] "The radiant visage, great wealth, bodily strength and all other things of this sort quickly perish" (Sallust, *Bellum Iugurthinum* 2.2).[213] "And what does Fortune not the more violently attack and crush, the more brilliantly it shines?" (Seneca, *Epistulae* 91.4).[214] For Horace, "All of life is only a little, no long-term plans are allowed. Soon night and half-remembered shapes and drab Pluto's walls will be closing in" (*Carmina* 1.4 lines 15–17).[215] For Ovid, "everything human hangs by a slender thread" (*Epistulae ex Ponto* 4.3.35).[216]

This infirmity often translated into a sense of doom. In a famous scene, Polybius reports the words that the general Scipio Aemilianus spoke to him when he watched Carthage burn: "Turning round to me at once and grasping my hand, Scipio said, 'A glorious moment, Polybius, but I have a dread foreboding that some day the same doom will be pronounced upon my own country'" (38.21.1).[217]

> Scipio, when he looked upon the city as it was utterly perishing and in the last throes of its complete destruction, is said to have shed tears and wept openly for his ene-

---

211. *praestatur laus virtuti, sed multo ocius / verno gelu tabescit.*

212. *res humanae fragiles caducaeque sunt.* See the sentiments of Sulpicius Rufus and Cicero, *Ad familiares* 4.5.4 and 4.6; Pliny, *Panegyricus* 55.8–9; Virgil, *Aeneis* 1.453ff., Petronius, *Satyricon* 34.

213. *igitur praeclara facies, magnae divitiae, ad hoc vis corporis et alia omnia huisce modi brevi dilabuntur.* The inscription on the sarcophagus of Publius Cornelius Scipio, the son of Africanus (ca. 180–82 B.C.E.) reads: "Death brought to pass that everything of yours was brief: honor, fame and virtue, glory and talent" (*mors perfecit tua ut essent omnia brevia: honos, fama virtusque gloria atque ingenium* [*Corpus Inscriptionum Latinarum*, vol. 1.2, no. 15 = *Inscriptiones Latinae Selectae*, vol. 1, no. 6]). "Human affairs, unstable and fickle as they are, always change for the worse" (*humanae res, quae fluxae et mobiles semper in advorsa mutantur* [Sallust, *Bellum Iugurthinum* 104.2, cf. 1.1]). The degree to which something was earnestly desired was the degree of its fragility. "The best of days are the first to flee for miserable mortals; diseases and bitter old age and suffering steal upon them, and then pitiless brazen death sweeps them away" (*optima quaeque dies miseris mortalibus aevi / prima fugit: subeunt morbi tristisque senectus / et labor, et durae rapit inclementia mortis* [Virgil, *Georgica* 3.66–68]). "Human affairs are unstable and fleeting, and no part of our life is so frail and perishable as that which gives the most pleasure" (*labant humana ac fluunt neque ulla pars vitae nostrae tam obnoxia aut tenera est quam quae maxime placet* [*Consolatio ad Marciam* 22.1]). Tacitus quotes the emperor Tiberius: "Everything is uncertain for a mortal; the higher he climbs the more slippery his path" (*cuncta mortalium incerta, quantoque plus adeptus foret, tanto se magis in lubrico* [*Annales* 1.72]). Petronius tells the deliciously horrible story of the man who invented unbreakable glass. When he demonstrated his miraculous invention, when "he had Jupiter by the balls," he was straightaway beheaded by the king. His sweet dream cracked like an egg (*Satyricon* 51). For the range of metaphorical associations of glass, see May Luella Trowbridge, *Philological Studies in Ancient Glass*, Urbana, Illinois, 1930, pp. 59–94.

214. *quid enim est, quod non fortuna, cum voluit, ex florentissimo detrahit? quod non eo magis adgrediatur et quatiat, quo speciosius fulget?* Cf. Seneca, *De ira* 2.31.5.

215. *vitae summa brevis spem nos vetat incohare longam. / iam te premet nox fabulaeque Manes / et domus exilis Plutonia.* Cf. Horace, *Carmina* 1.9, 1.11, 2.3, 2.11, 2.14, 3.29, 4.7; Steele Commager, "The World of Nature: Time and Change," chapter 5 of *The Odes of Horace*, Bloomington, Indiana, 1962, pp. 235–306.

216. *omnia sunt hominum tenui pendentia filo.* Cf. Seneca, *Ad Marciam* 22.1.

217. Paton trans.

mies. After being wrapped in thought for long, and realizing that all cities, nations, and authorities, must, like men, meet their doom, and that this happened to Ilium, once a prosperous city, to the empires of Assyria, Media, Persia, the greatest of their time, and to Macedonia itself, the brilliance of which was so recent, either deliberately, or the verses escaping him, said: "A day will come when sacred Troy shall perish, and Priam and his people shall be slain." And when Polybius, speaking with freedom to him, for he was his teacher, asked him what he meant by the words, they say that without any attempt at concealment he named his own country. (Appian, *Punica* 19.132)[218]

Pliny the Elder describes a display of precious myrrhine crystal that he saw in Nero's private theater. "I saw pieces of a single broken cup included in the exhibition. It was decided that these broken shards should be displayed in a kind of sepulcher, like the body of Alexander, as a testament to the sorrows of the age and the envy of Fortune" (*Historia naturalis* 37.7.19–20).[219] As Pliny explains, once it has been broken, rock crystal cannot be mended by any method whatsoever (37.10.29).[220] Just so, Catullus asserts, "Once night comes for us, it is night forever" (5.5–6).[221]

Last words *(ultima verba)* were compelling to the Romans, as they are to us— but not because they summed up or grasped the eternal essence of life. When Vespasian and Petronius make light of their own deaths, or when Seneca's Leonidas tells his doomed soldiers, "Eat your breakfast, for tonight we sup in Hell" (*Epistulae* 82.21),[222] we are affected by their words because they reveal the will of the speaker, the fantastic will of the doomed to let go of what there was the most extreme urgency to grasp.[223] The ability of the Roman gladiator to carry

218. Paton trans. See Diodorus Siculus 32.24; A. E. Astin, *Scipio Aemilianus,* Oxford, 1967, pp. 282–287. "Does Troy's fall makes us so proud and fierce? We Greeks are standing in the place from which Troy fell" (*Troia nos tumidos facit / nimium ac feroces? stamus hoc Danai loco, unde illa cecidit* [Seneca, *Troades* 264–266]). Compare the reflections on the vicissitudes of war and the instability of human affairs of the victorious Roman general Titus in Josephus, *Bellum Iudaicum* 3.396.

219. *vidi tunc adnumerari unius scyphi fracti membra, quae in dolorem, credo, saeculi and invidiamque Fortunae tamquam Alexandri Magni corpus in conditorio servari, ut ostentarentur, placebit.* Glass and mortality are juxtaposed in several tantalizing scenes in Pliny: when Nero received the news that all was lost, he broke two crystal cups as an act of spite toward his whole generation (*Historia naturalis* 37.10.29). Petronius, condemned to death by Nero, broke a precious myrrhine dipper out of spite for the emperor and his greed (ibid. 37.7.20).

220. *fragmenta sarciri nullo modo queunt.*

221. C. H. Sisson trans. slightly modified. *nobis cum semel occidit brevis lux, / nox est perpetua una dormienda.*

222. *"Sic commilitones, prandete tamquam apud inferos cenaturi."*

223. Cicero's Lacedaemonian tells the enemy Persian (who had boasted that the battling Spartans would not be able to see the sun for the multitude of Persian spears and arrows), "Then we will fight in the shade" (*E quibus unus, cum Perses hostis in colloquio dixisset glorians: Solem prae iaculorum multitudine et sagittarum non videbitis. In umbra igitur, inquit, pugnabimus [Tusculanae disputationes* 1.42.101]). See Herodotus 7.226. Compare Hannibal's joking at the sight of the army of Terentius, twice the size of his own

through with the "play" right up to the moment of death proved, perhaps more than anything, his terrifying courage. "How exalted his spirit!" *(quam elato animo est!)* Cicero exclaims at Theramenes's ability to jest while drinking the fatal poison (*Tusculanae disputationes* 1.40.96–97).[224] Again, you were what you could live without.

THE CHOREOGRAPHY OF THE IMMEDIATE

The Romans were wont to feel themselves burning in the focus of a giant spotlight. "Not only your army but all citizens, and almost all nations, have focused their eyes on you" (Cicero to Marcus Brutus in a letter from Rome dated June 43 B.C.E. [*Ad Brutum* 19.2 (= 1.9.2)]).[225] "The voices of their friends reminded them that their country and their country's gods, their parents, and their fellows at home and in the army had their eyes fixed on their right hands and on their swords" (Livy 1.25.1).[226]

Being in the spotlight created a self-consciousness so heightened that it could result, ironically, in a sense of unreality and disengagement. Confounded, exposed to the eyes of others, a Roman might find it difficult to act or speak at all. Plautus's Sosia, challenged by the bully Mercury, declares, "I'm afraid. I am altogether numb" (*Amphitruo* 335).[227] The young orator appearing before judges was, as might be expected of a youth of good breeding, paralyzed with shame and incapable of presenting the case he had prepared (Terence, *Phormio* 281–84).[228] The

---

(Plutarch, *Fabius Maximus* 15.2), and Oscar Wilde's famous joke about the wallpaper ("One of us has got to go"). Their words enabled the Romans not to pierce the darkness but to see it.

224. See the wonderful story of Björn Dufgusson's laughing death in battle in Richard Bauman, "Performance and Honor in Thirteenth-Century Iceland," *Journal of American Folklore* 99 (1986): 131–150. The Roman, like the Aztec or the Huron, wanted to see indomitable suffering. Inga Clendinnen says of the captured Nahua warrior: "Such a man presented to death before Huitzilopochtli's shrine crowning the temple pyramid ideally leapt up the steps shouting the praises of his city" (*Aztecs: An Interpretation*, Cambridge, 1991, esp. 93–94); "Cost of Courage," p. 69. See also Antony F. C. Wallace, *The Death and Rebirth of the Seneca* (New York, 1972, pp. 104–107; Bruce G. Trigger, *The Children of Aataentsic: A History of the Huron People to 1600*, Montreal, 1976, vol. 1, esp. p. 73; Barton, *Sorrows*, chapter 1.

225. *cum in te non solum exercitus tui, sed omnium civium ac paene gentium coniecti oculi sint.* "Today the world is on the lookout, watching every one of us to see how far he will observe his obligations and preserve the law" (*nunc autem homines in speculis sunt; observant quem ad modum sese unus quisque vestrum gerat in retinenda religione conservandisque legibus* [Cicero, *In Verrem* 1.16.46]).

226. *cum sui utrosque adhortarentur deos patrios, patriam ac parentes, quidquid civium domi, quidquid in exercitu sit, illorum tunc arma, illorum intueri manus.* As we say on my softball team: "No pressure!" Cf. Cicero, *Ad familiares* 2.12.2, 5.7.3; Sallust, *Bellum Iugurthinum* 85.5; Valerius Maximus 3.2.1; Tacitus, *Annales* 6.2 (= 5.7).

227. *Timeo, totus torpeo.*

228. *functus adulescentulist / officium liberalis; postquam ad iudices ventumst, non potuit cogitata proloqui: / ita eum tum timidum subito stupefacit pudor.*

great orator Crassus, Cicero tells us, went pale whenever he had to stand up to plead in court, his whole body trembling and shuddering. Indeed, when he was a young man first opening a case in court, he was so broken and debilitated by fear *(fractus ac debilitatus metu)*, so demoralized *(exanimatus)* that the judge took compassion on him and adjourned the hearing *(De oratore* 1.26.121).[229] A young man, put on the spot by the powerful Seneca, experienced a kind of stage fright. Blushing in confusion, he was unable to speak coherently (Seneca, *Epistulae* 11.1).[230] Cicero describes the reaction of the accuser Chaerea after Cicero had asked him an embarrassing question: "He blushes; he does not know what to answer; he can't come up with anything to say on the spot" *(Pro Roscio Commoedo* 3.8).[231] Livy's humble Bacchante, Faecenia Hispala, confronted with the censoring questions of the consul Spurius Postumius, is frozen and inarticulate. "So great a fear and trembling seized her in every part of her body that for a long time she could not speak" (39.12.5).[232]

There are many depictions of the anguished narcosis of exposure in modern literature: one might think of Hawthorne's Hester Prynne exposed for hours on the scaffold, or the handcuffed Oscar Wilde surrounded by a jeering mob at Clapham Junction railway station. Perhaps the most memorable description of this phenomenon in the Roman sources is Livy's lengthy dramatization of the Roman soldiers anticipating, experiencing, and reliving the appalling humiliations occasioned by their capture at the Caudine Forks (9.1–11). The agony stops time and paralyzes the Roman soldiers who emerge from the defile after passing under the yoke of their Sabine enemies.[233] They are silent and all but deaf and blind. They cannot bear the eyes of others; they cannot even bear the light (*pudor intuendae lucis* [9.7.3]).

Because unmediated embodiment was shocking, the man or woman in the spotlight had difficulty "being himself" or "being herself," and tended to lapse into confusion and stupefaction. For that reason, the Romans tended to frame contests as formalized and scripted dramas or games (whether the decorum of daily intercourse or the etiquette of the games, the law courts, and senate house). They relied on ritualization for the preservation of the face (and so of the *animus*).

229. Even the steadiest speaker, according to Seneca, was liable to sweat profusely, to tremble, quake and chatter when speaking in public *(Epistulae* 11.2).

230. The younger Fabia was "confused by the recent insult to her spirit" *(confusam eam ex recenti morsu animi* [Livy 6.34.8]).

231. *Erubescit, quid respondeat, nescit, quid fingat extemplo, non habet.*

232. *hoc ubi audivit, tantus pavor tremorque omnium membrorum mulierem cepit ut diu hiscere non posset.* Cf. Apuleius, *Metamorphoses* 3.12.

233. When the Romans try to describe the feeling of paralysis resulting from being, as we would say, "in a fix," they employ such phrases as "between the ax and the altar" *(inter sacrum et saxum* [Apuleius, *Metamorphoses* 11.28; Plautus, *Captivi* 617]), or "between the wolves and the hounds" *(hac lupi, hac canes* [Plautus, *Casina* 970]).

For Goffman, "One's face . . . is a sacred thing, and the expressive order required to sustain it is therefore a ritual one."[234] As Takie Lebra explains, "Face is most vulnerable in unpredictable situations. The most common means of keeping it safe, then, is to minimize the options and uncertainties that might arise in a situation. Ritualism is the answer."[235] The formalized game or rite was employed in ancient Rome when the desire to preserve the community was stronger than the desire to break the spirit of the opponent. Precisely because they alleviated shock, games were most effective precisely at moments of grief and terror.[236] Gladiatorial games and *decursiones funebres*, like funerals themselves, allowed for vigorous and ritualized activity at the very moment when one was most shocked by grief. Familiar and formalized behaviors facilitated action in emergencies, because, as the ethologist Irenäus Eibl-Eibesfeldt points out, "the more ritualized the behavior, the more easily it is released."[237]

234. "On Face-Work: An Analysis of Ritual Elements in Social Interaction," in *Interaction Ritual,* 5–45, p. 19.

235. *Japanese Patterns of Behavior,* Honolulu, 1976, p. 125. Mark Edward Lewis says of the Zhou period in Chinese history: "It was a world where . . . men showed that they treasured honor by fighting to the death over a single insulting word, and where elaborate social rituals were gradually erected to minimize the possibility of misunderstandings" (*Sanctioned Violence in Early China,* Albany, New York, 1990, p. 40).

236. For ritualized behavior, including plays and games, alleviating grief at funerals, relieving tensions caused by disturbances, or expiating improprieties or prodigies, see Erich Gruen, "The Theatre and Aristocratic Culture," in *Culture and National Identity in Republican Rome,* Ithaca, 1992, esp. pp. 183, 187; A. Van Gennep, *Rites of Passage,* trans. M. Vizedom and G. Caffee, Chicago, 1960, pp. 1–13, 146–165; Margaret Mead, "Ritual and Social Crisis," in *The Roots of Ritual,* ed. James D. Shaughnessy, Grand Rapids, Michigan, 1973, esp. pp. 89–90; Richard Katz, *Boiling Energy: Community Healing among the Kalihari Kung,* Cambridge, 1982; Jan C. Heesterman, *The Broken World of Sacrifice: An Essay on Ancient Indian Ritual,* Chicago, 1993.

237. "Ritual and Ritualization from a Biological Perspective," in *Human Ethology: Claims and Limits of a New Discipline,* ed. M. von Cranach, K. Foppa, W. Lepenies, and D. Ploog, Cambridge, 1979, p. 15. Inga Clendinnen discusses the ways in which ritual can release men from distracting nervousness. She follows Victor Turner who, in turn, follows Mihaly Csikszentmihalyi, who employs the word "flow" to describe

> the holistic sensation present when we act with total involvement . . . the state in which action follows action according to an internal logic which seems to heed no conscious intervention on our own part. . . . The rules simplify and focus, and above all facilitate the experience of intense but harmonious and fluent action. Turner saw an equivalent "flow" experience being achieved in ritual where, with self-consciousness reduced through drugs, vigil, chants or fasting, action and awareness fuse as attention centers on a limited stimulus field, in that only the "now" matters. ("Cost of Courage," p. 86)

See Milhaly Csikszentmihalyi and Isabella Selega Csikszentmihalyi, *Optimal Experience: Psychological Studies of Flow in Consciousness,* Cambridge, 1988; Victor Turner, "Variations on a Theme of Liminality," in *Secular Ritual,* ed. Sally F. Moore and Barbara G. Myerhoff, Amsterdam, 1977, pp. 48–52. For Clendinnen, this is an accurate description of the experience of the sacrificial victims in Aztec culture, who would otherwise have been debilitated with terror. Ritual brings them into the now and takes them through it. For the notion of "flow," see also the remarks by Paul Richards in *Key Debates in An-*

When the Roman soldiers first ascertained that they were surrounded and trapped in the Caudine Forks, they came abruptly to a halt, a stupor and a sort of torpor having seized their limbs. For a long time the soldiers stood in silence, immobilized, observing one another, each imagining the other to be more in command of his senses (Livy 9.2.10–11).[238] Spontaneously, without having been given orders, they launched into the Roman soldier's daily and arduous rite of building a stockade. The enemy mocked them and they mocked themselves, knowing full well the inanity of building a fortress within a cage (9.2.12–14).[239] Still, the automatic and formalized behavior provided a relief from stupor. It allowed them to move and to show energy.[240] The Romans, like Sartre's Roquentin, needed to suffer in rhythm.[241]

The most reliable and effective rules of the game were axiomatic and unquestioned. To the extent that the *religiones* of the Romans, however dangerous and complex, were givens, submission to them was no more humiliating or debilitating than for a baseball player to submit to the three-strike rule or a high-wire artist to yield to the laws of gravity. So Cicero, when speaking of the body and its involuntary functions, asserts that the acts of elimination and sex are necessities. They cannot be avoided and thus are not a cause of shame in themselves.[242] But the voluntary mentioning of the associated bodily parts and their activities was invariably shameful (Cicero, *De officiis* 1.35.127). Only what was subject to the will was shameful or honorable.[243] Decorum, etiquette, the strictures and subterfuges

---

thropology, ed. Tim Ingold, New York, 1966, pp. 123–128, 134, 139–40. The swimmer and Olympic gold medalist Pablo Morales, at a conference at Stanford University titled "The Athlete's Body" (May 12, 1995), described the effects of extremely ritualized behavior (swimming), in even the most highly tense and competitive situation (the Olympic Games), as allowing him to be "lost in focused intensity." Similarly, Karl Wallenda described the sense of tranquility he experienced in breathtakingly dangerous situations through the rigidly disciplined and repeated physical acts of walking the high wire.

238. *sistunt inde gradum sine ullius imperio, stuporque omnium animos ac velut torpor quidam insolitus membra tenet, intuentesque alii alios, cum alterum quisque compotem magis mentis, ac consilii ducerent, diu immobiles silent.*

239. *sua ipsi opera laboremque irritum, praeterquam quod hostes superbe increpabant, cum miserabili confessione eludentes.* Not just energy but *effective* energy was required to preserve one's honor. "To struggle in vain and to gain nothing by wearying oneself, except hatred, is the extreme of dementia" (*frustra autem niti neque aliud se fatigando nisi odium quaerere extremae dementiae est* [Sallust, *Bellum Iugurthinum* 3.3]). See chapter 4.

240. Livy offers us a similar example of automatic behavior being deployed at a moment of shock: "The Gauls, as if the miracle of their sudden victory had stupefied them, at first stood fixated with fear, as if unable to comprehend what had occurred to them. Then they feared an ambush. Then, according to their custom, they fell to collecting the spoils of the slain and erecting piles of arms" (*Gallos quoque velut obstupefactos miraculum victoriae tam repentinae tenuit, ipsi pavore defixi primum steterunt, velut ignari quid accidisset: deinde insidias vereri: postremo caesorum spolia legere armorumque cumulos, ut mos eis est, coacervare* [Livy 5.39.1]).

241. "Il faut souffrir en mesure" (Sartre, *La Nausée*, Paris, 1938).

242. The "natural functions" are not a cause of shame, provided that they are accomplished as secretly as possible.

243. Cf. Seneca, *De beneficiis* 5.5.1.

of formalized and ritualized behaviors, insofar as they were accepted as necessary and inevitable, helped to relieve both the shock of embodiment and the anguish of a heightened self-consciousness.

Closely related to the shock-relieving function of rituals was the shock-relieving function of roles. The Latin *persona* was not only the mask but also the part expressed by that mask. Latin *professio*, aside from being an open avowal, was the affirmation of the role or part presented by the *persona*—and the challenge presented by that affirmation. Horace's Lollius fears, for example, that, having professed himself a friend, he might appear only as a wit, a *scurra* (*Epistulae* 1.18.1–2).[244]

It was the discipline and training, the habituation to a particular role or roles, that gave one the ability to be truly present at the moment of truth. How is it that stalwart gladiators endure the death blow? How is it they offer their necks without flinching? "They are well trained" *(bene instituti sunt)*, Cicero explains. "Such is the power of exercise, of practice, of habit!" (*Tusculanae disputationes* 2.17.40–41).[245] And so the good parent, out of love for the child, acted as a trainer, endlessly manufacturing trials for the child (Seneca, *De providentia* 2.5).[246] The Elder Cato, good father that he was, subjected his frail son to the extremes of heat and cold and made him swim the wildest and most swiftly flowing stretches of the Tiber (Plutarch, *Cato maior* 20.4).[247] "Do you imagine that the Spartans hate their children, whose spirits they test by the administration of public whippings? Their own fathers exhort them to endure bravely the blows of the lash and call on them, lacerated and half dead, to keep offering their wounds for further wounding" (Seneca, *De providentia* 4.11).[248]

Seneca imagined that those who were not trained and fortified by the discipline of philosophy would crack when the torturer commanded them to stretch forth their hands or when death drew near (*Epistulae* 82.7–8).[249] And so Epictetus attributed to his training the casual, insouciant way that Agrippinus met his exile (Arrian, *Epicteti dissertationes* 1.1.28–32).

---

244. *si bene te novi, metues, liberrime Lolli / scurrantis speciem praebere, professus amicum.*

245. *tantum exercitatio, meditatio, consuetudo valet.*

246. Cf. Virgil, *Aeneis* 9.603–608.

247. The father's testing began in infancy. On the *dies lustricus* or *nominalia*, the child was subjected to a succession of ritual dangers. Until these trials were endured, the child had no being. Until the *nominalia* he was, according to Plutarch, "more like a plant than an animal" (*Quaestiones romanae* 102 [*Moralia* 288C]). Cf. Festus-Paulus p. 364, Dacerius ed.; Macrobius, *Saturnalia* 1.16.36.

248. *numquid tu invisos esse Lacedaemoniis liberos suos credis, quorum experiuntur indolem publice verberibus admotis? ipsi illos patres adhortantur, ut ictus flagellorum fortiter perferant et laceros ac semianimes rogant, perseverent vulnera praebere vulneribus.* The Spartan "whipping contest" was notorious for the deaths that resulted. It was a kind of training in expendability, a very cruel kindness on the part of the father.

249. *cum securos aliquis casus expertus est, exprimitur sera confessio. magna verba excidunt cum tortor poposcit manum, cum mors proprius accessit.*

Many Roman stories express admiration for those able to preserve their roles under great stress. Livy tells of the dauntless Gaius Fabius Dorsuo, who at the time of the Gallic sack nonchalantly descended from the besieged Capitol, in the midst of the enemy, to perform the family's traditional rites (5.46.1–3). He tells of the brave *seniores* who faced the invading Gauls dressed in their finery, with their emblems of office, sitting like statues on their curule chairs in the vestibules of their houses (5.41.1–3).[250] In Appian's account of the capture of Rome by Marius and Cinna, Gnaius Octavius, the consul of 87 B.C.E., refused to flee. Instead he withdrew to the Janiculum with the remnants of his force and there, sitting in the full regalia of his office, calmly awaited death (*Bellum civile* 1.8.71).[251] Livy's consul Horatius continued dedicating the temple of Jupiter even when news came of the death of his son (2.8.7–8).[252] Seneca's Paulus proceeded with his triumph despite the loss of one son and the imminent loss of another—whose deaths he interpreted publicly as the price he had paid to the envy of the gods for his Roman victories. "Behold the greatness of his spirit: he congratulated himself on his bereavement!" (Seneca, *Ad Marciam* 13.3–4).[253] Courageous Cornelia, the oft-bereaved mother of the Gracchi, continued graciously to open her house and to entertain guests after the murder of her two beloved sons (Plutarch, *Gaius Gracchus* 19). The bravery of Sertorius earned him hideous wounds, but "those who saw what he had lost saw, at the same time, the proof of his bravery" (*Sertorius* 4). The empty chariot of Paulus, the dry eyes of Cornelia, the mutilations of Sertorius revealed the courage their performances had cost them. I am reminded of Erving Goffman's wireless operator: "He politely declines to leave his sinking ship and goes down while coolly improvising repairs on the transmitter, gamely driving himself even though his hands are burned. [He] combines in his deed almost all that society can ask of anyone. He transmits an important message even though his S.O.S. may not get through."[254]

Going on with the show, then, was not a sign of delusion but a supremely defining moment for Roman society as well as for the men and women who could

250. Compare the Romans' admiration for women and men able to preserve their roles in the stress of sudden exposure.

251. Herodotus tells the wonderful story of the great citharode Arion: The pirates who determined to throw him into the sea allowed Arion one last chance to put on his full regalia and perform. Dressed in his finery, and standing on the rowing benches, Arion performed what he thought was his last song. After his song ended, he threw himself into the sea (1.24.4). Gregory Bateson tells an equally charming story of an Iatmul hunter caught by a giant crocodile who, with the help of his dog and his wife, put on his legbands, shell girdle, mother-of-pearl crescent, and headdress of parrot skins and bird-of-paradise feathers to await the inevitable (*Naven*, Stanford, 1958, pp. 158–159).

252. According to Josephus, Pompey admired the fortitude of the Jews and their priests who continued to sacrifice at the altars of the Temple in Jerusalem even while the soldiers of the victorious Pompey cut them into pieces (*Bellum Iudaicum* 1.148,150).

253. *Vides quam magno animo tulerit: orbitati suae gratulatus est!*

254. "Where the Action Is," p. 229.

play their roles with grace, honoring their obligations even while threatened with death or chaos.[255] The tremendous calm and deliberation with which Tacitus's Valerius Asiaticus committed suicide, taking scrupulous care—like Cato of Utica or the emperor Otho in similar situations—for others, moving his pyre lest it singe the trees, demonstrated his ability to play his role to the end (*Annales* 11.3.2). It kept alive the play in which he had a part and through which he lived.[256] One can compare the polite "thank you" that Julius Canus mustered in reply to his condemnation to death by Phalaris, servant of Caligula. The centurion who came to drag him to his execution found him playing chess. Canus blithely bid his guard to check the state of the game—in which he was ahead—lest his opponent should later claim to have won (Seneca, *De tranquillitate* 14.4–7). It is the very absurdity, the impossibility and unnaturalness of Julius Canus's behavior that renders it ferocious. He saves nothing, clings to nothing, grasps at nothing, and in doing so asserts the magnificence of his spirit and the potency, the reality of the code by which he lives. The gladiator who bared his throat to the death-blow, who adhered to the etiquette of the arena to the moment of his death, was an actor who turned what might be a farce into a supremely transcendent moment.[257] Just as the artificiality, the "unnaturalness," of his acts made the "true" man, so the theatricality, the "unnaturalness," of his acts allowed for the vivid reality of that world in which for an hour the Roman strutted and fretted.

THE BONDS OF COMPETITION

Modern competition is described as the fight of all against all,
but at the same time it is the fight of all for all.
GEORG SIMMEL, *CONFLICT*[258]

The most closely bound unit, the family, was also, necessarily, the focus of competition: one emulated, above all, one's ancestors and kin. The inscriptions from the

255. Cato the Elder, "like a champion athlete," continued to observe the rules of his training and maintained his self-discipline to the very end of his life (Plutarch, *Cato Maior* 4.2–3). The Younger Cato continued playing "the game" even when no one else would or could (Seneca, *De constantia sapientis* 2.2). The honorable person played by the rules of the game even when no one could see him; a man of integrity was one with whom you could play "Odds and Evens" (casting fingers, *micatio*) in the dark (Cicero, *De officiis* 3.19.77; *De finibus* 2.16.52; Petronius, *Satyricon* 44).

256. "Honor, that is, this readiness regardless of price to uphold the code by which he lives" (Goffman, "Where the Action Is," p. 254).

257. See Seneca, *Epistulae* 30.8. The gladiator's highly dramatic and ritualized gesture of baring the throat was often used by Romans in mortal situations when there was no time to stage their deaths more elaborately. See Cicero, *Pro Sestio* 37.80; Seneca Rhetor, *Suasoriae* 6.17; Seneca, *Agamemnon* 971–976; Petronius, *Satyricon* 101.1; Tacitus, *Annales* 1.53.8 (Sempronius Gracchus); *Historia* 1.41 (Galba). It signaled a willed but defiant submission.

258. That is, for the attention, the business, the love, the praise of all. Georg Simmel, *Conflict*, trans. Kurt H. Wolff, in *Conflict and the Web of Group Affiliations*, Glencoe, Illinois, 1955, p. 62; cf. p. 64.

tomb of the Scipiones offer wonderful illustrations of intergenerational competition. The following words were carved on the sarcophagus of Gnaeus Cornelius Scipio Hispanis around the year 130 B.C.E.: "By the way I lived my life I added to the achievements of my family. I aimed at equaling the deeds of my ancestors....I succeeded in obtaining public esteem so that they rejoice that I was born to them. My honor ennobled the stock."[259] The inscription on the sarcophagus of Publius Cornelius Scipio reads: "If you had been allowed to have a long life, you would have easily outshone the glory of your ancestors."[260] "You had a brave man for a grandfather; see to it that you are braver" (*avom fortem virum habuisti: vide ut sis fortior* [Seneca Rhetor, *Controversiae* 10.2.16]).[261] Sallust's Marius complains of the lazy and corrupt nobles that the glory of their ancestors serves as a brilliant searchlight in which their own lack of industry and energy is glaringly exposed (*Bellum Iugurthinum* 85.21–23).[262]

After the family, the most intense circle of competitors was lovers and friends, friends being, as Sallust explains, those who wanted the same things (*quos omnis eadem cupere, eadem odisse, eadem metuere* [*Bellum Iugurthinum* 31.14–15]).[263] Cicero speaks of his admiration for Marcus Claudius Marcellus, *aemulus, imitator, socius,* and *comes:* "I could not persuade myself, nor did I consider it right for me, to pursue my old path of life when he who had been the rival and imitator of my studies and my labors had been separated from me, considering him, as I did, a sort of comrade and companion" (*Pro Marcello* 1.2). Livy laments "that poor judgment of ours which makes us all so loath to be outdone by those closest to us" (6.34.7).[264] This rivalry also confirmed a social bond, for, as Alvin Gouldner explains, "The contestant wants most the plaudits of those with whom he is in the most intense competition."[265] Moreover, as Bourdieu points out, "To challenge someone is to

---

259. *virtutes generis mieis moribus accumulavi progeniem genui. facta patris petiei. / maiorum optenui laudem ut sibei me esse creatum laetentur. stirpem nobilitavit honor. Corpus Inscriptionum Latinarum,* vol 1.2, no. 15 = *Inscriptiones Latinae Selectae,* vol. 1, no. 6.

260. *sei in longa licu[i]sset tibi utier vita / facile facteis superases gloriam maiorum (Corpus Inscriptionum Latinarum,* vol. 1.2, no. 10 = *Inscriptiones Latinae Selectae,* vol. 1, no. 4).

261. Plautus's young Lysiteles challenges his friend Lesbonicus to live up to the *fama* they had won by their *virtus* and shames him with the reproach that he is unworthy of his ancestors (*Trinummus* 642ff.). "What can be more splendid than the youth who can say to himself: 'I surpassed my father in benefits'?" (*Quid eo adulescente praeclarius qui sibi ipsi dicere poterit..."patrem meum beneficiis vincere"* [Seneca, *De beneficiis* 3.38.3]). For competition with the ancestors and within the family, see Juvenal, *Satirae* 8; Livy 6.34.6–11 (the sisters Fabia); Cicero, *De officiis* 1.32.116; Valerius Maximus 3.5.1–4; Velleius 2.116.4; Apuleius, *Metamorphoses* 4.28–6.24 (the sisters of Psyche); Donald Earl, *The Moral and Political Tradition of Rome,* London, 1967, p. 26; John Lendon, *Empire of Honour,* p. 39.

262. *maiorum gloria posteris quasi lumen est, neque bona neque mala eorum in occulto patitur.* "Der praktische Ausdruck solcher Anschauung ist das '*Brute dormis'*" (Knoche, "Der römische Ruhmesgedanke," pp. 428–430).

263. For lovers as competitors, see Petronius, *Satyricon* 19.4–20.4; Apuleius, *Metamorphoses* 2.17.

264. *malo arbitrio quo a proximis quisque minime anteiri volt.*

265. *Enter Plato,* pp. 53–54. See Simmel, *Conflict,* pp. 43–45.

acknowledge that he is a man, an acknowledgment which is the prerequisite for any exchange."[266] "To make someone a challenge is to credit him with the dignity of a man of honour, since the challenge, as such, requires a riposte and therefore is deemed capable of playing the game of honour, and of playing it well. From the principle of mutual recognition of equality in honour there follows a first corollary: the challenge confers honour."[267]

But there was another and stronger sort of bonding effected by the good contest: the Roman was radically present in a role or game in which life or reputation was at risk. In preserving one's role to the end of the ordeal, one demonstrated both "sincerity" and "authenticity" in their Roman senses. Radical presence was sincere in the sense that one held nothing back, that everything one had was at stake in one's role.[268] Sincerity was the positive version, the vivifying version of self-exposure: will.

The perception of sincerity created mutual sympathies within Roman culture.[269] The Romans identified with a role that was voluntary. When they had the sense that someone was doing something *ex anima*, they had the sense that someone was "authentically" there, that he or she had "earned" their role. However silly and superficial you might consider a circus act, it is hard not to feel a powerful bond with the man or woman on the high wire without a net. Compare the emotions that Ernest Hemingway associated with the dangerous *faena* of the Spanish bullfighter,

> that takes a man out of himself and makes him feel immortal while it is proceeding, that gives him an ecstasy, that is, while momentary, as profound as any religious ecstasy; moving all the people in the ring together and increasing in emotional intensity as it proceeds, carrying the bullfighter with it, he playing the crowd through the bull and being moved as it responds in a growing ecstasy of ordered, formal, pas-

266. "The Sense of Honor," *Algeria 1960*, trans. Richard Nice, Cambridge, 1979, pp. 99–100.

267. Bourdieu, *Outline*, p. 11. Conversely, all forms of exchange can be interpreted as competitive. As Eibl-Eibesfeldt points out, shaking hands (one of the principal symbols of contractual obligations for the Romans) was both a form of exchange and a kind of contest. "This form of establishing contact includes a demonstration of strength and enables people to size each other up. In this respect the greeting undoubtedly contains an element of aggression: shaking and squeezing hands is often a kind of sporting contest" (*Love and Hate*, New York, 1971, p. 182). "Every exchange contains a more or less dissimulated challenge" (Bourdieu, *Outline*, p. 14).

268. Bourdieu says of contests of honor among the Kabyle: "The most profitable strategies are usually those produced on the hither side of all calculation, and in the illusions of the most 'authentic' sincerity.... These strategies without strategic calculation procure an important secondary advantage for those who can scarcely be called their authors—the social approval accruing from apparent disinterestedness" (*Outline*, p. 214 n. 2).

269. See Goffman, "Where the Action Is," pp. 184–185. The Roman rites that framed the contest were "methektic" in the sense employed by Jane Ellen Harrison. Harrison distinguished between methektic rites and mimetic rites. Methektic rites were ceremonies that were intensely sympathetic and cooperative: "the expression, the utterance of a common nature participated in, rather than the imitation of alien characteristics" (*Themis: A Study of the Social Origins of Greek Religion* [Cleveland, 1912], 1962, p. 125).

sionate, increasing disregard for death that leaves you, when it is over and the death administered to the animal that has made it possible, as empty, as changed, and as sad as any major emotion will leave you.[270]

One might also compare the Roman sensibility to the radical subjectivity of Zen, the warrior's Buddhism, with its fragile sense of all that is and its ideal of keeping nothing in reserve, of expressing everything fully.[271] I think the Romans of the Republic would have understood the notion of *sunyata:* emptiness as fullness.

It was for the vivid, translucent emotions of bonding that a Roman audience witnessed with pleasure a great performance in the ordeal.[272] The highest values of any person or state are not only indicated but created by what people within that community are willing to suffer or die for. The values of the community—indeed the very existence of the community—were formed in Rome by those who were willing to risk all.[273] As long as there were men like Mucius Scaevola, Marcus Curtius, or Publius Decius Mus, there would be a Rome. But after Cannae, in Livy's history, there were despairing patricians who wanted to abandon a Rome and an Italy doomed to be conquered by the Punic Hannibal. "This news, horrible in itself, and coming as a new sort of atrocity on top of so many previous disasters, stunned the fugitives from the battle of Cannae into a kind of numbed stupor of amazement" (Livy 22.53.6).[274] It was the young Publius Cornelius Scipio, the future conqueror of Hannibal, who called for bold action. He swore a great oath (an *exsecratio*) never to abandon the city and made the others swear likewise (22.53.7–13).[275] They would protect the city of Rome at the cost, if need be, of their lives. A Rome without a Horatius at the bridge, without a Camillus or a Publius Cornelius Scipio at the walls, was unthinkable.[276] *Moribus antiquis res stat Romana virisque,* Ennius wrote in his *Annales* (= Cicero, *De republica* 5.1.1): "It is by her ancient traditions, *mores,* and by her men, *viri,* that Rome stands."

---

270. *Death in the Afternoon,* New York, 1932, pp. 206–207. See also Bennassar, *Spanish Character,* pp. 235–245. These emotions are related to Mihaly Csikszentmihalyi's notion of the "flow" experience.

271. See Daisetz Suzuki, "The Role of Nature in Zen Buddhism," in *Zen Buddhism: Selected Writings of D. T. Suzuki,* Garden City, New Jersey, 1956; *Zen and Japanese Culture,* Princeton, 1959, p. 349; cf. pp. 51, 226, 286. Ruth Benedict spoke eloquently of the Japanese notions of sincerity. For the Americans, the plane of the kamikaze was the "idiot bomb," *baka;* for the Japanese it was the "cherry blossom," *oka* (*The Chrysanthemum and the Sword,* Boston, 1946, pp. 213–219).

272. See especially Seneca, *De providentia* 2.8–12; Cicero, *Ad familiares* 5.12.5; Valerius Maximus 9.12.4–7; Tacitus, *Annales* 4.33; Peter Schunck, "Römische Sterben," Ph.D. diss., Heidelberg, 1955, pp. 15–17.

273. It was the mother and her seven sons of Second and Fourth Maccabees, and Leonidas and his three hundred Spartans, who sacralized the laws of the Jews and the Spartans respectively.

274. *Quod malum, praeterquam atrox, super tot clades etiam novum, cum stupore ac miraculo torpidos defixisset.*

275. The powerful attachment of the Romans of the Republic to the very physical city and its walls is expressed in the stories of Horatius, Camillus, and Scipio. Horace's beautiful, tragic *Epode 16* on the abandonment of the city still speaks to this deep attachment.

276. For Silius's Minucius, Fabius was the champion and the wall: "Fabius is our country, and the walls of Rome rest on his shoulders alone" (*hic patria est, murique urbis stant pectore in uno* [*Punica* 7.743]).

CHAPTER FOUR

Stone and Ice

The Remedies of Dishonor

"What happens to you here is forever," O'Brien had said.
GEORGE ORWELL, *NINETEEN EIGHTY-FOUR*[1]

Being was ephemeral, but nonbeing was absolute. Valor was glass and fire, but humiliation was stone and ice. The captured Jewish generals were, according to Josephus, displayed on the triumphal floats of Titus and Vespasian frozen in the postures in which they had been taken (*Bellum Iudaicum* 7.139–147).[2] Ovid's prostrate and defeated Phineus was turned to stone by the victorious Perseus in the very act of begging for his life (*Metamorphoses* 5.210–235). Every day in the slave's life was an exhibition of defeat; as Reginald Haynes Barrow expressed it, "To enslave an enemy rather than to slay him was a device to reap his labor, but it was also a way of enjoying a perpetual triumph over him."[3] In the words of the tennis star Billy Jean King, "Victory is fleeting, but losing is forever."

---

1. *Nineteen Eighty-Four,* New York, 1963, p. 128.

2. Frozen images of humiliation, naked, bound, and defeated figures, were a common sight in Rome, especially in the Empire. A few examples: C. H. V. Sutherland, *Roman Coins,* New York, 1974, no. 351: a sesterces of Titus (80–81 C.E.) inscribed with *Judea capta,* showing a captive with his hands behind his back; no. 355: a denarius of Trajan (107–111 C.E.) with a bound Dacian; *Inscriptiones Latinae Selectae,* vol. 3.2, no. 8995: an inscription honoring Cornelius Gallus, surmounted by a relief showing a mounted cavalryman trampling a prostrate enemy. Suetonius describes a similar relief (*Nero* 41.2). See Jean Gagé, "La théologie de la Victoire Impériale," *Revue Historique* 171 (1933): 1–43, esp. pp. 28–31; A. C. Levi, *Barbarians on Roman Imperial Coins and Sculpture,* New York, 1952; Richard Brilliant, *Gesture and Rank in Roman Art,* New Haven, 1963, pp. 72–74, 96–98, 109–110; Paul Zanker, *The Power of Images in the Age of Augustus,* trans. Alan Shapiro, Ann Arbor, 1988, pp. 187, 230–232.

3. *Slavery in the Roman Empire,* New York, 1928, p. 2. The soldier, once defeated and captured, was irremediably dishonored. "Let them speak however fiercely, the spirit of the conquered has been diminished" (*et quamquam atrociter loquerentur, minorem est apud victos animum* [Tacitus, *Historia* 3.1]). "Wool died with purple never regains the hue it once has lost, . . . nor true *virtus,* once lost, cares to be restored to the diminished spirit" (*neque amissos colores / lana refert medicata fuco, / nec vera virtus cum semel excidit, /*

Abasement stopped time; it stupefied and petrified.[4] The Capuan nobles who witnessed the retreat of the Roman soldiers from their humiliations at the Caudine Forks judged by their paralytic silence that the Samnites had won "a victory not only brilliant but perpetual" (Livy 9.6.1–13).[5] When Apuleius's Lucius, tried in a kangaroo court by the people of Hypata, realized that he had been totally exposed and his *persona* destroyed, he was frozen and turned to stone *(fixus in lapidem steti gelidus)*—"indistinguishable from any of the statues or columns that stood in the theater in which he was being tried" *(Metamorphoses* 3.10).[6] Afterwards, taken by his host to the baths, Lucius recounts: "To escape the eyes and the laughter of the people we met, I walked close to my host's side, trying to conceal myself. On account of my shame *(rubor)*, I cannot recall how I washed, how I dried, how I returned home. I was out of my mind, branded and stupefied by the stares, the nods, the pointed fingers of everyone we passed" (Apuleius, *Metamorphoses* 3.12).[7]

Petronius's lusty Encolpius, proved impotent at a critical moment, blushed for shame *(perfusus ego rubore manifesto)* and came apart *(totoque corpore velut luxato)*. He was confounded, "like a man horror-stricken by an apparition" *(Satyricon* 128).[8] Ovid's lover, failing to rise to a similar challenge, declared that he lay inert, like the trunk of a fallen tree, a spectacle, a useless weight. "It could not be determined whether I was a body or a shadow" *(Amores* 3.7.15–16).[9] He was *vanus, cassus, inanis,* an empty shell of a man.

THE BAD CONTEST

To excel a rival is enough; to destroy him is too much.
PUBLILIUS SYRUS 678, FRIEDRICH ED.[10]

Where the rules of the game were arbitrary or unknown, where there were no limits to the scope or intensity of the contest, or where the contestants were too

---

curat reponi deterioribus [Horace, *Carmina* 3.5.26–29]). The color purple was the color of the blush, the color of the sense of shame. For the blush see part 3.

4. The defeated and enslaved was, like Shakespeare's Othello, a "fixed figure for the time of scorn to point his slow unmoving finger at" (4.2.53–55).

5. *victoriam non praeclarum solum sed etiam perpetuam.*

6. *at ego, ut primum illam laciniam prenderam, fixus in lapidem steti gelidus nihil secus quam una de ceteris theatri statuis vel columnis. nec prius ab inferis emersi quam Milon hospes accessit.* . . . Compare the story of the Aetolian ambassadors who, threatened with humiliation by the Roman general Manius Acilius Glabrio, were paralyzed with horror and embarrassment (Polybius 20.10.8–9).

7. *at ego vitans oculos omnium, et. . . risum obviorum declinans, lateri eius adambulabam obtectus. nec qui laverim, qui terserim, qui domum rursum reverterim, prae rubore memini sic omnium oculis nutibus ac denique manibus denotatus impos animi stupebam.*

8. *ego contra damnatus et quasi quodam visu in horrorem perductus.*

9. *truncus iners iacui, species et inutile pondus, / et non exactum, corpus an umbra forem.*

10. *sat vincere est inimicum, nimium est perdere.*

unequally matched, the contest turned caustic and brutal; rather than anneal, it charred and calcinated. In this chapter I draw, in rather broad strokes, the collapse of conditions for healthy competition in ancient Rome and the various strategies devised by the Romans for creating a new emotional economy and redefining their spirit. I attempt to explain why, in the course of Roman history, the worst imaginable spiritual condition for an ancient Roman—petrifaction, the cold stony unbeing of dishonor—inverts and becomes the ideal and honorable condition of the Roman soul, the ultimate remedy for dishonor—salvation. This is the sad chapter.

There had always been destructive and unequal competitions in Rome: near the praetor's tribunal in the forum stood an ancient statue of the pipe-player Marsyas, flayed alive by his rival musician Apollo, a naked reminder of the "scraping" that awaited one in a contest with a god.[11] Marsyas could not take on Apollo any more than the slave Sosia could take on Mercury. "Cease to compete with me" *(desine mecum certare)*, the rich patron warned the client who, in a futile attempt to achieve parity, dressed and anointed himself beyond his means (Horace, *Epistulae* 1.18.29–31). One of the most poignant of these unequal confrontations was that between Apuleius's destitute market gardener and the Roman soldier determined to "requisition" the gardener's ass. The gardener's spirited resistance to the Roman soldier inevitably cost him both his ass and his life (*Metamorphoses* 9.39–42). As the Stoic and former slave Epictetus admonished his hearers: "You ought to treat your whole body like a poor loaded-down donkey as long as it is possible, as long as it is allowed; and if it be commandeered and a soldier lay hold of it, let it go, do not resist or grumble.—If you do, you will get a beating and lose your little donkey just the same" (Arrian, *Epicteti dissertationes* 4.1.79).[12] In a contest of force between very unequal contestants, as Cervantes puts it, "Whether the pitcher hits the stone, or the stone hits the pitcher, it's bad for the pitcher."[13]

There had ever been bad competitions between god and human, master and slave, adult and child.[14] (When Plautus's Alcesimarchus tried to challenge his slave to a strenuous trial, the slave wisely replied: "I have no desire to be known as

---

11. Marsyas was the *stultitiae maximum specimem* for contending with a god *taeter cum decoro, agrestis cum erudito, belua cum deo* (Apuleius, *Florida* 1.3) Cf. Livy 38.13.6; Horace, *Satirae* 1.6.120; Ovid, *Fasti* 6.706–708; Statius, *Thebais* 4.183–186.

12. Oldfather trans. I owe the juxtaposition of these passages to Fergus Millar, "The World of the Golden Ass," *Journal of Roman Studies* 71 (1981): 63–75, pp. 67–68. Gellius reports a fragment of a speech by Gaius Gracchus to illustrate the tyrannical and brutal behavior of Romans outside of the city of Rome: a herdsman of Venusia made a joke at the expense of a Roman youth to the slaves who bore him in a litter through the countryside. The young Roman halted the litter and had the shepherd beaten to death on the spot with the thongs of the litter (*Noctes Atticae* 10.3).

13. This is the gist of the fable of the two jars in the Fables of Avienus (*Minor Latin Poets* XI); cf. Arrian, *Epicteti dissertationes* 3.12.12; Babrius, *Fabulae* 193, Crusius ed. = Aesop, *Fabulae* 422, Halm ed.

14. See, for example, Plautus, *Cistellaria* 23–35; Horace, *Epistulae* 1.18.21–31.

a *vir fortis*" [*Cistellaria* 231–232].)[15] But although there had always been bad contests in Rome, it was, above all, in the period of the collapse of the Republic and the civil wars that literate Romans came to describe the bad or destructive competition with increasing frequency. In the *Pro Quinctio* of 81 B.C.E., Cicero anticipates that Hortensius, the opposing counsel and advocate for Naevius, will argue that while Rome was under the thumb of Marius's henchmen, it was impossible for Naevius to challenge Alfenus (the well-connected Marian agent of Cicero's client Quinctius) and thus to proceed against Quinctius (21.68).[16] But now that the Sullan forces were in command and backing up Naevius with their overwhelming strength, Cicero argues, it was likewise impossible for Quinctius, fighting for his status as a citizen as well as his property, to proceed against an opponent who so outweighed him in power (22.72–73).[17]

In the late Republic and early Empire, after the loss of a level playing field, the most bitter complaints concerning the contest were that "those who least demonstrate *virtus* are those who win honor." The glory, Sallust's Marius asserts, goes to some, the labors to others. "They are not deluded," he complains, "who anticipate the conjunction of two very disparate things: the pleasure of cowardly idleness and the rewards of *virtus*" (*Bellum Iugurthinum* 85.20).[18] "Many have attained the insignia of *virtus* who have no *virtus*" (Cicero, *Ad familiares* 3.13.1).[19] Sallust's Catiline has seen "men honored who were not worthy of honor" (*Catilina* 35.3).[20] To many Romans it seemed that the words and signs of honor had become severed, abstracted from their physical and emotional bases, from the strenuous exertions and generous expenditures of life and energy that had defined them. *Virtus* was no longer *virtus*—and yet there was no other word to use. "Long ago," Sallust

15. Alcesimarcus: *Potine tu homo facinus facere strenuom?* Servus: *Aliorum affatim est / qui faciant. sane ego me nolo fortem perhiberi virum.*

16. *semper id clamitat* [Naevius] . . . *non fuisse Naevio parem certationem cum Alfeno illo tempore, illis* [the Marians] *dominantibus.*

17. *aderunt autem homines nobilissimi ac potentissimi, ut eorum frequentiam et consessum non modo P. Quinctius, qui de capite decernit, sed quivis, qui extra periculum sit, perhorrescat. Haec est iniqua certatio, non illa, qua tu contra Alfenum equitabas, huic* [Quinctius] *ne ubi consisteret quidem contra te locum reliquisti.*

18. *ne illi falsi sunt, qui divorsissumas res pariter expectant, ignaviae voluptatem et praemia virtutis.* Ruthless ambition *(ambitio)* now receives the rewards of virtue (Sallust, *Catilina* 52.22). Cf. *Bellum Iugurthinum* 85.37–38, 42–43.

19. *insignia enim virtutis multi etiam sine virtute adsecuti sunt.* "Meanwhile, those citizens who have done the most to deserve well of the state are indeed miserable, when other men not only forget their illustrious deeds, but even suspect them of crimes" *(miseros interdum cives optime de re publica meritos, in quibus homines non modo res praeclarissimas obliviscuntur, sed etiam nefarias suspicantur* [Cicero, *Pro Milone* 23.63]).

20. *non dignos homines honore honestatos videbam.* Cf. Juvenal, *Satirae* 8; Apuleius, *Metamorphoses* 7.2. When Seneca's Phaedra wants to kill herself to preserve her honor, her nurse advises her, "Despise your reputation. Fame . . . is better to the one who deserves worse, worse to the good" *(contemne famam; fama vix vero favet, / peius merenti melior et peior bono* [*Phaedra* 269–270]).

laments, "we lost the true words for things" (*iam pridem equidem nos vera vocabula rerum amisimus* [*Catilina* 52.11]).[21]

PASSING THE LIMITS

There was no custom. There was no law.
TACITUS, *ANNALES* 3.28.2[22]

Fortune did not come to the Romans with both hands full. With the rapid conquest of the Mediterranean beginning in the second century B.C.E., Rome went from a society where the rules of the game were givens, *res confessae*, to a society of greatly expanded possibilities where the rules governing competition became unclear or unenforceable. Plutarch, speaking of the time of the Elder Cato (mid-second century B.C.E.), explains: "The Republic had grown too large to preserve its purity, and the very domination that Rome exercised over so many realms and peoples brought it into contact with, and obliged it to adapt itself to, an extraordinary diversity of customs and patterns of living" (*Cato Maior* 4.2).[23]

The Romans, having gained their "empire without end," entered a kind of Nietzschean world where the rules of the contest and the traditions of the ancestors could no longer be taken for granted. After the Romans destroyed Carthage in 146 B.C.E., according to Sallust, "nothing was sacred" (*nihil pensi, neque sancti* [*Bellum Iugurthinum* 41.9]). Nothing was set apart, nothing tabooed, nothing too highly charged to tamper with. "What remains of those venerable traditions on which the Roman commonwealth was grounded?" asks Cicero. "They have been, we see, so obliterated that they are no longer cherished—indeed they are unknown" (*De republica* 5.1.2).[24] In 22 C.E. the emperor Tiberius addressed a letter to the senate in which he expressed his despair of controlling the luxurious excesses of the wealthy Romans through sumptuary legislation. At one time, to be sparing had been esteemed. Why? "Because each citizen had practiced self-control, and because we were all citizens of the same city—nor indeed were the temptations as great (as they are now) when our dominion was confined to Italy. But with our foreign victories we learned to consume the substance of others; with the civil

---

21. The Romans, ever given to ambiguity and paradox, now sometimes feel that words have lost their "true" meaning. Cf. "The name of *virtus* shall be given to unholy evil" (*sceleri nefando / nomen erit virtus* [Lucan, *Bellum civile* 1.667–68]); Juvenal, *Satirae* 8.30–38; Chaim Wirszubski, "*Audaces:* A Study in Political Phraseology," *Journal of Roman Studies* 51 (1961): 12–22; Paul Plass, *Wit and the Writing of History*, Madison, 1988, p. 4. The loss of a sense of reality leads to the notion of an abstract "truth."

22. *non mos, non ius.* Tacitus is speaking of the last stormy years of the Republic.

23. For cultural relativism brought to Rome by the Greek arch-sceptic Carneades in 155 B.C., see Cicero, *De republica* 3.5.8–9; Lactantius, *Institutiones divinae* 5.14.3–5. Cf. Cicero, *De republica* 3.10.17.

24. *Quid enim manet ex antiquis moribus, quibus ille* [Ennius] *dixit rem stare Romanam? quos ita oblivione obsoletos videmus, ut non modo non colantur, sed iam ignorentur.*

wars we learned to consume our own" (Tacitus, *Annales* 3.64).[25] The *agon* without limits was a cannibal feast.

The pulsing web of bonds and obligations that had constituted Roman Republican society—the venerable and *irreplaceable* Roman *religiones*—no longer embraced and realized the physics of the universe, but appeared as somewhat quaint artifacts that increasingly had an origin, a history, an evolution. Seneca spoke of the age of Cato Uticensis, the last generation of the Roman Republic, "when the old credulity had been thrown off" *(excussa antiqua credulitate [De constantia sapientis* 2.2]). "It has not escaped me, judges, that the old moral *exempla* are now reckoned fairytales" (Cicero, *In Verrem* 2.3.78.182).[26]

Cicero and Livy, without ever losing their romantic attachment to the ancient cultic forms, begin to sound like the cynical Athenian sophist Critias when they excuse Roman *religio* as a "necessary lie," a "pious falsehood" instituted by Numa to maintain civil order. "I think that augural law was originally established out of an esteem for divination, but that later it was maintained and preserved for the utility of the state" (Cicero, *De divinatione* 2.35.75).[27] This cynicism developed apace in the Empire.[28] Men who relied on traditional beliefs were criticized by Marcus Aurelius, on the authority of the Greek philosopher Heraclitus, as "children obeying their parents" (4.46). He labels the beliefs of the common man, by the authority of the Athenian Socrates, "Lamiae," the witches employed to frighten children (11.23).

Roman culture (like all cultures) had always been a necessary lie, a pious and mutual falsehood, but with the acceleration of Roman contacts and conquests, its deceptive theatricality begins to be decried: the *facies* is a façade, the *species* is specious; it is a sham, a conspiracy; it cannot bind or fool the truthsayer who stands self-consciously aloof from complicity in the fraud.[29]

---

25. *cur ergo olim parsimonia pollebat? quia sibi quisque moderabatur, quia unius urbis cives eramus; ne inritamenta quidem eadem intra Italiam dominantibus. externis victoriis aliena, civilibus etiam nostra consumere didicimus.* In the good old days before the rise of shameless ambition and violence *(ambitio et vis),* Tacitus believed, the laws were few and simple; *modestia* and *pudor* governed Rome. The more corrupt Rome became, the more numerous and more confusing the laws *(Annales* 3.26–27).

26. *non me fugit, iudices, vetera exempla pro fictis fabulis iam audiri atque haberi.* Shame used to be a strong enough *vinculum* for the law—now it would not be taken seriously (Livy 10.9.6).

27. *existimoque ius augurum, etsi divinationis opinione principio constitutum sit, tamen postea rei publica causa conservatum ac retentum.* Cf. *De divinatione* 2.24.51–53, 2.33.70, 2.60.125, 2.72.148, *De natura deorum* 3.1.5–6; Livy 1.19.4–5.

28. Consider the cynical skepticism Augustine attributes to Seneca's (lost) *De superstitione (De civitate dei* 6.10).

29. In the Roman forum, "As if in a war of all against all, men simulate goodness while plotting to entrap one another." *(bonum simulare virum se, / insidias facere ut si hostes sint omnibus omnes* [Lucilius, frag. 1145–51, Warmington ed.]). Ambition without restraint, like avarice, causes mortal men to become false "and to have the face rather than the spirit of a good man" *(Ambitio multos mortales falsos fieri subegit, . . . magisque voltum quam ingenium bonum habere* [Sallust, *Catilina* 10.5; cf. 54.6]). *Aurum atque ambitio specimen virtutis virique est* (Lucilius frag. 1194.5, Warmington ed).

PHANTOM OF LIBERATION

Freedom is an expense, freedom exhausts. . . . We see why slaves always win in the long run.
Masters, to their defeat, manifest themselves, drain themselves of their existence, express
themselves: the unconstrained exercise of their gifts, of their advantages, reduces them to the state
of phantoms. Freedom will have devoured them.

E. M. CIORAN, *DRAWN AND QUARTERED*[30]

As a result of the collapse of the traditional limitations, the erasure of the scripts
or scores of Roman social and psychological life, it was increasingly difficult to al-
leviate the shock of embodiment. The lack of reliable rules and shared unconscious assumptions often hobbled speech and action. And so immobility and stupor are as frequently depicted as violence in the literature of the great
heterogeneous Roman Empire. When Horace confronts his fellow citizens with
the enormity and unfathomability of the Roman civil wars, the Romans are
speechless. "A white pallor bleaches their faces, and their stricken minds are stupefied" (*Epodi* 7.16).[31] Tacitus's self-conscious and conscience-wracked tyrant
Tiberius begins a letter to the senate with the words: "If I know what I should
write to you, *patres conscripti*, or in what manner I should write or what I should not
write at all at this time, may the gods destroy me more effectively than I feel myself perishing daily" (*Annales* 6.12.1 = 6.6.1).[32]

---

30. *Drawn and Quartered,* trans. Richard Howard, New York, 1983, pp. 180–181.

31. *tacent, et ora pallor albus inficit / mentesque perculsae stupent.* The shock of civil war was described by
Lucan in terms of the obliquity, emotional paralysis, impotence, speechlessness, and dishonor it engendered in the community and the individual:

> When the Romans understood by what horrible disasters the faith of the gods would be con-
> firmed, a paralysis *(ferale iustitium)* prevailed throughout the city. Honor hid itself in plebeian
> dress, and no purple attended the *fasces*. At that moment the people suppressed their lamenta-
> tions, and a great sadness without a voice spread everywhere. Just so, households are stunned
> and silent at the moment of death, before the body is laid out and lamented, and before the
> mother with her hair unbound bids the arms of her maids to beat their harsh laments, at the
> moment when she presses to herself the limbs stiffening with departing life, and the inanimate
> face, and the eyes still menacing in death. She feels no fear—nor yet grief: in distraction she
> broods over the corpse, and marvels at her loss. (*Bellum civile* 2.16–28)

See Carlin Barton, *The Sorrows of the Ancient Romans,* Princeton, 1993, p. 104.

32. "*quid scribam vobis, patres conscripti, aut quo modo scribam aut quid omnino non scribam hoc tempore, di me
deaeque peius perdant quam perire me cotidie sentio, si scio.*" Cf. Suetonius, *Tiberius* 67. For the juxtaposition of
the extremes of violence and passivity during the civil wars, see Tacitus's appalling account of the
street fighting in Rome between Vitellius and Vespasian during the Saturnalia of 69 c.e. (*Historia* 3.83).
Bradford Lewis writes perceptively on the extremes of violence and passivity in Virgil in "The Rape of
Troy: Infantile Perspective in Book II of the *Aeneid*," *Arethusa* 7 (1974): 103–113. The absence of sufficient and powerful "given" rituals makes it hard, in contemporary American culture, not to be overwhelmed by the intensity of one's emotions or to respond to even slight challenges with anything but
expletives. The formalized behaviors that would mediate between violence and passivity are lacking in
our culture. We respond to humiliation by shooting one another or by watching television. See Tim
Hunter's brilliant and all but unbearable film *The River's Edge* (1986).

Where they were not arbitrarily dictated, boundaries and obligations became, equally arbitrarily, a matter of personal will and desire. Once, when a soothsayer reported that a sacrificial beast had been found to have no heart—traditionally an unlucky omen indeed—Caesar replied: "The omens will be more favorable when I wish them to be" (Suetonius, *Iulius* 77).[33] Pliny the Younger, writing in the first century of the Empire, had to decide how seriously to take the ancient office of tribune of the plebs. "Is it an empty shadow, a title without honor? Or is it a sacrosanct power?" He concludes with the assertion: "Everything depends on *your* idea of the tribunate and what mask *you* intend to wear" (*Epistulae* 1.23.1, 4).[34]

When, as a result of the imperial expansion of Rome, the spiritual walls around the city were irreparably breached, *urbanitas,* originally the ways and manners peculiar to those who lived within the walls of the city of Rome, took on the connotation of our modern "urbanity" or "cosmopolitanism."[35] The citizen of Rome became a citizen of the world.[36] And because, for the cosmopolite, limits, like definitions, had to be chosen, morality and adhesion to particular traditions and limits required a prodigious act of will. Preserving a sense of being, of identity, thus became a continuous—and ultimately exhausting—assault on the will. As a result, the enervating power of unrelieved good fortune became as common a theme in Roman literature as the annealing power of adversity. "Success," as Sallust points out, "wears out the souls even of wise men" (*Catilina* 11.8).[37]

For the Romans of the late Republic and early Empire, too much relied on the will. As in a play by Seneca, there were not enough areas of life where one could submit; there was no psychic rest, no catharsis. It is much easier, as Mary Douglas points out, to maintain a sense of one's own existence, of the expressiveness of one's words and actions, in a world with stubborn bonds and traditions than in a world without them, however burdensome those bonds.[38]

---

33. *eoque arrogantiae progressus est, ut haruspice tristia et sine corde exta quondam nuntiante, futura diceret laetiora cum vellet.*

34. *inanem umbram et sine honore nomen an potestatem sacrosanctam?...plurimum refert quid esse tribunatum putes, quam personam tibi imponas.*

35. See Otto Lutsch, "Die *Urbanitas* nach Cicero," *Festgabe für Wilhelm Crecelius,* Elberfeld, 1881, pp. 80–89; Edwin Ramage, *Urbanitas: Ancient Sophistication and Refinement,* Norman, Oklahoma, 1973.

36. Or rather, kings of the world. Abroad, Roman peasant soldiers were little tyrants. Roman aristocrats, as Kroll points out, were gods and kings (*Die Kultur der ciceronischen Zeit,* vol. 1, Leipzig, 1933, pp. 19–22).

37. *secundae res sapientium animos fatigant.* "Immoderate good fortune destroys the spirit" (*immoderata felicitas [animum] rumpit* [Seneca, *Epistulae* 39.4]). For the moral dangers of success see Cato the Elder in Gellius, *Noctes Atticae* 13.25.14; Polybius 6.18.5, 6.57.5–9; Cicero, *De officiis* 1.26.91; Sallust, *Catilina* 10.1–6, 11.8; *Bellum Iugurthinum* 41.4–9; Livy 9.18.1, 42.62.1–4; Ovid, *Fasti* 209–217; Velleius 2.1.1; Seneca, *Epistulae* 94.61–62; Josephus *Bellum Iudaicum* 2.250; Pliny, *Naturalis historia* 33.53.149–150; Tacitus, *Historia* 1.15; Florus 1.34.19, 1.47; Plutarch, *Cato maior* 27.1–3; Augustine, *De civitate dei* 1.30–31.

38. *Natural Symbols,* New York, 1970, esp. p. 51. In reaction to the *bad* contest, modern Europeans and Euro-Americans often attempt to minimize competition and discriminations (and thus hierarchy

In the late Roman Republic and early Empire, precisely because boundaries had become an act of will (and thus of honor), *not* to choose, simply to submit to a system of taboos or boundaries, was experienced as a lack of will and a dishonor.[39] If cosmopolitanism and relativism liberated, they also debilitated, because one's will was incessantly challenged, and because one felt that one should not, given one's freedom, feel so frustrated.[40] (One can compare the effects of evolutionary theory on modern European and American thought. The undermining of the Enlightenment view of human nature set in motion a great maelstrom of possibilities, of hopes, and desires—including the desire to be free of all restraining, imprisoning instincts—which, in turn, engendered feelings of impotence. As an instinct-free creature, one feels impotent precisely because one feels that everything is possible, and that therefore one's limitations, one's inability to be and have everything, are the result of one's own inadequacy.)[41] The Romans were, in the words of Erik Erikson, "victims of an overgrown and insatiable potentiality."[42] Their own effective energies had turned against them. "Rome," Ho-

---

and envy, particularly when directed against themselves). But attempts to have differences without competition or comparisons have produced, as a paradoxical side-effect, a yearning for identity and a sense of honorlessness and nonbeing. Fortunately or unfortunately, it is by comparisons and discriminations that we locate ourselves; it is by discriminations that we exist.

39. One's station feels like a prison only when one feels one could escape it provided one had the will. Aging, for instance (in so far as it mutilates the body), did not seem to me to be a dishonor until I read in *People* magazine the ways in which the entertainer Cher has, through exercise, determination, and plastic surgery, preserved her youthful appearance. Perhaps I too could have plastic surgery and simply do not have the will. If that is so, growing old is a shame and disgrace, and evidence that I lack effective energy. As Freud explained, "It is easier to submit to a remorseless law of nature, to the sublime Anangke, than to a chance which might perhaps have been escaped" (*Beyond the Pleasure Principle*, trans. James Strachey, New York, [1920] 1961, p. 39). In Robert Bresson's beautiful film *Un condamné à mort s'est échappé* (1956), there is an older prisoner, Blanchet, who, as long as his fate is beyond his power to affect, feels no degradation. The new prisoner Fontaine's determined preparations for escape from the impregnable prison act as a reproach to the older man who had "made his peace" with inevitable imprisonment and death. He experiences the very suggestion of the possibility of escape as a humiliation. Similarly, Etty Hillesum, having made her peace with the irresistible powers that commanded the transport camp and with the inevitability of her death at the hands of the Nazis, felt peace and strength. Not surprisingly, she reacted with indignation when a young Jew bolted from the cattle cars, and she blamed the reprisals of the Nazis not on the Nazi commandant but on the rebel who attempted to escape his "fate" (*An Interrupted Life: The Diaries of Etty Hillesum, 1941–43*, New York, 1981, p. 259).

40. See Barton, *Sorrows*, chapter 2 and part 2.

41. Clifford Geertz: "One of the most significant facts about us may finally be that we all begin with the natural equipment to live a thousand kinds of life but end having lived only one" ("The Impact of the Concept of Culture on the Concept of Man," *The Interpretation of Cultures*, New York, 1973, p. 45). It is not very surprising that contemporary "cultural constructionism" is a radical relativism that nevertheless often leads also to a type of determinism, the individual and his or her experience of the world being shackled by his or her culture's existing "chains of signification."

42. "Childhood and Tradition in Two American Indian Tribes," *The Psychoanalytic Study of the Child* 1 (1945): 341. The Roman's increasing sense of futility may have been compounded by the coincidence

race says sadly, "collapses from her own strength" (*suis et ipsa Roma viribus ruit* [*Epodi* 16.2]).

The feeling of triumph is the feeling of a vivified will, of effective energy; but effectiveness is always relative to a code. The imperial triumphs of the Roman Republic had been purchased with the attenuation or destruction of the codes that made these triumphs meaningful, the traditions by which these activities could be framed and interpreted. Ennius had written in the middle years of the Republic that the man whose task is ordained *(cui quod agat institutumst)* delights his heart and soul *(mentem atque animum delectat suum)* by devoting himself totally and actively to what must be done. But with no determined goals, the spirit floundered. He imagined the emotions experienced by Agamemnon's soldiers stalled at Aulus by the dead calm: They were neither at home nor at war, neither *domi* nor *militiae;* they could neither act nor use their leisure effectively, and so they felt only barely alive. "Our spirits drift aimlessly, we live but more or less" (*incerte errat animus, praeterpropter vitam vivitur* [Gellius, *Noctes Atticae* 19.10.12]).[43]

Like surfers, the Roman conquerors of the Mediterranean rode the crest of a great wave only to be subducted by the undertow. The enormous increase in wealth and the potentialities set in motion by their victories brought with them a sense of liberation from the old restrictions but also a sense of deprivation, a *taedium vitae,* a dulling of the senses, a feeling of confusion, corruption, entrapment, and loss.[44] As Horace asserts of the perjured man: "To be sure, the shamelessly acquired wealth grows apace. Still, there is ever something indefinable lacking to this damaged wealth of his" (*Carmina* 3.24.59–64).[45] There was no winning a game without rules; freedom without limits was, ultimately, a total loss. As Seneca declares, "There is no following wind for a man without a port" (*Epistulae* 71.3).[46]

---

of the growth of the empire and the growth of literacy (the "Empire of Signs")—with the concomitant development of a sense of history. "The best defense against civil war," asserts the Elder Seneca, "is forgetfulness" (*optima civilis belli defensio oblivio est* [*Controversiae* 10.3.5]). An accumulated wealth of knowledge about the past, especially when its endless variety and contradictions are documented, can create a sense of anomie. "From the standpoint of the individual intellectual, of the literate specialist, the vista of endless choice and discoveries offered by so extensive a past can be source of great stimulation and interest; but when we consider the social effects of such an orientation it becomes apparent that the situation fosters...alienation" (Jack Goody and Ian Watt, "The Consequences of Literacy," *Comparative Studies in Society and History* 5 [1963]: 334–335). The Romans' nostalgia and sense of loss in the last century of the Republic—as well as their alienation from one another—can be connected with the development of the sense of the past as different from the present.

43. See Jean-Marie André, *L'otium dans la vie morale et intellectuelle Romaine,* Paris, 1966, p. 18.

44. See Barton, *Sorrows,* chapter 2.

45. *scilicet improbae / crescunt divitiae: tamen / curtae nescio quid semper abest rei.*

46. *ignoranti, quem portum petat, nullus suus ventus est.*

The Romans sensed that the joke was on them. To be unbound, unobligated, in Latin was to be *immunis*. But to be *immunis* was also to be unfortified. The *immunes* were free, but they lacked vitality; they were idle, inactive, inert, contributing nothing. The Romans were conquerors who, paradoxically, found themselves diminished. The more they had, the more cheated they felt. Sallust's Memmius addresses the assembled Romans: "You, the Roman people—unconquered by your enemies, rulers of all peoples—have all you can do to barely retain your *animus*" (*Bellum Iugurthinum* 31.20).[47]

Without a code, what could "really" exist? Without clear boundaries, what was left of the commonwealth? "The Republic is nothing," Julius Caesar was accused of saying, "a mere name without a body—without a visage" (Suetonius, *Julius* 77).[48] " 'Republic.' We retain the word, but we have long since lost the thing itself" (Cicero, *De republica* 5.1.2).[49] "I return to our miserable—or rather nonexistent—Republic" (Cicero, *Ad Atticum* 14.13.6).[50] "We have lost, my dear Pomponius, not only all the sap and blood, but even the complexion and the unspoiled visage of our city" (*Ad Atticum* 4.18).[51] "What are we, after all, or what can we be, at home or abroad?" (*Ad Atticum* 13.10.1)[52] After this, if "Rome" was to have any "real" existence at all, it would have to be as an abstraction divorced from the immediacy and physicality of the city and the people in it: the transcendent goddess Roma.

The ability of the Romans to keep some version of the Republic alive, and to limp along (like the zombies in a movie by George Romero) during the century of sporadic civil wars that ended with Actium, was due (just as in Romero's *Dawn of the Dead,* where men and women haunt the same shopping mall when dead as they did when alive) to the Roman devotion to formalized and ritualized behavior.[53] Even the greatest rogues, like Sulla, Pompey, Caesar, and Octavian held to forms as long as they could. One can compare Roman formalism in this period with the National Socialists' obsession with *Ordentlichkeit.*

---

47. *vos autem, hoc est populus Romanus, invicti ab hostibus, imperatores omnium gentium, satis habebatis animam retinere. Nam servitutem quidem quis vostrum recusare audebat?* (Here, *animus* is the mere breath of life). Tiberius Gracchus addresses the plebs: They have conquered the world and what do they have? Nothing (Plutarch, *Tiberius Gracchus* 9.5). Like the plebs, the aristocracy that had conquered the world felt they had less, in so many ways, than they had started with. Somehow both the rich and the poor had been cheated of the fruits of the victory.

48. *nihil esse rem publicam, appellationem modo sine corpore ac specie.*

49. *rem publicam verbo retinemus, re ipsa iam pridem amisimus.* See all of 5.1. (October 54 B.C.E.)

50. *redeo enim ad miseram seu nullam potius rem publicam.* (April 44) Cf. *Ad Quintum fratrem* 3.4.1.

51. *amisimus, mi Pomponi, omnem non modo sucum ac sanguinem, sed etiam colorem et speciem pristinam civitatis.* (October 54) Cf. *De officiis* 1.11.35.

52. *quid enim sumus aut quid esse possumus? domin an foris?* (June 45 B.C.E.)

53. For an interpretation of the end of the Republic that emphasizes continuities, see Erich Gruen, *The Last Generation of the Roman Republic,* Berkeley, 1974.

STOPPING AT NOTHING

Aut Caesar aut nullus.[54]

The threat that the powerful man would turn against his own people or open the vendetta in defense of his own honor hung over Rome as it did over all warrior cultures.[55] In the Roman contest culture, the margin had ever been thin between a flame and a conflagration; the contest easily crossed over into civil strife.[56] "Natures that have innate vigor produce wrath, and being hot and fiery they have no room for anything weak and feeble, but their energy is defective...and unless such natures are quickly tamed, what was a disposition to bravery becomes recklessness and temerity" (Seneca, *De ira* 2.15.2).[57] The *vir fortis ac strenuus* easily became the rogue male. The audacity of the brave warrior shaded into ferocity, his constancy into contumacy.[58] The proud and envious, men and women like the Scipiones or Marius, Fulvia or Ovid's Aglauros, were liable to turn on their own.[59] These renegades include the would-be tyrants of

54. The wonderful, if apocryphal, motto of Cesare Borgia.

55. Inga Clendinnen remarks of the Aztec warrior: "Explosions of anger, paralyzing eruptions of rage, transformations from the stillness of perfect control to furious violence—great Aztec warriors would seem to be uncomfortable people to be with. And lesser warriors had less control. Young men kept at a pitch for war and trained to a style of touchy arrogance were hard to maintain peaceably in a city" ("The Cost of Courage in Aztec Society," *Past and Present* 107 [1985]: 64). For the overbearing hero in medieval Icelandic culture, see Richard Bauman, "Performance and Honor in Thirteenth-Century Iceland," *Journal of American Folklore* 99 (1986): 141–142. See the remarks made by Peter Matthiessen on the danger that the great *kains*, the touchy warriors of the Kurelu of New Guinea, posed to their own people (*Under the Mountain Wall*, New York, 1962, pp. 100–101), and by Pierre Bourdieu on the *amahbul* among the Kabyle ("The Sense of Honor," in *Algeria 1960*, trans. Richard Nice, Cambridge, 1979, p. 95). For the tendency of the Athenian contest system to produce the "rogue male," see Alvin Gouldner, *Enter Plato*, New York, 1965, pp. 41–77.

56. As John Lendon observes, "A man needed the power to hurt to defend his honour, to protect himself against slights and humiliations" (*Empire of Honour*, Oxford, 1997, p. 106).

57. *ingenia natura fortia iracundiam ferunt nihilque tenue et exile capiunt ignea et fervida, sed imperfectus illis vigor est...nisi cito domita sunt, quae fortitudini apta erant, audaciae temeritatique consuescunt.*

58. See Timothy J. Moore, *Artistry and Ideology: Livy's Vocabulary of Virtue*, Frankfurt am Main, 1989, pp. 19–23; Robert A. Kaster, "The Shame of the Romans," *Transactions and Proceedings of the American Philological Association* 127 (1997): 16–17.

59. For the rogue male in ancient Rome, see Kroll, *Die Kultur der ciceronishen Zeit*, vol. 1, pp. 10–15; Ulriche Knoche, "Der römische Ruhmesgedanke," in *Römische Wertbegriffe*, ed. Hans Oppermann, Darmstadt, 1967, pp. 435–436, and "Der Beginn des römischen Sittenverfalls," in *Vom Selbstverständnis der Römer*, Heidelberg, 1962, pp. 92–123; Wirszubski, "*Audaces*," pp. 12–22; A. W. Lintott, "The Tradition of Violence in the Annals of the Early Roman Republic," *Historia* 19 (1970): 12–24; Robin Seager, "*Populares* in Livy and the Livian Tradition," *Classical Quarterly* n.s. 27 (1977): 377–382; Erich Gruen, "The Exercise of Power in the Roman Republic," in *City-States in Classical Antiquity and Medieval Italy: Athens and Rome, Florence and Venice*, ed. Anthony Molhe, Kurt Raaflaub, and Julia Emlin, Stuttgart, 1991, pp. 251–267; Augusto Fraschetti, "Roman Youth," trans. Camille Naish, in *A History of Young*

the Republic: Spurius Cassius, Spurius Maelius, Marcus Manlius Capitolinus, the Scipiones, the Gracchi, Drusus, Verres, and Sulla, to name but few.[60] The man who took the competition seriously, a Coriolanus, a Catiline, or a Caesar, might have the temerity to overturn all the laws of man and god to secure preeminence for himself.[61] The man who stopped at nothing, like a fire out of control, would at last consume his own people.[62] Sallust describes the contest by which cities are destroyed: "[It is] when men will defeat other men by any means whatsoever, and when the defeated are bitterly intent on vengeance" (*Bellum Iugurthinum* 42.4).[63]

In the Roman contest culture, the greatest threat to Roman society was never the external enemy but rather the rogue male, the *rex*, the tyrant who was the one

---

People in the West, ed. Giovanni Levi and Jean-Claude Schmitt, Cambridge, Mass., 1997, p. 70. For examples of rogue females, see Tacitus, *Annales* 2.55.5 (Plancina), 6.31.3 (= 6.25.3) (Agrippina the Elder). For competition in Rome getting out of hand, see Polybius 6.57.5–9; Lucan, *Bellum civile passim* esp. 1.143–157; Tacitus, *Annales* 3.28. One can trace the escalation of competition in the negotiations and subsequent confrontation between Tiberius Gracchus and the tribune Octavius or in the maneuvers and negotiations between Caesar and Pompey that led to the outbreak of the war between them.

60. One might think of the claim made by Plutarch's Cato that "Cato owed less to the Roman people than the people owed to Cato" (*Cato Maior* 14.3), or the cavalier and high-handed way that Lucius and Publius Scipio treated the attempts made to make them account for the wealth that they garnered from their conquests. Cf. Alan E. Astin, *Cato the Censor*, Oxford, 1978, pp. 58, 61–62.

61. Cicero decries the audacity of Julius Caesar who, to gain the preeminence that he had wrongheadedly conceived for himself, perverted every law of man and god (*temeritas C. Caesaris, qui omnia iura divina et humana pervertit propter eum, quem sibi ipse opinionis errore finxerat, principatum* [Cicero, *De officiis* 1.8.26]). Gregory Bateson, in an imaginary dialogue between a father and daughter, illustrates the tendency of the contest to be undermined by a desire to win that is stronger than the desire to play:

> *Father:* I don't mind—not much—winning or losing. When your questions put me in a tight
>   spot, sure, I try a little harder to think straight and to say clearly what I mean. But I don't
>   bluff and I don't set traps. There is no temptation to cheat.
> *Daughter:* That's just it. It's not serious to you. It's a game. People who cheat just don't know
>   how to *play*. They treat a game as though it were serious.
> *Father:* But it *is* serious.
> *Daughter:* No, it isn't—not for you it isn't.
> *Father:* Because I don't even want to cheat?
> *Daughter:* Yes—partly that.

("Metalogue: About Games and Being Serious," in *Steps to an Ecology of Mind*, New York, 1972, pp. 14–15)

62. The film director Werner Herzog offers a brilliant and deliciously horrible depiction of the ambitious maverick warrior destroying his own people in *Aguirre: The Wrath of God* (1972).

63. *quae res plerumque magnas civitatis pessum dedit, dum alteri alteros vincere quovis modo et victos acerbius ulcisci volunt*. Sallust laments: "Even the 'new men' who were accustomed, formerly, to surpass the nobility through their virtue, now strive for power and honors by stealth and robbery" (*etiam homines novi, qui antea per virtutem soliti erant nobilitatem antevenire, furtim et per latrocinia potius quam bonis artibus ad imperia et honores nituntur* [*Bellum Iugurthinum* 4.7]). For the bad contest without rules see 3, 8.1–2, 31.9, 41–42.

consistently demonized character in Roman culture.[64] After the expulsion of the kings in the late sixth century B.C.E., the Romans were wont to find "kings" in their most brilliant men. "The trouble," Cicero declares, "is that it is in the greatest souls and in the most splendid temperaments that we usually find lusts for civil and military authority, for power and glory springing up" (*De officiis* 1.8.26).[65] "In competitions where it is not possible for many men to excel simultaneously, contention is liable to be so fierce that it is extremely difficult to preserve the sanctity of society" (loc. cit.).[66] Cicero's great man was in a slippery position *(locus sane lubricus)*: "In proportion to the loftiness of his spirit, a man is easily driven by the desire for glory to commit injustices" (*De officiis* 1.19.65).[67]

> It is a hateful thing that audacity and the desire for dominance grow so easily out of elation of the soul. . . . As each excels in the greatness of his spirit, so he desires to be the most powerful man—or rather the only powerful man. But it is a difficult thing, when you wish to be preeminent over everything, to preserve that sense of balance that is the most important quality of justice. When a man cannot suffer to be restrained by argument or by any public or legitimate bond, bribers and partisans appear in the Republic who desire to maximize their resources and attain superiority by force rather than remain equals by justice. (*De officiis* 1.19.64)[68]

64. Livy's Scipio says, "The name 'king'—elsewhere prestigious—is in Rome intolerable" (*regium nomen, alibi magnum, Romae intolerabile esse* [27.19.4]). "Romans cannot bear even to hear the name 'king'" (*nomen regis audire non poterat* [Cicero, *De republica* 2.30.52]).

65. *Est autem in hoc genere molestum, quod in maximis animis splendidissimisque ingeniis plerumque existunt honoris, imperii, potentiae, gloriae cupiditates.* While the crimes committed in their zeal by the tribunes Tiberius and Gaius Gracchus, Saturninus, and Publius Sulpicius Rufus were unforgivable, Cicero is nevertheless willing to attribute to these men weighty motives arising from the injury felt by an *animus virilis* (*gravis tamen et cum aliquo animi virili dolore coniuncta* [*De haruspicum responsis* 21.44, cf. 19.41]). In a generous mood, Cicero surmises that Antony has turned against the Republic, "not for any low motives, for I never saw anything sordid or base in you, . . . but I fear that, ignorant of the true road to glory, you think it glorious to be more powerful alone than everybody else and to be feared by your fellow citizens" (*Vereor ne ignorans verum iter gloriae gloriosum putes te unum posse quam omnes et metui a civibus tuis* [*Philippicae* 1.13.33—14.33]).

66. *nam quicquid eius modi est, in quo non possunt plures excellere, in eo fit plerumque tanta contentio, ut difficillimum sit servare sanctam societatem.*

67. *Facillime autem ad res iniustas impellitur, ut quisque altissimo animo est, gloriae cupiditate: qui locus est sane lubricus.* "Great things are a rung to still greater, and when men attain what they never hoped for, they embrace hopes more improbable" (*gradus a magnis ad maiora fit, et spes improbissimas complectuntur insperata adsecuti* [Seneca, *De clementia* 1.1.7]).

68. *Sed illud odiosum est, quod in hac elatione et magnitudine animi facillime pertinacia et nimia cupiditas principatus innascitur. . . . Ut quisque animi magnitudine maxime excellet, ita maxime vult princeps omnium vel potius solus esse. Difficile autem est, cum praestare omnibus concupieris, servare aequitatem, quae est iustitiae maxime propria. Ex quo fit, ut neque disceptatione vinci se nec ullo publico ac legitimo iure patiantur, existuntque in re publica plerumque largitiores et factiosi, ut opes quam maximas consequantur, et sint vi potius superiores quam iustitia pares.*

Cicero addresses that wildfire Julius Caesar: "Your spirit has never been content with the confines wherein nature has cribbed our lives" (*Pro Marcello* 9.27).[69] But, unfortunately, the man who would be *dominus* was for that very reason *indomitus*, out of control, *effrenatus*, unleashed.[70] Lucan's Caesar, like Seneca's Alexander, is *acer et indomitus*, violent and out of control (*Bellum civile* 1.143–157).[71]

One of the signs of the collapse of the Roman contest culture was, paradoxically, the increasing admiration for and cult of victory and the charismatic victor. As I tried to show in chapter 3, it had never been winning that made the Republic a grand game, a "real" game. The heroic mythology of the Republic belonged, above all, to Curtius, Lucretia and Mucius, Horatius and Regulus, Decius Mus and Spurius Postumius, prodigies of willful self-sacrifice.[72] But as the rules of the game became harder to preserve in the late Republic, as the stakes grew higher, the more frequent was the appearance—and glorification—of the *man not prepared to lose*. As the careful studies of Jean Gagé, Victor Weinstock, and J. Rufus Fears have revealed, it was the civil strife and civil war of the last century of the Republic that brought claims for victory and invincibility to full development.[73] Scipio Africanus suggested the way, but it was, above all, Sulla and Pompey, the great warlords of the crumbling state, who emphasized and advertised their victories on statues, standards, trophies, crowns, and coins and offered them as reasons for games and festivals.[74] The godhead Victoria, formerly associated with the guardians of the Republic, Jupiter and the Dioscuri, began to appear as the com-

---

69. *iste tuus animus numquam his angustiis quas natura nobis ad vivendum dedit contentus fuit.* Horatius Tergeminus, victorious against the Curatii, slew his own sister. Romulus the wall-builder destroyed his own brother. The oft-tested Hercules annihilated his own family. Appius Claudius the law-giver, like Pompey and Augustus, broke the laws he himself made. Each was, to use a phrase of Tacitus, "author and subverter of his own laws" (*suarum legum auctor idem ac subversor* [*Annales* 3.28]). Compare the story Plutarch tells of Augustus (*Regum et imperatorum apophthegmata,* Augustus 9 [*Moralia* 207D]). For Pompey as the rogue, see Dio 40.56; Lily Ross Taylor, *Party Politics in the Age of Caesar,* Berkeley, 1949, p. 151. For Caesar as the rogue, see Lucan, *Bellum civile,* esp. 1.143–50.

70. As J. Hellegouarc'h observes, Verres was called *tyrannus* "simplement parce qu'il exerce sans contrainte sa libido" (*Le vocabulaire latin des relations et des partis politiques sous la République,* Paris, 1963, p. 562).

71. For Philip and especially Alexander as the rogues and models for the great warlords and the emperors, see Seneca, *Epistulae* 94.62–63; *Naturales quaestiones* 3, *praefatio* 5; Livy 9. 18.1–5; Gagé, "La théologie de la Victoire impériale," pp. 29, 39.

72. See Carlin Barton, "Savage Miracles: The Redemption of Lost Honor in Roman Society and the Sacrament of the Gladiator and the Martyr," *Representations* 45 (winter 1994): 41–71.

73. Gagé, "La théologie de la Victoire impériale," p. 3; Stefan Weinstock, "*Victor* and *Invictus,*" *Harvard Theological Review* 50 (1957): 224–225; J. Rufus Fears, "The Theology of Victory at Rome: Approaches and Problems," *Aufstieg und Niedergang der römischen Welt,* vol, 2.17.2, Berlin, 1981, pp. 736–826.

74. "La mystique de la Victoire et de la Félicité se développe et se fixe dans le culte de Vénus Victrix—ou Genetrix—qui n'a pas été moins chère à Pompée qu'à César et qui prépare directement, à travers les *ludi Victoriae* de Sylla, le règne impérial de la *Victoria Augusti*" (Gagé, "La théologie de la Victoire Impériale," p. 4).

panion of Sulla, intimately associated with his person.[75] "One by one," Fears observes, "the elements of the ideological framework of the Roman state were being detached from associations with the concept of collective authority in the *res publica* and were being transformed into extensions of the personality of individual charismatic dynasts."[76] It was Pompey, not the Roman people or Jupiter Optimus Maximus, who was "Conqueror of all Nations" (Cicero, *In Pisonem* 16).[77] "If Pompey was the *invictissimus civis,* Caesar wanted to become the *deus invictus.* The title of *victor omnium gentium* was applied to both. . . . Augustus accept[ed] the new meaning of victory and stressed the cult of *Victoria* perhaps more than Caesar did."[78]

When news of Julius Caesar's victory at Munda reached the city of Rome in 45 B.C.E., the senate granted to Caesar the *praenomen imperatoris;* "Victorious General" should henceforth be his first name, a permanent and inalienable part of his personal being (rather than a spontaneous gift of his soldiers). He should, henceforth, always wear the laurel wreath of victory and be attended by lictors with laurels on their *fasces.* He should wear the triumphal garb at all public functions, and his ivory statue should be carried, with those of the other high gods, in the *pompa circensis.* And Weinstock explains that the permanent *imperator* was the permanent *victor:* "All victories had now become Caesar's victories."[79] Victory became profoundly personalized. In his speech on behalf of Marcellus, Cicero explicitly refutes those who suggest that victory in war is the common achievement and honor of the Roman army and the Roman people: "This glory, Gaius Caesar, which you have recently acquired, no one shares with you. All of it, as great as it is (and it is undeniably very great)—all of it, I say, is yours. No credit belongs to centurion, to prefect, to cohort, to squadron. Not even the mistress of human destinies, Fortune herself, claims any partnership in this glory. She yields it to you; she confesses it to be yours—wholly and personally" (*Pro Marcello* 2.1–7).[80]

Caesar is, he says elsewhere, "the one true *imperator* in the whole world" (*Pro Ligario* 7).[81] From the time of Caesar's nephew Augustus, the emperor would be the perpetual (and increasingly exclusive) conqueror.[82]

---

75. Fears, "The Cult of Virtues and Roman Imperial Ideology," *Aufstieg und Niedergang der römischen Welt,* vol. 2.17.2, Berlin, 1981, p. 879.

76. Ibid., p. 882; cf. pp. 875, 877, 888, cf. "Theology of Victory at Rome," pp. 787–89, 794.

77. Fears, "Cult of Virtues," p. 884.

78. Weinstock, "*Victor* and *Invictus,*" pp. 236–237.

79. Ibid., p. 103; cf. pp. 107–111; Léon Halkin, *La supplication d'action de graces chez les romains,* Paris, 1953, p. 79. Cf. Suetonius, *Julius* 76.1, 45.4; Dio 43.44.2.

80. *At vero huius gloriae, C. Caesar, quam es paulo ante adeptus, socium habes neminem: totum hoc, quantumque est, quod certe maximum est, totum est, inquam, tuum. Nihil sibi ex ista laude centurio, nihil praefectus, nihil cohors, nihil turma decerpit; quin etiam illa ipsa rerum humanarum domina Fortuna, in istius societatem gloriae se non offert: tibi cedit, tuam esse totam et propriam fatetur.*

81. *cum ipse imperator in toto imperio populi Romani unus esset.*

82. Gagé, "La théologie de la Victoire," p. 27; cf. pp. 27, 31.

Gagé labels the growth of the "theology of victory" "une véritable transformation des croyances."[83] Fears observes that, "When men came to believe that the charisma of victory no longer resided in the collective entity of the *res publica* but rather in the figure of an individual leader, communal authority and republican government were doomed and monarchy the only reality."[84]

There were, however, Romans like Sallust and Cicero who pointed out the close connection between victory and tyranny, *victoria* and *dominatio*.[85] In February 49 [B.C.E.] Cicero referred to the long duration of Caesar's *victoria et dominatio* (*Ad Atticum* 7.22.1).[86] Sallust's Catiline enlists as rebels against the state those whose parents had been proscribed, whose property had been confiscated, and whose civil rights had been curtailed "by the victory of Sulla" (*quorum victoria Sullae parentes proscripti, bona erepta, ius libertatis inminutum erat* [*Ad Atticum* 37.9]).[87] And it is out of scorn for his domination that Catullus refers to Julius Caesar as "the one and only victorious general" (*imperator unicus* [29.11, 54A.7]). These Roman authors understood that what made the victory of the great warlords unparalleled was that it was a victory over their own people as well as the enemy, and that it was precisely their unequaled felicity that legitimated their infractions of law and custom.[88] If the blood of the expendable man, going down to defeat and death for the commonwealth, had been the seed of the health and spirit of the *res publica*, the desire to prevail over and at the expense of the community created great, hemorrhaging wounds through which poured the vitality and health of the commonwealth. Great victories destroy competition. Great victories are tragic in a contest culture.

What could be done to curb the renegade male, to end unchecked competition? "What hope of liberty remains if it is permitted to them to do whatever

83. Ibid., p. 3.

84. "Theology of Victory at Rome," p. 824. "The theology of victory justified the *de facto* abolition of the republic and the creation of a personal monarchy" (p. 752; cf. p. 790).

85. Sallust, *Catilina* 21.4, 37.6,9; Cicero, *Ad Atticum* 7.22.1; Weinstock, "*Victor* and *Invictus*," pp. 220–221. Fears points out that the *dominatio* of the great warlords rested on and was justified by their victories ("Theology of Victory at Rome," pp. 795). "Sulla...appears as the formative figure in the personalization of the theology of victory at Rome, and, to the degree that the principate rested upon a political mythology of victory, it is no exaggeration to state that in ideological terms charismatic monarchy at Rome became a reality under Sulla" (p. 796).

86. Weinstock notes that it was not the idea *victoria uti* that was new but its application to fellow citizens ("*Victor* and *Invictus*," p. 221).

87. Catiline reminded some of his fellow rebels of the spoils they had obtained by the victories of Sulla (*admonebat...multos victoriae Sullanae, quibus ea praedae fuerat* [*Catilina* 21.4]). Many of Catiline's rebels, "remembering the victories of Sulla" (*memores Sullanae victoriae*), anticipated becoming rich and powerful at the expense of their fellow citizens (37.6).

88. Gagé, "La théologie de la Victoire," p. 3; cf. pp. 32, 35–41. It was Pompey's personal and perpetual *felicitas* that qualified him for extraordinary commands (Cicero, *Pro lege Manilia* 16.47–17.50). Cf. Fears, "Cult of Virtues," p. 882.

they please, and if they have the power to do what is permitted to them, and if they have the audacity to do what they have the power to do, and if what they have the audacity to do they proceed to do, and if, finally, what they do is acceptable to you?" (*Auctor ad Herennium* 4.35).[89] Radical antidotes were needed. But the Republican "body politic" would suffer as much from the cure as the disease; the so-called *senatus consultum ultimum,* the response of the Roman senate to the Gracchan "tyranny," was a form of martial law—martial "law" being, of course, no law at all, but the vendetta set loose. And the courts set up to try the followers of the Gracchi had no built-in limitations save the exhaustion of the prosecutors' lust for vengeance (*non lex, verum lubido eorum finem fecit* [Sallust, *Bellum Iugurthinum* 31.7]).[90] Caesar may have opened civil war to protect his honor, but the "remedial" tyrannicide of Brutus and Cassius only reopened the civil war.

EYE TO EYE WITH LEVIATHAN

For he is not a man, as I am, that I might answer him, that we should come to trial together.
There is no umpire between us, who might lay his hand upon us both.
JOB 9.32

"Imagine that the man who might act shamelessly is not only callous but also pre-eminently powerful—as was Marcus Crassus, as is now our Pompey, to whom we must give thanks for behaving with restraint—for he could be as iniquitous as he wished with impunity" (Cicero, *De finibus* 2.18.57).[91] Beginning in the period of the civil wars, whether there were to be any rules at all depended on the arbitrary will of the great gangsters of the dying Republic, the great rogue males. The powers of the warlords, and those of their successors, the emperors, were rendered the more potent by their obscurity, paralyzing the will of others. "How could I contend against Pompey himself, the one who can do anything?" (*unus ille omnia possit, cum illo ipso contenderem?* [Cicero, *Ad Quintum fratrem* 3.4.2]). "Remember that I am permitted to do anything to anybody," Caligula replied to his scolding grandmother (Suetonius, *Caligula* 29.1).[92] Seneca addresses "Caesar, to whom all things are permitted" (*Ad Polybium* 7.2),[93] "Caesar who can do anything" (*De clementia*

89. *nam quae reliqua spes manet libertatis, si illis et quod libet licet, et quod licet possunt, et quod possunt audent, et quod audent faciunt, et quod faciunt vobis molestum non est?*
90. Compare the *lex de imperio Vespasiano* that legalized absolution; it was a sort of *senatus consultum ultimum* writ large. See *Corpus Inscriptionum Latinarum,* vol. 6, no. 930.
91. *sed finge non solum callidum eum qui aliquid improbe faciat, verum etiam praepotentem, ut M. Crassus fuit, ... ut hodie est noster Pompeius, cui recte facienti gratia est habenda; esse enim quam vellet iniquus poterat impune.*
92. *"memento," ait, "omnia mihi et in omnis licere."* Cf. 32.3.
93. *Caesar ... cui omnia licent.*

1.8.5).[94] The will of the king was law, and the will of the king was, like the *senatus consultum ultimum,* no law at all.[95]

The writers of the civil wars and early Empire respond to a world increasingly resembling that of the servants and sycophants of Plautus or Terence. The enormous inequality of power between himself and Julius Caesar made it impossible for the knight Laberius (106–43 B.C.E.) to refuse Caesar's request to degrade himself and perform as a mime at Caesar's public shows. "How could I, a mere man, say 'no' to him whom the gods themselves deny nothing?... I left my household gods today a Roman knight; I shall return a mime. In very truth, today I have lived a day too long" (Macrobius, *Saturnalia* 2.7.3).[96] The relations between Caligula and the audience at the theater may have been hostile, Dio explains, but the contest between them was not an equal one; the people could talk and gesture, whereas Gaius could destroy them (59.13.4).[97]

---

94. [*Caesar*] *qui omnia potest.*

95. "The desires of kings, as they are violent, are often fickle and at variance with themselves" (*regiae voluntates ut vehementes sic mobiles, saepe ipsae sibi advorsae* [Sallust, *Bellum Iugurthinum* 113.1]). For the *regia libido,* see Tacitus, *Annales* 6.48.3 (= 6.42.3). Cf. 5.3.1, 6.7.2 (= 6.1.2). The defeated Pompey, touching down in Egypt, quotes Sophocles: "Whoever comes to traffic with a king is slave to him, however free he come" (Plutarch, *Regum et imperatorum apophthegmata,* Pompeius 15 [*Moralia* 204E]; cf. Plutarch, *Pompeius* 78.4, Appian, *Bellum civile* 2.12.85; Dio 42.4.4).

96. *et enim ipsi di negare cui nihil potuerunt,*
   hominem me denegare quis posset pati?
   ...eques Romanus e Lare egressus meo,
   domum revertar mimus, ni mirum hoc die
   uno plus vixi quam vivendum fuit.

See Barton, *Sorrows,* pp. 117–119.

97. Tacitus's Domitian was afraid of and eliminated any contest that he could lose. "As was his way, Domitian greeted the news of Agricola's achievements (although the latter did not, in his despatches, augment them in any way by boasting) with a smile on his face that concealed the anxiety in his breast. For the emperor was conscious that he himself was being ridiculed for his recent and counterfeit triumph over the Germans." Domitian had, Tacitus explains, purchased slaves whose clothes and hair had been altered to make them look like German prisoners of war.

But here was both a real and a major victory—with enemies slain in the thousands.... It was the very thing Domitian feared the most: the name of a "private" person exalted above that of the prince. The repression of oratorical and civic skills, and the honor given to them, would have been in all in vain if another usurped military glory. Moreover, while he might dissimulate with regard to almost everything else, there was no denying that the valor of a good general was "imperial."

Domitian would bide his time, waiting until the fame of Agricola's achievements and his popularity with the soldiers had died down before he avenged himself on the too-successful commander. (*Hunc rerum cursum, quamquam nulla verborum iactantia Agricolae auctum, ut Domitiano moris erat, fronte laetus, pectore anxius excepit. inerat conscientia derisui fuisse nuper falsum e Germania triumphum.... Id sibi maxime formidolosum, privati hominis nomen supra principis adtolli: frustra studia fori et civilium artium decus in silentium acta, si militarem gloriam alius occuparet; cetera utcumque facilius dissimulari, ducis boni imperatoriam virtutem esse* [*Agricola* 39.1–3].) For the inability of the Roman emperors to endure an equal contest, see Seneca, *Epistulae* 94.65; Dio 57.19.3; Lendon, *Empire of Honour,* pp. 108–113.

To the extent that, by the early Empire, the contest had degenerated to a *ludibrium*, a farce, the most degrading of all competitions were those with the emperor himself:

> A gladiator... against whom Caligula was fencing with a wooden sword deliberately fell to the ground; whereupon Caligula drew an iron dagger, stabbed him to death, and ran about waving the palm-branch of victory. (Suetonius, *Caligula* 32.2)[98]

> Nero inaugurated the Neronia, a festival of competition in music, gymnastics, and horsemanship.... At the prize-giving Nero descended to the orchestra stalls where the senators sat, to accept the laurel-wreath for Latin oratory and verse which had been reserved for him by the unanimous vote of all the distinguished competitors. (Suetonius, *Nero* 12.3)[99]

> Commodus descended into the arena and cut down all the domestic animals that approached him and some that were led up to him or that were brought to him in nets. (Dio 73.19.1).

> For among other things that we did, we would shout out whatever we were commanded, and especially these words continually: "Thou art lord and thou art first, of all men, most fortunate. Victor thou art and thou shalt be; from everlasting, Amazonian, thou art victor." (Ibid. 73.20.2).[100]

> He [Commodus] had once got together all the men in the city who had lost their feet as the result of disease or some accident, and then, after fastening about their knees some likenesses of serpents' bodies, and giving them sponges to throw instead of stones, had them killed with blows of a club, pretending they were giants. (Ibid. 73.20.3).[101]

Plautus could have written the script for many of the encounters between the emperors and their subjects in the early Empire. In a scene eerily reminiscent of the confrontation between the slave Sosia and the god Mercury in the *Amphitruo*, the senator Julius Montanus quarreled with the disguised emperor Nero at night

---

98. *murmillonem e ludo rudibus secum battuentem et sponte prostratum confodit ferrea sica ac more victorum cum palma discucurrit.*

99. *instituit et quinquennale certamen primus omnium Romae more Graeco triplex, musicum gymnicum equestre, quod appelavit Neronia.... deinde in orchestram senatumque descendit et orationis quidem carminisque Latini coronam, de qua honestissimus quisque contenderat, ipsorum consensu concessam sibi recepit.* For Nero's bad contests, see Shadi Bartsch, *Actors in the Audience: Theatricality and Doublespeak from Nero to Hadrian*, Cambridge, Mass., 1994, pp. 1–35. "A paterfamilias who said that a Thracian gladiator was a match for the *murmillo*—but not for the giver of the games (Domitian), the latter caused to be dragged from his seat and thrown into the arena against dogs, wearing a placard that said: 'A fan of the Thracians who spoke impiously'" (*Patrem familias, quod Thraecem murmilloni parem, munerario imparem dixerat, detractum spectaculis in harenem canibus obiecit hoc titulo: "impie locutus parmularius"* [Suetonius, *Domitianus* 10.1]).

100. Foster trans. Compare the people's victory chants for Nero the unconquered citharode (Dio 62.3–5). The senators competed, according to Tacitus, in congratulating Nero on surviving the plots of his mother, whom he had recently murdered (*Annales* 14.12.1).

101. Fortis trans.

on the streets of Rome. Like Plautus's Mercury, Nero was slumming, playing the street shark. And, as in the encounter between of Mercury and Sosia, there was a semblance of an equal contest. But Montanus (like Job, or Winston Smith, or Sosia) had no idea what he was dealing with; it was less a game than a trap. Or, rather, if it was a game for the emperor, it was a trap for his subject, like the challenge issued by the patron to his clients to tell him the truth in Persius's First Satire (1.53ff.). (The powerful man, demanding to "hear the truth" about himself from his clients or subjects, knows full well that the unrelieved domination of the patron defines and limits the "truth.")[102] The "contest" between Nero and Montanus ends in exactly the way as that between Job and Yahweh, Winston Smith and Big Brother, Sosia and Mercury, Marsyas and Apollo, the market gardener and the Roman soldier.[103] In the violent confrontation in the street, it was Montanus who prevailed; nevertheless, it was Montanus who lost his life (Tacitus, *Annales* 13.25.1–3; Dio 61.9.2–4). According to Tacitus and Dio, if only Montanus had not recognized Nero and not apologized, the emperor would have let him live. But it was as difficult for poor Montanus as it was for Lewis Carroll's Alice to know by what rules one was playing when one played with a despot.

When the rules and outcome of every contest were decided not in an arena between relative equals but by the arbitrary will of the emperor (or his agents), the most coveted signs of public recognition *(honores)* became cruel jokes. Pliny the Younger tells us that the senate, in accordance with the proposal of the emperor, decreed a triumphal statue to Vestricius Spurinna, "an honor granted to many who have never engaged in a battle, never seen a camp nor even heard the sounds of a trumpet except in the theater" *(Epistulae* 2.7.1).[104] Claudius, according to Tacitus, granted the triumphal insignia to Curtius Rufus for exhausting his troops in the excavation of a silver mine. On this occasion, Tacitus tells us, the soldiers wrote to the emperor beseeching him, not without sarcasm, not to put a general in charge of an army—unless, of course, that general had been given triumphal honors in advance *(Annales* 11.20).[105] Dio accuses Tiberius of granting triumphal honors even to his informers. As a result, he tells us, several men who

---

102. See Barton, *Sorrows,* p. 143. Seneca declares that it was impossible for Maecenas or Agrippa to speak frankly to Augustus (Seneca, *De beneficiis* 6.32.4). The "truth" created in a very unequal contest was belied rather than validated by the agonistic framework.

103. The ostensibly equal contest where the cards are nevertheless stacked is perhaps the most embittering contest of all. See the hideous phony contests that open Ralph Ellison's *Invisible Man,* New York, 1947.

104. *Vestricio . . . triumphalis statua decreta est non ita ut multis qui numquam in acie steterunt, numquam castra viderunt, numquam denique tubarum sonum nisi in spectaculis audierunt.* Claudius and Nero granted *triumphalia* arbitrarily to quaestors and equites and not always for military service *(nec utique de causa militari* [Suetonius, *Nero* 15.2; *Claudius* 24]). On the trivialization of military honors, see Susan Mattern, *Rome and the Enemy: Imperial Strategy in the Principate,* Berkeley, 1999, pp. 200–201.

105. For a slightly different version, see Suetonius, *Claudius* 24.3.

were worthy of such honors refused them, for they did not want to be thought equal to those who received them (58.4.8). Thus, not so strangely, illustrious men declined the "honor" of commanding an army (Tacitus, *Annales* 6.33.3 [= 6.27.3]). Tacitus ascribes a lull in activity on the Rhine to the attitude of the generals who, with the triumphal insignia so vulgarized, anticipated more honor from inaction than from action (*Annales* 13.53).[106]

The honor of magistracies was similarly debased. Tiberius granted his nephew, the future emperor Claudius, the consular regalia. When the latter urgently requested the actual position of consul, Tiberius replied to him in a note: "I have already sent you forty gold pieces for the Saturnalia" (Suetonius, *Claudius* 5).[107] Pliny comments, sadly, that men despised even the consulship when elected to it (*Panegyricus* 63.3–4). Such titles, he declares, are empty, *mimica* and *inepta* (*Epistulae* 7.29.3). He comments on the honors given by Claudius and a servile senate to the freedman Pallas: "Who is so crazy as to desire advancement through his own and his country's dishonor, in a state where the chief privilege of its highest office is that of being the first to pay compliments to Pallas in the Senate?" (*Epistulae* 8.6.3).[108]

The perception that a player was more intent on winning than preserving the rules of the game reduced the competition to a farce. So, in our own culture, when a player takes the contest too seriously, when winning becomes an end in itself and not the excuse for playing, the other players are wont to remind the too-serious contestant ironically that "it's just a game." When one or more players is unwilling to lose, the quality of participation suffers for all players. When something external, something beyond the game becomes more important than the playing, the game becomes "just a game." The code by which the participants live begins to seem frivolous and vacuous; their commitment to the rules of the game is weakened, if not destroyed. In such circumstances it is difficult to be graceful.

---

106. Because of his *malignitas* and *superbia,* Caligula deprived illustrious Roman families of names and insignia of honor that they already possessed (Suetonius, *Caligula* 35.1). While Domitian ruled, being worthy of honor only imperiled one (Tacitus, *Agricola* 41).

107. *Tiberius patruus petenti honores ornamenta detulit; sed instantius legitimos flagitanti id solum codicillis rescripsit, quadraginta aureos in Saturnalia et Sigillaria misisse ei.* Under Claudius, Tacitus asserts, the quaestorship, once a reward for merit (*virtutis praemium*), was virtually put up for auction (*Annales* 11.22). For Claudius's debasement of Roman magistrates, see Suetonius, *Claudius* 24. According to D. W. T. C. Vessey, "The mockery is overt; Rome's traditional honors have been debased and prostituted under the monarchy" ("Thoughts on Tacitus's Portrayal of Claudius," *American Journal of Philology* 92 (1971): 396.

108. *Sed quis adeo demens, ut per suum, per publicum dedecus procedere velit in ea civitate, in qua hic esset usus florentissimae dignitatis, ut primus in senato laudare Pallantem posset?* Petronius's awful poet Eumolpus announces, "I am a poet, and a poet of no mean talent, I like to hope, at least if any credit can be placed in the crowns of honor that favoritism confers even on the unworthy" ("*Ego,*" inquit, "*poeta sum et ut spero, non humillimi spiritus, si modo coronis aliquid credendum est, quas etiam ad immeritos deferre gratia solet*" [*Satyricon* 83]).

FROM TRIAL TO TORTURE

"What is there that suffering cannot overcome?"
SENECA, *HERCULES OETAEUS 1279*[109]

Mikhail Bakhtin remarks that for the individual, isolated body, "death is only death, it never coincides with birth, old age is torn away from youth, blows merely hurt without assisting in an act of birth."[110] Death cannot define life if one is not expending one's life for anything or anyone. In April 58 B.C.E. Cicero laments to Atticus, "I have missed the most honorable time to die. Now when death comes, it will not heal but only end my pain" (*Ad Atticum* 3.7).[111]

When the contest was too often or too irremediably lost, or when the odds against winning were too enormous or too consistent, tests became *supplicia*, tortures. Instead of invigorating, they debilitated. Instead of confirming, they mutilated the spirit. In the words of the Republican Caecilius Balbus, "When there are no effects, labor grows more weighty" (*Sententiae* 189, Friedrich ed.).[112] Contests, *labores*, were, for the powerless (like the slaves Apuleius's Lucius sees grinding flour in the bakery) sufferings, *aerumnae*.[113] Outside the good contest sufferings could be at best punishments, *piacula*.

The contest with a *competitor*, Cicero tells us, is different from that with an *inimicus* (*De officiis* 1.12.38). The competitor held back; for the competitor there were still taboos and limitations.[114] With the enemy there were no boundaries and no bonds. Where the competitor tested one's spirit, the enemy would go to any length, including torture, to break one's spirit. In Seneca's scorching and beautiful *Trojan Women*, Andromache engages the victorious Achaeans in a war of wit and will for the life of

109. *quid non possit superare dolor?*

110. *Rabelais and His World*, trans. Helene Iswolsky, Austin, Texas [1964] 1984, p. 322.

111. *Cuius [mortis] oppetendae tempus honestissimum praetermissum est: reliqua temporis sunt non iam ad medicinam, sed ad finem doloris.*

112. *ubi nullus est effectus, gravior est labor.* Lucretius compares the ineffective labor *(durus labor)* of Sisyphus in hell to that of the ineffective politician (*De rerum natura* 3.998–1002). "It is one thing to labor," Cicero says, "another to suffer" (*Aliud est enim laborare, aliud dolere* [*Tusculanae disputationes* 2.15.35]). "Who," Aeneas asks of the night his city fell, "could match our toils with tears?" (*quis / ...possit lacrimis aequare labores?* [*Aeneis* 2.361]). Compare Aeneas's agonies with the happy labors of Dido building her city.

113. Ruth Benedict remarks on the negative effects of relentless competition in Japan: when the fear (and likelihood) of shame was greater than the pleasure of competing, competition could be felt keenly as aggression and result in melancholy, depression, and lowered rather than heightened performance (*The Chrysanthemum and the Sword*, New York, 1946, pp. 153–155).

114. Seneca shows his awareness of the value of the limited contest when he offers his advice on child-rearing: "In contests with his equals we should not suffer the child either to be vanquished or to get angry. We should see to it that he acts amiably toward those with whom he is wont to contend, in order that he become accustomed not to want to injure but only to win" (*In certaminibus aequalium nec vinci illum patiamur nec irasci: demus operam ut familiaris sit iis cum quibus contendere solet, ut in certamine adsuescat non nocere velle sed vincere* [*De ira* 2.21.5]).

her son. Seneca's "tyrant" Ulysses reminds the pathetically outmatched Andromache, struggling to hide from him the secret whereabouts of Astyanax, "The agony of being flogged and burned and racked will compel you to speak aloud, however unwilling, what you now conceal; it will dig out those things hidden deep in your breast. Necessity is more powerful than piety" (*Troades* 578–581).[115] Seneca's angry Theseus threatens the old nurse who is defending Phaedra with her silence: "With whips and bonds the old woman can be made to reveal whatever she declines to utter. Chain her! Let the force of the scourge extract the secrets of her mind" (*Phaedra* 882–885).[116] As Tacitus remarks, "There is nothing that cannot be obtained by torture or the promise of reward" (*Annales* 15.59.4).[117] Torture was the contest without condition. If the ordeal made citizens, the rack made subjects.[118]

In these circumstances there was no advantage in adversity. Tacitus, in the *Agricola*, chides the empty and contumacious displays of freedom of the suicidal rebels who died in resistance to the power of the emperors. He complains that "many became famous under the emperors by a death that was stubborn and self-advertising but useless to the Republic" (*plerique per abrupta sed in nullum rei publicae usum ambitiosa morte inclaruerunt* [42.4–5]).[119] These impetuous Romans were like those rebel Jews who were moved (according to the Jewish general Josephus, who collaborated with the Roman generals Vespasian and Titus) by "an unreasonable hope of freedom" *(elpis alogistos eleutherias)* to their fatal rebellion against the Roman governor Florus in 66 C.E. (*Bellum Iudaicum* 2.346).[120] Like suicide in our culture—and for similar reasons—their deaths were stillborn.

A STONE OF HOPE

Does he love his children? Good, I've got him!
The target for the wound is exposed.
SENECA, *MEDEA* 549–550[121]

At all times in Roman culture, in order to preserve the spirit, nothing apart from that spirit could be preserved. To have anything that one would not expend, to cling to

---

115. *verberibus igni omnique cruciatu eloqui / quodcumque celas adiget invitam dolor / et pectore imo condita arcana eruet / necessitas plus posse quam pietas solet.*

116. *verbere ac vinclis anus / altrixque prodet quidquid haec fari abnuit. / vincite ferro, verberum vis extrahat / secreta mentis.*

117. *cruciatui aut praemio cuncta pervia esse.*

118. See Page duBois, *Torture and Truth*, New York, 1991, for the evolution, in ancient Greek culture, of the touchstone, *basanos*, to the ordeal that revealed the truth and demonstrated the absolute sovereignty of the torturer.

119. Cf. Tacitus, *Annales* 16.22.

120. Compare the "sheer opposition," the contumacy *(philen parataxin)* of Marcus Aurelius's Christians (11.3) and the *pertinacia et inflexibilis obstinatio* of Pliny's Christians (*Epistulae* 10.96.3).

121. *sic natos amat? / bene est, tenetur, vulneri patuit locus.*

anyone or anything made humiliation inevitable. The bonds of love, in particular, held one hostage. Argyrippus's unwillingness to renounce his lover Philaenium (like the miser Euclio's unwillingness to part with his gold in the *Aulularia*) led directly to a long series of humiliations for both (Plautus, *Asinaria* esp. 127–157, 243–248, 646–731). Old Lysimachus's infatuation with Casina led as inevitably to his abasement (Plautus *Casina* 724–741) as Andromache's determination to save Astyanax resulted in cruel humiliations for her (Seneca, *Troades* esp. 410–425). Virgil's Aeneas was compelled by his bonds to father and son to outlive his courage: "Not long ago, there was no rain of missiles nor line of Greek soldiers massed in opposition that could move me. Now I am frightened by every breeze and startled by every sound, anxiously uncertain, and fearing alike for my companion and my burden" (*Aeneis* 2.726–728).[122]

The doomed Piso, in the aftermath of his unsuccessful conspiracy against Nero, loaded his will with "repulsive flattery of Nero" (*foedis adversus Neronem adulationibus*) in hopes of providing for his beloved wife (Tacitus, *Annales* 15.59). Why did Seneca's knight Pastor endure to be so horridly mocked by the emperor who killed his son? Because he had another son (*De ira* 2.33.3–4). If men or women of honor made very "unnatural" parents, "natural" parents were, by necessity, humble. According to Dio, when the Bastarnae invaded Thrace and attacked people who were under treaty to the Romans in 29 B.C.E., Crassus did his best to annihilate them. They were the more easily defeated, Dio tells us, because "they wished to save their wives and children" (51.24.4).

The desire to save one's own life (however "natural" or altruistic the reasons) resulted, in all periods of Roman history, in the worst humiliations. Tacitus speaks of "the hope of life, which is wont to break even great spirits" (*spe vitae, quae plerumque magnos animos infringit* [*Historia* 5.26.1]). "You must always fear," says Publilius Syrus, "when you desire to be safe." (*Metuendum est semper, esse cum tutus velis* [359, Friedrich ed.]). When Seneca's caged, befouled, and mutilated Telesphorus of Rhodes declares, "Where there's life there's hope," he is echoing Terence's slave Syrus (*modo liceat vivere est spes* [*Heautontimorumenos* 981]).[123] It was hope (and so slavery) that the clemency of Julius Caesar offered to the Romans.[124] Bru-

122. *et me, quem dudum non ulla iniecta movebant*
   tela neque adverso glomerati ex agmine Grai,
   nunc omnes terrent aurae, sonus excitat omnis
   suspensum et pariter comitique onerique timentem.

Cf. Seneca, *Epistulae* 56.12–14. Seneca's Hercules (*Hercules furens* 1314–41), Oedipus (*Phoenissae* 288–319), and Seneca himself (*Epistulae* 78.2) outlive their honor for love of parents or children. Ovid's Tereus was made vulnerable by his son Itys; Philomela and Procne were able to avenge themselves on Tereus by serving him up the flesh of his son (*Metamorphoses* 6.424–674). The nurse who convinced Phaedra that she, Phaedra, was her only comfort was instrumental in bringing about the latter's loss of honor (Seneca, *Phaedra* 250 ff., esp. 267–70).

123. Telesphorus: *Epistulae* 70.6–7, *De ira* 3.17.3–4.

124. Cf. Cicero, *Pro Marcello* 1.2, *Pro Ligario* 10.31–32, *De rege Deiotaro* 13.38.

tus warns old Cicero that if, by the gift of Octavian, they should live, keep their wealth, and be styled "consulars," it will be they, and not Octavian, who will have paid a high price, indeed, the highest of all prices (*Ad Brutum* 25.5).

Not one's child, nor oneself, but the rogue male became, by a very simple twist of fate, the unique and ultimate inexpendable being, the highest value of the culture. Cicero addresses Julius Caesar: "Is there a man so ignorant of his situation, so unversed in public affairs, so without thought for his own well-being or that of the community, that he does not realize that his own salvation is bound up with yours, and that on your life alone, Caesar, hangs the life of all?" (*Pro Marcello* 7.22).[125] Virgil's bees, conceived under Augustus, understood that the health of the hive depended on the health of their "king." With him, they were of one mind; if anything should happen to the "king," the bees would "break their faith" and tear the hive to pieces. Moreover, it was for the "king" bee—and not for the hive—that the bees exposed their bodies to the risks of battle and sought a glorious death (*Georgica* 210–218). For the sake of the "good" emperor, Seneca declared, "The people would throw themselves in an instant against the assassins' swordpoints; they would lay their bodies beneath his feet if his path to safety could be paved with slaughtered men; they guard his sleep by nightly vigils, they defend his body with an encircling barrier, they make of themselves a rampart against assailing dangers" (*De clementia* 1.3.3).[126] One owes *everything* to Caesar *(totum te Caesari debes)*: he is dearer to you than your own life (*carior tibi spiritu tuo* [Seneca, *Ad Polybium* 7.3–4]). To Nero, he says, "You are the soul of your state" (*tu animus rei publicae tuae es* [*De clementia* 1.5.1]). "The king is the bond through which the Republic coheres, the very breath of life which these many thousands draw, who, on their own, would only be a burden to themselves and the prey for others if the Mind of the Empire should be withdrawn" (*De clementia* 1.4.1).[127] The Roman people, he explains, will be free from danger just as long as they submit to the rein; if ever they should break away from obedience to the king, the fabric of the empire would fly into many parts and the end of Roman rule would coincide with the end of her people's submission to the prince (*De clementia* 1.4.2–3). The

125. *Nam quis est omnium tam ignarus rerum, tam rudis in re publica, tam nihil umquam nec de sua nec de communi salute cogitans qui non intellegat tua salute contineri suam et ex unius tua vita pendere omnium?* Cf. 7.21–25, 10.32. Cicero had already made similar, if somewhat milder claims, for Pompey (*Pro lege Manilia* 16.48).

126. *Obicere se pro illo mucronibus insidiantium paratissimi et substernere corpora sua, si per stragem illi humanam iter ad salutem struendum sit, somnum eius nocturnis excubiis muniunt, latera obiecti circumfusique defendunt, incurrentibus periculis se opponunt.* For the dependence of the state on the well-being of the charismatic leader, see Jean Béranger, *Recherches sur l'aspect idéologique du Principat,* Basel, 1953, pp. 169–218; Fears, "Theology of Victory," p. 799. For the sacrosanctity of the emperor, see Livy, *periochae* 116; Suetonius, *Julius* 76.1; Appian, *Bellum civile* 2.16.106.

127. *ille est vinculum, per quod res public cohaeret, ille spiritus vitalis, quem haec tot milia trahunt, nihil ipsa per se futura nisi onus et praeda, si mens illa imperii sbtrahatur.* Cf. 1.4.2.

worship of the emperor and of victory was, in the words of Jean Béranger, "la consécration du droit du plus fort."[128]

As so often in Roman life and thought, extremes invert. In the most profound paradox of Roman history then, the rogue male was transformed into the Roman emperor/god who then became every subject's point of honor, the one whose life all were bound to save and protect,[129] to whose health they pledged themselves. (It was a more atrocious crime, Cicero asserts, to kill the *parens patriae* than one's own father [*Philippicae* 2.13.31]).[130] And at the same time, the indispensable, the essential emperor, like the essential child, would be every subject's "Achilles' heel"—the target for the wound. The humility of the devoted subject was as necessary and inevitable as the humility of the devoted parent.

But the result of valuing anything more highly than one's honor (including, or especially the emperor or god), however selfless the motive, was humiliation. Recall Livy's story of the soldiers who returned home alive but disgraced from the Caudine Forks. While still trapped in the gorge, the soldiers had been persuaded to live through their terrible humiliations by the argument that Rome would be defenseless if they died. They would live and so be of further service to the state (9.4.8–16). But when, according to Livy, the Romans heard of the surrender and the peace made by Postumius at the Caudine Forks, they were more disturbed than they had been by the news of the soldiers' peril. The people spontaneously, without the command or authorization of the magistrates, went into deep mourning. All action was suspended; they closed their shops; a *iustitium* reigned in the forum. Such contempt did the Romans feel for the soldiers and their officers who had chosen to live that they wished to deny them admission to city and home *(negare urbe tectisve accipiendos).* The soldiers entered the city at night, hiding themselves in their own homes so that, on the following day, not one of them could be seen in public (Livy 9.7.6–11).[131] Similarly, when Plutarch's Antony fled the battle

---

128. *Recherches sur l'aspect idéologique du Principat,* p. 242.

129. Andreas Alföldi discusses the Augustan denarius issued with the inscription *s(enatus) c(onsulto) ob r(em) p(ublicam) cum salut(e) imp(eratoris) Caesar(is) Augus(ti) cons(ervatam):* "Dann ist die *conservatio rei publicae* schon zu einer sekundären Konsequenz des Heils des Staatsleiters herabgesunken" (*Der Vater des Vaterlandes in römischen Denken,* Darmstadt, 1971, p. 71). Cf. H. Mattingly, *Roman Imperial Coinage,* vol. 1, London, 1923, p. 17, no. 90. For pledging oneself to the health of the warlord or emperor, see Alföldi, *Der Vater des Vaterlandes,* p. 97; Fears, "Cult of Virtues," p. 883.

130. *est atrocius patriae parentem quam suum occidere.* Cf. 13.10.23. The king is held more dear than those to whom we are bound by personal ties (Seneca, *De clementia* 1.4.3).

131. The German chieftain Maroboduus, driven from his homeland, took refuge with the Romans. He had been an illustrious general, according to Tacitus, but when he died his splendor had been diminished by his too-great desire to live (*multum imminuta claritate ob nimiam vivendi cupidinem* [*Annales* 2.63.5]). In Livy's account there were ten Roman survivors of Cannae who refused to honor their oath to return to Hannibal. They were allowed, after a heated debate and narrow vote in the senate, to remain in Rome. However, under the next censors, they were so overwhelmed by every conceivable brand of ignominy that some of them committed suicide, and the remainder did not dare for the rest

of Actium to pursue Cleopatra, he could not bear to be seen by the woman from whom he could not bear to be parted; after boarding Cleopatra's ship, he spent three days alone in the prow (*Antony* 67.4). On returning to Alexandria, he built for himself a lonely dwelling in the sea on a mole constructed for him out from the Pharos promontory (*Antony* 69.4).[132]

THE REMEDIES OF DISHONOR: SERVICE

One effective remedy for servitude was to turn it into service—by a simple pirouette of one's emotions. If, like Sartrian existentialists, the heroes and heroines of the Republic had chosen terror over slavery,[133] Tacitus entertained the possibility of walking a path between terror and slavery, between stubborn contumacy and ugly servility, a path free from both self-display and danger (*Annales* 4.20.5).[134] He hoped that "it was possible to be a great man even in the service of a bad prince, and that *obsequium* and modesty, provided they were attended by vigorous activity, could bring one praise" (excelling that given to those rebels who earned fame by their stubborn, self-displaying, useless deaths described in *Agricola* 42.4).[135] Domitian was, Tacitus thought, pacified to some degree by his father-in-law Agricola, in whom "there was no willfulness, no empty, ostentatious display of freedom to provoke fame and ruin" (*Agricola* 42.3).[136]

Unfortunately, the desire to be "useful," to serve the state or the emperor (once the state was embodied in the emperor) made it hard for Tacitus and his father-in-law Agricola to "keep face." The path of compromise, he discovered (like Seneca before him and Thomas More after him), was less a path than a minefield. Service to the king easily slipped into servitude; the adviser to the

---

of their lives to enter the forum, or indeed to appear in the streets during daylight. (*ceterum proximis censoribus adeo omnibus notis ignominiisque confectos esse ut quidam eorum mortem sibi ipsi extemplo consciverint, ceteri non foro solum omni deinde vita sed prope luce ac publico caruerint* [22.61.9].)

132. Isolation (like abstract and decontextualized thought) breeds the longing for intimacy and for death (which are the same, as Georges Bataille points out in *Erotism* [trans. Mary Dalwood, San Francisco, 1986]). Imprisonment, even enslavement—to one's god or one's mistress—becomes increasingly attractive, a sort of complete and final surrender that would end the constant insult of living in an arbitrary world where one is asked to make oneself. For a similar crisis of intimacy in the Athenian contest culture, see Gouldner, *Enter Plato*, chapter 2.

133. "In a choice between terror and slavery, one chooses terror" (*Situations*, trans. Benita Eisler, New York, 1965, p. 216; cf. Frank Kermode, *The Sense of an Ending*, Oxford, 1966, p. 112).

134. *inter abruptam contumaciam et deforme obsequium pergere iter et deforme ambitione ac periculis vacuum.*

135. *posse etiam sub malis principibus magnos viros esse, obsequium ac modestiam, si industria ac vigor adsint, eo laudis excedere, quo plerique per abrupta sed in nullum rei publicae usum ambitiosa morte inclaruerunt.* Tacitus's formulation is part of a radical reformulation of the tradition values of self-control. Here he paints a capitulation as a traditional act of balance.

136. *non contumacia neque inani iactatione libertatis famam et fatumque provocabat.*

tyrant easily became his tool.[137] And useful men, like good parents, could not throw away their lives without ceasing to be instrumental to their king, their god, their country, or their children.[138]

THE REMEDIES OF DISHONOR: PETRIFACTION

For me Troy died long since, when Achilles lashed his chariot, axle shuddering,
with the weight of Hector's corpse.....Now I am rigidly impervious to horror;
I absorb each new blow and feel nothing.
ANDROMACHE IN SENECA, *TROADES* 412–17[139]

When the moment of truth became the "hour of lead," when competition was insupportable, then paralysis, the desire to hide, and the desire to be insensitive and autonomous became widespread cultural phenomena. With the loss of the good contest and the rules that framed it, cold, callous, brazen shamelessness became a cure for shame.[140] Servius Sulpicius reminds Cicero, inconsolable at the death of his beloved daughter Tullia, of their far greater losses: Having lost *patria, honestas, dignitas, honores,* "what spirit, trained in these times, ought not to become insensitive?" (Cicero, *Ad familiares* 4.5.2 [45 B.C.E.]).[141] Cicero himself, in the same baleful

---

137. For a detailed study of Seneca's agonizing moral dilemmas as "the adviser to the king," see Carlin Barton, "*Vis Mortua:* Irreconcilable Patterns of Thought in the Literature of the Neronian Period," Ph.D. diss., Berkeley, 1985.

138. For the notion of *utilis servitus,* see Hermann Strassburger, "Poseidonios on Problems of the Roman Empire," *Journal of Roman Studies* 55 (1965): 40–53, esp. pp. 45, 48.

139. Ahl trans. *Ilium vobis modo, / mihi cecidit olim, cum feras curru incito / mea membra raperet et gravi gemeret sono / Peliacus axis pondere Hectoreo tremens. / tunc obruta atque eversa quodcumque accidit / torpens malis rigensque sine sensu fero.*

140. "Too much shaming does not result in a sense of propriety but in a secret determination to get away with things when unseen, if, indeed, it does not result in deliberate shamelessness" (Erik Erikson, *Identity, Youth, and Crisis,* New York, 1968, p. 110). "The shame-prone person is on the brink of behaving in an unfeeling or inhuman way....He longs for the easy escape into object narcissism [Kinston's "shamelessness"] and not uncommonly gives into this longing" (Warren Kinston, "A Theoretical Context for Shame," *International Journal of Psychoanalysis* 64 [1983]: 218). Cf. Leo Rangell, "The Psychology of Poise," *International Journal of Psychoanalysis* 35 (1954): 316. Bertram Wyatt-Brown points out that shamelessness was a kind of salvation for the enslaved ("The Mask of Obedience: Male Slave Psychology in the Old South," *American Historical Review* 93 [1988]: 1228–1252). That they had been shamed was one of the reasons why, in the Nazi death camps, the Kapos and collaborators were often more brutal than the SS. The reason Stella Goldschlag turned against her fellow Jews in the first place was that she was already ashamed of being a Jew and could not bear further humiliation. Her biographer Peter Wyden's attempts to shame her into confessing that she betrayed her fellows only made her carapace the harder (*Stella,* New York, 1992). For an extensive discussion of the desensitization of the shamed, see James Gilligan, *Violence: Reflections on a National Epidemic,* New York, 1997.

141. *qui non in illis rebus exercitatus animus callere iam debet.* Cicero bids Atticus: "I ask you to consider what I should do now, for my troubles have rendered me blunt and stupid" (*Tu quaeso, cogita quid deinde, nam me hebetem molestiae reddiderunt* [*Ad Atticum* 9.17.2]). Of violence in Rome: *his quidam iam inveteratis, patres conscripti, consuetudine obduruimus* (*Philippicae* 2.42.108). *aures nobis calliscerent ad iniurias* (Cato apud Non-

year, remarks to his friend Atticus: "What could be more dishonorable? But now we harden ourselves to these humiliations and shed our humanity" (*Ad Atticum* 13.2 [May 45 B.C.E.]).[142] Even earlier, Cicero had written to Caelius, "Your letter would have caused me great grief if reason itself had not already dispelled all burdensome thoughts, and had not my spirit, from lasting despair, hardened itself against any new sorrows" (*Ad familiares* 2.16.1 [May 49 B.C.E.]).[143] In the *Tusculanae disputationes* he speaks of the endurance, the *patientia* of those who, having suffered much, bear more easily whatever happens to them and harden themselves against fortune. He quotes a line of Euripides' *Phrixus:* "If this mournful day were the first to dawn for me, had I not long sailed in such a sea of troubles, then there would be reason for anguish like that felt by a colt when the reins are first imposed and he bridles at the first touch of the bit. But now, broken by miseries, I am numb" (*Tusculanae disputationes* 3.38.67).[144]

THE REMEDIES OF DISHONOR: A ROCK FEELS NO PAIN

> *Cast out of your heart whatever torments it, and if it cannot otherwise be extracted,*
> *tear out your heart along with it.*
> SENECA, *EPISTULAE* 51.13[145]

The Stoics (even while they said that *honestas* was the sole good) asserted that nature compelled humans to seek the things conducive to life (Cicero, *De finibus* 4.28.78).[146] With the ideal of survival or salvation came the idealization of "natural" man and of "*living* according to nature."[147] Natural man did not have to prove he was a man, and so he did not need the contest. But the life of a "natural man" was, paradoxically, the life of a rock. Commitment to life made the nonbeing of dishonor unbearable. When the Romans begin to talk about saving

---

ius, vol. 1, p. 128, Lindsay ed.). *vale puella. iam Catullus obdurat* (Catullus 8.11–12). Cf. Tacitus, *Annales* 1.6.3, 3.15.4, *Historia* 4.59.2. For the gradual hardening and harshening of the Roman character, see Schunck, "Römisches Sterben," Ph.D. diss., Heidelberg, 1955, pp. 30–32.

142. *Quid enim indignius? sed iam ad ista obduruimus et humanitatem omnem exuimus.*

143. *Magno dolore me affecissent tuae litterae, nisi iam et ratio ipsa depulisset omnes molestias, et diuturna desperatione rerum obduruisset animus ad dolorem novum.*

144. *Si mihi nunc tristis primum illuxisset dies,*
Nec tam aerumnoso navigavissem salo,
Esset dolendi causa, ut iniecto eculei
Freno repente tactu exagitantur novo:
sed iam subactus miseriis obtorpui.

145. *Proice quaecumque cor tuum laniant, quae si aliter extrahi nequirent, cor ipsum cum illis revellendum erat.*

146. *honestum sit solum id bonum esse, ... appetitionem rerum ad vivendum accomodatarum a natura profectam.*

147. The ideal of "natural" man is one of the main sources of notions of ontological rather than existential gender characteristics.

things, when they begin to talk about salvation, the stone—once the image of cal-lousness and stupidity—became an ideal. There was a hardness of the spirit, like a hardness of the body, that, when it was burned, could not feel it. (*eam . . . animi duritiam, sicut corporis, quod cum uritur non sentit* [Cicero, *De domo sua* 36.97].)[148] "Stand by a stone and slander it: what effect will you produce? If a man listens like a stone, what advantage has the slanderer?" (Arrian, *Epicteti dissertationes* 1.25.29). It was a desperate strategy to preserve both life and honor.

The loss of the good contest helps to explain the reception in Rome of the Cynic or Stoic *anaideia* (shamelessness), *apatheia* (apathy), and *autarkeia* (indepen-dence): "Surround yourself with philosophy, an impregnable wall; though fortune assault it with her many engines, she cannot breach it. The spirit that abandons external things stands on unassailable ground; it vindicates itself in its fortress; every weapon hurled against it falls short of its mark" (Seneca, *Epistulae* 82.5).[149]

It is not just the philosophers who are influenced by this thinking: for Sallust (himself the sensitive object of calumny), the good man is ultimately self-made and autonomous. Nothing and no one can touch his spirit: "The uncorrupted, eternal spirit, governor of the human race, acts and possesses everything and is not itself possessed" (*Bellum Iugurthinum* 2.3).[150] "He has no need of fortune who is incapable of either giving or snatching away probity, industry, and the other hon-orable skills" (*Bellum Iugurthinum* 1.3).[151] The miserable Ovid, banished by Augus-tus, writes from the shores of the Black Sea: "My *ingenium* is my companion and my resource. Caesar has no jurisdiction over it" (*Tristia* 3.7.47–48).[152] "Beyond the last inner tunic, which is this poor body of mine, no one has any authority over me at all" (Arrian, *Epicteti Dissertationes* 1.25). Seneca imagines Socrates's reaction to insults: "The hardness of a stone is felt by no one more than the one striking it. I present myself no differently than the lonely rock in the sea: on all sides there is commotion; I am continually buffeted, but not for that reason do they move that rock nor consume it—though the battery continue through the aeons" (*De vita beata* 27.3).[153]

---

148. There is "an inhuman hardness that counterfeits endurance" (*patientiam* [*imitatur*] *duritia imma-nis* [Cicero, *De partitione oratoria* 81]).

149. *Philosophia circumdanda est, inexpugnabilis murus, quem fortuna multis machinis lacessitum non transit. In insuperabili loco stat animus, qui externa deseruit, et arce se sua vindicat, infra illum omne telum cadit.*

150. *animus incorruptus, aeternus, rector humani generis agit atque habet cuncta neque ipse habetur.*

151. *probitatem, industriam, aliasque artis bonas* [*fortuna*] *neque dare neque eripere quoiquam potest.* See Werner Eisenhut, *Virtus Romana: Ihre Stellung im römischen Wertsystem,* Munich, 1973, p. 51 and n. 136.

152. *ingenio tamen ipse meo comitorque fruorque; / Caesar in hoc potuit iuris habere nihil.*

153. *Duritia silicis nullis magis quam ferientibus nota est. Praebeo me non aliter quam rupes aliqua mari destituta, quam fluctus non desinunt, undecumque moti sunt, verberare, nec ideo aut loco eam movent aut per tot aetates crebro in-cursu suo consumunt.*

Shamelessness—in the form of apathy and autonomy—was raised to a high virtue among the Epicureans, Cynics, and Stoics of the Empire.[154] Caligula was wont to say that there was nothing in his own nature more to be praised and approved that his Stoic immobility *(adiatrepsia)*. That, Suetonius explains, was his word for shamelessness *(inverecundiam)* (Gaius 29.1). "Saint" Cato does not respond to insult; he does not blush; he does not defend himself; he does not play the game; it is beneath him. Everything might move around him, but Seneca's Cato is unmoved *(Epistulae* 104.30).[155] "Through it all," according to Velleius, "he was nearer in spirit to the gods than to other human beings" (2.35.2).[156] "It is possible," asserted the sad emperor Marcus Aurelius—affirming his greatest fear as if it were his greatest hope—"to become an entirely godlike man and yet not be recognized by anyone" *(Meditations* 7.67).[157]

THE REMEDIES OF DISHONOR: THE ARMOR OF HYPOCRISY

When Brutus heard of the murder by Tarquin of the Roman aristocrats, and that one of the victims was his own brother, he determined that Tarquin would not perceive anything in his spirit worthy to be feared, nor anything in his condition worthy to be desired. And so Brutus, looking for safety in contempt when there was too little in the law, strategically feigned stupidity.
LIVY 1.56.7[158]

"If you wish to make progress," Epictetus suggests, "you must be content in external matters to seem a fool and a simpleton; do not wish men to think you know anything."
ENCHEIRIDION 13

154. The wise man was a stone: "As the hardness of certain stones is impervious to steel, and adamant cannot be cut or ground or worn down, but, on the contrary, blunts whatever assails it, as certain substances cannot be consumed by fire, but, though encompassed by flame, retain their hardness and their shape; as certain cliffs, projecting into the deep, break the force of the sea, and though lashed for countless ages, show no trace of this savagery, just so the spirit of the wise man is solid, and has gathered so much strength that it is no less safe from injury than these things that I have mentioned" (*Quomodo quorundam lapidum inexpugnabilis ferro duritia est nec secari adamas aut caedi vel deteri potest sed incurrentia ultro retundit, quemadmodum quaedam non possunt igne consumi sed flamma circumfusa rigorem suum habitumque conservant, quemadmodum proiecti quidam in altum scopuli mare frangunt nec ipsi ulla saevitiae vestigia tot verberati saeculis ostentant: ita sapientis animus solidus est et id roboris collegit, ut tam tutus sit ab iniuria quam illa quae rettuli* [Seneca, *De constantia sapientis* 3.5, cf. 6.8]). Cf. Marcus Aurelius 4.49.1.

155. *nemo mutatum Catonem totiens mutata in re publica vidit.* Cf. *Epistulae* 95.71. For winning by not playing (the "snub gambit"), see Barton, "Savage Miracles."

156. *per omnia ingenio diis quam hominibus proprior.*

157. Farquharson trans.

158. *L. Iunius Brutus . . . iuvenis longe alius ingenio quam cuius simulationem induerat. is, cum primores civitatis, in quibus fratrem suum, ab avunculo interfectum audisset, neque in animo suo quicquam regi timendum neque in fortuna concupiscendum relinquere statuit contemptuque tutus esse ubi in iure parum praesidii esset. ergo ex industrua factus ad imitationem stultitiae.*

The face became a façade.[159] The *persona* went from being primarily expressive to primarily defensive.[160] In Tacitus's world, all (including the emperor) were compelled to hide behind the façade of their faces. To give just a few examples: Piso Licinianus emerged from the palace carrying with him the great and dangerous secret of his adoption by the elderly Emperor Galba. The pressure of all eyes was immediately upon Piso, who, according to Tacitus, betrayed no emotions. Nothing could be read from the opaque expression on his face: no turbulence, no exaltation, nothing (*Historia* 1.17).[161] Piso's face became a mask: he was forced to hide behind it, and at the same time the mask allowed him to preserve his life— for a time.[162] "At Rome, consuls, senators and knights were rushing into slavery. The more illustrious one was, the prompter to hypocrisy. They composed their faces carefully so that they would not betray cheerfulness at the departure of the prince nor sorrow at his arrival, blending their tears with joy, their regrets with adulation" (Tacitus, *Annales* 1.7.1–2).[163] As for Livy's Brutus under Tarquinius or Suetonius's Claudius under Caligula, the mask, even a dishonorable one—or I should say *especially* a dishonorable one—relieved and assuaged embarrassment and humiliation, defended against an unbearable "now" that would crush you.[164] When Tacitus's Nero poisoned his rival Britannicus, the stricken Octavia, having learned to hide her every emotion *(omnes adfectus abscondere)* looked upon the death throes of her brother and all her hopes with a brazen face (*Annales* 13.16).[165] The thick-skinned would survive. "Dissimulation is often more effective than revenge,"

---

159. According to A. Ernout and A. Meillet, *facies* was "the appearance, the thing presented to view" "jusqu'à l'époque impériale, où, par une restriction comparable à celle de *figura*, il se spécialise dans le sens de 'façade'" (*Dictionnaire étymologique de la langue latine*, Paris [1932] 1985, p. 211).

160. For a similar phenomenon in the life of poor African-American youths, the hardening of the mask and the resulting inner distancing and isolation, see "The Genesis of Black Masking" and "The Negative Side of Being Cool" in Richard Majors and Janet Mancini Billson, *Cool Pose: The Dilemmas of Black Manhood in America*, New York, 1992 , pp. 40–45, 55–66. For defensive theatricality and masking in unequal power relations, see Bartsch, *Actors in the Audience*, pp. 1–35; James C. Scott, *Domination and the Arts of Resistance*, New Haven, 1990.

161. *Pisonem ferunt statim intuentibus et mox coniectis in eum omnium oculis nullum turbati aut exultantis animi motum prodidisse.*

162. Cf. Seneca, *De ira* 3.15.2–3.

163. *At Romae ruere in servitium consules, patres, eques. quanto quis inlustrior, tanto magis falsi ac festinantes, vultuque composito ne laeti excessu principis neu tristiores primordio, lacrimas, gaudium, questus adultationem miscebant.* Cf. 11.38. For hypocrisy before the tyrant, see Pliny, *Panegyricus* 2.2, 2.5, 3.4, 66.3; Barton, *Sorrows*, pp. 39–40.

164. Paul Zanker depicts the Romans as escaping from the confused and tormented late Republic into an idealized Greek Never-Never Land. When they could no longer play at being Romans, playing at being Greek may have allowed them to feel something, to escape the numbness that resulted from "the collapse of the integral system of values among the Roman upper class" (*The Power of Images*, p. 31). The visible aspects of this collapse Zanker describes very well.

165. Compare the reaction of the young Gaius Caligula to the damnation of his mother and the murder of his brothers (Tacitus, *Annales* 6.26.1 [= 6.20.1]).

Seneca asserts. "The blows of the powerful must be borne not patiently merely, but even with a cheerful face. The powerful strike again, if they think that they have once struck home" (Seneca, *De ira* 2.33.1).[166] "It is the endurance of the ox and of the horse obedient to the rein that I would recommend," he says elsewhere in the same work (2.16.2).[167]

A king did not want to see the expression of the spirit, the will, in his subject's face, any more than a master wanted to see will in his slave's face: "First of all, I want to see a clearer expression on your face when you talk to me; it is stupidity for you to scowl at one who is more powerful than you are" (Plautus, *Casina* 281–283).[168] Just as the master could dictate the face to be worn by his slave, or the patron by his client, the emperor could dictate the face to be worn by his courtier. And if one could not take off one's mask, it petrified.[169] The role-playing that had no end, like the game that had no temporal limits, was slavery.[170] The person *compelled* to speak and act a formalized script felt "inane." In the prologue of Persius's first satire, the parasite and client, compelled to speak at the dinner party of the rich patron, describes himself as a "magpie" or "puppet." As time went on, even—or should I say especially—the victorious Roman elite came to know, profoundly, the experience of the defeated and the dependent.[171]

THE REMEDIES OF DISHONOR: THE REMOVABLE FACE

Erik Erikson explains that there is a limit to a child's or an adult's individual endurance in the face of repeated humiliations, and to his belief in the judgments of

---

166. *saepe autem satius fuit dissimulare quam ulcisci. Potentiorum iniuriae hilari vultu, non patienter tantum ferendae sunt: faciunt iterum, si se fecisse crediderint.* Cf. Barton, "*Vis Mortua*," p. 71.

167. *Patientiam laudaverim boum et equorum frenos sequentium.*

168. *Primum ego te porrectiore fronte volo mecum loqui: / stultitia est ei te esse tristem, cuius potestas plus potest.* Cf. Horace, *Epistulae* 1.18.86–95. For slaves whipped for giving their masters insolent looks, see Seneca, *De ira* 3.24.2.

169. Compare Tacitus's description of the face of Marcus Cluvius Rufus, "who had left his government in Spain and came up with Vitellius after his departure from Lugdunum. He wore a look of joy and congratulations, but was anxious at heart, for he knew he was the object of accusations" (*Digressum a Luguduno Vitellium Cluvius Rufus adsequitur omissa Hispania, laetitiam et gratulationem vultu ferens, animo anxius et petitum se criminationibus gnarus* [*Historia* 2.65.1]). Like Aeneas, he wears hope in his face but despair in his heart (*spem vultu simulat, premit altum corde dolorem* [Virgil, *Aeneis* 1.208–209]). *obnixus curam sub corde premebat* (ibid. 4.332). *animi dolorem vultu tegere* (Cicero, *In Verrem* 1.8.21). *abscondunt gemitus et pectora laeta / fronte tegunt* (Lucan, *Bellum civile* 9.1105–8). *et magnos ficto premit ore timores* (Statius, *Thebais* 11.233). *ut Domitiano moris erat, fronte laetus, pectore anxius* (Tacitus, *Agricola* 39.1).

170. Compare the party that does not end in Luis Buñuel's *Exterminating Angel* (1962), or the dismal soirée at the Japanese ambassador's house in Lima, Peru, that went on for four long months in the winter of 1996–1997, when the house was surrounded by rebels.

171. Recent work of Barbara Kellum on the image of Actium as it was employed by freedmen shows with what glee many of them greeted the revolution that brought down the elite.

those who belittle him. "Occasionally, he may turn things around, become se-cretly oblivious to the opinion of others, and consider as evil only the fact that they exist."[172] The revolt against unbearable humiliation often took the form of disengagement. The hardened skin is the disposable skin; it could be applied and peeled off like papier-mâché or painted on and washed off like greasepaint. The subject, like the dependent, delighted in being *callidus*, wily as well as hard; he or she enjoyed being a Vertumnus or a *versipellis*, a protean creature who changed his or her skin to suit the moment.[173] Tacitus's aristocrats often adopted the survival strategy of Plautus's slaves: metamorphosis. It is important to add, however, that if being a trickster made one like the slaves in Plautus or Petronius, it also made one like a god.[174] Jupiter was, of course, the ultimate *versipellis* (Plautus, *Amphitruo* 123).[175] Like the god, the slave was not attached to his face. To borrow a phrase from Jerome: "either a stone or a god" (*vel saxum vel deus* [*Epistulae* 133.3.5]).[176]

Protean shamelessness gave one a kind of handicap in unequal power relation-ships. It was this shameless indifference that had given the slaves of Plautus and Terence a certain advantage over their masters. The Elder Cato, insulted by an infamous and dissolute man, complained: "Any fight between us is an unequal one: you are so hardened that you can utter calumny as easily as you hear it, whereas for me it is both unusual to hear and unpleasant to speak" (Plutarch, *Cato Maior* 9.7).

THE REMEDIES OF DISHONOR: NO CONTEST

To struggle in vain and to obtain, by exhausting oneself, nothing but loathing,
is an act of insanity.
SALLUST, *BELLUM IUGURTHINUM* 3.3[177]

172. *Identity, Youth, and Crisis*, p. 111.

173. For Vertumnus, the god who presided over the changing of the year and could assume any shape he pleased, see Horace, *Satirae* 2.7.8–14.

174. The slave and the king (or god)—both outside the balancing systems—were liable to be iden-tified, as, in the Roman physics, extremes were liable to invert.

175. For the king as a *versipellis*, see the stories of the disguised kings and their minions foraying into the world of slaves and muledrivers, from Antony and Cleopatra through Commodus: Tacitus, *Annales* 13.25.1–3, 13.47; Suetonius, *Nero* 26.1–2, *Otho* 2.1; Plutarch, *Antony* 29.1–2; Dio 61.8.1, 61.9.2–4; Gellius, *Noctes Atticae* 6.11.4–6; *Scriptores historiae Augustae, Commodus* 3.7.

176. *Corpus Scriptorum Ecclesiasticorum Latinorum*, vol. 56.

177. *frustra autem niti neque aliud se fatigando nisi odium quaerere extremae dementiae est.* "Sisyphus also ap-pears in this life before our eyes, athirst to solicit from the people the lictor's rods and cruel axes, and always retiring defeated and full of gloom: for to solicit powers, an empty thing, which is never granted, and herein always to endure hard toil, that is to push laboriously up a steep hill the rock that still rolls down again from the top." Rouse trans.

(*Sisyphus in vita quoque nobis ant oculos est*
qui petere a populo fasces saevasque secures

Whatever assaults fortune may launch against you, if you are unable to face them, you may escape by running away.
CICERO, *TUSCULANAE DISPUTATIONES* 5.41.118[178]

If you do not wish to fight, you are permitted to flee.
SENECA, *DE PROVIDENTIA* 6.7[179]

Children, when things do not please them, say, "I will not play anymore"; so, when things seem to you to reach that point just say, "I will not play anymore," and so depart, instead of staying to make moan.
ARRIAN, *EPICTETI DISSERTATIONES* 1.24

Otium, vacatio, immunitas, withdrawal, leisure, the absence of tension and disturbance, became values in Roman society at the moment when it became impossible to maintain one's being by contest and when the isolation of withdrawal was less painful than the humiliation that came with the active negotiation of one's honor.[180] "Whoever said that the best course was to set sail, and then denied that one should navigate that sea in which shipwrecks were wont to occur and frequent and sudden storms arose, driving the captain against his course—I think that he forbids me to lift anchor, even while he praises navigation" (Seneca, *De otio* 8.4).[181] In the words of Zvi Yavetz, "From the time of Augustus, there begins a period in which the *primores civitatis* themselves often regarded *inertia* as *sapientia*."[182]

The senate and the courts having ceased to function, Cicero's leisure was, he says, the result not of a yearning for repose but of the frustration of activity. It was

---

imbibit et semper victus tristisque recedit.
nam petere imperium quod inanest nec datur umquam
atque in eo semper durum sufferre laborem,
hoc est adverso nixantem trudere monte
saxum quod tamen e summo iam vertice rursum volvitur et plani raptim petit aequora campi.
[Lucretius, *De rerum natura* 3.995–1002])

178. *sic iniurias fortunae, quas ferre nequeas, defugiendo relinquas.* "Enough of labor!" the exhausted and beastialized Lucius cries, "Enough of peril!" (*Sit satis laborum, sit satis periculorum* [Apuleius, *Metamorphosis* 11.2].) For the utter banality and futility of the contest, see also Marcus Aurelius 5.33.

179. *si pugnare non vultis, licet fugere.* "A contest with one's equals is hazardous, with a superior mad, with an inferior degrading" (*Cum pare contendere anceps est, cum superiore furiosum, cum inferiore sordidum* [*De ira* 2.34.1]).

180. André points out that, in its earliest appearances, *otium* was not withdrawal or leisure, but rather a particular sphere of activity, most commonly agricultural activity—which was distinguished from the sphere of military activity. But in the period being discussed it came to mean "temps creux consacré librement au loisir" (*L'otium,* p. 22).

181. *si quis dicit optimum esse navigare, deinde negat navigandum in eo mari in quo naufragia fieri soleant et frequenter subitae tempestates sint, quae rectorem in contrarium rapiant, puto hic me vetat navem solvere, quamquam laudet navigationem.*

182. *Plebs and Princeps,* Oxford, 1969, p. 9. Cf. Tacitus, *Agricola* 6.3.

not the rest, he says, owed to a man who once secured for the city a rest from civil strife (*De officiis* 3.1.2).[183] He wrote philosophy while, under the rule of one man, he languished in retirement (*cum otio langueremus* [*De natura deorum* 1.4.7]). Cicero's withdrawal from politics was an anesthetization of his spirit: "That part of my spirit, where once wrath resided, has grown numb. Now only my personal and domestic affairs please me" (*Ad Atticum* 4.18 [Oct. 54 B.C.E.]).[184] "*Otium*, leisure," Seneca explains, "begins to be a necessity for us because that thing we would prefer to *otium* nowhere exists" (*De otio* 8.3).[185]

The ideal of a stable, permanent, benevolent *status quo,* a state free from the endless equilibrations, the tensions and disturbances of the Republican balancing systems, an *otium commune*, a *pax civilis*, appears in Cicero's thought simultaneously with the perception that the tensions of public life had become insufferable.[186] *Virtus,* the active principle par excellence, congeals into patience, endurance, passive resistance; it began to be used of internal qualities, even those unseen or unacknowledged.[187] It looks more and more like our "virtue." But the idea that one could have *virtus* in *otium*, that one could have *virtus* without the strenuous expenditure of energy, without contest, without witnesses, was nothing short of a revolution in Roman values.[188]

THE REMEDIES OF DISHONOR: AN ABSTRACT LIFE

You are a little soul carrying around a corpse.
MARCUS AURELIUS QUOTING THE FORMER ROMAN SLAVE EPICTETUS, *MEDITATIONS* 4.41

Honor, in ancient Rome, had always been "sightliness," *decus, honestas.*[189] Dishonor had ever been unsightly, a *dehonestamentum* (something that disfigured), a

---

183. *Nostrum otium negotii inopia, non requiescendi studio constitutum est.... otio fruor non illo quidem quo debeat is qui quondam peperisset otium civitati.*

184. *Locus ille animi nostri, stomachus ubi habitabat olim concalluit; privata modo et domestica nos delectant.* "If we cannot enjoy the Republic, it is stupid not to enjoy our private affairs" (*si re publica non possis frui, stultum est nolle privata* [Cicero, *Ad familiares* 4.9.4]). Withdrawal to the country becomes the cure for the miseries and humiliations of being a client (Horace, *Epistulae* 1.18; cf. Columella 1 *praefatio* 10).

185. *incipit omnibus esse otium necessarium, quia quod unum praeferri poterat otio, nusquam est.*

186. See, especially Chaim Wirszubski, "Cicero's *cum dignitate otium*: A Reconsideration," *Journal of Roman Studies* 44 (1954): 1–13; Wegehaupt, *Die Bedeutung und Anwendung von dignitas,* pp. 53–60, 62–63, 77; J. P. V. D. Balsdon, "*Auctoritas, dignitas, otium,*" *Classical Quarterly* n.s. 10 (1960): 46–50.

187. Cf. Cicero, *Tusculanae disputationes* 2.26.63–64; Arrian, *Epicteti dissertationes* 1.10.

188. In Rome *virtus* often begins to stand for, or is replaced by, the notion of *honestas.* See Anthony A. Long, "Cicero's Politics in *De officiis,*" in *Justice and Generosity: Studies in Hellenistic Social and Political Philosophy,* ed. André Laks and Malcolm Schofield, Cambridge, 1994.

189. Cf. Servius, *In Aeneida* 1.289: *veteres...honestum pro specioso ponebant*: Nonius, vol. 2, p. 501, Lindsay ed.: *honor, gratia, pulchritudo; Scholia Bembina in Terentium,* ed. J. F. Mountford, London, 1934, *Eunuchus* 132: *maiores nostri honestum dicebant pulchrum;* Drexler, "Honos," in Oppermann, *Römische Wertbegriffe,* pp. 459–60.

dedecus (blemish), something *turpis* (unsightly, ugly), *pravus* (crooked, misshapen), *foedus* (foul, filthy). But when one could not defend one's honor, embodiment itself became ugly and enervating. When one could not resist the injury, when one could not battle the corruption, one was tempted to remove an "essential being" from the social and physical world, to sheath it, as it were, in asbestos. The excruciating sense of an unbearable immediacy unrelieved by effective rules and rituals resulted in an intense desire to remove the *animus* from the contest, to break the spell of self-conscious embodiment. One was tempted to say: "This is not real. This is not really happening to me."[190] The divorce of the *animus* from the body, the "mind/body split,"[191] and the notion that the body was an unsightly prison gained ground simultaneously in ancient Rome with the notion that the contest had become trivial. It was as if, in this period, one might relegate the ugliness of dishonor to the visible and palpable which one could then slough off and discard. The withdrawal into the self that we associate with an abstract or transcendental Truth or Reality was a way of saying, "You can't see me. I am not what I see in your eyes." This tactic was both a relief from the problem of face and an abandonment of face.

We are not accustomed to thinking of the abstract thinker as shameless but rather as autonomous (insofar as he or she is obedient to God or Reason). But the abstract thinker *was* shameless insofar as he or she did not submit his or her truth to common consent; Reason and Truth were ways of creating a reality over which one was totally sovereign—while totally submissive to God or Reason.[192] The abstract thinker could have a reality without others, a being without others.[193] If

---

190. Cf. Erving Goffman, "Embarrassment and Social Organization," *American Journal of Sociology* 62 (1956): 271 and n. 11.

191. For the idea of the body as the *vinculum,* the *onus* of the *animus,* see Cicero, *Tusculanae disputationes* 1.31.75, *De republica* 6.15.15. When you extract the *animus* from the body while preserving it as the center of energy, the spirit becomes an image of both freedom and formlessness. Disdain for public opinion coincides with both the separation of *virtus* from *fama* and—at least in Sallust—with the separation of the *animus* and the *corpus.* (See Eisenhut, *Virtus Romana,* p. 50: *vis corporis, virtus animi*). Virgil's *fama,* the blind, many-eyed, many-mouthed *dea foeda* is a wonderful depiction of public opinion as an increasingly blind voyeur (*Aeneis* 4.174–197). It could be argued that Marx's radical materialism, in a converse but related development (with its separation of a material base from an ideological superstructure), resulted ultimately from his perceptions of the unfair and unequal contest between a factory worker and a factory owner.

192. "Seneca versucht, den vollkommenen Menschen mit dem vollkommenen römischen Manne gleichzusetzen. Dessen Wert wird nun freilich nicht mehr durch die römische Bürgergemeinde legitimiert, sondern allein durchs eigene Gewissen" (Knoche, "Der Beginn des römischen Sittenverfalls," p. 101).

193. Indifference becomes the emotional prerequisite for speaking truly. In the *Acts of Peter,* as Maud Gleason points out, it is the talking corpse—the thing (for one cannot say man or person) for whom nothing at all is at stake—that is the voice of truth. See "Truth Contests and Talking Corpses," in *Classical Constructions of the Body,* ed. James I. Porter, Ann Arbor, 1999, pp. 287–313.

doubt was the central socializing emotion of the ancient Romans,[194] certainty and *veritas,* abstract transcendental "Truth," appeared as the symptom of social collapse.

CONCLUSIONS: ONCE WERE WARRIORS

Wretched is our fate, that we were not born into the age of the Punic Wars,
That we were not the men who fought at Cannae and the Trebia!
LUCAN, *BELLUM CIVILE* 2.45[195]

The Romans had long believed that the man was not alive who thought only of living. (*Non vivit, qui nil cogitat nisi vivere* [Caecilius Balbus, *Sententiae* 138, Friedrich ed.].)[196] At his last stand against Antony, Cicero declared, "Life does not consist in the breath of life; there is no life at all in the slave" (*Non enim in spiritu vita est, sed ea nulla est omnino servienti* [*Philippicae* 10.10.20]). He continues:

> All other nations endure slavery, but our city cannot.... We have been trained and our minds imbued by our ancestors to refer all our acts and thought to the standard of *dignitas* and *virtus*. So glorious is the recovery of liberty that in regaining liberty we must not shrink even from death. If immortality were to follow our flight from present peril, it would seem we should shrink from it the more as a perpetuation of servitude. While day and night and on every side danger surrounds us, it is not the part of a man, least of all a Roman, to hesitate to surrender the breath he owes to nature to his fatherland.[197]

But Cicero, until he found the courage to turn his ship about and take the blow broadsides, trimmed his sails to the tyrants' winds. In a letter to Publius Lentulus written in 54, Cicero justified his submission to Pompey. "*Obsequium,*" he claims, "is the art of navigating in a storm" (*Ad familiares* 1.9.21). And Cicero was not the only trimmer. The "studiously insouciant Caelius" (to use the words of Shackleton Bailey) lectured Cicero in 50 B.C.E.: "I'm sure it does not escape you that in civil dissensions one should take the more honorable side as long as the struggle is carried on with civility and not with weapons, but when it comes to war one

---

194. For doubt as a central socializing emotion and product of socializing, see Jean L. Briggs, "Living Dangerously: The Contradictory Foundations of Value in Canadian Inuit Society," *Politics and History in Band Societies,* ed. Eleanor Leacock and Richard Lee, Cambridge, 1982, esp. pp. 121–122.

195. *O miserae sortis, quod non in Punica nati / Tempora Cannarum fuimus Trebiaeque iuventus!*

196. "It is my opinion that all men need to consider either their mortality or their immortality" (*Etenim omnes homines arbitror oportere aut immortalitatem suam aut mortalitatem cogitare* [Pliny, *Epistulae* 9.3.2]).

197. *Omnes nationes servitutem ferre possunt, nostra civitas non potest.... Quodsi immortalis consequeretur praesentis periculi fugam, tamen eo magis ea fugienda videretur, quo diuturnior servitus esset. Cum vero dies et noctes omnia nos undique fata circumstent, non est viri minimeque Romani dubitare eum spiritum, quem naturae debeat, patriae reddere.* "I am guilty of no sin except that I did not forfeit my life when I forfeited my honors" (*peccatum est nullum nisi quod non una animam cum ornamentis amisimus* [Cicero, *Ad familiares* 14.4.5 (April 58 B.C.E.)]).

should choose the stronger side and reckon the safer course the better" (*Ad Familiares* 8.14.3).[198]

As the rules became easier to break and less and less guilt was associated with breaking them, it became harder for Romans to sacrifice or risk their lives to uphold them. As a result, death lost its life-affirming value. When death lost its value, life became an abstraction, what Clifford Geertz calls a "bloodless universal."[199] But, as Seneca points out to Lucilius, no one is willing to die for a syllogism (*Epistulae* 82.21–24). A "virtuous" and absolute god arose, but it was an abstract god over a naked rock.

How reluctant the Romans were to give up being fragile, ephemeral humans even to become gods of adamant is made ever so poignantly clear in the writings of men like Cicero, Sallust, Lucan, Seneca, and Tacitus. Perfect and superterrestrial understanding was no compensation for the loss of community (Cicero, *De amicitia* 22.23.87–88).[200] Even while they praised withdrawal from an untenable public life, they dreaded appearing to others as inactive and inert.[201] Peaceful autonomy (minding one's own business) and imperviousness to shame played their flat but poignant counterpoint to the tense and fiery bass of the ancient warrior values. Cicero wrote philosophy because withdrawal was necessary for survival; he delivered his fatal attacks on Antony because, in his heart, finally, he still ached for glory. Cicero wrote to Brutus at the end of both of their lives: "This is what I want you to understand: my soul is on the front line, and I seek no quarter" (*Ad Brutum* 1.2–3 [= 2.1.2–3]).[202]

---

198. *illud te non arbitror fugere, quin homines in dissensione domestica debeant, quamdiu civiliter sine armis certatur, honestiorem sequi partem: ubi ad bellum et castra ventum sit, firmiorem: et id melius statuere, quo tutius sit.*

199. I have discussed elsewhere (*Sorrows,* chapter 2) the solution adopted by some Romans: like Nietzsche, some Romans tried to impose strict voluntary boundaries on themselves, to build, like the Romans trapped at the Caudine Forks, a sort of fortress within a cage. The great ascetic movements that took hold in Rome at this time, which demanded the submission of the individual to a tight circle of bonds, required relentless exercise of the will.

200. *Si quis in caelum ascendisset naturamque mundi et pulchritudinem siderum perspexisset, insuaven illam admirationem ei fore, quae iucundissima fuisset, si aliquem cui narraret habuisset.*

201. "But I believe that there will be those who, because I have determined to pass the rest of my days far from political life, will label my difficult and useful work as *inertia;* certainly those who think that the greatest work is to court the masses and cultivate their influence at dinner parties" (*atque ego credo fore qui, quia decrevi procul a re publica aetatem agere, tanto tamque utili labori meo nomen inertiae inponant, certe quibus maxuma industria videtur salutare plebem et conviviis gratiam quaerere* [Sallust, *Bellum Iugurthinum* 4.3]). Sallust protests that he can serve the Republic more successfully in his (own) *otium* than in the *negotium* of others (4.4). Cf. Cicero, *Tusculanae disputationes* 1.3.5, *De officiis* 1.6.19, 3.1.1, *De republica* 1.2.2; Seneca *Epistulae* 8.1–2. "Tout l'effort des tenants de la vie contemplative consiste à discuter la notion équivoque de *nihil agere:* à démontrer que l'inaction est pure apparence au niveau des grands esprits" (André, *L'otium,* p. 40). As Wirszubski points out, the emphasis in Cicero's phrase *cum dignitate otium* was on the *dignitas;* Cicero wanted to preserve a peaceful public order in which his political prestige and influence could continue to operate ("Cicero's *cum dignitate otium,*" pp. 10, 12).

202. *illud est quod te velim habere cognitum, meum quidem animum in acie esse, neque respectum ullum quaerere.* Cf. *Ad Brutum* 7 [= 1.3].

Cicero's use of *honestas, decus,* or *fortitudo* to replace *virtus,* of *virtus* to translate Greek *arete,* of *persona* to translate Greek *prosopon,* or of *veritas* for Greek *ta onta* or *aletheia* did not drive out the more ancient and traditional uses of these words. Rather, Roman notions of honor were increasingly compelled to exist in two simultaneous, incompatible frames.[203] To quote Miriam Griffin:

> Cicero's own choice of *honestum*... as the Latin equivalent for the Greek *to kalon* (the morally beautiful) reveals an assumption that he makes explicit in the first of the *Paradoxa Stoicorum:* there, after saying that our ancestors agreed with the Stoics that only *quod rectum et honestum et cum virtute est*... is good, he enumerates deeds of those Roman paragons that demonstrate their beliefs that the only thing in life worth seeking is what is worthy of praise and renown (*quod laudabile esset et praeclarum*). The Romans could not accept that the conduct of the individual should not be governed in any way by the estimate of others.[204]

Francis Sullivan observes that the gradual dissolution of his earlier ideas about fame did not drive out his yearning for glory: *honestas,* which was meant to be an end in itself, never succeeded in being so; it remained the means to the end of *vera gloria. Veritas* became Cicero's way, ironically, of preserving all the ancient Roman values by inverting them. The ancient warrior values survived, but now only in an individualized, internalized, ultimately unassailable form. Cicero wanted a glory that could not be taken from him.[205]

The Roman Stoics, like the early Christians, like the love poets, never stopped wanting to be warriors. Froma Zeitlin remarks on the protagonist of Petronius's mock epic of the Neronian period: "Encolpius, the anti-hero in a world in which heroism is dead, persists in the fantasy of viewing his life in heroic terms and gauging his responses accordingly. He is an outsider, like all picaros, because of his loss of place in the social hierarchy. But he is even more of a psychic outsider, who by persisting in living in a vanished mode, can never come to terms with the world."[206] Is Juvenal so different?

> Be a good soldier, a good guardian, an incorruptible judge; if summoned as a witness in some dubious and uncertain case, even if the tyrant Phalaris himself should command you to lie, and, bringing up his bull [his notorious instrument of torture], to dictate the perjury he would have you tell, count it an abomination to prefer life to

203. See Francis A. Sullivan, "Cicero and *Gloria,*" *Transactions and Proceedings of the American Philological Society* 72 (1941): 382–391; Christopher Gill, "Personhood and Personality: The Four-*Personae* Theory of Cicero, *De Officiis* I," *Oxford Studies in Ancient Philosophy* 6 (1988): 169–199. For the simultaneous operation of irreconcilable frames of value in Seneca and Lucan, see Barton, *"Vis Mortua."*

204. "Cynicism and the Romans: Attractions and Repulsion," in *The Cynics,* ed. R. Bracht Branham and Marie-Odile Goulet-Cazé, Berkeley, 1996, p. 196.

205. See Sullivan, "Cicero and *Gloria*"; Gill, "Personhood and Personality."

206. "Petronius as Paradox: Anarchy and Artistic Integrity," *Transactions and Proceedings of the American Philological Association* 102 (1971): 631–684.

honor, and to lose, for the sake of living, the reason to live. The man who deserves to die is already dead, even if he is eating a hundred oysters from Guarana and bathing in a whole cauldron of Cosmus's perfumes. (*Satirae* 8.79–86)[207]

In the third book of Seneca's *De ira*, the tutor and sometimes vicar of the emperor Nero tells the story of the tyrant Cambyses and his friend and adviser Praexaspes. It is a story designed by Seneca to demonstrate that contest and confrontation can be avoided, that the most violent emotions can be suppressed, and that one can protect oneself from the tyrant with an impenetrable mask of apathy. In the story, Praexaspes admonishes the wild Cambyses that drunkenness is a disgrace in a king, a man who "is followed by the eyes and ears of all" *(omnium oculi auresque sequerentur)*. Cambyses, bristling, fastens on the words of his adviser as a challenge. He declares that he will demonstrate that he is ever in control of his hands and eyes. Defying the pleas of his adviser, he continues to drink, bidding Praexaspes introduce his son into the room. Cambyses draws his bow and, calling out his intended mark, shoots the son of Praexaspes in the chest. Tearing open the breast of the corpse, the tyrant reveals to the boy's father that the arrow had penetrated the heart. Turning to his adviser he asks, "Is my hand not sufficiently steady?" Praexaspes calmly replies: "Apollo himself could not have made a more unerring shot."

Seneca's Praexaspes was meant to be the hero of this tale, another wise man like the philosopher Stilpo who, when his fatherland had been conquered and his daughters had been raped by the soldiers of Demetrius Poliorcetes, was able, through his imperturbable indifference, to deny the victory to the mighty Demetrius.[208] But even the Stoic author, finally, cannot bear the consequences of his own philosophy. He cries out at this point: "May the gods damn him—a slave more in his soul than in his condition!" *(Dii illum male perdant animo magis quam condicione mancipium!* [3.14.3]) Praexaspes ought, he declares, to have challenged the king into giving still another demonstration of his skill upon the person of the father! Seneca sedately concludes: "The point under discussion is clear: it is possible to suppress anger" (3.14.4).

207. *esto bonus miles, tutor bonus, arbiter idem*
        integer: ambiguae si quando citabere testis
        incertaeque rei, Phaleris licet imperet ut sis
        falsus et admoto dictet periuria tauro,
        summum crede nefas animam praeferre pudori,
        et propter vitam vivendi perdere causas.
        dignus morte perit, cenet licet ostrea centum
        Guarana et Cosmi toto mergatur aeno.

208. *At ille victoriam illi excussit et se urbe capta non invictum tantum sed indemnem esse testatus est (De constantia* 5.6–7). If the ancient ideal was to make of oneself a target, to say, in effect, "Here I am, come and get me," the Stoic ideal was to declare, "I am not what you see; you can't get me because I'm not here at all."

From this anguished and telling story several things can be seen: first, it is not an equal contest. Cambyses shoots the son of Praexaspes as casually as Commodus shoots the animals led to him for slaughter; there is no challenging the king and living. (The tanks would roll right over you.) Second, Seneca continues to see even these unequal contests as basic tests of the quality and existence of one's being. Even while teaching his listeners how to preserve their being by withdrawing from the contest behind an impenetrable mask of indifference, he is also teaching them that the mask of indifference is never impenetrable enough; the arrow of contempt always hits its mark.

Not so paradoxically, it is from the pen of the Stoic philosopher Seneca that we get perhaps the most beautiful moment of truth in all of Roman literature. In Seneca's *Agamemnon*, the gods strike the Achaean soldiers returning home from the Trojan War with a cataclysmic storm. One ship founders on another. The sailors can do nothing to calm the storm or save themselves. The living envy the dead. The prayers of those who beseech the gods (insatiate of evil) are cut short by death. In the darkening night, only unconquered Ajax continues to fight (*solus invictus malis / luctatur Ajax* [532–533]). He is glanced by one and then struck by another bolt of lightning aimed at him with deliberate malice by the goddess Athena, affronted by the death-defying resistance of the lone mortal.

> And still Ajax struggles. Scorched, but unmoved, Ajax stands out from the deep like a sheer rock, cleaving the wild sea and breaking the waves on his chest. Clasping his ship in his hand he draws the flames behind him. And Ajax is illuminated. He causes all the sea to shine.[209]

209. *nil ille motus, ardua ut cautes, salo*
 ambustus extat, dirimit insanum mare
 fluctusque rumpit pectore et navem manu
 complexus ignes traxit et caeco mari,
 conlucet Ajax, omne resplendet fretum. (539–543)

PART TWO

Confession and the Roman Soul

A tension, a dilemma for the person of honor in ancient Rome had ever been the need to display oneself to others while simultaneously preserving an inviolate and protected sphere, the source and power of one's will, the *animus*, the effective energy at the core of one's being—what Sallust calls the *dux atque imperator vitae* (*Bellum Iugurthinum* 1.3).

It was above all one's word that realized, that reified one's spirit in the world. Varro defined *loquor*: "When what is in the spirit is brought forth in speaking" (*cum in animo quo habuit extulit loquendo* [*De lingua latina* 6.56]). One could have no *ius*, no *libertas*, no sphere of free or effective operation that did not rest, finally, on the vitality of the voice. The voice, moreover, conveyed the particularity of one's existence. As Pliny explains, "There are as many voices as there are mortals, and each person's voice is as distinctive as his face" (*Naturalis historia* 11.112.271).[1] Pliny goes on to say that the ability to express the spirit *(explanatio animi)* was what distinguished a human being from a wild beast. And the ability to articulate the spirit distinguished one human from another as surely as it distinguished humans from other animals.

Even while the voice, in humans, played a great part in the presentation of the self, in the expression of one's "face" (*vox in homine magnam voltus habet partem* [Pliny, loc. cit.]), the Romans were as aware as Voltaire or Talleyrand that speech also concealed feelings, that it disguised as well as displayed the hidden *animus*. "The submissive slave, who," according to the fabulist Phaedrus, "dared not say what he willed, translated his personal feelings into fables and eluded the charge of

---

1. *totidemque sunt hae quot in rerum natura mortales, et sua cuique sicut facies.*

calumny under the guise of jesting" (3, *prologus* 34–37).[2] The aristocratic orator calculated his words as carefully as the slave. However expressive, Roman rhetoric, like Roman poetry, was concurrently an elaborate system of strategic obfuscation, self-conscious moves in a delicate chess game. "I am not dissimulating when I declare that I am ignorant of those things which, even if I knew, I would dissimulate ignorance of" (Cicero, *De domo suo* 46.121).[3]

And so Roman speech was not simple; it was filled with ironies and innuendoes, ambiguities, feints, parries, and "second intentions."[4] Good speaking, in Rome, was a gambit. Good speaking was effective, stimulating, provocative. Good speaking was musical, polyphonic, resonant; every utterance elicited another in an unending movement.[5] Its purpose was never simply to arrive at the end. To pause, perhaps; but always to remain "in play." It was the Roman's way of "singing the world," to borrow a phrase from Merleau-Ponty.[6]

Because of the active role of the voice in defining, expressing, and protecting the spirit, confession (*fateor, confiteor*, from *for*, to speak), insofar as it was the suppression or appropriation by one person of another's person's voice, was a humiliation, perhaps the ultimate one, for a Roman. Confession was the move to end all moves; it was checkmate, the end of the game.

In chapter 5 I attempt to sketch, synchronically and panoptically, the notions and emotions of confession in ancient Rome and their relationships to Roman notions of the spirit and the breaking of the spirit.[7] In chapter 6 I discuss some of

---

2. *servitus obnoxia / quia quae volebat non audebat dicere, / affectus proprios in fabellas transtulit, calumniumque fictis elusit iocis.*

3. *Non dissimulo me nescire ea, quae etiam si scirem, dissimularem, ne aliis molestus . . . viderer.*

4. Compare the type of competitive speech Pierre Bourdieu found among the Kabyle in Algeria, which plays "on the equivocations, innuendoes and unspoken implications of verbal or gestural symbolism to produce ambiguous conduct that can be disowned at the slightest sign of withdrawal or refusal, and . . . maintain[s] uncertainty about intentions that always hesitate[s] between playfulness and seriousness, abandon and reserve, eagerness and indifference" (*Outline of a Theory of Practice*, trans. Richard Nice, Cambridge, 1977, p. 10).

5. *Ratio*, before it translated Greek "reason," was, like *sapientia*, the shrewd calculation of the pros and cons in any situation. For some of the ways in which this aspect of Roman thought operated, see especially Paul Plass, *The Game of Death in Ancient Rome*, Madison, 1995.

6. *The Phenomenology of Perception*, trans. C. Smith, London, 1962, p. 187. As I argued in *The Sorrows of the Ancient Romans* (Princeton, 1993), we have made our Romans altogether too solemn and self-consistent (on the model of our own notion of "honorable"). Rather, the Romans' verbal culture, in its playful and (to us) disconcerting counterpoint, was very like that Roman visual culture described so perceptively by Barbara Kellum. See, for example, "Sculptural Programs and Propaganda in Augustan Rome: The Temple of Apollo on the Palatine," in *The Age of Augustus*, ed. R. Winkes, Providence, 1985, pp. 169–176; "What We See and Don't See: Narrative Structure and the *Ara Pacis Augustae*," *Art History* 17 (1994): 26–45; "The Phallus as Signifier: The Forum of Augustus and Rituals of Masculinity," in *Sexuality in Ancient Art*, ed. Natalie Boymel Kampen, Cambridge, 1996, pp. 170–183.

7. For the history of confession in general, see Marcel Mauss, "L'histoire de la confession," in *Oeuvres*, vol. 2, Paris, 1969, pp. 640–642; Henry Charles Lea, *A History of Auricular Confession and Indulgences*

the historical aspects of Roman confession and the remedies for the irremediable: the consolations for a broken spirit and the redemption of honor by confession, submission, and the redefinition of the soul. I try to show how, after "spilling their guts," the ancient Romans were empty vessels ready to be filled up with a very different voice and spirit.

in the Latin Church, vol. 1, Philadelphia, 1896; C. M. Roberts, *A Treatise on the History of Confession until It Developed into Auricular Confession, A.D. 1215,* London, 1901; Edward Peters, *Torture,* New York, 1985, p. 46; Michel Foucault, *History of Sexuality,* vol. 1, trans. Robert Hurley, New York, 1980, esp. pp. 18–24, 58–68; Foucault, "Technologies of the Self," in *Technologies of the Self,* ed. Luther H. Martin, Huck Gutman, and Patrick H. Hutton, Amherst, 1988, pp. 17–49.

CHAPTER FIVE

The Spirit Speaking

Who conquers is not the victor unless the conquered confesses.

ENNIUS, *ANNALES* 493, VAHLEN ED.[1]

In the *Metamorphoses*, Ovid's Phineas submits to Perseus, who has overpowered him with the help of the Gorgon's head: "He turns his face away, and, stretching forth obliquely suppliant arms and hands that confess defeat, says: 'Perseus, you win. Remove those monsters of yours, those petrifying Medusa-heads—whatever they are, take them away, I beg you!...I am content to yield. Grant me nothing, mightiest of men, save this my life. The rest be yours'"(5.214–222).[2] "The Romans," according to Cincinnatus, "did not require the blood of the Aequi. The latter would be allowed to depart, but they would be sent under the yoke in order

---

1. *qui vincit non est victor nisi victus fatetur.* Servius, commenting on this line, remarked that "Varro and others declared the Trojans unconquered *(invictos)* because the Trojans were taken by ambush; they affirmed that it was those who surrendered themselves to the enemy who were defeated" (*Varro et ceteri invictos dicunt Troianos, quia per insidias oppressi sunt: illos enim vinci adfirmant qui se dedunt hostibus* [*In Aeneida* 11.306]). Compare the remark of the late fourth- to early fifth-century Claudian: "No victory subjugates the enemy save that which the enemy confesses from the spirit" (*victoria nulla quam qua confessos animo quoque subjugat hostes* [*De sexto consulato Honorii*, l. 248, K.A. Muller ed.]). The Roman commander ordered the Volscians to surrender their generals, lay down their arms, and, "confessing themselves defeated, to yield to his authority" (*fatentes victos se esse et imperio parere* [Livy 4.10.3]). Cf. Caesar, *Bellum civile* 1.84.5; Livy 36.45.6; Stefan Weinstock, "*Victor* and *Invictus*," *Harvard Theological Review* 50 (1957): 219–220.

2. *avertitur atque ita supplex*
   confessasque manus obliquaque bracchia tendens
   "vincis" ait, "Perseu! remove tua monstra tuaeque
   saxificos vultus, quaecumque ea, tolle Medusae,
   tolle precor!...non cessisse piget; nihil o fortissime, praeter
   hanc animam concede mihi, tua cetera sunto!"
   Cf. Ovid, *Amores* 1.2.19–22. Compare this scene of surrender to that in Livy 7.31.3.

that they might finally confess aloud that they were a people subjugated and dominated" (Livy 3.28.10).[3]

In both Ovid and Livy, the defeated and suppliant enemies were exposed to further shaming. They were made into spectacles, eternally in the case of poor Phineas, caught in stone in the act of begging for mercy: "And now in marble was fixed the cringing attitude: the face of cowardice, the look of submission, the hands of supplication" (5.234–235).[4]

The Romans did not confess defeat in war, as Hannibal learned after the battle of Cannae in 216 B.C.E.[5] "Surrender," Livy reminds his audience, "is vile and ignominious" (*foeda atque ignominiosa deditio est* [9.4.14]).[6] "Neither these disasters nor the defections of their allies ever moved the Romans to breathe a word about peace... so great was the *animus* in the city at that time" (Livy 22.61.13–14).[7] The soldiers trapped at the Caudine Forks in 320 B.C.E. deprived the victorious Samnites of the sweetest part of their victory by refusing to confess defeat. Indeed, the Romans had the nerve to send legates to the Samnites to suggest a *pax aequa* (a settlement based on acknowledged equality of rights) or, failing that, to provoke the enemy into

3. *sanguinis se Aequorum non egere; licere abire, sed ut exprimatur tandem confessio subactam domitamque esse gentem, sub iugum abituros.*

4. *sed tamen os timidum vultusque in marmore supplex / submissaeque manus faciesque obnoxia mansit.*

5. The Roman tradition was to impose rather to seek a settlement, *pacem dare* not *pacem petere*. See Friedrich Klingner, "Virgil und die Idee des Friedens," in *Römische Geisteswelt: Essays zur lateinischen Literatur,* Stuttgart, 1979, esp. p. 616. The only terms of settlement worthy of the Romans were for the enemy to surrender and yield to the former's discretion *(Romaiois epitrepein)* (Appian, *Iberica* 13.79). One should go to any length to avoid surrender. "Courage knows no yielding to calamity" *(non novit virtus calamitati cedere* [Publilius Syrus 402, Friedrich ed.]). Cato the Younger addresses the Italians of Utica about to surrender to Julius Caesar: "Prayer belonged to the conquered and the craving of grace to those who had done wrong; but for his part he had not only been unvanquished all his life, but was actually a victor now" (Plutarch, *Cato minor* 64.5). On the reluctance of Cato to be a suppliant, see also Seneca, *De providentia* 2.10. Seneca was proud of the fact that even under the tyranny of Messalina and Narcissus he never played the clinging suppliant *(non e manibus ullius supplex pependi* [*Naturales quaestiones* 4A, *praefatio* 16]). In Seneca's words: "Even if he falls, he fights on his knees" *(etiam si cecidit de genu pugnat* [*De providentia* 2.6]). Cf. Cicero, *Pro rege Deiotaro* 13.36; Horace, *Carmina* 2.7.9–12.

6. On *deditio,* see Schulten, "*Dediticii,*" in Pauly-Wissowa, *Paulys Realencyclopädie der classischen Altertumswissenschaft,* vol. 4.2, Stuttgart, 1901, cols. 2359–2363; Eugen Täubler, *Imperium Romanum: Studien zur Entwicklungsgeschichte des römischen Reichs,* Leipzig, 1913, pp. 14–28; Emil Seckel, *Über Krieg und Recht in Rome,* Berlin, 1915, pp. 18–19; Alfred Heuss, *Die völkerrechtlichen Grundlagen der römischen Aussenpolitik in republikanischer Zeit,* Leipzig, 1933, esp. pp. 60–77; Bruno Paradisi, *"Deditio in fidem,"* Studi di storia e diritto in onore di Arrigo Solmi, Milan, 1941, pp. 285–324; André Piganiol, *"Venire in fidem,"* Revue internationale des droits de l'antiquité 5 (1950): 339–347; Erich Gruen, "Greek *pistis* and Roman *fides,*" Athenaeum 60 (1982): 50–68.

7. *Nec tamen eae clades defectionesque sociorum moverunt ut pacis usquam mentio apud Romanos fieret.... quo in tempore ipso adeo magno animo civitas fuit.* See the scene staged by Livy in the Carthaginian senate (23.12.17–13.2); Jean-Paul Brisson, "Les mutations de la Seconde Guerre Punique," *Problèmes de la Guerre à Rome,* Paris, 1969, pp. 42–43.

giving battle.[8] But the Samnite general Pontius decreed firmly, "The war is finished. And since not even conquered and captured do the Romans know how to confess their condition, they would be sent under the yoke, unarmed, and with a single garment" (Livy 9.4.3).[9] Nor did the Romans of the Republic confess in criminal trials.[10] "Confession," according to Cicero, "is both base and dangerous" (*In Verrem* 2.3.71.165).[11] "There is nothing worse than confession," Quintilian states (*Institutio oratoria* 5.13.8).[12] The *confessus* was a suppliant *(supplex)*, someone who bent at the knees,[13] and *confessio* was inseparable from *deprecatio*, the *postulatio ignoscendi*, the plea

---

8. Compare the audacious response of Quintus Cicero to the Gauls, who, having besieged him in his winter camp, offered him lenient terms. It was not the practice of the Romans to accept terms from an enemy in arms; but if the Gauls laid down their arms he would intercede with Caesar on their behalf! (*Non esse consuetudinem populi Romani accipere ab hoste condicionem: si ab armis discedere, se adiutore utantur legatosque ad Caesarem mittant: sperare pro eius iustitia, quae petierint impetraturos* [Caesar, *De bello Gallico* 5.41].) See also the case of Publius Licinius, defeated by Perseus of Macedon in 171 B.C.E. When the enemy sent envoys to impose a settlement, the vanquished Licinius advised the victor to submit his case to Rome (Polybius 27.8; Livy 42.62.7,12–15; Plutarch, *Regum et imperatorum apophthegmata*, Licinius [*Moralia* 197E–F]).

9. *Tum Pontius debellatum esse respondit: et quoniam ne victi quidem ac capti fortunam fateri scirent, inermes cum singulis vestimentis sub iugum missurum.*

10. "Le droit pénal romain ne reconnaît aucune place à l'aveu" (Yan Thomas, "*Confessus pro iudicato:* L'aveu civil et l'aveu pénal à Rome," *L'aveu: Antiquité et Moyen Age*, Rome, 1986, p. 99; cf. pp. 97, 106, 109). In my discussion of the judicial aspects of confession I am deeply indebted to the article by Thomas and to that by Jean-Michel David, "La faute et l'abandon: Théories et pratiques judiciares à Rome à la fin de la République," also in *L'aveu*, pp. 69–87.

11. *turpis enim est et periculosa confessio.*

12. *nihil erit peius quam confessio.*

13. "Le supplex est pour les Latins en même temps *deditus*" (Gérard Freyburger, "Supplication grecque et supplication romaine," *Latomus* 47 (1988): 524. For the meaning of *supplicium*, see Theodore Mommsen, *Römisches Strafrecht*, Leipzig, 1899, pp. 916–917 n. 5; Émile Benveniste, *Le vocabulaire des institutions indo-européennes*, vol. 2, Paris, 1969, pp. 245–252; Gerhard von Beseler, "Bindung und Lösung," *Zeitschrift der Savigny-Stiftung für Rechtsgeschichte: Romanistische Abteilung* 49 (1929): 418; Richard Heinze, "*Supplicium*," *Vom Geist des Römertums: Ausgewählte Aufsätze*, ed. Erich Burck, Darmstadt, 1960, pp. 29, 35–36. For visual examples, see especially Richard Brilliant, *Gesture and Rank in Roman Art*, New Haven, 1963, pp. 78, 92, 103, 120, 122, 152. The attitude of the *supplex* and that of the *deditus* were the same: kneeling with arms outstretched to receive the bonds. Compare Ovid's conquered lover, surrendering to Cupid. "I confess! I am your new prize, your booty. I stretch forth my defeated hands, submissive to your commands. There is no need of war; I entreat for peace and pardon" (*En ego confiteor! tua sum nova praeda, Cupido; / porrigimus victas ad tua iura manus. / nil opus est bello, veniam pacemque rogamus* [*Amores* 1.2.19–20]). The captive or criminal also bent at the knees, as Mommsen points out, to receive the deadly blow of the ax, and so the word *supplicium* came to be a synonym first for capital punishment and then for any type of punishment (*Strafrecht*, pp. 916–917 n. 5). Mommsen, like most modern scholars, derives *supplicare* from *plicare*, to bend (compare *simplex, duplex*), but Festus derived it from *placare*, to conciliate (pp. 402, 403, 206, 207, Lindsay ed). As Heinze emphasizes, the Romans often construed *supplicium* as a form of "satisfaction," "compensation," "atonement," especially *supplicationes* of thanksgiving to the gods ("*Supplicium*," pp. 30–31). In the words of Publilius Syrus, "It is enough of a penalty when the offender comes on his knees" (*poenae sat est qui laesit cum supplex venit* [497, Friedrich ed.]). See the remarkable story of Lucius Piso, pardoned because, while he was prostrate on the ground kissing

for mercy. Terence's Sostrata confesses to her husband: "My Chremes, I sinned, I confess. I give in. Now I entreat you that there might be some refuge for my foolishness in your justice" (*Heautontimorumenos* 644–645).[14] "One confesses that he has sinned and seeks mercy for his crime" (Cicero, *Pro Murena* 62).[15]

"*Deprecatio* is a last resort," Quintilian asserts, "and most deny that this type of defense can ever to be introduced in court" (*Institutio oratoria* 7.4.17).[16] According to a fourth-century student of Quintilian, "If one has exhausted all other means of defense, there remains the *deprecatio*, when, confessing to having acted both badly and willingly, we are left with nothing but our prayers" (Gaius Julius Victor 3.8.35–36, K. Halm ed.).[17] One confessed only if one had lost heart, if there were no more moves one could make.[18]

---

the feet of the judges, a sudden storm arose and his mouth filled with mud. His accusers judged that this hideous humiliation was in itself a sufficient punishment *(satis iam graves eum poenas sociis dedisse arbitrati sunt)* and sought no further reparations (Valerius Maximus 8.1.6).

14. *Mi Chremes, peccavi, fateor. Vincor. nunc hoc te obsecro / ut meae stultitiae, in iustitia tua sit aliquid praesidi.*

15. *Fatetur aliquis se pecasse et sui delicti veniam petit.* "Spare, I beseech you, the man who has confessed" (*Parce, precor fasso* [Ovid, *Heroides* 16.11]). See Plautus, *Aulularia* 731–739, 752, 789–795, *Miles gloriosus* 540–574, *Mercator* 983–997; Lucilius apud Nonius p. 193, Lindsay ed.; *Rhetorica ad Herennium* 1.14.24, 2.17.25; Cicero, *De inventione* 1.11.15; 2.34.104, *Pro Ligario* 1.1, 5.13; Livy 39.12.8; Ovid, *Metamorphoses* 9.545–48, 561; Petronius, *Satyricon* 130; Quintilian, *Institutio oratoria* 5.13.5–6, 7.4.18; Sidonius Apollinaris, *Epistulae* 4.23.1. When Isidore, bishop of Seville, wrote in the seventh century, confession and the plea for mercy were still indistinguishable in the popular mind *(Sed nunc iam utrumque vocabulum sub una designatione habetur: nec distat vulgo utrum litaniae an exomologesis dicantur* [*Etymologiae* 6.80–81]). For the close relationship between *deditio* and the plea for mercy, see Ernst Bux, "*Clementia Romana*," *Würzburger Jahrbücher für die Altertumswissenschaft* 3 (1948): 209.

16. *Ultima est deprecatio, quod genus causae plerique negarunt in iudicium unquam venire. Deprecatio* left no room for defense. "*Deprecatio* is the plea that contains no defense of the deed but only a request for pardon" *(Deprecatio est in qua non defensio facti, sed ignoscendi postulatio continetur* [Cicero, *De inventione* 2.34.104]). "The cause of a confessed defendant *(confessus)* must not be defended," Ovid declares in one of his many pleas to Augustus for mercy *(non est confessi causa tuenda rei* [*Tristia ex Ponto* 2.2.54]). "We must deny or justify what has been done or raise the question of competence; for there are almost no other methods of defense available in the courts apart from these. The plea for mercy, which is in no sense a method of defense, should be used very rarely, and only before judges who are not limited to some precise form of verdict" *(aut negandum aut defendendum aut transferendum: extra haec in iudiciis fere nihil est. Deprecatio quidem, quae est sine ulla specie defensionis, rara admodum et apud eos solos iudices, qui nulla certa pronuntiandi forma tenentur* [Quintilian, *Institutio oratoria* 5.13.4–5]). Even in speeches such as the *Pro Ligario* and *Pro Deiotaro*, pleaded in Caesar's house, Cicero employed some forms of defense as well as pleas for mercy. See Holly Montague, "Advocacy and Politics: The Paradox of Cicero's *Pro Ligario*," *American Journal of Philology* 113 (1992): 559–574.

17. *Rhetores Latini Minores*, Leipzig, 1863, p. 381. *Si omnia defecerint, superest deprecatio, in qua et male et sponte nos fecisse confessi nihil aliud quam preces allegamus.* According to Cicero, "*Deprecatio* occurs when the defendant both confesses that he has deliberately sinned and yet implores to be forgiven; which type of defense can happen only very rarely" *(Deprecatio est cum et peccasse et consulto peccasse reus se confitetur et tamen ut ignoscatur postulat; quod genus perraro potest accidere* [*De inventione* 1.11.15]). See Thomas, "*Confessus pro iudicato*," p. 105 n. 65.

18. For the absolute quality of *deditio*, see Täubler, *Imperium Romanum*, pp. 16, 20; Appian, *Punica* 9.64: *hoti meden autois estiv idion.* The Aetolians did not understand how absolutely the Romans considered the *confessi* to be crushed (Polybius 20.9–10, 36.4.1–4; Livy 36.27–28).

It was more honorable to exhaust all possible means of defense, including lying and blaming others even for one's manifest crimes. Plautus's slave Tranio thinks that "the game is up" *(manifesta res est)* when both the moneylender (on whose loans he and Philolaches have been luxuriating) and Theopropides (the father of Philolaches) are in sight. Though Tranio is tormented by conscience, he does not for one moment think of confessing.[19] Menaechmus, faced by his wife with his manifest and conspicuous misdeeds, brazens it out. Even when he starts to falter, he continues to offer excuses rather than sue for pardon (Plautus, *Menaechmi* 602–657).[20] Libanus is prepared to deny shamelessly the crimes he will commit. "I'll say up and down and stick stubbornly to 'I didn't do it.' I'll swear right and left" (Plautus, *Asinaria* 322).[21] Giving surety would be a confession, Cicero asserts, and Quinctius will not pass judgment on himself—a judgment heavy indeed *(quod iudicium gravissimum est)*. He refuses to condemn himself and so chooses to risk all in a trial, a *sponsio (Pro Quinctio* 9.32). "If I were to catch you in the act, if my eyes were forced to behold your shame, just deny that I clearly saw what I clearly saw—my eyes will yield to your words. . . . Only let your tongue remember, 'I did not do it!' " (Ovid, *Amores* 3.14.43–46, 48).[22] "She does not sin who can deny that she has sinned; only the confessed fault brings dishonor" *(Amores* 3.14.5–6).[23]

To throw oneself on the mercy of the court was a form of surrender in despair, of madness.[24] The Romans believed that to accuse oneself was a form of *demen-*

---

19. "Nothing is more miserable than a guilty conscience such as the one possessing me. But that being the case, let's just get on with our obfuscations" *(nihil est miserius quam animus hominis conscius, / sicut me habet. verum utut res sese habet, / pergam turbare porro: ita haec res postulat* [*Mostellaria* 536–689, esp. 544–545]). Cf. Terence, *Andria* 633–638. For Roman notions of guilt and conscience, see chapters 7 and 8.

20. See the long list of excuses that the proprietor of a farm should expect from his steward: he has been diligent, but the slaves have not been well; the weather has been bad; the slaves have run away; he has had to carry out public works (Cato, *De agricultura* 2.2).

21. *pernegabo atque obdurabo, periurabo denique.*

22. *si tamen in media deprensa tenebere culpa,*
    et fuerint oculis probra videnda meis,
    quae bene visa mihi fuerint, bene visa negato!
    concedent verbis lumina nostra tuis.
    . . . sit modo "non feci" dicere lingua memor.

23. *non peccat, quaecumque potest peccasse negare, / solaque famosam culpa professa facit.* "What you are doing, go on doing; only deny that you have done it; do not be ashamed to speak with modest words in public" *(quae facis haec facito: tantum fecisse negato, nec pudeat coram verba modesta loqui!* [Ovid, *Amores* 3.14.15–16, cf. 3.14.27–28]).

24. "Renoncer à se défendre pour se sauver est cependant dénoncé comme une tactique du désespoir" (Thomas, *"Confessus pro iudicato,"* p. 103). Cf. Appian, *Bellum civile* 2.3.15, cf. 1.2.14. "Il est plus honorable d'épuiser auparavant tous les rebondissements grâce auxquels un crime qui n'est ni nié ni même justifié peut être mis au compte d'un tiers qui n'en est pas l'auteur" (Thomas, *"Confessus pro iudicato,"* p. 103). Cf. Quintilian *Institutio oratoria* 5.13.7.

tia.[25] "Confession is entirely of that nature that he who confesses himself may appear insane" (Pseudo-Quintilian, *Declamationes minores* 314.7, Shackleton Bailey ed.).[26] As Guiliana Lanata has observed, to pronounce against oneself, to accuse oneself without the pressure of necessity was to go against both the instinct of self-preservation and the code of honorable behavior; it was a sign of mental disturbance. The confession made on one's own account was attributed to a fool.[27] For the Romans, as for Bourdieu's Kabyle, if a man did not respond to a challenge (whether a gift or offense) when it appeared to others that he still had the ability to respond, "he is in a sense choosing to be the author of his own dishonour, which is then irremediable. He confesses himself defeated in the game that he ought to have played despite everything."[28]

The *confessus* in criminal trials, like the *confessus* in war, was liable to further humiliation. To the extent that the judge operated within and was bound by the rule of law, confession resulted automatically in punishment.[29] "A *confessus* is like a *iudicatus* (someone who had been condemned by a judge), since he is condemned, in a certain way, by his own judgment" (*confessus pro iudicato est qui quoddammodo sua sententia damnatur* [Ulpian, *Digesta* 42.2.6.1]).[30] Pseudo-Quintilian's magistrate de-

---

25. "What insanity is this, to confess by the light of day things hidden by the night, to refer openly to the deeds committed in secret?" (*quis furor est, quae nocte latent, in luce fateri / et quae clam facias facta referre palam?* [Ovid, *Amores* 3.14.7–8]). In Plautus's *Cistellaria*, the love-crazed Alcesimarchus, in a fragmentary confession scene, appears to plead repeatedly for mercy, offering to make restitution and undergo punishment. At the same time, his "madness" is well-established in the wonderful song that begins act 2 (203–229). Livy's African prince Syphax confesses to Scipio that he had sinned and that he had been insane (*tum ille peccasse quidem sese atque insanisse fatebatur* [30.13.10]). Pliny laments to Trajan the *amentia* of the confessing Christians (*Epistulae* 10.96.4). Cf. Tertullian, *Apologeticus* 1.13, 27.2–3, 49.1, 50.4.

26. *Ea natura est omnis confessionis, ut possit videri demens qui de se confitetur.*

27. "Ma pronuntiare contra se, accusare se stessi senza necessità, venir meno al naturale istinto di conservazione e di decoro, è già di per sé segno di squilibri mentale, la confessione autentica è quella che l'accusatore strappa alle negazioni del colpevole mediante le torture del carnefice; in caso contrario, ogni confessione sul proprio conto può per sua natura essere legittimamente attribuita a un folle" (Guiliana Lanata, "Confessione o Professione? Il Dossier degli Atti dei Martiri," in *L'aveu*, p. 138; cf. p. 140). "Un aveu aurait été pour lui [Cicero], comme pour tout orateur judiciaire, une manifestation inadmissible d'impuissance" (Thomas, *"Confessus pro iudicato,"* p. 72; cf. pp. 99, 104, 106); David, "La faute et l'abandon," pp. 71–72.

28. *Outline of a Theory of Practice,* trans. Richard Nice, Cambridge, 1979, p. 13.

29. "A Rome, à la fin de la République, avouer un crime était quasiment impossible. D'abord parce que certaines règles de droit faisaient que qui confessait était assuré d'être condamné" (David, "La faute et l'abandon," p. 69). "L'aveu du crime aurait inévitablement conduit à l'exécution capitale, par une sorte d'automatisme comparable à celui que postule, en droit civil, la règle *'confessus pro damnato'* " (Thomas *"Confessus pro Iudicato,"* p. 100; cf. pp. 89–90, 97).

30. Cf. Dionysius 3.22.5; Curtius Rufus, *Historia Alexandri magni* 6.11.14; Petronius 130. This principle operated especially in civil cases (*si qui de debito quocumque modo confessus docetur, ex ea re actio creditori non datur, sed ad solutionem compellitur* [Paulus, *Sententiae* 2.1.5]). Whether *confessio* resulted automatically in punishment only in certain phases of the trial is a matter of controversy. See Nevio Scapini, *La confessione nel Diritto Romano,* vol. 1, Turin, 1973.

clares, "I was not only allowed, I was obliged to execute the *confessus,* even against my own wishes" (*Declamationes minores* 314.4).[31] As Sallust's Cato explains: "According to the ways of our ancestors, from the confessed, as from men caught in the act of capital crimes, punishment must be exacted" (*Catilina* 52.36).[32]

BENDING

We spare the dediticii.
PETRONIUS, *SATYRICON* 107[33]

The Romans of the late Republic, like the Greeks, believed that the defeated and suppliant should be respected, that submissive behavior should evoke the force of self-restraint, the *fides* of the powerful. "To crush a suppliant is not an act of valor but of cruelty" (Publilius Syrus 682, Friedrich ed.).[34] Not to destroy, when one could do so easily, was a noble act.[35] Sallust's general Quintus Marcius Rex responds to the pleas for help of the Catilinarian conspirator and general Gaius Manlius: "Whatever it is that they seek to obtain from the senate, let them put down their weapons and proceed to Rome as suppliants. The senate of the Roman people has always acted with such mildness and pity that no one has ever sought assistance from it in vain" (*Catilina* 34.1).[36] "One should meet an armed enemy with a hostile spirit; it is best to show a very gentle spirit toward the defeated" (Livy 33.12.9).[37] According to the emperor Claudius, "It had pleased the

---

31. *Ergo non solum licuit mihi occidere confessum, sed etiam, si nollem, necesse fuit.* Cf. 314.8–9.

32. *de confessis sicuti de manufestis rerum capitalium, more maiorum supplicium sumundum.*

33. *dediticiis hostibus parcimus.*

34. *suplicem non est opprimere virtus, est crudelitas.* Catullus abhors the inhuman hardness and cruelty of the lover despising the suppliant (60). Cf. Seneca, *De clementia* 1.18.1–3.

35. Again: "The greatest praise a man can receive is that 'he could injure, but he chooses not to.'" (*Nocere posse et nolle laus amplissima est* [Publilius Syrus, 397, Friedrich ed.]). Cf. Freyburger, "Supplication," pp. 521–523.

36. *si quid ab senatu petere vellent, ab armis discedant. Romam supplices proficiscantur: ea mansuetudine atque misericordia senatum populi Romani semper fuisse, ut nemo umquam ab eo frustra auxilium petiverit.* Cf. Tacitus, *Annales* 2.10. The Romans of the late Republic and early Empire imagined a time when Rome consistently treated the suppliant well: "Judges, all of you are well aware that the Roman people, formerly reckoned very lenient even to their enemies, now cruelly oppress one another" (*Vestrum nemo est quin intellegat populum Romanum, qui quondam in hostes lenissimus existimabatur, hoc tempore domestica crudelitate laborare* [Cicero, *Pro Roscio Amerino* 53.154, cf. 52.150]). "Truly, our Roman ancestors exercised their domination in peace because they ruled by benefits rather than by fear, and they preferred to pardon rather than to avenge the injuries they endured" (*in pace vero quod beneficiis magis quam metu imperium agitabant et accepta iniuria ignoscere quam persequi malebant* [Sallust, *Catilina* 9.5; cf. 12.4]). "Apart from their very ancient custom of sparing the defeated, the Romans gave exceptional proof of their clemency by the peace that they gave to Hannibal and the Carthaginians" (*Romanos praeter vetustissimum morem victis parcendi praecipuum clementiae documentum dedisse pace Hannibali et Carthaginiensibus data* [Livy 33.12.7]). Cf. Livy 31.31.1–16, 37.45.7–8.

37. *cum armato hoste infestis animis concurri debere, adversus victos mitissimum quemque animum maximum habere.*

ancestors to show as much forbearance to a suppliant as they showed persistence against a foe" (Tacitus, *Annales* 12.20).[38]

But, as Cicero reminds us, the Romans were inclined to despise the timid suppliant and those who begged for their lives (*Pro Milone* 34.92). Indeed, Cicero pleads for mercy for Milo on the grounds that Milo is *not* pleading for it. "As we are wont to have more sympathy for those who do not ask for it than for those who urgently implore it, how much more sympathy, then, ought we to have for our most stalwart citizens."[39] Plautus's Sosia, beaten on the street by the bully Mercury, surrenders and begs for mercy *(tuam fidem obsecro!)*. But the beating goes on just the same (*Amphitruo* 373). The eloquent protagonist of the *Testamentum Porcelli* pleads with his master: "Whatever I have done, whatever sins I have committed, whatever pots I may have broken with my toes, I beseech you, Master Cook, to spare my life, spare the pig who begs." But the cook has no pity and executes the poor penitent pig.[40] The prophetic mission of the Romans may have been "to tame the proud and spare the submissive" (*Aeneis* 6.853).[41] But when Virgil's Turnus was on his knees, vanquished, and, in the sight of his people, extended his right hand and beseeching gaze in supplication to Aeneas, the latter showed him no mercy (*Aeneis* 12.930–931, 936–937).[42] Neither did he spare good Queen Dido, even when she begged.

Tacitus asserts that "human beings are wont to hate those whom they have injured" (*Agricola* 42.3).[43] "Cruelty is not broken," Publilius Syrus declares, "but fed by tears" (114, Friedrich ed.).[44] It was *because* Pastor asked for clemency on behalf

---

38. *verum ita maioribus placitum, quanta pervicacia in hostem, tanta beneficentia adversus supplices utendum.* According to the Roman general Flamininus, "Good men *(agathous andras)* ought to be stern and hot-blooded in combat, noble and high-minded if worsted, but moderate, mild, and benevolent when they conquer" (Polybius 18.37.7). Cf. Cicero, *De officiis* 1.11.33–35; Livy 7.31.7, 30.42.17, 36.27.6–8, 37.6.6, 37.45.7–8, 42.62.11; Matthias Gelzer, "Römische Politik bei Fabius Pictor," *Hermes* 68 (1933): 129–166, esp. 137, 164–165; Weinstock, "*Victor* and *Invictus*," p. 220; Nathan Rosenstein, *Imperatores Victi: Military Defeat and Aristocratic Competition in the Middle and Late Republic*, Berkeley, 1990, p. 116. For examples of Romans respecting the suppliant, see W. Dittenberger, *Sylloge Inscriptionum Graecarum*[3], vol. 2, Leipzig, 1917, no. 618 = Robert Sherk, *Roman Documents from the Greek East*, Baltimore, 1960, no. 35; Terence, *Andria* 282–298; Caesar, *De bello civile* 3.98; Cicero, *Pro Marcello* 4.12; Livy 5.27, 7.30–31, 26.49.7–10; Piganiol, "*Venire in fidem*," pp. 342–343.

39. *eorumque nos magis miseret qui nostram misericordiam non requirunt, quam qui illam efflagitant, quanto hoc magis in fortissimis civibus facere debemus.*

40. W. Heraeus ed., in Petronius, *Saturae*[6], F. Buecheler ed., Berlin, 1922, pp. 268–269: *Si qua feci, si qua peccavi, si qua vascella pedibus meis confregi, rogo, domine coce, vitam peto, concede roganti.* On the "Testament of the Pig," see David Daube, *Roman Law*, Edinburgh, 1969, pp. 77–81.

41. *parcere subiectis et debellare superbos.*

42. *humilis, supplex, oculos dextramque precantem / protendens.... Victum tendere palmas, / Ausonii videre.*

43. *proprium humani ingenii est odisse quem laeseris.* Compare Seneca: "Those whom they injure they also hate" (*quos laeserunt et oderunt* [Seneca *De ira* 2.33.1]).

44. *crudelis lacrimis pascitur non frangitur.* The postures of submission (making oneself low and small like a child) may have evolved from the appeasement behaviors designed to inhibit aggression in other

of the son who had offended Caligula that the emperor ordered his son to be immediately led out to execution—"as if he had been admonished" (Seneca, *De ira* 2.33.3).[45] It was *because* he begged for pardon that Nero ordered Julius Montanus to destroy himself; if he had not asked for it, his life would have been spared him (Tacitus, *Annales* 13.25; Dio 61.9.3–4). Brutus wrote to Cicero in May 43 that he feared that compliance with the powerful only provoked them to do worse: "To refrain from bearing down on the unfortunate I judge more honorable than to endlessly concede to the powerful what may inflame their greed and arrogance" (*Ad Brutum* 10.2 [= 1.4.2]).[46]

When Cicero himself, accused by Clodius of putting Lentulus and Cethegus to death without a trial, put on the weeds of the accused, the *vestis sordida*, defiled with squalor and dirt, and supplicated those he met in the street, his pleas met with derision (Appian, *Bellum civile* 2.3.15).[47] When, in 37 B.C.E., the Hasmonean Antigonus threw himself at the feet of Antony's general Sosius, the latter, far from pitying Antigonus's changed condition, burst into uncontrollable laughter, called him "Antigona," and put him into irons before executing him (Josephus, *Bellum Judaicum* 1.353, 357).[48] In 173 B.C.E. the Ligurian Statellates, after surrendering un-

---

primates. See Irenäus Eibl-Eibesfeldt, *Love and Hate: The Natural History of Behavior Patterns,* trans. Geoffrey Strachan, New York, 1971, pp. 174–178; Walter Burkert, *The Creation of the Sacred: Tracks of Biology in Early Religions,* Cambridge, Mass., 1996, pp. 85–86. But the zoologist Thelma Rowell, in a fascinating article, discusses "provocative cringing." She explains that the behaviors evolved to hinder aggressive behaviors often, ironically, have the effect of triggering them. "Cringing, fleeing, fear-grinning are extremely potent stimuli eliciting attack behavior in primates" ("The Concept of Social Dominance," *Behavioral Biology* 11 [1974]: 131–154). As any hunter or general or lover knows, running away can incite the chase. Cato, at the battle of Emporiae in 195 B.C.E., has his cohorts simulate flight in order to induce the enemy to pursue (Livy 34.14–16). Horatius Tergeminus, by his strategic flight, lures the three Curiatii into pursuing him (Livy 1.25.7–12). In short, the motives for aggression can arise in the behaviors of the submissive.

45. *rogante patre ut salutem sibi filii concederet, quasi de supplicio admonitus duci protinus iussit.*

46. *Multo equidem honestius iudico magisque quod concedere possit res publica miserorum fortunam non insectari quam infinite tribuere potentibus, quae cupiditatem et arrogantiam incendere possint.* As Brent Shaw shows, in an illuminating study of the notion of "passive" endurance, while it may be easy to discern who is mutilating and who is being mutilated in the torture scenes of the last century of the Republic and the first centuries of the Empire, it is very complicated to discern who is calling the shots in these scenes ("Body/Power/Identity: Passions of the Martyrs," *Journal of Early Christian Studies* 4 [1996]: 269–312).

47. "Not being ashamed to annoy people who knew nothing about the business,... his doings excited laughter rather than pity by reason of his unseemly aspect.... When Clodius interrupted Cicero's supplications on the street with contumely, Cicero gave way to despair and, like Demosthenes, went voluntarily into exile" (Horace White trans.). In 58 B.C.E., when Clodius published his bill "banning from fire and water" anyone who had put a Roman citizen to death without trial, Cicero personally appealed to Pompey for help. "Years later he wrote Atticus that when he lay at Pompey's feet, the latter did not even ask him to get up" (Shackleton Bailey, *Cicero,* London, 1971, p. 62). Compare the fate of the suppliant Phaedra before Hippolytus (Seneca, *Phaedra* 666–712).

48. Compare Scipio Africanus's insulting treatment of the suppliant Hasdrubal, son of Gisgo, in Polybius (38.20.1–6). Compare also Maecenas's poetic plea for mercy (*Fragmenta Poetarum Latinorum,*

conditionally and imploring the *fides populi Romani*, were deprived of arms, their strongholds were destroyed, and they and all their belongings were sold into slavery by the Roman general Popilius Laenas (Livy 42.8).[49]

The Roman response to the supplication of the defeated could not be calculated.[50] And it was, I would argue, the very arbitrariness and unpredictability of the response of the conquerors that demonstrated the fullness of their power. (Here it is important to point out that the word *fides*, like *dicio*, indicated the fullness of power or the restraint of that power—or both simultaneously.) The *dediticii* who surrendered into the *fides* of the victorious general surrendered into his discretion, as the *indices*, the informers, surrendered into the *fides publica*.[51] Those who confessed and surrendered hoped for the best but expected the worst. The Capuans addressed the Roman senators: "We have given everything into your power and that of the Roman people. Whatever we shall afterwards suffer, we will suffer as your *dediticii*" (Livy 7.31.4).[52]

Morel ed., Stuttgart, 1975, frag. 4, p. 102) with Seneca's sneering commentary on it (*Epistulae* 101.10–12). Brutus reacts equally harshly to what he perceives as the shame of Cicero's supplication (Cicero, *Ad Brutum* 17.6 [= 1.17.6], 25.8, 11 [= 1.16.8, 11]). For more humiliations of the suppliant, see Plautus, *Asinaria* 682–731, *Cistellaria* 458ff., *Mercator* 983–997; Sallust, *Bellum Iugurthinum* 91.5–7; Livy 9.1.3–10; Propertius 2.14.13–14; Suetonius, *Augustus* 13.2. Compare the sentiments expressed in Seneca, *De ira* 1.2.4, *De tranquillitate* 11.5, *Epistulae* 7.5; Lactantius, *Institutiones divinae* 6.20.

49. This time the senate reacted with consternation: "The senators thought it atrocious that the Statellates ... having surrendered into the *fides* of the Roman people—so many thousands of innocent people imploring the *fides* of the Roman people—should have been brutalized and destroyed by every example of extreme cruelty. No one ever afterwards would dare to surrender themselves" (*Atrox res visa senatui Statellates ... deditos in fidem populi Romani omni ultimae crudelitatis exemplo laceratos ac deletos esse, tot milia capitum innoxiorum fidem implorantia populi Romani, ne quis umquam se postea dedere auderet* [42.8.5–6]).

50. André Piganiol believes that prior to the second century B.C.E., *fides* involved the victorious Romans in mutual obligations with their defeated, but that after that date the Romans were as likely to insult and injure the surrendered as not (*"Venire in Fidem,"* pp. 339–347). For Sallust, the cruel treatment of the suppliant began with Sulla (*Catilina* 11.7, 12). After reviewing the evidence, Fritz Hampl came to the conclusion that the Romans of the early Republic, like many American Indians, determined whether to incorporate or destroy, to adopt or cruelly dispose of their defeated enemies on a case-by-case basis and that there was neither a moral imperative to be merciful nor a reproach attached to brutality (" 'Stoische Staatsethik' und frühes Rom," in *Das Staatsdenken der Römer*, ed. Richard Klein, Darmstadt, 1973, esp. pp. 121–122). Heinze came to a similar conclusion after surveying the portrayals of supplication in Roman literature (*"Supplicium,"* p. 30). For the difficulty of attributing a single range of motivations or behaviors to Roman treatment of the defeated in war, see the introduction to Gruen, *The Hellenistic World and the Coming of Rome*, Berkeley, 1984. See also Bux, *"Clementia Romana,"* pp. 212, 215–216; John Rich, "Fear, Greed and Glory: The Causes of Roman War-Making in the Middle Republic," in *War and Society in the Roman World*, ed. John Rich and Graham Shipley, New York, 1993, pp. 38–68; Adam Ziolkowski, *"Urbs direpta*, or How the Romans Sacked Cities," pp. 69–91 of the same collection.

51. See Polybius 20.9; Livy 8.18, 36.27.8, 36.28.4–9; Sallust, *Catilina* 47.1, 48.4; David, "La faute et l'abandon," pp. 76–87.

52. *omnia in vestram, patres conscripti, populique Romani dicionem dedimus, quidquid deinde patiemur, dediticii vestri passuri.*

The Romans' contempt for the suppliant often extended to their own defeated.[53] "Life is not to be bought at any price. . . . I would not be brought to that confession of vile weakness" *(illa turpi infirmitatis confessione non veniam)*, Seneca remarks in disgust, commenting on the famous words of the caged and mutilated Telesphorus of Rhodes: "Where there's life there's hope" *(Epistulae* 70.7).[54] On the contrary, Seneca relates with approval the practice of the ancient Spartans: "The Spartans forbid their citizens to contend in the *pancratio* (which included both wrestling and boxing) and boxing events, where the confession of the defeated exposed his inferiority. . . . Since the Spartans considered it of great moment that their citizens be undefeated, they removed them from those contests in which neither the judge nor the outcome itself established the victor, but the voice of the one yielding and begging to surrender" (Seneca, *De beneficiis* 5.3.1).[55]

The Romans did not confess because they did not want to live at the whim and will, at the mercy of another. "Marcus Cato," the elder Seneca's Labienus tells us, "the most brilliant of the men swept away by the storm of civil war, could have lived by the kindness of Caesar—if he had been willing to live by the kindness of anyone" *(Controversiae* 10.3.5).[56] In the last days of his life, Marcus Brutus exclaims in a letter to Cicero, "I would rather not exist than to exist on the sufferance of Octavian" *(Ad Brutum* 25 [= 1.16]).[57] "I am not a man to supplicate another," he says later in the same letter (25.8 = 1.16.8).[58]

BREAKING

If he doesn't confess nimbly . . . let's slice off a few parts with a saw.
PLAUTUS, *PRAEDONES* 219 (FROM A FRAGMENT PRESERVED BY CHARISIUS)[59]

For the plebeian as for the patrician, the effective voice had its seat and source, its *sedes,* in a secret and inviolable sphere. And until the Roman was free from the

---

53. Consider the fate of Hannibal's Roman captives (Livy 22.59.1–61.1; Polybius 6.58). In Livy, the soldiers who had survived Cannae to be relegated to Sicily remark on the arbitrariness of the Romans' treatment of their own defeated: while they were degraded and "banished" to Sicily, their general Varro was welcomed home and warmly thanked (25.6.7–9). Josephus tells a poignant story of a Roman soldier who, having been captured by the rebel Jews, made a daring and difficult escape. While his bravery was acknowledged and he escaped being put to death by Titus for being captured in the first place, he was nevertheless degraded and dismissed *(Bellum Iudaicum* 6.362). Cf. Valerius Maximus 5.8.4; Horace, *Carmina* 3.5.13–40.

54. *non omni pretio vita emenda est. Quaedam licet magna licet certa sint, tamen ad illa turpi infirmitatis confessione non veniam.*

55. *Lacedaemonii vetant suos pancratio aut caestu decernere, ubi inferiorem ostendit victi confessio. . . . Cum invictos esse Lacedaemonii cives suos magno aestimarent, ab iis certaminibus removerunt, in quibus victorem facit non iudex nec per se ipse exitus, sed vox cedentis et tradere iubentis.*

56. *M. Cato, quo viro nihil speciosius civilis tempestas abstulit, potuit beneficio Caesaris vivere, si ullius voluisset.*

57. *atqui non esse quam esse per illum praestat.*

58. *Ego vero . . . is sum, qui non modo non supplicem, sed etiam coerceam postulantes ut sibi supplicetur.*

59. *si non strenue fatetur ubi sit aurum / membra exsecemus serra.*

threat of arbitrary corporal punishment or physical violation, he or she could have no protected sphere or portion, no *ius*, no *libertas*. The acts that established the immunity of the plebs from the capricious coercion of the magistrates, like those that instituted the secret ballot, established them as truly existing, as having being. According to Richard Saller, "The plebs symbolically established their *libertas* with the *lex Valeria* and in the second century the *leges Porciae* which gave citizens the right of protection from the magistrate's arbitrary use of the rods."[60] ("The law of Porcius removed the threat of the rod from the body of any Roman citizen.... The law of Porcius wrested the liberty of the citizens from the lictor" [Cicero, *Pro Rabirio perduellionis* 4.12].)[61] In the same section of the same Ciceronian speech, as Saller points out, the orator claimed that the infliction of beatings *(flagella)* and death on a citizen amounted to the loss of *libertas*. Later still, Tacitus interprets the limitations placed on the coercive powers of German kings and generals, particularly their inability to inflict floggings, *verbera*, as a sign of the Germans' *libertas* (*Germania* 7.1–2).[62]

Confession was the speech of those who had succumbed to the power of another.[63] It was the speech of those who had lost or abandoned the defense of their spiritual boundaries, the speech of those under compulsion *(confessio coacti ... verbum est* [Seneca Rhetor, *Controversiae* 8.1]).[64] To quote the fourth-century lexicogra-

---

60. *Patriarchy, Property, and Death in the Roman Family*, Cambridge, 1994, p. 140, cf. p. 72. Sandra Joshel points out that the freeborn Roman had physical integrity but the slave did not (*Work, Identity, and Legal Status at Rome: A Study of the Occupational Inscriptions*, Norman, Oklahoma, 1992, pp. 150, 155).

61. *Porcia lex virgas ab omnium civium Romanorum corpore amovit.... Porcia lex libertatem civium lictori eripuit.* Cf. Cicero, *Pro Cornelio* 1 fr. 50.

62. "Corporal Punishment, Authority, and Obedience," in *Marriage, Divorce, and Children in Ancient Rome*, ed. Beryl Rawson, Oxford, 1991, pp. 144–243. Saller perceptively relates this idea to Georg Simmel's notion of the "ideal sphere," the impenetrable "sphere ... placed around a man by his honor" (ibid. pp. 152–153). (Cf. *The Sociology of Georg Simmel*, ed. and trans. Kurt Wolff, Glencoe, Illinois, 1950, p. 321). Cf. Erving Goffman, "On Face-Work: An Analysis of Ritual Elements in Social Interaction," in *Interaction Ritual: Essays on Face-to-Face Behavior*, New York, 1967, esp. p. 19; Saller, *Patriarchy, Property, and Death*, p. 135; Carlin Barton, "Savage Miracles; The Redemption of Lost Honor in Roman Society and the Sacramentum of the Gladiator and the Martyr," *Representations* 45 (winter 1994): 45 and n. 15. See also the Kabyle notion of *essor* in Bourdieu, "The Sentiment of Honour in Kabyle Society," in *Honour and Shame*, ed. J. G. Peristiany, Chicago, 1974 [1966], pp. 217–218.

63. See esp. Plautus, *Epidicus* 680–731.

64. "Overwhelmed, I am compelled to confess" (*Superata fateri cogor* [Ovid, *Metamorphoses* 9.545]). "Now that they had wrung a confession from the conquered" (*postquam confessionem victos satis expresserunt* [Livy 36.45.6]). "Tiberius Caesar extorted from the Dalmatians a definite confession of submission such as that which Augustus had wrested from Spain" (*At Tiberius Caesar quam certam Hispanis parendi confessionem extorserat parens Illyriis Dalmatisque extorsit* [Velleius Paterculus 2.39.3]). For other examples of extorting confession, see Livy 7.30.9; Seneca, *De clementia* 1.1.7 (ironically), *Epistulae* 82.7; Suetonius, *Galba* 10.5.

pher and grammarian Nonius Marcellus: "To confess is the act of someone forced and under constraint" (vol. 3, p. 700, Lindsay ed.).[65] "One is driven to confess by madness, another by drunkenness, another by mistake, another by grief, another by torture. No one declares against himself unless someone or something compels him" (Isidore, *De differentiis* 1.31.232).[66] Indeed, according to the Elder Seneca, "There is no confession unless the accuser elicits it, the accused denies it, the torturer extorts it" (*Controversiae* 8.1).[67] Those who confessed surrendered an inviolate sphere, the source of their voice, the force of their "word." Confession was the act of someone whose spirit had been broken, someone whose *animus* was *fractus;* someone who, as we say in English, had "cracked."[68] When, in 345/344 B.C.E. the Capuans, with tears and entreaties, surrendered into the *dicio* of the Romans, "the *patres* were greatly disturbed at the fickleness of human fortune: that a people so formidable in their wealth, so illustrious for their luxury and arrogance, should be so broken in spirit *(adeo infractos gereret animos)* that they would surrender themselves and all their possessions into the power of another state" (Livy 7.31.6).[69] It was the *animus fractus* of the woman bereaved of both husband and child that drove her to confess herself guilty of sacrilege (Seneca Rhetor, *Controversiae* 8.1). The spirits of those not fortified by philosophy would crack, Seneca imagined, when the torturer commanded them to stretch forth their hands or when death drew near. He believed that they would, as we say, "spill their guts" (*Epistulae* 82.7).[70] "She confessed under torture. Who is there who possesses such strength of spirit, so firm and solid a mind that she could not be vanquished by pain, nor yield to burning brands, or groan beneath the blows of the lash?" (Pseudo-Quintilian, *Declamationes minores* 272.10).[71]

The voices of the *confessi* were no longer their own. Words were "put in their mouths." The *confessi* were, according to Varro, "those who say what is demanded

---

65. *confiteri necessitatis et coactus.*

66. *Patrologia Latina*, ed. J. P. Migne, vol. 83, Paris, 1862. *Furore impulsus est; alius ebrietate, alius errore, alius dolore, quidam quaestione. Nemo contra se dicit nisi aliquo cogente.* "To confess is an act, not of will, but of a spirit compelled" (*fateri...coacti est animi non voluntatis* [loc. cit.]). Cf. Seneca, *Epistulae* 53.6, 71.29; Ulpian, *Digesta* 48.18.1.23, 27.

67. *non est confessio nisi cum accusator eruit, negat rea, tortor expressit.*

68. "What is evil in torments and in other things that we label hardships? It is, I believe, that the mind sags, bends and collapses" (*Quid est in tormentis, quid est in aliis, quae adversa appellamus mali? Hoc ut opinor, succidere mentem et incurvari et succumbere* [Seneca, *Epistulae* 71.26]).

69. *Commoti patres vice fortunarum humanarum, si ille praepotens opibus populus, luxuria superbiaque clarus,...adeo infractos gereret animos ut se ipse suaque omnia potestatis alienae faceret.* Cf. Livy 36.28.6: *tum fracta Phaeneae ferocia Aetolisque aliis est.*

70. *cum securos aliquis casus expertus est, exprimitur sera confessio. Magna verba excidunt cum tortor poposcit manum, cum mors proprius accessit.* Cf. *Epistulae* 71.29, 53.6. Elsewhere, however, Seneca makes it clear that everyone had his or her breaking point. Cf. *Hercules Oetaeus* 1279.

71. *confessa est cum torqueretur. ubi tantum robur animi, ubi tam firmam solidamque mentem quae non dolore vincatur, non ignibus cedat, non verberibus ingemsicat?*

of them" (*qui fati id quod ab his quaesitum* [Varro, *De lingua Latina* 6.55]). Quintus Curtius Rufus tells the story of the torture of Philotas to obtain evidence of a conspiracy against Alexander the Great: after experiencing atrocious pain in silence, Philotas, unable to endure, promised to confess, provided the torture were stopped. The torment having ceased, Philotas addressed the inquisitor: "Tell me what you want me to say" ("*Cratere,*" inquit, "*dic quid me velis dicere!*" [*Historia Alexandri Magni* 6.11.18]).The young and wild Titus Manlius held the tribune Marcus Pomponius at swordpoint and threatened to slay him if he did not swear according to the terms that he would dictate *(nisi in quae ipse concepisset verba iuraret).* The tribune, broken with fear, swore by the words imposed on him (*adiurat in quae adactus est verba* [Livy 7.5.5]). In the ancient Roman formula of unconditional surrender, the *deditio in fidem (in dicionem)* preserved in Livy, the words of the surrender were dictated by the victor (1.38.2).[72] The victor was the ventriloquist, the defeated his dummy.[73]

Perhaps the Latin idiom *verba dare* (to fool, deceive, and humiliate) can be explained by the Roman association of humiliation with putting words into the mouth of another.[74] As Erich Segal points out, Plautus's Palaestrio, in the process of trapping his master, the braggart warrior, also succeeds in putting his own words into the soldier's mouth. "Three times the slave 'instructs' his master on how best to get rid of the girl Philocomasium.... Finally, the soldier parrots the slave's advice as if it were his own idea."[75]

72. The king asked the *legati* and *oratores* of Collatia: "Do you surrender yourselves and the people of Collatia, town, lands, water, boundary markers, shrines, and all provisions and utensils divine and human, into my power and that of the Roman people?" "We do." "I accept the surrender." ("*Deditsne vos populumque Collatinum, urbem, agros, aquam, terminos, delubra, utensilia divina humanaque omnia in meam populique Romani dicionem?*" "*Dedimus.*" "*At ego recipio.*") Livy's Spurius Postumius speaks of the formula for the surrendering of a city: "What if the Samnites, with the same arrogance with which they extorted this solemn promise (of capitulation) from us, had compelled us to pronounce the formal words of those surrendering their cities?" (*An, si eadem superbia, qua sponsionem istam expresserunt nobis Samnites, coegissent nos verba legitima dedentium urbes nuncupare?* [9.9.5]); Schulten, "*Dediticii*"; Paradisi, "*Deditio in Fidem,*" pp. 289–290. "Dans le procès, le *confessus* ratifie verbalement les mots qu'un autre a déjà prononcés. Comme on le lit dans les glossaires, avouer, c'est homologuer" (Thomas, "*Confessus pro iudicato,*" p. 90). See G. Goetz, *Thesaurus glossarum emendatarum* (vol. 6 of *Corpus Glossariorum Latinorum*), Amsterdam, 1965, s.v. *confessio: homologia, ex homologesis;* s.v. *confiteor: homologo, exomologoumai sunomologo.*

73. And so the slave, the defeated one, who lived at the sufferance of another, was a "talking tool" as well as a tool that talked (*instrumentum vocale* [Varro, *De re rustica* 1.17.1]). "It is a confession of servitude to do what you are ordered to do" (*confessio servitutis est iussa facere* [Seneca Rhetor, *Suasoriae* 5.2.4]).

74. For example, Plautus, *Miles gloriosus* 353, 576, 1434; *Captivi* 786; *Cistellaria* 484; *Epidicus* 92–93, 521, 614; *Menaechmi* 131; *Mostellaria* 925.

75. Segal goes on to discuss the way in which Shakespeare's Othello increasingly echoes Iago as the latter's sinister control over his general increases (*Roman Laughter: The Comedy of Plautus,* New York, 1971, p. 208 n. 55). Mnesilochus is urgently in need of the help of his slave Chrysalus to procure money to redeem his courtesan, and so he is at the mercy of Chrysalus, who is then able to dictate word for word the letters Mnesilochus writes to his father (Plautus, *Bacchides* 729–760, 983–1035, esp. 1018). Cf.

In America, we have the expression "Say uncle!" When we already have our little brother in a hammerlock, when we have physically overwhelmed him, we will ask him to confess with the word "uncle." Until he has said "uncle," the victory is incomplete and the vanquished maintains his honor. So it was possible for the Roman *not* to win and yet not be destroyed *in animo*—but *not* when he or she was forced to admit it aloud. The vocal confession for the Romans was—as it is for us—the ultimate defeat. To quote Livy: "The spirit of a man was considered broken for all time from whom the confession had been extorted that [and here we have the kind of confession that was put into the mouth of the defeated] 'he had been overcome, not by craft or by accident, but in a just and pious confrontation of arms' " (42.47.8).[76]

The point of our "uncle" is precisely that it is a nonsense word. The same applies to the confession of the ancient Romans. Whether or not the words had logical content, it was their sheer arbitrariness that was the cutting edge of the confession.[77] This arbitrariness was the nonsense, the whimsy at the fluttering heart of Roman notions of power. The Romans were as aware as we are that the truth produced by torture was often invented on the spot. "It is often possible to know or intuit what the inquisitor wants to hear, and the tortured man understands that when he has said this, his pain will cease" (*Auctor ad Herennium* 2.7.10).[78] "Reliance should not always be placed in torture...it is a delicate and dangerous business and one which can be deceptive. For many, by their endurance or their toughness under torture, are so contemptuous of it that the truth can in no way be squeezed out of them. Others have so little endurance that they would rather tell any kind of lie than suffer torture. And so they confess arbitrarily, incriminating not only themselves but others as well" (Ulpian, *Digesta* 48.18.23).[79] Calpurnius explains: "A voluntary confession is a suspi-

---

Curculio 369. Sandra Joshel points out how frequently Messalina's agents or Claudius's own freedmen are depicted as putting words into his mouth, making him into a stock figure of Roman comedy ("Female Desire and the Discourse of Empire," *Signs* 21 [1995]:56–57). Cf. D. W. T. C. Vessey, "Thoughts on Tacitus's Portrayal of Claudius," *American Journal of Philology* 92 (1971): 385–409, esp. p. 404; Sheila Dickison, "Claudius: *Saturnalicius Princeps*," *Latomus* 36 (1977): 634–647, esp. p. 643. Claudius's dependence on his freedman Pallas is exemplified by the use of Pallas's arguments in the speech he gave before the senate urging the adoption of Nero (Tacitus, *Annales* 12.25).

76. *eius demum animum in perpetuum vinci, cui confessio expressa sit se neque arte neque casu, sed conlatis communibus viribus iusto ac pio esse bello superatum.* Cf. 7.31.4.

77. Paul Chodoff points out that during the Korean War, American civilian and military prisoners of the Chinese, even when they were ready to confess, often had no idea what to confess and had to wait until their captors informed them. They were frequently made to fabricate, under close guidance, long, elaborate, and spitefully nonsensical confessions ("Effects of Extreme Coercive and Oppressive Forces: Brainwashing and Concentration Camps," in *American Handbook of Psychiatry*, ed. Silvano Arieti, vol. 3, New York, 1966, pp. 388–390).

78. *quod denique saepe scire aut suspicari possit, quid quaesitor velit audire: quod cum dixerit, intellegat sibi finem doloris futurum.*

79. *quaestioni fidem non semper...habendam....etenim res est fragilis et periculosa et quae veritatem fallat. Nam plerique patientia sive duritia tormentum ita tormenta contemnunt, ut exprimi eis veritas nullo modo possit. Alii tanta*

cious one; you might label such a confession of crime 'the voice of pain' " (*Confessio voluntaria suspecta est. Confessionem sceleris appellas vocem doloris* [34.5]).

REQUIRED SPEECH

If one could not speak *ex animo*, one could still flatter, but flattery (at least in one of its aspects) is a form of confession. The flatterers *(adulatores, assentatores, kolakes)* spoke as slaves do to masters, according to Lucian *(Nigrinus* 23).[80] The flatterers said what was required of them; their speech had no force or content. There is a wonderful—and excruciatingly extended—scene in Plautus's *Asinaria* in which, on account of Argyrippus's desperate need for the money in the possession of his slaves Libanus and Leonida, the slaves are able to demand—indeed *dictate*—the silliest and most shameless flattery ("Call me your little sparrow, hen, quail; call me your lamb, your kid, your calf"), as well as to demand supplication and other increasingly vile and humiliating acts of submission from Argyrippus and his courtesan Philaenium (646–731). Plautus's slave Sosia, having been whipped into submission by Mercury, is addressed by the god: "I'm Sosia—not you.... And now—what do *you* call yourself?" Sosia replies, "I'm no one but who you tell me to be" (*Amphitruo* 379–382).[81] Plautus's parasite Peniculus bids Menaechmus: "Knock my eyes right out the back of my skull if I utter any word that you don't tell me to.... In accordance with your wishes, I affirm, I deny" (Plautus, *Menaechmi* 156–157, 162).[82] Terence's parasite Gnatho declares of his patron, "If he denies it, I deny it. If he assents, I assent" (*Eunuchus* 250–253).[83] Horace's fawning parasite repeats the words of his patron: "The one man, excessively prone to servility, a jester of the lowest couch, so attends the rich man's nod, so echoes his speech and picks up his words as they fall, that you would think him a schoolboy repeating his lessons to a stern master, or the mime who acted the 'second part' " (*Epistulae* 1.18.10–14).[84]

---

sunt impatientia, ut quodvis mintiri quam pati tormenta velint; it fit, ut etiam vario modo fateantur, ut non tantum se, verum etiam alios criminentur. Cf. 48.18.24–25.

80. "When you see someone cringing before or fawning on another against his real opinion, you can say with confidence that this is no free man" (Arrian, *Epicteti dissertationes* 4.1.55). See Ramsay MacMullen, *Roman Social Relations, 50 B.C. to A.D. 184,* New Haven, 1974, p. 116. The flattery directed at the freedman Pallas (*a rationibus* to Claudius) by the senate sends Pliny the Younger into paroxysms of indignation. For him the flattery was proof of the senate's enslavement (*Epistulae* 7.29; 8.6).

81. Mercury: *ego sum, non tu, Sosia.... qui nunc vocare?* Sosia: *Nemo nisi quem iusseris.*

82. Peniculus: *Oculum ecfodito per solum / mihi Menaechme, si ullum verbum faxo nisi quod iusseris.... id enim quod tu vis, id aio atque id nego.*

83. *eorum ingenia admiror simul*
    quidquid dicunt laudo: id rursum si negant, laudo id quoque.
    neqat quia, nego: ait, aio: postremo imperari egomet mihi
    omnia adsentari.

84. *alter in obsequium plus aequo pronus et imi*

Like the *damnati* of Publilius Syrus, the tongues of the flatterers had sound but not strength (142, Friedrich ed.).[85] Merely speaking before a master emptied a person's words of their power and turned the speaker into a fool or a knave.[86] For Tacitus, the emperor's unwillingness to hear anything save flattery made Domitian's fifteen-year domination a "reign of silence" (*Agricola* 2.3, 3.1–2).

THE STRATEGIC CONFESSION

Cicero, how slight you must have judged a crime to which you confessed!
SENECA RHETOR, *CONTROVERSIAE* 10.3.3[87]

The confession, while rare in criminal proceedings in the Republic, was common in civil suits, especially in the "confession of debts" *(confessio aeris)*, where confession functioned in its contractual aspect, creating a contingent and contextual truth. As Yan Thomas remarks with regard to civil cases, "The reality of the facts to which one confessed made little difference, the institution of confession resembling a verbal contract producing obligations."[88] Plautus's Periphanes declares: "I gave you that thirty minae for my daughter, did I not?" Epidicus responds: "I so confess" (*Epidicus* 703).[89]

Verba concepta, solemn and ritual utterances, along with oaths and other forms of contract, consent, and consensus, often took the form of echoed or exactly repeated words and phrases.[90] The question-and-answer contract, the *stipulatio*, was

---

> *derisor lecti sic nutum divitis horret,*
> *sic iterat voces et verba cadentia tollit,*
> *ut puerum saevo credas dictata magistro*
> *reddere vel partis mimum tractare secundae.*

(The *stupidus* was the mime who got slapped, the mime who echoed the *derisor*.) Juvenal mocks with bitterness the mimicry of the servile, flattering Greeks (*Satirae* 3.73–74, 86–108).

85. *Damnati lingua vocem habet, vim non habet.*

86. For the self-deprecation and self-hatred that can result from "reciting the script as given," see Bertram Wyatt-Brown, "The Mask of Obedience: Male Slave Psychology in the Old South," *American Historical Review* 93 (1980): 1230.

87. *M. Tulli, quam leve iudicasti crimen de quo confessus es!* In other words, if Cicero confessed to Caesar that he had fought on the side of Pompey, it must have been because he felt no guilt at doing so.

88. "Peu importe d'ailleurs, à cet égard, la réalité des faits que l'on avoue, puisque l'institution s'apparente à une sorte de contrat verbal producteur d'obligations" (Yan Thomas, "*Confessus pro iudicato*," p. 94; cf. 89–97). "L'aveu fait naître une obligation verbale et abstraite" (p. 94). "La *confessio* civile, par sa nature contractuelle, est empreinte de liberté" (p. 109).

89. *"Dedin tibi minas trigenta ob filiam?" "Fateor datas."* For confession in civil cases, see Kipp, "*Confessio*," in Pauly-Wissowa, *Realencyclopädie*, vol. 4.1, Stuttgart, 1900, cols. 864–870; Scapini, *La confessione*.

90. Plautus's Jupiter, assuming the role of a repentant husband, implores his indignant "wife" Alcmena for pardon. To indicate the depth and sincerity of his submission, he offers to swear according to her dictates (*arbitratu tuo ius iurandum dabo* [*Amphitruo* 931–932]). Cf. *Mercator* 789–791. For *verba concepta*, see Plautus, *Rudens* 1332–1349; Livy 2.1.9, 7.5.5; Horace, *Epistulae* 1.1.14; Pliny, *Panegyricus* 64.1–4;

created by mimesis. "*Spondesne? Spondeo. Datisne? Dabo.*"[91] Just so, the soldier's repetition of the dictated *sacramentum*, like the consul's oath, created a binding contract without the loss of honor.[92] Here "confession" is well translated by the Greek *homologein*.

Res confessae were the givens, the undisputed premises of any argument or situation.[93] And when Velleius says that "by the confession of all, Quintus Catulus was *princeps senatus*" (Velleius Paterculus 2.43.3),[94] or when Cicero asserts that "he would be crazy *not* to confess that Caesar's achievements were greater than almost anyone thought possible" (*Pro Marcello* 2.6), confession is here shameless and consensual, a form of covenant, of common sense.[95]

Various forms of submission and voluntary self-exposure could be used to cement community in ancient Rome. The tribune of the plebs, for example, had to be easily accessible and keep his doors open. The candidate for office was a suppliant; he "professed himself" *(se profiteri)*[96] and was expected to be available to all by day and by night, and not only through the doors of his house, but through his open expression, the door to the spirit *(vultu ac fronte quae est animi ianua)*.[97] The candidates for the decemvirate, in Livy's history, made the rounds humbly soliciting *(suppliciter petentes)* the votes of the plebs (3.35.1–2). According to Cicero, Laterensis's failure at the polls was due to his unwillingness to humble himself before the people. They would, he asserts, remind the proud man of established usage and the example of ancestral precedent. "They would say that they have always desired to be asked, to be supplicated" (*Pro Plancio* 5.12).[98] The people speak di-

---

Gellius, *Noctes Atticae* 2.24.2; Émile Benveniste, *Le vocabulaire des institutions indo-européennes,* vol. 2, pp. 117–118.

91. It is possible that the *stipulatio* bond, like the *tessera* bond, was conceptualized as something in two pieces (the *stipula* or the *tessera*) that fit together, and that, as in the case of the handshake, it was the mirroring/fitting function that produced the bond.

92. *Vocati sumus ad militiam Dei vivi iam tunc, cum in sacramenti verba respondemus* (Tertullian, *Ad martyras* 3.1, *Corpus Christianorum,* Series Latina, vol. 1).

93. Seneca, *Epistulae* 113.15; Quintilian, *Institutio oratoria* 5.12.2, 5.14.13.

94. *Q. Catulus, omnium confessione senatus princeps.*

95. *quae [victoriae] quidem ego nisi ita magna esse fatear, ut ea vix cuiusquam mens aut cogitatio capere possit, amens sit.* Cf. Plautus, *Miles gloriosus* 661–662; Seneca *Epistulae* 108.12, *De clementia* 1.1.7–8; Pseudo-Seneca, *Octavia* 252; Cornelius Nepos, *Hannibal* 1.1. The willingness to be silent while another spoke or to let another speak for you was a closely related form of contract or confession. Cf. Virgil, *Aeneis* 1.148–153; Valerius Maximus 3.7.3; Plutarch, *Cato minor* 44.3–4; Lucian, *Demonax* 64; Robert Gore, *The Legend of Cato Uticensis from the First Century B.C. to the Fifth Century A.D.,* Brussels, 1987, p. 26.

96. Cf. *Corpus Inscriptionum Latinarum,* vol. 8.4, no. 25808b: *L. Octavio Felici Octaviano . . . professori aedilitatis;* Sallust, *Catilina* 18.3.

97. *Commentariolum petitionis* 11.44; Zvi Yavetz, "*Existimatio* and *Fama,*" appendix to *Julius Caesar and his Public Image,* London, 1983, p. 218.

98. *te ille ad sua instituta, suorumque maiorum exempla revocabit: semper se dicet rogari voluisse, semper sibi supplicari.*

rectly to Laterensis: "I suggest that you learn to supplicate a little more earnestly if you would attain the high honors equal to your merit" (5.13; cf. 20.50).[99] In this case, the humility of the candidate was a kind of strategic feint, a gambit, a posture of submission. "I know, fellow citizens, how election to a post of authority seems to change most men's characters. As candidates they are *industrios, supplices, modicos.* Once elected they become insolent and slothful," Sallust's Marius declares (*Bellum Iugurthinum* 85.1).[100] The degree to which a candidate was willing to perform this strategic and symbolic homage was the degree to which he was willing to be obliged, to be indebted to those he entreated. Those Roman aristocrats who did not want to be bound or obligated to the people found this submission galling.[101] Not even as defendants in capital trials before the people would the Claudii, notorious for their contempt of the plebs, put on the suppliant's weeds or ask for mercy (Suetonius, *Tiberius* 2.4).[102]

Calling on one's fellow Quirites for help or mercy, the *fidem implorantia*, could be, like appealing to one's fellows as judges (*provocatio*), a type of confession (as well as a challenge) that cemented obligations. "The legates from the province of Baetica were calling upon my *fides*, pleading the bond of patronage" (*implorantes fidem meam . . . adlegantes patrocini foedus* [Pliny *Epistulae* 3.4.4]).

Confession, then, could be a way of entrusting, of honoring others, of voluntarily admitting them into one's secret or protected sphere.[103] When Terence's tormented old Menedemus confessed his merciless treatment of his son to his neighbor Chremes, it was by way of binding them together in friendship (*Heautontimorumenos* 159). When the great orator Crassus confessed to nervousness, the audience felt complimented by his self-deprecation and reacted with indulgence—as they might to the man who blushed (Cicero, *De oratore* 1.26.119–122).[104] Indeed, to evoke the same sympathy, Cicero confessed to being unnerved (*Pro rege Deiotaro* 1.1).

---

99. *Sed amplissimos honores ut pro dignitate tua consequare, condiscas, censeo, mihi paullo diligentius supplicare.* Cicero's words reveal the resentment that he himself felt at even this strategic self-abasement. When Plutarch's Elder Cato, candidate for the office of censor, saw the other candidates soliciting and flattering the people, he admonished them that they should elect not the most pliable but the most inexorable man to the office, who would be a stern physician and give them a thorough cleansing (*Cato maior* 16; *Regum et imperatorum apophthegmata;* Cato 22 [*Moralia* 199B]).

100. *Scio, ego, Quirites, plerosque non isdem artibus imperium a vobis petere et, postquam adepti sunt gerere: primo industrios, supplices, modicos esse, dein per ignaviam et superbiam aetatem agere.* Livy's once-humble candidates for the decemvirate become the tyrannical *decemviri* in his extended account in book 3.

101. Cicero boasted that he obtained the consulship not by continuously beseeching the people (i.e., not by flattery and subservience) but as the reward owed to his *dignitas*, his worthiness (*nec diuturnus precibus sed dignitate impetratus* [*De lege agraria* 2.3]).

102. *ne capitis quidem quisquam reus apud populum mutare vestem aut deprecari sustinuerat.* Cf. Livy 2.61.5–7.

103. Cf. Plautus, *Cistellaria* 120–148, 170; Terence, *Heautontimorumenos* 159.

104. Augustus's confession to the senate of Julia's scandalous behavior, like Claudius's confession to the praetorian guard of his marriage problems with Messalina, may have been conceived of as acts of courtesy to those groups. See Suetonius, *Augustus* 65.2–3; Seneca, *De beneficiis* 6.32.1–2; Suetonius,

In general, the great man needed to expose himself.[105] He needed to demonstrate his accessibility, opening the doors to his clients each morning. Prestige, for the Roman, was not a house ringed with razor wires, cameras, and alarms, but the *domus frequentata*, dilating to embrace the world.[106] As in the nudity of the heroic statue of the Imperator, or that of the fighting Gaul, one could gain rather than lose honor by "laying oneself open."[107] Augustus was thought to behave with the grace of a Republican grandee when he opened his morning audiences to all and behaved sociably to those who came with petitions, or when he made the rounds of the tribes with his candidates for office and supplicated the people according to the traditional formulas (*supplicabat more sollemni* [Suetonius, *Augustus*

Claudius 26.2. In publishing the shame of his daughter and granddaughter and insisting on their punishment, Augustus may have been following the *exemplum* of the elder Brutus. Like Brutus, Augustus would not respond to the supplications of the people on behalf of his offspring. Cf. Tiberius's exposure of the "crimes," along with the death and suffering of Drusus (Tacitus, *Annales* 6.24). The "confessions" of the monarchs are, not surprisingly, hard for the authors of these accounts to interpret. See chapter 6.

105. See especially the excellent article by Andrew Wallace-Hadrill, "*Civilis Princeps*: Between Citizen and King," *Journal of Roman Studies* 72 (1982): 32–48. Wallace-Hadrill is mistaken only in that he believes this pattern first arose in the Empire.

106. For the revealing as well as the concealing functions of the Roman aristocratic house, see T. P. Wiseman, "Competition and Co-operation," in *Roman Political Life 90 B.C.–A.D. 69*, Exeter, 1985, pp. 14–15; Yvon Thébert, "Private Life and Domestic Architecture in Roman Africa," in *A History of Private Life*, ed. Philippe Ariès and George Duby, vol. 1, Cambridge, Mass., 1987, pp. 313–409; Andrew Wallace-Hadrill, *Houses and Society in Pompeii and Herculaneum*, Princeton, 1994, pp. 3–37; Saller, *Patriarchy, Property, and Death*, pp. 91–92.

107. Whatever the great man said was shared openly: "So many slaves attended him, so many freedmen and clients, that whatever he said became the talk of the town" (*quidquid dixerit rumor sit* [Seneca Rhetor, *Controversiae* 5.2]). MacMullen, *Roman Social Relations*, p. 107. The good emperor not only was accessible but revealed his secret wealth and made it common property (*nunc secretas illas et arcanas ac sub te primum communes opes* [Pliny, *Panegyricus* 34.3]). When the generals at their triumphs, when Metellus, Cato, Pompey, Caesar, Antony, Augustus, Vespasian, or Antoninus Pius tolerated the verbal freedom of those less powerful, they gained prestige. Socrates and Antisthenes gained prestige, according to Seneca, by taking ribbing (*De constantia* 18.5). For the *patientia* of Metellus, Cato, and Pompey under lampoons and accusations, see J. B. Mayor, *Thirteen Satires of Juvenal*, London, 1872 (*Satirae* 1.153). Cf. Suetonius, *Tiberius* 28, *Vespasianus* 13–14; Lucian, *De morte Peregrini* 18 (Antoninus Pius was above responding to the abuse and ridicule of the Cynic Peregrinus). For the "snub gambit" in Rome, see Barton, "Savage Miracles," pp. 58–59. For more on the salutary effects of voluntary self-humiliation and ritual ridicule, see Barton, *Sorrows*, part 2. The good master encouraged others to speak freely. "In a free city the mind and the tongue must be free" (*in civitate libera linguam mentemque liberas esse debere* [Suetonius, *Tiberius* 28]). In both Tacitus's and Suetonius's accounts, the positive assessment of the emperors depends, to a large extent, on the degree of the emperors' openness and accessibility as well as on the degree of both frankness and secrecy granted to their subjects. (On the other hand, the greater the power, the more insidious the secrecy of the powerful.) However, the strategy of the powerful of exposing themselves to the weak could backfire. Demaenetus's confession of his domestic problems to his slave Libanus, while eliciting the good will of his servant, also resulted in Libanus's feeling contempt for his master (Plautus, *Asinaria* 60, 109–114).

53.2, 56.1]). He acted with magnanimity when, the people insistently offering him the dictatorship, "he knelt before them and, throwing back his toga to expose his naked breast, implored them to desist" (*Augustus* 52).[108]

Pliny extols Trajan: "It is to your great glory, Caesar...to act while a prince no differently from a commoner, while an emperor no differently from a subject. I do not know, I really do not know, which is more splendid: to have taken the consular oath with no precedent before you, or to have taken the oath dictated to you by another" (*Panegyricus* 64.3–4).[109] Like supplication, confession could be a gift, an act of liberality and respect toward one's fellows. The consul Tiberius Gracchus, having initially insisted on his innocence, afterwards confessed to having committed an error that invalidated the consular elections over which he had presided. His admission inspired Cicero not with loathing, but with admiration: "A man," Cicero says, "of the greatest wisdom and, I might even venture to say, far surpassing all others, preferred to confess an offense that he might have concealed rather than that the transgression should adhere to the Republic" (*De natura deorum* 2.4.11).[110]

The general Spurius Postumius confessed responsibility for the degrading (i.e., solicited and negotiated) peace with the Samnites at the Caudine Forks in 320 B.C.E.: "We are sureties, bondsmen, sufficiently *locupletes* in that which belongs to us, in that which we can offer—our bodies and our spirits" (Livy 9.9.18).[111] The adjective *locuples* implies both wealth and the ability and willingness to give security, to be responsible by reason of one's wealth. The confession of responsibility,

---

108. *dictaturam magna vi offerente populo genu nixus deiecta ab umeris toga nudo pectore deprecatus est.*

109. *Ingens, Caesar et par gloria tua....idem principem quod privatum, idem imperatorem quod sub imperatore. Nescio iam, nescio, pulchriusne sit illud quo praeeunte nullo, an hoc quod alio praeeunte iurasti.* "The greater your power, the greater the restraint you need to exercise" (*quo plus potestis, eo moderatius imperio uti debetis* [Livy 34.7.15]). "The greater we are, the more humbly must we behave" (*quanto superiores simus, tanto nos geramus summissius* [Cicero, *De officiis* 1.26.90]). "The more power you possess, the more you must bear patiently" (*quo plura possis, plura patienter feras* [Seneca, *Troades* 254]). Although the honorable needed to have dependents, to be followed by a large retinue, having dependents was most honorable when they were voluntary, when the patron or master risked losing control over them. See MacMullen, *Roman Social Relations*, p. 194 n. 56 (with bibliography); Orlando Patterson, *Slavery and Social Death*, Cambridge, Mass., 1982, esp. pp. 81, 83; Lila Abu-Lughod, *Veiled Sentiments: Honor and Poetry in a Bedouin Society*, Berkeley, 1986, pp. 104–105, 117, 165.

110. *Vir sapientissimus atque haud sciam an omnium praestantissimus peccatum suum quod celari posset confiteri maluit quam haerere in re publica religionem.* The *indices*, the "stool-pigeons" who had confessed and surrendered into the *fides publica*, and by whose information the *res publica* was saved, might, like Faecenia Hispala, be honored and rewarded and their prestige and position in the state augmented and enlarged. See David, "La faute et l'abandon," p. 84. Tiberius's willingness to expose the horrors of his treatment of his grandson Drusus was interpreted as evidence of his *confidentia* and greeted with *admiratio* as well as *pavor* (Tacitus, *Annales* 6.24.4).

111. *Samnitibus sponsores nos sumus rei satis locupletes in id quod nostrum est, in id quod praestare possumus, corpora nostra et animos.*

the self-diminishing act of Postumius, simultaneously enlarged him. "The name of Postumius was on everyone's lips," Livy tells us. "They exalted him to the sky with praise" (*Postumius in ore erat; eum laudibus ad caelum ferebant* [9.10.3]).[112]

Vulnerability could be a greater and more effective strategy than arms: Veturia and Volumnia succeeded against the rebel Coriolanus where the Roman envoys had failed. "Men . . . could not defend the city with their swords; women might better succeed with tears and entreaties" (Livy 2.40.2).[113] The warring Sabines and Romans respected the women (the daughters of the Sabines, now Roman matrons) who came between them as suppliants and claimed responsibility for the war. "Turn your anger against us. We are the cause of strife" (Livy 1.13.3).[114]

As both Cicero and Quintilian point out, one could always utilize confession partially and peripherally, so long as the aim was tactical and served the immediate goal of winning the point or the case.[115] And so Plautus's miser Euclio, having discovered his grandfather's hidden treasure, is not ashamed to confess his penury to his maidservant (*Aulularia* 88). Cicero employs the *deprecatio* as one of the ways, together with *obiurgatio, admonitio,* and *promissio,* to correct the opinions of an audience. "The plea for mercy," he tells us, "is a weak one—but on occasion a useful one" (*Deprecatio . . . est infirmum sed nonnumquam utile* [*De oratore* 2.83.339]). Pliny recounts that Licinianus, a senator of praetorian rank, confessed to adultery with the Vestal Virgin Cornelia in anticipation of mercy. Pliny speculates that Licinianus may have been innocent and may have confessed (strategically) in anticipation of mercy (*Epistulae* 4.11.11).[116]

There was a fine line, in ancient Rome, between the words and acts that articulated and protected society and the soul, and those that destroyed and silenced both. It was very like the line that often appears, among humans and primates, between friendly greeting behavior and submission.[117] The nod, the bow, the doffing of the hat, the offering the hand, the formulaic repetition of the word

112. When Sthennius, commander of the Mamertines, confessed to Pompey that the blame for the Mamertines having sided with Marius against Sulla was his alone and that the punishment should fall on him alone, Pompey set free both Sthennius and his city (Plutarch, *Regum et imperatorum apophthegmata,* Pompey 3 [*Moralia* 203D]). The same story with slightly different names appears in Plutarch, *Pompey* 10.6.

113. *quoniam armis viri defendere non possent, mulieres precibus lacrimisque defenderent.*

114. *in nos vertite iras; nos causa belli, nos vulnerum ac caedium viris ac parentibus sumus.* This strategy worked when and if the aggressor recognized and accepted common bonds. Gandhi's strategy of passive resistance was effective against the British in India because, as P.A. Brunt points out, British imperialism was "crippled" by its notion of a common humanity ("Reflections on British and Roman Imperialism," *Comparative Studies in Society and History* 7 [1965]: 267–285, esp. p. 281).

115. Compare the notion of "defeated we conquer" discussed in chapter 3.

116. *Si comitium et virgas pati nollet, ad confessionem confugeret quasi ad veniam.*

117. See Eibl-Eibesfeldt, *Love and Hate,* pp. 175–178.

"hello" when someone else says "hello": these are simply the limited and strategic forms of the behaviors that could also signal concession, defeat, and a broken spirit.[118] It was only in the pliable network of reciprocal boundaries and limitations, the equilibrations involved in simultaneously both revealing and concealing, that these behaviors bound and did not break.

118. It was the close resemblance of the confession of the defeated to the contractual guarantee *(stipulatio)* that misled scholars like Jhering, Täubler, and Seckel to think that *deditio in fidem* was a form of contract or treaty; they forgot that *fides* as the unlimited power, the will and discretion of the victorious general, was a sort of mirror image of the *fides,* the self-restraint, of the party to a contract.

CHAPTER SIX

Confession and the Remedies of Defeat

The Roman centurion says, "I say to one 'Go,' and he goes; to another
'Come,' and he comes, and to my slave 'Do this,' and he does it."
MATTHEW 8.9

As soon as little Octavian began to talk, Suetonius tells us, it chanced that the frogs were making a racket at his grandfather's country house. He bade them be silent, "and they say that since then no frog has ever croaked there" (*Augustus* 94.7). Juvenal's willful mistress says: "This is what I want; this is what I order. Let my will be its own argument" (*Satirae* 6.223).[1] The greatest force of the soul that a Roman could imagine was effective speech.

For us the voice is an airy, disembodied phenomenon. But for the Romans it was the airiness of the really real. The immediacy and embodiment of one's will, one's spirit in the world was accomplished, above all, through the force of one's own speech—and through the words spoken about one by others, one's *fama.*[2]

The Romans may have been down-to-earth, but they were not "materialists." It was difficult for the Romans to trace our line between "physical" and "spiritual"; in speaking, the body was "spiritualized" and the spiritual "embodied." The culture of the voice "charged," "vivified" the spirit, like the loud war-cry cultivated by Cato.[3] It was physical exercise and demanded discipline and control.[4] According to Seneca, speech was the grooming, the adornment of the soul (*oratio cultus animi est* [*Epistulae* 115.2]). And just as the gods and the dead would cease to

---

1. *hoc volo, sic iubeo, sit pro ratione voluntas.*

2. One could argue that, in our culture, the failure to cultivate the voice has resulted in the separation of the soul from the voice and from the "breath." We are not "in" our words. We can separate our voices from our words and from our life-spirits.

3. The Romans cultivated the loud war-cry: Plutarch, *Regum et imperatorum apophthegmata*, Cato 7, 23 (*Moralia* 198E, 199C), *Cato maior* 1.6, 9.4; *Coriolanus* 8.3; Alan Astin, *Cato the Censor*, Oxford, 1978, p. 37.

4. Speaking was strenuous exercise. See Aline Rouselle, "Parole et inspiration: Le travail de la voix dans le monde romain," *History and Philosophy of the Life Sciences* 5 (1983): 129–157; Maud Gleason, *Making Men: Sophists and Self-Presentation in Ancient Rome*, Princeton, 1994.

exist, for all intents and purposes, when they ceased to be cultivated, so one's living spirit would cease to exist when it ceased to be tended. The soul of a Roman was like the rose of Saint-Exupéry's prince: it was the time you wasted on it that made it precious.

The *promissum* (from *promitto,* to send forth, project) was the most powerful commitment of the spirit to the voice. The force of one's will, in ancient Rome, was realized above all in one's vow, one's oath. (In English the identity is still so close that "word" and "promise" can be used interchangeably.) "I will not change what once I have spoken," Plautus's Nicobulus declares (*Bacchides* 1202).[5] Plautus's Demaenetus says of his slave Libanus: "He would prefer to die a miserable death than not to carry out what he had promised" (*Asinaria* 121).[6] One's word bound one tightly, but it also liberated one insofar as voluntarily binding oneself concentrated, channeled, and focused the energy of one's spirit. One's word, provided it was binding, sacralized one's spirit.

The voice guaranteed and delimited not only the individual spirit but the collective liberties of all citizens. The defining rights of *commercium* and *connubium* rested, finally, on the citizen's right to make promises, covenants, and on the respect afforded these contracts by others. The right to vote (*suffragium,* from *frangere,* to break into sound) was the right of the citizen to cry aloud, to contribute his voice.[7] The plebeian organs of government, like their magistracies, rested, finally, on the oath that sacralized their tribunes, sworn at the time of their first secession to the Mons Sacer in 494 B.C.E. (Livy 2.32).

The soul-enhancing speech, the "free" speech of the Republic, was not unconstrained; it was not speaking without hesitation or saying anything that came into one's mind whenever and wherever one felt like it (as is our freedom of speech). On the contrary, the more powerful, the weightier one's words, the *less* freedom (in our sense) of speech or movement one could have.[8] The greater the authority one aspired to give one's words, the more formalized, the more circumscribed, the more choreographed one's speech and behavior needed to be.[9] The patrician

---

5. *Quod semel dixi haud mutabo.*

6. *moriri sese misere mavolet, / quam non perfectum reddat quod promiserit.* The "honorable" speech of the Republic was not the telling of a truth that was in the mind of god or attesting to a preexistent reality (although it became so in the time of Cicero); it was not "spilling the guts" but setting up for one's word a challenge or ordeal in the form of an oath or promise.

7. See Lily Ross Taylor, *Roman Voting Assemblies from the Hannibalic War to the Dictatorship of Caesar,* Ann Arbor, 1966, pp. 2, 85.

8. Margarete Bieber has documented in great detail the association of unrestrained motion and speech with *levitas* and servility. See *The History of the Greek and Roman Theatre,* Princeton, 1961, with the remarkable collection of illustrations there.

9. The man of honor at Rome was thus restrained in the same way as the man of honor among Bourdieu's Kabyle: "The 'man of worth' *(argaz el' 'ali)* must constantly be on his guard, he must watch his words, which 'like bullets fired from a rifle, don't come back'; the more so because his every act and

Claudia could not casually insult the plebs in 246 B.C.E. because her status was too high and her words were too weighty (Suetonius, *Tiberius* 2.3; Gellius, *Noctes Atticae* 10.6). Just so, the emperor Claudius could not, like a plebeian, allow his left hand to be carelessly exposed (Suetonius, *Claudius* 21.5). Roman speech and gesture could be free or "immune" *(immunis)* only when they were inconsequential. Only the fool, the insane, Greeks, slaves, and actors—those whose word was considered weightless—had freedom of speech in our sense.[10]

As Arnaldo Momigliano points out, freedom of speech (again in our sense) was not an ideal in Rome until the collapse of the Republic and the beginning of the Empire: "Liberty is nowhere explicitly associated with freedom of speech in Republican Rome.... The Romans never had a proper translation of *parrhesia* [the uninhibited speech of the Greeks]."[11] Rather, speaking, like all actions in ancient Rome, drew its meaning from being part of a scripted score or game, a contest, with all the conditions that entailed: rules, limitations, witnesses, an equal opponent.[12] Good speech was appropriate to one's role and expressive of one's *persona*. Above all, the well-trained and sharpened tongue was formidable, like the sword of a great fencer—even when it rested in its scabbard.

It was the mastery of the rules and the script and the wit, grace, and elegance of one's performance that made the shell of one's words shimmer like mother-of-

---

his every word commit the whole group" ("The Sense of Honor," *Algeria 1960*, trans. Richard Nice, Cambridge, 1979, p. 111, cf. p. 112).

10. Kenneth Greenberg, in speaking of the antebellum South, explains that while the master's word was binding, the slave's was not: "Whites assumed that slaves lied all the time—and that their lies were intimately connected to their position as slaves.... At one level, masters expressed repeated exasperation over the deceit of slaves. But, on another level, masters welcomed the chance to catch their slaves in lies. Their own honor and the respect accorded their words could then stand in favorable contrast to the dishonored condition of their slaves" ("The Nose, the Lie, and the Duel in the Antebellum South," *American Historical Review* 95 [1990]: 65).

11. Review of Laura Robinson, *Freedom of Speech in the Roman Republic*, in *Journal of Roman Studies* 32 (1942): 124.

12. There were no trustworthy oaths between men and lions; the speech that passed between humans of very unequal power relations was not binding. Rich Megadorus rightly assumes that poor Euclio will think that he is being sported with, made a fool of, when he offers to marry the poor man's daughter (Plautus, *Aulularia* 205–206, cf. 219–222). The Roman attitude toward promises was not unlike that described by Guido Ruggiero (*Binding Passions: Tales of Magic, Marriage and Power at the End of the Renaissance*, Oxford, 1993, p. 64): given a sufficient social distance between the man who promised marriage with the goal of obtaining sexual favors and the woman who granted sexual privileges in return for that promise, "courts and community were often predisposed to accept the claim that the man was not serious in his attentions. Moreover the woman and her family—especially her family, with their greater experience of social realities—were expected to be aware of the fact that the word of a man in such circumstances, no matter how serious it might sound, was not serious." Consider the attitude of the patricians to the promises made to the plebs by Publius Servilius and Manius Valerius in Livy's account of the class struggles of the early Republic in 495–494 B.C.E. (2.24.6, 2.27.1–4, 2.30.6–7, 2.31.5–11).

pearl. The most satisfying speaking, for a Roman, occurred when the expressive and protective aspects of speech operated like alternating currents in the flow of one's experience and so were all but indistinguishable from one another. Speech was most demoralizing, most constricting, most "dispiriting," when what you wanted to say and what you were compelled to say were far removed from one another, when speech became only the means to the end of survival. This utilitarian subordination of speech to survival happened automatically when survival became a person's highest priority; it took the joy and spirit out of speaking.[13]

While the Republic endured, the tension, the dilemma for the person of honor had been the simultaneous need to expose oneself and the desire to maintain a controlled and secret sphere, to preserve the secret source and power of one's word. But for the subject, as for the parasite and slave, the dilemma was the inverse; like Orwell's Winston Smith, the Romans of the Empire imagined themselves as neither enjoying the dignity of an inviolate spirit nor acting and speaking openly. "In the senate," Tacitus said, "it was hard to keep the proper measure in anything, since silence might seem rebellious and free speech suspect" (*Historia* 1.85).[14] Whenever his fellow senators raised their voices to flatter the emperor Nero, Thrasea Paetus would be silent or curtly assent. When word came that Nero had executed his own mother and the senators vied with one another to put forward resolutions to honor the emperor, Thrasea left the house without saying a word, "for he could not say what he would and would not say what he could" (Dio 62.15.2). (Nevertheless, his silence before Nero, like that of the tortured Epicharis before Nero's inquisitors or of Apuleius's poor market gardener before the Roman soldier, was taken as an insupportable insult and a challenge to authority.)[15] Cicero was compelled to sacrifice the "dignity" of his retirement and deliver a long flattering speech to Caesar because he feared that his silence might be interpreted as disapproval or despair (*Ad familiares* 4.4). Speaking of life under an autocrat, Seneca remarks, "It is often so far from being advantageous to avenge one's injuries that it is disadvantageous even to confess them" (*De ira* 2.33.2).[16] When both speech and silence were shackled, one's voice could neither express nor protect one's soul. Tacitus's Galba explains to his heir-designate Piso

---

13. Under the domination of Pompey and Caesar, Cicero has lost the power to speak weighty or effective words. He can still make noise, but it counts for nothing. "The ability to speak with dignity in the senate and freedom in dealing with public affairs has been lost to me forever—to me and to everyone—for either we must agree with this clique and so be altogether without weight, or disagree with them in vain" (*dignitas in sententiis dicendis, libertas in republica capessenda, ea sublata tota, sed nec mihi magis quam omnibus. Nam aut assentiendum est nulla cum gravitate paucis, aut frustra dissentiendum* [*Ad familiares* 1.8.3]). Cf. 4.14.1.

14. *coacto vero in curiam senatu arduus rerum omnium modus ne contumax silentium, ne suspecta libertas.*

15. Tacitus, *Annales* 14.12, 15.57, 16.21–29; Apuleius, *Metamorphoses* 9.39–42; Chaim Wirszubski, *Libertas as a Political Idea at Rome During the Late Republic and Early Principate*, Cambridge, 1960, p. 139.

16. *saepe adeo iniuriam vindicare expedit, ut ne fateri quidem expediat.*

that one agrees without any feeling when one agrees with a prince (*adsentatio erga quemcumque principem sine adfectu peragitur* [*Historia* 1.15]). Spirit and passion must be disengaged from speech if one were to survive in this very unequal contest.

Moreover, under the warlords of the civil war period, as under the emperors, all were liable to violations, to the breaking of the spirit formerly reserved for slaves and those unprotected by the laws.[17] Henceforward the Roman aristocrat might wear his purple stripes on his back as well as on his toga. Cicero dreamed of the young Octavian wielding a *flagellum,* the whip used for punishing slaves (Suetonius, *Augustus* 94.9).[18]

Insofar as "voluntary" speech existed under the emperors, it was at the sufferance of the man who had the ability arbitrarily to destroy it. "In the end, as with everything else in the principate, it was up to the *princeps,* in each particular case, to draw the line in the sand" (D. C. Feeney).[19] Insofar as there was no acknowledged

---

17. For the torture of free men and women (particularly those charged with *maiestas,* treason), see Arcadius Charisius, *Digesta* 48.18.10.1; Suetonius, *Augustus* 27.4, *Caligula* 27.3–4; Tacitus, *Annales* 11.22.1, 15.56–57; Dio 57.19.2, 60.15.6; Pseudo-Quintilian, *Declamationes minores* 269. See Theodor Mommsen, *Römisches Strafrecht,* Leipzig, 1899, pp. 405–406; Fritz Schulz, *Principles of Roman Law,* Oxford, 1936, pp. 207–208; Yan Thomas, "*Professus pro iudicato:* L'aveu civil et l'aveu pénal à Rome," in *L'aveu: Antiquité et Moyen Age,* Rome, 1986, pp. 97–99; Peter Garnsey, "Why Penalties Became Harsher: The Roman Case, Late Republic to Fourth Century Empire," *Natural Law Forum* 13 (1968): 151 and n. 41. For torture as an expression of tyranny, see Ammianus Marcellinus 14.9.5–9. For a concise summary of the humiliations of the senatorial aristocracy under the emperors, see Keith Hopkins and Graham Burton, "Ambition and Withdrawal: The Senatorial Aristocracy under the Emperors," in *Death and Renewal: Sociological Studies in Roman History,* vol. 2, Cambridge, 1983, pp. 176–177. There is much evidence among American slaveholders for calculated methods of destroying the spirit by attacking the body. See Frederick Douglass, *Narrative of the Life of Frederick Douglass, an American Slave,* Boston, [1845] 1985, chapter 10, pp. 65–73; Bertram Wyatt-Brown, "The Mask of Obedience: Male Slave Psychology in the Old South," *American Historical Review* 93 (1988): 1249 n. 78. For Nazi strategies for breaking the spirit, see Bruno Bettelheim, "Individual and Mass Behavior in Extreme Situations," *Journal of Abnormal Social Psychology* 38 (1943): 417–452; Paul Chodoff, "Effects of Extreme Coercive and Oppressive Forces: Brainwashing and Concentration Camps," in *American Handbook of Psychiatry,* ed. Silvano Arieti, vol. 3, New York, 1966, pp. 394–402; Terrence Des Pres, *The Survivor: An Anatomy of Life in the Death Camps,* Oxford, 1976, p. 60.

18. "*Servilia verbera* were particularly distinguished by the use of the *flagellum,* the whip" (Richard Saller, *Patriarchy, Property, and Death in the Roman Family,* Cambridge, 1994, p. 138). "Since *verbera* were fit for slaves, to suffer *verbera* symbolically put a free man in the servile category and so degraded him" (p. 137).

19. "*Si licet et fas est:* Ovid's *Fasti* and the Problem of Free Speech under the Principate," in *Roman Poetry and Propaganda in the Age of Augustus,* ed. Anton Powell, London, 1992, p. 8. According to Otto Steen Due, "The strength of his [Augustus's] power enabled him to permit a certain freedom of speech but he arbitrarily and unpredictably reserved for himself the right of determining the limit of it, and in his later years he was narrowing those limits" (*Changing Forms: Studies in the Metamorphoses of Ovid,* Copenhagen, 1974, p. 174 n. 92). "The *libertas* of the empire was only what the autocrat voluntarily conceded to his subjects.... Since the execution of Cicero no man had been free to speak against the dynast with power of life and death except to the extent that he permitted it" (Andrew Wallace-Hadrill, "*Civilis Princeps:* Between Citizen and King," *Journal of Roman Studies* 72 [1982]: 38). See A.J. Boyle, "Introduction: The Roman Song," *Roman Epic,* London, 1993, p. 16 n. 11.

or consensual boundary protecting speech it was not *libertas* at all, but slavery. Indeed, "free" speech, insofar as it was tolerated or encouraged by an emperor, was indistinguishable from empty flattery.[20] Anyone who has read Cicero's Caesarian speeches, Lucan's *Laus Neronis*, or the *Panegyricus* of Pliny realizes the impossibility of the speaker's position. This was what I think of as "the paradox of nonbeing."

The extremes inverting, an identical problem was created by too much and too little freedom, the problem of how to speak effectively and expressively without the script, the code, and the traditions that protected the spirit. How could one live without limitations? What move could one make after checkmate? The remainder of this chapter concerns the metamorphosis, the conversion of the dead soul, the broken spirit, into the protagonist of a new and ongoing drama. It emphasizes the diachronic adjustments, the historical counterpoint, to the synchronic patterns discussed in chapter 5.

THE FIRST STRATEGY: THE FATHER CONFESSOR

Even for a great fault a little punishment satisfies a father.

(pro peccato magno paulum supplici satis est patri.)

TERENCE, *ANDRIA* 903

As Cicero and Quintilian note, a person who confessed could only hope for mercy, and only from a judge with wide powers of discretion.[21] And the widest powers of discretion belonged, in the Roman imagination, not to the magistrate but to the *pater.*[22] Submission to the father, supplication of the father was not only

---

20. Questioned by Tiberius, the senator Valerius Messalla avowed that his proposals to honor the recently deceased Augustus were indeed voluntary and spontaneous *(consilio suo, sponte).*This assertion of one's freedom of speech was, Tacitus adds cynically, the only form of adulation left *(ea sola species adulandi supererat) (Annales* 1.8.5). The problem of speaking freely to a despot is one that vexes Cicero. See, for example, *Ad Atticum* 13.51; *Pro Ligario* 2.6, 8.23. For the *angusta et lubrica oratio* of the poets trying to speak "freely" under Augustus, see Jasper Griffin, "Augustus and the Poets: *Caesar Qui Cogere Posset,"* in *Caesar Augustus: Seven Aspects,* ed. Fergus Millar and Erich Segal, Oxford, 1984.

21. Cicero, *De inventione* 2.33.105; Quintilian, *Institutio oratoria* 5.13.5, 7.4.18.

22. On the power of the *pater,* see E. Sachers, *"Patria potestas,"* in Pauly-Wissowa, *Paulys Realencyclopädie der classischen Altertumswissenschaft,* vol. 22.1, Stuttgart, 1953, cols. 1046–1175; R. Yaron, *"Vitae necisque potestas," Tijdschrift voor Rechtsgeschiedenis* 30 (1962): 243–251; John Crook, *"Patria Potestas," Classical Quarterly* n.s. 17 (1967): 113–122; David Daube, *Roman Law: Linguistic, Social and Philosophical Aspects,* Edinburgh, 1969, pp. 75–93; Andreas Alföldi, *Der Vater des Vaterlandes im römischen Denken,* Darmstadt, 1971; Yan Thomas, *"Vitae necisque potestas:* Le père, la cité, la mort," in *Du châtiment dans la cité: Supplices corporels et peine de mort dans le monde antique,"* Rome, 1984, pp. 499–548; William V. Harris, "The Roman Father's Power of Life and Death," in *Studies in Roman Law in Memory of A. Arthur Schiller,* ed. Roger S. Bagnall and William V. Harris, Leiden, 1986, pp. 81–95; W. K. Lacey, *"Patria Potestas,"* in *The Family in Ancient Rome,* ed. Beryl Rawson, Ithaca, 1986, pp. 121–144; Emiel Eyben, "Fathers and Sons," in *Marriage, Divorce, and Children in Ancient Rome,* ed. Beryl Rawson, Oxford, 1991, pp. 114–173; Saller, *Patriarchy, Property, and Death,* pp. 102–153.

proper, it was due. "No controversy was shorter than that between a father and a son" (Livy 1.50.9).[23] Not the Roman god but the Roman *pater*, with his right to give and to take life (the *ius vitae necisque*), resembled the Pauline God, both in the absoluteness of his power and in his commitment to mercy. As Lacey points out, "the *paterfamilias* was in a more autocratic position that the *consul*—not that this is surprising, since the *paterfamilias* was expected to be checked by the affection which he felt for his family."[24] "I love Glycerium—I confess. And if in this I have sinned, I confess to having sinned. To you, my father, I surrender myself. Punish me, order me as you will" (Terence, *Andria* 896–899).[25]

Terence's Clitophon asks pardon of his father Chremes in the presence of Chremes's friend and neighbor Menedemus:

Clitophon: Father, I beseech you to forgive me.
Menedemus: Chremes, forgive him.
Clitophon: If you want me to continue living, father, forgive me.
Chremes: I will do so, on condition that he does what I think is fair.
Clitophon: Father, give me your orders! I will do all that you ask.

[*Heautontimorumenos* 1049–1055][26]

To a modern eye, the paucity of evidence for the exercise of the *ius necis*, the right of a father to slay his own child, makes the *patria potestas* appear negligible. But, as Thomas and Saller point out, the father's *ius vitae necisque* was less a description of social reality than a definition or ideal of power—an ideal of the completeness of power *(summa potestas)*.[27] "Il n'existe ni conditions ni limites à ce pouvoir," to quote Thomas.[28] It was precisely the counterpoise of the most powerful restraints to the broadest imaginable powers that, in the Roman mind, made

---

23. *nullam breviorem esse cognitionem quam inter patrem et filium.* Tacitus's emperor Tiberius acquits the son of Piso of any charges stemming from the civil war on the grounds that "a son could not have refused a father's orders" (*Tiberius adulescentem crimine civilis belli purgavit, patris iussa nec potuisse filium detrectare* [*Annales* 3.17.1]).

24. *"Patria Potestas,"* p. 133.

25. *ego me amare hanc fateor, si id peccarest, fateor id quoque. / tibi pater me dedo. Quidvis oneris inpone, impera.*

26. *Pater obsecro mi ignoscas. / da veniam Chremes. . . . Si me vivom vis, pater, ignosce. . . . ea lege hoc adeo faciam, si facit quod ego hunc aequum censeo. / pater, impera! faciam omnia.*

27. See Thomas, *"Vitae necisque potestas,"* pp. 500, 512, 545; Saller, *Patriarchy, Property, and Death,* p. 117. Death at the hands of the father, *nex*, was conceived as a particularly harsh and terrible death because, as Thomas indicates, it was bloodless (pp. 509–510): it did not allow the atonement of shedding one's blood. See Chapter 8 n. 11.

28. *"Vitae necisque potestas,"* p. 501. Cf. Dionysius of Halicarnassus 2.26. Cicero equates by parallel the command of the father over a child to that of a master over a slave or that of a general over a soldier (Cicero, *Tusculanae disputationes* 2.21.48, cf. 2.22.51) or that of a king over his subjects (Cicero, *De re publica* 3.25.37). Yaron offers fascinating comparisons with Hittite, Neo-Assyrian, Canaanite, and Hebrew notions of complete power as the right to kill coupled with the prerogative of mercy (*"Vitae necisque potestas,"* pp. 246–248).

the *patria potestas* the most highly charged force the Romans could conceive.[29] It demonstrated, like the *fides* of the honorable, both the unlimited fullness of strength and its strictest restraint.[30] The father, with his right to kill *(ius necis)*, lifting in his hands the newborn and helpless infant *(filiam, filium tollere)*, exercising his prerogative of mercy *(ius vitae)*, was the very model of the Roman man of honor, the man who could do harm, but chose not to.[31] On the relationship of a father and child, Seneca remarks, "A father would be slow to sever from himself his limbs" *(De clementia* 1.14.3).[32]

The father was the only person to whom one could surrender absolutely and retain one's honor and one's soul.[33] Indeed, this submission was a condition of honor in ancient Rome. Sandra Joshel comments on the "filiations" in Roman inscriptions: " 'The son of' was evidence of his submission to the authority of a father, which brought with it a rightful place in society and marked him as an individual with a family of origins."[34] "There is no power of words or genius that can express how beneficial, how laudable, how unforgettably fixed in the memory of man is the ability to say: 'I obeyed my parents, I yielded to their rule, and, whether it was just or unjust and harsh, I showed myself obsequious and submissive' " (Seneca, *De beneficiis* 3.38.2).[35]

---

29. The *patria potestas* was at the center of a balancing of forces within the household and the state; but, as so often in Roman thought, the center is not fixed but elusive and arbitrary (in a neutral sense).

30. Thomas writes of the right of the father to kill his son: "On ne peut qu'être surpris de voir que, lorsqu'il est exceptionnellement attesté, son exercice ait toujours été reprouvé... un droit formellement énoncé et en même temps sacrilège" (*"Vitae necisque potestas,"* p. 512).

31. For the father as the source of the child's life, the one who causes to live, see Cicero, *Pro Roscio Amerino* 22.63, 26.71.

32. *Tarde sibi pater membra sua abscidat.*

33. Sandra Joshel remarks, "The liabilities of the son or daughter in paternal power were similar to the slave's, although they were not so drastic and had different repercussions. The child's position was considered an honorable one, because obedience was owed to a father, not a master" (*Work, Identity, and Legal Status at Rome: A Study of the Occupational Inscriptions,* Norman, Oklahoma, 1992, p. 27). On the similarities between the positions of slaves and sons, see J.A. Crook, *Law and Life of Rome 90 B.C.–A.D. 212,* Ithaca, p. 56. Crook points out that everything the son had was in the power of the father; in this he was like the slave, and, I would add, like the surrendered enemy, the *deditus.* See Daube, *Roman Law,* pp. 85, 79.

34. *Work, Identity, and Legal Status,* p. 35, cf. 32, 36. The father, like the monarch, embodied or symbolized the family as a whole. Children and members of the family participated vicariously in and shared the honor of the father to the extent that they attuned themselves fully to his will and identified with his person. See Julian Pitt-Rivers, "Honour and Social Status," in *Honour and Shame,* ed. J. G. Peristiany, Chicago, 1966, p. 36.

35. *Nulla vi verborum, nulla ingenii facultate exprimi potest, quantum opus sit, quam laudabile quamque numquam memoria hominum exiturum, posse hoc dicere: "parentibus meis parui, cessi imperio eorum, sive aecum sive inicum ac durum fuit, obsequentem submissumque me praebui."* Seneca goes on: "In only one thing was I stubborn—the resolve not to be outdone by them in benefits" *(ad hoc unum contumax fui, ne beneficiis vincerer).* For the absolute submission of the son to the father, see Cicero, *Pro Roscio Amerino* 14.37.

And so, while the master needed to coerce and to break his slave *(coercet et frangit)*, the children followed the father out of a readiness, a promptness to obey *(oboediendi facilitatem)* (Cicero, *De republica* 3.25.37). Service to a father was not servitude.

The actions of a parent and a tyrant might be identical, but the motivations, the emotions ascribed to them were very different. One could presume on the goodwill of the father. "The father's power... consults for the interests of his children with the utmost forbearance and subordinates his own interests to theirs" (Seneca, *De clementia* 1.14.2).[36] The parent, forced to act severely, feels keenly the pain of the punishment he inflicts. "After a harsh decision, the parent is himself saddened, for he virtually lays the punishment on himself that he exacts from his child" (Ovid, *Epistulae ex ponto* 2.2.117–118).[37]

The special nature of the father is illustrated by Livy's and Plutarch's wonderful story of the young and impetuous Minucius, master of horse to the dictator Fabius Maximus. During the war with Hannibal, Minucius was elevated to a joint dictatorship with Fabius by a Roman populace impatient with Fabius's lingering war of attrition; they were weary of Fabius's "rope-a-dope" tactics and longed for a knockout punch. Minucius obliged them with a prompt and disastrous pitched battle from which he was only rescued by Fabius.

In the first of a series of elaborately staged scenes, Minucius confesses his incapacity to lead. Minucius then conducts his troops to the camp of Fabius where, planting the standards of his legions and with his own soldiers as witnesses, he surrenders to Fabius. Minucius addresses Fabius as *parens*:

> "I call you by the name of Father, because it is the most honorable that I can use, and yet even a father's kindness is not so great as the kindness I have received from you. My father gave me life, but to you I owe the salvation of not only this life but the lives of all the men under me.
>
> "Dictator, on this day you have won two victories, one over Hannibal through your bravery, and the other over your colleague through your generalship and generosity. With the first you saved our lives, and with the second you taught us a lesson, and if Hannibal overcame us to our disgrace, your superiority has been to our salvation and our honor."

---

36. *potestatem patriam... est temperantissima liberis consulens suaque post illos reponens.*

37. *Parens... / qui cum triste aliquid statuit, fit tristis et ipse / cuique fere poenam sumere poena sua est.* It is Piso's indulgence of the troops that earns him the popular title of "Father of the Legions" (Tacitus, *Annales* 2.55). The parent was contrasted with the master or tyrant. Pliny praises Trajan: "We speak not of a master but a parent" *(non de domino sed de parente loquimus* [Pliny, *Panegyricus* 2.3]). See Cicero, *De domo sua* 35.94; Livy 2.60.3, 4.42.1–7; Dio Chrysostom 1.22. Alföldi emphasizes throughout his work the emotional associations the Romans had with the notion of *pater* (*Der Vater des Vaterlandes*, esp. pp. 41–46). It was because Augustus renounced the fullness of powers acknowledged to be his that he was granted the *corona civica* (acknowledging him as *servator/conservator* of the state [Augustus, *Res gestae* 34; Alföldi, *Der Vater des Vaterlandes*, p. 68]).

Then, according to Plutarch, he embraces "Father" Fabius and kisses him, and the soldiers on both sides follow his example, "so that the whole camp was filled with rejoicing and tears of happiness" (Plutarch, *Fabius Maximus* 13).[38]

"Our ancestors," Cicero declares, "did not call those men whom they justly obeyed 'lords' and 'masters'—nor 'kings' even—but 'custodians of the fatherland,' but 'fathers,' but 'gods'" (*De republica* 1.41.64).[39]

Here it is important to explain that, in Roman thought, the father was a savior *(servator/conservator)* and, conversely, the savior was a father. Andreas Alföldi points out that the oak-leafed *corona civica*, bestowed by a soldier on another who, to save him, had risked his own life in battle, permanently marked the saved as the "son" and the savior as the "father."[40] Accordingly, in Silius's poetic version of the story of Minucius and Fabius, Minucius's soldiers loudly proclaim Fabius to be "their honor, their salvation, their parent" *(decus, salus, parens* [*Punica* 7.732–735]).[41]

Chremes explains to Menedemus (sick with remorse for having been hard and unmerciful to his son) that the father should be the one whom the son trusts in everything: "Act in such a way that your son will feel that you are his father. Act in such a way that he can dare to entrust you with all things, that it will be from you that he will seek and beseech all things" (Terence, *Heautontimorumenos* 925–926).[42] It is because sons can rely, finally, on the mercy of their fathers that the sons of Plautus and Terence can get away with so much in Roman comedy. Because she can presume on the indulgence of her father, the daughter of Marcus Fabius Ambustus confesses to him her envy of her sister's patrician marriage. Her father encourages her to speak, consoles her, bids her be of good cheer, and then arranges to satisfy her by advancing her plebeian husband (Livy 6.34.7–10).[43] Philocrates,

---

38. See Livy 22.29–30.6; Valerius Maximus 5.2.4; Pliny, *Historia naturalis* 22.5.10; Silius Italicus, *Punica* 7.705–8.3, 9.565–67. Compare Livy's account of the relationship between the merciful "father" Lucius Papirius Cursor, *dictator,* and his disobedient "son" Quintus Fabius Maximus Rullianus, the *magister equitum* (8.30–35).

39. *Non eros nec dominos apellabant eos, quibus iuste paruerunt, denique ne reges quidem, sed patriae custodes, sed patres, sed deos.* Walter Burkert, after rehearsing the many versions of "Lord" or "Master" given to the gods in the ancient Near East and Greece, remarks, "It is surprising that the expressions of power and lordship are much less obtrusive in the language of Roman religion. *Dominus* got its prominence only with Christianity, translated from *kyrios.*" Rather, he notes, "The important gods are called *pater*" (*Creation of the Sacred,* pp. 81–82).

40. *Der Vater des Vaterlandes,* pp. 49–59. See Polybius 6.39.6–7; Livy 6.14.4–8; Cicero, *Ad Atticum* 9.10.3; *Phillipicae* 2.5.12.

41. In recognition of the benefits that he had received from Publius Cornelius Lentulus, Cicero hails him as *parens, deus, salus nostrae vitae, fortunae, memoriae, nominis* (*Post reditum ad populum* 5.11).

42. *Fac te patrem esse sentiat; fac ut audeat / tibi credere omnia, abs te petere et poscere.*

43. It is only because and to the extent that mercy or indulgence could be presumed on that confession could be strategic. Relying on the mercy of his father, and under the guidance of his slave Chrysalus, Mnesilochus concocts a phony epistolary confession to bilk his father Nicobulus: "I am ashamed to come into your sight, father; I have heard that you know of my wicked behavior. . . . I con-

entrusting his fate and future redemption to his slave Tyndarus, says, "I could almost call you my own father, if I dared. You are a second father to me, after my own" (Plautus, *Captivi* 238–239).[44] Given their identity in age, we would be more likely to say, "You are like a brother to me." But because of the completeness of the trust, the completeness of the dependency, and Philocrates's certainty that his slave will not seek compensation or try to humiliate him for this dependency, Tyndarus is cast as the father rather than the friend or brother.

The relationship of a parent to a child was not strictly reciprocal; the Roman child (like the Japanese) would always be in debt to the parent, but the parent would not demand repayment in full.[45] The parent would hold back, hesitating to break the spirit of the child.[46] "Nothing humiliating or servile should be endured

---

fess that I acted stupidly. But I pray, father, if I erred through foolishness, do not desert me.... Now if I have the right, I beseech you, I beg you to give me two hundred gold coins."

Pudet prodire me ad te in conspectum pater:

tantum flagitium te scire audivi meum.... Stulte fecisse fateor. Sed quaeso, pater, ne me, in stultitia si deliqui,
deseras.

... Nunc si me fas est obsecrare abs te, pater,

da mihi ducentos nummos Philippos te obsecro. (*Bacchides* 1007–1026)

44. *Pol ego si te audeam, meum patrem nominem: / nam secundum patrem tu es pater proximus.* Pseudippus addresses his slave: *Mi anime, mi Trachalio, mi liberte, mi patrone potius, immo mi pater!* (Plautus, *Rudens* 1265–1266). Cf. Segal, *Roman Laughter,* pp. 111–112). "You, Milo, were able to recall me to my country. Will I be unable to retain you in that country? What answer will I give to my children who consider you a second father?" (*Quid respondebo liberis meis, qui te parentem alterum putant?* [Cicero, *Pro Milone* 37.102]). No decision of the senate was ever welcomed by the plebs with such rejoicing as the one to institute pay for military service. "A crowd gathered at the senate house, and men grasped the hands of the senators as they departed, declaring that they were rightly called 'fathers'" (*Concursum itaque ad curiam esse prensatasque exeuntium manus et patres vere appellatos* [Livy 4.60.1]).

45. In the contest of mutual beneficence, "We are almost always defeated by our parents" (*A parentibus fere vincimur* [Seneca, *De beneficiis* 5.5.2]). Nevertheless, "It is not a dishonor to be defeated by a parent in bestowing benefits" (*Non est tamen turpe vinci beneficiis a parente* [ibid. 5.5.3]).

46. "Classical Roman authors, far from advocating the virtues of corporal punishment for children and slaves alike, condemned the use of the whip on children precisely because it was important to differentiate children from slaves" (Saller, *Patriarchy, Property, and Death,* p. 14; cf. Plutarch, *De liberis educandis* 12 [*Moralia* 8F]). You break a slave; you do not break a child—at least, as Saller observes (following the work of Lawrence Stone and Steven Ozment), not until the Christianization of Europe. "Rather than an evolution from paternal severity to indulgence, the evidence suggests a continuing debate about how to manage the right balance" (Saller, p. 145). Saller points out that the essential mode of socialization employed by the parent was the granting or withholding of praise (p. 142). "The aim was to imbue the child with a sense of both his honorable position and the shame that would contribute to self-restraint" (p. 151). Seneca's parent tries to instill in the child a proper sense of balance by the application of both severity and indulgence, since "the spirit increases by permissiveness and diminishes through servitude" (*crescit licentia spiritus, servitute comminuitur* [*De ira* 2.21.3]). For the difficulty of this balancing act, see Emiel Eyben, "Fathers and Sons," pp. 125–136. The greatest moral problem for parents was to avoid the Roman tendency to overindulge their children (Quintilian, *Institutio oratoria* 1.2.6–8; Seneca, *De ira* 2.21.6; Tacitus, *Dialogus* 29.2).

by the child; never should it be necessary for him to beg" (Seneca, *De ira* 2.21.4).[47] The parent, especially the father, acted as the guarantor, the bulwark, of the *libertas*, the *ius*, the *animus* of his progeny.

While the father had the acknowledged right to kill his son, the Romans could hardly imagine a more pathetic situation, a more terrible emotional double bind, than for a father to have to do so. It was only reasons of state that drove men like Brutus the Elder, Aulus Postumius Tubertus, or Titus Manlius Torquatus to sacrifice their own sons. The sacrificial aspects of these executions did not make them any less harrowing to the Romans.

> The consulship imposed on a father the duty of imposing the death penalty on his sons, and the man who should have been spared even the sight of their suffering was the man whom Fortune appointed to exact it.... The sons of Brutus were stripped, scourged with rods, and beheaded. And the whole time, the people watched closely the expression on the father's face—where they might clearly read the father's soul—as he administered the public penalty. (Livy 2.5.8)[48]

> The rest could not endure to look upon that sight, but it is said that the father neither turned his gaze away, nor allowed any pity to soften the stern wrath upon his countenance.... He had done a deed which it is difficult for one either to praise or to blame sufficiently. For either the loftiness of his virtue made his spirit incapable of suffering, or else the magnitude of his suffering made it insensible to pain. In either case his act was not a trivial one, nor a human one, but either like a god or a beast. (Plutarch, *Publicola* 6.3–4)[49]

47. *nihil humile, nihil servile patiatur: numquam illi necesse sit rogare suppliciter.* As Burkert remarks, "Animals are normally programmed not to attack their own children" (*Creation of the Sacred*, p. 86).

48. *poenae capiendae ministerium patri de liberis consulatus imposuit, et qui spectator erat amovendus, eum ipsum fortuna exactorem supplicii dedit.... Nudatos virgis caedunt securique feriunt, cum inter omne tempus pater voltusque et os eius spectaculo esset eminente animo patrio inter publicae poenae ministerium.*

49. Perrin trans. Everyone, according to Livy, was horrified at so shocking a command *(exanimati omnes tam atroci imperio)*, and the spectators reacted with extreme dismay (8.7.21–22, cf. 8.12.1). Dionysius finds it extraordinary that Brutus not only humiliated his own sons with a public execution but stayed to watch that execution. Every spectator wept save Brutus (5.8.3–6). See the similar story told of Aulus Postumius, which Livy is loath to credit (4.29.5). William Harris believes that the *ius vita necisque* was evidence for the severity of the *pater* (or at least the autocratic *pater*), but his own arguments and the evidence that he offers tell a very different story ("The Roman Father's Power of Life and Death," pp. 87–88, 90–95). Harris notes that in several cases where a father killed a son, the father acted in his capacity as magistrate and felt obliged to suppress his natural compassion (p. 86). "The ideal magistrate carries out his duties whatever the personal sorrow it may cost him, ... the magistrates are above paternal indulgence and above favoritism" (p. 90). See Yaron, "*Vitae necisque potestas*," p. 243; A. W. Lintott, "The Tradition of Violence in the Annals of the Early Roman Republic," *Historia* 19 (1970): 19–20; Saller, *Patriarchy, Property, and Death*, pp. 121–122; Wilfried Nippel, *Public Order in Ancient Rome*, Cambridge, 1995, pp. 31–32. Yaron compares these stories to the story in 1 Samuel: Saul had forbidden by oath the taking of food before evening, and his son Jonathan, unaware of his father's command, had eaten honey. Saul, resorting to oracles to establish the identity of the guilty person, declared that he would put the culprit to death, "even if it be Jonathan" (14.34–45).

Even as he pronounced the death penalty against his son, the general Torquatus, Livy tells us, was moved not only by admiration for his son's bravery but by "the instinctive love of a parent for his children" (*ingenita caritas liberum* [8.7.18]).[50]

The arbitrarily or unnecessarily cruel father and the mother without mercy (often the *noverca*, the stepmother) were prodigious figures in Roman literature.[51] Livy notes that Lucius Manlius's cruelty extended even to his son Titus Manlius (the future Torquatus), whom, on account of his intellectual slowness, he kept imprisoned in a squalid rural workhouse, and this merciless behavior was a charge against him. He should have nurtured and encouraged the son rather than try to crush his spirit (Livy 7.4.4–7). Cicero argues that a son could assume the loving tenderness of his father. It would take many and terrible faults to make a father disown a son. A father would have to forget that he was a father; he would have to overcome nature itself *(naturam ipsam)* and his intrinsic love for his child *(amorem illum penitus insitum)* (*Pro Roscio Amerino* 19.53).[52] When, in the course of a hypothetical court case, a father is charged with bidding his suppliant daughter to kill herself, the father's advocates excuse his behavior with arguments to the effect that she should have known he did not mean it; it was just a figure of speech; she should have come back a little later when he had calmed down; she was not sufficiently sincere in her supplication; and so on. The Roman orators assume that her death was an unnecessary tragedy, that in the end the father would have been merciful to his daughter (Seneca, *Controversiae* 10.3). The good parent was, as Ovid remarks, thunder without lightning (*Epistulae ex ponto* 2.2.117–118).[53]

FATHER OF THE FATHERLAND

Now, patient reader, mark well and listen intently to the speech delivered by Cicero before the victorious Julius Caesar in 46 B.C.E.:

> Often, Caesar, I pleaded cases together with you while the progress of your career kept you in the forum, but *never* after this fashion: "Forgive him. He went astray. He slipped. He never thought. If ever again." *That is the tone one adopts towards a parent, but to a jury we say:* "He did not do it. He never considered it. The witnesses are false.

50. For the *patrius affectus*, the *animus patrius*, see Cicero, *Pro Roscio Amerino* 16.46; Valerius Maximus 4.1.5.

51. That he killed his own son to make room for a new marriage is one way of asserting the monstrosity of Catiline (Sallust, *Catilina* 15.2). For other Roman reactions to parental cruelty, see Cicero, *Pro Cluentio* 9.27–28; Seneca, *De clementia* 1.15.1, 1.16.3; Orosius 5.13.17–18, 5.16.8; Marcian, *Digesta* 48.9.5: *patria potestas in pietate debet, non atrocitate consistere.* For the stepmother, see Seneca, *Controversiae* 4.6, 9.5; Quintilian, *Institutio oratoria* 2.10.5; Virgil, *Georgica* 2.128; Jerome, *Epistulae* 54.15.

52. The man would forgive his errant son unless his father's heart had become rock-hard *(scopulis durior aut adamantibus rigidior)* (Sidonius Apollinaris 4.23.2). For a father merciful even to the son who tried to kill him, see Seneca, *De clementia* 1.15.2.

53. *Sed placidus facilisque parens veniaeque paratus / et qui fulmineo saepe sine igne tonat.*

The charge is invented." ... *So we speak to a jury.* ... *But I plead before a father:* "He blundered. He acted thoughtlessly. He is sorry. I throw myself upon your clemency. I beg you to pardon his sin. I implore your mercy." (*Pro Ligario,* 10.30)[54]

Here Cicero makes the sharpest imaginable distinction between the meaning of confession and the plea for mercy in the courts of the Republic, where Cicero and Caesar competed or collaborated as relative equals, and Caesar's court, where Caesar was the "father." As Thomas points out, "It was dishonorable to confess because it was dishonorable to admit oneself vanquished. It was in the face-to-face judicial jousting, the oratorical contest engaged in *by equals,* that the confession was adjudged degrading."[55] But in June 46 B.C.E., Cicero wrote to the stubborn Marcus Marcellus, pleading with him to confess the defeat of the Republican cause and to return home from his proud, self-imposed exile in the expectation of clemency: "We are defeated," Cicero confessed. "Or, if *dignitas* cannot be defeated, we are, to be sure, broken and prostrate" (*Ad familiares* 4.7.2).[56] He admonished the unbending Marcellus that "if it is the part of a great soul not to approach the conqueror as a suppliant, avoid being the arrogant man who spurns the mercy of that same victor" (*Ad familiares* 4.9.4).[57] King Deiotarus, he declares, would be not only ungrateful but insane to feel any resentment against Caesar, who has mercifully allowed the king to retain his title and part of his kingdom (*De rege Deiotaro* 13.38).[58] "You have," Cicero says to Julius Caesar, "what every prosecutor most desires: a defendant who confesses" (*Pro Ligario* 1.2).[59]

---

54. *Causas, Caesar, egi multas, equidem tecum dum te in foro tenuit ratio honorum tuorum, certe numquam hoc modo:* "*Ignoscite, iudices, erravit, lapsus est, non putavit, si umquam posthac.* ... " *Ad parentem sic agi solet: ad iudices:* "*Non fecit, non cogitavit, falsi testes, fictum crimen.*" ... *Ad iudicem sic, sed ego apud parentem loquor:* "*Erravit, temere fecit, paenitet; ad clementiam tuam confugio, delicti veniam peto, ut ignoscatur oro.*"

55. "*Confessus pro iudicato,*" p. 113, emphasis mine. "Il n'était pas honorable d'avouer, parce qu'il était honteux de s'avouer vaincu. C'est dans le face à face de la joute oratoire, entre égaux, que la *confessio* était jugée dégradante." Cf. p. 110.

56. *Victi sumus igitur, aut, si vinci dignitas non potuit, fracti certe et abiecti.* Cf. *Ad familiares* 4.9.4. Even Fortune had to confess herself defeated by Caesar (*Pro Marcello* 2.7). Cicero is willing to confess not only Ligarius's but also his own faults before Caesar because he can presume on Caesar's clemency (*Pro Ligario* 3.8).

57. *si fuit magni animi non isse supplicem victori, vide ne superbi sit aspernari eiusdem liberalitatem.* Cf. *Ad familiares* 4.7, 8 and Marcellus's reply at 4.11.

58. *Non modo tibi non suscenset—esset enim non solum ingratus, sed etiam amens—verum omnem tranquillitatem et quietem senectutis acceptam refert clementiae tuae.*

59. *habes quod est accusatori maxime optandum, confitentem reum.* Compare the words of Petronius's "Polyaenos," caught, as it were, in inaction by his mistress: "I confess, my Lady, to my many sins. ... You have a defendant who confesses. I deserve whatever punishment you order. I have been a traitor, killed a man, profaned a temple. Demand my punishment for these crimes. If you decide on execution, I will come with my sword; if you are contented with a flogging, I will run naked to my Lady" (*Fateor me, domina, saepe peccasse.* ... *Habes confitentem reum: quicquid iusseris, merui. Proditionem feci, hominem occidi, templum violavi: in haec facinora quaere supplicium. Sive occidere placet, ferro meo venio, sive verberibus contenta es, curro nudus ad dominam* [*Satyricon* 130]). "He begs, he confesses, he is prepared to atone. What more can you want?" (*Orat confitetur purgat. Quid vis amplius?* [Terence, *Phormio* 1035]).

"Confession of one's faults," says Seneca, writing under Nero (the emperor who condemned him to death), "is the sign of a sound mind" (*Epistulae* 53.8).[60]

THE REIGN OF MERCY

Let them surrender into our discretion.... Whatever we grant to them they will then take in the light of a favor and not of a bargain.... When they surrender into our control, and we take away their arms, and when their persons are in our possession and they see that there is nothing that they can call their own, their spirits will be tamed and they will welcome as a gift whatever we allow them to have.

APPIAN, *PUNICA* 9.64[61]

The expectation of mercy was a necessary condition for the confession, and mercy could be offered only by those with wide powers of discretion, *"be it a con-queror, be it a father—or that combination of the two that is a prince,"* to use the words of Thomas (*"Confessus pro iudicato,"* pp. 102–103).[62] The world of the citizen had been formed in contravention to the absolute and unlimited powers implied in the *patria potestas*. Under the Republic, the relationship of a man in his role as a citizen to a man in his role as a son had been a tense, problematical one. (There was nothing more important for the Roman sense of honor than not being "fixed," and in the Republic, as in the plays of Plautus, there had been room to maneuver between roles and relationships, between alternative realities, between alternative

---

60. *vitia sua confiteri sanitatis indicium est.*

61. Horace White trans. (with modifications). "He was back in the Ministry of Love, with everything forgiven, his soul white as snow. He was in the public dock, confessing everything, implicating everybody.... O stubborn self-willed exile from the loving breast! Two gin-scented tears trickled down the sides of his nose. But it was all right, everything was all right. The struggle was finished. He had won the victory over himself. He loved Big Brother" (George Orwell, *Nineteen Eighty-Four: Text, Sources, Criticism*, ed. Irving Howe, New York, 1963, p. 131).

62. Emphasis mine. "Il n' y a de *confessio* que parce que la grâce en est attendue. Grâce qui ne s'espère jamais d'un tribunal saisi sur accusation; mais soit d'un vainqueur, soit d'un père, soit de ce mélange des deux qu'est un prince." (Thomas, *"Confessus pro iudicato,"* pp. 102–103); cf. David, "La faute et l'abandon," p. 72. "It is a plea for mercy when the defendant confesses the crime and premeditation, yet begs for compassion. In the courts this is rarely practicable, except when we speak in defense of one whose good deeds are numerous and notable.... Such a cause, then, is not admissible in the courts, but is admissible before the senate, or a general, or a council" (*Deprecatio est cum et peccasse se et consulto fecisse confitetur, et tamen postulat ut sui misereantur. Hoc in iudicio fere non potest usu venire, nisi quando pro eo dicimus cuius multa recte facta extant.... Ergo in iudicium non venit, at in senatum, ad imperatorem et in consilium talis causa potest venire* [*Auctor ad Herennium* 1.14.24, Caplan trans.). "When one is addressing the senate, the people, the emperor or any other authority in a position to offer clemency, the plea for mercy has its place" (*In senatu vero et apud populum et apud principem et ubicumque iuris clementia est habet locum deprecatio* [Quintilian, *Institutio oratoria* 7.4.18]). I would add to this list of judges with wide powers of discretion the beloved (and her servants). In Ovid's *Metamorphoses*, the desperate and suppliant Iphis confesses his love for Anaxarete to the latter's nurse in hopes of merciful treatment (14.703–709); cf. Petronius, *Satyricon* 130.

scripts.) As a citizen, Fabius Maximus (to whom Minucius had surrendered) decided to give way before his own son the consul.[63]

But with the collapse of the Republic and the reestablishment of the monarchy, the Romans were cast as children of a *pater* with an unlimited and unmitigated *ius vitae necisque*. Seneca imagines the emperor speaking to himself: "I am the arbiter of life and death for all people *(ego vitae necisque gentibus arbiter)*; every individual lot and condition is in my hand. What fortune chooses to assign to each mortal, she proclaims through my tongue" *(De clementia* 1.1.2).[64] As Alföldi points out, the title *pater patriae*, along with the role of savior and the *corona civica*, became imperial monopolies.[65] But now the father who saved you was simultaneously the conqueror who had brought you to your knees.[66] Indeed, the image of the state on its knees as supplicant to the merciful *pater* was impossible to distinguish from the image of the enemy on its knees as *deditus* to the victorious *imperator*. The fine line between the child and the captive, service and servitude, grew much finer. The emperor was, to use an image of Seneca, a father—with a whip. "What then is the prince's duty? It is that of the good parent who corrects his children gently at times, at times with threats—and occasionally even with the blows of a whip.... The duty of the father is the same as that of the prince, whom we have been led to call—and not in empty flattery—'Father of his Country' " *(De Clementia* 1.14.1–2).[67]

Saller comments astutely on this passage, "Seneca must justify the use of physical coercion by the emperor who as *pater patriae* was certainly not going to give up the disciplinary use of force."[68] The Romans understood that the perpetual victor needed the perpetually vanquished to prove the fullness of his power and his mercy.[69] And so, in his lapidary testament, Augustus emphasizes his clemency—

---

63. For the father ordered by the lictors to pay reverence to his son the consul, see Livy 24.44.10; Plutarch, *Fabius Maximus* 24.1–2; Quadigarius apud Gellius, *Noctes Atticae* 2.2.13; cf. Pomponius, *Digesta* 1.6.9.

64. *Ego vitae necisque gentibus arbiter, qualem quisque sortem statumque habeat, in mea manu positum est; quid cuique mortalium fortuna datum velit, meo ore pronuntiat.* The emperor has the power both to give and to take life *(dandi auferendi vitam potens* [*De clementia* 1.21.2]).

65. *Der Vater des Vaterlandes*, pp. 71, 97.

66. For a detailed study of the idea and image of the *pater* (and its associations with clemency, care, and salvation) as the basis for Caesar's and later Augustus's ideological program, see Alföldi, *Der Vater des Vaterlandes*, pp. 41–97, and the sources extensively cited there.

67. *Quod ergo officium eius est? Quod bonorum parentium, qui obiurgare liberos non numquam blande, non numquam minaciter solent, aliquando admonere etiam verberibus.... Hoc, quod parenti, etiam principi faciendum est, quem appellavimus patrem patriae non adulatione vana adducti.*

68. *Patriarchy, Property, and Death*, p. 146 n. 47.

69. "Il est dans la logique de la mystique du perpétuel vainqueur d'exiger, comme preuve de son efficacité, de perpétuels vaincus. Il y aurait lieu, en effet, d'ajouter aux images de la Victoire impériale qui peuplent la numismatique du 1er au IVe siècle les nombreuses représentations de ses victimes" (Jean Gagé, "La théologie de la Victoire impériale," *Revue Historique* 171 [1933]: 28; cf. pp. 29–31).

and the murderous threat behind it: "As victor, I spared all citizens who sought my mercy, and all foreign peoples—when I could in safety—I preferred to pardon than to exterminate" (*Res gestae* 3.1–2).[70] Seneca remarks of Augustus "the mild prince" *(mitis princeps)*, "I am loath to call clemency what was, rather, the exhaustion of cruelty" (*De clementia* 1.11.2).[71] And when the Pseudo-Senecan Octavia bids Nero to be clement in the manner of Augustus, *patriae parens*, Nero cynically retorts with a long account of the bloody atrocities that preceded the sheathing of Augustus's sword (*Octavia* 472–532).[72] His audience might have recalled that Julius Caesar and Sulla were also flattered with the titles "savior" and "father."[73] Or that, in 43 B.C.E., in the midst of the reign of terror instigated by their proscriptions, the triumvirs were given the *corona civica* as "saviors" of the state.[74] Ruthless violence and tender mercy were two sides of the same princely face. In September 217, the people at the circus cried out to the emperor: "Oh Jupiter, as a master you were angry; as a father take pity on us!"[75] The following dialogue takes place in the Pseudo-Senecan *Octavia:*

Nero: To exterminate his enemy is the greatest virtue of a leader.
Seneca: To save his citizens is still a greater virtue in the Father of the Fatherland.
 (443–444)[76]

As Thomas points out, the increased reliance on confession by the subjects of the emperors can be correlated to the increased application of torture, the development of the inquisitorial procedure, and the emergence of the emperor, freed from the restraints of the law, as judge.[77] Now, when there was no safety in tradi-

---

70. *victorque omnibus veniam petentibus civibus peperci. Externas gentes quibus tuto ignosci potuit conservare quam excidere malui.* On the connection between clemency and victory, see Rufus J. Fears, "The Theology of Victory at Rome: Approaches and Problems," *Aufstieg und Niedergang der römischen Welt,* vol, 2.17.2, Berlin, 1981, p. 808.

71. *Ego vero clementiam non voco lassam crudelitatem.*

72. Horace describes Augustus: "Formerly belligerent but now mild to the fallen foe" *(bellante prior, iacentem / lenis in hostem* [*Carmen saeculare* 51]).

73. *Sulla* 34.1; cf. Fears, "The Cult of Virtues and Roman Imperial Ideology," *Aufstieg und Niedergang der römischen Welt,* vol, 2.17.2, Berlin, 1981, p. 880. For Caesar as *pater patriae* and savior of the citizens, see *Corpus Inscriptionum Latinarum,* vol. 9, no. 34; Dio 44.4.4–5; Appian, *Bellum civile* 2.16.106. For Cicero as *parens patriae,* see Pliny the Elder, *Naturalis historia* 7.30.117. For Brutus as *publicus parens,* see Florus 1.3.5.

74. Dio 47.13.3. For Augustus as *servator mundi,* see Propertius 4.6.37; Fears, "Theology of Victory," pp. 812, 814; "Cult of Virtues," p. 910.

75. Dio 78.20.2. The title "Father" should signal that the emperor loves his subjects as a father loves his children, and that the subjects respect and honor the emperor as they would a father. Now, however, it only signals the absolute power that the emperors have over all of us (Dio 53.18.3).

76. *Extinguere hostem maxima est virtus ducis. / —Servare cives maior est patriae patri.*

77. In the inquisitorial procedure, the prosecutor and judge were one and the same (as opposed to the accusatorial and contest system that dominated in the Republic). See Thomas, "*Confessus pro iudicato,*" pp. 97–99, 106–107. Mark Gustafson remarks on the "elasticity" of the imperial system of *cognitio*

tional laws, one was prompt to be contemptible, quick to throw oneself on the mercy of the judge.[78] According to Thomas, "Faire avouer est devenu un moyen de procédure inquisitoriale."[79]

Justice, that dynamic and perpetually unstable Roman system of distribution and retribution, had been, in the Republic, a contest for relative equals. Under the domination of a master or king there could be no reliance on *aequitas* however conspicuous her mask. In the words of Macrobius, "Power, should it invite— should it even supplicate—compels" (*Saturnalia* 2.7.2).[80] "It is hard," declares Publilius Syrus, "to refuse the supplication of a superior" (660, Friedrich ed.).[81] Cicero quotes Plato: "A tyrant's entreaties *(ton turannon deeseis)* partake of the nature of compulsion *(anagkais)*" *(Ad Atticum* 9.13). The Romans feared the indulgence of the king as the poor miser Euclio feared the indulgence of his rich neighbor Megadorus: "In one hand he holds out a loaf of bread; in the other a stone" (Plautus, *Aulularia* 195–196).[82] "No one," Dio remarks, "believes that those who have the power to use compulsion are acting honestly when they give judgment, but all men think they are led by a sense of shame to spread out before the truth a mere semblance and illusive picture of a constitutional government, and under the legal name of a court of justice are but satisfying their own desires" (52.7.4).[83]

Under the emperors, whatever justice existed was by way of mercy. And so it was a short step from Ligarius's trial in the house of Caesar to Valerius Asiaticus's trial in the bedroom of Messalina (Tacitus, *Annales* 11.2). It was a another short step to the "trial" where, according to Suetonius, Gaius glanced at the prisoners lined up before him, and gave the order, "Kill every man between that bald head and the other over there" *(Caligula* 27.1). The *indulgentia principis* was *l'acte gratuit.* David Daube discusses the paradoxes of such "grace" *(gratia):* "Gratuitous" (in

---

extra ordinem, which left the judge, unhindered by any law, to prescribe any penalty he saw fit ("'*Inscripta in fronte*': Penal Tattooing in Late Antiquity," *Classical Antiquity* 16 [1997]: 88).

78. Some examples of the resort to confession under the emperor as inquisitor appear in Tacitus, *Annales* 3.67 (the trial of Gaius Silanus under Tiberius); Cicero, *Pro Marcello, Pro Rege Deiotaro, Pro Ligario* (Caesar as judge); Pliny, *Epistulae* 4.11.11.

79. "*Confessus pro Iudicato,*" p. 99.

80. *Sed potestas, non solum si invitet, sed etiam si supplicet, cogit.* See Carlin Barton, *The Sorrows of the Ancient Romans,* Princeton, 1993, pp. 118–119. One can think of Augustus on his knees to the Roman people (Suetonius, *Augustus* 52).

81. *durum est negare cum superior supplicat.*

82. *altera manu fert lapidem, panem ostentat altera.* John Lendon remarks of the relationship of gratitude created when a rich man does a favor for the poor man: "All the inferior could do was to be 'grateful,' that is, he could remember and hold himself in readiness to repay forever" (*Empire of Honour,* Oxford, 1997, p. 66). On the "grateful man," see Seneca, *De beneficiis* 5.3.3–4.1.

83. Cary trans.

French *gratuit*)...can signify on the one hand 'free of charge,' 'munificent,' on the other 'senseless,' 'absurd.' "[84]

Mercy, Andrew Wallace-Hadrill explains, was the renunciation of power, and the power that you renounced was your gift.[85] The Roman emperors were aware that the giver of mercy was infinitely more powerful than the guarantor of justice.[86] "A slave can kill a king—or a snake, or an arrow; but no one has saved the life of another who was not greater than the one he saved" (Seneca, *De clementia* 1.21.1).[87] "One can take the life of a superior, but one can never give it except to an inferior" [*De clementia* 1.5.6]).[88] In the words of Paul Veyne, "To give is the royal gesture par excellence."[89] Petronius's Trimalchio *tyrannus* repeatedly threatens his servants with dire punishments in order to have the satisfaction of granting the clemency his guests have pleaded for (*Satyricon* 49.6, 52.4, 54.1).[90] Brutus complains to Cicero that Antony, like Octavian, wanted them to seek their salvation from him, so that they might have safety at his sufferance, "that our lives should be in his gift, that we should hold our positions at his pleasure" (*Ad Brutum* 25.4 [= 1.16.4]).[91]

---

84. " 'Suffrage' and 'Precedent,' 'Mercy' and 'Grace,' " *Tijdschrift voor Rechtgechiedenis* 47 (1979): 243. Cf. Daube, *Roman Law,* p. 118f. "I will be gracious to whom I will be gracious" (Exodus 33.19).

85. *"Civilis Princeps,"* pp. 38–39, 42–43.

86. "Liée à la victoire, la clémence est aussi affaire de souveraineté. *'Ubicumque sui iuris clementia est'* (Quintilian, *Institutio oratoria* 7.4.18): par cette formulation juridique, Quintilien fonde le droit de grâce sur l'autonomie d'un pouvoir dont l'indépendance à l'égard d'autrui est la condition même de son exercice sur ses subordonnés" (David, "La faute et l'abandon," p. 107).

87. *Regem et servus occidit et serpens et sagitta: servavit quidem nemo nisi maior eo, quem servabat.*

88. *vita enim etiam superiori eripitur, numquam nisi inferiori datur.* "The powerful grows more powerful by forgiving much" (*multa ignoscendo fit potens potentior* [Publilius Syrus 350, Friedrich ed.]). "Le *confessus* fait de son adversaire, auquel il s'abandonne, un sauveur" (Thomas, "*Confessus pro iudicato*," p. 104). "Son humiliation même charge son vainqueur du bienfait attendu de la grâce" (p. 105). For the victory of the donor over the recipient, see Marcel Mauss, *The Gift: Forms and Functions of Exchange in Archaic Societies,* trans. Ian Cunnison, New York, 1967, esp. p. 72; Richard Saller, *Personal Patronage under the Early Empire,* Cambridge, 1982, pp. 8–11, 17–39; Joshel, *Work, Identity, and Legal Status,* p. 117.

89. *Le pain et le cirque: Sociologie historique d'un pluralisme politique,* Paris, 1976, p. 228. "The king is the 'giver' par excellence....By definition he gives more than he receives..." (Pierre Bonte, " 'To Increase Cows, God Created the King': The Function of Cattle in Intralacustrine Societies," in *Herders, Warriors, and Traders,* ed. P. Bonte and John G. Galaty, Boulder, Colorado, p. 74). "In Burundi the term *bugabire* is derived from the root *kugaba,* which means 'to give freely,' 'to own in full,' but also 'to distribute,' 'to dominate,' 'to rule.' In the same way the root *gusaba* means both 'to ask,' 'to pray,' but also 'to pay homage,' 'to be subject of' " (p. 73).

90. See Barton, *Sorrows,* pp. 118–119.

91. *salutem ab se peti, precariam nos incolumitatem habere.* Cicero speaks of the reluctance of soldiers to award the *corona civica* to men who have saved their lives in battle: "Even common soldiers are reluctant to confess, by the bestowal of the civic crown, that they have been saved by another—not that it is humiliating to have been shielded in battle and rescued from enemy hands—but they shrink from the overwhelming burden of being under the same obligation to a stranger as they are to a parent" (*At id etiam gregarii milites faciunt inviti, ut coronam dent civicam et se ab aliquo servatos esse fateantur, non quo turpe sit protectum in acie ex hostium manibus eripi...sed onus beneficii reformidant, quod permagnum est alieno debere idem quod parenti* [*Pro Plancio* 30.72]). "Diese Verpflichtung ist grundlegend wichtig auch für das Verständnis der

"All Roman citizens," Seneca declares, "were compelled to confess that they were happy under Nero" (Seneca, *De clementia* 1.1.7).[92]

Like the Pauline god, the all-powerful and merciful emperor might not only forgive you but might not even impute to you your sins. "Certainly," Augustus remarked to the confessed patricide, "You did not slay your father" (*certe patrem tuum non occidisti* [Suetonius, *Augustus* 33.1]). Seneca's *bonus iudex* with his *potestas vitae necisque* is not concerned with retribution or the vendetta but is governed solely by his own prudence and his concern for the *salus*, the health of the state. He will be merciful, provided that mercy does not threaten the health of the state that he himself embodies (*De ira* 1.19.5–8).

When the *imperator* becomes the *pater*, he no longer has to conquer in order to assert complete control; he has only to forbear. "We believe Augustus a god, and not because we are ordered to do so; he was a good prince, and we confess that he well deserved the name of *parens* for no other reason than that he did not avenge with cruelty even personal insults" (Seneca, *De clementia* 1.10.3).[93] The merciful emperor had only to forbear using the full measure of his power. And so the emperor Tiberius allowed a decree to be passed in recognition of his remarkable clemency toward his daughter-in-law Agrippina in not having had her strangled and her body cast out on the Gemonian steps (Suetonius, *Tiberius* 53.2).[94] By the *indulgentia Trimalchionis*, Petronius's mock tyrant framed his rude lateness as a form of clemency (*Satyricon* 33); he was so very beneficent that he did not to forbid his guests to pass gas, urinate, or defecate. "We thanked him for his generosity and indulgence" (*Gratias agimus liberalitati indulgentiaeque eius* [47]).

Alföldi traced the evolution of the Roman notion of the "savior" from the soldier who rescued another soldier from the enemy at great risk, to an abstract and inherent quality of the emperor involving no risk whatsoever.[95] "The civic crown," Pliny tells us, "that glorious decoration for military valor has now for a long time been the sign of the emperor's clemency—ever since, owing to the civil wars, not to kill a fellow citizen came to be to seen as worthy of merit" (*Naturalis historia* 16.3.7).[96]

---

bindenden Kraft des Begriffes *parens (pater) patriae*. Er erweist sich nämlich, daß es sich hier nicht nur um einen Ehrentitel des Monarchen handelt, sondern um die stärkste Verpflichtung der Ganzheit ihn gegenüber" (Alföldi, *Der Vater des Vaterlandes*, p. 50).

92. *omnibus tamen nunc civibus tuis et haec confessio exprimitur esse felices.*

93. *Deum esse non tamquam iussi credimus; bonum fuisse principem Augustum, bene illi parentis nomen convenisse fatemur ob nullam aliam causam, quam quod contumelias quoque suas . . . nulla crudelitate exsequebatur.*

94. Cf. Tacitus, *Annales* 6.25. "I saw, in the time of Gaius Caligula, tortures, I saw burnings, and I knew that . . . men who were merely killed were considered examples of the emperor's mercy" (*Videbam apud Gaium tormenta, videbam ignes, sciebam . . . ut inter misericordiae exempla haberetur occisi* [*Naturales quaestiones* 4A, *praefatio* 17]).

95. *Der Vater des Vaterlandes*, p. 74.

96. *civicae coronae, militum virtutis insigne clarissimum, iam pridem vero et clementiae imperatorum, postquam civilium bellorum profano meritum coepit videri civem non occidem.*

And the emperors knew that in a universe where mercy reigns, only the fool protests his innocence. A merciful emperor, like a merciful god, ruled over a universe of the guilty.[97] The exiled Ovid addresses *mitissime Caesar*: "It is indeed just—I don't deny that I have deserved my punishment—shame has not fled so far from my face. But if I had not sinned, what room would there be for your mercy?" (*Tristia* 2.29–31)[98]

THE NEW FREEDOM

You order us to be free: we shall be; you order us to speak what we feel in public: we shall express ourselves.
PLINY, *PANEGYRICUS* 66.4[99]

Words could not define one when there were no *fines*, no limits. One's voice became (like that of Ovid's Echo or Horace's parasite) sound and nothing more: the barking of the Cynic dog, the braying of Apuleius's ass, the wailing of the infant (the *infans*, the child without speech). Pliny affirms the common saying that "the living voice is that which affects others" (*ut vulgo dicitur viva vox adficit* [*Epistulae* 2.3.9]). One could invert this statement and say that the voice that affected others was the living voice. When one's voice had no effective force, neither had one's soul. Seneca, speaking of the *libertas promiscua* of the Cynic street preachers, declared that it detracted from the *auctoritas* of the great man to preach to passersby unheeded (*Epistulae* 29.1–3). When the voice met with no response, when it did not "count" for others, the voice was nothing but air, *vox et praeterea nihil*. The Roman *animus* went from being the energy at the core of one's existence to the last vestige of animation. When Phineas begs Perseus to grant him nothing save his *animus (nihil praeter hanc animam concede mihi)*, the life that he begs for—the life that anyone begs for—is mere life, breath and nothing more. "Just because you've saved me," explains Seneca, "doesn't mean you're my savior" (*si servasti me, non ideo servator es* [*De beneficiis* 2.18.8]).[100]

97. "*Clementia* is superfluous unless a crime has been committed, and is the only virtue that has no place among the innocent" (*nisi post crimen supervacua est* [*clementia*] *et sole haec virtus inter innocentes cessat* [Seneca, *De clementia* 2.1]). Cf. 2.3.1.

98. *illa quidem iusta est, nec me meruisse negabo / non adeo nostro fugit ab ore pudor / sed nisi peccassem, quid tu conceded posses?* Compare 1 John 1.8–10: "If we confess our sins he is faithful and just, and will forgive our sins and cleanse us from all unrighteousness. If we say we have not sinned, we make him a liar." For the mercy of the emperor, see especially Lothar Wickert, "*Princeps*," in Pauly-Wissowa, *Realencyclopädie*, vol. 22, cols. 2234ff. with bibliography; Paul Plass, *The Game of Death in Ancient Rome*, Madison, 1995, pp. 163–167.

99. *Iubes esse liberos: erimus: iubes quae sentimus promere in medium: proferemus.* Cf. Sandra Joshel, "Female Desire and the Discourse of Empire: Tacitus's Messalina," *Signs* 21 (1995): 66.

100. See Barton, *Sorrows*, pp. 118–119.

Libertas, once embracing the entire sphere of one's acknowledged rights, coalesced into the notion of free speech, *libertas loquendi,* in the early Empire. Free speech became the very definition of *libertas* because in trying to save one's soul, one's word was the last thing that one surrendered. And "free" speech became, paradoxically, a totally unconstrained, uninhibited speech at the moment when a Roman's speech was furthest from expressing his or her will, when the function of speech was overwhelmingly to guard the breath of life.[101] Tacitus, complaining of the submissiveness of his generation, remarks, "The spying of imperial informers has deprived us even of the give-and-take of conversation. We should have lost memory as well as voice, had forgetfulness been as easy as silence" (*Agricola* 2.3).[102] And so Tacitus's definition of the *felicitas temporum* was "to think what one willed and to say what one felt" (*sentire quae velis* and *quae sentias dicere* [*Historia* 1.1]).

When the script, the score, was gone, "freedom" of speech became the arbitrary, whimsical speech of the king or the fool *(aut rex aut fatuus).* Rather than the display and definition of a bounded and limited "turf," *libertas* became one's unboundedness, one's lack of restraint.[103] At precisely the moment when one could no longer defend one's *libertates* or *iura* in their ancient sense, one's soul cried out for complete emancipation. This new "freedom of speech" makes its appearance in the *licentia theatricalia* of the public spectacles, in the *parrhesia* of the Cynic and Stoic, in the literary underground, in the graffiti scratched on the city walls, and in the outspoken calumnies of the poor man clinging for immunity to the emperor's statue (Tacitus, *Annales* 3.36).[104]

According to Ovid, the poet (like the lover, the slave, and the pauper) had no *fides.* He could not be a reliable witness; but he surrendered his gravity and dignity in return for the freedom to speak (*Amores* 3.12.19–20). Ovid was willing, like Horace, to give up having weighty words in return for immunity of speech. But just as the new ideas of virtue never drove out the old, so the new "freedom of speech" never drove out the older and incompatible ideal of effective speech. Hence there

---

101. Cicero contrasts "free speech" *(libertas loquendi)* with *verecundia (Ad familiares* 9.22.1).

102. *adempto per inquisitiones etiam loquendi audiendique commercio. memoriam quoque ipsam cum voce perdidissemus, si tam in nostra potestate esset oblivisci qua tacere.* For the condemned, despairing of life, taking back their freedom of speech, see Suetonius, *Augustus* 13.2.

103. One can follow this development in Wirszubski's *Libertas.*

104. "Les Pompéiens écrivaient sur les murs pour publier leur esprit, leurs idées, leur culture; ils s'exprimaient, ils ne se 'défoulaient' pas. Quelle belle psychologie des graffiti vésuviens il y aurait à faire! Quelle attitude extrêmement moderne avaient ces Pompéiens qui écrivaient sur les murs sans se cacher, pour 'prendre la parole'! Les actuels graffiti de New York ont retrouvé cela" (Paul Veyne, "Le folklore à Rome et les droits de la conscience publiques sur la conduite individuelle," *Latomus* 42 (1983): 4.

was confusion and anguish over the possible meaning of speech. Spontaneous, untrammeled speech was now considered the only "free" speech, but such speech often seemed indistinguishable from empty verbiage or, worse, from flattery, a confession of defeat. It was ineffective, and no one listened. It was the *libertas insanae vocis.*[105]

Totally uncensored and unhindered speech could be totally frustrated speech (the four-letter speech one hears so often on the streets of America): it was both the antithesis and the mirror of the dictated speech of the *confessus.* One could not and cannot use speech to protect and express one's spirit if that speech is untrained, undisciplined, or uncultivated. (It is hard for a modern American to understand why free speech can not only feel like no speech at all but actually reduce the ability of speech to either express or protect. We share with the Romans of the civil war period and the early Empire both the ideal of uncensored and uncontrolled speech and a sense that we have lost "authentic" speech.)

The Elder Seneca says of Titus Labienus, a man who savaged all ranks and persons indiscriminately, "His *libertas* was such that it surpassed the definition of *libertas*" (*Controversiae* 10, *praefatio* 5).[106] Tacitus remarked on those who made empty displays of *libertas* in a futile effort to undermine the principate (*Annales* 16.22). Such a man was Favonius, the close companion and emulator of Cato Uticensis, whom Plutarch accused of exaggerating the *parrhesia* (frank speech) of Cato into *akairia* (unseasonableness) and *authadeia* (insolence) (*Pompey* 60).[107] Similarly, Plutarch's Brutus the Younger castigates the free-speaking Favonius as a *haplokuna* (a mere dog), and *pseudokuna* (a false Cynic), or *pseudokatona* (a false Cato) (*Brutus* 34.3–5).[108] The verbal behavior of aristocrats begins to resemble that of the slaves in Plautus and Terence.

That the discipline of the voice, through oratorical exercises and show declamations, went on long after the political effectiveness of speaking was gone, long after the advocate had became an actor or a professional speaker, illustrates the lasting power of the ancient ideal of speech. But the strongest evidence of the persistence of the ancient ideal, paradoxically, is offered by those who, when faced with the necessity of crying "uncle," chose to say nothing.

---

105. Cf. Publilius Syrus 292, Friedrich ed.: *Insanae vocis numquam libertas tacet.*

106. *Libertas tanta ut libertatis nomen excederet.*

107. "I cannot feel any sympathy with those who would rather lose their heads than their chance to turn a fine phrase" (*non possum misereri qui tanti putant caput quam dictum perdere* [Seneca Rhetor, *Controversiae* 2.4.13]).

108. Miriam Griffin, "Cynicism and the Romans: Attraction and Repulsion," in *The Cynics,* ed. R. Bracht Branham and Marie-Odile Goulet-Cazé, Berkeley, 1996, p. 193.

THE SECOND STRATEGY: THE *INFITIANS*

"Tell the secret!" Epictetus's Tyrant demands.
"I refuse to tell, for this is in my power!"
"But I will chain you."
"What do you say? Chain me? My leg you will chain, yes, but not my will.
No, not even Zeus can conquer that."

ARRIAN, *EPICTETI DISSERTATIONES* 1.1.23

Under the domination of another, not speaking became the minimum of liberty. One spoke because there was no safe silence before a master. Seneca's Creon beseeches Oedipus: "Let me be silent. Can less liberty be sought from a king?" Oedipus replies: "Often more than speech, mute liberty injures king and kingdom" (*Oedipus* 523–525).[109]

And so, conspicuous among the heroes and heroines of the early Empire was the *infitians,* the one who ostentatiously refused to confess, the man or woman who, like the heroes of Samuel Beckett, could not or would not bend at the knees. Among the prodigies of silence were the rustic of Termestino, the woman of Liguria, the servant of Marcus Antonius the orator, Thrasea Paetus, Leaena, and Anaxarchus. The most memorable, perhaps, was the valiant freedwoman Epicharis, who, alone of the conspirators against Nero, refused to break under torture and reveal the names of her fellows. According to Tacitus, she was an *exemplum* all the more glorious in that the very freeborn and aristocratic men protected by her silence rushed to confess their crime and implicate one another (*Annales* 15.57).[110] Just so, Pliny's prostitute Leaena, on the rack, refused to betray the tyrannicides Harmodius and Aristogeiton. Anaxarchus, tortured for a similar reason, "bit off his tongue and spat the only hope of betrayal in the tyrant's face" (*Historia naturalis* 7.23.87).[111] Like Tacitus's Plautius Lateranus, they died "full of

---

109. Cr. to O.: *Tacere liceat. ulla libertas minor / a rege petitur?* O. to Cr: *saepe vel lingua magis / regi autque regno muta libertas obest.*

110. Compare the story of the rebellious peasant of Termes in Spain, who, caught and tortured by the Romans, would not confess (*Annales* 4.45), and the silent and smiling defiance of the Jew of Jotapata taken prisoner and crucified by the Romans (Josephus, *Bellum Iudaicum* 3.321).

111. [Leaena] *quae torta non indicavit Harmodium et Aristogeitonem tyrannicidas,...* [Anaxarchus] *qui simili de causa cum torqueretur praerosam dentibus linguam unamque spem indici in tyranni os expuit.* Pliny, *Naturalis historia* 34.19.72: [Leaena] *excruciata a tyrannis non prodidit.* Cf. Ammianus Marcellinus 29.2.11; Apuleius, *Metamorphoses* 7.2. Cicero's Zeno of Elea is offered to his audience as an example of the man who endures every torment rather than divulge the names of his accomplices in the plot to overthrow tyranny (*Tusculanae disputationes* 2.22.52). The young servant of the orator Marcus Antonius, despite brutal torment, did not betray his master (Valerius Maximus 6.8.1). "The age," as Tacitus remarks at the beginnings of the *Historia,* "was not altogether sterile of *virtus;* there were examples of the fidelity of servants contumacious even in the face of torments" (*contumax etiam adversus tormenta servorum fides* [1.3]). Cf. Ammianus Marcellinus 14.9.6. Interestingly, the young Gaius, *civilis princeps,* "awarded eight thousand gold pieces to a freedwoman who, though put to extreme torture, had not revealed her patron's guilt" (*Caligula* 16.4).

constant silence" (*plenus constantis silentii* [*Annales* 15.60.2]). As Brent Shaw remarks on the author of Fourth Maccabees: "The active agents of domination can be forced...to admit their defeat and to confess the superior power of the tortured body."[112]

This was the strategy of those who would not play the new game, the game without rules, the game of God's grace or the emperor's clemency. It was the strategy of those who at all costs preserved the secret and hidden self. It was the eloquent voice of no voice at all. But there was still another strategy employed by Romans faced with overwhelming odds, one employed at all times in Roman history, both republican and imperial: confession, active willed confession, profession.

THE THIRD STRATEGY:
PROFESSION (OR, THE TALKING CURE)

"Shameless!"	*"Yup."*
"Scoundrel!"	*"True."*
"Whipped slave!"	*"And why not?"*
"Tomb-robber!"	*"Sure."*
"Gallowsbird!"	*"Good."*
"Friend-swindler!"	*"That's me."*
"Parricide!"	*"Go on."*
"Sacrilegious!"	*"I confess."*

PLAUTUS, *PSEUDOLUS* 360FF.[113]

Nonius Marcellus remarks: "This is the difference: to profess is an act of will, to confess the act of someone under compulsion; therefore it is more honorable to profess than to confess."
NONIUS MARCELLUS, VOL. 3, P. 700, LINDSAY ED.[114]

Marcus Terentius, accused of being the friend of Sejanus, declares: "However events should fall out, I will confess that I was the friend of Sejanus, that I strove

---

112. "Body/Power/Identity: Passions of the Martyrs," *Journal of Early Christian Studies* 4 (1996): 278. Cf. "The Passion of Perpetua," *Past and Present* 139 (1993): 3–45, esp. p. 19.

113. *Impudice!*   *itast.*
    Sceleste!   *dicis vera.*
    Verbero!   *quippini?*
    Bustirape!   *certo.*
    Furcifer!   *factum optume.*
    Sociofraude!   *sunt mea istaec.*
    Parracida!   *perge tu.*
    Sacrilege!   *fateor.*

The scene goes on for quite a while in this vein. Cf. the lines from the *fabula togata* of Titinius, the *Varus*, fr. 3, verse 137 (*Comicorum Romanorum Fragmenta*, ed. Otto Ribbeck, Leipzig, 1898).

114. *hoc distat, quod profiteri voluntatis est, confiteri necessitatis et coactus....honestius profiteri quam confiteri.* Cf. Pseudo-Quintilian: "There is no one so ignorant of the nature of speech that he does not know that

to be, and that, having attained his friendship, I rejoiced" (Tacitus, *Annales* 6.14–15.1 [= 6.8–9.1]).[115] The impenitent Pontia proclaims: "'I did it. I confess. I served aconite to my children. The deed, having been detected, is known to all. I did it on my own.' 'What, you most savage viper! You killed two at a single meal?' 'And seven too, had there been seven!'" (Juvenal, *Satirae* 6.638–692).[116] Plautus's Libanus gleefully confesses to perjury, perfidy, and thievery (*Asinaria* 558–566). Terence's Sannio admits, "I'm a pimp, the common bane of youth, I confess, a perjurer, a pestilence" (*Adelphi* 188).[117] Compare the same playwright's confession at the beginning of the *Heautontimorumenos*: "As to the malicious rumors with which he has been mangled—that he has combined many Greek plays and written few Latin ones—he doesn't deny having done this; moreover, he does not repent, and he will do it again" (*prologus* 16–19).[118]

Antony avowed without hesitation the relationship with Cleopatra of which Octavian accused him (Suetonius, *Augustus* 69.2). When, according to Suetonius, Caesar was blamed for elevating lowly friends to high places, "He openly pro-

---

declaring is different from confessing. Declaration is an act of will and of a spirit not subject to coercion; confession is extracted by force with great pain" (*Enuntiare vero aliud esse quam confiteri nemo adeo ignarus est loquendi ut nesciat. Enuntiatio voluntatem habet et animum non coactum, confessio expressam dolore multo necessitatem* [*Declamationes minores* 272.5, Shackleton Bailey ed.]). "To profess is an act of one's own free will. But to confess is the act, not of will, but of a spirit compelled" (*profiteri proprii arbitrii est, fateri autem coacti est animi non voluntatis* [Isidore, *De differentiis* 1.31.232 (J. P. Migne, *Patrologia Latina*, vol. 83, Paris, 1862)]).

115. *sed utcumque casura res est, fatebor et fuisse me Seiano amicum, et ut essem expetisse, et postquam adeptus eram laetatum.* Cicero professes to his friendship with Caesar's assassins (*Philippicae* 2.13.31). Messala Corvinus professes to having fought on the Republican side in the civil war (Tacitus, *Annales* 4.34).

116. *Set clamat Pontia, "Feci.*
  Confiteor. Puerisque meis aconita paravi:
  quae deprensa patent: facinus tamen ipsa peregi."
  "Tune duos una, saevissima vipera cena?
  tune duos?" "Septem, si septem forte fuissent."

Plautus's Sosia shamelessly confesses that he hid while his master Amphitryon waged war against the Teleboians (*Amphitruo* 199–200). Cf. the scene of defiant confession in Afranius's *Compitalia* (*Comicorum Romanorum Fragmenta*, fr. 1, lines 25–29).

117. *Leno sum, fateor, pernicies communis, adulescentium, periuris, pestis.*

118. *nam quod rumores distulerunt malevoli,*
  multas contaminasse Graecas, dum facit
  paucas Latinas: id esse factum hic non negat
  neque se pigere et deinde facturum autumat.

Compare the confessions of Petronius's Encolpius: "I fled from a court of justice, I cheated in the arena, I killed my host" (*effugi iudicium, harenae imposui, hospitem occidi* [*Satyricon* 81.3]); "I confess, my Lady, to my many sins…I have been a traitor, I killed a man, I violated a temple" (*fateor me, domina, saepe peccasse…proditionem feci, hominem occidi, templum violavi* [130.1–4]). See the very interesting article by Gareth Schmeling, "*Confessor Gloriosus*: A Role of Encolpius in the *Satyrica*," *Würzburger Jahrbücher für die Altertumswissenschaft* 20 (1994/1995): 207–224.

fessed that if he had made use of the resources of brigands and cutthroats in defending his dignity, he would have rewarded them also in such a way" (*Iulius* 72.1).[119] Sallust's Marius, scorned by the aristocracy, was pleased to confess that he was unable to arrange a fashionable dinner party, that he did not keep in his entourage an actor or a gourmet cook (*Bellum Iugurthinum* 85.39).[120]

To avoid violation, one erected boundaries. But, paradoxically, when dishonored or faced with the inevitability of dishonor, it was exactly those most vulnerable parts of oneself that one aggressively exposed, like Cyrano's or Vatinius's nose.[121] There was nothing, Suetonius tells us, apart from being taunted as a poor lyre-player, that Nero resented more than being called by his family name Ahenobarbus. "With regard to the name that was cast in his teeth as an insult, he professed that he would resume it and give up that name that was his by adoption" (*Nero* 41.1).[122] And so Cicero, ridiculed for his name ("Chickpea"), dedicated to the gods a silver goblet inscribed with the words Marcus Tullius and the image of a pea (Plutarch, *Regum et imperatorum apophthegmata,* Cicero 1–2 [*Moralia* 204E]).[123]

One could humiliate another by denuding oneself. The act of challenging another often involved a kind of exhibitionism: sticking out the tongue, looking in the eye, exposing one's nakedness.[124] The Romans might betray, in insult, the very parts and aspects of themselves that shame hid or inhibited, like the Roman soldier who, from the parapets of the Temple, bared his ass at the Jews assembled

119. *professus palam, si grassatorum et sicariorum ope in tuenda sua dignitate usus esset, talibus quoque se parem gratiam relaturum.* Augustine condemns the worshippers of the Mother of the Gods: "As part of their rites they profess this sickness, this crime, this depravity, that even men of vicious habits can hardly be compelled to confess under torture" (*Hic morbus, hic crimen, hoc dedecus habet inter illa sacra professionem, quod in vitiosis hominum moribus vix habet inter tormenta confessionem* [*De civitate dei* 6.8]).

120. Vespasian, son of a municipal tax collector, not only did not conceal his former lowly condition but even paraded it (Suetonius, *Vespasianus* 12).

121. Vatinius defiantly mocked the very physical deformities that his enemies reproached him with (Seneca, *De constantia sapientis* 2.17.3).

122. *Nihil autem aeque doluit* [Nero], *quam ut malum se citharoedum increpitum ac pro Nerone Ahenobarbum appellatum, et nomen quidem gentile, quod sibi per contumeliam exprobraretur, resumpturum se professus est deposito adoptivo.*

123. Cf. Plutarch, *Cicero* 1.3–8. Was the outlandish tomb of the baker Marceius Vergilius Eurysaces, like that of Petronius's Trimalchio, a "profession," a way of echoing the Roman elite that was at the same time a way of thumbing his nose at it? We are tempted to interpret Trimalchio's behavior as simply a flattering but grossly inept imitation of Roman elite behaviors. But I think it would be very much in tune with Petronius's own thinking, and with what little we know of his actions, to interpret Trimalchio's behavior as an insult as well as a mimesis, a profession as well as a confession. For this kind of impudent mimesis, see Barbara Kellum's work on images of Actium as they appear in the art of freedmen, "The Play of Meaning: The Visual Culture of Ancient Roman Freedmen and Freedwomen" (forthcoming).

124. The Roman defendant stripping to the waist to show his scars in a court enacted just such a form of aggressive self-exhibition. At the moment I am writing there is a fashion among youthful "skinheads" for shaving the head as a form of aggressive self-exposure à la Gabriele D'Annunzio.

for Passover (Josephus, *Bellum Iudaicum* 2.224).[125] The third finger, the *digitus infamis*, was a visual pun for aggressively exposing oneself aimed at insulting and violating the eyes of another,[126] not unlike the little Roman *cacans*, the erect penis or the female genitals that aggressively drove away the violating eye.[127] The Roman prostitutes, *professae feminae* (Ovid, *Fasti* 4.866), put to shame by having to confess their names to the aediles, redeemed their honor by aggressively professing their wares in the street and by dancing naked at the Floralia.[128] The witch Meroe and her sister Panthea insulted the spying Aristomenes by lifting up their dresses and pissing on him (Apuleius, *Metamorphoses* 1.13). As Pierre Bourdieu says, "A woman challenges or insults by 'pulling up her skirt.'" Bourdieu relates it to the insulting language of "pissing on" or "soiling."[129] Like the opening of the gates of Janus, all forms of self-exposure presented a challenge, from saying "hello," to looking in the eye, to presenting to another one's empty and unarmed hand.

Tacitus tells the tale of the exemplary courage of a Ligurian woman who concealed her son from the troops of Otho ravaging the defenseless towns of northern Italy. When the soldiers, believing her money to be hidden along with her son, tortured her and demanded that she reveal the hiding place, she responded by exposing herself *(uterum ostendens latere)*. Neither additional terrors nor death itself could alter her *constantia* (Tacitus, *Historia* 2.13).[130] With this same aggressive-

---

125. Cf. Horace, *Satirae* 1.9.69, 1.8, esp. 46–47. Being exposed involuntarily was a deep shame for a Lakota, while voluntarily exposing oneself was a powerful insult (Mari Sandoz, *Crazy Horse: The Strange Man of the Oglalas*, Lincoln, Nebraska, [1942] 1969). Freud's "talking cure" was "profession" rather than "confession"; it was not a plea for mercy but a sort of homeopathic reaction against the shaming pressure of the superego, a way of despising one's degradation. See Scheler, "Der 'Ort' der Schamgefühls und die Existenzweise des Menschen," *Schriften aus den Nachlass*, vol. 1 = *Gesammelte Werke*, vol. 10, Bern, 1957, p. 114.

126. Cf. Seneca, *De constantia sapientis* 5.1.

127. See Barton, *Sorrows*, part 2. How easily these signs of aggressive defiance could appear as signs of submission can be discerned from Irenäus Eibl-Eibesfeldt's discussion of the bared buttocks outside old fortresses and gateways in Europe and on Japanese protective amulets (*Love and Hate*, New York, 1971, p. 178).

128. Tacitus tells the story of Vistilia, the daughter of a praetorian family, who in 19 C.E. advertised her venality on the aediles' list, "according to the procedure of our ancestors, who believed that the unchaste were sufficiently punished by the profession of their disgrace" (*Vistilia praetoria familia genita licentiam stupri apud aediles vulgaverat more inter veteres recepto, qui satis poenarum adversum impudicas in ipsa professione flagitii credebant* [*Annales* 2.85.1–2]). Cf. Suetonius, *Tiberius* 35.2: *lenocinium profiteri coeperant*.

129. "Sense of Honor," p. 106 n. 12. For the Spartan mother exposing herself to her cowardly sons in insult, see Plutarch, *Lacaenarum apophthegmata* 4 (*Moralia* 241B). See the remarkable photographs in Irenäus Eibl-Eibesfeldt, "The Myth of the Aggression-Free Hunter and Gatherer Society," in *Primate Aggression, Territoriality, and Xenophobia*, ed. Ralph B. Hoolaway, New York, 1974, pp. 452–454, and the story told by Nisa in Marjorie Shostak's *Nisa: The Life and Words of a !Kung Woman*, Cambridge, Mass., 1987, p. 259. In Paul Verhoeven's movie *Basic Instinct* (1992), the character played by Sharon Stone, indignant at being questioned, aggressively exposes herself during her police interrogation.

130. *auxit invidiam praeclaro exemplo femina Ligur, quae filio abdito, cum simul pecuniam occultari milites credidissent eoque per cruciatus interrogarent ubi filium occuleret, uterum ostendens latere respondit, nec ullis deinde terroribus aut morte constantiam vocis egregiae mutavit.*

ness, Agrippina bared her womb to the soldiers sent by Nero to slay her (Tacitus, *Annales* 14.8).[131] Seneca's Hecuba commands the distraught and defeated Trojan women to strip in anticipation of their violation. To quote Ahl's wonderful translation, "Open your dresses, bare your arms, knot the sleeves around your thighs, let your legs give open access to your wombs. There is no chastity when you're a slave; you wear a veil for marriage, not for rape!" (*Troades* 88–91).[132]

Voluntarily exposing oneself was a powerful act in that it always exposed the naked will. One might even say it *forged* the will.[133] When nothing protected his entrails save the spears stuck in his bones, Lucan's Scaeva blasted the soldiers of Pompey: "Why, fools, are you wasting your light javelins and arrows? They can never reach my vital powers!" (*Bellum civile* 6.196–197).[134] The more of himself Scaeva exposed, the less protection he afforded himself, the greater the *animus* revealed.

Lucretia became not less but more invigorated when she was violated and confessed it.[135] The confession of the violation subsumed even the violation in an act

---

131. *iam in mortem centurioni ferrum destringenti protendens uterum 'ventrem feri' exclamavit multisque vulneribus confecta est.* Cf. Pseudo-Seneca, *Octavia* 369–372.

132. *veste remissa substrnge sinus*
     uteroque tenus pateant artus
     cui coniugio pectora velas
     captive pudor?

For an ancient Greek parallel, see Michael N. Nagler, "Towards a Generative View of the Oral Formula," *Transactions and Proceedings of the American Philological Association* 98 (1967): 269–311, and Paul Friedrich, "Sanity and the Myth of Honor," *Ethos* 5 (1977): 281–305. For the notion of cutting off one's nose to spite the other's face, see Barton, "Savage Miracles: The Redemption of Lost Honor in Roman Society and the Sacrament of the Gladiator and the Martyr," *Representations* 45 (winter 1994): 49–50; A. W. Lintott, *Violence in Republican Rome*, Oxford, 1968, p. 16 (on *immitere/ summittere capillos*, the Roman practice of allowing the hair to grow long and disheveled, and wearing dirty or shabby clothes to shame another). Cf. J. M. Kelly, *Roman Litigation*, Oxford, 1966, pp. 49–50. M. P. Baumgartner relates certain practices of self-mutilation in contemporary American prisons to Indian "sitting dharma" and Irish forms of fasting and the "dirty protest" of the IRA hunger strikers ("Social Control from Below," in *Toward a General Theory of Social Control*, ed. Donald Black, vol. 1, Orlando, 1984, esp. pp. 317–18, 330–331).

133. I direct the reader to Peter Cattaneo's brilliant movie *The Full Monty* (1997), in which the protagonists, after enduring a long series of destructive humiliations, redeem their honor in a daring act of self-exposure and self-humiliation.

134. *Quid nunc, vaesani, iaculis levibusve sagittis / perditis haesuros numquam vitalibus ictus?* For the Jewish version of Scaeva, see Eleazar at Jotopata: "He leapt down and, seizing the head of the battering ram under the noses of the enemy, carried it back to the wall without turning a hair. A target now for all his foes, and with no armor to protect his body from the rain of missiles, he was pierced by five shafts; but, paying not the slightest regard to them, he climbed the wall and stood there for all to admire" (Josephus, *Bellum Iudaicum* 3.229–31). Compare the thrilling death scene of the Japanese hero Benkei in the tales of Yoshitsune. His will is so fierce that he is still standing, defiantly exposing himself to the missiles of the enemy, long after he is dead and defenseless (*Yoshitsune: A Fifteenth-Century Japanese Chronicle*, trans. Helen Craig McCullough, Tokyo, 1966, p. 288).

135. Cf. Ovid's mistress in the *Amores* 3.14.

of will. When Lucretia announced that she had been raped, her confession became an act of defiance, a way of despising her degradation.[136] So the ravaged Philomela threatened her tormenter: "Casting shame aside, I myself would tell the world what you have done. If I ever have the chance, I will go amongst the people and tell it." (Ovid, *Metamorphoses* 6.544–548).[137] Before the Etruscan chieftain Porsena can even begin torturing the Roman Mucius into confessing, he professes: "I am a Roman, my name is Mucius. I came, an enemy, to kill mine enemy" (Livy 2.12.9).[138]

In Sextus Propertius, the man "diseased with love" is willing to submit to a cruel cauterization, the agony of knife and fire—provided he is allowed the liberty to speak as his anger wills him to. The lover's confession of anger would be a relief, a sort of exorcism or purification, worth the price of the torture (1.1.27–28).[139]

"I not only confess, I profess!" *(hic ego non solum confiteor, verum etiam profiteor)* Cicero declares in a fragment preserved by Nonius Marcellus (vol. 3, p. 700, Lindsay ed.). In the *Pro Caecina*, Cicero patterns his opponent's response to the pressure to confess on that of the man who confesses with a readiness that suggests that he is not merely confessing but actually professing (9.24).[140] The tribune and conspirator Subrius Flavus, when pressed, "embraced the glory of confession" *(confessionis gloriam amplexus)*. Asked by Nero why he had joined the conspiracy against the emperor, he replied unapologetically, "I hated you," and proceeded to an outspoken attack on Nero as the murderer of his mother and sister, a charioteer, an actor, and an arsonist (Tacitus, *Annales* 15. 67). It is in this spirit that the "demented" Christians stubbornly, aggressively, and repeatedly confessed to the Roman governor Pliny, rejecting his mercy (*Epistulae* 10.96.3–4).[141]

---

136. There is willful aggression in Ovid's confession and submission to Love (*En ego confiteor!* [*Amores* 1.2.19]). It is more exhibitionism than shame. Like the deliberate blush, confession and begging for mercy could be a form of cynical manipulation. Consider Paris's begging mercy from Helen (Ovid, *Heroides* 16).

137. *ipsa pudore*
proiecto tua facta loquar: si copia detur,
in populos veniam: si silvis clausa tenebor
implebo silvas et conscia saxa movebo;
audiet haec aether et si deus ullus in illo est!

Compare Ovid's lover, who threatens to confess his adultery aloud in public if his mistress allows her husband to kiss her at a dinner party (*Amores* 1.4.38–40).

138. *"Romanus sum,"* inquit, *"civis, C. Mucium vocant. Hostis hostem occidere volui."* Notice the assertion of equality. One can compare the degraded Laberius's challenge to Caesar: "He must fear many whom many fear" *(necesse est multos timeat quem multi timent* [Macrobius, *Saturnalia* 2.7.4]).

139. *fortiter et ferrum patiemur et ignes, / sit modo libertas quae velit ira loqui.* But if he would not be able to speak as he willed, then he is unwilling to endure it.

140. *quid confitetur, atque ita libenter confitetur, ut non solum fateri sed etiam profiteri videatur?*

141. "I have asked them in person whether or not they were Christians. To those who confessed, I repeated the question a second and third time, threatening them with punishment. Those who persisted, I ordered to be led out to execution; for, whatever it is that they are confessing, their tenacious

If confession was the act of a broken will and the loss of one's spirit, profession could be evidence of both aggressiveness and sincerity, sincerity being the positive, the vivifying version of foolish self-exposure.[142] Vibulenus Agrippa, having been condemned to death by Tiberius in 36 C.E., was both aggressive and "sincere" when he drank his lethal dose of poison in full view of the senate (Tacitus, *Annales* 6.40).[143] Everything that perfect Cato did was *amabile, conspicuum, mirabile,* exposing himself and putting his life to the test (*obtulit in discrimen vitam suam* [Cicero, *Pro Sestio* 28.61]). Boundaries and limits defined and delineated one, but radical presence was unbounded; radical presence was "sincere" in the sense that it was exposed and defenseless. This radical defenselessness could, paradoxically, cloak the naked soul in an aura of privacy in the same way that the brutal exposure of Hawthorne's Hester Prynne on the scaffold acted as a sort of apotheosis, revealing to the audience only an enigmatic person possessing a great secret.[144]

Finally, and ultimately, confession could be a revelation, an apotheosis. "My gracious mother, never before so brilliant to behold, offered herself to my eyes, in pure radiance gleaming through the night, confessing herself a goddess—in beauty and stature such as she is wont to appear to the lords of heaven" (*Aeneis* 2.589–591).[145] Compare Ovid: "And now the god, having put off the deceptive

---

and inflexible obstinacy ought to be punished" (*Interrogavi ipsos an essent Christiani. confitentes iterum ac tertio interrogavi supplicium minatus. perseverantes duci iussi. Neque enim dubitabam, qualemque esset quod faterentur, pertinaciam certe et inflexibilem obstinationem debere puniri*). "Quegli imputati confessavano troppo, confessavano reiteratamente, confessavano testardamente sempre la stessa cosa, anche quando doveva apparire chiaro che il magistrato avrebbe preferito sentirsi dare risposte diverse" (Giuliana Lanata, "Confessione o professione?? Il dossier degli Atti dei Martiri," in *L'aveu: Antiquité et Moyen Age,* Rome, 1986, p. 135). Compare Minucius Felix: "Our rejection of the remnants of sacrifice and cups of the libations is not a confession of fear but an assertion of true liberty" (*quod vero sacrificiorum reliquias et pocula delibata contemnimus, non confessio timoris, sed verae libertatis adsertio* [*Octavius* 38.1]).

142. Speaking *simplicissime* was valued by the Romans. See Tacitus, *Historia* 1.15. The Japanese, as concerned as the Romans to preserve a secret self, nevertheless, like the Romans, admired the complete vulnerability and exposure of the sincere. See chapter 3, pp. 78–79.

143. Cf. Suetonius, *Tiberius* 61.4; Dio 58.21.4.

144. Compare Jerome's description of the penitent noble Roman matron Fabiola, who, publicly confessing herself guilty (of a second marriage), exhibited herself in the porch of the Lateran with hair unbound, face livid and swollen with weeping, and neck and hands unwashed. Fabiola incited the wonder of Jerome, who declared that such tears and lamentations would cleanse the soul from any sin (*errorem publice fateretur ... Quae peccata fletus iste non purget? quas inveteratas maculas haec lamenta non abluant? Petrus trinam negationem trina confessione delevit* [Jerome, *Epistulae ad Oceanum* 77.4 = *Epistulae,* J. Labourt ed., vol. 4, Paris, 1954]). Cf. Henry Charles Lea, *A History of Auricular Confession and Indulgences in the Latin Church,* vol. 1, Philadelphia, 1896, p. 21. So Jean-Jacques Rousseau, by the admissions and the painful story of his public exposure and humiliation that introduce the *Confessions,* disarms his readers and creates an impression of courage, candor, and sincerity.

145. *cum mihi se, non ante oculis tam clara videndam / obtulit et pura per noctem in luce refulsit / alma parens, confessa deam qualisque videri caelicoles et quanta solet.*

image of the bull, confessed himself, and reached the fields of Crete" (Ovid, *Metamorphoses* 3.1–2).[146]

CONCLUSIONS: REMEDIAL SPEECH

Being indebted to, being liable to punishment by, being at the mercy of, being subservient to, and cringing before are all distilled into the wonderful Latin word *obnoxius*. For us, it is only the failure to repay a debt that invokes any feeling of guilt, liability, or servility; but for the Romans, it was the debt itself that humiliated and chained one.[147] "To accept a benefit, according to Publilius Syrus, "is to sell your freedom" (48, Friedrich ed.).[148] To owe one's life to someone was an almost unbearable burden for a Roman, whether a slave or an aristocrat. As Jasper Griffin explains, to be beholden to someone more powerful made the Roman feel like a *meretrix*, a prostitute. The benefits of a great man made you feel cheap, worthless, embarrassed, a sponger.[149] Seneca warns his fellow Romans that continually reminding a man of the services you have rendered him—and so of the debt he owes you—crushes his spirit (*lacerat animum et premit frequens meritorum commemoratio* [*De beneficiis* 2.11.1]). He describes the man who, having been saved from the proscriptions of Octavian by a friend of the latter, exclaims, when faced with the arrogance of his benefactor: "'Give me back to Caesar!' 'I saved you. I snatched you from death.' 'Your service, if I remember it of my own free will, is truly life; if I remember it at yours, it is death.... If I had had to march [as a captive] in a triumph, I would have had to march only once!'" (*De beneficiis* 2.11.1).[150] Caesar was murdered because, according to Florus, "his very power to convey benefits was oppressive to free men" (2.13.92).[151]

One hated to live at the sufferance of another; but one always lived at the sufferance of one's *pater*.[152] When you were a helpless, voiceless infant, you lived be-

---

146. *Iamque deus posita fallacis imagine tauri / se confessus erat Dictaeque rura tenebat.*

147. I agree with those who argue that it was not the failure to repay the debt that enslaved the *nexus* but the debt itself. See Georges Dumézil, *Mitra-Varuna*, trans. Derek Coltman, New York, [1948] 1980, pp. 99–104; Jacques Imbert, "'*Fides*' et '*Nexum*,'" *Studi in onore di Vincenzo Arangio-Ruiz*, Naples, 1952; Moses Finley, "Debt Bondage and the Problem of Slavery," *Economy and Society in Ancient Greece*, Middlesex, England, 1981, esp. p. 158. Veyne, speaking of the benefits bestowed by the emperors on provincials: "Les cadeaux de l'étranger peuvent être des symboles de dépendance...acceptation a la signification d'une promesse d'obéissance" (*Le pain et le cirque*, p. 229).

148. *Beneficium accipere libertatem est vendere.*

149. "Augustus and the Poets," p. 196, cf. 203–204.

150. "*Ego te servavi, ego eripui morti.*" "*Istud, si meo arbitrio memini, vita est: si tuo mors est.*" ... "*Semel in triumpho deductus essem!*" Cf. Lendon, *Empire of Honour*, p. 69. "A trifling debt makes a debtor, a large one makes an enemy" (*Leve aes alienum debitorem facit, grave inimicum* [Seneca, *Epistulae* 19.11]). For Romans hating to be obligated by benefits, see also Cicero, *Pro Plancio* 30.73.

151. *Quippe clementiam principis vicit invidia, gravisque erat liberis ipsa beneficiorum potentia.*

152. Here it is important to remember that *pater* and *mater* were titles rather than biological functions: one could be a *pater* without having children. In the same way that *virtus* evolves into "manli-

cause your father willed it, you lived because of his mercy and his love. You could never, with honor, escape that particular debt. But one could turn slavery into sonship by embracing the glory of *obsequium,* by confessing to the father and asking for indulgence. (It remained infinitely preferable to be a son than a slave.) If the emperor monopolized the title *pater patriae,* it was with the collaboration of his subjects. The Roman people conspired in the exaltation of the great renegade males because it allowed them to save something of their honor.[153] Paradoxically, it was because Rome had such a Spartan code of valor, and not because the Romans had lost all sense of shame, that they slipped so very quickly into fawning sycophancy.[154] They got on their knees to a father in a desperate effort to avoid getting on their knees to a conqueror.

When the youthful Cicero began speaking in a world dominated by the lethally dangerous Sulla, he pleaded indulgence for his youth *(ignosci adulescentiae meae).* Why had he and not older and more important men risen to defend Roscius? The words of the more august, he explained, were too highly charged for them to speak. "No word of theirs can pass unnoticed, owing to their rank and dignity, and no rashness of speech can be allowed in their case owing to their age and ripe experience; whereas, if I speak too freely, my words will either be ignored, because I have not yet entered public life, or pardoned owing to my youth" (Cicero, *Pro Roscio Amerino* 1.1–3).[155] To redeem his honor, the elderly ex-consul Cicero resumed the strategy of the youth, begging indulgence of a father. In the year after the assassination of Julius Caesar, Brutus scolded Cicero: "You thank Octavian on behalf of the Republic ever so submissively and abjectly *(tam suppliciter ac demisse)....* Acknowledge what you have said, and deny that these are the prayers that a servant addresses to a king!" *(Ad Brutum* 25.1 [= 1.16.1]).[156] But

---

ness," *pater* evolved into "father." The Romans described by Orosius in the fourth book of his *Historiae adversus paganos* gave a name to the manifestation of a particular power or energy; the Roman gods did not preexist the manifestation of their power. Similarly, it was the power of the *pater* (the *ius vitae necisque*), like the effective energy of the *vir,* that came first, that "entitled" him.

153. See Alföldi, *Der Vater des Vaterlandes* p. 96.

154. In reading, over the years, about the American warrior chiefs Crazy Horse, Pontiac, Chief Joseph, and Osceola, I have been struck with the radical change in their behavior after their final defeat. Whatever else they were fighting for, they were fighting for their spirits and so they would, like wild horses, continue fighting until totally broken and exhausted. But once defeated, they were, like the Roman aristocrat, defeated forever and docile, so heartbreakingly so that it is hard to imagine they had ever fought.

155. *ceterorum neque dictum obscurum potest esse propter nobilitatem et amplitudinem neque temere dicto concedi propter aetatem et prudentiam: ego si quid liberius dixero, vel occultum esse, propterea quo nondum ad rem publicam accessi, vel ignosci adulescentiae poterit.*

156. *Sic enim illi gratias agis de re publica, tam suppliciter ac demisse.... verba tua recognosce et aude negare servientis adversus regem istas esse preces!*

Cicero was attempting to convert ignominious groveling into honorable homage.[157] He knew, just as Brutus did, what the alternatives were. In the trenchant words of Walter Burkert, "Worship means exalting the superiors to whom we bend in veneration; and the higher they are raised the less we are forced to bow down ourselves."[158]

Augustus was shown on contemporary coins extending a hand to raise the suppliant Republic from its knees.[159] It was an image, simultaneously, of salvation and degradation. Humiliation was the price of salvation. Henceforward the spirit, the soul, would be a gift that came from outside. It would no longer be made in the contest, no longer realized in effort, no longer earned by labor, certainly no longer deserved, but allowed and suffered by the father.[160] So the spirit of Apuleius's Lucius, redeemed after long suffering (inflicted by Isis) has its source no longer in his own (broken) will but in that of merciful Isis, his savior. Henceforth, so long as Lucius demonstrates total obedience, devotion, and gratitude, Isis will guarantee his soul and speech. The price of Lucius's life in this world and the next will be, henceforward, gratitude.[161] How, Seneca asks, does one attain old age in the court of a king? "By accepting the injury and saying 'Thank you'" (*De ira* 2.33.2).[162]

The Emperor's *clementia* made his subjects guilty.[163] It convicted those he pardoned. With the fall of the Republic, the Romans, like Josephus and the Jews

157. According to Paul Chodoff, in his discussion of the "confessions" of American soldiers and pilots by the Chinese during the Korean War, the confession often constituted a "conversion," after which the confessed not only ceased to resist but began to cooperate enthusiastically ("Effects of Extreme Coercive and Oppressive Forces," pp. 385, 388–392). Similarly, in Rome, to confess might imply a sacrifice of will or a change of conviction.

158. *Creation of the Sacred*, p. 91.

159. For the aureus of C. Lentulus (12 B.C.E.), see Paul Zanker, *The Power of Images in the Age of Augustus*, trans. Alan Shapiro, Ann Arbor, 1988, p. 91. For other images of the emperor extending his hand to the suppliant, see Richard Brilliant, *Gesture and Rank in Roman Art*, New Haven, 1963, pp. 74, 124, 150; Freyburger, "Supplication grecque et supplication romaine," *Latomus* 4 (1988): 517, 520–521.

160. One result of this shift in Roman thought is manifest in modern Western culture: a prisoner of war, a "victim," can be an honorable person, because our souls are ontological rather than existential. We imagine that they are not a product or creation of our will, and so they are untouched by defeat; or, rather, our souls are not at stake in our victory or defeat. Our spirits can be detached from our persons. The difference between ancient Roman and modern Western concepts of the prisoner of war resembles that between the Japanese and British attitudes in Nagisa Oshima's brilliant film *Merry Christmas, Mr. Lawrence* (1983).

161. Lucius, in return for his salvation, will owe assiduous obedience to Isis all of his life (*Metamorphoses* 11, esp 11.6).

162. *Cum illum quidam interrogaret, quomodo rarissimam rem in aula consecutus esset, senectutem: "iniurias," inquit, "accipiendo et gratias agendo."*

163. See Eugeniusz Konik, "*Clementia Caesaris* als System der Unterwerfung der Beseigten," in *Forms of Control and Subordination in Antiquity*, ed. Toru Yuge and Masaoki Doi, Leiden, 1988, pp. 226–238.

whom the Romans conquered—like all subject peoples, if they were to live in a world where mercy reigned—had to learn to blame themselves. They had to become sinners. *Peccavimus omnes,* Seneca declares in his essay on the clemency of the king (*De clementia* 1.6.3). "Consider," he says, "how great would be the loneliness and the desolation of Rome if none should be left but those whom a strict judge would acquit" (*De clementia* 1.6.1).[164] "Who is the man so bold as to profess himself innocent by every law?" (*De ira* 2.28.2)[165] "We have been punished. Let us consider not what we suffer, but what we have done. Let us deliberate on our past. If we are frank with ourselves, we will impose on ourselves a still stiffer fine" (*De ira* 2.27.4).[166]

If the Roman emperor based his power on his role as *pater patriae,* if the Romans based their empire on the notion of *patrocinium,* it was because, in the Roman mind, no other relation allowed the paradoxical coexistence of the soul with total unconditional surrender.[167] It was an all-powerful God, who could be a stern judge but who, instead, acted as a merciful father, a God who could maintain his honor and still respect the suppliant, that allowed for the Pauline positive vision of the Christian as suppliant and "*confessus.*"[168] Lactantius says of the Christian God: "He alone should be called *pater* who has the true and perpetual power of life and death" (*solus pater vocandus est qui habet vitae ac necis veram et perpetuam potestatem* [*Di-*

---

164. *quanta solitudo ac vastitas futura sit, si nihil relinquitur, nisi quod iudex severus absolverit.*

165. *Quis est iste qui se profitetur omnibus legibus innocentem?* Again: "If everyone with a depraved and evil nature should be punished, then no one would be exempt from punishment" (*Si puniendus est cuicumque pravum maleficiumque ingenium est, poena neminem excipiet* [*De ira* 2.31.8]).

166. *Adfecti sumus poena: succurrat non tantum quod patiamur sed quid fecerimus, in consilium de vita nostra mittamur; si modo verum ipsi nobis dicere voluerimus pluris litem nostram aestimabimus.* "Even if you have done no wrong, you are capable of it" (*etiam si nihil mali fecisti, potes facere* [*De ira* 3.26.5]). Cf. 2.28.1,3,8, 3.26.4.

167. For the notion of *patrocinium orbis,* see Cicero, *De officiis* 2.8.27; Dio 53.18.3; Ernst Badian, *Foreign Clientelae, 264–70 B.C.,* Oxford, 1958; Hermann Strassburger, "Poseidonius on Problems of the Roman Empire," *Journal of Roman Studies* 55 (1965): 40–53, p. 45; Friedrich Klingner, "Vergil und die römische Idee des Friedens," in *Römische Geisteswelt: Essays zur lateinischen Literatur,* Stuttgart, 1979, pp. 614–644; N.M. Horsfall, "Virgil, History and the Roman Tradition," *Prudentia* 8 (1976): 73–89; Erich Gruen, *The Hellenistic World and the Coming of Rome,* Berkeley, 1984, pp. 158–200. As Alföldi points out, beginning with Augustus the emperor increasingly becomes the father and savior not just of Rome, but of the world (*Der Vater des Vaterlandes,* pp. 71–73).

168. For the importance, during the first three centuries of Christianity, of the theme of *misericordia divina* and its association with the *deprecatio* of the weeping penitent, abased in sackcloth and ashes, see H. Pétré, "*Misericordia:* Histoire du mot et de l'idée du paganisme au christianisme," *Revue des études latines* 12 (1934): 380–82. There were, similarly, all-powerful and merciful female deities: "Nurturing Venus, we two tearfully entreat you, as on our knees and clasping this altar of yours, to receive us into your custody and preserve us" (*Venus alma, ambae te obsecramus / aram amplexantes hanc tuam lacrumantes, genibus nixa, / nos in custodiam tuam ut recipias et tutere* [Plautus, *Rudens* 694–696]). Compare Apuleius's merciful Isis, "Parent of the natural world, mistress of every element" (*rerum naturae parens, elementorum omnium domina),* to whom the broken Lucius surrenders (*Metamorphoses* 11.5).

vinae institutiones 4.4.11]).[169] But I cannot emphasize enough that the soul that was redeemed was the very inverse of the ancient Roman soul; the *animus* that was "saved" by the Emperor, by Isis, or by the Christian God filled a vessel that, like the flayed skin of Marsyas, had been emptied of its will.[170]

Given the history of Roman confession, its connections to the breaking of the will, the loss of the voice, and mimesis, it is not surprising that a millennium later, at the time of the Fourth Lateran Council of 1215, auricular confession became an obligation, simultaneously with both the elevation of torture as the "queen of proofs" *(regina probationum)* and the start of the catechetical movement. Torture, confession, and the rote responses of the catechism were all forms of discipline based on the same principle of unconditional surrender of the spirit demonstrated by verbal submission and echoing. And what made torture the "queen of proofs" was the notion that truth, that reality was no longer created in the daily give-and-take of social and psychological life but arose in the will of an all-powerful God.

One could refuse salvation, save the spirit, and spit out one's tongue in the face of power. But there was still a third strategy: When Amphitryon threatened to cut the tongue of his slave Sosia, the latter replied, "I am yours. Therefore, whatever you do I accommodate myself to and desire. However, there is no one who can in any way deter me from saying what was done here" *(Amphitruo* 557–560).[171]

We have the notion that confession is good for the spirit; that it is cleansing, purifying. We draw a clear distinction between the humiliating confessions of the tortured soldier or political prisoner and the salutary confessions of the sinner to her priest or the patient to his psychoanalyst. The first is involuntary, the second voluntary; the first the rupture, the second the redemption of the spirit.[172] But I have attempted to show that our positive and purifying "confession" *is* the breaking of the spirit as the Romans understood it, metamorphosed into the sinner confessing to the father, while the Roman's "profession" was, like Freud's talking

---

169. See Thomas, *"Vitae necisque potestas,"* in *Du châtiment dans la Cité: Supplice corporels et peine de mort dans le monde antique, collection de l'École française de Rome,* no. 79, Rome, 1984, 499–548, p. 508.

170. This is a "soul" not unlike that described by Michel Foucault: "It is produced permanently around, on, and within the body by the functioning of a power that is exercised on those punished—and, in a more general way, on those one supervises, trains and corrects, over madmen, children, at home and at school, the colonized, over those who are stuck at a machine and supervised for the rest of their lives" *(Discipline and Punish: The Birth of the Prison,* trans. Alan Sheridan, New York, 1979, p. 29).

171. *Tuos sum,*
   proinde ut commodumst et lubet quidque facias
   tamen quin loquar haec uti facta est hic,
   numquam ullo modo me potes deterrere.

172. In the first volume of *The History of Sexuality,* Foucault notes the way in which these two forms of confession produce the modern compulsion to "say everything," to leave nothing unsaid and to abjure the hidden and secret self. But while the confession and the profession both produce a self-exposing, self-violating speech, their motivations are inversions of one another.

cure, a reaction against the breaking of the spirit and a refusal to assume the guilt that would justify the submission.[173]

The new value put on confession, submission, and the plea for mercy were, then, radical inversions of the ancient warrior values of the Romans. Nevertheless, this revaluation of values did not drive out the power or the memory of those old values, which continued to assert themselves mightily. And even the inversions were, in one aspect, desperate attempts to preserve the ancient Roman ideals of honor when the conditions that had fostered them were hopelessly gone.

173. But, as Helen Block Lewis and Thomas Scheff have pointed out, the pressure on an unwilling subject to speak in a "therapeutic" situation can be felt as an attempt to break the spirit and compel one to confess.

PART THREE

On the Wire

The Experience of Shame in Ancient Rome

The very law that condemned her...held her up through the terrible ordeal of her ignominy.
NATHANIEL HAWTHORNE, *THE SCARLET LETTER*

To have a sense of honor in ancient Rome was to have a sense of shame. Latin shame—*pudor*—embraced a set of finely calibrated and counterpoised emotions ranged along a balance bar pivoting on the fulcrum of the blush. Every man or woman of honor in ancient Rome walked a high wire, simultaneously supported and aggravated by the great ballast-weight of these emotions.

Shame was a restless and relentless agitation, a sort of mild vertigo. Shame was, again, a skill, a discipline that allowed one to sway rather than stagger over the abyss that was inexpiable dishonor. To move, to live while balancing this burden required energy, grace, and skills finely honed in the course of a lifetime.[1] A fall meant disgrace, the extremes of autonomy and dependency: isolation and dissolution.

The ancient Romans did not distinguish a passive, defensive shame from an active, aggressive honor.[2] Nor did they, as some modern Mediterraneanists (such

---

1. "Ganz allgemein ist die echte Scham stets auf die Empfindung eines positiven Selbstwertes aufgebaut" (Scheler, "Der 'Ort' des Schamgefühls, und die Existenzweise des Menschen," *Gesammelte Werke,* vol. 10, Bern, 1957, p. 100. For Scheler, shame not only socializes but also plays an integral part in creating a functioning, unified sense of self. He points out that one's psyche and one's sense of shame collapse together [p. 113]).

2. Here are just a few of the many instances where Latin *pudor* might be translated into something close to our all-embracing "honor": Terence's father Micio: *pudore et liberalitate liberos / retinere satius esse credo quam metu (Adelphi* 57–58). *meus pudor, mea existimatio, mea dignitas in discrimen adducitur* (Pliny, *Epistulae* 2.9.1). Paris, having mocked Helen for her prudish *rusticitas,* replies: *rustica sim sane, dum non oblita pudoris* (Ovid, *Heroides* 17.13). *pudoris dignitas* (Petronius, *Satyricon* 106). *servare iudicum pudorem* (Quintilian, *Institutio oratoria* 11.1.78). Cf. Plautus, *Stichus* 322; Lucilius fr. 992, Krenkel ed.; Virgil, *Aeneis* 4.27.

as Jacob Black-Michaud or Bruce J. Malina) have done, reserve a positive honor for males and leave females with a negative, shame.[3] Rather, the force of Roman shame was, for both the soldier and the maiden, the sum of two complex sets of opposing drives and inhibitions.

On the one hand were the "orders" of shame: Roman *pudor* comprised the fear that inhibited one from transgressing one's bonds and the remorse that one felt as a result of transgressing. On the other hand were the "disorders" of shame; Roman *pudor* encompassed the more extreme and destabilizing emotions that "unhinged," that "offset," that alienated one human being from another: irremediable inadequacy and inexpiable guilt.

The socializing or integrating emotions of shame were those countervailing emotions that *could* be indulged or rectified; they could be satisfied, made right. Movement in one direction could be compensated for by movement in the other direction. The balance of these emotions allowed for the freedom of a person's being within the community.[4] The desocializing or disintegrating emotions of shame were those that could not be rectified. The impossibility of expiating one's sins or correcting one's inadequacies shattered one's equilibrium and the communal system of social reciprocities; if it did not result in suicide or self-exile, it could evoke shamelessness or erupt in the vendetta.

The *simultaneous* operation of these very different, apposed rather than opposed emotions constituted the Roman sense of shame. We have a tendency to think in antinomies. To understand Roman honor it is necessary to think in terms of balancing, of fluid continuities and reciprocities. For us, honor and shame, like autonomy and dependence, internality and externality, form abstract dichotomies.[5] For the ancient Roman, honor *was* shame, and shame demanded a deft and elegant movement be-

---

3. "Women have no honour. But they do have 'shame' in sexual modesty, the feminine counterpart of and complement to honour, which they and their menfolk must do their utmost to defend....But whereas honour is positive and cumulative, shame is negative, absolute,...cannot be increased and can be demonstrated, as it were, only in the breach" (Jacob Black Michaud, *Cohesive Force: Feud in the Mediterranean and the Middle East*, Oxford, 1975, p. 218). The simplicity of this binary dualism is effectively undermined by Unni Wikan in her article "Shame and Honour: A Contestable Pair," *Man* n.s. 19 (1984): 635–652. For an explanation of the principally negative associations of "shame," for modern Europeans, see Scheler, "Der 'Ort' des Schamgefühls," pp. 98–99.

4. For an excellent summary of the socializing effects of shame, see David Ausubel, "The Relationship between Shame and Guilt in the Socializing Process," *Psychological Review* 62 (1955): 378–390. See also Bruce J. Malina, *New Testament World: Insights from Cultural Anthropology*, Atlanta, 1981, pp. 44–45, and John Braithwaite, *Crime, Shame, and Reintegration*, Cambridge, 1989, pp. 71–83.

5. The distinctions between "shame cultures" and "guilt cultures" developed by the anthropologists Margaret Mead, Ruth Benedict, and Clyde Kluckhohn grew out of the tendency in Western thought to make a radical break between internal and external. Guilt was the response to standards that were internalized. Shame was the response to criticism or ridicule by others; it was externalized. "True shame cultures rely on external sanctions for good behavior, not, as true guilt cultures, on an internalized conviction of sin" (Benedict, *The Chrysanthemum and the Sword*, New York, 1946, p. 323). As Helen Merrell Lynd points out, these distinctions assume that guilt is somehow more internalized (and

tween inhibition and exhibition, contraction and expansion, dependence and autonomy.[6] At the same time, shame could precipitate a fatal disturbance of all systems of poise and balance. Roman shame kindled the spirit while it threatened to consume it.

Both the poised and the poisoned emotions of shame were expressed in the body. They were felt and seen on the core of one's social being, the face, the *imago animi*.[7] Even more particularly, they were manifested on the skin, the delicate and penetrable barrier through which the ancient Romans contacted the world and one another.[8] The *pudor* of interdependence was expressed, above all, in the blush. The disorders of shame were also expressed on the face, in the red, hard, brazen face that severed the ancient Romans from the world and one another.

The following chapters deal with what are, in many ways, the least dramatic but nevertheless the deepest levels of Roman honor, the molten core, the marrow in the bones of the Roman social structure. In the following chapters I attempt to trace the Romans' elaborate economy of shame. Because the basic patterns endured relatively unchanged throughout the entire period I discuss in this book, the analyses in these chapters appear more static and synoptic, more functional and less historicized than those in parts 1 and 2. The historical significance of these patterns is great, however, and I attempt to indicate this significance both in the conclusion to part 3 and in the general conclusion to the book.

---

therefore more refined, more "advanced") than shame, and that one would not feel shame if one were not exposed to the expressed scorn of others. The separation of shame from guilt also assumed a deep and basic separation of oneself from others and that others were related to oneself principally as critics and not as supporters or mirrors (*On Shame and the Search for Identity*, New York, 1956, p. 21). A different understanding of shame and guilt arises if the lines between internal and external are blurred or redrawn (as they must be when speaking of ancient Rome), and if the ways in which inhibition and transgression operate as a system, for the preservation of both the single person and the community, are reassessed. For critical reconsiderations of the early anthropological formulations of shame and guilt, see especially Millie R. Creighton, "Revisiting Shame and Guilt Cultures: A Forty-Year Pilgrimage," *Ethos* 18 (1990): 279–307. See also the works of the psychologist David Ausubel, the historian John Demos, and the criminologist John Braithwaite.

6. The ancient Greeks distinguished *aidos* from *aischyne*, as the French distinguish *pudeur* from *honte* and the Germans *Scham* from *Schande*. But the Romans, in a way that is important for understanding the reciprocal patterns of their thought, used the same words for both ranges of emotion.

7. Cicero, *Orator* 18.60; Seneca, *Epistulae* 11.10 *(animum ante se ferens vultus)*; Juvenal, *Satirae* 9.18–20. For Silvan S. Tomkins, "affect is primarily facial behavior" ("The Primary Site of the Affects: The Face," *Affect, Imagery, Consciousness*, vol. 1, New York, 1962, pp. 204–242). Cf. Tomkins, "Shame," in *The Many Faces of Shame*, ed. Donald L. Nathanson, New York, 1987, pp. 133–161. Seneca believed that, while anger was the most difficult emotion to hide, all strong emotions stamped themselves on the body, especially on the face. Lust and fear and boldness, indeed, all strong feelings, "moved" the face *(Nec ignoro ceteros quoque affectus vix occultari, libidinem metumque et audaciam dare sui signa et posse praenosci, neque enim ulla vehementior intrat concitatio, quae nihil moveat in vultu [De ira 1.1.7])*. At the same time, Seneca seems to say that the outward manifestations of all emotions except anger can be concealed (ibid. 1.1.5).

8. For the skin as mediating between the internal and external worlds, see Mark Gustafson, "'Inscripta in fronte': Penal Tattooing in Late Antiquity," *Classical Antiquity* 16 (1997), esp. p. 91.

CHAPTER SEVEN

The Poise of Shame

Shame is a discipline of great power.
CICERO, *DE REPUBLICA* 4.4.6[1]

Pudor and *verecundia* were the inhibiting emotions.[2] "Shame hesitates," *tardat pudor* (Catullus 61.79). "Shame impedes," *pudor praepedit* (Livy 9.6.4). "Shame blocks," *pudor opstat* (Juvenal *Satirae* 3.60).[3] *Pudor* was the shyness that caused one to draw back before another, the fear or respect that caused one to make way for another even when one was within one's rights, one's *libertas* or *ius*. *Pudor* caused the citizen to retreat before the consul's lictors.[4] It caused the worshiper to veil his or her head before the gods.[5] It caused Statius to give way to Virgil.[6]

Pudor was the emotion that constrained speech, that bridled the tongue.[7] "I'm too ashamed to say the other things that I saw him do," Plautus's Lydus declared, having caught his pupil Pistoclerus in the house of the courtesan Bacchis (*Bac-*

---

1. *magnam habet vim disciplina verecundiae.*

2. They were *impedimenta.* Cf. Scheler, "Der 'Ort' des Schamgefühls und die Existenzweise des Menschen," *Gesammelte Werke,* vol. 10, Bern, 1957, p. 88 and n. 1.

3. "It is the function of *verecundia* not to give offense" (*verecundiae* [*partes sunt*] *non offendere* [Cicero, *De officiis* 1.28.99]). *commemorationem verecundia impedivit* (Cicero, *Ad Atticum* 1.17).

4. The lictors walked in line before the magistrates to guarantee that the people made way for them. See Kübler, "*Lictor*," in Pauly-Wissowa, *Realencyclopädie der classischen Altertumswissenschaft,* vol. 13.1, Stuttgart, 1926, cols. 507–512, esp. 512. In a line from the poetic narrative of his consulship, Cicero expresses respect behavior as "ceding": *Cedant arma togae* (*De officiis* 1.22.77).

5. "Who is this man who dares to greet Aesculapius with an uncovered head?" (*Quis hic est qui operto capite Aesculapiam salutat?* [Plautus, *Curculio* 389]).

6. *Thebais* 12.816–817. According to Valerius Maximus, the people, made self-conscious by the gaze of Cato, blushed to call for (*postulare erubuit*) the mimes' customary nude dance at the Floralia of 55 B.C.E. (Valerius Maximus 2.10.8; cf. Seneca, *Epistulae* 97.8; Martial 1, *praefatio*).

7. *pudet dicere* (Terence, *Heautontimorumenos* 1041–1042). *muta pudens est* (Lucretius, *De rerum natura* 4.1164). *pudet dicere* (Cicero, *Pro Quinctio* 25.79). *dicere puduit* (Ovid, *Heroides* 4.10). *pudet effari* (Petronius, *Satyricon* 119.19). [*vox*] *in metu et verecundia contracta* (Quintilian, *Institutio oratoria* 11.3.64). Cf. Cicero, *Pro Quinctio* 11.39; Seneca, *Phaedra* 602–603.

chides 481).[8] Ovid's blushing Lucretia was cut short, in the narration of her violation, by shame (*Fasti* 2.815–824).[9] When Plutarch's Younger Cato scolded his loot-
ing cavalry, "All were silent out of shame and went away with downcast eyes"
(*Cato Minor* 65.3).[10] "I'm ashamed," Cicero says, "even to speak of shame" (*De legibus* 1.19.50).[11]

THE GENEROUS INHIBITION

Who steals another's modesty loses his own.
PUBLILIUS SYRUS 455, FRIEDRICH ED.[12]

I feel shame, therefore we exist.[13]

Shame was the ability, the willingness to be awed or intimidated by others.[14] It
was a kind of gift one gave to others; by withdrawing before another person or a
god, one augmented the portion of that person or god.[15]

The philosopher Max Scheler speaks eloquently of the *Beseelung*, the animation, the "ensouling" of others that we accomplish through our own shame, and
the *Entseelung*, the "desouling," the depriving others of their spirit effected by our
shamelessness.[16] We have the capacity to veil another with our own shame; we
can dress another's nakedness in an aura of chastity. In the locker room of my
gym there is an unwritten law: although the temptation is great, no woman ever
stares or even looks directly at the body of another woman. No woman remarks

8. *nam alia memorare quae illum facere vidi dispudet.* The soldiers of Vitellius, running amok in Rome,
were guilty of *inhonesta dictu,* things too shameful to say (Tacitus, *Historia* 2.93).

9. Cf. Ovid, *Metamorphoses* 9.515: *si pudor ora tenebit.*

10. The noisy and seditious crowd is shamed into silence before the man "weighty by reason of his
piety and services" (Virgil, *Aeneis* 1.151–53). When Antony retreated from Parthia, according to
Plutarch, he was so dejected by shame and melancholy that he was unable to make the customary
speech of encouragement to the army but sent Domitius Ahenobarbus to do it for him (*Antony* 40.5).

11. *pudet etiam loqui de pudicitia.*

12. *Pudorem alienum qui eripit perdit suum.*

13. The phenomenologists modified *cogito ergo sum* to *pudeo ergo sumus.* See Emmett Wilson Jr.,
"Shame and the Other: Reflections of the Theme of Shame in French Psychoanalysis," in *The Many
Faces of Shame,* ed. Donald L. Nathanson, New York, 1987, p. 169. Wilson discusses the especial impor-
tance of "intersubjectivity" for the philosophers Franz Brentano, Edmund Husserl, Max Scheler,
Jean-Paul Sartre, and Maurice Merleau-Ponty.

14. Scheler's *Verschüchterheit* ("Der 'Ort' des Schamgefühls," p. 88). " 'Shyness,' as the derivation of
the word indicates in several languages, is closely related to fear" (Charles Darwin, *The Expression of the
Emotions in Man and Animals,* Chicago, [1872] 1965, p. 330). According to the *Oxford Universal Dictionary,*
"shy" derives from the Teutonic root **skeuhw*—to fear, to terrify.

15. "*Cultus* und *verecundia* sind Synonyma zu *honos,*" Friedrich Klose, *Die Bedeutung von* honos *und*
honestas, Breslau, 1933, pp. 122–123; cf. pp. 24, 83. "*Dignitas* is the possession of an authority (or office)
meriting respect, honor and reverence" (*dignitas est alicuius honesta et cultu et honore et verecundia digna auctoritas* [Cicero, *De inventione* 2.166]).

16. "Der Ort des Schamgefühls," esp. pp. 87, 101.

on the body of another woman, either to compliment or disparage her. Dressed, we eagerly comment on and examine each other's clothing, but we glance at one another's naked bodies through a foggy haze. The secrets of any woman who enters the dressing room are safe. Every woman knows that her own honor, her integrity, is ultimately a product of this inhibition. This deliberate not-seeing of the naked critterliness of one another is an indulgence that we pass from one to another, from eye to eye.[17] The result of this shared self-discipline, this mutual *fides*, is a feeling of security, camaraderie, and freedom.[18] The woman who insists on privacy, who undresses behind a door, experiences only the privative aspects of that privacy, depriving herself of this gift.

As Scheler points out, one of the rewards for our own shame, for treating other persons and things with reverence, for restraining our own desire to look, to invade with our eyes, is that we find ourselves in a world with depth, in a world where the visible surface, the façade *(facies)* or mask *(persona)*, expresses an infinite profundity. "It is our reverence that first allows us to glimpse into the deep well of worth in the world, whereas shamelessness must ever content itself with a world whose value is 'skin deep.' "[19]

That the Romans, with their communal baths (and communal toilets), were subject to such temptations and inhibitions is suggested by the *apotropaia* on the walls of the baths that diverted the leering eye; by Seneca's and Martial's singling out for scathing ridicule those who, like Hostius Quadra, Cotta, Maternus, or Philomusus, went to the baths to look;[20] by the traditional sanctions against fathers bathing with sons and sons-in-law;[21] and by Petronius's hilarious scene in which

---

17. In the words of Unni Wikan, "The person's own honour, in the sense of value both in her own and other's eyes…requires that she or he honour others" ("Shame and Honour: A Contestable Pair," *Man* n.s. 19 [1984]: 641). Wikan explains that consciousness of the reciprocity of honor encourages Omani women to indulge and reincorporate the transgressors of their own stringent social code.

18. Anthropologists (such as Jean Briggs, Richard Lee, and Nurit Bird) studying band societies, where there is little privacy and humans are subject to relentless mutual surveillance, have often remarked on the respectful "civil inattention" they afford one another. See Robert Redfield, *The Primitive World and Its Transformations*, Harmondsworth, 1968, p. 32; Peter Wilson, *The Domestication of the Human Species*, New Haven, 1988, p. 27.

19. "[So]…lässt auch die Ehrfurcht erst die Werttiefe der Welt erblicken, wogegen der Ehrfurchtslose sich immer nur mit der Flächendimension ihrer Werte begnügen muss" ("Der 'Ort' des Schamgefühls," p. 101; cf. p. 87).

20. Seneca, *Naturales quaestiones* 1.16; Martial 1.96, 1.23, 11.63. For the dangers to bathers from the uninhibited eye, see Katherine M. D. Dunbabin, "*Baiarum grata voluptas*: Pleasures and Dangers of the Baths," *Papers of the British School at Rome* 57 (1989), esp. pp. 18, 33–46; John Clarke, "Hypersexual Black Men in Augustan Baths; Ideal Somatypes and Apotropaic Magic," in *Sexuality in Ancient Art*, ed. Natalie Kampen et al., Cambridge, 1996, pp. 184–198.

21. "According to our own customs, grown sons do not bathe with their fathers, nor sons-in-law with their fathers-in-law" (*Nostro quidem more cum parentibus puberes filii, cum soceris generi non lavantur* [Cicero, *De officiis* 1.35.129]). Cicero describes this inhibition as *verecundia*. Cf. Valerius Maximus 2.1.7; Plutarch, *Cato maior* 20.5. The Romans were much more sensitive than the Greeks about being naked:

the patrons of the bathhouse surround the irresistibly well-endowed Ascyltos to stare and applaud (*Satyricon* 92). According to Dio's Empress Livia, naked men were, to chaste women, not a bit different from statues. She said this, I should add, to save the lives of the men who, having accidentally encountered her while they were undressed, were to be put to death for this violation of her eyes (58.2.4).

Cicero remarks on the great honor that a jury paid to Metellus Numidicus, when the latter was brought to trial, by declining even to glance at his account books (*Ad Atticum* 1.16). "The whole jury averted their eyes from the tablets lest they seem to be in doubt concerning the veracity of their contents" (Valerius Maximus 2.10.1).[22] They showed Metellus deference by refusing to scrutinize him, by taking his word at face value. So one showed honor to the defenseless dead by dressing and decorating the corpse rather than exposing it to the eyes and abuse of the living. And so Tiberius upbraided the friends of Germanicus who exhibited the naked body of the dead prince (in order to reveal the traces of poisoning on the corpse). The emperor accused them of letting the vulgar touch Germanicus's dead body with their eyes *(contrectare vulgi oculis)*—and so violate and contaminate it (Tacitus, *Annales* 3.12.7).[23]

In Latin, the *verenda* were those parts of the body to be regarded with awe or reverence, the *pudenda* the parts to be protected by shame. The genitals were the "shameful" parts of the body only when the boundaries enforced by *pudor* were breached (which violation could be accomplished simply by staring or speaking). The person with a sense of shame was acutely aware of the potential for his or her most sacred parts to become the most shameful parts. As the social psychologist Kurt Riezler points out, "*Pudenda* and *veneranda* imply each other. Behind every *pudendum* is hidden a *venerandum.*"[24] The Romans were conscious of the paradox of the sacred; it was the shame that made the holy.[25]

"The original act of disgrace: to strip one's body naked before one's fellow citizens" (*flagiti principium est nudare inter cives corpore* [Cicero, *Tusculanae disputationes* 4.33.70]). See Larisa Bonfante, "Nudity as a Costume in Classical Art," *American Journal of Archaeology* 93 (1989): 543–570.

22. *totum consilium ab earum contemplatione oculos avertit, ne de aliqua re, quae in his relata erat, videretur dubitasse.*

23. Some things should not be seen. Hippolytus, having heard his stepmother Phaedra's shameful confession of love, reprimands the sun for enduring the sight (*Phaedra* 677–678). Catullus remarks of the vicious extravagance of Mamurra: "Who is able to watch this? Who can endure it—except the shameless, the voracious and the gambler?" (*Quis hoc potest videre, quis potest pati / nisi impudicus et vorax et aleo?* [29.1–2]). "Wanton Rome, will you look at this and bear it?" (*Cinaede Romulus, haec videbis et feres?* [29.5]).

24. "Comment on the Social Psychology of Shame," *American Journal of Sociology* 48 (1942–1943): 464. The genitals were *sanctissima pars corporis* (Cicero, *Post reditum in senatu* 5.11); the *viscus sacer* (*Corpus Inscriptionum Latinarum*, vol. 1.2, no. 2520.33; *pars tegenda* (*Priapea* 1.7; Ovid, *Metamorphoses* 13.479–80); *velanda* (Pliny, *Epistulae* 6.24.3); *secreta* (Ammianus Marcellinus 28.1.28). Cf. Isidore, *Etymologiae* 11.1.102, Lindsay ed; J. N. Adams, *The Latin Sexual Vocabulary*, Baltimore, 1982, p. 56.

25. To quote Nietzsche: "Shame exists wherever there is a 'mysterium,'" *Human, All Too Human*, trans. Marion Faber, Lincoln, Nebraska, 1984, p. 69 no. 100.

The persistence of this paradox helps to explain the gender split, in much modern thought, between a man's honor and a woman's shame. With reference to the Kabyle society of Algeria, Pierre Bourdieu explains, "A man should never be asked about his wife or sister: this is because woman is one of those shameful things (the Arabs say *lamra'ara*, 'woman is a shame') that one never mentions without apologizing and adding 'saving your respect,' and also because woman is for man the sacred thing above all others, as is shown by the phrase customarily used in pledging an oath: 'May my wife be taboo to me'...or 'may my house be taboo' ('if I fail to do such-and-such')."[26] "The Elder Cato used to say," according to Plutarch, "that the man who struck his wife or child laid violent hands on the holiest of things" *(tois hagiotatois hierois prospherein tas cheiras [Cato maior 20.1]).* Romulus, Plutarch also observed, legislated a series of prohibitions against violating the eyes, ears, and space of women in order to honor them *(eis timen* [loc. cit.]).[27] By not uttering any indecent word in their hearing, by not appearing naked in their sight, and by giving them the right of way in the street, men could insure themselves against the shame with which women threatened them. They could, by their inhibition, make the *pudenda* the *veneranda (Romulus* 20.3).[28]

Concomitantly, *reverentia* or *observantia* could be not only an inhibition in the eyes but an "observing," a particularly accepting or affirming look. Cicero speaks of *"observantia* by which we revere and cultivate those whom we recognize as preceding us in age or wisdom or honor or in any form of worthiness" *(De inventione* 2.66).[29] In Livy's extended account of the humiliation of the Roman army at the Caudine Forks, the Capuan allies try to reanimate the deeply dispirited Roman soldiers, who had arisen from the defile like zombies from a crypt, with their *voltus benigni,* their healing, embracing, annealing gazes. Livy sharply contrasts the way the Capuans looked at the Romans with the way the victorious Samnites, with

---

26. "The Sense of Honor," *Algeria 1960,* trans. Richard Nice, Cambridge, 1979, pp. 124–125. Women are, in the words of Anton Blok, "the most precious and most vulnerable part of the patrimony of men" ("Rams and Billy-Goats: A Key to the Mediterranean Code of Honour," *Man* n.s. 16 [1981]: 434).

27. Cf. Valerius Maximus 2.1.5; Festus-Paulus p. 142, Lindsay ed. For the inviolability and privileges of *matronae,* see Amy Richlin, "Carrying Water in a Sieve: Class and the Body in Roman Women's Religion," in *Women and Goddess Traditions in Antiquity and Today,* ed. Karen L. King, Minneapolis, 1997, pp. 346–350.

28. It is ironic that some of the "erasure" of women from our sources comes not from contempt but from respect. The Romans did not mention the name of a proper woman except *causa honoris,* that is, unless the intention to honor her was very clear. Otherwise, to mention her name was to besmirch it. See Cicero's comments on the expression *praefari honorem (= dicere honorem)* that polite Romans used to excuse mention of *aliquid de Aurelia or Lollia (Ad familiares* 9.22.4). Cicero is not embarrassed, for instance, to name the dishonorable women who were involved sexually with Verres, but he declines to mention the Roman matrons *(In Verrem* 5.13.34).

29. *observantia, per quam aetate aut sapientia aut honore aut aliqua dignitate antecedentes reveremur et colimus.* For the benevolent, kindly gaze, see also Seneca, *De clementia* 1.19.8.

their scornful *voltus superbi*, regarded the Roman soldiers who went under the yoke and through the gauntlet of their taunts and blows (9.6.8, 9.5.8).[30]

SHAME AND COMMITMENT

Shame was the emotion of relatedness. One had shame before someone (or the thought of someone) to whom one wished to be bound, with whom one wished to be associated or identified: the gods,[31] one's ancestors or elders,[32] one's parents,[33] one's master,[34] one's spouse,[35] one's siblings,[36] one's fellow citizens,[37] one's friends,[38] one's lover,[39] or one's children.[40] Conversely, a bond or shared identity awakened

30. In Tim Robbins's 1995 film *Dead Man Walking*, Sister Helen Prejean is determined to counteract the "desouling" looks of many of the witnesses of the execution with her own "ensouling" look. She bids the doomed man, in the seconds before his death, to keep his eyes focused on her own. Her look admits, accepts, respects.

31. *divum pudor* (Silius, *Punica* 1.58). *deum me hercle atque hominum pudet* (Plautus, *Trinummus* 912). *pudet deorum hominumque* (Livy 3.19.7). *parentis, vitrici, deorum verecundia* (Livy 39.11.2).

32. According to Cicero, it is the part of the young to show deference to their elders (*est igitur adulescentis maiores natu vereri* [*De officiis* 1.34.122]). Cf. Juvenal, *Satirae* 13.54–59; Gellius, *Noctes Atticae* 2.15.1–2; Stanley F. Bonner, *Education in Ancient Rome*, Berkeley, 1977, pp. 6–7. For the close relationship of *pudor* and *verecundia* to *pietas*, see Richard Saller, *Patriarchy, Property, and Death in the Roman Family*, Cambridge, 1994, pp. 106–112.

33. *parentis, vitrici, deorum verecundia* (Livy 39.11.2). In a letter that Mnesilochus and his slave Chrysalus have concocted, Mnesilochus affects shame before his father Nicobulus: *Pudet prodire me ad te in conspectum, pater. / tantum flagitium te scire audivi meum* (Plautus, *Bacchides* 1007–1008); *patris pudor* (Terence, *Andria* 262); *patris conspectum vereri* (*Phormio* 315), *Heautontimorumenos* 119–20; Quintilian, *Institutio oratoria* 6.3.64.

34. Martial's fifth book of epigrams is so proper that a client could laugh over it with his master without embarrassment (5.2).

35. Plautus, *Epidicus* 173–177 (here the dead wife).

36. *a caro fratre verenda soror* (Ovid, *Amores* 3.7.22).

37. "Are you not at all ashamed before the people?" (*nihilne te populi veretur?* [fragment of the dramatist T. Quinctius Atta, quoted by Nonius, vol. 3, p. 797, Lindsay ed.]). Cf. Plautus, *Trinummus* 738–740; Cicero, *De oratore* 1.26.120–122.

38. *amicos observantia...retineret* (Cicero, *Pro Quinctio* 18.59).

39. Terence, *Andria* 279–280.

40. *revereor filium* (Plautus, *Epidicus* 173). According to Pliny the Younger, whenever her pantomime troop performed, the grandmother of Quadratus, out of affection and *reverentia* for her grandson, sent him to his room (*non amore eius magis quam reverentia* [*Epistulae* 7.24.4–5]). *maxima debetur puero reverentia* (Juvenal, *Satirae* 14.47). For reverence shown to children, see also Plutarch, *Cato maior* 20.2, 5; Cicero, *De officiis* 1.35.129; Pseudo-Quintilian, *Declamationes minores* 340.13, Shackleton Bailey ed.; Stanley F. Bonner, *Education in Ancient Rome*, Berkeley, 1977, p. 8; Thomas Wiedemann, *Adults and Children in the Roman Empire*, New Haven, 1989, p. 25. Wiedemann speculates that the child is revered because he is "marginal," closer to the gods, both *infans* and ominous. But perhaps Roman parents also showed reverence toward their children for the same reason that we show reverence to naked women in the locker room: to "ensoul," to sacralize these naked and vulnerable creatures, and to inhibit our adult temptation to violate or harm them.

one's sense of shame. Although the Roman soldiers trapped at the Caudine Forks were enraged by the incompetence of their generals, they nevertheless lowered their eyes when those generals were stripped and driven under the yoke and through the gauntlet of jeering Samnites. "Every Roman soldier, forgetting his own condition, averted his eyes from that degradation of so great a majesty, as from a spectacle too horrid to behold" (Livy 9.5.13–14).[41] Their pity for and their willingness finally to be bound to their generals was expressed in their shame at their generals' humiliation. Cicero writes of Pompey's unpopularity and self-loathing: "And just as the sculptors Apelles or Protogenes, if they had seen their Venus or Ialysus smeared with dirt, would, I imagine, have been grief-stricken, so I myself could not but feel great sorrow at seeing the idol on whose adornment I had lavished all the colors of my art suddenly disfigured" (Ad Atticum 2.21.4).[42]

Shame committed one to those before whom one withdrew. Plautus's Philo-laches declares his beloved freedwoman Philematium a woman "sensitive to shame…with a noble sense of shame" (pudico ingenio) when he accidentally over-hears her affirm her gratitude and profound sense of obligation to him (Mostellaria 206). One felt shame not only before those to whom one was bound but before the bonds themselves: before one's promises, contracts, and engagements.[43] When, in 463 B.C.E., Rome was simultaneously infested by the plague and by her inveterate enemies the Aequi and the Volsci, pudor obliged Rome's formal allies (the Hernici and the Latini) to come to the military aid of Rome (Livy 3.7.4).[44] Virgil's Achilles blushed (erubuit) to break the iura and fides owed the suppliant (Aeneis 2.541–42). Ovid's Medea felt pudor at the thought of her debt to her father and her country (Metamorphoses 7.38–73, esp. 72–73).[45]

---

41. suae quisque condicionis oblitus ab illa deformatione tantae maiestatis velut ab nefando spectaculo averteret oculos.

42. Sic ego hunc omnibus a me pictum et politum artis coloribus subito deformatum non sine magno dolore vidi.

43. "He was held to his word by the fear of the shame he would feel at failing to do what he had promised" (pudor omittendi quae promiseram tenuit [Quintilian, Institutio oratoria 12, praefatio 1]). Cicero indig-nantly asserts, "Could anything be more shameless than tax-farmers repudiating their contract?" (Quid impudentius publicanis renuntiantibus? [Ad Atticum 2.1.8]). See also Silvan Tomkins, "Shame," in The Many Faces of Shame, ed. Donald L. Nathanson, New York, 1987, p. 153; Helen Block Lewis, "Shame and the Narcissistic Personality," ibid., p. 108.

44. Interim Hernici Latinique pudore etiam, non misericordia solum moti, si nec obstitissent communibus hostibus infesto agmine Romanam urbem petentibus nec opem ullam obsessis sociis ferrent, coniuncto exercitu Romam pergunt. For the disgrace incurred for failing to protect one's friends, see Caesar, De bello Gallico 7.10.

45. Pudor could be the bond itself. "I feel the flickering of the ancient flame. But I would rather that the earth gape to its depths for me, or that the almighty father hurl me with his bolt to the shades—the pale shades and the deepest night of Erebus—before, O Pudor, I violate you or loosen your bonds."

(adgnosco veteris vestigia flammae.
sed mihi vel tellus optem prius ima dehiscat
vel pater omnipotens adigat me fulmine ad umbras,
pallentes umbras Erebi noctemque profundam,
ante, Pudor, quam te violo aut tua iura resolvo. [Aeneis 4.23–27])

As shame was vicarious, so it was contagious. "If my son is taken in adultery, I blush" (Seneca, *De beneficiis* 5.19.5).[46] "Consider again and again," Horace advises his client, "what sort of person you commend to your patron, lest the other's failings strike you with shame" (*Epistulae* 1.18.76–77).[47] In Plautus's *Bacchides*, Pistoclerus's tutor Lydus, livid with anger, complains of the shame that his pupil is bringing on everyone around him: "You are making your father and me, your friends and relatives, into the carriers of your disgrace (380–381).[48] "We feel ourselves blushing prodigiously with shame," Pliny asserts, "even for the men of former time" (*Naturalis historia* 36.2.4).[49]

Ironically, the restraints or obligations before which one blushed might be the *honores* bestowed on one by others—the gifts or benefits that constrained one until they were requited. Horace, by *not* writing epic poetry, avoided the blushing misery of having to receive the tribute to his genius of other poets' bad verse (*Epistulae* 2.1. 266–267).[50] When alarming reports came from Tusculum in 456 B.C.E. that the Aequi had invaded, the recent military services of the Tusculan people to Rome made the Romans ashamed of their delay in sending aid (Livy 3.31.3).[51]

How did shame bind? In the homeopathic emotional economy of the ancient Romans, voluntarily holding back or restraining oneself was a form of sharing one's portion that created a debt-bond. Cicero imagines the "shy" Naevius hesitating to approach Quinctius, a man "respectful of you, a man with a sense of shame" *(tui observantem, pudentem)*. Naevius, Cicero asserts, must have been inhibited by his fear of losing Quinctius's good opinion. The *pudor* of Quinctius evoked, in turn, the *pudor* of Naevius (*Pro Quinctio* 11.39).[52] When Livy's Valerius,

---

46. *si filius meus in adulterio deprensus erit, erubescam. . . .*

47. *qualem commendes etiam atque etiam aspice, ne mox / incutiant aliena tibi peccata pudorem.*

48. *tuom patrem meque una, amicos, adfinis tuos / tua infamia fecisti gerulifigulos flagiti.*

49. *ingens ista reputantem subit etiam antiquitatis rubor.* Cf. Plautus, *Curculio* 502–504; Terence, *Adelphi* 264 *Heautontimorumenos* 1037; Livy 39.15.13; Pseudo-Seneca, *Octavia* 639–43; Pliny, *Epistulae* 8.6.17. For the contagion of dishonor, see also Léon Pommeray, *Études sur l'infamie en droit romain*, Paris, 1937, p. 14; John Lendon, *Empire of Honour*, Oxford, 1997, pp. 45, 103–105; Helen Merrell Lynd, *On Shame and the Search for Identity*, New York, 1956, pp. 53–56, 59–60. Max Scheler points out that those whom you can shame are those with whom you share fellow-feelings. To say, "You make me feel shame," is to say, "I identify with you." See "Der 'Ort' des Schamgefühls," p. 81 and n. 1. See also Erving Goffman, "Embarrassment and Social Organization," *American Journal of Sociology* 62 (1956): 265, 268.

50. *nec prave factis decorari versibus opto / ne rubeam pingui donatus munere.* Silius describes the unrestrained grief and tears of Scipio (the future Africanus) when he heard in 212 B.C.E. that both his father and his uncle were dead in Spain. "No sense of shame before his honors and military command restrained him: his piety raged against the cruelty of heaven, and his grief refused all consolation" (*non ullus honorum / militiaeve pudor: pietas irata sinistris / caelicolis furit atque odit solacia luctus* [*Punica* 13.390–392]).

51. *trepidi nuntii ab Tusculo veniunt Aequos in agro Tusculano esse. Fecit pudorem recens eius populi meritum morandi auxilii.* Cf. 39.49.2.

52. While Cicero is being ironic and implying that Naevius is in fact shameless, he nevertheless sketches the reciprocal nature of *pudor* as he understood it functioning.

out of regard for the people, lowered the *fasces* in their presence, when he tore down his house and reconstructed it on a lower level so that they might observe and scrutinize him, he cemented the identification between himself and the people. His reverence toward the people was, in turn, acknowledged and rewarded by them with the name Publicola, "benefactor of the people" (2.8).[53]

SHAME AND MEASURE

Shame was the calibrating, the measuring emotion.[54] The person with a sense of shame was a person with a delicate sense of balance; he or she was "scrupulous," the *scrupulus* being the smallest weight that could move a scale.[55] (I should emphasize that, in the Roman imagination, the person who was *scrupulus*, like the person who was *religiosus*, was constantly anxious.[56]) To have shame was the quality of a modest *(modestus)*, a continent *(continens)*, a temperate *(temperans)*, an innocuous *(innocens)* man or woman, perpetually assessing his or her own value and limitations in relation to others.[57] The Elder Pliny tells the famous story of the competition be-

---

53. The respectful behavior of the Etruscan enemy Porsenna toward Mucius prefigured both the lifting of his siege and his seeking of a treaty with Rome (Livy 2.12–13). In the *Res gestae*, Octavian's surrender of complete control over the *res publica* demonstrated his wish to be considered a part of, and not above or in possession of, the state. This withdrawal was rewarded by the title Augustus, "the Augmented" (34.1–2). For the reciprocal nature of shame, see Robert Kaster, "The Shame of the Romans," *Transactions and Proceedings of the American Philological Association* 127 (1997): 9.

54. *Modestus* comes from *modus*, the measure or standard of behavior.

> C'est la "mesure," mais non une mesure qui soit une dimension propre des choses, pour "mesurer" le latin emploie un verbe distinct, *metior*. Par *modus* on exprime une mesure imposée aux choses, une mesure dont on est maître, qui suppose réflexion et choix, qui suppose aussi décision. Bref, ce n'est pas une mesure de *mensuration*, mais de *modération*, c'est-à-dire une mesure appliquée à ce qui ignore la mesure, une mesure de limitation ou de contrainte. C'est pourquoi *modus* a plutôt un sens moral que matériel, *modestus* est dit "celui qui est pourvu de mesure, qui observe la mesure"; *moderari*, c'est "soumettre à la mesure (ce qui y échappe)"

(Émile Benveniste, *Le vocabulaire des institutions indo-euopéennes*, vol. 2, Paris, 1969, pp. 127–128). For shame as *das haarscharfe Masswerkzeug*, see Scheler, "Der 'Ort' des Schamgefühls," p. 80.

55. Compare our "punctilious" attention to the details or niceties of behavior, from Latin *punctillum*, little point.

56. See, for example, Cicero, *Pro Roscio Amerino* 2.6; *Pro Cluentio* 28.76; *De haruspicum responsis* 5.11; *Ad Atticum* 1.18.2; 2.4.1; Terence, *Andria* 940–942; *Phormio* 954, 1019; *Adelphi* 228; Suetonius, *Claudius* 37.1; Pliny, *Epistulae* 3.17.2; 6.8.7. Walter Otto points out that being *religiosus* involved a delicate balancing act. The man who was excessively anxious was the *superstitiosus*—a little out of his mind (literally, "standing above himself." We would say he was "beside himself"). One can compare Latin *superstitio* to Greek *ekstasis*, standing outside oneself, but the terms have different valances. For the Romans, to be ecstatic was to be a little too far out of one's mind, a little too far off balance ("*Religio* und *Superstitio*," *Archiv für Religionswissenschaft* 12 [1909]: 532–554; 14 [1911]: 406–422).

57. *moderator cupiditatis pudor* (Cicero, *De finibus* 2.34.113). While the great—but modest—orator Lucius Crassus possessed a pair of extravagantly expensive goblets, he never actually used them. His *verecundia* prevented him from such ostentatious display (Pliny, *Naturalis historia* 33.53.147).

tween the illusionist painters Zeuxis and Parrhasius. Zeuxis painted a cluster of grapes; Parrhasius painted a curtain. Zeuxis's painting deceived the birds who attempted to pluck the grapes. Proud of the verdict of the birds, Zeuxis demanded that the curtain be drawn and the painting of his rival Parrhasius displayed. "Zeuxis, grasping his error, conceded the palm to his rival with *ingenuus pudor:* while he had fooled the birds, Parrhasius had fooled him" (*Naturalis historia* 35.36.65).[58] Zeuxis's moderate measure of himself (presumably coincident with, or even more modest, than that of his audience) brought him credit. It rendered him creditable, trustworthy. He was not arrogant; he did not take for himself more than he was thought to deserve. So Gellius described Caesellius Vindex, an exceptionally learned man willing to admit his ignorance, as "a man of noble integrity" (*homo ingenuae veritatis* [*Noctes Atticae* 20.2.2]).[59] One's shame created a debt-bond, a favorable balance of credit, when society would give you more than you took for yourself.

WILLINGNESS TO BE WITNESSED

Roman honor was, to use a phrase of Sandor Feldman, "a readiness to be ashamed."[60] "If I leave anything undone, I shall confess to having committed a crime and covered myself with disgrace," Cicero says when he wants to assure Appius Claudius that he is committed to acting honorably and doing everything possible to assist him (*Ad familiares* 3.10.2).[61] Those with a sense of shame demon-

---

58. *atque intellecto errore concederet palmam ingenuo pudore, quoniam ipse volucres fefellisset, Parrhasius autem se artificem.*

59. Horace apologizes to Augustus for not writing heroic poetry: "If only I had strength equal to my desire! But your majesty cannot be expected to receive light poetry, and my *pudor* forbids me to attempt a task that is beyond my strength to bear" (*si quantum cuperem possem quoque: sed neque parvum / carmen maiestas recipit tua, nec meus audet / rem temptare pudor quam vires ferre recusent* [*Epistulae* 2.1.257–259]). Here Horace's "confession" is a submission meant to honor and so to bind Augustus to himself.

60. "Blushing, Fear of Blushing, and Shame," *Journal of the American Psychoanalytic Association* 10 (1962): 371. Wikan's female informers in Omani Sohar, labeled as *yistiḥi* the emotion that kept them from doing dishonorable acts. "It could, in some contexts, be translated as having the power to be shamed by one's acts ("Shame and Honor," pp. 647, 650 n. 19).

61. *si quid a me praetermissum erit, commissum facinus et admissum dedecus confitebor* (May 50 B.C.E.). For the weight attached to a commitment to confess in Roman society, see part 2. Among the Japanese of the early twentieth century, according to Benedict, a willingness to be shamed formed part of the complex Japanese notion of honor:

> A borrower may pledge his *giri* to his name when he asks for a loan; a generation ago it was common to phrase it that "I agree to be publicly laughed at if I fail to repay this sum." If he failed, he was not literally made a laughingstock; there were no public pillories in Japan. But when the New Year came around, the date on which debts must be paid off, the insolvent debtor might commit suicide to "clear his name." New Year's Eve still has its crop of suicides who have taken this means to redeem their reputations. (*The Chrysanthemum and the Sword,* p. 151)

Just so, an unpaid debt was a shame in Rome. For *pudor aeris alieni* as a motive for suicide among the Romans, see *Digesta* 49.14.45.2.

strated their willingness to be shamed by calling on witnesses to their words or acts. Cicero called on the judge Aquilius and his counselors to commit to memory the limitations to which he, Cicero, had committed himself in his defense of Quinctius (*Pro Quinctio* 10.35–36). When the enemy Etruscans had taken the Janiculum and the Roman soldiers were fleeing in terror and confusion, Livy's Horatius Cocles "stood his ground and called on god and man as witnesses" (Livy 2.10.3).[62] Calling on spectators—or judges, for they were inseparable notions in the Roman mind—of an oath or an action was a Roman's way of saying, "Go ahead: put me in the spotlight. My words and my actions will stand the test of your scrutiny." The presence of witnesses made every act into an ordeal. Shame was a test.

SHAME BEFORE ONESELF

Cato thought it especially necessary for every man to respect himself
(heauton aideisthai), *since no man is ever separated from himself.*
PLUTARCH, *REGUM ET IMPERATORUM APOPHTHEGMATA*, CATO 9 (*MORALIA* 198F)[63]

Plautus's tutor Lydus scolds his truant student Pistoclerus (amusing himself in the house of the courtesan Bacchis) for having had no shame before himself or before his old tutor (*neque mei neque te tui intus puditumst factis quae facis* [*Bacchides* 379]). The honorable controlled themselves even when they could not be seen; the honorable judged themselves even when others did not. Plautus's slave Palinurus, as tutor of his young master Phaedromos, advises him to live and love as if always in the eyes of others: "If you're wise, you'll so give your love that it won't be to your disgrace if the people should come to know what it is you love" (*Curculio* 28–29).[64]

Each man, to use a phrase of Juvenal, has his own witness in his breast (*suum in pectore testem* [*Satirae* 13.198]). "With himself as his own judge, no guilty man is absolved—even if he has won his cause by the favor of a corrupt praetor" (*Satirae* 13.2–4).[65] There could be, Cicero explained, no excuse for that Gyges of the story,

---

62. *Qui* [*Horatius*] *positus forte in statione pontis cum captum repentino impetu Ianiculum atque inde citatos decurrere hostes vidisset trepidamque turbam suorum arma ordinesque relinquere, reprehendans singulos, obsistens obtestansque deum et hominum fidem testabatur nequiquam deserto praesidio eos fugere.* In Plautus's *Mercator,* Charinus accuses Eutychus of faithlessness (and, by implication, shamelessness) for calling on the gods as witnesses when the gods are clearly absent (i.e., when they clearly have abandoned his cause [625–627]). For the *fetiales* calling upon divine witnesses, see Livy 1.32.7.

63. "The Noble Soul has reverence for itself" (Die vornehme Seele hat Ehrfurcht vor sich [Friedrich Nietzsche, *Beyond Good and Evil,* trans. R.J. Hollingdale, London, 1990, p. 215 no. 287]). In the words of Leon Wurmser, "I am ashamed in front of myself" (Ich schäme mich vor mir selbst [*The Mask of Shame,* Baltimore, 1981, p. 48; cf. p. 51]).

64. *Ita tuom conferto amare semper, si sapis, / ne id quod ames populus si sciat, tibi sit probro.*

65. *se / iudice nemo nocens absolvitur, improba quamvis / gratia fallaci praetoris vicerit urna.* Cf. 192–195; Seneca, *Phaedra* 159–164. Cicero argues that *conscientia* is a more effective deterrent than the gods. The

who took advantage of his magic ring to make himself invisible so that he might act shamelessly (De officiis 3.19.78). The good man or woman, he suggests, was someone with whom you could play "Odds and Evens" in the dark (De officiis 3.19.77).[66]

The Roman incorporated the example of others as a sort of "ego ideal": "I tell my son to look into the lives of all others as if into a mirror and to take from others a model for himself" (Terence, Adelphi 415–416).[67] And so Seneca advises Lucilius to choose a venerable man of outstanding qualities and to keep him ever before his mind's eye as an inhibitor:

> We should have high regard for a particular good man and keep him ever before our eyes, so that we might live as if he were always watching and judging us. . . . Most sins would disappear if there were a witness of the man about to sin. The will (animus) should have someone to fear, by whose authority even one's most guarded secrets would be still more carefully hidden.[68] He is a happy man who is able to amend the faults of another, not only when he is present, but when he is merely thought of! And he is a happy man who can so fear another that at just the thought of this other he can compose and regulate himself. Who can so venerate another will soon be worthy of veneration. So pick a Cato. And if he seems a bit too rigid to you, pick a man of gentler spirits—a Laelius. Choose one whose life and speech and soul-baring face has pleased you. Always present him to yourself as custodian or exemplum. (Epistulae 11.8–10)[69]

---

man who is not inhibited by his own self-consciousness will not be afraid of the gods. And so the man who is accustomed to lie will be likely to perjure himself (Pro Roscio Commoedo 16.46). No one can trust a man who has no dangerous conscience; self-respect was the prerequisite of mutual respect.

66. For an example of blushing even when one is not is the presence of others, see Cicero, Ad Atticum 15.4.

67. inspicere tamquam in speculum in vitas omnium / iubeo atque ex aliis sumere exemplum sibi. "It is the part of a young man to show reverence to his elders and to elect for himself the best and most highly approved of them, in order that he might advance by their counsel and authority" (Est igitur adulescentis maiores natu vereri exque iis deligere optimos et probatissimos quorum consilio atque auctoritate nitatur [De officiis 1.34.122]). Cf. Lendon, Empire of Honour, p. 47.

68. This is a very interesting sentence. Although its meaning is not altogether clear to me, this sentence suggests that the inner authority would be your friend, your ally in maintaining your secrets; it would not expose and "desoul" you. Just as one could endow or deprive others of spirit by the way in which one regarded them, so one could "ensoul" or "desoul" oneself by the way in which one watched oneself. How does one reverence oneself? I suggest that it is by cultivating oneself, by respecting one's own role and persona, by acting as if one were on stage. Men and women fought the Entseelung of the death camps of World War II by maintaining their posture, by sewing on their buttons and washing themselves with filthy water, by not suffering themselves (in contrast to Seneca's Telesphorus of Rhodes) to be contemptible in their own eyes.

69. Aliquis vir bonus nobis diligendus est ac semper ante oculos habendus, ut sic tamquam illo spectante vivamus et omnia tamquam illo vidente faciamus. . . . Magna pars peccatorum tollitur, si peccaturis testis adsistit. Aliquem habeat animus, quem vereatur, cuius auctoritate etiam secretum suum sanctius faciat. O felicem illum, qui non praesens tantum, sed etiam cogitatus emendat! O felicem, qui sic aliquem vereri potest, ut ad memoriam

It is important to realize that *pudor* as a form of self-regarding was also a form of self-splitting; one was both the watched and the watcher. Thus, if a Roman had a sense of integrity, it was built, paradoxically, on the dividing of the self.[70] Cicero speaks of the self-control needed to resist shameful reactions to pain: "I'm not exactly sure how to say it, but it is as if we would be two people: one who commanded and one who obeyed" (*Tusculanae disputationes* 2.20.47).[71] The person with a sense of shame endured this splintering of the self. Ovid's young Medea, torn between her love of Jason and her obligations to her father, "spoke to herself, and before her mind's eye stood Righteousness, Piety, and Shame" (*Metamorphoses* 7.72–73).[72]

As shame was a delicate system of reciprocities, so Roman notions of transgression had two complementary aspects: taking more than your share and/or not repaying what had been given to you. Both were forms of debt, which were disequilibrations: both the arrogant person and the debtor were using or holding what rightfully belonged to another. Because they were controlling part of another's sphere, they were, in effect, intruding into that sphere.[73] Restitution, repayment, and expiation were necessary to heal the wounds of transgression.[74] Apart from being the inhibitor, *pudor* was the guilt, the expiatory suffering, of the transgressor.

Social grace, in ancient Rome, required one to orient and reorient oneself as constantly and delicately as a musician in a string quartet. No one apprised of the

---

quoque eius se conponat atque ordinet! Qui sic aliquem vereri potest, cito erit verendus. Elige itaque Catonem. Si hic tibi videtur nimis rigidus, elige remissioris animi virum Laelium. Elige eum, cuius tibi placuit et vita et oratio et ipse animum ante se ferens vultus: illum tibi semper ostende vel custodem vel exemplum.

Here we have the internalized "ego ideal" of psychologists such as Melanie Klein and Helen Lewis, rather than the hostile "superego" of Freud.

70. For the instability of the notion of the self in societies where the self is construed interdependently, see Wilhelm Kroll, *Die Kultur der ciceronischen Zeit*, vol. 1, Leipzig, 1933, pp. 5–6; Barbara Kellum, "The Play of Meaning: The Visual Culture of Ancient Roman Freedmen and Freedwomen" (forthcoming)," ms. p. 21; Clyde Kluckhohn, "The Moral Order in the Expanding Society," in *The City Invincible*, ed. Carl H. Kraeling and Robert M. Adams, Chicago, 1960, pp. 395–396; Seiichi Morisaki and William B. Gudykunst, "Face in Japan and the United States," in *The Challenge of Facework*, ed. Stella Ting-Toomey, Albany, 1994, pp. 60, 62–63.

71. *Quamquam hoc nescio quo modo dicitur, quasi duo simus, ut alter imperet, alter pareat.*

72. *dixit, et ante oculos rectum pietasque pudorque / constiterant.*

73. For an illuminating discussion of the relationship of Japanese notions of guilt to the nonrepayment of debts, see Takie Sugiyama Lebra, "The Social Mechanisms of Guilt and Shame: The Japanese Case," *Anthropological Quarterly* 44 (1971): 241–255.

74. "Longtemps...les moeurs et les lois ne font aucune différence entre le voleur et le debiteur" (P. Huvelin, "Magie et droit individuel," *L'année sociologique* 10 [1905–1906]: 14; cf. p. 22). As Helen Merrell Lynd points out, the Old English root of the word "guilt" carries the double meaning of guilt and debt. German *schuldig*, "guilty," also means owing a debt, duty, or obligation (*On Shame*, pp. 23–24). See chapter 8.

precision of Roman shame could imagine the Romans as existing in a comfortable and primitive unselfconscious. A Roman was, ironically enough, more like Dostoevsky's fidgety Underground Man than his complacent Zverkov, more like Nietzsche than his Blond Beast.

THE ARMOR OF SHAME

Be this our wall of bronze, to have no guilt at heart, no wrongdoing to turn us pale.
HORACE, *EPISTULAE* 1.1.60–61[75]

If shame caused one constant anxiety and occasional anguish, it was also a force field or membrane that protected one, Cicero's *firmissimum praesidium pudoris* (*Pro Sulla* 77).[76] Our English "shame" evolved from an Indo-European *skam* or *skem*, which means "to hide," from which we get our word "skin."[77] (Compare English "hide," which embraces both the notions of "a covering" and "to conceal.")[78] Roman shame also acted as a hide; it was the veil of pink cloaking the acute sensibility of the man or woman with a sense of the sanctity of his or her being.[79] The masking of a person in the name of decorum and decency was a *pia dissimulatio*.[80] Cicero offers examples of this pious dissimulation: "Whoever is rather inclined to pursue pleasure, provided he be not one of the herd (for there are those who are human in name only)—whoever is, then, a little more erect, even if he should be in the power of desire, will hide it and cloak his appetites for the sake of shame (*verecundia*)" (Cicero, *De officiis* 1.30.105).[81] It is *vere-*

75. *hic murus aeneus esto, / nil conscire sibi, nulla pallescere culpa.*

76. For *modestia* as a covering, see Plautus, *Mostellaria* 162–163. For *verecundia* and *virtutis modum* as coverings, see ibid. 139–140. For the protective aspects of shame, see Scheler, "Der 'Ort' des Schamgefühls," pp. 80–81; Wurmser, *Mask of Shame*, p. 48.

77. A sense of shame was one's "hide." "The root of the English 'shame' and the German '*Scham*' is the Gothic word '*Schama*,' which signifies cover and which is also the root of the German '*Hemd*,' shirt, and the English and French 'chemise'" (Kurt Riezler, "Comment on the Social Psychology of Shame," *American Journal of Sociology* 48 [1942–1943]); cf. Wurmser, *Mask of Shame*, p. 29. One can compare the protective aspects of shame to the notion of "personal" space, with its territorial aspects, as articulated by ethologists. "The power sphere around a person resembles territory in animals" (Wurmser, *Mask of Shame*, p. 62).

78. Donald L. Nathanson, "A Timetable for Shame," in Nathanson, ed., *Many Faces of Shame*, New York, 1987, p. 8.

79. *famae pudor* (Cicero, *De provinciis consularibus* 6.14). *honorum / militaeve pudor* (Silius, *Punica* 13.390). Cicero uses the phrases *pudor existimationis* (*In Verrem* 2.2.16.40).

80. Debra Hershkowitz has remarked that "all dissimulation, when it specifically refers to deception, is considered 'bad' in the Roman conception of the terms; when it is concealed under other banners, like 'decorum' or 'self-control,' however, it is a cardinal virtue" ("*Dissimulare etiam sperasti?* The Poetics of Dissimulation," [unpublished manuscript, p. 3]).

81. *si quis est paulo ad voluptates propensior, modo ne sit ex pecudum genere (sunt enim quidam homines non re, sed nomine), sed si quis est paulo erectior, quamvis voluptate capiatur, occultat et dissimulat appetitum voluptatis propter verecundiam.*

cundia, according to Cicero, that causes men and women to hide their genitals and bodily functions: "The shame of men has imitated that very diligent fabrication of nature: what nature has hidden, sane men themselves remove from sight and take care to obey the necessities of nature as secretly as possible" (*De officiis* 1.35.127).[82] A sense of shame was a kind of surgical mask that one wore both to protect oneself and to avoid infecting valuable others with the painful emotions of shame.[83]

THE AGGRESSION OF SHAME

Brutus, art thou asleep?
PLUTARCH, *BRUTUS* 9.6[84]

While shame was a discipline, it was also a stimulus. *Pudor* inhibited, but it also impelled one beyond one's limitations.[85] And if the bond *(religio, obligatio)* was the hinge of these two impulses, the motion around the fulcrum was evoked by the bond itself. For the Romans, as for Sigmund Freud or Max Scheler, any barrier was a tease. The very existence of a prohibition evoked the desire to cross it, in the way that the closed blinds of the bedroom invite the voyeur.[86] Cicero commends Solon for not instituting any punishment for patricide, "lest he seem not so much to prohibit as to suggest. How much wiser than we were our ancestors! For they understood that nothing could be so sanctified that it would not be periodi-

---

82. *Hanc naturae tam diligentem fabricam imitata est hominum verecundia. Quae enim natura occultavit, eadem omnes qui sana mente sunt, removent ab oculis ipsique necessitati dant operam ut quam ocultissime pareant.* Compare Max Scheler's "objective shame phenomenon": the evolution from plants to mammals demonstrates a tendency to make less prominent and obvious the organs of reproduction ("Der 'Ort' des Schamgefühls," pp. 74–75).

83. "Blushing...comes at the time when hypocrisy and concealment are adopted as an adjustment to the environment" (Feldman, "Blushing, Fear of Blushing, and Shame," p. 381).

84. "On the statue of his ancestor Brutus—the Brutus who overthrew the power of the kings, there was written: 'O that we had thee now, Brutus!' and 'O that Brutus were alive!' Moreover, the praetorial tribunal of Brutus himself was daily found covered with such writings as these: 'Brutus, art thou asleep?' and 'Thou art not really Brutus.'" For a complex and fascinating reading of Brutus's motives for slaying Caesar, and in particular Caesar's relentless shaming of Brutus, see Thomas Africa's wonderful "The Mask of an Assassin: A Psychohistorical Study of M. Junius Brutus," *Journal of Interdisciplinary History* 8 (1978): 599–626.

85. *pudor* encouraged the soldiers to take heart, to stand their ground and not to retreat or panic: *pudor ire retro* (Statius, *Thebais* 8.522); *vertere terga pudor* (Silius, *Punica* 4.329).

86. For the psychological relationship of prohibitions to transgressions, see Freud's brilliant essay, "Taboo and the Ambivalence of Emotions," *Totem and Taboo,* trans. A.A. Brill, [1913] 1918, esp. pp. 42–48. To put Freud's theory in its simplest form, no incest inhibition would be necessary if we did not have a strong inclination to violate those who are nearest and most vulnerable to us. See also Scheler's "Der 'Ort' des Schamgefühls," esp. pp. 83–84, 101–102, and Jean Briggs's fascinating "Living Dangerously: The Contradictory Foundations of Value in Inuit Society," in *Politics and History in Band Societies,* ed. Eleanor Leacock and Richard Lee, Cambridge, 1982, pp. 109–131.

cally violated by audacious acts" (*Pro Roscio Amerino* 25.70).[87] Indeed, a sense of shame was *only* brought into play by the desire to trespass. Ovid's Medea feels *pudor* when she thinks of her obligations to her father and her country—*because* she is in love with Jason and aching to elope with him (*Metamorphoses* 7.72–73).

We tend to distinguish the idea of yielding or of giving way from that of transgressing, inhibition from exhibition, the shame of inadequacy from the guilt of violation. But for the Romans, with their logic of complementarities, these are inseparable aspects of *pudor.* Self-control, insofar as it required constant and critical self-scrutiny, combined in constant tension the constraining and stimulating aspects of shame.[88] (Shame, like the contest, ordered and arranged Roman life but always threatened to disrupt it.)

The contrapuntal nature of Roman honor resulted in the elaboration of another very important theme, one that is generally absent from our (conscious) definitions of honor: although shame provided the restraint necessary for the preservation of all contracts and bonds, no Roman was credited with a sense of shame unless he or she was also credited with the desire and means to transgress those same contracts and bonds. In the words of Publilius Syrus, "The highest praise that one can give a man is that he is capable of doing harm but chooses not to" (397, Friedrich ed.).[89] "The good man wishes it to be remembered that he spared when he could have destroyed" (Cicero, *Pro Quinctio* 16.51).[90]

Cicero remarks, "Integrity deserves no praise if no one has either the power or the will to corrupt it" (*In Verrem* 1.16.46).[91] And so the ability to violate was admired even when the violation was criminal. As Juvenal asserts, "Even those who do not want to kill anyone want to have the power to do so" (*Satirae* 10.96–97).[92] The impotent man got no credit for continence. Rather, self-control was most to be praised where it was least expected. "To the degree that moderation is more rare in kings, to that degree it is the more to be lauded" (Seneca, *De ira* 2.23.3).[93] The following exchange takes place in Seneca's *Trojan Women:*

87. *Sapienter fecisse dicitur, cum de eo nihil sanxerit quod antea commissum non erat, ne non tam prohibere quam admonere videretur. Quanto nostri maiores sapientius! Qui cum intellegerent nihil esse tam sanctum quod non aliquando violaret audacia.*

88. For the difficulty for the Romans in distinguishing free act from obligation, *liberalitas* from *officia,* see David Daube, *Roman Law: Linguistic, Social and Philosophical Aspects,* Edinburgh, 1969, pp. 118–119.

89. *nocere posse et nolle laus amplissima est.*

90. *bonus... mavult commemorari se, cum posset perdere, pepercisse.*

91. *nulla est enim laus ibi esse integrum ubi nemo est qui aut possit aut conetur corrumpere.*

92. *qui nolunt occidere quemquam / posse volunt.*

93. *Quo rarior autem moderatio in regibus, hoc laudanda magis est.* "The greater the power they possess owing to their energy and their rank, the less they ought to show how great it is" (*quo plus propter virtutem nobilitatemque possunt, eo minus, quantum possint, debent ostendere* [Cicero, *Pro Quinctio* 2.9]). "The greater our superiority, the more humbly we should act" (*quanto superiores simus, tanto nos geramus summissius* [*De officiis*

Pyrrhus: No law spares a captive....

Agamemnon: Shame forbids what the law does not.

Pyrrhus: To the victor is permitted whatever he pleases.

Agamemnon: The more freedom a man has to indulge his desires, the less it becomes him to do so. (333–336)[94]

Cicero praises Caesar for having "vanquished victory" (*ipsam victoriam vicisse videris*
[*Pro Marcello* 4.12]). He accomplished this paradoxical feat by overcoming himself
(*animum vincere, iracundiam cohibere, victoriam temperare* [*Pro Marcello* 3.8; cf. 1.1].) "He
conquers twice," Publilius Syrus declares, "who, in victory, conquers himself" (64,
Friedrich ed.).[95]

Dignitas was worthiness of *honor*. To have *dignitas*, in ancient Rome, one had, at
the very least, to live up to one's bonds and obligations. In that sense it was not
unlike our English "dignity," which implies self-possession or self-containment.
But Roman *dignitas* was a less static and more ambiguous notion than our "dignity." For the Romans, *dignitas* involved one actively and aggressively in a system
of social reciprocities. Deserving crossed easily into demanding. As Cicero says,
"dignity demands" (*dignitas poscit* [*Pro Quinctio* 7.28]). And so *dignitas* was both a
containment and a title to expand (and so infringe on another's territory).[96]

1.26.90]). Compare the discussion on power between Oscar Schindler and Amon Goeth, commandant
of the Nazi labor camp, in Steven Zaillian's screenplay for Steven Spielberg's *Schindler's List* (1993):

Goeth: Control is power. That's power.

Schindler: Is that why they fear us?

Goeth: We have the fucking power to kill; that's why they fear us.

Schindler: We have the power to kill arbitrarily. A man commits a crime he should know better. We have him killed and we feel pretty good about it or we kill him ourselves and feel
even better. That's not power, though, that's justice. That's different than power. Power is
when we have every justification to kill and we don't.

Goeth: You think that's power?

Schindler: That's what the emperors had. A man stole something. He's brought in before the
emperor. He throws himself down on the ground. He begs. He knows he's going to
die....and the emperor pardons him. He lets him go.

94. *Lex nulla capto parcit aut poenam impedit.*
   Quod non vetat lex, hoc vetat fieri pudor.
   Quodcumque libuit facere, victori licet.
   Minimum decet libere cui multum licet.

95. *Bis vincit qui se vincit in victoria.* "This is the virtue of Caesar and the glory of Caesar: that the
hand that conquered was the same that sheathed the sword" (*Caesaris haec virtus et gloria Caesaris haec est:
illa, qua vicit, condidit arma manu* [Propertius 2.16]). "That they were able to conquer such a general of
the enemy made them illustrious; but it made them more illustrious, by far, that they were not willing
to do so" (*Claros illos fecerat tantum hostium ducem vincere potuisse: sed multo clariores fecit, noluisse* [Valerius
Maximus 6.6.2]). Cf. Seneca, *De clementia* 1.21.3.

96. On the demands of *dignitas*, see Ramsay MacMullen, "Personal Power in the Roman Empire," in *Changes in the Roman Empire*, Princeton, 1990, esp. pp. 190–197 and p. 352 n. 14 (with the
sources discussed there); Helmut Wegehaupt, "Die Bedeutung und Anwendung von *dignitas* in den

I can illustrate this aspect of Roman honor by a modern example (even while we tend not to define honor in this way): in our own culture, one way of strengthening, of galvanizing our will is by denying ourselves something we earnestly desire. So a person (not unlike myself) might swear off chocolate. But if she is to derive any feeling of increased efficacy from such willful self-deprivation, she must subject her resolve to an ordeal, a temptation, a contest. She might, for instance, deliberately pass by the candy machine on the way to her office. If she desires a candy bar but cannot procure one because she does not have enough money, she will not feel empowered by passing the dispenser. If she wants the candy bar but comes away without one because she does not know how to work the machine, she will leave the machine not with a feeling of increased energy but with embarrassment and a feeling of inadequacy. The optimum conditions for the enhancement of her willpower require that she approach the machine with both the necessary change and full knowledge of how to work the machine. In other words, she must have both the desire and the ability to transgress in order to gain credit for continence in her own or others' eyes. The strongest evidence, finally, of her ability to transgress is the experience, the fact of transgressing.

The ostentatious constrictions that Cicero put on the time and subject of his oration in the *Pro Quinctio* would have meant little if his audience did not believe he easily could have ignored them.[97] Scipio's gallant protection of the chastity of the lovely captive offered him by the soldiers at New Carthage would have earned him less credit if he did not have a reputation as a womanizer—and if he could not have taken her with impunity (Livy 26.50).[98] The restraint of Pompey later in his life would not have garnered the respect it did if the Romans did not have a vivid memories of him as an *adulescentulus carnifex,* a teenage butcher.[99] (Likewise for Augustus, that other youthful monster.)[100] One needed to be self-controlled, but one also needed to reveal to others the cost of that control.

Schriften der republikanischen Zeit," Ph.D. diss., Breslau, 1932, esp. pp. 22, 37–39, 42–42, 73–74, 77; Chaim Wirszubski, "Cicero's *cum dignitate otium:* A Reconsideration," *Journal of Roman Studies* 44 (1954): 12; J. P. V. D. Balsdon, "*Auctoritas, Dignitas, Otium,*" *Classical Quarterly* n.s. 10 (1960): 44–46; Levi Robert Lind, "The Tradition of Roman Moral Conservatism," *Studies in Latin Literature and History,* vol. 1, Brussels, 1979, p. 25; T. P. Wiseman, "*Conspicui postes tectaque digna deo:* The Public Image of the Aristocratic and Imperial Houses in the Late Republic and Early Empire," in *L'urbs: Espace urbain et histoire,* Rome, 1987, p. 393.

97. *Pro Quinctio* 10.35–36.

98. Cf. Polybius 10.19.3–6 (*philogunen onta Popliov*); Valerius Maximus 4.3.1, 6.7.1; Frontinus, *Strategemata* 2.11.5; Gellius, *Noctes Atticae* 7.8.3; Plutarch, *Regum et imperatorum apophthegmata,* Scipio Maior 2 (*Moralia* 196b).

99. Cf. Helvius Mancia fr. 1 (*Oratorum Romanorum Fragmenta,* Malcovati ed.).

100. Cf. Seneca, *De clementia* 1.9.1, 1.11.1–2. In her wonderful article "Perusinae Glandes and the Changing Image of Augustus," *American Journal of Ancient History* 2 (1977): 151–171, Judith Hallett makes the point that Augustus committed adultery not out of passion but out of policy; he needed to appear as the code-breaker as well as the code-maker. Jasper Griffin, in an equally fine article, presents the

DEBILITATING SHAME

The man or woman who never broke the rules was despised. The mildness of a mild man, like the poverty of the poor man, met with little respect.[101] Modesty unbroken, Plutarch observes in his essay "On Bashfulness," prevented people from setting and defending any limits; it made them unable to say no. Persons with too great a sense of inhibiting shame were easy marks; out of fear of offending others they could be cowed into acting against their own will and judgment. In other words, they could be shamed into acting shamefully (*De vitioso pudore* [*Moralia* 530A]).[102]

There are those, Cicero tells us, who are so fearful of offending others that they are afraid to say what they believe, even when they have something important to say (*De officiis* 1.24.84).[103] Terence's Charinus declares (in reference to Pamphilus, who he thinks has betrayed him): "The worst kind of men are the ones who, in the pressure of circumstances, haven't the courage to say no. And, afterwards, when the time comes to do what they have promised, the pressure of necessity exposes them" (*Andria* 629–632).[104]

Quintilian warns his fellow Romans against inordinate modesty:

> I say with some reluctance ... that even modesty—a fault which is nevertheless an amiable one easily giving rise to virtues—is on occasion an impediment to those virtues. ... It is not probity that is the object of my criticism, but that modesty which is a form of fear deterring the soul from doing what it should, and resulting in confusion of mind, regret that our task was ever begun, and sudden silence. For who can hesitate to number among the faults a feeling that makes man ashamed to do what is right? (*Institutio oratoria* 12.5.2–3)[105]

---

stereotype of the man of action who tended to transgress as a type of hostile propaganda ("Propertius and Antony," *Journal of Roman Studies* 67 [1977]: 17–21). If it was hostile propaganda, it was also very close to the ideal. As Ronald Syme points out, "The old Republic knew that vice and energy are not incompatible" (*Tacitus*, vol. 2, Oxford, 1958, p. 545).

101. The inability of poor people to be generous when they willed made their frugality worthless. Only the voluntary poverty of the rich (or potentially rich) was respected. The ability to give was closely related, in the Roman emotional economy, to the ability to transgress.

102. Because he could not say no to Messalina, Tacitus's Claudius was despised. See Sandra R. Joshel, "Female Desire and the Discourse of Empire: Tacitus's Messalina," *Signs* 21 (1995): 50–82.

103. *Sunt enim qui, quod sentiunt, etsi optimum sit, tamen invidiae metu non audeant dicere.*

104. *immo id est pessumum hominum genus*
   denegandi modo quis pudor paulum adest;
   post ubi tempust promissa iam perfeci
   tum coacti necessario se aperiunt.

105. *Invitus mehercule dico ... ipsam verecundiam, vitium quidem sed amabile et quae virtutes facillime generet, esse interim adversam. ... non probitatem a me reprehendi, sed verecundiam, quae est timor quidem reducens animum ab iis, quae facienda sunt; inde confusio et coepti paenitentia et subitum silentium. Quis porro dubitet vitiis adscribere adfectum, propter quem facere honeste pudet?*

Cicero suggests that the "excessively bashful" Naevius was unable to do the right and honorable thing (that is, to inform Quinctius of the debt from his inheritance that the latter owed him):

> You were unwilling or afraid to call on one who was your relative, who had great respect for you, a worthy and modest man, and older than yourself. More than once (as is often the case) after you had plucked up courage and determined to mention the money, when you approached him, having carefully prepared what you intended to say, on a sudden, you, the nervous man of virgin modesty, drew back; at once words failed you; when you wanted to call on him for the money, you did not dare to do so, for fear that he might feel hurt to hear you. (*Pro Quinctio* 11.39)[106]

Livy provides another example of this debilitating shame. When a portentous dream appeared to the plebeian Titus Latinius, he was driven by the will of Jupiter to bring his vision to the attention of the magistrates. "But while his spirit was certainly not free from religious scruples, bashfulness before the majesty of the magistrates overcame his fear of the gods—lest he should depart an object of sport in the mouths of men. As a result, he delayed for a long time, which delay cost him dearly, for within a few days his son had died" (2.36.3).[107]

Brutus was praised by Plutarch because "no flattery could induce him to grant an unjust petition, and that susceptibility to shameless importunity *(ten hupo ton avaischuntos liparounton hettan)*, which some call 'bashfulness' *(dusopeisthai)*, he regarded as most disgraceful *(aischisten)* in a great man" (*Brutus* 6.9). The person unable to endure the painful and negative emotions of shame could have no integrity; he or she could not endure the contest.[108] The person both restrained and honored was the one whom others feared, but the person of honor had to be not only sensitive to shame but also willing to suffer it.

---

106. *Hominem propinquum, tui observantem, virum bonum, pudentem, maiorum natu nolebas aut non audebas appellare, saepe, ut fit, cum ipse te confirmasses, cum statuisses mentionem de pecunia facere, cum paratus meditatusque venisses, homo timidus virginali verecundia subito ipse te retinebas; excidebat repente oratio; cum cuperes appellare, non audebas, ne invitus audiret.*

107. *Quamquam haud sane liber erat religione animus, verecundia tamen maiestatis magistratuum timorem vicit, ne in ora hominum pro ludibrio abiret. Magno illi ea cunctatio stetit: filium namque intra paucos dies amisit.*

108. For an excellent example of Caesar's balancing of his reputation for ferocity with his reputation for clemency, see *De bello gallico* 8.44.1. Innutiaq, the fascinating father in Jean Briggs's *Never in Anger* (Cambridge, Mass., 1970), was doubly feared because he had never completely lost his temper, and yet everyone had seen—in small doses—his passionate lapses of self-control. Elizabeth Marshall Thomas's Toma, the super-self-controlled leader of a band of San foragers, flew, only once, into a legendary rage. "The people said: After that everyone knew how angry Toma could be, so from that day on he never had another fight" (*The Harmless People*, New York, [1958] 1989, p. 183).

THE AGE OF IMMEDIACY

It was to produce the controlled but dangerous man and to build the mutual trust that would enable such a man to endure shame that the Romans, like other peoples governed by shame, accorded special liberties to the child (not unlike those accorded the child by the Japanese, Inuit, San, Navajo, or Iroquois). In Rome, it appears to have been the adolescent who was given the widest scope. It was not unbecoming to the young, Pliny believed, to lead rather confused and turbulent lives. "A quiet and well-ordered life does older men honor, but not so much the young, in whom a certain amount of confusion and irregularity are not misplaced" (*Epistulae* 3.1.2).[109] "That time of life is accustomed to find favor rather than meet with opposition" (Cicero, *De officiis* 2.13.45).[110] In both the *Bacchides* and the *Asinaria*, to give just two examples, Plautus's wayward youths are able to presume on the indulgence of the father for their escapades: Pistoclerus meets with indulgence from his father Philoxenus as Argyrippus does from his father Demaenetus. "If I speak too freely," the brave young orator declares, "I will be pardoned owing to my youth" (Cicero, *Pro Roscio Amerino* 1.3).[111] Perhaps this immunity enabled adolescents to gain a feeling of self-mastery—and not just constriction—as they gained self-control.[112] Everyone knew you were capable of

---

109. *nam iuvenes confusa adhuc quaedam et quasi turbata non indecent.* Cf. Plutarch, *An seni respublica gerenda sit* 19 (*Moralia* 794A).

110. *nonmodo non invidetur illi aetati verum etiam favetur.*

111. *ego si quid liberius dixero...ignosci adulescentiae poterit.* "Dans les cités romaines, la jeunesse était considerée comme un groupe à part, qui avait des droits à part" (Paul Veyne, "Le folklore à Rome et les droits de la conscience publique sur la conduite individuelle," *Latomus* 42 [1983]: 29). Augustus was willing to humor the youthful Julia, but not the adult. For the indulgence granted the transgressions of youth, see Terence, *Andria* 443–444; Cicero, *Pro Caelio* 12.28, 18.42–43, 31.76–77; Livy 3.12.7; Quintilian, *Institutio oratoria* 1.3.3ff.; Emiel Eyben, *Restless Youth in Ancient Rome,* trans. Patrick Daly, London, 1993, esp. pp. 16–24, 78–80; A. W. Lintott, "The Tradition of Violence in the Annals of the Early Roman Republic," *Historia* 19 (1970): 24–29.

112. According to Anthony Wallace, the permissive child-rearing of the Iroquois had as its goal (interestingly enough from a Euro-American point of view) the cultivation of autonomous responsibility in the adult (*The Death and Rebirth of the Seneca,* New York, 1972, pp. 30–39). In Roman as in Iroquois child-rearing, the laissez-faire attitude of the adults was consistent with the setting up of strenuous ordeals. Cato the Elder's fond fixation on his son from infancy was not inconsistent with his setting strenuous ordeals for that same son. The Iroquois, like the Romans, placed a high value on "self-overcoming." Compare Erik Erikson on Sioux child-rearing: "The Sioux baby is permitted to remain an individualist...while he builds unequivocal trust in himself and his surroundings. Then when strong in body and confident in himself, he is asked to bow to a tradition of unrelenting public opinion....He is forced into a stern tradition which satisfies social needs....As long as he is able to conform he feels free" ("Childhood and Tradition in Two American Indian Tribes," *The Psychoanalytic Study of the Child* 1 [1945]: 344). By the late republic, this strategic indulgence had become problematic. As in modern American culture, the fear of the renegade male had become so great that more stringent methods of child-rearing, with a greater emphasis on obedience to authority, were cultivated. It was the Romans of the "decadence" who admired and cultivated the image of the father as martinet.

breaking the rules, because they had seen you do it every day as a child.[113] You knew you could get away with it, because you had. Concomitantly, everyone knew the cost, in willpower, of your growing self-control.[114]

The freed slave, having seldom experienced this indulgence, found it imperative to demonstrate that he or she could transgress. Plautus's slave Toxilus complains about the assertive insolence of *libertini:* "But this is the way with a lot of freed slaves: if they don't cross their patron, they don't think they're free enough or good enough or respected enough—unless they've done this, unless they've been impertinent to him, unless they've proved ungrateful to their benefactor (*Persa* 838–840)."[115]

REVEALING THE COST OF CONTROL: THE BLUSH

To stand on a chair mounted two-high on a shoulder bar 40 feet in the air is a laudable stunt.
It will earn a modicum of applause. Take away the net and the handclaps will rise by one
decibel. Now, wobble the chair to its ultimate degree and the act becomes sensational.

KARL WALLENDA[116]

Self-control gained its positive value, paradoxically, from its impossibility; for self-control to have social value, it needed to be belied.[117] This is the reason that Cicero and Quintilian recommend that the orator appear nervous and not fully under control. To be sincere was to be so totally in one's role that one was not safe

---

113. Children were often thought of as shameless. "[Children] would make rude noises at passersby; they would chase peculiar adults, like Horace's poet, along the streets; they would pluck the beard of a venerable philosopher; and a favorite game would be to stick a coin firmly in the mud, and then wait to see if an adult would try to pick it up" (Wiedemann, *Adults and Children in the Roman Empire,* p. 24; cf. p. 25); Horace, *Ars poetica* 455–56, *Satirae* 1.3.133–34, *Epistulae* 1.16.163–65; Petronius, *Satyricon* 92; Seneca, *De ira* 2.10.1–2. According to the *Digesta, infantes* (here formally below the age of seven) were coupled with lunatics, neither being held liable for homicide under the late Republican *lex Cornelia de sicariis et veneficiis* (48.8.12; cf. all of book 4).

114. Jean Briggs brilliantly describes with what anguish Inuit children learned self-restraint. She follows the miseries of little Raigili and Saarak as each was replaced by a new infant and their formerly unlimited self-indulgence thoroughly thwarted (*Never in Anger*). For similar experiences in other cultures where children were given great freedom, see Dorothea Leighton and Clyde Kluckhohn, *Children of the People: The Navaho Individual and His Development,* New York, [1947] 1969; Marjorie Shostak, *Nisa: The Life and Words of A !Kung Woman,* Cambridge, Mass., 1981.

115. Nixon trans. *sed ita pars libertinorum est: nisi patrono qui adversatust, / nec satis liber sibi videtur nec satis frugi nec sat honestus, / ni id effecit, ni ei male dixit, ni grato ingratus repertust.* See Pliny, *Epistulae* 9.5; Ramsay MacMullen, *Roman Social Relations, 50 B.C. to A.D. 184,* New Haven, 1974, pp. 113, 197 n. 76.

116. Quoted by Ron Morris, *Wallenda: A Biography of Karl Wallenda,* New York, 1976, p. 110. Morris frequently alludes to the highly skillful and practiced vulnerabilities that the Wallendas built into their high-wire acts to evoke the empathy of the audience.

117. One of the most important functions of Bedouin poetry, according to Lila Abu-Lughod, is that it reveals, by its unbridled passion and its transgressions, the enormous price of one's self-control and shame (*Veiled Sentiments: Honor and Poetry in a Bedouin Society,* Berkeley, 1986, esp. pp. 244–253).

there. When men and women walked the high wire of Roman honor, they needed to wobble.[118]

In this delicate physics of honor, the pivotal mechanism was the blush. The blush and sensitivity to shame were so inextricably linked in Roman thought that the words *pudor* and *rubor,* shame and redness, were often used together or interchangeably. "Purple shame," according to Ovid, "appeared on her guilty face (*Amores* 2.5.34).[119] Achilles "grew red" *(erubuit)* before he respected the rights of the suppliant Priam (Virgil, *Aeneis* 2.540–41).

Pliny the Elder describes the cheeks of the face as "the seat of shame." "It is here, in particular," he says, "that the red of the blush is revealed" (*Naturalis historia* 11.58.157).[120] The one sensitive to his or her "face," the *delicatus* with the *os molle,* the *imbecilla frons,* was liable to blush.[121] Like Ovid's artless Hippolytus or Seneca's virginal Theseus,[122] young men and women whose masks, whose *personae,* were not sufficiently tempered were especially liable to the blush.[123] (Notice that, in Roman sources, males are as likely to blush as females.) "Indeed, the blush appears particularly in youths in whom there is greater heat and a more tender brow" (Seneca, *Epistulae* 11.3).[124] In the case of Lucilius's young friend, the blush occurred, according to Seneca, "not on account of the infirmity of his mind, but from the unexpectedness of the situation which, even if it does not deeply impair the inexperienced youth, nevertheless is wont to move those who are prone to blush by a natural tendency of the body" (*Epistulae* 11.5).[125]

118. In contrast, in modern American society, there is generally the expectation that the honorable man or woman controls himself or herself consistently and at all times, without a lapse.

119. *conscia purpureus venit in ora pudor.*

120. *pudoris haec sedes: ibi maxume ostenditur rubor.* For *pudor* on the face, see Ovid, *Tristia* 2.30.

121. For the *imbecilla frons,* see Quintilian, *Institutio oratoria* 12.5.4.

122. "A bashful blush colored his [Hippolytus's] golden face" *(flava verecundus tinxerat ora rubor* [Ovid, *Heroides* 4.72]). "Golden shame tinged his [Theseus's] face" *(ora flavus tenera tinguebat pudor* [Seneca, *Phaedra* 652]). Compare Lygdamus's description of the youthful and blushing god (Tibullus 3.4.29–34).

123. Juvenal's servant is a simple, noble-spirited lad: *ingenui vultus puer ingenuique pudoris* (*Satirae* 11.154). Martial claims that his fifth book of epigrams could be read by *matronae, pueri virginesque.* Which book "Germanicus could, without a blush, read in the presence of maiden Athena" (*ore non rubenti / coram Cecropia legat puella* [5.2.7–8]). Martial assumes that the man would blush to violate the sensitivity of the young woman.

124. *Magis quidem in iuvenbus apparet, quibus et plus caloris est et tenera frons.* "Finally we have to mention a frequently cited characteristic which the Romans believed typical of an exemplary youth, namely diffidence *(pudor, verecundia),* of which blushing *(iuvenalis rubor)* is the symptom" (Eyben, *Restless Youth,* p. 40). Cf. Horace, *Epistulae* 17.2.21–22; Sidonius Apollinaris, *Epistulae* 1.2.3; Nicolaus of Damascus, *Vita Caesaris* 13.

125. *Non accidit hoc ab infirmitate mentis, sed a novitate rei, quae inexercitatos, etiamsi non concutit, movet naturali in hoc facilitate corporis pronos.*

One was particularly liable to blush when one was not trained to receive attention: "He was not prepared to talk, and, having been apprehended suddenly, the blush suffused his face from deep within his spirit" (Seneca, *Epistulae* 11.1).[126] Just being looked at by her new husband was enough to cause the bride to blush and lower her eyes in shame (Ovid, *Amores* 2.5.36).[127]

The blush could be evoked by an excess of positive as well as negative attention.[128] Indeed, the regard of the more powerful or prestigious might invoke the embarrassment or blush of the subject unable to return the look of his or her superior. In Plautus's *Asinaria* the poor man is not only embarrassed but deeply suspicious of the kindly and equal treatment afforded him by his rich neighbor. We might describe the poor man's anxiety as fear of being patronized. The respect shown him by his rich neighbor threatens to make him even more hopelessly in debt to, and so more vulnerable to, an already more powerful man.

Even one's own self-consciousness could cause one to blush. Her intense interest compels Virgil's Lavinia, listening to her mother plead with Turnus, to blush deeply (*Aeneis* 12.64–66). When Ovid's Medea comes suddenly and unexpectedly into the sight of Jason, "her cheeks grew red, her whole face burned with the blush" (*Metamorphoses* 7.78).[129]

THE LAW OF SHAME

Actors on the stage, who mimic the emotions, who portray fear and anxiety, who represent sadness, imitate bashfulness by keeping their head down, lowering their voices, and keeping their eyes fixed and rooted on the ground.[130] *They cannot, however, muster a blush; for the blush can neither be repressed nor induced. Wisdom offers us no defense or advantage against it; for the blush comes or goes unbidden. It is a law unto itself.*

SENECA, *EPISTULAE* 11.7[131]

126. *Non enim ex praeparato locutus est, sed subito deprehensus . . . adeo illi ex alto suffusus est rubor.* For blushing as a reaction of the unprepared, see Wurmser, *Mask of Shame*, p. 52. In Roman thought as in ours, it is difficult to distinguish inadequacy from unpreparedness. See Lynd, *On Shame*, pp. 30, 32–34.

127. *sponso visa puella novo.* Cf. Tibullus 3.4.30–32. For blushing at the look of another, see Ovid, *Amores* 2.8.15–16.

128. See Goffman, "Embarrassment," p. 266.

129. *erubuere genae, totoque recanduit ore.* Compare Catullus's maiden, blushing self-consciously at the sudden and simultaneous appearance of her mother and her lover's gift (65.19–24).

130. This is exactly how Terence's Chaerea, pretending to be a slave and a eunuch, feigns modesty (*Eunuchus* 579–580).

131. *Artifices scaenici, qui imitantur adfectus, qui metum et trepidationem exprimunt, qui tristitiam repraesentant, hoc indicio imitantur verecundiam: deiciunt enim vultum, verba submittunt, figunt in terram oculos et deprimunt. Ruborem sibi exprimere non possunt; nec prohibetur hic nec adducitur. Nihil adversus haec sapientia promittit, nihil proficit; sui iuris sunt, iniussa veniunt, iniussa discedunt.* He would try to train himself out of blushing but would fail: *His illum, quantum suspicor, etiam cum se confirmaverit et omnibus vitiis exuerit, sapientem quoque sequetur* [the blush] (11.1).

As Charles Darwin explained, "Blushing is not only involuntary; but the wish to restrain it, by leading to self-attention, actually increases the tendency."[132] While the Romans yearned for and idealized autonomy and self-mastery, the blush was one of the most important socializing mechanisms in ancient Rome precisely because it was involuntary. It was not subject to the will. The blush could not be mastered.[133]

Pudor and *pudeo* come from a root *(pu, pav)* meaning "to strike."[134] The blush struck you. It was the *signum pudoris,* the mark that the community (or nature, insofar as she was the benevolent overseer of the community) stamped on the face of a man or woman who belonged to it.[135] The blush enabled the cultural norms (or "nature," insofar as it was thought to embody or enforce these cultural norms) to triumph ultimately over the will of even a powerful mortal.[136] Our "real men" don't blush, but in ancient Rome even the "heavies," the *gravissimi,* as Seneca points out, were subject to the blush:

> Certain even very constant men, when in the public eye, break out in a sweat, just as if they were fatigued and overheated. The knees of others, when they are about to speak, begin to tremble; I know of those whose teeth chatter, whose tongues falter, whose lips quiver. Training and experience can never eradicate this propensity; nature exerts her power and by this weakness makes herself felt by even the strongest man.[137]

132. *Expression of the Emotions,* p. 310. For the involuntary nature of the blush, see also Thomas Burgess, *The Physiology or Mechanism of Blushing,* London, 1839, pp. 169–170; Lynd, *On Shame,* p. 33.

133. According to the Christian Gregory of Nazianzus,

> In time gone by... glory fell to the most dishonorable and dishonor to the noblest as these distinctions changed hands without justice.... The Lord God..., slow to anger, spoke these words: "It is not right that good and bad should enjoy the same repute; this would only increase evil. Therefore I will bestow a goodly token whereby you may tell who is evil and who is good." So saying, he reddened the cheeks of those who were good, causing the blood to flow beneath their skin as shame arose in them; especially in the female kind did he implant a deeper blush, inasmuch as they are weak of nature and tender of heart. But as for the evil, he made them hard and insensitive within, and that is why they are not in the least affected by shame. (*Poemata Moralia, Patrologia Graeca,* Migne ed., vol. 37.3, pp. 898–899)

Similar arguments are made by Burgess, *Physiology or Mechanism,* pp. 24–26, 49, 179–180, and by Darwin, *Expression of the Emotions,* p. 336. For more on the social advantages of blushing, see Goffman, "Embarrassment," pp. 270–271; Vieda Skultans, "Bodily Madness and the Spread of the Blush," in *The Anthropology of the Body,* ed. John Blacking, London, 1977, esp. p. 152.

134. Compare Sanscrit *paviram* or Latin *pavio, tripudium,* and *repudium.*

135. "Just see if any blush, the sign of *pudor,* appears on his face!" (*vide num eius color pudoris signum usquam indicat* [Terence, *Andria* 878]). Sandor Feldman believes that the development of a sense of shame represented the adoption, the incorporation into oneself, of what had originally been felt as an involuntary imposition ("Blushing, Fear of Blushing, and Shame," p. 381).

136. According to the ethologist Irenäus Eibl-Eibesfeldt, the evolutionary advantages of blushing for the survival of the human group may have fostered the development of highly vasculated skin parts and special presenting movements in humans ("Ritual and Ritualization from a Biological Perspective," in *Human Ethology: Claims and Limits of a New Discipline,* ed. M. von Cranach, K. Foppa, W. Lepenies, and D. Ploog, Cambridge, 1979, p. 14).

137. Cf. Cicero, *De oratore* 1.26.120–121.

I know that the blush, too, is like this, spreading suddenly over the faces of even the most dignified men. While youths are most likely to blush, nevertheless the blush touches even the veteran and the old. (Seneca, *Epistulae* 11.2)[138]

Seneca offers Pompey the Great, the great warlord of the dying republic, as an example: "Nothing was more tender than the face of Pompey; he blushed whenever he was in public, especially in assemblies" (*Epistulae* 11.4).[139]

Insofar as blushing was involuntary, the blusher felt his or her will overcome. He or she was patently, manifestly not autonomous.[140] For just that reason, the person with the ability to blush was sane and able to be trusted within a society.[141] The blush was the *color ingenuus,* the free-born, noble, innocent, and sincere complexion (*ingenuus pudor* [Catullus 61.79]).[142] Ovid's lover recommends himself to Cythera with a description of his blushing modesty, his crimson shame, as the concomitant of his trustworthiness, his naked simplicity, and his decency (*Amores*

138. *Quibusdam etiam constantissimis in conspectu populi sudor erumpit, non aliter quam fatigatis et aestuantibus solet, quibusdam tremunt genua dicturis, quorundam dentes colliduntur, lingua titubat, labra concurrunt. Haec nec disciplina nec usus umquam excutit, sed natura vim suam exercet et illo vitio sui etiam robustissimos admonet. Inter haec esse et ruborem scio, qui gravissimis quoque viris subitis adfunditur. Magis quidem in iuvenibus apparet,... nihilominus et veteranos et senes tangit.*

139. *Nihil erat mollius ore Pompei; numquam non coram pluribus rubuit, utique in contionibus. Fabianum, cum in senatum testis esset inductus, erubuisse memini. et hic illum mire pudor decuit.*

140. Goffman says of the embarrassed person:

He demonstrates that, while he cannot present a sustainable and coherent self on this occasion, he is at least disturbed by the fact and may prove worthy at another time. To this extent, embarrassment is not an irrational impulse breaking through socially prescribed behavior but part of this orderly behavior itself. Flusterings are an extreme example of that important class of acts which are actually quite spontaneous and yet no less required and obligatory than ones self-consciously performed. ("Embarrassment," pp. 270–271)

141. See Burgess, *Physiology or Mechanism,* p. 134; Darwin, *Expression of the Emotions,* p. 49; Skultans, "Bodily Madness," p. 153. The Papuan informant of the anthropologist Andrew Strathern spoke about the relationship between shame and trustworthiness among the native peoples of the Mount Hagen area of the Western Highlands district of New Guinea: "'All sensible people,' he added, 'will feel this *pipil* [shame]. If someone does not, his relations will tell him "you have no shame on your skin, you are crazy.... People have shame on their skin, but you have none. If you had a soul *(min)* as other people have, it would have given you a good social attitude *(noman kae,* the *noman* is thought to be inside a person's chest and to guide his thoughts, feelings and actions). But you have no *min,* and so you do not feel shame"'" ("Why Is Shame on the Skin?" in Blacking, *Anthropology of the Body,* esp. pp. 103–104).

142. The *ingenuus* was freeborn, a member of society, and also frank, transparent, noble. (Conversely, hiding or being brazen and deceitful were associated with servility; it was the behavior ascribed to slaves in Plautus.) Juvenal's young servant was "a lad with an ingenuous face and ingenuous modesty, such as those ought to be who are clothed in brilliant purple" *(ingenue vultus puer ingenuique pudoris / quales esse decet quos ardens purpura vestit* [Juvenal, *Satirae* 11.154–55]). The blush was the *ingenuus color* (Propertius 1.4.13)—evoked, according to Vitruvius, by one's shame at soliciting something suspect *(ingenuus color movetur pudore petendo rem suspiciosam* [*De architectura* 6, *praefatio* 5]). "A kindly nature with a generous hand gave him the gift of a pure spirit and a face ardent with modest blood—and what better thing can nature, more careful, more potent than any guardian, bestow upon a youth?"

(castum ingenium vultumque modesto
sanguine ferventem tribuit natura benigna

1.3.13–14).[143] Seneca was able to deduce from the blushing collapse of self-control of Lucilius's young friend "how much of will and of character he possessed, how far he had progressed" (11.1).[144] The youthful emperor Domitian's persistent flush was taken as the mark of his goodness and modesty: "On the day that Domitian first entered the senate, he spoke briefly of his absent father and brother and of his own youth, and since, at that point, his *mores* were unknown, his frequent blushing was interpreted as modesty" (Tacitus, *Historia* 4.40).[145] Pliny the Younger interprets the emperor Trajan's blush as a sign of his transparent sincerity: "While he listens to these words of praise, tears well up in his eyes and the blush of shame appears on his cheeks, for he recognizes that these words are addressed to himself and not to 'The Prince'" (*Panegyricus* 2.8).[146] Trajan's loss of control demonstrated that the ruler was liable to, answerable to those he ruled. Trajan revealed by his tearful blush the cost to his own autonomy that he was willing to pay to his people.[147] In the man or woman who blushed, the very weakness revealed the strength of social bonds; it was a confession of subordination that cemented society.

---

larga manu. quid enim puero conferre plus
custode et cura natura potentior omni? [Juvenal, *Satirae* 10.300–303])

143. *nulli cessura fides, sine crimine mores / nudaque simplicitas, purpureusque pudor.*

144. *in quo quantum esset animi, quantum ingenii, quantum iam etiam profectus, sermo primus ostendit.* Plutarch tells us that Cato the Elder liked to see young men blush rather than turn pale. "For to fear one's commanders when at close quarters with the enemy is a sign of bravery and of obedience to authority as well. Therefore Plato tries to establish the habit of fearing blame and disgrace more than toils and dangers, and Cato used to say that he liked people who blushed better than those who blanched" (Plutarch, *Quomodo adolescens poetas audire debeat* 10 [*Moralia* 29E]). See also *Cato Maior* 9, *Regum et imperatorum apophthegmata*, Cato 6 (*Moralia* 198E), *De vitioso pudore* 1 (*Moralia* 528F). One could, by blushing, hint at the fury (rather than the fear) behind one's self-control. "It is more serviceable for a youth to blush than to turn pale" (*erubescere est utilius iuvenem quam pallescere* [Caecilius Balbus, *Sententiae* 61, Friedrich ed.]). That the same fear and awe that produced the red face could produce the white is attested by Plautus, *Menaechmi* 610. But blanching was considered closer to the pallor of death than the red of blood. "*Aidos . . .* is defined as a fear of ill-repute, and is brought to pass in a way similar to the fear of danger; for those who feel shame blush, while those who fear death turn pale" (Aristotle, *Nicomachean Ethics* 4.9.1–3, 1128b 10–12). For pallor associated with fear or death, see Macrobius, *Saturnalia* 7.11.7; with death, Virgil, *Aeneis* 1.354, Petronius, *Satyricon* 63. With disgrace: Horace, *Carmina* 3.5.26–30. "Once, when Caesar was told that Antony and Dolabella were plotting revolution, he said that it was not the fat and long-haired fellows that troubled him but those pale and lean ones, meaning Brutus and Cassius" (Plutarch, *Brutus* 8.1). In Pliny's description of Domitian, he was said to have a "feminine pallor" of the body even while having a permanently red face (*superbia in fronte, ira in oculis, femineus pallor in corpore, in ore impudentia multo rubore suffusa* [*Panegyricus* 48.4]).

145. *Quo die senatum ingressus est Domitianus, de absentia patris fratrisque ac iuventa sua pauca et modica disseruit, decorus habitu; et ignotis adhuc moribus crebra oris confusio pro modestia accipiebatur.*

146. *Ad quas ille voces lacrimis etiam ac multo pudore suffunditur; agnoscit enim sentitque sibi, non principi dici.*

147. The ideal of autonomy must be belied. While the ideal is to be as fully in one's role as possible, the value of the *persona* comes from its occasionally falling away, revealing the *nuda simplicitas* of the actor.

THE PAIN OF SHAME

Blushing was not a pleasurable experience. It was a troubled commotion of the mind, a "change of color" *(mutatio coloris)*[148] and confusion *(confusio)*,[149] a disorder, anarchy, uncertainty in one's face and body.[150] Latin *confusio* resembled Greek *paralysis:* it was a sort of liquidating of the body; the limbs lost their tensile strength. Those who blushed felt as if they needed to "collect" themselves *(se colligere* [Seneca, *Epistulae* 11.1]). The blusher was torn in different directions, wounded, invaded; he or she fell apart, came unglued.[151] Virgil's Lavinia blushed "as if someone had stained [*violaverit*] Indian ivory with a bloody dye" *(Aeneis* 12.67–68).[152] The Roman of honor was simultaneously a tiger on a leash and a bug under glass.

The pain of shame (like its pleasure) was self-awareness. As in the Hebrew story of Adam and Eve, the sense of shame was the concomitant of the loss of innocence and fall into self-consciousness.[153] *Conscius rubor,* Catullus calls it (65.24). "Shame," Helen Lynd explains, "interrupts any unquestioning unaware sense of self."[154] In the words of Donald L. Nathanson (following Charles Darwin and Silvan Tomkins): "Self-consciousness is a cognate for shame."[155] Macrobius met the young poet Servius at a dinner party. When it was the latter's turn to speak, Servius blushed and betrayed the intensity of his discomfort. His table companion Disarius encouraged him: "Go ahead, Servius—you are the most learned not only of your peers but of all men. Wear a bold face. Banish the diffidence your

---

148. Cicero, *Pro Cluentio* 54.

149. *Confusio* is from *fundo,* to pour out, to empty, to emit freely (as blood or tears), to let go. For the psychosomatic symptoms of blushing and embarrassment, see Burgess, *Physiology or Mechanism,* esp. pp. 131–135; Darwin, *Expression of the Emotions,* pp. 317, 322–325; Goffman, "Embarrassment," pp. 264, 266.

150. *oris confusio pro modestia accipiebatur* (Tacitus, *Historia* 4.40).

151. Susan Miller points out that the blusher's feeling of distraction is created, in part, by increasing exposure as he or she attempts to slip into hiding (*The Shame Experience,* Hillsdale, New Jersey, 1985, pp. 38–39).

152. *Indum sanguineo veluti violaverit ostro / si quis ebur.* On the violence of the metaphor, see R. O. A. M. Lyne, "Lavinia's Blush: Virgil, *Aeneis* 12.64–70," *Greece and Rome* 30 (1983): 55–64. Lyne points out that the allusion in Virgil's metaphor is to Menelaus's wound in the *Iliad* 4.141ff. I owe this citation to Jim O'Hara.

153. "That feeling: 'I am the center of the universe!' arises very sharply when one is suddenly overtaken by shame, when one stands dazed in the midst of a breaking wave and feels oneself bedazzled, blinded as if by a great eye that looks at us and through us from all sides" (Friedrich Nietzsche, *Daybreak,* trans. R. J. Hollingdale, Cambridge [1881] 1997, no. 352). "In this moment of self-consciousness, the self stands revealed. Coming suddenly upon us, experiences of shame throw a flooding light on what and who we are and what the world we live in is" (Lynd, *On Shame,* p. 49).

154. *On Shame,* p. 20.

155. "A Timetable for Shame," in Nathanson, *Many Faces of Shame,* p. 26. "Experiences of shame are called self-consciousness" (Lynd, *On Shame,* p. 19). See Scheler, "Der 'Ort' des Schamgefühls," pp. 51, 68–69. For Scheler, individualization, limitation, self-consciousness, and consciousness of choice are coincident. See also Wurmser, *Mask of Shame,* p. 51.

blush betrays. Speak freely to us whatever comes to your mind." Servius, still in-capacitated by shame, could not emit a word despite his friend's repeated exhor-tations. Finally, he asked the question: "What happened to me? How does the red of the body arise from the shame of the soul?" (*Saturnalia* 7.11.1–3).[156]

The continence requisite for all social life was the source of individual self-attention and self-definition. At the same time, the impossibility of disengagement could effectively alienate and "disembody" consciousness. But, as I discussed ear-lier, this acute self-consciousness could also be cured by disciplined and formal-ized behaviors.[157] In her famous book on Japanese culture, Ruth Benedict dis-cussed "the 'expert' self-discipline, in which they [the Japanese] train themselves with such persistence to eliminate the 'observing self' and get back to the direct-ness of early childhood."[158]

THE INDULGENCE OF SHAME

If the blush was a mark imposed by the group, this mark did not necessarily dis-figure; it could ornament, like the red face of the *triumphator.* "I recall that Fabi-anus, when he was summoned to testify in the senate, blushed, and this shame ad-mirably became him" (Seneca, *Epistulae* 11.4).[159] The blush represented a loss of self-control, and so was indeed a fault *(vitium),* but a Roman audience found the blush an endearing imperfection: the blusher could trust in, could presume on, the goodwill of the larger society.[160] The community redeemed the honor, lost by blushing, of the man and woman who blushed—*because* they blushed.[161]

---

156. *naturali pressus ille verecundia usque ad proditionem coloris erubuit. Et Disarius: Age, Servi, non solum adulescen-tium, qui tibi aequaevi sunt, sed senum quoque omnium doctissime, commascula frontem, et sequestrata verecundia quam in te facies rubore indicat.... Cumque diutule tacentem crebris ille exhortationibus excitaret: Hoc, inquit Servius, ex te quaero, quod mihi contigisse dixisti, quae faciat causa, ut rubor corpori ex animi pudore nascatur?* See Eyben, *Restless Youth,* p. 41.

157. See chapter 2 and chapter 3.

158. *The Chrysanthemum and the Sword,* p. 289. This is related to Mihaly Csikszentmihalyi's notion of "flow"; see chapter 2.

159. *Fabianum, cum in senatum testis esset inductus, erubuisse memini, et hic illum mire pudor decuit.* For *vere-cundia* as an *ornamentum,* see Cicero, *Pro Roscio Amerino* 149, *De officiis* 1.27.93, *De amicitia* 22.82; Ovid, *Amores* 1.8.35.

160. Did the blush evolve as a way of controlling the confrontational impulse, as a signal of ap-peasement and apology? See Cristiano Castelfranchi and Isabella Poggi, "Blushing as Discourse: Was Darwin Wrong?" in *Shyness and Embarrassment: Perspectives from Social Psychology,* ed. W. Ray Crozier, Cambridge, 1990, esp. pp. 240–248. See the discussion of appeasement gestures in Irenäus Eibl-Eibesfeldt, *Ethology: The Biology of Behavior,* New York, 1970, pp. 129–134; *Love and Hate: The Natural His-tory of Behavior Patterns,* trans. Geoffrey Strachan, New York, 1971, pp. 174–178; and Frans de Waal, *Peace-Making among Primates,* Cambridge, Mass., 1989. See also the chapter on "Shame, Blushing and Hidden Secrets," in Jeffrey Masson and Susan McCarthy, *When Elephants Weep: The Emotional Lives of Animals,* New York, 1995, pp. 179–191.

161. "Qualities exerted with apparent fearfulness receive applause from every voice and support from every hand. Diffidence may check resolution and obstruct performance, but it compensates its

For this reason the Romans were not as ashamed of being ashamed as we are. (Compare the reception given to the emperor Trajan's tears and that given to the tears of the American presidential candidate Edmund Muskie in the New Hampshire primary of 1972, which disqualified him, in the eyes of Americans, from a position of leadership.) The Romans did not, in general, have to "break" to blush or weep. Their awareness of the positive and socializing aspects of shame may help to explain why the Romans of the Republic tolerated well-timed and periodic displays of emotions that we do not. The Romans did not have to perpetually display a "stiff upper lip."[162] They indulged in public displays of embarrassment and weeping that we do not.[163] A nervous modesty, a revelation that one was sensitive to the eyes of one's observers, was as expected of the accomplished orator at the commencement of his speech as it was of the young man at the outset of his speaking career. According to Cicero's Crassus, "Even the best orators appear impudent and arrogant if they do not begin their pleading with due shyness and seem nervous at the beginning" (*De oratore* 1.26. 119).[164] "I turn pale," he declares, "at the outset of every speech, and quake in every limb and in all my soul" (*De oratore* 1.26.121).[165] Quintilian thought that the man about to begin a

embarrassments by more important advantages; it conciliates the proud, and softens the severe, averts envy from excellence, and censure from miscarriage" (Samuel Johnson, "The Nature and Remedies of Bashfulness," *The Rambler* no. 159 [Tuesday, September 24, 1751], in *The Works of Samuel Johnson*, vol. 3 [Troy, New York, 1903], p. 292). For the collaboration of others in protecting the face of the shamed, see Goffman, "Embarrassment," pp. 267–268; Mark R. Leary and Sarah Meadows, "Predictors, Elicitors, and Concomitants of Social Blushing," *Journal of Personality and Social Psychology* 60 (1961): 254–262.

162. "It is important to stress that Roman culture allowed, gave opportunities for, and at funerals even encouraged, the public expression of grief" (Keith Hopkins and Melinda Letts, "Death in Rome," *Death and Renewal: Sociological Studies in Roman History*, vol. 2, Cambridge, 1983, p. 221). See also Ramsay MacMullen, "Romans in Tears," *Classical Philology* 75 (1980): 254–255. For reasons similar to those discussed here, the Japanese, according to Takeo Doi, were, until recently, not as ashamed as Westerners of manifesting shame. (Consider the geysers erupting from the eyes of men and women in the *Tale of Genji*, and from the warriors and their women in the *Tale of the Heike, Yoshitsune*, and other medieval Japanese warrior stories.) Doi believes that Western influence has made the Japanese increasingly ashamed of feeling ashamed and less able to *amaeru*, to presume upon, to trust in the goodwill of others (*The Anatomy of Dependence*, trans. John Bester, Tokyo, 1973, pp. 108, 119, 121).

163. For Augustus's public tears, see Suetonius, *Augustus* 58.2. For those of Titus, see Suetonius, *Titus* 10.1; Dio 66.26.1. See the reactions of Cicero to the tears of Gaius Marcellus (*Pro Marcello* 4.10). Caracalla won popular favor for crying or averting his eyes when criminals were thrown to wild animals (*Historia Augusta, Caracalla* 1.5).

164. *Mihi etiam quique optime dicunt, . . . nisi timide ad dicendum accedunt, et in exordienda oratione perturbantur, paene impudentes videntur.* See Seneca, *Epistulae* 11.2–4.

165. *in me ipso saepissime experior, ut exalbescam in principiis dicendi, et tota mente, atque omnibus artubus contremiscam.*

speech should hesitate, sigh, pat his head, or wring his hands with anxiety (*Institutio oratoria* 11.3.158).[166]

It was hard to be anything by oneself in ancient Rome. Challenging and maintaining the face was a collaborative effort. Limited shaming and invoking the blush formed part of a cultural inoculation against the shame that could destroy and "desoul" one.[167]

THE STIMULUS OF SHAME

One was ashamed, in ancient Rome, of being smaller than one's allotted share, of not being able to fill up the space granted to one. A Roman might be ashamed of not filling his or her ancestors' shoes, of not achieving his or her own or others' expectations. He or she might be ashamed of being poor, of being needy, of being dependent.[168] Above all, a Roman was ashamed of being ineffective or impotent, of not fulfilling the demands of his or her role. A *grammaticus* would blush for shame at a slip of the tongue (Seneca, *Epistulae* 95.9). A Roman soldier would blush to be accused of not being able to bear the hardship of a long winter campaign (Livy 5.6.5). When, in 449 B.C.E., the Roman cavalry dismounted and fought on foot in order to rescue from the Sabines the beleaguered Roman infantry, the latter were ashamed not only that they had to be rescued but also that the cavalry had assumed their role and showed themselves better foot soldiers than they were (Livy 3.62.8–9).[169] However, so long as these shortcomings were seen as surmountable, as temporary or expiable inadequacies, the shame that

166. The orator should look emotionally exhausted at the end of his oration (11.3.147). On the demonstration of emotions expected of the orator, see Fritz Graf, "Gestures and Conventions: The Gestures of Roman Actors and Orators," in *A Cultural History of Gesture*, ed. Jan Bremmer and Herman Roodenburg, Ithaca, 1991, pp. 36–58. Compare Confucius's directions for appearing sincere (*Analects* 10.3–6).

167. "That bashfulness...which prevents disgrace, that short temporary shame which secures us from the danger of lasting reproach, cannot be properly counted among our misfortunes" (Johnson, "Nature and Remedies of Bashfulness," p. 292). See Goffman, "Embarrassment," p. 270 n. 10; Scheler, "Der 'Ort' des Schamgefühls," p. 115.

168. "In the following year [455 B.C.E.], in the consulships of Titus Romilius and Gaius Veturius, the tribunes frequently urged the law (to open the Aventine to settlement) in every *contio*, saying that they would be ashamed, and their numbers augmented in vain, if this matter lay dead for the two years of their service, as it had in the five proceeding years" (*Insequente anno T. Romilio C. Veturio consulibus legem omnibus contionibus suis celebrant: pudere se numeri sui nequiquam aucti, si ea res aequo suo biennio iaceret ac toto superiore lustro iacuisset* [Livy 3.31.2]). When, in 219 B.C.E., word came of Hannibal's capture of Saguntum, the news caused shame to the Romans who had not met their treaty obligations to the Saguntines (*pudor non lati auxilii* [Livy 21.16.2]). "The Romans were at last seized with shame that Saguntum was in the power of the enemy" (*verecundia Romanos tandem cepit, Saguntum... sub hostium potestate esse* [Livy 24.42.9]).

169. *pudore deinde animos peditum accendunt. Verecundiae erat equitem suo alienoque Marte pugnare, peditum ne ad pedes quidem degresso equiti parem esse.*

they engendered was endurable and often served as a goad to achievement. The young Scipio Aemilianus was ashamed to be spoken of as a quiet and indolent man, but when he confessed that shame to Polybius, the latter responded: "I admire you when you say that you are pained to think that you are of a milder character than becomes members of this family; for that shows that you have a high spirit" (31.23.9–24.4).[170] Scipio's display of shame not only met with indulgence but impelled him to improve himself.[171]

Mild shaming could be a form of challenge, "trial by taunting," as Goffman calls it. Cornelia never let her sons Tiberius or Gaius Gracchus forget that she was the daughter of Scipio Africanus. She reproached them because she was not yet known as the mother of the Gracchi (Plutarch, *Tiberius Gracchus* 8.5). A degree of disregard, of chiding and teasing taught one poise and self-control.[172] The result of Cornelia's teasing was, according to Thomas Africa, that "both sons were confident to the point of arrogance."[173]

Insofar as Rome was a contest culture, mocking and teasing formed one of the most common and insistent forms of the ordeal, whether it be the coarse jests aimed, during his wedding, at the bridegroom or the mocking derision aimed, during his triumph, at the general.[174] The endless shaming, the ranking behavior that Plautus's slaves suffer from each other, was not unlike the ritual provocation of the modern "Dozens" that taught slaves and free African Americans to be "cool."[175] Inuring to shame helped to inhibit violence within a culture without a

---

170. Paton trans.

171. For examples of shaming as a spur, see Livy 25.37.10–11; Frontinus, *Strategemata* 4.1.1; Tacitus, *Historia* 3.2.

172. "It is no wonder that trial by taunting is a test that every young person passes through until he develops a capacity to maintain composure" (Goffman, "Embarrassment," p. 267). Ruth Benedict points out that teasing threats of rejection and separation were used beginning early in a Japanese child's life to encourage the development of expert self-discipline, a discipline reinforced by "hazing" in secondary schools and the army. At the same time this teasing also made youths extremely sensitive to insult and fearful of ostracism (*The Chrysanthemum and the Sword*, pp. 261–264, 273–274, 287–288). Likewise, exceptional self-control appears to have been the goal of the type of mild and insistent shaming among the Inuit described by Jean Briggs in an unpublished paper, "Out of the Garden of Eden: Morality Play in the Life of a Canadian Inuit Three-Year-Old." A similar type of emotional "coolness" or "awayness" was the end result of types of taunting in Balinese culture. See Gregory Bateson and Margaret Mead, *Balinese Character: A Photographic Analysis*, New York, 1942, pp. 26, 32–34, 131, 148, 151, 204. Teasing was a particular method of socialization that produced an adult able to demonstrate a heightened degree of control over his or her emotions while preserving a degree of inner autonomy.

173. "Mask of an Assassin," p. 604.

174. For the variety of teasing invective in Rome, see Thomas Cole, "In Response to Nevio Zorzetti, 'Poetry and Ancient City: The Case of Rome,'" *Classical Journal* 86 (1991): 379.

175. In the African-American teasing game known as "the Dozens," the ability to endure shaming was one of the qualities required of the winner. The one who preserved his "cool" at all costs was admired. To lose one's composure and to lash out was to lose. It is not surprising that this provocative be-

central peacekeeping force and helped to desensitize the Roman to the shaming of the enemy and the stranger.[176]

In his essay "On Bashfulness," Plutarch prescribes just such a "discipline" in enduring mild social discomfort and shame as a remedy for excessive shyness, and therefore for submissiveness (*De vitioso pudore* [*Moralia* 530E–533F]). "Taunting" would steel one against the ability of others to cow the spirit. "It is well," he says, "to choose a time when children are full of confidence to put them to shame by rebuke, and then in turn to cheer them up by praises, and to imitate the nurse who, when they have made their babies cry, in turn offer them the breast for comfort" (Plutarch, *De liberis educandis* 12 [*Moralia* 9A]).[177]

The work of a modern psychologist, Solomon Asch, throws a searching light on the ancient Roman "physics of shame." In a well-known experiment, Asch tested the ability of one lone subject to affirm his judgment against a unanimous majority of confederates.[178] In an apparently simple test of perception that was in fact a test of independence and sensitivity to shame, three-quarters of the subjects tested by Asch altered some or all of their own correct judgments to coincide with the deliberately erroneous judgments expressed aloud by the confederates. While almost all the subjects felt discomfort (often acute) in the course of the experiment, a minority were able to resist the desire to conform and be accepted. The social psychologist Thomas Scheff, in turn, discussed the results of Asch's experiment and Asch's subsequent interviews with the subjects.[179] He suggested

---

havior would continue to be practiced in a threatened subculture that relies to a great degree on the masking of one's emotions. "This teasing game promotes the toughening of emotional sensitivity, and the inhibiting of impulses toward physical aggression. Frustrated outgroup aggression is safely channeled into the ingroup. In this, the formalized game of 'the Dozens' has social value to a group subjected to suppression, discrimination and humiliation" (Samuel Sperling, "On the Psychodynamics of Teasing," *Journal of the American Psychoanalytical Association* 1 [1953]: 470).

176. The Roman who could not endure the enemy's taunting, like the son of Titus Manlius Torquatus, endangered the whole army as well as the hierarchy of command. Fabius Maximus, the famous "Hesitator" of the Hannibalic War, had to ignore shaming by his fellow Romans as well as by the enemy.

177. The Inuit, as described by Jean Briggs, were, like the Romans, a culture without a central peace-keeping force. Inuit "teasing" behavior was a way of accustoming the child to endure low levels of shame even while imparting to the child that she could presume on the affection of the adults. The mother and grandmother of a small girl repeatedly shamed her until she cried and then told her that she should not "take things seriously"; of course they loved her! She knew that! ("Out of the Garden of Eden"). For moderate shaming and reintegration, see also Leighton and Kluckhohn, *Children of the People,* pp. 32–36, 42, 51–52, 55, 58, 105, 170–171, 235. Cf. the careful balancing mechanisms of child-rearing that Seneca prescribes in *De ira* 2.21.1–8.

178. Solomon Asch, "Studies of Independence and Conformity: A Minority of One against a Unanimous Majority," *Psychological Monographs* 70 (1956): 1–70.

179. Thomas J. Scheff, "Shame and Conformity," in *Microsociology: Discourse, Emotion and Social Structure,* Chicago, 1990, esp. pp. 89–95.

that those who were able to maintain their self-esteem and affirm their own judgments against the group were those who were able to endure, to "manage" a degree of shame. They could act despite their embarrassment. Those who were intimidated, who caved in, were those who could not tolerate even mild degrees of shame.

Asch emphasized (in his comments on his interviews with the subjects) that those who had most frequently succumbed to the pressure to blend invisibly into the group were precisely the ones who, when confronted with the purpose of the test, were likely to deny or radically underestimate the extent of their collaboration and exaggerate their independence. In other words, those excessively sensitive to shame were, paradoxically, those most likely to deny that they felt ashamed at all and to insist on their autonomy.[180] Scheff explains this response very ably in terms of the "spiral of shame."[181] Those who could not bear the shame of exclusion also could not bear the shame of inadequacy implied by their collusion. It was clear both from Asch's experiment and the subsequent interviews with the subjects that those who most feared and rejected the emotion of shame were least capable of acting in accordance with their own will.

In Rome, loving, nurturing, and cultivating seem to have involved perpetual mild shaming and teasing. The lover affronted, called the beloved by animal names: "my little dove," "my little veal," "my little goat" (e.g., Plautus, *Asinaria* 666–667; *Casina* 134–138). But the difference between the teasing of the *amicus* and the *inimicus* was that the former was prepared to pay for his or her teasing, while the latter was not. The former was a reciprocal relationship; the latter was not. The benevolent teaser was prepared to atone for the violation.

At the time I am writing, the idea is popular in the United States that no one should ever be shamed. We forget that teasing and mild shaming are among the most important socializing mechanisms of society—*provided that trust is there and that the teaser is prepared to exchange roles with the teased.* When reassurance and reintegration are part of the process, teasing and mild shaming are not only forms of communication, they are forms of communion.

---

180. Our modern American insistence on autonomy and our high degree of conformity (and terror of exclusion) are not unrelated. They are two aspects of the same excessive sensitivity to shame and the yearning to be loved and included. "It is an extremely paradoxical idea, but it seems possible that the very desire of the Japanese for *amae* [to be able to presume on the love and acceptance of others] leads them to deny it when they find it difficult to satisfy that desire in practice" (Doi, *Anatomy of Dependence*, pp. 112–113).

181. On the spiral of shame, see T.J. Scheff, "The Shame-Rage Spiral: Case Study of an Interminable Quarrel," in *The Role of Shame in Symptom Formation*, ed. H. Lewis, Hillsdale, N.J., 1987, pp. 109–149. Such a spiral of shame was indicated by Darwin. He believed that the wish to restrain the blush led to increased self-attention, which actually aggravated the tendency to blush. See Darwin, *Expression of the Emotions*, p. 310. See also Sandor Ferenczi, "Embarrassed Hands," in *Further Contributions to the Theory and Technique of Psychoanalysis*, New York, [1926] 1953; Tomkins, "Shame," p. 155.

SHAME AND BALANCE

Mild shaming stimulated one's yearning for acceptance and approval;[182] it encouraged one to "take heart," to overreach oneself.[183] It was by taunting that Acestis spurred Entellus to box with Dares. Having been knocked to the ground, he rose to fight more ferociously (*Aeneis* 5.386–402, 453–455).[184] At the Battle of Orchomenus in 85 B.C.E., the general Sulla threw himself from his horse, seized a standard, and, driving through the ranks of his retreating soldiers, cried aloud, "O Romans, when men ask you where you betrayed your commander, tell them it was at Orchomenus" (Plutarch, *Sulla* 21.2). According to Appian, "When the officers saw his peril, they darted from their ranks to his aid, and the troops, moved by a sense of shame, followed and drove the enemy back in their turn" (*Mithridates* 49). Everyone followed him, Frontinus tells us, out of shame (*cuius rei pudore universi eum secuti sunt* [*Strategemata* 2.8.12]); this was the beginning of Sulla's victory.[185] Like the many challenges that took the form "if you are a man," these forms of shaming were designed to prod and stimulate to action.[186]

Like a good athletic coach, the general taunted his own soldiers as he did the enemy. Livy's consul Titus Quinctius Capitolinus addressed the men who, in 446 B.C.E., on account of civil strife in Rome, had not gone out to meet the attacks of the Aequi and the Volsci: "I have no consciousness of crime, fellow Quirites, and yet I appear before you feeling the greatest shame. Of this you are well aware— and it is this that will be handed down to posterity: that the Aequi and Volsci (who

---

182. "For guilt the antidote is forgiveness; shame tends to seek the healing response of acceptance—acceptance of the self despite its weaknesses, defects and failures" (Andrew P. Morrison, "Shame and the Psychology of the Self," in *Kohut's Legacy: Contributions to Self Psychology*, ed. Paul E. Stepansky and Arnold Goldberg, Hillsdale, N.J., 1984, p. 87).

183. Cf. Livy 3.62.1, 8; Tacitus, *Annales* 2.13. Speaking of the Ilongot horticultural and hunting population of the Northern Luzon, the Philippines, Michelle Rosaldo comments, "As children learn to speak, the verbal challenges of adults are seen to 'shame' them in a way that motivates the acquisition of new skill and knowledge. Verbal wit, fine dress, productive skill are all, Ilongot claim, things that the young acquire because they envy the accomplishments of peers and would not have their fellows' excellence stand to 'shame' them" ("The Shame of Headhunters and the Autonomy of Self," *Ethos* 11 [1983]: 144). "In ambition the person endeavors to overcome shame by objectively improving the value of the self. One may say it is the instinctual drive of exhibition modified by shame" (Wurmser, *Mask of Shame*, p. 51).

184. *at non tardatus casu neque territus heros / acrior ad pugnam redit ac vim suscitat ira. tum pudor incendit viris.* The attitudes expressed in this behavior are closely related to those discussed in chapter 3 ("defeated, we prevail").

185. Sulla used a similar strategy when he marched on Rome in 88 B.C.E. against Marius: "Sulla's forces were beginning to waver when Sulla seized a standard and exposed himself to danger in the foremost ranks, so that out of regard for their general and fear of disgrace (*atimia*), they might rally at once" (Appian, *Bellum civile* 1.7.58). See Frontinus, *Strategemata* 4.1.1.

186. See chapter 3.

are hardly equal opponents to the Hernici) came under arms to the walls of Rome in the fourth consulship of Titus Quinctius unavenged!" (Livy 3.67.1).[187]

There is an important difference, however, between the enemy's and the general's reproaches: the good general, like the good parent, also praises his troops; he lifts their spirits up as well as he depresses them. In 449 B.C.E., the consul Horatius used shame (as well as praise) to spur his soldiers into battle against the Sabines: "The consul provided for every contingency, extolling the brave, and upbraiding those who fought without energy. Having been scolded, they at once began to acquit themselves like men—shame proving as powerful an incentive to them as praise to the others" (Livy 3.63.3).[188] Good shaming, then, was a form of contest that followed certain rules. Benevolent shaming was accompanied by a sense of inhibition on the part of the person doing the shaming. Indeed, teasing could be a way of proving that one could do harm but that one chose not to, a chance to demonstrate that one could be aggressive and yet hold back, allowing the person exercising the restraint to feel magnanimous. Good shaming, moreover, was done to someone's face and not behind the back (which was a form of theft). Indeed, mild teasing, because the teased person was aware that the teaser was holding back, could feel like deference. (Bad shaming had no limits and no inhibitions; the shamer went for the jugular.)

The person giving way, who showed *verecundia* and *reverentia* to others, was entrusting them with part of herself. She depended on them to watch over her, or that part of her, that she had given them in trust. She trusted them to respond to her, to "answer" to her. When someone she trusted called her a worm, she knew that the humanness they had taken from her was a loan she made to them, a trust that they needed to treasure and guard and give back. Allowing someone to tease you was like opening your house to a guest; if the teaser accepted your hospitality *as a gift*, then you, the person teased, were the richer for it.

I cannot emphasize enough how important this behavior was in a contest culture, a sometimes brutally competitive, hierarchical society in which one's status and being were perpetually tested. Why did Plautus's slaves and lovers perpetually tease one another, and why did his audience enjoy the teasing? Why were the senator, the father, and the soldier "roasted" in Roman comedy or at the triumph? Because there was safety in the teasing: you could be bald or a worm and still be all right; you could be lacking and inadequate and be indulged for it.

---

187. "*etsi mihi nullius noxae conscius, Quirites, sum, tamen cum pudore summo in conspectum vestrum processi. Hoc vos scire, hoc posteris memoriae traditum iri: Aequos et Volscos, vix Hernicis modo pares, T. Quinctio quartum consule ad moenia urbis Romae impune armatos venisse!*" For the important role of shame in Roman military campaigns, see Kaster, "Shame of the Romans," pp. 17–18.

188. *Consul providere omnia, laudare fortis, increpare sicubi segnior pugna esset. Castigati fortium statim virorum opera edebant tantumque hos pudor quantum alios laudes excitabunt.*

Moreover, in the Roman's potlatch mentality, tolerance of shaming and teasing could be referred to the ideal of *liberalitas:* giving away and giving way were potentially indistinguishable. Tolerance of ridicule and teasing could turn a loss, an inadequacy, into a superabundance, an overflowing. The ridicule that the *imperator* endured from his soldiers at his triumph was not just a way of bringing him back down to earth; it was also a way for his soldiers to prove the trust and love that they had for him.[189] Good teasing was like being naked together in the baths or the gym—it expressed a willingness to be bound to one another, to be obligated to one another for one's humanity.[190] Vespasian earned Suetonius's admiration for his good-humored tolerance of men such as the taunting Cynic Demetrius (Suetonius, *Vespasianus* 13). Likewise, Antoninus Pius gained stature in Lucian's eyes for patiently enduring the jibes of the Cynic Peregrinus; Lucian interpreted his tolerance as arising from his generous spirit (*De morte Peregini* 18).

Positive forms of shaming were ways of creating a good contest even, or especially, when the contest was unequal. Taking turns did not create equality, and yet it was a way of equalizing the competition between master and slave, general and soldier, man and woman, parent and child, and even god and human. It was as if the two principles that organized the Roman government, *par potestas* (power limited by collegiality) and *potestas ad tempus* (power limited in time), also organized the Romans' emotional life. If the good contest involved *par potestas*, benevolent shaming helped to create equality by the application of the principle *potestas ad tempus*.

But shaming had to be administered judiciously.[191] If you fail to correct your friends at all, Cicero admonishes his hearer, you let them plunge headlong into an uncontrollable fall. But, Cicero goes on, "Careful calculation and attention must be applied in this matter, that your admonitions be without acerbity, that your re-

---

189. I suspect, although I am by no means certain, that this is the explanation both for the giving of ridiculous nicknames like "Warty," "Gimpy," and "Baldy" to Roman aristocrats and to the adoption of these as permanent *cognomina* by aristocratic families. Cf. Plutarch, *Cicero* 1.3. Although I disagree, in part, with Anthony Corbeill's explanation, I refer the reader to his very interesting discussion on Roman names in *Controlling Laughter: Political Humor in the Late Roman Republic*, Princeton, 1996, pp. 57–97.

190. When my students, on the last day of my first teaching job, gleefully recited a list of the most ridiculous statements I had made during the year, I was amused and touched—because I trusted them, and because they trusted me. Indeed, it was their way of expressing how much they trusted me. Conversely, I suggest that the concern for "civility" and "political correctness" in contemporary American culture are the result of the absence of mutual trust, resulting from excessive shaming without reincorporation. The shaming that Nathan McCall found unendurable from whites, because he did not trust them, he found endurable from his black peers (*Makes Me Wanna Holler*, New York, 1994).

191. This is a point made repeatedly by John Braithwaite in *Crime, Shame, and Reintegration*, Cambridge, 1989.

buke lack viciousness" (*De amicitia* 24.89).[192] Make sure, Seneca urges, that a person is left something to lose; a man with an irremediably ruined reputation was exempt from further shaming (*De clementia* 1.22.1). Our forefathers, Cicero asserts, intended the censor's power to inspire fear, not to punish for life (*Pro Cluentio* 43.120).[193] This moderation in shaming was exactly what Julius Caesar did not observe when he succeeded in strong-arming himself into the provincial assignments he desired: "Elated with joy, he could not refrain from gloating a few days later before a packed senate, that having gotten what he desired despite the ill-will and complaints of his opponents, he would thenceforth leap on [*insultare*] their heads" (Suetonius, *Julius* 22.2).[194] Without trust, shaming was unbearable. Lack of mutual trust was a lack of mirroring, an unwillingness to play the same game by the same rules. When you gave way without trusting those to whom you were *entrusting*, the gift became an extortion, a theft, and created resentment and a desire for revenge.[195]

THE REDEMPTION OF THE SHAMED

The emotional equilibrations of shame and reintegration worked not just as a mechanism to correct inadequacy but also to expiate, to exact payment for transgression. In the Irish epic the *Táin Bó Cuailnge*, the precocious hero Cuchulain, like all great warriors, was a danger to his own people, returning to Emain still driven by the fury of battle. When he threatened to kill every man in his own fort, his people sent out the women—naked—to meet him. The sight of so many

---

192. *Omni igitur hac in re habenda ratio et diligentia est, primum ut monitio acerbitate, deinde ut obiurgatio contumelia caveat.* Too "penetrating" a shaming would result in hatred and anger. Moderate shaming guides and corrects the orator, just as the orator guides and corrects his audience, but "one must be careful not to arouse the disapproving outcries of the people, who are aroused...if a remark is thought to be harsh or arrogant or base or mean" (*vitanda est acclamatio adversa populi, quae aut orationis peccato aliquo excitatur si aspere, si arroganter, si turpiter, si sordide...dictum esse aliquid videtur* [*De oratore* 2.83.339]).

193. *Timoris enim causam, non vitae poenam in illa potestate* [*maiores nostri*] *esse voluerunt.* Cf. 43.120–22.

194. *Quo gaudio elatus non temperavit quin paucos post dies frequenti curia iactaret invitis et gementibus adversariis adeptum se quae concupisset, proinde ex eo insultaturum omnium capitibus.* Note the sexual insult. Consider Caesar's failure to rise for the senators who came as a body to offer him sacrosanctity, the dictatorship for life, and the title of *parens patriae* (Livy, *periochae* 116). It was not enough to win; Caesar needed to stigmatize his opponents. Cf. Lily Ross Taylor, *Party Politics in the Age of Caesar*, Berkeley, 1949, p. 135. For Caesar employing excessive shaming, see Tom Africa, "Mask of an Assassin," pp. 599–626. For Gaius Caligula's uses of excessive shaming (which, as in the case of Caesar, led directly to his assassination), see Seneca, *De constantia sapientis* 18.1.

195. See chapter 8. For Gresham Sykes, the very definition of a maximum security prison in the United States was a society totally without trust (*The Society of Captives*, Princeton, 1958, pp. 66–67). And James Gilligan, who worked in just such a prison, shows, with great acumen, the murderous effects of shaming in that situation (*Violence: Reflections on a National Epidemic*, New York, 1997).

bared breasts shamed Cuchulain and so broke his fury.[196] He hid his head, and this involuntary gesture of shame was the signal that he was once again vulnerable to his fellows. The men of Emain were at that moment able to seize the otherwise formidable hero and plunge him into a series of cold baths—the second of which instantly boiled and vaporized, so much heat was contained in the hero.[197]

As Georges Dumézil has suggested, Livy's Horatius Tergeminus was a sort of Roman Cuchulain, returning home from his battle with the Curiatii, still driven by the warrior's *furor*. The sight of his sister's grief for her betrothed (a fallen Curiatius) greased the flame, and Horatius plunged into his sister's breast the sword that slew the man she loved.[198] The clamorous debate within the city on whether to execute or congratulate the hero evinces the ambiguous feelings of every warrior society toward its own greatest killers. (The best hero in any warrior society was, finally, the dead one.)[199] The compromise that was reached was a ceremonial humiliation; Horatius was compelled to go under the yoke, to pass, with head covered, beneath the *tigillum sororium*—a shaming that was simultaneously an expiation and resocialization.[200]

196. "L'enfant [Cûchulainn] n'en est pas maître, au contraire c'est elle [*ferg*] qui le possède. Revenant à sa ville, avant d'exercer sa nouvelle qualité de protecteur, il constitue un danger public. Il faut donc refroidir, et c'est à quoi s'emploient les deux médications que le roi lui fait appliquer: le spectacle des femmes nues d'abord, qui le contraint à baisser les yeaux, puis l'immersion dans les cuves, qui le calme (*Horace et les Curiaces*, Paris, [1942] 1978, p. 41). "Il a dû servir principalement à purger de son trop-plein de *furor*, à réadapter à sa vie et à son milieu ordinaires en le rendant inoffensif le jeune homme" (p. 111; cf. p. 120).

197. *Táin Bó Cuailnge*, ed. and trans. Cecile O'Rahilly, Dublin, 1976. "En fermant ou en baissant les yeux, Cûchulainn cesse d'être en garde, il devient accessible à une saisie brusquée" (*Horace et les Curiaces*, p. 49). I strongly disagree with Dumézil when he interprets this movement of the eyes as contempt for the women and rejection of an attempt by the women to seduce him.

198. For the story of Horatius Tergeminus, see Ennius, *Annales*, lines 131–138; Livy 1.24–26; Dionysius 3.21, 22; Valerius Maximus 6.3.6, 8.1, *absoluti* 1; Cicero, *De inventione* 2.26.78–79; Aurelius Victor, *De viribus illustribus* 4; Festus, s.v. "*sororium tigillum*"; "*sub iugum missio.*"

199. At the beginning of the *Táin*, Medb desires to slay the Gailióin, her and Ailill's best warriors, because she suspects that the great warriors will inevitably become a danger to their rulers.

200. For Dumézil,

> Plutôt que d'un *piaculum*, ce geste a la figure d'un rite de désacralisation; les anciens le rapprochaient du rite d'affranchissement des captifs de guerre (Dionysius 3.22), et il paraît en effet moins propre à décharger le héros d'une souillure qu'à lui ouvrir le retour d'un monde à un autre, du surnaturel à l'ordinaire: les portes artificielles, ou inusuelles, ou secrètes, de même que les démarches anormales jouent souvent un grand rôle dans ce genre de "rentrées." (*Horace et les Curiaces*, pp. 112–113)

For James Frazer, the act of going under the yoke was performed to strip the foe of his malignant and hostile powers before dismissing him to his home. For Frazer, the gate functioned to draw mana— either good or bad—from those who passed beneath it (*Balder the Beautiful*, vol. 2, New York, 1935, pp. 193–194, cf. 168–192). For Henri Wagenvoort, the *iugum* was an improvised gate to effect a transition to an unwarlike and defenseless period of life. "Seen from the conqueror's standpoint, the action is a *piatio*, having the object of depriving unworthy bearers of their mana" (*Roman Dynamism*, Westport,

The victorious general who came home *exsultans* had to lay down his almost complete and unrestricted *imperium militiae* and his *dicio/fides,* to change clothes, to suffer ritual ridicule, to calm down.[201] The triumph, like all ceremonies that brought one extreme attention, shamed even as it honored. It is possible that the *lustratio* of the army and the passage through the Porta Triumphalis was a milder version of Horatius's going under the yoke—a form of mild shaming to lower the warrior's charge.[202]

CONCLUSIONS: THE BALANCING ACT

The honorable man or woman in ancient Rome, was, then, neither simple nor at peace. The Roman with a sense of shame was never free from the painful emotions of shame. "To have a sense of shame is, as it were, a servitude" (Publilius Syrus 490, Friedrich ed.).[203] Shame was a kind of irritating doubt that one wore beneath one's toga, like the hair shirt worn by Thomas More beneath his ermine robes. Before those people and obligations to whom and by which one was bound, the person with *pudor* never felt innocent.[204] The *castus* and *casta* in ancient Rome could never feel chaste and pure.[205] At the very least (or most), they always felt shame before themselves.

Conn., 1976, p. 155 and n. 6). These various positions are reconcilable if one understands the paradoxical aspects of *pudor:* all forms of punishment, expiation, and reintegration were forms of shaming. For the relationship of the *tigillum sororium* to the *porta triumphalis,* see W. Warde Fowler, "Passing under the Yoke," *Classical Review* 27 (1913): 48–51; H. S. Versnel, *Triumphus: An Inquiry into the Origin, Development and Meaning of the Roman Triumph,* London, 1970, pp. 132ff., 138. As Versnel rightly points out, the apotropaic and expiatory rites are not possible to disentangle.

201. It is so characteristic of this strange compensatory physics that when "the consul Varro came beaten and flying home, full of shame and humiliation, after he had so disgracefully managed their affairs, the whole senate and people went forth to greet him at the gates of the city, and received him with honor and respect" (Plutarch, *Fabius Maximus* 18.4–5).

202. "Even if we cannot say that the returning host was *sacer,* we know that it needed *lustratio,* and that it underwent this process immediately before passing through the *porta,*" (Fowler, "Passing under the Yoke," p. 50). Lua Saturni expiated, cleansed bloodshed in battle; to her were devoted the arms taken from the enemy (Livy 8.1.6, 45.33.1; Varro, *De lingua latina* 8.36; Gellius, *Noctes Atticae* 13.23.1). Cf. Kurt Latte, "Über eine Eigentümlichkeit der italischen Gottesvorstellung," *Archiv für Religionswissenschaft* 24 (1926): 253.

203. *Pudorem habere servitus quodammodo est.*

204. *Pudor* prevented Ovid from being so bold as to assert his innocence before Caesar: "Shame has not so far fled from my face" (*non adeo nostro fugit ab ore pudor* [*Tristia* 2.30]).

205. Only the shameless felt pure. As Sandor Feldman has acutely observed, the protective blushing of the "proper lady" was also a confession of prurient interest: "One could not in the presence of a lady say the words 'breast' or 'bathroom' or other words of that nature. Women had to blush in order to 'prove' their 'innocence'.... Thus they gave evidence of their chastity and at the same time revealed their interest in sexual matters" ("Blushing, Fear of Blushing, and Shame," p. 372).

The tension produced by the balancing act of Roman honor could be acute. Antoninus Pius's last words to his heir Marcus Aurelius was "equanimity." Marcus developed bleeding ulcers trying to maintain his equanimity.

To sum up and illustrate the balancing mechanisms of the blush, I retell Valerius Maximus's wonderful story of Antiochus, the son of King Seleucus, "smitten with a boundless love for his stepmother Stratonice. Knowing well with how shameful a torch he was being burned, he hid the impious wound in his chest with a pious dissimulation. These conflicting emotions—the desire to transgress and shame—locked within the same innards and nerves at last fatally exhausted him" (5.7, externa 1).[206]

The king's physician, planted at the bedside of Antiochus by the distraught father Seleucus, noticed that whenever Stratonice entered the room, the breath and pulse of the otherwise pale inanimate prince would quicken, and, with a great blush, the blood would rise to his face. The physician noticed, in addition, that the vital signs of the prince departed together with the queen. Divining the cause of Antiochus's consumption, the physician so informed Seleucus. The dénouement of Valerius's story exemplifies the Roman homeopathic "physics of the blush": "Seleucus did not hesitate to cede to his son his beloved wife." As Valerius explains: "He imputed his son's passion to the whim of fortune. But that his son was willing to hide this love even unto death, he imputed to his sense of shame" (5.7, externa 1).[207]

Antiochus was an honorable man. His bonds to his father and his commitment to the conventions of his culture ground him away with inner conflict.[208] He was, like every man and woman of honor in ancient Rome, a soul at white heat. His burning blush both betrayed and redeemed him. On the one hand, the blush exposed his lack of self-control. On the other hand, it revealed the terrible cost of that self-control, of his efforts to conform to his father's and his society's expectations. The involuntary blush triggered the love and even the gratitude of his father and reaffirmed the bonds between them. The beloved wife that King Seleucus would not suffer to be stolen from him, he willingly surrendered to his

---

206. *Seleuci regis filius Antiochus novercae Stratonices infinito amore correptus, memor quam improbis facibus arderet, impium pectoris vulnus pia dissimulatione contegebat. Itaque diversi adfectus iisdem visceribus ac medullis inclusi, summa cupiditas et maxima verecundia, ad ultimam tabem corpus eius redegerunt.*

207. *Qui carissimam sibi coniugem filio cedere non dubitavit: quod in amorem incidisset, fortunae acceptum referens, quod dissimulare eum usque ad mortem paratus esset, ipsius pudori imputans.* Terentius Varro, whose rash engagement of Hannibal led to the disaster at Cannae, refused, out of shame, the office of dictator later offered him. In the eyes of the Romans, Varro's display of *pudor* relieved him of his guilt for the great debacle and had the result that the defeat was attributed to the anger of the gods, while his modesty was attributed to his own will and character (*culpam maximae cladis effecitque ut acies deorum irae, modestia ipsius moribus imputaretur* [4.5.2]). See Kaster, "Shame of the Romans," p. 7.

208. Compare Virgil's Dido, Ovid's Byblis, and Seneca's Phaedra—before they give in to their illicit passions.

blushing son, underlining in the most dramatic way the equivalence of their identity despite their differences in age and status.

In the Roman imagination, the person with a sense of honor, then, had to be willingly frustrated, somewhat ineffectual, and not completely in control;[209] the person with a sense of shame, like a high-wire artist, experienced and tolerated constant tension and discomfort. It was the cost of being, but it came with profound consolations.

209. He or she was both the imperious voice of social authority (Freud's superego) and the more or less docile and obedient and submissive silent servant.

CHAPTER EIGHT

The Poison of Shame—and Its Antidotes

CYRANO: *It is my pleasure to displease. I love hatred.... The Spanish ruff I wear around my throat is like a ring of enemies: hard, proud, each point another pride, another thorn—so that I hold myself erect perforce, wearing the hatred of the common herd haughtily....*

LE BRET: *Tell this to all the world—and then to me say very softly that... she loves you not.*

EDMUND ROSTAND, *CYRANO DE BERGERAC*[1]

As there were orders of shame, so there were disorders of shame; Latin *pudor* embraced a range of emotions from a mild stimulation to a stunning panic.[2] The shame that animated a soul and a society could also destroy that same soul and society. The Roman who lost his or her poise might stagger headfirst into a spiraling descent from which there was no recovery, like a stunt pilot who has lost control of her plane or a high-wire artist who has lost a grip on her bar.[3]

In the following pages I describe the various attempts made by the Romans, at all times in their recorded history, to salvage something of their souls from the wreckage of their honor.

INCORRIGIBLE INADEQUACY

The most extreme and toxic version of shame was a feeling of insufficiency or incompetence that could not be rectified.[4] In 102 B.C.E., while serving as a legate under the consul Catulus, the son of Marcus Aemilius Scaurus fled before the victory charge of the Germans. His father sent word that he would prefer to see him dead than accused of a disgraceful flight. "If there remained any trace of shame in his breast, he would avoid the sight of the father he had humiliated" (Valerius

---

1. Trans. Brian Hooker, New York, 1923, p. 126.

2. See Leon Wurmser, *The Mask of Shame*, Baltimore, 1981, p. 52.

3. Modern notions of shame tend to revolve around the noxious aspects of shame discussed in this chapter. This is Freud's shame, the tyrannical censor and hostile suppressor, which compels humans to wear suffocating masks and crippling corsets.

4. For excellent descriptions of the more powerful emotions of inadequacy, see Wurmser, *Mask of Shame*, pp. 32–33, and James Gilligan, *Violence: Reflections on a National Epidemic*, New York, 1997.

Maximus 5.8.4).[5] The son's feelings of inadequacy were insupportable. "The young man, overwhelmed by the shame of ignominy, destroyed himself" (Frontinus, *Strategemata* 4.1.13).[6]

At the lowest point in his life, Cicero, having fled into exile, wrote to his wife Terentia and their children Tullia and Marcus:

> I am exhausted by grief...but I have no one but myself to blame. It was my duty either to avoid impending danger by taking the legation offered by Caesar, or to oppose it by the diligent marshaling of my resources—or to fall bravely. Nothing I could have done could have been more miserable, more dishonorable and unworthy of me than what I have done. And so I am consumed by shame as well as grief. Yes, I am ashamed to have been found wanting in the courage and foresight that my best of wives and dearest of children had the right to expect of me. (*Ad familiares* 14.3.1–2)[7]

Cicero, confounded by his own lack of will and energy, contemplated suicide. Virgil's Dido, shamed past mending by her betrayal of her vow to Sychaeus and by Aeneas's treachery, felt she had no recourse but to curse Aeneas and slay herself (*Aeneis* 4.20ff.).

More than death or dead failure, more than defilement, the Roman feared irremediable dishonor. Livy's Lucretia submitted to the shame of being raped by Tarquin not out of fear of death but because he threatened her with a shame she could not expiate even by her death (Livy 1.58.4–5). The inability to atone for their shame with their blood compounded the disgrace of the soldiers who survived their defeat at Cannae. They pleaded for the chance to fight and die (Livy 25.6).

Capital crimes, in ancient Rome, were those insults to the collectivity so great that they could not be indulged. They could not be corrected except by the elimination (through death or exile) of the offender. Of the "Bacchanalian affair" of 186 B.C.E., Valerius Maximus writes:

> When many women had been condemned by the senate, all of the condemned were punished by their relatives within their own homes, it being widely held that the deformity of the shame could be emended by the severity of the punishment. In accordance with the degree of shame [literally: the intensity of the blush *(quantum ruboris)*] that the women had caused the city by their immoral behavior, just so much of praise was incurred by their harsh punishment. (6.3.7)[8]

---

5. *si quid modo reliquum in pectore verecundiae superesset, conspectum degenerati patris vitaturum.*

6. *M. Scaurus filium, quod in saltu Tridentino loco hostibus cesserat, in conspectum suum venire vetuit. Adulescens verecundia ignominiae pressus mortem sibi conscivit.* Cf. *De viribus illustribus* 72.10.

7. *Conficior enim maerore...sed culpa mea propria est. Meum fuit officium vel legatione vitare periculum, vel diligentia et copiis resistere, vel cadere fortiter. Hoc miserius, turpius, indignius nobis nihil fuit. Quare cum dolore conficior, tum etiam pudore. Pudet enim me uxori meae optimae, suavissimis liberis virtutem et diligentiam non praestitisse.*

8. *Consimili severitate senatus postea usus Sp. Postumio Albino et Q. Marcio Philippo consulibus mandavit ut de his quae sacris Bacchanalium inceste usae fuerant, inquirerent. A quibus cum multae essent damnatae, in omnes cognati intra domos animadverterunt, lateque patens opprobrii deformitas severitate supplicii emendata est, quia, quantum ruboris civitati nostrae mulieres turpiter se gerendo incusserant, tantum laudis graviter punitae adtulerunt.*

In 140 B.C.E., Titus Manlius Torquatus condemned his son Decimus Iunius Silanus for extortion in the latter's provincial command with the words, "I judge you unworthy of the Republic and of my house; I order you to depart far from my sight." By the ostracism Torquatus indicated that no reconciliation was possible. Silanus, stricken by the severity of his father's banishment, "could no longer bear to see the light, and on the following night hanged himself" (Valerius Maximus 5.8.3).[9] As Richard Saller points out, *abdicatio* or *exheredatio*, expulsion from the *domus* of the father, was generally the worst punishment that a Roman father (even with his "right of life and death") meted out to an errant child.[10] It was, for a Roman, punishment enough.[11]

INEXPIABLE GUILT

> *"Happy are you, Hester, that wear your scarlet letter openly upon your bosom!*
> *Mine burns in secret."*
>
> NATHANIEL HAWTHORNE, *THE SCARLET LETTER*

The hideous complement of incorrigible shame was inexpiable guilt. For the person with a sense of shame, *conscientia* (the Latin word that, in one of its usages, comes closest in meaning to our word "guilt") was a sort of appalling super-self-consciousness.[12] "Nothing is more miserable than when what we have done causes us shame" (Publilius Syrus 432, Friedrich ed.).[13] "O silent torment, *animi conscientia*" (ibid., 443).[14] "He is crucified by *conscientia*, tormented by *pudor*" (Calpurnius Flaccus, *Declamationes* 49).[15] "Nothing is more miserable than an *ani-*

---

9. *"et republica eum et domo mea indignum iudico, protinusque e conspectu meo abire iubeo."* Tam tristi patris sententia perculsus Silanus, lucem ulterius intueri non sustinuit, suspendioque se proxima nocte consumsit. Here the transgression, because it resulted in the father's low esteem, could result in the same sense of inadequacy as impotence or insufficiency. Cf. Cicero, *De finibus* 1.7.24; Livy, *periochae* 54.

10. *Patriarchy, Property, and Death in the Roman Family,* Cambridge, 1994, p. 110. See also William Harris, "The Roman Father's Power of Life and Death," *Studies in Roman Law in Memory of A. Arthur Schiller,* Leiden, 1986, p. 86.

11. The death-giving power of the father, *nex,* as Yan Thomas points out, was a bloodless death ("*Vitae necisque potestas; Le père, la cité, la mort,*" in *Du châtiment dans la cité: Supplice corporels et peine de mort dans le monde antique, collection de l'École française de Rome,* no. 79, Rome, 1984, pp. 509–510). The condemnation by one's father was a harsher and more terrible death than that exacted in war or by the community, because to die without the shedding of one's blood was to die without atoning. There was no sacrifice involved in the bloodless death. Concomitantly, patricide was punished by a bloodless death. For blood as the means of atonement, see Frontinus, *Strategemata* 4.1.16.

12. For *conscientia* as "guilt," see, for example, Cicero, *In Verrem* 2.5.59.155; Pseudo-Quintilian, *Declamationes maiores* 1.10, 10.16, Hakanson ed.; Juvenal, *Satirae* 13.192–195.

13. *Nil est miserius quam ubi pudet quod feceris.*

14. *O tacitum tormentum animi conscientia!* It is the secret crimes which weigh on the conscience (*secreta...conscientiam premunt* [Seneca, *Naturales quaestiones* 1.16.3]).

15. *cruciatur conscientia, pudore torquetur.*

mus conscius such as the one possessing me" (Plautus, *Mostellaria* 544–545).[16] Ovid's poor Byblis, driven wild by her guilty desire for her brother, dreams of transgression and blushes even in her sleep (*Metamorphoses* 9.468–471).[17]

"But why should you suppose that they escape punishment whose minds are ever kept in terror by the consciousness of evil deeds which lashes them with unheard blows, their own souls ever shaking over them the unseen whip of torture? It is a grievous punishment, more cruel by far than any devised by the stern Caedicus or by Rhadamanthus, to carry in one's breast, by night and day, one's own accusing witness" (Juvenal, *Satirae* 13.192–198).[18] *Conscientia* was the unspeakable, the "guilty secret" that made one sweat to look another in the eye (those informers, those betrayers of the soul).[19] *Conscientia* was the freezing timidity that made one dread to blush, lest the loss of control that ought to reveal the soul's transparent innocence betray, instead, its dark secrets. It was the guilty knowledge of their enormities *(stuprorum sibi incestarumque noctium conscii)* that stopped the candidates for office from appearing in public. They could not bear the eyes of god or man (Pliny, *Panegyricus* 63.7–8). The nurse admonished Phaedra: even if heaven

---

16. *nihil est miserius quam animus hominis conscius, / sicut me habet.*

17. *Spes tamen obscenas animo demittere non est*
    ausa suo vigilans; placida resoluta quiete
    saepe videt quod amat: visa est quoque iungere fratri
    corpus et erubuit
    quamvis sopita iacebat.

Compare the *conscius amor* that burns the silent Phaedra in Ovid's *Heroides* 4.52.

18. *Cur tamen hos tu*
    evasisse putes, quos diri conscia facti
    mens habet attonitos et surdo verbere caedit
    occultum quatiente animo tortore flagellum?
    poena autem vehemens ac multo saevior illis
    quas et Caedicius gravis invenit et Rhadamanthus,
    nocte dieque suum gestare in pectore testem.

Compare Cicero: "It is their own evil deed, their own terror that torments them more than anything else; each of them is harassed and driven to madness by his own crime; his own evil thoughts and *conscientia animi* terrify him" (*Sua quemque fraus et suus terror maxime vexat, suum quemque scelus agitat amentiaque adficit, suae malae cogitationes conscientiaeque animi terrent* [*Pro Roscio Amerino* 24.67]). Tormented by *conscientia*, the son acquitted of his father's murder but, burning in his soul, is driven to confess (Pseudo-Quintilian, *Declamationes minores* 314.15–17, Shackleton Bailey ed.). "Even in the absence of law, *conscientia* punishes silently" (*sine lege muta poena est conscientia* [Publilius Syrus 683, Friedrich ed.]). *Conscientia* made one timid and untrusting (Cicero, *In Verrem* 2.5.29.74; Seneca, *De clementia* 1.13.3).

19. "As the face is the image of the spirit, so the eyes are the informers" (*Nam ut imago est animi vultus, sic indices oculi* [Cicero, *Orator* 18.60]). "Nature formed the *species oris* in such a way that she has represented in it the moral intentions hidden deep within *(reconditos mores)*. For the eyes speak only too clearly the way our souls have been emotionally affected. And that which we call our 'face' *(vultus)* betrays our moral intentions *(mores)*" (Cicero, *De legibus* 1.27). When Augustus accused Cinna of conspiring against his life, the guilty Cinna fell silent and dropped his eyes *ex conscientia* (Seneca, *De clementia* 1.9.10).

should keep her incestuous secret, "What of the ever-present penalty: the mind's trembling consciousness, and the soul filled with guilt and fearful of itself?" (Seneca, *Phaedra* 162).[20] Guilt that could not be shared could not be repaired; it would break any man or woman not made of stone.

VISUAL ASSASSINATION

Even Nero averted his eyes and did not deign to watch the outrages that he ordered.
The worst of our torments under Domitian was to see him with his eyes fixed upon us—
with our every sigh being registered against us.
TACITUS, *AGRICOLA* 45.2[21]

Toxic shaming occurred when one felt that there was no inhibition in the eyes of others, when the eyes of others would "desoul" you. Many of the most terrible dramas of Roman life had to do with the uninhibited and contemptuous observation of one person by another.[22] Tacitus's Germanicus, bitter with anguish, felt that he was being forced to die under the gloating eyes of his enemy Piso (*Annales* 2.70). The Roman soldiers trapped by the Samnites at the Caudine Forks were sent under the yoke "and, what was almost heavier to bear, before the eyes of the enemy" (Livy 9.6.3).[23] Ovid's rejected lover moans, "I have kept vigil lying like a slave before your shuttered doors. I have seen your wearied lover come forth from those doors...yet this is an easier thing to endure than being seen by him—may shame like that befall my enemies!" (Ovid, *Amores* 3.11a.12–15).[24]

To force another to watch you watching him with soul-withering contempt was a form of vivisection, a violence as penetrating, as mutilating, as any that one human being could inflict on another.[25] The brutality of the adolescent general Octavian is expressed, for Suetonius, in his ability not only to order but to observe coolly the execution of a father and son (*Augustus* 13.2).[26] Pliny the Younger glee-

20. *quid poena praesens conscius mentis pavor / animusque culpa plenus et semet timens?* Cf. lines 159–164.

21. *Nero tamen subtraxit oculos suos iussitque scelera, non spectavit. praecipua sub Domitiano miserariarum pars erat videre et aspici, cum suspiria nostra subscriberentur, cum denotandis tot hominum palloribus sufficeret saevus ille vultus et rubor, quo se contra pudorem muniebat.*

22. For the relationship between this penetrating gaze and the "evil eye," see Léon Pommeray, *Études sur l'infamie en droit romaine*, Paris, 1937, p.44; Carlin Barton, *The Sorrows of the Ancient Romans*, Princeton, 1993, part 2.

23. *Ita traducti sub iugum et quod paene gravius erat per hostium oculos.*

24. lines 14–15: *hoc tamen est levius, quam quod sum visus ab illo / eveniat nostris hostibus ille pudor!* At the triumph the plebs will be able to look at captives with their eyes averted *(vultus versus)* (Ovid, *Tristia* 4.2.23). The captives cannot meet the arrogant and uninhibited gaze of the spectators.

25. We are accustomed to think of men as the active penetrators and women as the passive receptors, but in ancient Rome (as with most cultures where the notion of the "evil eye" functions), the Roman's sensitivity to another's gaze allowed women to violate with as much damage as men.

26. Suetonius's Caligula compelled parents to observe the executions of their sons (*Gaius* 27.4). Plutarch describes the wonder and horror with which the Roman people watched the elder Brutus

fully asserts, "Nothing was so gratifying, nothing so worthy of our times as the chance we enjoyed of looking down at the informers prostrate at our feet, their heads forced back and faces upturned to meet our gaze" (*Panegyricus* 34.3).[27] The gaze without compunction signaled the loss of trust between the seer and the seen, the breakdown of a common bond. One can imagine the look on the face of Cicero when he says: "Your blood, Piso, I have never sought....But I wanted, rather, to see you abject, scorned, despised by your fellows, despaired of and abandoned even by yourself, a creature peering nervously about and quaking at every whisper, one without trust in itself, without a voice, liberty, or authority, without even the semblance of a consul, a shivering, trembling, fawning wretch— this have I desired to see....I have seen" (Cicero, *In Pisonem* 41.99).[28]

When others turned on one their basilisk stare, one's face became flint. When the fear of exposure became so great that one could not afford a wobble, when one could not afford to blush, the splitting of the self necessary for voluntary self-control became a laceration. Self-control became unbearable when there was no indulgence for the loss of it. As Seneca says in another context, "It is a torture to be constantly watching oneself and to fear being caught in other than one's usual role" (*De tranquillitate* 17.1).[29] Having just executed the knight Pastor's son on a trifling charge, the emperor Gaius invited the father to celebrate with him. He set guards to scrutinize the latter's every reaction. Gaius's cruelest instrument of torture was the smile carved on the bereaved father's face with the sharp edge of the emperor's gaze (Seneca, *De ira* 2.33.3–5).[30] Complete self-control becomes an ideal—and a necessity—precisely when all control of one's destiny is wrested from one.

It is important to remember that there were *no* particular behaviors that were, in and of themselves, shaming. Shaming could take any form: rudeness or meticulous politeness,[31] saying another's name aloud, serenading or clamor-

---

watching the public whipping and execution of his two sons (*Publicola* 6.3–4). Compare Procne observing the slaughter of her child (Ovid, *Metamorphoses* 6.642, 7.340–42).

27. Radice trans., slightly modified. *nihil tamen gratius, nihil saeculo dignius, quam quod contigit desuper intueri delatorum supina ora retortasque cervices.* To "despise" was to "look down on" (*despicere*).

28. *Numquam ego sanguinem expetivi tuum....Sed abiectum, contemptum, despectum a ceteris, a te ipso desperatum et relictum, circumspectantem omnia, quidquid increpuisset pertimescentem, diffidentem tuis rebus, sine voce, sine libertate, sine auctoritate, sine ulla specie consulari, horrentem, trementem, adulantem omnis videre te volui: vidi.*

29. *Torquet enim adsidua observatio sui et deprendi aliter ac solet metuit...non...iucunda vita aut secura est semper sub persona viventium.* Horace describes the misery of trying to present an appearance, a face that one cannot live up to, and that others can see through (*Epistulae* 1.18.21–36).

30. Frederick Douglass tells of the crippling effects of constant surveillance on the life of the slave in his *Narrative of the Life of Frederick Douglass, An American Slave, Written by Himself,* Boston, 1845, pp. 56–73.

31. Consider the politeness of the wealthy neighbor that embarrasses the poor man in Plautus' *Asinaria.* Jean Briggs describes the forms of exquisite politeness that attended her social ostracism from her Inuit hosts (*Never in Anger,* Cambridge, Mass., 1970).

ing,[32] refusing to mention another's name,[33] looking or not looking.[34] It could take the form of binding or loosing.[35] It could take the form of just saying the word "shame."[36]

The distinguishing quality of severe and alienating shaming was the lack (or perceived lack) of collaboration from others in maintaining one's face. The embarrassed person was the proverbial ass in the lion's skin.[37] Dining at the palace with the emperor, drinking toasts, wearing crowns and unguents might have been honors—in other circumstances. But they were profound humiliations to the knight Pastor because they compelled a grieving father to wear a mask of gaiety and gratitude (*De ira* 2.33.3–6).

32. *occentare* = *infame carmen cum certo nomine dicere* (*Corpus Glossarum Latinarum*, 5.228.30.31). *iam hercle ego illum nominabo* (Plautus, *Mostellaria* 587). Cf. Plautus, *Curculio* 683; *Menaechmi* 44–46; *Pseudolus* 554–555, 1145. One could shame a convicted man by the public announcement of the sale of his confiscated property (Cicero, *Pro Quinctio* 16.50). One could shame a debtor in default by placing a notice on the Columna Maenia (Wilfried Nippel, *Public Order in Ancient Rome*, Cambridge, 1995, p. 41 n. 36). For more on *occentatio, flagitatio*, and *convicium*, see chapter 2. In Ovid's *Heroides* 17.34, to speak a woman's name was in itself an indication that she had a bad reputation. Cicero has to explain that he is naming the consul *gratia honoris* (*Pro Quinctio* 7.28).

33. By the so-called *damnatio memoriae*, "the *praenomen* of the condemned man might not be perpetuated in his family,... images of him must be destroyed, and his name erased from inscriptions" (Adolf Berger, "Damnatio memoriae," *Encyclopedic Dictionary of Roman Law*, Philadelphia, 1953; cf. Braslof, "Damnatio memoriae," in Pauly-Wissowa, *Realencyclopädie der classischen Altertumswissenschaft* 4.2, Stuttgart, 1901, cols. 2059–2062. The *infamis*, according to Léon Pommeray, was originally the person or thing whose name was ominous to pronounce (*Études sur l'infamie*, pp. 16–17 and n. 5). It was considered an act of respect to be mentioned in the will of a friend or relative and a major insult to have your name omitted.

34. *culpant eum, conspicitur, vituperatur* (Plautus, *Curculio* 503). Alcmena turns her back and refuses to look at Amphitryon after he has wrongly accused her of unfaithfulness. "I have always hated to look at enemies" (*Ita ingenium meumst: / inimicos sempre osa sum optuerier* [*Amphitruo* 899–900]). The soldiers of Appius Claudius so despise their arrogant general that they refuse to look at him (Livy 2.58.8 [471 B.C.E.]). For the deprivation of a child of the *conspectus patris*, see Valerius Maximus 5.8.3–4; Seneca, *De clementia* 1.15.7; Cassiodorus, *Historia Ecclesiastica* 6.44.6–9; Yan Thomas, "*Vitae necisque potestas*," p. 538 and n. 79.

35. The *emancipatio* of a child could be a form of disowning. Unwillingness to bond with, not allowing intermarriage with, and/or not allowing or respecting a contract with *(commercium* and *connubium)* could be severe forms of insult and radical exclusion. (Consider the struggles over the *lex Canuleia* in the early Republic.) When none of their neighbors would give their daughters in marriage to the Romans, the latter felt justified in raping the daughters of the neighboring Sabines. In the United States, the reluctance of whites to intermarry with blacks has been a perpetual insult that black people have, at times, turned against whites.

36. "*O pudor!*" (Horace, *Carmina* 3.5.38). *propudium dicebant, cum maledicto nudare turpitudinem volebant, quasi porro pudendam* (Paulus apud Festus p. 227 M.). (Here the speaker intends to strip away what covers the shame.)

37. For the story of the ass in the lion's skin, see Babrius 139; Horace, *Satirae* 1.6.21–22. "The loss of identity one thought one had is in many ways more painful and disconcerting than the tortuous process of discovering identity" (Helen Merrell Lynd, *On Shame and the Search for Identity*, New York, 1956, p. 37).

SPORTING

For Sallust's Catiline, the worst scenario was to be "an object of sport for others' arrogance" *(alienae superbiae ludibrio [Catilina* 20.9]), like Apuleius's Lucius for the people of Hypata. In extreme forms of "desouling," the person doing the shaming treated the shamed as less than a full player in the former's "game";[38] the shamed discovered that he or she was being played with rather than playing.[39] Plautus's slaves defeat and humiliate their masters by pretending to play the masters' game while using them as pawns in their own, revealing, finally, that the latter were the playthings of their own slaves.[40]

Sharing in the emotions of shame characterized the human being. ("A human being is the only animal born sharing in shame and reverence" [Cicero, *De finibus* 4.7.18].)[41] And so one of the ultimate ways of shaming another was to deprive the other of his or her claimed status as a human being. It was a simple thing to do:

38. "He is present with them, but he is not 'in play'" (Erving Goffman, "Embarrassment and Social Organization," *American Journal of Sociology* 62 [1956]: 266). One is willing to take off one's clothes and reveal the most protected parts of one's body or mind to another within certain clearly and unambiguously defined perimeters. If the doctor and patient both know and voluntarily assume their roles, and these roles are clearly defined, the shame is limited. Just so, an actor can express shameful emotions qua actor and not feel shame. But if your gynecologist acts out of role, if she or he starts giggling and winking at you, you'll probably grab your sheet and run for the door. Your face depends on the other's face and on both adhering to their roles and the rules of the game. (See Scheler, "Der 'Ort' der Schamgefühls und die Existenzweise des Menschen," *Gesammelte Werke,* vol. 10, Bern, 1957, p. 79.) It is not having emotions but losing control of one's emotions, not having a body but losing control of the body, that overwhelms our sense of being. (Many modern psychologists associate the development of a "sense of shame" with the young child's desire for control over the excretory functions of urination [Piers and Singer] and or defecation [Erikson]. See Donald L. Nathanson, "A Timetable for Shame," in *The Many Faces of Shame,* ed. Donald L. Nathanson, New York, 1987, p. 39. I believe that the sensation of losing control can be experienced as a result of being observed or treated without inhibition.)

39. "We have acted on the assumption of being one kind of person living in one kind of surroundings and unexpectedly, violently, we discover that those assumptions are false. We had thought that we were able to see around certain situations and, instead, discover in a moment that it is we who are exposed, alien people in an alien situation can see around us" (Lynd, *On Shame,* p. 35). See Gilligan on the ceremony of "booking" in American prisons (*Violence,* pp. 153–154).

40. Scheler explains that you can be made to feel shame when your own particular experiences are redefined by others. You may feel that you have had a vision, but when others explain that you have had a lesion of the cerebral cortex, you may feel humiliated and ashamed. Suffering the "insult" of redefinition is one of the reasons why visits to the hospital or appearances at court can be so exquisitely shaming. By redefining your experiences, others demonstrate that they are not collaborating with you or playing your game but, rather, that you are playing their game whether you will or not ("Der 'Ort' des Schamgefühls," p. 79). See William James, *The Varieties of Religious Experience,* Glasgow, [1902] 1960, esp. pp. 35–38. Committing the "insult" of redefinition or interpreting is one of the contributing causes of the modern anthropologist's acute self-consciousness. See Amy Richlin, "The Ethnographer's Dilemma and the Dream of a Lost Golden Age," in *Feminist Theory and the Classics,* ed. Nancy Sorkin Rabinowitz and Amy Richlin, pp. 272–303.

41. [*homo*] *solum animal natum pudoris ac verecundiae particeps.* Cf. Cicero, *De officiis* 1.4.14, 1.30.105. See also Darwin and Scheler ("Der 'Ort' des Schamgefühls," pp. 67, 74) for shame as a particularly human

one need only discard one's inhibitions before him or her.[42] When the courtesans, the Bacchides, want to humiliate the old men Nicobulus and Philoxenus, they impudently talk about them as if they were not in their presence. When they are addressed by the old men, one sister says to the other, within the men's sight and hearing, "Certainly this is a prodigy: sheep are addressing us in the voice of humans!" (Plautus, *Bacchides* 1141).[43] Lysimachus and Pasicompsa, ridiculing the old lover Demipho, talk about him as a sheep (*Mercator* 524–526, 567, 574–575). Similarly, Libanus rides Argyrippus like a horse in the course of shaming him (Plautus, *Asinaria* 699–710).[44] Apuleius's Lucius the ass is, to be sure, the ultimate example of the crushing loss of one's human status.

Alternatively, the shamed might be treated as dead, lifeless, cold.[45] Plautus's humorless Lydus is so ashamed of his pupil Pistoclerus for carousing with a courtesan that he exclaims to Pistoclerus's father and friend: "My disciple, your friend, this man's son, has perished, for I declare that he has died for whom shame has died" (*Bacchides* 484–485).[46] When the Roman people heard of the humiliation and survival of the Roman soldiers at the Caudine Fork, they dressed themselves in mourning and declared a *iustitium*, a kind of public strike (Livy 9.7.7–8). Cicero paints a picture for us of the equally appalling public shaming of the man whose property was confiscated and sold at public auction: "He is not only banished from the number of the living, but, if it were possible, he would be relegated to a position lower even than that of the dead" (*Pro Quinctio* 15.49).[47]

The community might deny personhood to those they shamed by covering or wrapping the head, the focus of one's social being: "Lictor, tie his hands, cover his head, hang him from the Tree of Misfortune" (Cicero, *Pro Rabirio perduellionis reo* 4.13).[48] "A beam having been placed across the road, Horatius was sent under it

---

quality. This is an idea disputed by modern ethological studies. See Jeffrey Moussaieff Masson and Susan McCarthy, *When Elephants Weep: The Emotional Lives of Animals*, New York, 1995, esp. chapter 9, "Shame, Blushing and Hidden Secrets," pp. 179–191.

42. These behaviors are closely related to exposing oneself to shame another. See chapter 6.

43. *"Prodigium hoc quidemst: humana nos voce appellant oves."* Cf. 1121–1141.

44. The examiner Doktor Pannwitz looked at Primo Levi as he would a creature in an aquarium (*Survival in Auschwitz*, New York, 1961, p. 96).

45. Wurmser points out that contemning, despising, ignoring were forms of making "cold," of "cold-shouldering" (*Mask of Shame*, p. 81). "Certains modernes ont même pensé que l'*infamia* a peut-être un lien avec l'antique *sacratio*. Il est certain que, de même que le parricide était exclu de la cité, de même l'individu tombé dans le discrédit était en quelque sorte mis au ban de la société: cette 'marginalisation' apparaissait sans nul doute comme consécutive, de quelque façon à une sanction divine" (G. Freyburger, *Fides*, Paris, 1986, p. 49).

46. *mihi discipulus, tibi sodalis periit, huic filius, / nam ego illum periisse dico quoi quidem periit pudor.*

47. *is non modo ex numero vivorum exturbatur sed, si fieri potest, infra etiam mortuos amandatur.* Cf. 15.50.

48. *Lictor, conliga manus, … caput obnubito, arbori infelici suspendito.* "Go ahead, lictor, tie those hands that but a little while ago secured *imperium* for the Roman people. Go ahead, cover the head of the lib-

with his head covered, as if he were being sent under the yoke" (Livy 1.26.13).[49] The law ordered the head of the person who had murdered his parent to be wrapped (Paulus-Festus p. 170, Müller ed.).[50] While it was an act of reverence to cover one's own head voluntarily, it was an intensely shaming act to shroud the head of another.

If being a citizen in Rome was to have a share or a portion, the shamed were "cut" out.[51] Plautus's parasite Curculio warns the pimp Cappadox, "No decent man would dare to stand together with you in the forum. Whoever appeared by your side would be blamed, observed, vituperated; he would lose his wealth and his credibility, and even if he did nothing wrong, people would talk" (*Curculio* 502–504).[52]

SHAME AND THE SOUL

Oh, I'm burning with the horrible scandal of it; and I don't know what to do about it, or how
I can look my wife in the face—I'm so utterly destroyed! The whole disgraceful business is
out!... they have me by the throat, caught in the act.
PLAUTUS, *CASINA* 937[53]

If one could be molded and defined by shame, one could also be broken by it (*fractos pudore* [Cicero, *Tusculanae disputationes* 2.21.48]). The honor of Livy's Verginia was "hedged about, guarded by shame" (*pudore saepta* [3.44.4]).[54] But the maiden's *pu-*

---

erator of this city; hang him from the Tree of Misfortune" (*I, lictor, colliga manus, quae paulo ante armatae imperium populo Romano pepererunt. I, caput obnube liberatoris urbis huius; arbore infelici suspende* [Livy 1.26.11]). The Romans treated the honored dead as still living human beings and went to great lengths to preserve the latter's "face," dressing and painting and posing them, while the dishonored dead might be thrown into the river or into a common and open pit like so much garbage or sewage.

49. *transmisso per viam tigillo capite adoperto velut sub iugum misit iuvenem.*

50. *legem iubere caput eius obnubere qui parentem necavisset, quo est obvolvere.*

51. They were "cut and chewed," so to speak, by "Theon's tooth" ("backbiting"); calumny was cannibalism. For "cutting," see Harold Garfinkel, "Conditions of Successful Degradation Ceremonies," *American Journal of Sociology* 61 (1956): 421. "The experience of shame is in itself isolating, alienating, incommunicable" (Lynd, *On Shame*, p. 67). As Sandor Feldman points out, "The blusher is isolated. He feels like an outcast with no genuine relationship.... All blushers are 'self-centered'" ("Blushing, Fear of Blushing, and Shame," *Journal of the American Psychoanalytic Association* 10 [1962]: 377). Cf. Wurmser, *Mask of Shame*, pp. 52–53.

52. *nec vobiscum quisquam in foro frugi consistere audet, / qui consistit, culpant eum, conspicitur, vituperatur, / eum rem fidemque perdere, tam etsi nil fecit, aiunt.*

53. Lysidamus:

Maxumo ego ardeo flagitio
nec quid agam meis rebus scio
nec meam ut uxorem aspiciam
contra oculis; ita disperii.
Omnia palam sunt probra.... manufesto faucibus teneor.

54. Valerius speaks of the *matronale decus* protected by the *verecundiae munimentum* (2.1.5). Tacitus talks of the *mulieres saeptae pudicitia* (*Germania* 19).

dicitia, like the shell of a nut, could be broken and the kernel consumed. (*Qui e nuce nuculeum esse volt, frangit nucem* [Plautus, *Curculio* 55].) The soul was cut from the shamed to be consumed by another. Plautus's Hegio, when he realized that he had been made a fool of, declares, "They've done me...cleaned out the nut and left me with the shell for a memento" (*Captivi* 655).[55] Plautus's Ballio accuses Calidorus of being a lover "empty like a nut broken open" (*inanem quasi cassam nucem* [*Pseudolus* 371]). As Leon Wurmser explains, "Ultimately radical abandonment by the other means disappearance of the self."[56]

If *pudor* was one's hide, it could also flay. For the one who felt ashamed, the one with the *os oblitum,* the besmeared, befouled, dirt-defiled face,[57] the skin provided all the cover it did for Marsyas. Plautus's Olympio moans: "Where can I flee to? Where can I hide? How can I conceal this disgrace? I don't know!...I am now so ashamed and we're both such laughingstocks!" (Plautus, *Casina* 875–877).[58] According to the story told by Livy, the ten representatives of the Roman captives from Cannae who subverted their oaths to Hannibal were allowed to stay in Rome, but "they were so branded with every kind of stigma and ignominy by the next censors that some immediately put themselves to death, and the rest, for all their life afterwards, not only shunned the forum but almost the light and public" (Livy 22.61.9).[59] The soldiers who emerged from their humiliating ordeal at the Caudine Forks felt so hideously exposed that Livy describes their feelings as an inability to endure the light of day (*pudor intuendae lucis* [9.7.3]). Cicero writes to his friend Atticus from exile: "I shun my fellow creatures, I can hardly bear the light" (*Ad Atticum* 3.7).[60] To endure, to enjoy being visible, to accept, to sustain the rays of another's gaze, felt like basking in sunlight to a Roman, just as the inability to sustain the regard of others' eyes felt like quivering in darkness and death.

BEYOND THE PALE

To those who are utterly ruined, help comes as an insult.
PUBLILIUS SYRUS 45, FRIEDRICH ED.[61]

---

55. *nucleum amisi, retinui pignori putamina.* Here Hegio is referring both to himself as having been tricked and to the situation of holding the slave and having let slip the master.

56. *Mask of Shame,* p. 63.

57. For example, Plautus, *Curculio* 589; *os sublinere* (Plautus, *Mercator* 485, 538, 604, 631). The Roman might get his nose wiped (*me emunxisti mucidum* [Plautus, *Epidicus* 494]). We have the expression "Don't rub it in!"

58. *Neque quo fugiam neque ubi lateam neque hoc dedecus quo modo celem / tantum erus atque ego flagitio superavimus nuptiis nostris, / ita nunc pudeo atque ita inridiculo sumus ambo.*

59. *ceterum proximis censoribus adeo omnibus notis ignominiisque confectos esse ut quidam eorum mortem sibi ipsi extemplo consciverint, ceteri non foro solum omni deinde vita, sed prope luce ac publico caruerint.*

60. [April 29, 58 B.C.E.] *Odi enim celebritatem, fugio homines, lucem aspicere vix possum.* For esteem of one's fellows as light, see also Cicero, *Pro Quinctio* 23.73–74.

61. *Auxilium profligatis contumelia est.*

The "spiral of shame" was the concomitant of the sense that one could neither satisfy nor be satisfied.[62] Incorrigible inadequacy or inexpiable guilt could result in a kind of rampant shame, a spinning nose-dive into hell. One could lose the ability to orient oneself and calibrate one's behavior to the social situation. Fear of shaming could become so intense that one simply could not trust oneself or another human being.[63] And at this stage, ignominy could actually be increased by indulgence.[64] In Livy's story of the disaster at the Caudine Forks, the Capuans are prepared to let the defeated and shamed Romans presume upon their goodwill. They are generous and more than willing to cooperate in redeeming the Romans' honor. In addition to treating the defeated Romans with exquisite politeness and attending to all their bodily needs, they supply the generals with lictors and replace their uniforms and the insignia of their offices. Rather than reassure or reinvigorate the Romans, the sympathy and faithfulness of the Capuans exacerbates the Romans' sense of inadequacy and need. "Neither the friendliness of the allies nor their kindly looks and speech could elicit a word from the defeated Romans nor bring them to even raise their eyes or return the gaze of the friends who attempted to console them; shame beyond grief compelled them to flee the conversation and company of other men" (9.6.6–8).[65]

The aggravation of shame by sympathy helps to explain the rejection of Caesar's clemency by Cato, Brutus, or Domitius[66] and the ineffectiveness of Macrobius's reassuring praise for the poet Servius paralyzed with shyness (*Saturnalia* 7.11.2).

Moreover, the Roman might feel ashamed at feeling ashamed. The impotence of Ovid's lover was aggravated by the shame he felt at being impotent. "*Pudor* contributed to my predicament, for the *pudor* I felt at what happened [i.e., his in-

---

62. One can connect this impossibility of satisfaction to the fixations and fascinations described by Freud in *Totem and Taboo* and Doi in *The Anatomy of Dependence*. See Barton, *Sorrows*, chapter 3.

63. Gilligan reports on the "spiral of shame" in a maximum security prison: "They [the inmates] are ashamed even to reveal what shames them. And why are they so ashamed of feeling so ashamed? Because nothing is more shameful than to feel ashamed" (*Violence*, p. 111; cf. 117, 132–136). The more slight an inmate felt, the more easily he felt slighted (281 n. 7).

64. "This tendency for shame anxiety to spread from one situation to all situations makes it akin, even if not causally, to paranoid ideas" (Wurmser, *Mask of Shame*, p. 53). Shame and paranoia are inseparable in the functioning of an American prison. See Gilligan, *Violence*, esp. pp. 155–156, 281 n. 7. In this situation teasing can become not only insupportable but deadly dangerous.

65. *Neque illis sociorum comitas voltusque benigni et adloquia non modo sermonem elicere sed ne ut oculos quidem attollerent aut consolantes amicos contra intuerentur efficere poterant; adeo super maerorem pudor quidem fugere conloquia et coetus hominum cogebat.*

66. Cf. Cicero, *Ad Brutum* 25 (= 1.16) (July 43 B.C.E.); Seneca Rhetor, *Controversiae* 10.3.5; Seneca, *De providentia* 2.10; Plutarch, *Cato minor* 64.4–5. Lucan's Domitius, humiliated by Caesar's generosity, prefers to die rather than accept it (*Bellum civile* 2.505–525). Compare the rejection of mercy by Lucan's Vulteius (ibid., 4.507–512). Compare also the inability of Dostoevsky's Underground Man to accept the sympathy of Liza.

ability to maintain an erection] injured me further: it was the second cause of my trouble" (*Amores* 3.7.37–38).[67] Indeed, the weight of what James Gilligan calls "the Great Chain of Non-Being" could be compounded until it became insupportable.

The spiral of shame could produce a repulsive self-consciousness of and alienation from one's body, like that of Adam and Eve in Masaccio's painting "The Expulsion of Adam and Eve." "What is it?" the frantic Circe cried, shamed by her lover's impotence. "Do you find something offensive in my kiss? In my breath faint from fasting? Am I careless about my armpits?" She turned to her maid: "Speak to me, Chrysis, tell me the truth: am I unsightly or inelegant? Does some natural blemish disfigure my appearance? Don't deceive your mistress!" (Petronius, *Satyricon* 128).[68]

Society could not survive in this vortex of shame. The defeated and captured Roman soldiers, having emerged from the Caudine Forks as if from the grave, could not approach the walls of their allies the Capuans and ask for succor. They chose to prostrate their bodies "needing everything" alongside the road rather than accept any sympathy or help.

Four forms of relief possible from this anxiety were isolating withdrawal, impenetrable masking, brazen shamelessness, or rage.[69] In the words of Erving Goffman:

> There seems to be a critical point at which the flustered individual gives up trying to conceal or play down his uneasiness: he collapses into tears or paroxysms of laughter, has a temper tantrum, flies into a blind rage, faints, dashes to the nearest exit, or becomes rigidly immobile as when in a panic. After that it is very difficult for him to recover composure. He answers to a new set of rhythms, characteristic of deep emotional experience, and can hardly give even a faint impression that he is at one with the others in interaction. In short, he abdicates his role as someone who sustains encounters. The moment of crisis is of course socially determined: the individual's breaking point is that of the group to whose affective standards he adheres. On rare occasions all the participants in an encounter may pass this point and together

---

67. *huc pudor accessit: facti pudor ipse nocebat; / ille fuit vitii causa secunda mei.* "In addition to his other troubles, he has discredited his implicit claim to poise. He will feel he has cause, then, to become embarrassed over his embarrassment (Goffman "Embarrassment," p. 269, n. 7). For more on the spiral of shame, see Wurmser, *Mask of Shame*, pp. 43, 50, 53, 55.

68. *"Quid est?" inquit "numquid te osculum meum offendit? Numquid spiritus ieiunio marcens? Numquid alarum sum negligens [sudor puto]? . . . Dic, Chrysis, sed verum: numquid indecens sum? Numquid incompta? Numquid ab aliquo naturali vitio formam meam excaeco? noli decipere dominam tuam."* The limp that Spurius Carvilius earned in battle made him unwilling to be seen in public (Cicero, *De oratore* 2.61.249). Takeo Doi noticed that Japanese sensitivity to shame often translated into a feeling of repulsiveness before the eyes of others, the inability to meet the eyes of others, and the fear of bodily odor (*The Anatomy of Dependence*, trans. John Bester, Tokyo, 1973, pp. 104–109).

69. The alternative of submission and the abandonment of the self I have discussed in chapter 6.

fail to maintain even a semblance of ordinary interaction. The little social system they created in interaction collapses.[70]

THE REMEDIES OF SHAME: OBLIQUITY

*Some men take refuge so deeply in the shadows that they think to be
in wild disorder whatever is in light.*

POMPONIUS, QUOTED BY SENECA, *EPISTULAE* 3.6[71]

The shamed, the man or woman whose skin had been peeled away, looked for a more impenetrable hide. After being accused of electoral corruption, "who afterwards observed Publius Sulla except grieving, abject and stricken? Was there anyone who thought that he avoided the sight of men and the light of day from hate rather than from shame? He departed from your sight, and when he had the right to stay, he punished himself, as it were, with exile" (Cicero, *Pro Sulla* 74).[72] According to Tacitus, the emperor Tiberius flirted with the idea of appearing in Rome in 32 C.E. but decided against it. "Tiberius often landed at points in the neighborhood, visited the gardens by the Tiber, but went back to the cliffs and the solitude of the sea shore from shame at his crimes and lust" (*Annales* 6.7 [= 6.1]).[73] Titus Labienus, unable to support the shame of a condemnation, went so far as to wall himself alive in his ancestral tomb (Seneca, *Controversiae* 10, *praefatio* 7). Before throwing herself into the river, Ovid's Ilia covered her head and cried aloud, "Perish the face that bears the brand of shame and disrespect!" (*Amores* 3.6.78).[74]

---

70. "Embarrassment," p. 267.

71. *quidam adeo in latebras refugerunt, ut putent in turbido esse, quidquid in luce est.* Seneca is talking about men who withdraw from society and cannot trust anyone.

72. *Postea vero quis P. Sullam nisi maerentem, demissum adflictumque vidit, quis umquam est suspicatus hunc magis odio quam pudore hominum aspectum lucemque vitare? . . . afuit ab oculis vestris et, cum lege retineretur, ipse se exsilio paene multavit.* "Antony started from Capua on the tenth, sending word that shame prevented his visiting me, because he thought I was annoyed at him" (*Antonius autem VI Idus Capuam profectus est. Ad me misit se pudore deterritum ad me non venisse, quod me sibi suscensere putaret* [Cicero, *Ad Atticum* 10.15 (May 12, 49 B.C.E.)]).

73. *saxa rursum et solitudinem maris repetiit, pudore scelerum et libidinum.* After having caused to be read his letter denouncing to the senate the shameful misdeeds of his daughter Julia, Augustus long abstained, out of shame, from intercourse with other human beings (*abstinuitque congressu hominum diu prae pudore* [Suetonius, *Augustus* 65.2]). Ovid's Echo, spurned by Narcissus, lurks in the woods and hides her face behind the foliage (*spreta latet silvis pudibundaque frondibus ora / protegit* [*Metamorphoses* 3.393–394]). The Roman soldier beaten by the gardener, ashamed of his *inertia* and *impotentia*, hid from sight (Apuleius, *Metamorphoses* 9.41).

74. *desint famosus quae notet ora pudor!* The defeated consul Varro, home from Cannae, cannot lift his eyes to meet those of his fellow Romans (*deiectum attollere vultum / ac patriam aspicere . . . pigebat* [Silius, *Punica* 10.632–633]). For hiding from shame in death, see Yolande Grisé, *Le suicide dans la Rome antique,* Paris, 1982, esp. pp. 61–64, 67–68.

Servius's aphasia was a last-ditch strategy for preserving his self-control and self-sufficiency.[75] The silence of the shamed could be a fortress.[76]

THE REMEDIES OF SHAME: SHAMELESSNESS

In my opinion, they act foolishly who put captives in chains and who load
with fetters fugitive slaves. Heaping woe upon the woes of a miserable man only
increases his desire to flee and to offend.
PLAUTUS, *MENAECHMI* 79–83[77]

When the heart's past hope the face is past shame.
SCOTTISH PROVERB[78]

Pudor and *verecundia* were socializing emotions so long as they were relatively mild forms of fear or awe. But, as Seneca reminds us, "while a degree of fear restrains the spirit, when it is made too sharp and extreme it incites the prostrate to audac-

75. Donna Williams, in her remarkable autobiography, describes her autism as an effective and almost impenetrable defense against an unbearable sensitivity to the world, especially to the touch and gaze of other humans. She distinguishes the autistic person from the schizophrenic, who, she believes, has an inadequate and ineffective defense against invasion from the world and other humans (*Nobody Nowhere*, New York, 1992).

76. Cf. Plautus, *Bacchides* 981–983; [*Olympio*] *pudet dicere* (Plautus, *Casina* 897; cf. 900, 910). The words addressed by Menaechmus's wife to her "shameless" husband (actually his twin Menaechmus/Sosicles) show that the shamed were expected to be silent and to hide from those before whom they were shamed: "Aren't you ashamed to appear before my eyes, you scandal of a husband, with this garment [her *palla*, which he had stolen to give to his mistress]?" (*non te pudet prodire in conspectum meum, / flagitium hominis, cum istoc ornatu?* [708]). *Etiamne, impudens, muttire verbum unum audes aut mecum loqui?* Compare Lucretius: *muta pudens est* (*De rerum natura* 4.1164).

77. *homines captivos qui catenis vinciunt*
et qui fugitivis servis indunt compedes
nimis stulte faciunt mea quidem sententia.
nam homini misero si ad malum accedit malum,
maior lubido est fugere et facere nequiter.

78. Quoted by Lynd, *On Shame*, p. 33. For the destruction of the socializing instinct by excessive and irremediable shaming, see John Braithwaite, *Crime, Shame, and Reintegration*, Cambridge, 1989, esp. pp. 67–68; in Gilligan's violent and incarcerated patients, feelings of personal inadequacy led to narcissism, arrogance, and self-importance (*Violence*, p. 183). "Many of the violent criminals who fill our maximum-security prisons...desperately want to feel that they are big, tough, independent, self-assertive, self-reliant men, so as not to feel needy, helpless, frightened, inadequate, unskilled, incompetent, and often illiterate" (p. 127; cf. 103–132). "I have yet to see a serious act of violence that was not provoked by the experience of feeling shamed and humiliated" (p. 110). "Somehow the imprisoned criminal must find a device for rejecting his rejectors if he is to endure psychologically" (Gresham Sykes, *The Society of Captives: A Study of a Maximum Security Prison*, Princeton, 1958, p. 67). To quote a scholium on Aristotle, "They make a cult of shamelessness not as being beneath modesty *(aidos)* but as superior to it" (p. 23, Brandis ed.). They "refuse what is anyway refused and...love the inevitable" (Pierre Bourdieu, *Outline of a Theory of Practice*, trans. Richard Nice, Cambridge, 1979, p. 77).

ity and urges them to attempt anything." He goes on: "Extreme necessity hammers out a fierce valor. It is fitting therefore that fear leave some form of security and offer men more of hope than of peril" (*De clementia* 1.12.4–5).[79]

Ovid's Byblis with difficulty restrains her unspeakable desire for her brother. After an exhausting inner struggle, she loses control of herself and confesses her love to her brother, who repulses her in disgust. With no possibility of preserving her honor, Byblis becomes lawless. "Now," she declares, "I cannot help but commit a crime" (9.626).[80] Seneca's Phaedra, having exposed herself to disgrace past healing, dares herself to do worse. "Now it is too late for shame," she declares, "now we love crime" (*Phaedra* 594).[81] For Phaedra and Byblis, as for Sallust's Catiline, shamelessness helped to redress the injury—or at least anesthetize the pain. "No one," Seneca reminds us, "spares a ruined reputation; it is a kind of exemption from punishment to have no further room for it" (*De clementia* 1.22.1).[82] Those men or women who had nothing left to lose were, in the Roman mind, dangerous in the extreme.

Virgil's vigilant, many-eyed Fama could be too violating, too pitiless a censor (*Aeneis* 4.173–197). Loss of reputation without the possibility of redemption could result in the Roman's despising his or her degradation. It could result in the Roman being *effrenatus, dissolutus,* loosed from his or her moorings and from the mutual ties and obligations that bound him or her to other people. "To take no heed of what other people think of you is the part not only of an arrogant man but, to be sure, of a *dissolutus*" (Cicero, *De officiis* 1.28.99).[83] For Plautus, the shameless were those "who no longer cultivate either the laws or equity" (*Menaechmi* 580).[84] The shamed might despise other people's opinions of them. They might contemn the censorious Catones.[85]

---

79. *Temperatus enim timor cohibet animos, adsiduus vero et acer et extrema admovens in audaciam iacentes excitat et omnia experiri suadet....Acerrima virtus est, quam ultima necessitas extundit. Relinquat oportet securi aliquid metus multo plus spei quam periculorum ostentet.* See Livy 3.2.11. In the April 1877 edition of the *Atlantic,* B. O. Townsend noticed that "So often were the slaves whipped and humiliated before each other, often for no cause, that punishment came to be looked on as no disgrace" (quoted by Fox Butterfield, *All God's Children,* New York, 1995, p. 61).

80. *iam nequeo nil commisisse nefandum.*

81. *serus est nobis pudor / amavimus nefanda.*

82. *Nemo dignitati perditae parcit; impunitatis genus est iam non habere poenae locum.* For Eve Kosofsky Sedgwick, the shaming of the "queer child" without indulgence stimulates the gay man and woman to despise their degradation and to embrace autonomy, theatricality, and exhibitionism ("Queer Performativity: Henry James' *The Art of the Novel*," *GLQ* 1 [1993]: 1–16). For exhibitionism as a reaction to shame, see Scheler, "Der 'Ort' des Schamgefühls," p. 94; Wurmser, *Mask of Shame,* p. 86.

83. *Nam neglegere quid de se quisque sentiat non solum arrogantis est, sed etiam omnino dissoluti.*

84. *qui neque leges neque aequom bonum usquam collunt.*

85. As a remedy for excessive shyness, Samuel Johnson suggests that the bashful continually remind themselves: We are nobodies. No one cares about us. We'll soon be forgotten. And we don't care about them either! They are nobodies! ("The Nature and Remedies of Bashfulness," *The Rambler* no. 159 [Tuesday, September 24, 1759], in *The Works of Samuel Johnson,* vol. 3, Troy, New York, 1903,

In the war against the Volsci in 471 B.C.E., as a result of the complete break-down of trust between Appius and his troops, the arrogant general Appius Claudius could not shame his troops nor be shamed by them. Indeed, each seemed to glory in the contempt of the other:

> Appius's anger and indignation incited his ferocious spirit to vex the soldiers with harsh commands. But he was unable to dominate them by any violence, so deeply had the spirits of his soldiers drunk of the liquor of their contest with Appius. Everything they did they did slowly, lazily, negligently, stubbornly. Neither shame nor fear inhibited them. If Appius wished the troops to move more quickly, they deliberately slowed down; if he was present to exhort his troops in their labors, all the soldiers spontaneously relaxed their efforts. While they lowered their eyes in his presence, they cursed him under their breaths. (Livy 2.58.6–7)[86]

The anguish of shame demanded autonomy, or rather, to borrow a phrase from Michelle Rosaldo, "the autonomous posture."[87] As I pointed out earlier, only the shameless was *sui iuris*, a law unto himself or herself.[88] Cicero reflects on his public panegyric of Julius Caesar:

> There was also the fact (I might as well stop nibbling at what has to be swallowed) that I was not exactly proud of my palinode. But good night to principle, sincerity and honor!...It's time for me to love myself since they [the optimates] won't love me whatever I do. (Cicero, *Ad Atticum* 4.5.1–3)[89]

> With good will they could have kept me for the common [i.e., optimate] cause; instead, their malice has estranged me. For I must tell you that their venomous back-biting has pretty well succeeded in turning me away from my old long-established principles and brought me to the point, not indeed of forgetting my dignity, but of paying some attention to my salvation. (Cicero, *Ad familiares* 1.7.7)[90]

Cicero has crossed his own Rubicon. He is alone on the farther shore.

---

pp. 294–295). This was the strategy repeatedly employed by Cicero and the excessively sensitive Marcus Aurelius, as well as other Stoics and Cynics.

86. *Haec ira indignatioque ferocem animum* [of Appius] *ad vexandum saevo imperio exercitum stimulabat. Nec ulla vi domari poterat, tantum certamen animis imbiberant. Segniter, otiose, neglegenter, contumaciter omnia agere, nec pudor nec metus coercebat. Si citius agi vellet agmen, tardius sedulo incedere, si adhortator operis adesset, omnes sua sponte motam remittere industriam, praesenti voltus demittere, tacite praetereuntem exsecrari, ut invictus ille odio plebeio animus interdum moveretur.*

87. *Knowledge and Passion: Ilongot Notions of Self and Social Life*, Cambridge, 1980, p. 13.

88. Independence was the other side of *fides* as restraint: *fides* as completeness of power.

89. Shackleton Bailey trans. *Etiam (dudum enim circumrodo quod devorandum est) subturpicula mihi videbatur esse palinodia. sed valeant recta, vera, honesta consilia....Sed iam tempus est me ipsum a me amari, quando ab illis nullo modo possum.*

90. *qui nos, quos favendo in communi causa retinere potuerunt, invidendo abalienarunt; quorum malevolentissimis obtrectationibus nos scito de vetere illa nostra diuturnaque sententia prope iam esse depulsos, non nos quidem ut nostrae dignitatis simus obliti, sed ut habeamus rationem aliquando etiam salutis* [August 56 B.C.E.].

The humiliated might put over his or her skin a shell of "solitude and shadows and this protective covering of disgrace" (Cicero, *Pro Caelio* 20.47).[91] The one prone to blush would yearn for, strive for self-control and impenetrable masking; Seneca assumes that the young man who blushes will strive to rid himself of this *corporis vitium*.[92] He will aspire to be brazen *(expudoratus, callidus, impudens, durus, ferreus)*, as thick-skinned and crafty as Pliny's crocodile.[93] He would aspire to be secure, free from care *(securus)* like Virgil's shameless Pygmalion.[94] He would desire to feel no doubt, no need. He would want to sleep well, free from guilt.[95]

Dido interprets as a sign of Aeneas's shamelessness *("improbe!"* [*Aeneis* 4.386]) that he tells her he is leaving while wearing just such a clear and brazen face, a face without any sign of embarrassment or emotion, without a sigh, without even a lowered or softened gaze. Aeneas does not flinch; he does not blush or lose his cool (368–370). The masking of Aeneas, like that of the Stoic, Cynic, or modern street tough, had the goal of making one impenetrable. The arrogant, the petulant, the *perjuror,* the *faenator* could not be shamed.[96] Even when others could easily see beneath the defensive armor of his brazen face, Domitian was not embarrassed: "Domitian was a practiced dissembler; he would listen to his subjects' pleas for mercy with an insolently composed face, and when he granted mercy he

---

91. *solitudinem ac tenebras atque haec flagitiorum integumenta.*

92. It was in respect to the value of autonomy that the blush was a *vitium.* Cf. Seneca, *Epistulae* 11.2–3; Plutarch, *De vitioso pudore.* Seneca believes, in the case of the ingenuous young friend of Lucilius, that the effort to suppress the blush will be in vain *(Epistulae* 11.1).

93. For "hard" shamelessness, *duritia oris,* see Plautus, *Menaechmi* 708–710, *Miles gloriosus* 235; Catullus 42.17; Seneca, *Phaedra* 136–137, *De constantia* 2.17.3; Kaster, "The Shame of the Romans," *Transactions and Proceedings of the American Philological Association* 127 (1997): 14 and n. 34. See also the citations on "hardness" above (p. 74 and nn. 202 and 204). "There are persons who think that . . . animals are more or less brutish owing to their skin and bodily coverings, as for instance mollusks and tortoises, and that the hides of oxen and bristles of pigs obstruct the thinness of the air when being inhaled, and it is not transmitted pure and liquid; so also in man, when his skin being thicker and more callous, shuts it out—as if crocodiles did not possess both a hard hide and cunning!" *(sunt qui . . . putent . . . cute operimentisque corporum magis aut minus bruta esse, ut ostreas et testudines; boum terga, saetas suum obstare tenuitati immeantis spiritus, nec purum liquidumque tramitti; sic et in homine, cum crassior callosiorve excludat cutis—ceu vero crocodilis et duritia tergoris tribuatur et sollertia* [Pliny, *Naturalis historia* 11.92.226], Rackham trans.). See Richard B. Onians, *The Origins of European Thought about the Body, the Mind, the Soul, the World, Time and Fate,* Cambridge, 1954, chapters 1–4.

94. The person without shame, like Pygmalion, king of Tyre, *impius ante aras* is *securus (Aeneis* 1.349–350). For *expudoratus,* see Petronius, *Satyricon* 39.5.

95. For "toxic" shame producing complaisant apathy, see Gilligan, *Violence,* pp. 33, 36, 48, 51–53, 113.

96. *Petulans* (from *peto,* to aim for, strive, or seek to obtain): impudently or boisterously aggressive, self-assertive, unruly, wanton, immodest. *Petulantia:* impudence, boldness, rudeness, effrontery. Plautus's Mnesilochus derides himself for being *petulans* and for being *indomitus, sine modo et modestia, sine bono iure atque honore* and *impos animi (Bacchides* 612–614).

suffered himself to be thanked, and did not even blush at the malice that was beheld behind the benefit" (Tacitus, *Agricola* 42.2).[97]

Aulus Gellius tells the story of Lucius Veratius, a man who had no respect for other men nor for the laws, a shameless, crazy man *(homo improbus atque inmani vecordia)* who took pleasure in slapping the faces of free men in the street. Fined for his scandalous behavior, he gladly and repeatedly paid the fine but did not cease the act. Like the Cynic,[98] Veratius exulted in being free from shame (*Noctes Atticae* 20.1.13).[99]

THE REMEDIES OF SHAME: RAGE

There are those who are never more to be feared than when they blush. For it is as if all shame fled their bodies. Sulla was at his most violent just when the blood invaded his face.
SENECA, *EPISTULAE* 11.3[100]

Who is not bent by shame will not be broken by fear.
PUBLILIUS SYRUS 494, FRIEDRICH ED.[101]

One writhed within shame as one would within a hair shirt; it was an irritant that one was tempted to throw off. Because *pudor* and *verecundia* were ways of giving way before others, of letting others into one's own sphere, they required one to endure perpetual boundary insecurities and anxieties. But excessive giving way could make one feel like a creditor and cause one to want retribution, to demand indemnification. To quote Clyde Kluckhohn, "There is a point at which 'shyness' grades into resentment."[102] The excessively shamed felt that something was owed them.[103] The person with an acute sense of shame was volatile and liable to venge-

---

97. *qui* [Domitian] *paratus simulatione, in adrogantiam compositus, et audiit preces excusantis et, cum adnuisset, agi sibi gratias passus est, nec erubuit beneficii invidia.* Cf. 45.2.

98. The lover, like the Cynic, was shameless in Roman thought. Ovid's adulterous lover gives himself to those enemies of shame, night, wine, and love: *nox et Amor vinumque nihil moderabile suadent; / illa [nox] pudore vacat, Liber Amorque metu* (*Amores* 1.6, esp. 59–60). Compare Shakespeare: "Thou know'st the mask of night is on my face; / Else would a maiden blush bepaint my cheek / For that which thou hast heard me speak tonight" (*Romeo and Juliet* 2.2). For the *furor* of Dido in love, Dido *amens*, see *Aeneis* 4.69, 4.92, 4.465, 4.433. Dido's *furor* will not be hindered by concern for *fama: Quam simul ac tali persensit peste teneri / cara Iovis coniunx nec famam obstare furori* (4.91–92).

99. *L. Veratius fuit egregie. Is pro delectamento habebat, os hominis liber manus suae palma verberare.* Compare Aristotle's description of the Celts as *mainomenos*, "crazed," and *analgetos*, "lacking in normal sensitivity" (*Nicomachean Ethics* 1115b 25). See H.D. Rankin, *Celts and the Classical World*, London, 1987, pp. 55–59, 67–68.

100. *Quidam numquam magis, quam cum erubuerint, timendi sunt, quasi omnem verecundiam effuderint. Sulla tunc erat violentissimus, cum faciem eius sanguis invaserat.*

101. *Pudor quem nondum flectit, non frangit timor.*

102. *Children of the People: The Navaho Individual and His Development*, New York, [1947] 1969, p. 105.

103. One of the results of excessive shaming in our own culture is identity with the "victim," who is conceived of as the person or persons to whom something is "owed." The identification with the

ful rage.[104] Plautus's elderly Demipho, pressured by the taunting of young Lysi-machus, collapses, confesses, and pleads for help and forgiveness. But when his sub-mission meets with further shaming, Demipho erupts into fury (*Mercator* 983–999).[105]

It was the morbid depth of the humiliation suffered by the Roman soldiers trapped at the Caudine Forks that required the destruction of the Samnites who had humiliated them (Livy 9.7.4, 9.12.1–4). It was the ineradicability of the brand-ing imposed on many slaves by their Sicilian masters that contributed to the fero-cious outbreak of the First Sicilian Slave War.[106]

Just so, the inability to repay one's debts made one want to destroy the creditor. If the Romans emphasized the role of indebtedness in the civil wars, it was not a result of a modern appreciation for economic motives but of an ancient economy of shame. (In the Roman mind no material base could be abstracted from an ethi-cal and emotional superstructure.) The Romans understood, better than we do, that a man with no hope of repaying his debts or atoning for his transgressions would no longer feel bound or obligated to his creditor or his victim. Calling in a debt that could not be repaid dissolved the debtor's bonds of gratitude and obliga-tion.[107] Because the Aequi had repeatedly violated their treaties with the Romans

victim, Doi suggests, allows one to engage in violent reactions without guilt: the victim can, like Sallust's Catiline, take revenge with a clear conscience (*Anatomy of Dependence*, p. 162). Nietzsche's "Blond Beasties," victimized by the victims, can take revenge without having to feel guilty. As Wilhelm Stekel observed in *Sadism and Masochism: The Psychology of Hatred and Cruelty* (New York, 1929), sadism arises out of the unful-filled desire to dominate. The "victim" (the shamed man or woman freed from shame) may easily be-come a sadist. See Andrew P. Morrison, "Shame and the Psychology of the Self," in *Kohut's Legacy: Contri-butions to Self Psychology*, ed. Paul E. Stepansky and Arnold Goldberg, Hillsdale, N.J., 1984, pp. 71–90, esp. p. 87; James Gilligan, "Beyond Morality: Psychoanalytic Reflections on Shame, Guilt and Love," in *Moral Development and Behavior*, ed. T. Likona, New York, 1976, pp. 144–158. Doi believes that the feeling of victimization is "the spirit of the modern age" (*Anatomy of Dependence*, p. 26). Doi, it seems to me, is map-ping out in his wonderful book the Japanese equivalents of the psychological complexities of Dosto-evsky's Underground Man and Nietzsche—and of the Romans of the civil war and early Empire.

104. In our culture, an ideal of equality accompanied by radical competitive inequality results in intense feelings of incorrigible inadequacy that find expression in shamelessness, rage, and/or apathy. So long as we maintain this ideal of equality, attempts to abolish "handicapping" (such as affirmative action, preferential hiring, and special scholarships for the disadvantaged) and to create one great (and impossibly unequal) pool of competitors aggravate the spiral of shame. (Paradoxically, status shame is often alleviated by creating smaller and more equal pools of competitors, that is, a hierarchy.) As Gilli-gan repeatedly points out, violence temporarily relieves the shame of inadequacy, and, at least in our society, the punishment involves less pain than do feelings of inadequacy.

105. For additional examples of bashfulness turning into anger, see Plutarch, *De vitioso pudore* 15 (*Moralia* 534D).

106. Cf. C. P. Jones, "Stigma: Tattooing and Branding in Graeco-Roman Antiquity," *Journal of Ro-man Studies* 77 (1987) 139–155.

107. See Thomas Africa, "The Mask of the Assassin: A Psychohistorical Study of M. Junius Bru-tus," *Journal of Interdisciplinary History* 8 (1978): 616. The unpayable debt that one owed to one's parents and ancestors should not, of course, ever be called in.

and so despaired of being able to atone for their guilt, they fought the Romans with desperate courage in 465 B.C.E. (Livy 3.2.11).[108] The son who successfully pursued his incestuous love for his mother came increasingly to feel an implacable hatred for his father. When the latter, having discovered his son's crime, tortured him to death, the son met the whip with a dumb, hollow, unmoving grief. There was nothing that he could do to set things right, and so he felt no remorse. "Fortunate," Pseudo-Quintilian proclaims, "are those who are conscious of a wrong they need to correct and put right" (*Declamationes maiores* 17.13, Hakanson ed.).[109]

Cicero gloated after Caesar's assassination. Shackleton Bailey explains:

> Cicero had solicited and accepted generous treatment from the man he now vilified—and resented it. Was it not Caesar, as he had written to Atticus in 48, who had robbed him not only of what he had, but of what he was? It was Caesar, not Cicero, who had lived Achilles' slogan "Far to excel, out-topping all the rest," and whose success in wicked courses had reduced the premier consular of 62 to something like a sycophant—not only of Caesar but of Caesar's creatures. "You must be polite to him," he wrote to Atticus anent Caesar's secretary Faberius, from whom he needed a financial accommodation, "though these fawnings are little less than criminal."[110]

Profound and inexpiable shame made one feel "pinned"—self-absorbed, but also, since one's *persona* was broken, empty, *inanis*, without being.[111] Excessive shame produced an extreme and insupportable self-consciousness, a radical self-alienation, which in turn spawned a deep hatred of those who made one ashamed.[112] Publilius Syrus phrased it succinctly: "To make a friend blush is to lose him" (576, Friedrich ed.).[113]

---

108. *quod...*(sc. *eos*) *conscientia contracti culpa periculi et desperatio futurae sibi postea fidei ultima audere et experiri cogebat.* Here "the courage of despair" is attributed to those outside the community, those beyond the pale.

109. *felices qui habent in conscientia sua quod debeant emendare, corrigere.*

110. *Cicero,* London, 1971, p. 228.

111. Darwin, even while he remarked that "idiots rarely blush" (*The Expression of the Emotions in Man and Animals,* Chicago, [1872] 1965, p. 310), also remarked that some of the insane were particularly liable to blush (p. 313). This apparent paradox may be the result of the fact that excessive shame often results in no shame at all.

112. For the *furor* growing from insult, see Statius, *Thebais* 2.319ff.; Virgil, *Georgica* 3.226–241; Debra Hershkowitz, "Sexuality and Madness in Statius," *Materiali e discussioni per l'analisi dei testi classici* 33 (1994): 124–126.

> Two investigators (Kaufman and Heims 1958) have described interestingly how certain delinquent adolescents may seek experiences in which they can be hostile and aggressive because the very act of feeling angry has self-delineating effects. They noted that many of these aggressive-acting adolescents felt "opened up" and vulnerable and uncertain of their personal limits unless they could get angry.... One is reminded of the typical Camus character who feels dead and without identity and only glimpses himself as a bounded entity when he explodes in an act of violence. (Seymour Fisher, *Body Consciousness,* New York, 1974, p. 25)

See L. Kaufman and L. Heims, "The Body Image of the Juvenile Delinquent," *American Journal of Orthopsychiatry* 28 (1958): 146–159.

113. *Ruborem amico excutere amicum est perdere.*

Transgression might not, in itself, imply any anger on the part of the transgressor, but his self-conscious vulnerability to the eyes and opinions of others might invoke rage: "Whenever the burning Lucilius thundered, attacking as if with a drawn sword, the hearer blushed whose mind was cold with consciousness of crime, and he sweated from a breast silent in its guilt—*hence anger and tears*" (Juvenal, *Satirae* 1.165–168).[114] According to Juvenal, "There's no audacity like that of wives caught in the act; their very guilt makes them angry and insolent" (Juvenal, *Satirae* 6.284).[115] "Conscious of her own secret sins, she turns on her husband fiercer than a tigress who has lost her cubs. She fakes a sigh. She hates his boys or weeps over some imagined mistress" (*Satirae* 6.270–72).[116] "Well, what good was the steady resolve of Hippolytus or Bellerophon? Phaedra blushed as though repelled with scorn. Stheneboea glowed with no less fury. Both goaded themselves into a fury; for a woman is never so savage as when her hatred is stimulated by shame" (*Satirae* 10.324–329).[117]

Pudor and *ira* were paired in ancient Rome. It was as common a notion in ancient Rome as it is in modern psychology that shame leads to rage and revenge.[118] "Shame and rage goad them into conflict" (Virgil, *Aeneis* 9.44).[119] One could wound men into war (*lacessere ad pugnam* [Livy 2.45.3]). "I die. I am ashamed; it is an outrage for a man of my age to be made a fool of twice; the more I think of it, the more I burn" (Plautus, *Bacchides* 1089–1092).[120]

Shame and rage were so intimately connected in Roman thought that the word *pudor* could stand not only for the insult but for the fury it evoked:

114. *ense velut stricta quotiens Lucilius ardens*
  infremuit, rubet auditor cui frigida mens est
  criminibus, tacita sudant praecordia culpa
  inde ira et lacrimae.

115. *nihil est audacius illis / deprehensis: iram atque animos a crimine sumunt.*

116. *tum gravis illa viro, tunc orba tigride peior, / cum simulat gemitus occulti conscia facti; / aut odit pueros aut ficta paelice plorat.*

117. *quid profuit immo*
  Hippolyto grave propositum, quid Bellerophonti?
  erubuit nempe haec ceu fastidita, repulsa,
  nec Stheneboea minus quam Cressa, excanduit et se
  concussere ambae. mulier saevissima tunc est,
  cum stimulos odio pudor admovet.

Initially acutely self-conscious and embarrassed at her lover's impotence, Petronius's Circe, like Virgil's scorned Juno and Dido and Catullus's scorned Ariadne, turns her shame to wrath. For Quintus Pompeius hiding guilt under indignation, see Cicero, *De finibus* 2.17.54.

118. See Herennius's advice to Pontus in Livy 9.3.12–13.

119. *conferre manum pudor iraque monstrat.* Cicero fears that Pompey's shame might give way to wrath (*Ad Atticum* 2.21.4). Cf. Cicero, *Pro Caelio* 21; Livy 34.4.12; Tacitus, *Annales* 1.4.3.

120. *Perii, pudet: hocine me aetatis / ludos bis factum esse indigne! / magis quam id reputo, tam magis uror.* "Never, by god, will she laugh at me alive!" (*numquam edepol viva me inridebit* [Plautus, *Bacchides* 515]).

Horatius Cocles, surveying the leaders of the Etruscans with menacing eyes, taunted the enemy, now singly, now all at once. He charged them with being in servitude to an arrogant king. Forgetful of their own liberty, they had come to attack the freedom of others. For a long time they hesitated, each regarding the others and expecting another to begin the battle. *Pudor* finally moved the line and, taking up the clamor, they hurled their weapons from all sides against a single enemy. (Livy 2.10.8–9)[121]

In 482 B.C.E., in the midst of civil strife at Rome, the enemy Veians molested the Romans with insults. The Roman generals Marcus Fabius and Gnaeus Manlius, fearful of fighting against two enemies at once (the Veians and their own mutinous Roman troops), kept the soldiers within the walls of the camp and allowed the enemy to tease, taunt, and disparage the Roman soldiers until *odia externa* could conquer *odia domestica:* "When the Veians shouted out their insults under the very walls and gates, the consuls welcomed it. Now indignation, now *pudor* filled the hearts of the unthinking multitude and distracted them from their quarrels with each other; they did not want to let the enemy depart with their insults unavenged" (Livy 2.45.5).[122]

In 468 B.C.E. the Roman soldiers pursued the Volscian enemy up steep hills, against the good sense of the consuls. The consuls prevented their troops from falling apart by chiding both their temerity and their timidity, driving out fear with shame. They knew that fury and the desire to vindicate their honor would attend that shame, that inhibiting *pudor* could become an aggressive rage that overcame any fear: "Then the left wing of the Roman army was nearly overcome, had not the consuls dispelled their fear by exciting a sense of shame as they were retreating, chiding at the same time their audacity and their cowardice" (Livy 2.65.4).[123]

THE REMEDIES OF SHAME: THE DELIBERATE BLUSH

If you cannot get rid of the family skeleton, you may as well make it dance.
ERIK ERIKSON, *IDENTITY, YOUTH, AND CRISIS*

Paradoxically, the blush itself could act as a remedy for shame, a "hide": "Natural Philosophers assert that nature, being moved by shame, spreads the blood

---

121. *Circumferens inde truces minaciter oculos ad proceres Etruscorum nunc singulos provocare, nunc increpare omnes: servitia regum superborum, suae libertatis immemores alienam oppugnatum venire. Cunctati aliquamdiu sunt, dum alius alium, ut proelium incipiant circumspectant; pudor deinde commovit aciem, et clamore sublato undique in unum hostem tela coniciunt.*

122. *Haec* [the insults of the Veians] *cum sub ipso vallo portisque streperent, haud aegre consules pati; at imperitae multitudini nunc indignatio, nunc pudor pectora versare et ab intestinis avertere malis; nolle inultos hostes.*

123. *Sic prope oneratum est sinistrum Romani cornu, ni referentibus iam gradum consul increpando simul temeritatem, simul ignaviam, pudore metum excussisset.* Livy 8.7.8: *seu ira, seu detractandi certaminis pudor.*

before herself as a veil" (Macrobius, *Saturnalia* 7.11.5).[124] The blush could be a mask, worn strategically or even cynically, designed to convince others of one's simplicity, modesty, and scrupulousness, as in Ovid's *Amores*, where the witch Dipsas urges Ovid's lover to be shameless and to blush strategically. The false blush, she explains, is advantageous; the true one is a hindrance (1.8.35–36).[125] "They are innocuous and bashful in order that they might hear themselves praised; they blush so that they can gain a good reputation" (Cicero, *De legibus* 1.19.50).[126] Tacitus talks of "the blush, by which he [Domitian] steeled himself against shame" (*Agricola* 45.2).[127] According to Pliny, "There was arrogance, in his brow, wrath in his eyes, a feminine pallor in his body, and, in his face, impudence masked by high color" (*Panegyricus* 48.4).[128] One could argue that the orator's feigned timidity,[129] like the painted-on blush of the wanton,[130] like Phaedra's show of modesty in Seneca's tragedy, was not a sign of sensitivity to but a fortification *against* the feeling of shame.[131] "She (Daphne, beloved of Apollo) abhorred the wedding torch as if it were an evil. Fastening her coaxing arms about her father's neck, and with her lovely face suffused with the blush of modesty, she would say, 'Allow me, dearest father, to enjoy perpetual virginity'" (Ovid, *Metamorphoses* 1.483–487).[132] With the goal of cementing her independence, the antisocial Daphne puts on a seductive show of vulnerability and softness. She is making her father play her game. She uses the blush to elicit the in-

124. *Dicunt etiam physici, quod natura pudore tacta ita sanguinem ante se pro velamento tendat.* Macrobius goes on to compare the blush to a blushing man putting his hands before his face.

125. *Decet alba quidem pudor ora, sed iste / si simules prodest, verus obesse solet.*

126. *innocentes ergo et verecundi sunt, ut bene audiant, et ut rumorem bonum colligant, erubescunt.*

127. *rubor, quo se contra pudorem muniebat.*

128. *superbia in fronte, ira in oculis, femineus pallor in corpore, in ore impudentia multo rubore suffusa.*

129. "The man who is going to speak should show signs of nervousness when rising to his feet, change color, and make it clear that he feels the risk. If these symptoms do not occur spontaneously, it will be necessary to simulate them" (*Neque ego ... nolo eum, qui sit dicturus, et sollicitum surgere et colore mutari et periculum intelligere; quae si non accident, etiam simulanda erunt* [Quintilian, *Institutio oratoria* 12.5.4]). For deliberate or encouraged shows of "breaking down," see Seneca Rhetor, *Controversiae* 7.4.6 (*de industria vocem infringere et vultum deicere*); Seneca, *Epistulae* 11.7; Cicero, *De oratore* 2.47.196.

130. For Gregory of Nazianzus, the painted blush was "the red of the shameless woman who knows not how to blush" (*touto gar estiv ereuthos anaideies avereuthou. Rubor enim ille est impudentiae, quae erubescere nescit* [*Patrologia Graeca* vol. 37 p. 899]). For the *rubor fucatus*, see Cicero, *Orator* 23.79. I owe these associations to Daniel Bridgman.

131. Barbara Kellum has reminded me of the scenes in Robert Redford's *Quiz Show* (1994) where the character played by John Turturro demonstrates how he was taught to sweat and grimace in order to cynically evoke the audience's sympathy.

132. *illa velut crimen taedas exosa iugales*
    pulchra verecundo suffunditur ora rubore
    inque patris blandis haerens cervice lacertis
    "da mihi perpetua, genitor
    carissime," dixit, "verginitate frui!"

dulgence of her father,[133] relying on the Romans' tendency to respond to the blush with tenderness.[134]

CONCLUSIONS: THE LOSS OF TRUST

Nowhere is trust certain.

(nusquam tuta fides.)

VIRGIL, *AENEIS* 4.373

According to Helen Merril Lynd, shame involves the fear of a sudden break in a trustful relationship or a sudden break of trust in general and in the overall meaningfulness of one's existence.[135] With the loss of a face-to-face culture, the ability to presume upon the goodwill and collusion of others (Doi's *amaeru*) was lost to the Romans.[136] The increasing size and complexity of Roman society, the attenuation of the inherited patron-client relationship, and above all the civil wars, had the effect of heightening the extreme aspects of shame, unrelieved by the reassurance of others. One who cannot trust cannot endure shame. Shame becomes heightened to the point of unbearability when one can no longer presume upon the collusion of others in the maintenance of one's face, when one cannot rely on the shame in others' eyes.[137]

When the Romans complain about their "decadence," they are not lamenting their loss of a sense of shame but the loss of the *fides* that made a sense of shame not only endurable but expressive and even enjoyable. The angry vortex of shame filled the abyss left by mutual trust. The wreck of the delicately balanced

133. Compare the apparently submissive but very aggressive and manipulative flattery of the slaves in the *Miles gloriosus* of Plautus.

134. For aggressive blushing, see Tacitus, *Agricola* 45; Pliny, *Panegyricus* 48.4; Seneca, *Epistulae* 11.4. Like blushing, supplication could be as cynical and self-serving as Paris begging for mercy from Helen in Ovid's *Heroides* 16.

135. See Wurmser, *Mask of Shame*, p. 52. Modern anthropology, with its acute self-consciousness about seeing and being seen, about acting and speaking, together with its narcissism, its egoism, and inflated sense of power, is a result of Westerners' loss of mutual trust within their own culture. They are *dissoluti*, freed from their moorings. They have lost a sense of the other as fair opponent (and thus are unsure both of their own being and that of the other).

136. For Rome "outgrowing" shame, see Kaster, "Shame of the Romans," p. 17. "Alistair Reid has pointed out that having a sense of identity is having 'good faith'" (Lynd, *On Shame*, p. 267 n. 50).

137. Doi believes that postwar Japan increasingly resembles Tönnies's *Gesellschaft* and that there is not sufficient opportunity to *amaeru* (a kind of limited and tolerated transgression, in which one can "presume" upon the tolerance and mercy of others); or else that society has become so complex that the rules by which one can *amaeru* with ease have been lost. The result, in Japan, is increased anxiety (and shame) in dealing with others (Doi, *Anatomy of Dependence*, p. 119). "In a modern age of 'freedom, independence and self,' the sense of solidarity with others that comes from *amae* is ultimately no more than a mirage" (p. 121).

mechanisms of shame was well on its way when Romans begin to associate trust with the past.[138]

The apotheosis of the gangster male and the complementary reduction of honor to honesty (frozen and full-time self-control) occurred simultaneously in ancient Rome; they were mirrored phenomena reflected in the dark pool of intolerable shame.[139] Extremes invert in Roman thought, and there was nothing as revealing of this paradoxical and mirroring inversion as the cynical, deliberate blush. The deliberate blush was the *extreme* self-control of the man or woman deeply alienated from the nexus of social bonds. While calculated self-control was essential for the existence and preservation of social ties, too much self-control was destructive and antisocial. No one could trust the man or woman who risked nothing in speaking or acting, whose face was impenetrable. The man or woman with the painted-on blush was the exact counterpart of the man or woman who did not blush at all. The excessively self-possessed became, like the unblushing red-faced Domitian, inscrutable, treacherous, alone.[140]

The Roman ideal was, according to Cicero, to possess an imperturbable poise, a presence of mind, not to be thrown off one's stride, to be aware of and prepared for all possible events and mishaps (*De officiis* 1.23.80).[141] This desire for self-mastery and autonomy was accentuated during the turmoil of the civil war. But, paradoxically, the delicate moral balancing system of the ancient Romans demanded that one never realize the highest ideals of the culture, that one never be "the complete man." Like the fullness of power implied in the *patria potestas*, like being *sui iuris*, a law unto oneself, one constantly aspired to autonomy, hoping all the time never to achieve it. Like Horace's Fortunate Isles or Cavafy's Ithaca, it might seem a salvation to those tossed on the rough seas of the Roman civil wars, but to those who arrived it would always prove a desolation.

138. For instances of the absence of trust in Tacitus, see *Annales* 4.69–70, 6.13 (= 6.7), 6.25 (= 6.19).

139. The development of the "rebel" figure in the early empire (in Seneca, in Lucan, and in early Christian thought) is a direct result of the changes in Roman notions of honor. Lucan's rebel is utterly intolerant of shame. Lucan himself is, in many ways, the spiritual mirror image of his villain Caesar.

140. Paradoxically, with the increasing idealization of hardness and self-control in Roman culture, the involuntary blush becomes "feminine." So long as a "sense of shame" was the quality of a "socialized" man, men and women blushed equally.

141. *Fortis vero animi et constantis est non perturbari in rebus asperis nec tumultuantem de gradu deici ut dicitur, sed praesenti animo uti et consilio nec a ratione discedere.*

CHAPTER NINE

Conclusions
Choosing Life

In contemporary American culture, the "honorable" person is "honest and true," someone who is above all consistent. He or she is conscientious, predictable, stable, solid, "four-square," a "rock," a "brick." He or she is committed to a code that admits no exceptions, like the Orioles' Cal Ripken, a person who never takes a vacation from the game that he or she plays.

The "honorable" man or woman is simple in the way a child or a worshiper is simple. Their simplicity, like an arctic icebreaker, clears a path through the pack ice of ritual and the muck of embodiment.

The "honorable" person is an "integrated psychic whole," not an actor or hypocrite. He or she is "authentic" and unadulterated in his or her being and identity, in harmony with his or her inner nature. The "honorable" have a guiding and unifying conscience rather than a fracturing self-consciousness. They can sleep at night. ("There is no pillow like a clear conscience.")[1] They have smooth complexions and steady eyes. They are without sinister secrets and vices.

The "honorable" tell the truth.

Although dependable, the "honorable" person is independent. He or she serves diligently and is frequently a "workaholic" (like Cal Ripken) and an altruist (like Sophie Scholl, the heroine of the White Rose resistance movement against the Nazis in Munich, 1942–1943), but this service is not servitude. Honorable people serve only their own autonomous consciences.

The "honorable" do not throw temper tantrums, "break" into tears, or succumb to other strong emotions; they do not sulk on the beach like Achilles or

---

1. Hans Kohut's heroic characters are true to their "nuclear selves." They are in a state of peaceful stability and clarity. See the wonderful example of Sophie Scholl in Kohut's essay "On Courage," in *Self-Psychology and the Humanities: Reflections on a New Psychoanalytic Approach,* ed. Charles B. Strozier, New York, 1985, pp. 5–50.

brood like Brutus. They do not presume upon the goodwill or indulgence of others. The "honorable" are not ashamed.

Finally, the "honorable" have "dignity": a dispassionate demeanor, faultless self-possession, and a private reserve of security that ensures their autonomy even while allowing their faithful and voluntary submission to the laws of their code.[2]

What is "honorable" in our Euro-American culture is also "just," and there is a perfect consonance between justice and the just and honorable person. Moreover, justice is a state rather than a process, an equilibrium rather an equilibration (the benevolent state being a "fixed" one). We feel that to live in perpetual tension and confusion is to live in corruption. When we are unable to resolve contradictions, we feel not only that something is deeply wrong with us but also that we are dishonorable and unjust. We feel distressed, for instance, that we cannot finally determine if we are all equal or all different. Likewise, we feel disconcerted that we cannot resolve the radically different social and psychological demands of hierarchy and equality. It is hard for us, emotionally, to conceive of a culture idealizing a tense and never-ending balancing act.

For us, truth and reality, like the laws of physics, simply are. The honorable and the intelligent do not pretend to make the world. Truth and reality are not products of their wills. Reality is, and humans adjust themselves to it—or else.

Our notions of honor seem self-evident, positive, and morally unambiguous to us. I have written this book in part because I think that it is possible to see through the lens of ancient Roman society the obliquities of our own notions of honor.

Roman honor, especially that of the Republic, was built on a very different set of assumptions from our own: on fluid notions of balancing, on reciprocities and compensations. Within the restless Roman dynamics, no one's position was fixed except that of the enslaved and the defeated, and even they, in their own spheres, often strove to live by the reciprocities of honor. What Ernestine Friedl says of the Greek peasants of modern Vasilika could be easily applied to the ancient Romans: "If it were necessary to describe the villagers' feelings with respect to each other and the world in one word, that word would be 'tension.'"[3]

2. Clifford Geertz points out how peculiar and unique within the world's cultures is our Western conception of the person as a more or less integrated, motivational, and cognitive universe organized into a distinctive whole and set against other such wholes and against its social and natural background ("From the Native's Point of View: On the Nature of Anthropological Understanding," in *Culture Theory: Essays on Mind, Self, and Emotion*, ed. Richard A. Schweder and Robert A. LeVine, Cambridge, 1984, pp. 123–136).

3. She continues: "In Vasilika, when one walks through the field and asks how the work is going, the common response is... 'We are wrestling.'... The villagers can amplify with further comments on their perpetual contest with soil, weather and machinery....The sense of contest, of struggle, of agony, of a kind of pushing and pulling—is also a feature of a large number of encounters with other human beings" (*Vasilika: A Village in Modern Greece*, New York, 1962, pp. 75–76). Cf. Alvin Gouldner, *Enter Plato*, New York, 1965, p. 47.

Intolerant of shame and its discomforts, modern Euro-Americans are slow to understand a culture in which many of the most compelling stories explored or exploited the disjunctions between emotional life and the codes governing behavior. When we read that Brutus and Torquatus slew their sons or that Aeneas left behind his beloved Dido, we want to imagine Brutus and Torquatus as men of conscience bravely and dutifully following a code that dictated that fathers should be severe to their sons, and that Aeneas was dutifully bowing to the will of the gods rather than pursuing his own selfish desires. We do not want to think that the very point of these stories is the terrible choice, the anguish of a father having to follow a code that conflicted with a father's intense feelings for a child, or the agony of a man whose duty to the gods conflicted with his commitment to the woman whom he loved.[4] We do not want the double-bind to be "real." We do not want irresolvable paradoxes to be at the heart of our spiritual lives. We want the choice to be clear to Brutus and Torquatus and Aeneas, and the heroes to be spiritually in harmony with the choices they have made and the demands of the code by which they have lived. Then they could be heroes by our definition. But the person of honor, the person with a sense of shame, in ancient Rome had to be willingly frustrated, somewhat ineffectual, and not completely in control. The honorable man and woman in ancient Rome continually experienced and tolerated a high degree of discomfort and disorganization; they were ashamed in avoidance of greater shame.[5] There could be no resolution to this paradox.

The "sincere" Roman was not simple and childlike. On the contrary, insofar as a Roman was *scrupulosus* or *religiosus,* he or she was afflicted with relentless low-grade anxiety. Indeed, the "sincere" Roman was the one who could not quite preserve the integrity of his or her *persona,* the man who blushed like Pompey or cried like Trajan. Beneath the necessary but frangible mask of the trustworthy, the socialized, the honorable person, one could glimpse the chafing confusion, even the anguish. A Roman inferred the pain beneath Cornelia's hospitable smile and detected the grief that accompanied Aemilius Paullus triumphing in an empty chariot. Moreover, Roman honor, with its conflicting bonds and obligations, not only allowed a complex emotional life; it actually necessitated lapses and transgressions from the bonds and obligations. Romans of honor were, as portrayed by the

---

4. The Japanese, like the Romans, experience, examine, and exploit the disparities between the code and their emotional life. For the cleavage between *giri* (duty) and *ninjo* (human feeling) in Japanese thought, see Donald Keene's introduction to his translation of *Chushingura: The Treasury of Loyal Retainers,* New York, 1971, pp. 18–19.

5. Bourdieu, speaking of the Kabyle, remarks on "the unceasing vigilance one needs to exert so as to be 'carried along' by the game without being 'carried away' beyond the game, as happens when a mock fight gets the better of the fighters" (*Outline of a Theory of Practice,* trans. Richard Nice, Cambridge, 1979, p. 10). The kind of security for which we yearn from our culture is impossible to find in a society governed by reciprocity and the vendetta.

Romans themselves, silly, witty, tricky, fiery, volatile, petulant, dangerous, even when socially skilled. The very behaviors that for a modern Westerner signal shallowness and the absence of a complex inner life are, in fact, the evidence for it.

Roman men and women might stick stubbornly and willfully to their word and their promise, but they did not necessarily tell the truth. Rather they spoke the lines—and between the lines. Rather than be transparent, the Romans, particularly those of the Republic, were involved in a delicate counterpoint between display and concealment. They were willful, unnatural, and theatrical, more like Maria Callas and Karl Wallenda than Sophie Scholl and Cal Ripken.

CONFIDENCE LOST

Roman history can be construed, in one of its various aspects, as the story of a culture long governed by the sense of balance (or the sense of shame, which was the sense of balance) in which the highest value was placed on the will *(animus)*, manifested in moderation and self-overcoming, and whose operation depended above all on mutual trust and recognition. Beginning in the civil war period, this culture radically changed to one ideally governed from a stable center and by fixed laws, in which the highest value was placed on obedience to those laws; it became a culture whose operation depended, above all, on each individual's surrender to, and identification with, the will of the king and god (the sources of the law), a culture that saw the separation of the spiritual from the social as the necessary condition for a rich inner life (or, indeed, for any inner life at all).

In his work on policing Rome, Wilfried Nippel emphasizes the personal aspects of Roman public "government" during the Republic: magistrates had to face the citizenry in person and could not avoid the risks of physical confrontation. In dealing with disturbances they had to rely on the power of their bodily presence and their eloquence, their personal dignity and authority, rather than on threats or coercion.[6] While a sense of shame was—and ever will be—an infinitely more effective method of policing a culture than force, preserving order was still a very risky business in ancient Rome. And so it was mandatory for the Romans of the Republic, as it was in all cultures without a central peacekeeping force, to have an elaborate etiquette and an exquisite sensitivity to the eyes and opinions of one another. At the same time, to prevent shame from dismantling the culture (as it always threatened to do), and to keep the code of formalized behavior from becoming a straitjacket, several other conditions had to apply: first, and above all, there needed to be mutual trust: not only a heightened sensitivity to but collabo-

---

6. "Policing Rome," *Journal of Roman Studies* 74 (1984): 21, 23. "Lictors could only fulfil their tasks with the magistrates present. This means that they could not relieve the magistrate of the physical confrontation with the addressees of his orders" (ibid., p. 22). Cf. Cicero, *Brutus* 56f.

ration in the maintenance of each other's "face"—what one might call tact.[7] Second, shaming needed to form part of a rhythm of expiation and reintegration, of teasing and indulgence, for all but the most reprobate within the culture.[8] Third, there had to be outlets, opportunities for withdrawal, for shamelessness—even fury—both within and without the society. Submission to the strictures and formalities of shame, to the codes of honor, could never be full-time. The Romans' acute sensitivity to shame was relieved by periodic, permissible impertinence. The bashful, blushing Romans could be roistering rakehells in youth, in war, and on the Saturnalia. Indeed, it was the Romans' vigilant sense of shame within the society that allowed for the development of a ruthless imperialism, like that of the Japanese in China or the British in North America.[9] "All-Honored Honest Roman Brutus" could be "Brutus the Loan Shark" in the provinces.[10]

THE LOSS OF MEDIOCRITY

Roman imperial expansion severely strained the delicate balancing mechanisms of shame. With the rapid Roman expansion of the second century B.C.E. came the loss of the face-to-face culture. The population of Rome became large, heterogeneous, and less clearly delimited. In the *imperium sine fine*, the lines were obscured between the insider (with whom you observed limitations and whose spirit

7. On tact, see Kurt Reizler, "Comment on the Social Psychology of Shame," *American Journal of Sociology* 48 (1942–1943): 459.

8. Nathan Rosenstein, in his *Imperatores Victi: Military Defeat and Aristocratic Competition in the Middle and Late Republic* (Berkeley, 1990), emphasizes the surprising degree to which even defeated Roman generals and their offspring were reintegrated into Roman society. Rosenstein's Romans are like Frans de Waal's male chimpanzees, who fight frequently, hard, and occasionally viciously but also easily forget and re-ally (*Peace-Keeping among Primates*, Cambridge, Mass., 1989, pp. 48–78).

9. According to Michelle Rosaldo, the tendency of the Ilongot to feel shame and inadequacy was alleviated by the energy and force felt in head-hunting and raiding; the externalized aggression allowed for the balanced and cooperative everyday life of the Ilongot within the kinship group ("The Shame of Headhunters and the Autonomy of Self," *Ethos* 11 [1983]: 144–145). Jules Henry's aggressive Kaingang, like Rosaldo's headhunters, make radical distinctions between those inside and those outside. See Rosaldo, *Knowledge and Passion: Ilongot Notions of Self and Social Life*, Cambridge, 1980; Henry, *Jungle People*, New York, 1941, esp. pp. 49–51.

10. There is a Japanese adage: "The traveller easily discards his sense of shame" (quoted by Seiichi Morisaki and William B. Gudykunst, "Face in Japan and the United States,"in *The Challenge of Facework*, ed. Stella Ting-Toomey, Albany, 1994, p. 64). The authors report on experiments carried out in Japan similar to Solomon Asch's experiment (in which a lone subject was isolated and shamed by a group of confederates—see chapter 5). They discovered that when the confederates were members of the Japanese subject's "in-group," the conformity of the isolated subject was even higher than in Asch's experiment with Western subjects; but when the confederates were strangers, conformity was lower than in Asch's studies. They conclude that where "face" (i.e., self-identity) is established by intersubjectivity, shame has a greater force for compelling conformity than in a culture where one is ideally autonomous. At the same time, once out of the "in-group," the subjects' shame was considerably lower.

you did not break) and the outsider (with whom there were no limitations and whose spirit you could and would break). The Romans lost a clear and intuitive sense of the "we," the unquestioned distinction between those with whom one ate and those whom one ate. The enemy, the Not-Us who helped forge their identity, came to be included in Cicero's all-embracing *humanitas*. It is poignant, but not accidental, that the notion of "humanity" appears in Rome during the century of intermittent but psychologically and socially devastating civil wars.

As a result of the dissolution of mutual trust during the civil wars and the institution of the monarchy, the Romans of the ruling classes, feeling themselves conquered and enslaved, begin to feel themselves as much outsiders as their conquered peoples, as much strangers in a strange land, as Virgil's Aeneas, Petronius's Encolpius, Apuleius's Lucius, the emperor Marcus Aurelius, or the apostle Paul.[11]

The loss of clear distinctions between insiders and outsiders created, furthermore, a profound sense of incorrigible guilt, of *conscientia*, a super-self-consciousness. The more the Romans began to see themselves through the eyes and speak to themselves through the mouths of their conquered, through a Pontic Mithridates or a British Galgacus, the more the Romans lost their ability to manage shame.[12] Expelled from the magic circle of an all-justifying cultural narcissism, they began to feel both the pain of compassion and the numbing indifference that results from the recognition of the Other as someone whom they now enclosed under the umbrella of "humanity," even while the formal methods were lacking by which they could expiate their transgressions against that Other. They had already killed or broken the spirit of many of those with whom they now felt a bond.[13] "I wish they had not destroyed Corinth," Cicero laments (*De officiis* 1.11.35).

Thus when the Romans talk about themselves as a fallen people and complain about their corruption, it is not because they have lost their sense of shame. On the contrary, shame is there, virulent, festering, but now it cannot be managed. The sphere of their shame has been enlarged and intensified without the alleviation of mutual trust and indulgence. The debilitating aspects of shame have been so

11. For the sensation of defeat and enslavement expressed in the literature of the late Republic and early Empire, see, for example, Sallust, *Catilina* 20.6–7; Tacitus, *Annales* 3.65, *Agricola* 2.3; Sandra Joshel, *Work, Identity, and Legal Status at Rome: A Study of the Occupational Inscriptions*, Norman, Oklahoma, 1992, p. 151; Elizabeth Keitel, "Principate and Civil War," *American Journal of Philology* 105 (1984): 306–325.

12. Cf. Sallust, *Historiae*, fr. 4.17; Tacitus, *Agricola* 30. For compassion and the breakdown of Roman intersubjective identity, see Barton, "The Cost of Compassion in Ancient Rome" (in preparation).

13. I am reminded of the cosmopolitan South African Laurens van der Post's poignant and profoundly sympathetic portrait of the Bushmen set against his family's deeply callous attitudes toward the native San they had helped to exterminate. If they had dared to think of the Bushmen as humans, remorse would have destroyed them (*The Lost World of the Kalahari*, New York, 1958, esp. pp. 55–56).

greatly augmented and intensified that they frequently invert and produce a hard brutishness. We have lost, Cicero declares, speaking under Sulla's dictatorship in 80 B.C.E., "the faculty of forgiveness" *(ignoscendi ratio [Pro Roscio Amerino* 1.3]).

Fides (the paradoxical, reciprocal, and intersubjective Roman system of power and its restraint) had, according to Lucan, writing in the first century of the Common Era, long since vanished from the Roman scene *(Bellum civile* 2.242–243). He traced this death back to the moment when Sulla and Marius, like vampires, were admitted armed within the city walls (9.204–206). The civil wars were, of course, the ultimate dismal example of the collapse of good faith in the Republic, the civil wars brought about by men who could not be shamed as their ancestors Horatius Tergeminus or Marcius Coriolanus had been shamed. Marius, Pompey, Caesar, and Augustus admired, rather, the Macedonian Alexander, despite—or because of—his lapses in self-control:[14] Alexander, the perfect ideal of the renegade male, the man who rejected the bonds and limitations of his society and even "home" itself, the man who was willing to be a stranger in a strange land, the man who aspired to be a king (and there was no antidote to a king), the man who could break every rule and still not feel ashamed, the ideal and the anti-ideal of the Roman aristocracy in the collapsing Republic.

THE NEED TO LIVE

Let us live; for captives this suffices.
SENECA, *TROADES* 975–976[15]

The Japanologist Maurice Pinguet quotes Sakaguchi Ango's "Darakuron" ("Essay on Decadence," 1946) concerning the despair and anomie in Japan after the war:

> It is a grandiose image of man which ending the war has vouchsafed us: sixty- and seventy-year-old generals dragged before the tribunals instead of committing *seppuku!* Japan is defeated, *bushido* [the code of the samurai] is no more; but our decadence is the true womb whence man has at long last been born. Living is a progressive imperfection: is there any quicker and more convenient way to save mankind than that natural process? *Harakiri* does not appeal to me.

Pinguet comments:

> You give yourself to life, which gives itself to you, and accept it for what it is: a gradual wearing away, a deterioration, dispersion, forgetting; and also a birth, a flowering, a becoming. Sakaguchi's view of the future, formulated when his people were in the deepest pit of distress, takes us back to the intuitions of the Buddhist Greater Vehicle:...that salvation must be in this world, that you can save yourself here and

---

14. See Stefan Weinstock, "*Victor* and *Invictus*," *Harvard Theological Review* 50 (1957): 211–247.
15. *Quod captis sat est vivamus.*

now if you can see yourself and accept yourself as you really are: a fallen being perhaps, but ready for redemption—which is metamorphosis, the law of life.[16]

The Romans were compelled by the circumstances of history to reject the death-
centered warrior ethos of the Republic. But they discovered that they could have
the purifying, simplifying sincerity of choosing death even while choosing life, if
choosing life was equated with the death of the self to the world (and one's body
in the world).

THE NEED TO WIN

When an archer is shooting for nothing
He has all his skill.
If he shoots for a brass buckle
He is already nervous.
If he shoots for a prize of gold
He goes blind
Or sees two targets—
He is out of his mind!
His skill has not changed. But the prize
Divides him. He cares.
He thinks more of winning
Than of shooting—
And the need to win
Drains him of power.
CHUANG TZU[17]

The greatest source of power for the ancient Romans had been their willingness,
singly and as a group, to compete strenuously, but not in order to win, not to survive. The most powerful social bonds in ancient Rome were a precipitate of the
blood the Romans were willing to expend so prodigally for one another generation after generation; no law, no god, no victory, no pride in family or race or status could ever so clarify or crystallize the spirit. The will, the willingness, on
behalf of the collectivity to lose everything, to become nothing, had kept self-
consciousness and shame from being too excruciating, too alienating.

But when Roman generals began fighting for themselves, and to win, when
their soldiers begin fighting for their generals and their pay (rather than for their
homes, their lands, and the altars of their ancestors), the ultimate source of mutual trust within the culture was lost. When the Romans *needed* to win, shame and
its attendant self-consciousness became unbearable.

---

16. *Voluntary Death in Japan,* trans. Rosemary Morris, Cambridge, 1993, pp. 265–266.
17. Quoted in Thomas Merton, *The Way of Chuang Tzu,* San Francisco, 1969, p. 107. I owe this citation to Larry Meredith.

Moreover, because the Romans imagined themselves as a people who had once lived by the slogan "Victory or death," survival itself became a source of embarrassment during and after the civil wars.[18] Many Romans, like Cicero or Laberius, felt they had outlived their honor. By continuing to live, they advertised their submission. Survival was a voluntary confession of servility, a confession that their wills had been broken; it was saying "Uncle." On the other hand, like the Japanese following World War II, the Roman could now embrace life and its entropy and evolution, its complexity, corruption, dissolution, its flowerings and rebirths.

By a profound paradox that is, nevertheless, easy to understand, the Romans, beginning in the period of the civil wars, begin to long for and idealize stability. Although a few, like Petronius and Ovid, may gleefully have embraced the metamorphoses, most ancient Romans found it as difficult as modern Americans to surrender joyously to the flux. They tended to think of themselves, like Aeneas or Lucius, as wandering in search of a safe place, a rock in which to hide, a permanent, secure reality in which they could be like that reality: permanent, secure, a rock.

If historians have long had the notion that Rome "fell," it is a notion based on the metaphor of an original firm, stable, solid structure that collapsed or disintegrated. I would argue that if Rome had a fall, it was a fall *into* a world dominated by exactly that metaphor, that moral ideal.

THE INFANTILIZATION OF ROME

Modern thinkers, from Jean-Jacques Rousseau to Max Scheler, often posit a complete, free, and infinitely expansive—if inarticulate—human origin. Psychologists often imagine the speechless infant as feeling omnipotent and only gradually awakening to limitations and differentiations. Shame, for Max Scheler (as for Rousseau, Dostoevsky, and Helen Block Lewis), was the product of the frustration of an essential or original emotional and physical wholeness by the limitations of our bodies and our societies. For the Romans of the early and middle Republic, there had been no original wholeness, but only an original limitation. In the beginning were the walls— the breachable walls. As Chaim Wirszubski explains, the *libertas* of the Republic was a product not of an unlimited freedom, but of qualified restraints and limitations.[19]

I suggest that the very appearance of the ideal of an original completeness, an original autonomy, simplicity, authenticity, and an original or ideal absence of ten-

18. "A man has lost his life who owes it to another; and whoever, having been cast down from high estate at his enemy's feet, has awaited the verdict of another on his life and throne . . . is a lasting spectacle of another's virtue" (*perdidit enim vitam, qui debet, et quisquis ex alto ad inimici pedes abiectus alienam de capite regnoque sententiam expectavit, in servatoris sui gloriam vivit. . . . Adsiduum enim spectacultum alienae virtutis est* [Seneca, *De clementia* 1.21.2]).

19. Chaim Wirszubski, *Libertas as a Political Idea at Rome During the Late Republic and Early Principate*, Cambridge, Mass., 1960.

sion, in both ancient and in modern thought, follows from the breakdown of trust and the elevation of life to the ultimate value. The religious and legal systems of ancient Rome, as well as the stories and *exempla* of the Republic, reveal a contest culture with all its attendant emotional and social frictions. There is, however, nothing to suggest the secure and tension-free community that Sallust, writing in the period of the civil wars, imagined existing in the early or middle Republic. This peaceful original Roman state of Sallust's was less a reflection of history than a response to it. Sallust created a sort of simple, clear, undifferentiated Roman identity that was therefore unlimited, unbound, and unselfconscious—the proto-type of our "honest" man. Retrospectively, Roman identity became, for Sallust, as for us, ontological rather than existential. It was no longer a result of anxiety, conflict, balancing. The Romans of the late Republic and early Empire begin to construct, retroactively, an ideal of an integrated psychic whole *(honestas),* for both the community and the individual. For the Romans, as for us, the ideal of the "honest" man was an expression of nostalgia for an imaginary past integrity, an imaginary past wholeness that was, simultaneously, comfortably compatible with—indeed a mirror image of—a present infantile dependency and shameless-ness. The conjunction of the ideas that one could have unlimited autonomy (like empire without end) and, at the same time, exercise *complete* self-control resulted from the collapse of the compensatory physics of the culture. This is the reason that in Roman thought the Golden Age looks so much like the Apocalypse, the re-turn of Saturn looks so much like the Saturnalia out of bounds.[20]

CLOSING THE CIRCLE

The more "limitless" and abstract Rome became, the fewer people one trusted. The more the distinctions between insiders and outsiders broke down, the smaller the circle one clung to for the maintenance of one's sense of self. Sometimes all that was left was one's daughter, one's buddy, one's old freedman, one's sweet-heart, one's pet eel. As in the huge, amorphous United States, people increasingly relied on their intimates for their identity.[21] (And henceforward, as in America, only in sporting contests, war, or calamity would the Romans have a sense of

---

20. See Carlin Barton, *The Sorrows of the Ancient Romans,* Princeton, 1993, part 2.

21. There is an inverse proportion between the collective power and competency of the group and the power and competency of the individuals within it. Compare the person driving across the continent in a '61 Volkswagen (with its famous Fix-it Manual tucked under the seat) with the person who rides strapped in his or her narrow seat in a roaring Boeing 747. The first (possessing maximum competency) has to be active, endlessly engaged in repairing and adjusting the car; the second (with access to the power produced by the collectivity) has to adjust, quietly and constantly, to situations be-yond his or her control. The members of a San foraging band, so powerless as a group, nevertheless possessed much broader control and competence over their lives than members of a settled farming community, not to mention members of a powerful modern bureaucratic state.

identity in which shame was, at least temporarily, bearable.) Cicero complained to Atticus in January 60 B.C.E. that all that was left to him was his immediate family (*Ad Atticum* 1.18). Macrobius's Crassus had his lamprey.[22] Caesar, his biographer Matthias Gelzer surmises, had no friends at all.[23]

It is possible that the cult of romantic love, of a personal God, and of "Pyladean" friendship, as well as the keeping of pets in the late Republic and early Empire, was the result of this "crisis of intimacy" in Rome. One still needed a sphere where one could submit, where one could presume upon the love and indulgence of another.[24]

THE GOOD CONSCIENCE

Each man will have to bear his own load.

GALATIANS 6.5

Virtue rests not on others' judgments but on the witness of one's own conscience. But let everyone prove his own work, and so he shall have glory in himself only, and not in his neighbor.

AUGUSTINE, *DE CIVITATE DEI* 5.2

Some of the most important developments in Roman thought in the late Republic and early Empire, developments that were to have lasting effects on European thought, concerned ways of maintaining one's being without the support of others; ways of having self-consciousness without being alienated from oneself, of having honor apart from shame, hope apart from fear, life apart from death, soul apart from will.

In the world where one could not take the rules of the game for granted, where one could not presuppose the goodwill of others, one was required to sustain one's honor without either competition or collaboration. Cicero in the *De legibus* scolds his imaginary audience for wanting shame and modesty to meet with praise. One must act without seeking recognition, he asserts. One must maintain one's spirit without the collusion of others: "But what shall we say of sobriety, moderation, and self-restraint, of modesty, shame and chastity? Is it for fear of disgrace that we should not be wanton, or for fear of the laws and the courts?"

---

22. For Lucius Crassus, see Macrobius, *Saturnalia* 3.15.3–5; Barton, *Sorrows*, p. 67 and n. 89.

23. *Caesar: Politician and Statesman*, trans. Peter Needham, Oxford, 1968, pp. 331–333.

24. The roles played by romantic love and love for pets in modern America may be similar to those they played in Rome of the late Republic and Empire. Americans' sentimentalism, our love for pets and young children—anything soft and cuddly—is, in part, a result of the unfulfilled desire to submit, a desire to presume upon the love of another that is impossible in the broader culture, where one's being is not cared for. Love of love, in our culture, as in ancient Rome, is not a contradiction but a concomitant of our violence and mutual mistrust.

(*De legibus* 1.19.50).[25] "There is," he declares, "no audience for virtue with greater authority than 'conscience'" (*nullum theatrum virtuti conscientia maius est* [*Tusculanae disputationes* 2.26.63]).[26]

The Roman notion of *conscientia* did not have to change greatly to shift from the nightmarish alienation of secret and inexpiable guilt to the autonomous, positive, guiding "conscience." The Romans had rarely, before the influence of the Stoics, identified the personal will with the deity. But when one attuned one's will, one's *animus,* to that of the master, emperor, or god, the *animus* became a deity. This is what we think of as the psychological basis for "conscience" as a "higher form" than shame, and it forms the basis for the modern conception of a "guilt culture" as opposed to, and superior to, a "shame culture." After Rome was garrisoned by the emperors like a defeated city, there developed, in Rome, the notion of an authority higher than public scrutiny. In response to this authority, the Romans, like Socrates before them, developed a "little inner voice," a *bona conscientia,* a friendly or benevolent "conscience," in our sense. The Romans began putting respect for that authority over common consent and common opinion. Like Socrates's "little inner voice," *conscientia* was infallibly right *because* one submitted to it unconditionally, *because* it was given complete and consistent authority. This complete and consistent authority, in turn, enabled it to shield one from the public opinion that would shame one. The man or woman of conscience, in possession of the truth, need have no shame before his or her peers. A Roman could end the tension between self and society by redefining the bonds. One could be totally independent, even while totally dependent, by linking one's gears completely with the "higher authorities."

THE HONEST MAN

The best thing is to want what is right (the honesta) *and not to stray from the path.*
SENECA, *PHAEDRA* 140–141[27]

Consistency of behavior over a long time is the most important criterion of a good vassal.
EIKO IKEGAMI[28]

With the loss of the rules and conditions of the good contest, the entire language of honor "imploded" and had to be "reconstructed." *Virtus,* the effective energy, the

---

25. *Quid vero de modestia, quid de temperantia, quid de continentia, quid de verecundia, pudore pudicitiaque dicemus? infamiaene metu non esse petulantis an legum et iudiciorum?*

26. "You bid me avoid the mob, to withdraw and be content with my conscience?" ("*Tu me,*" inquis, "*vitare turbam iubes secedere et conscientia esse contentum?*" [Seneca, *Epistulae* 8.1]).

27. *Honesta primum est velle nec labi via, / pudor est secundus nosse peccandi modum.*

28. *The Taming of the Samurai: Honorific Individualism and the Making of Modern Japan,* Cambridge, Mass., 1995, p. 26.

valor and potency that made one a *vir*, exsanguinated until, in Cicero's day, it was reborn as temperance, sobriety, chastity. *Virtus* tends increasingly to describe obedience or endurance rather than vigor or potency. *Virtus* is, moreover, frequently replaced by *honestas, fortitudo,* or *patientia,* words that stress control and consistency. *Pudor* is superseded by *verecundia* for the reason that it implies all of the inhibitions and none of the assertions, all of the constraint and none of the bile or volatility of shame. In short, honor becomes "honesty," total self-control, complete, unblushing submission to the conscience (or the god or king represented by that conscience), without support, without compensation or reward.[29] Cicero defines *honestum* as "that action which, in and of itself, without bringing the actor any advantage or reward or profit, ought by right to be praised" (*De finibus* 2.14.45).[30] The new "honest" man served the truth rather than made it. Lucan's Cato was the *rigidi servator honesti,* the preserver of a rectitude unbending (*Bellum civile* 2.389). But, as I pointed out in the chapters on *pudor,* total control was the inversion and mirror image of extreme shamelessness: the "honest" man, like the most dangerous criminal, could not be shamed by the opinion of others. This new notion of honor unblushing, which we have inherited from the Romans of the civil war period and the Empire, explains why we think of honor as the antithesis of shame.

That willfulness, unpredictability, craftiness, and whimsy were defined out of honor was perhaps the single greatest revaluation of values that took place in the course of Roman history. The new "honest" man was not tense and dangerous.[31] He was a man who could not be shamed and yet, simultaneously, posed no threat. The honest man allowed himself no Saturnalia; nor, conversely, was he given the opportunity to presume upon others' indulgence. The honest man had all the aspects of *fides* as self-restraint but none of the aspects of *fides* as fullness of power. Indeed, the second meaning of *fides* starts to fade, leaving only the aspects of *fides* as trust or fidelity. The "honest" man's *dignitas* was no longer his presumptive claim to honor but rather an autonomous well of reserve. The tiger was declawed, the fire extinguished.

NATURAL MAN AND NATURAL WOMAN

The new "honest" man or woman did not wear a mask. Nor was he or she split into the master/slave whom one sees in Plautus's *Captivi* or the man/woman of Cicero's *Tusculanae disputationes.* He or she was required to be wholly, consistently,

---

29. Paradoxically, the creation of a code that was "complete" is one of the best pieces of evidence for the priority of emotional experience in the generation of symbolic systems of ancient Rome.

30. *quod tale est detracta omni utilitate sine ullis praemiis fructibusve per se ipsum passit iure laudari. Honestum* is a fixed ontological property: Cicero, *De officiis* 1.4; *Tusculanae disputationes* 2.58.

31. Southern honor underwent a similar transformation in the wake of the defeat of the South in the Civil War. According to Bertram Wyatt-Brown, "Honor in the antebellum North became akin to respectability, a word that included freedom from the licit vices that once were signals of masculin-

and transparently one or the other, man or woman, master or slave. Increasingly the honorable man or woman became "ontologically" rather than "existentially" male or female.[32] While the man and woman of *virtus* were most "unnatural," the new "honorable" man and woman, like good Stoics, were at one with their natures as with their god, and that nature/god was eternal and internal.[33]

One of the advantages to this emotional autonomy was that one could, all by oneself, return to the time before the Fall. David Ausubel and Lawrence Kohlberg outline the development from childhood to adulthood in the following way: The dependent child evolves from implicit acceptance of axiomatic truth to a reasoned acceptance of functionally necessary norms growing out of interpersonal relations as an independent member of adult society.[34] Going from the Roman Republic to the monarchy, from honor to honesty, was reversing this process. The Romans were indeed becoming like little children; the voluntary assumption of absolutes and absolute authority, of dependence on the mercy of the father and the indulgence of the prince, allowed one to maintain one's honor once mutual trust was gone. The Romans were "essentialized" even as they were infantilized. They were getting ready to enter the Kingdom of Heaven.

THE DOWNSIDE OF UPSIDE DOWN

If men regard him as foolish or ignorant, he pays them no heed. In one word, he keeps watch and guard on himself as his own enemy, lying in wait for himself.
EPICTETUS ON THE SAGE, *ENCHEIRIDION* 48

Peter Berger and Fox Butterfield echo a common notion when they argue that if we are to rid our culture of violence, we need to rid ourselves of the notion of "honor"—and replace it with a self-contained and independent "dignity," a no-

---

ity.... Honor in Yankeedom had become another word for domestic and civic virtue" (*Honor and Violence in the Old South*, Oxford, 1986, p. 20). For Wyatt-Brown's illuminating distinctions between "honor" and "honesty," see p. 23.

32. This, of course, only aggravates the shame of the person who feels split. A man or woman is ashamed of being (or being like) both a man and a woman or being (or being like) both free and enslaved. The identity problems of modern "hyphenated" Americans are closely related to this ideal of honor as integrity, purity of identity.

33. The shift in Roman thought from an existential to a ontological personhood can be traced in Cicero. According to Cicero, there is a *persona*—and what is appropriate to it—in a play (with the implication that there are many different roles that a person might play). But nature has assigned to humans a *persona* distinct from and superior to that of animals (implying that there is *one* persona for a human being, a proper role for a human, as opposed to an animal, and that one can speak about what is proper to that *persona* as decorum [*honestas*]) (*De officiis* 1.28.97–98).

34. Ausubel, "Relationship between Shame and Guilt in the Socializing Process," *Psychological Review* 62 (1955): 384; Kohlberg, "Moral Stages and Moralization," in *Moral Development and Behavior: Theory, Research and Social Issues*, ed. Thomas Likona, New York, 1976, pp. 31–53.

tion that self-respect and moral guidance comes from within, from one's "conscience."[35] They do not consider the possibility that it is exactly these notions (of "dignity" and "conscience") that makes shame such an unbearable and destructive force in our culture.[36]

There were some very negative side-effects of the Romans' remedies for excessive shame. Because the new "conscience" was not occasional or situational, it could be more relentless than the old. The *speculator sui censorque*, to use a phrase of Seneca's, could be a brutal and unforgiving judge.[37] The "god who sees every secret thing and hears what is buried in silence," to borrow a phrase from Josephus,[38] the omniscient "conscience" that followed one around everywhere and relentlessly demanded submission, was just as likely as the merciful emperor or merciful god to be cruel, to wield the whip. The new "conscience" was not so different from the ancient shaming mechanisms of the culture, except that, being asocial, it lacked the moderating, the relieving, the compensatory and reciprocal aspects—the humor and whimsy and vacillations—that characterized their socialized forms. People who measured their actions by the rule of their consciences were less liable to have a sense of humor and often less likely to forgive.

The self-consciousness of shame could be unbearably aggravated by identifying one's inner eye with a higher authority who watched one without blinking. Like Job before the God who had conquered Leviathan, or Apuleius's Lucius before the omniscient and omnipotent Isis, the Roman could be ashamed of his or her unlimited inadequacies before his or her divine and limitless desires and aspirations. Charles Segal explains: "The vulnerability of the human body stands out all the more in contrast to the god's absolute power [and] invulnerability."[39] The emperor Marcus Aurelius, in the solitude of his tent on the Danube, watches and

35. See the introduction, n. 33.

36. For the negative and destructive aspects of a notion of human dignity defined from within the individual, see Helmut Wegehaupt, "Die Bedeutung und Anwendung von *dignitas* in den Schriften der republikanischen Zeit," Ph.D. diss., Breslau, 1932, p. 39.

37. For self-scrutiny and self-examination in Seneca, see *De ira* 3.36.1–3, *De brevitate vitae* 10.3, *Epistulae* 56.9–10. For the relentless gaze of the eye of God, connected with a regime of harsh self-watching and an extreme sensitivity to shame, see John Demos, "Shame and Guilt in Early New England," in *Emotion and Social Change*, ed. Carol Z. Stearns and Peter Stearns, New York, 1988, esp. p. 76.

38. *Bellum Iudiacum* 5.413.

39. "Ovid's Metamorphic Bodies: Art, Gender, and Violence in the Metamorphoses," *Arion* 5 (1998): 32. Compare Scheler's formulation: "Er schämt sich in letzter Linie seiner selbst und 'vor' dem Gott in ihm" (Scheler, "Der 'Ort' des Schamgefühls und die Existenzweise des Menschen," *Gesammelte Werke*, vol. 10, Bern, 1957, p. 69). Jacques Salvan formulates one of the consequences of Kierkegaard's God being not an "object" but an "alter ego," a Thou, an absolute subject: "Before God, one can only feel guilty of standing, finite and contingent, before the Infinite. Our finitude is our metaphysical sin and we experience it in various kinds of anguish" (*To Be and Not to Be: An Analysis of Jean-Paul Sartre's Ontology*, Detroit, 1962, p. xviii). In Sartre's super-self-conscious existential philosophy, one's consciousness is split from one's being. One sees oneself as both the center of the universe and as a shamefully contingent being (ibid., p. xiii). And this splitting itself is a cause of anguish.

criticizes himself relentlessly, as unforgiving of himself as Dostoevsky's Underground Man. The supremely powerful emperor and wretchedly impotent mortal describes his own soul, the soul of an evil man: "A black, feminine heart; the heart of a wild beast of the field, that of a child, lazy and unreliable, stupid and deceitful, the heart of a tyrant" (4.28). "Whose soul," he asks, "inhabits me at the moment? Is it a little child's, a youngster's, a woman's, a tyrant's, that of a beast of burden or a wild animal?" (5.11). Marcus's internal critic is more severe than any Cato. As a result, the delicate negotiations between roles and aspects of the self that anciently and ideally molded and formed the personality are experienced by Marcus as a loss of being, a chaos of the self.

The result of censorious self-examination, then, could be shame past mending. Just as the Roman census was a form of invasion of privacy, self-censorship could be a form of irremediable self-violation. One could strip oneself naked, pry into one's own deepest secrets, insult oneself.[40] One could skin oneself, "desoul" oneself, and in so doing prepare the empty vessel ready to receive God's grace.

THE OUTSIDE OF THE INSIDE

The result of the aggravation of one's shame at not being a simple, clear, integrated being was that one wanted desperately to be outside oneself, outside one's own body and consciousness. As Rudolf Otto explains, Roman *superstitio*, being "above" oneself (the Latin version of Greek ecstasy, being "outside" oneself), had, in the delicate balancing mechanisms of the Republic, been seen as a dangerous and antisocial excess of *religio*, an extreme and unnecessary anxiety or scrupulousness.[41] But while the Romans of the early and middle Republic had resisted it, it came as a relief in the period of the civil wars and the Empire. Increasingly the Romans were lured away from the "heroic middle" to forms of asceticism and excess that I have described at length elsewhere.[42]

What the psychologist Takeo Doi says of the modern Japanese could be applied to the Romans of the late Republic and early Empire: The unsatisfied will to submit (which is also the narcissistic desire to be loved and taken care of, to be at the center of the universe) leaves the modern Japanese in that extremely unsatisfying and endlessly demanding world of duty obligation *(giri)* in which one is forever inadequate. One of the effects of shame without indulgence on the Japa-

---

40. We have, in two thousand years, grown accustomed to this paradigm of "conscience," of "honor," of "honesty," and of the "soul," but it is new to modern Japan, as it was new to the Romans two millennia ago. And so, as Ruth Benedict says, reaction to shame in modern Japan leads less often now to the vendetta than to paralysis and self-destruction. "In the modern era law and order and the difficulties of managing a more interdependent economy have sent revenge underground or directed it against one's own breast" (*The Chrysanthemum and the Sword,* New York, 1946, p. 164).

41. Walter Otto, *"Religio* und *Superstitio,"* Archiv für Religionswissenschaft 12 (1909): 533–554.

42. See Barton, *Sorrows.*

nese, according to Doi, is workaholism and/or liability to fascination: an inability to be satisfied with oneself, and, simultaneously, an attempt to get outside oneself, a type of autofascination, the "obsessive-compulsive" behavior in which one loses oneself.[43] Being "fixated" was the mirror image and inversion of being turned to stone; its embrace offered some relief from the state of nonbeing.

OUR ROMAN INHERITANCE

Modern ideals of honor are ideals of salvation, a salvation necessitated not by the threat of death, paradoxically, but by "choosing life," with its endless devouring, its endless melting away, its endless undermining; they are an attempt to find an indissoluble—a true and fixed—core of being in the endless metamorphosis of powerlessness by embracing that flux as if it were a perfect stillness, by acting as if a runaway train or planet hurtling through space were firmly anchored in a sort of cosmic cement.[44] Our notions of honor are attempts to be in total control because we have no control, to be trusting like a child because we trust no one, to save ourselves and the world because we can save no one and nothing even by our deaths. It is an attempt to be as pure and complete as the man or woman who has chosen death without actually being dead—by willing not to will. The ideal of the stable, simple, autonomous, honorable human being of our culture bespeaks the long, tormented history it has sought to efface and overcome; it articulates a ferocious hope, and silences a terrible pain.

TRUE HONOR

In these modern times, character and honor depend upon a man's own life and conduct; not upon what another may say of him. So long as the individual maintains his character spotless he has in his possession a more powerful weapon than a pistol with which to defend his reputation—the weapon of truth. Armed with truth and backed up by common sense, he is well nigh invulnerable.

SAVANNAH SUNDAY MORNING NEWS, APRIL 24, 1894[45]

43. *The Anatomy of Dependence*, trans. John Bester, Tokyo, 1973, pp. 112–113. I discuss this phenomenon at length in *The Sorrows of the Ancient Romans*, especially chapter 3. Freud (in *Totem and Taboo*) and Doi (in *The Anatomy of Dependence*) both deal extensively with the phenomenon of fixations that can result from the frustrations of shame. Doi describes *toraware* (obsession, preoccupation, fascination) as characteristic of the compulsive type (the person who can't satisfy himself until—, who won't be satisfied unless), one of the more autonomous types of individuals in Japanese society "permeated through and through with *amae*" (pp. 109–110). Doi attributes the Japanese willingness to submerge themselves in work as an expression of this inability to be fulfilled (p. 111). He sees the whole society as afflicted with an insatiable hunger.

44. Compare the total freedom and total determinism of post-structuralism and "social constructionism."

45. Quoted in Edward Ayers, *Vengeance and Justice: Crime and Punishment in the Nineteenth-Century American South*, Oxford, 1984, p. 272.

A special value, in our Euro-American culture, is attached to the demonstration of independence from others and to freedom from controlling emotions and affects. To show emotions or dependence is considered weak.[46] To appear "flustered" in our society is considered evidence of debility, inferiority, low status, moral guilt, defeat, and other unenviable attributes.[47] Modern Westerners are afraid of feeling the emotions of shame and intolerant of expressing them; as a result, the fear of shame intensifies the experience of shame. Modern Westerners become ashamed of feeling ashamed and thus are swept into a spiral of shame, making shame so fearful that it is impossible to endure either independence or dependence.[48]

In modern fractionalized, "balkanized" American society, mutual trust, the presumption of the goodwill of others—so essential for the good contest, the enabling competition, and for comfortable joking and teasing relations—is so fragile as to seem a mirage. As a result, shame has become increasingly insupportable in America; we would rather endure isolation and insensibility than suffer shaming. Not so paradoxically, when we do shame another, it is crude and brutal. We stigmatize, we break each other's spirits. And so we are simultaneous rogues and puritans (or prurient puritans), free and/or slaves (or free conformists), with little in between. In our culture, even mild shaming produces rage, and severe shaming can produce, as James Gilligan has documented so horrifyingly, cataclysmic violence. Our terror of shame leads to the desire for apathy, autonomy, and shamelessness (if not also passivity, rage, and a desire for revenge). We are terrified by our strongest emotions because we have no traditions, no "way" strong enough to manage them, to channel, bridle, or inhibit them.

Paul Veyne observes, "We might say that they [the Romans] lived in the tension between envy and amity, while we, since the advent of Christianity, live, or believe that we live, in the tension between humility and pride."[49] Veyne's obser-

---

46. See Leo Rangell, "The Psychology of Poise," *International Journal of Psycho-Analysis* 35 (1954): 318. "Patients with anxiety," he remarks, "are often less concerned and tortured by the anxiety itself than by the question 'does it show?'"

47. See Erving Goffman, "Embarrassment and Social Organization," *American Journal of Sociology* 62 (1956): 266.

48. It is under Western influence, Doi believes, that the Japanese have begun to feel ashamed of expressing shame; their own society is increasingly less accepting of behavior that expresses embarrassment and inadequacy (*Anatomy of Dependence,* pp. 108–109). Doi spoke of his *shinkeishitsu* patients who suffered from excessive sensitivity to others, showed enormous restraint and difficulty in relationships, and found it hard to trust in the benevolence of others (p. 102). "This kind of patient is in a state of mind where he cannot *amaeru* even if he wants to" (p. 103). Doi explains the Japanese notion of *taijin kyofu,* fear of others: "fear of blushing, fear of meeting the other's gaze, anxiety concerning their own body odor" (p. 104). "This type of patient becomes strongly aware of feelings of restraint *(kigane)* and difficulty *(kodawari)* in the course of treatment" (pp. 104–105).

49. "Disons que ces gens-là vivaient dans la tension de l'envie et d'amitié, alors que, depuis le christianisme, nous vivons ou croyons vivre dans celle de l'humilité et de l'orgeuil" ("Le folklore à Rome et les droits de la conscience publique sur la conduite individuelle," *Latomus* 42 [1983]: 12).

vation of the difference in Roman tensions and modern ones is astute. I would add that the Roman tension between envy and friendliness—or, perhaps better, envy and generosity—was a constant and everyday tension that had the potential to regulate and bind a culture. The Christian (and our) much harsher (and so insufferable) tension was between two extreme emotions that, for the Romans of the Republic, desocialized and destabilized. Typically, the two poles, the two extremes were easily inverted, the most abject humility and the greatest arrogance being indistinguishable. I would only argue that the Romans of the period of the civil wars and the early Empire had already begun to feel this unbearable tension and the consequent desire to live in a state of perfect and imperturbable peace in which one was in serene, right relationship to god, king, and nature.

LA CHUTE

You cannot imagine the sense of personal dishonor I feel at living in the Rome of today.
CICERO, *AD FAMILIARES* 7.30.1–2 (JANUARY 44 TO MARCUS CURTIUS AT PATRAE)

Honor was the sum of the great algebraic system of counterforces on which Roman Republican society was maintained. If, in the Roman mind, there was a fall from grace, it was not, as in the Christian tradition, a fall away from an absolute obedience to God or king or conscience, but a fall from the high wire, a tumble from the delicate balancing systems that had sustained them and suppressed violence for so many centuries within their culture. Like the Wallendas after their great fall in Detroit, the Romans had trouble pinpointing the moment of the collapse. But the crumbling was not an instant's act. The overseas expansion, the growth of literacy, of skepticism and relativism, the influx of captured wealth, people, and ideas all served to disequilibrate the Romans and send them spinning out toward the rim of a universe nearer to our own. In this new world one needed to repair oneself as best one could, alone—with god, emperor, or Maltese lapdog. Yet there remained for the Romans, even after the adoption of radically new ideas of honor, a nostalgia for life on the edge, for the Roman way.

And, like the Romans of the early Empire, we are walking on the coals of a fire that is not yet out.

We think we have, we aspire to have, self-respect without shame, life without death, a soul without a will. I think we can learn from the ancient Romans both why we think this way and why it is not possible. We still feel for the man with the white shirt standing before the tanks in Tiananmen Square. We cannot, any more than the ancient Romans, live without honor—even if honor cannot set a leg, even if it cannot buy breakfast, even if it cannot turn back the tanks.

The Sentiment and the Symbol

Symbols and Their Discontents

This world is not this world.
Robert Jay Lifton

In dealing with the emotions, being a modern Euro-American, it was necessary for me to abandon the linear and dichotomous tendencies of modern thought and to locate and straddle the vague border between words and sensations, between the vast repository of inarticulate experience and the comparatively small—but still huge—distillate of symbols and symbolic actions.[1] Moreover, I was compelled to do this for my own culture simultaneously with that of the ancient Romans—a mental act requiring the elasticity of Plastic Man. On the following pages I struggle to articulate some of the knotty theoretical and philosophical issues raised by my approach to Roman emotional life.

The anthropologist Clifford Geertz believes that without symbolization, human action would be meaningless chaos. "Undirected by culture patterns—organized systems of significant symbols—man's behaviour would be virtually ungovernable, a mere chaos of pointless acts and exploding emotions, his experience virtually shapeless. Culture, the accumulated totality of such patterns, is not just an ornament of human existence but...an essential condition for it."[2] "The accumulated fund of significant symbols...are thus not mere expressions, instrumentalities, or correlates of our biological, psychological, and social existence; they are the prerequisites of it."[3] "Men without culture...would be unworkable mon-

---

1. Paul Ekman analyzes in excellent fashion the broad spectrum of "body language," from the bodily manipulations that the person may be unaware of or unable to control to the "emblem" that deliberately functions as a sign ("Biological and Cultural Contributions to Body and Facial Movements," in *The Anthropology of the Body*, ed. John Blacking, London, 1977, pp. 39–84).

2. "The Impact of the Concept of Culture on the Concept of Man," *The Interpretation of Cultures*, New York, 1973, p. 46. Cf. "The Growth of Culture and the Evolution of Mind," ibid., esp. pp. 77, 81; Blacking, "Towards an Anthropology of the Body," p. 15.

3. Geertz, "The Impact of the Concept of Culture," p. 49.

strosities with very few useful instincts, fewer recognizable sentiments, and no intellect: mental basket cases."[4] "Without the guiding patterns of human culture, man would, quite literally, not know how to feel."[5]

Humans without a symbolic system would be totally incarnated and totally incarcerated, like Jean-Marc-Gaspard Itard's wild child or like the young Helen Keller before she learned the use of signs. But like the wild boy of Aveyron or the child Helen Keller, they would not be without a body, emotions, and depth. It is only from a comfortable distance that dumb creatures look dumb.[6] When we get close enough, we realize, as R. D. Laing or Jacques Lacan might explain, how like the deaf and dumb, how like schizophrenics or autistic children we all are: every statement and every silence is both a poem and a subterfuge.

FEAR OF SHAME: THE PRICE OF ABSENTMINDEDNESS

No wonder how I lost my wits;
Oh! Caelia, Caelia, Caelia sh———!
JONATHAN SWIFT[7]

We humans pay a high cost for our speech. Any understanding of the necessity of symbolic systems for humans must be accompanied by the knowledge that our antidotes to chaos—like those of the Romans—have crippling side-effects. Our symbolic worlds are also forms of obscurity, like Brutus's rod of cornel wood, defying the animal realities of our own and other lives. In the words of Edward Hall, "Culture hides much more than it reveals, and strangely enough what it hides, it hides most effectively from its own participants."[8] Culture is a kind of collective lie or shared misunderstanding.[9] "The function of culture," Terrence Des Pres declares, "is to negate the primal facts of nothingness and death."[10] Naming Tiamat

---

4. Ibid., p. 49.

5. Ibid., p. 47.

6. "Children initiate social relationships within weeks or even within hours of birth, and these relationships are complex and nuanced long before even the most primitive sentences are produced during the second year of life" (Alfred Gell, *Key Debates in Anthropology,* ed. Tim Ingold, New York, 1996, p. 162).

7. "Cassinus and Peter" (1731), *The Writings of Jonathan Swift,* ed. Robert A. Greenberg and William B. Piper, New York, 1973, pp. 547–550.

8. *The Silent Language,* New York, 1959, p. 39. The inarticulate emotions of the ancient Romans (and perhaps of every culture) resemble the ancient Pythagorean's "music of the spheres," to which humans are so accustomed that they do not hear it. The Romans are like the inhabitants of Catadupa, who, Cicero tells us, are deaf, from long habituation, to the roaring cataracts of the Nile (*De republica* 6.18.19).

9. "The essence of human culture is the capacity to lie collectively" (comment by Chris Knight, *Key Debates,* p. 177). "The discourse of culture may have more to do with misunderstanding than with shared understanding" (comment by David Parkin, ibid., p. 185).

10. *The Survivor: An Anatomy of Life in the Death Camps,* Oxford, 1976.

binds and tames her only so long as we turn our eyes away. When we look back we find that she has been waiting, licking her whiskers, honing her basilisk glare. The more we cling to symbolic systems, the more we confide our future and our honor to particular codes and signs, the more complexity seems like chaos; the more we confide in the light of that obscurity, the darker, more abysmal, becomes the inarticulate. The more fiercely we resist being stripped of all meaning, all identity, the more we are subject to what Des Pres calls "the excremental attack," the violation that reduces us to dirt.

With the purpose of depriving him of his majesty, of dishonoring and "demystifying" the dead emperor, Seneca's *Apocolocyntosis* describes Claudius's death: "The last words heard from the emperor came after he had emitted a loud noise from that end of his which spoke with the most ease: 'Oh dear! Oh dear! I think I've shit on myself!'"[11] Like Claudius, we all die beshitting ourselves. However great we reckon the need (in Lear's words), every one of us is Caelia, every one Claudius. Our symbolic systems, our historical myths, exactly like those of the Romans, from the simplest to the most subtle, protect us like gauzy and diaphanous diapers.[12]

Anyone who has read Helen Keller's youthful autobiography can attest to the unendurable frustration and confusion experienced by a human being without access to her society's language. At the same time, many who have read her famous story find her attempts to articulate her inarticulate experience the most riveting parts of her book. And for Helen herself, the key and keenest moment, the defining moment of her young existence ("the most important day I remember in all my life"), occurred on that day when, at the pumphouse, her teacher Anne Sullivan first convinced her of the nature of the sign: "I stood still, my whole attention fixed upon the motion of her fingers. Suddenly I felt a misty consciousness as of something forgotten—a thrill of returning thought; and somehow the mystery of language was revealed to me. I knew then that 'w-a-t-e-r' meant that wonderful cool something that was flow-

---

11. *Ultima vox eius haec inter homines audita est, cum maiorem sonitum emisisset illa parte, qua facilius loquebatur: "vae me, puto, concacavi me"* (*Apocolocyntosis* 4).

12. Every expression is simultaneously a repression; it is the very use of symbolic systems that makes for the suppressed "unconscious," the beast that cannot speak. To the extent that one defines or limits human reality to human discourse, one raises a nightmare incubus of inarticulate biology. The two visions reinforce one another; the first elicits the second. When Roland Littlewood, for example, attempts to demonstrate just how completely our world is constructed and limited by language, he does so, ironically, by stripping away the veil of language which defines our "health" as human beings (not unlike Swift's lover looking into Caelia's chamberpot). The radical "social constructionist" speaks: "We are disease, not just in the sense that we share certain nucleotide sequences with bacteria, but also that we are descended from among the limited and selected survivors of innumerable epidemics in which survival was determined by antigenic complementarity with bacteria or other micro-organisms" (comment, *Key Debates*, p. 122).

ing over my hand. That living word awakened my soul, gave it light, hope, joy, set it free."[13]

The most vivid of all moments were, for the Romans, as for Helen Keller, spent on that fine line between a totally immediate, embodied universe and a symbolized one. It was at that moment, trembling on that dizzy wire, that the Romans, like little Helen, truly had their world and lived it too. The spirit, for the Romans, the precious *animus,* existed fully only on this edge: the *animus* was at once the very visceral, animal breath of life and the realization, the reification, the hypostatization of the living spirit in speech.[14]

THE DOUBLE AGENT, OR, A RADICAL RELATIVIST TALKS ABOUT THE REALLY REAL

Two times two makes four is no longer life, gentlemen, but is the beginning of death.
FEODOR DOSTOEVSKY[15]

Issues of honor are deeply involved in the very style and the perspectives I have adopted in this book about honor. The notion that all our ideas, including those about the body and the emotions, are products of the symbolic systems of our culture, rather than "facts," and that our notions reveal to us the ultimate contingency of all our ideas rather than an ultimate truth, is a very modest way of looking at the universe. It removes any privileged perspective and renders the human being incapable of self-satisfied existential security; one cannot mistake one's own notions for those of one's species. This Western philosophical position has confounded our sense of what a "human being" is or should be. In these ways, to assert that the experience of human beings is socially constructed is a very humble position. But looked at from another angle, the notion that all our ideas, including those about the body and the emotions, are products of the symbolic systems is an arrogant philosophical position.[16] The same philosophic position that subjects all human reality to human arbitration leaves very little room for inarticulate, secret, accidental, capricious, or unique experience.[17] When taken consistently, rather than straddling the line, it draws a deep dividing line between humans and

---

13. *The Story of My Life,* New York, [1902] 1961, p. 34. Afterward Helen gives herself over so completely to the language of contemporary literature, including its visual imagery, that she occludes not only her blindness and deafness, but also the particularity and extraordinary quality of her experience.

14. See especially chapters 5 and 6 (on confession and profession).

15. *Notes from Underground,* trans. Ralph E. Matlaw, New York, 1960, pp. 30–31.

16. Paul Richards abhors "the appalling arrogance (or so it seems to me) of the notion that, as Berger and Luckmann have it, 'people make themselves'" (comment, *Key Debates,* p. 124). See Peter L. Berger and Thomas Luckmann, *The Social Construction of Reality,* Garden City, New York, 1966.

17. And as Nancy Partner warns us, what humans can totally make, they can totally unmake ("No Sex, No Gender," *Speculum* 68 [1993]: 419–443).

other animals and removes humans from their bodies and from the evolutionary and biological processes that brought their species into being.[18] In many ways it is an extreme statement of mind over body, one more earnest attempt to free humans from a world in which they are determined beings, to assert the will and dignity of humans against a world in which they are enslaved by original sin or their genes.[19] When Karl Marx spoke about the "self-generation of the species," and when Michel Foucault proclaimed that "man" "would be erased like a face drawn in sand at the edge of the sea," they wanted to liberate their hearers from a notion of man as a defined and determined being.[20]

By claiming that the human is all culture and not nature, one is liberated and trapped at the same time.[21] One can compare the effects of evolutionary theory on modern European and American thought. The undermining of the Enlightenment

18. "Arguments based on fish, birds and other animals are strictly for them. They have no relevance for man....Man is man because he has no instincts, because everything he is and has become he has learned, acquired from his culture, from the man-made part of the environment, from other human beings" (M. F. Ashley Montagu, "The New Litany of 'Innate Depravity,' or Original Sin Revisited," in *The Human Revolution*, New York, 1965, pp. 8–10). Cf. Ashley Montagu, *Man and Aggression*, London, 1968, in which he takes on the ethologists of innate human aggressiveness: Robert Ardrey and, to a lesser degree, Konrad Lorenz.

19. The anthropologists, in accepting the ideology of a socially constructed world, were reacting, in part, against the evolutionary determinism, the "twitching automatons," of the sociobiologists and the kind of "demystification" of human narcissism or dignity implied in Richard Dawkins, *The Selfish Gene*, Oxford, 1978 (humans being just the gene's way of making another gene). (Both Montagu and Geertz, two of the key spokesmen for this position, tended automatically to use the word "lower" when they used the word "animals.") They were also acting against the genetic determinism that led to Nazism and the haughty excesses of European colonial rule. Likewise, many feminists seeking to undermine the biological determinism that justified male dominance have argued that men and women are not born but are socially created. See Barbara Gold, "But Ariadne Was Never There in the First Place: Finding the Female in Roman Poetry," *Feminist Theory and the Classics*, ed. Nancy Sorkin Rabinowitz and Amy Richlin, 1993, p. 79; Steven Seidman, *Contested Knowledge: Social Theory in the Postmodern Era*, Oxford, 1994, pp. 236–240, 245, 250; Amy Richlin, "Towards a History of Body History," in *Inventing Ancient Culture: Historicism, Periodization, and the Ancient World*, ed. Mark Golden and Peter Toohey, New York, 1997, esp. pp. 21–22.

20. See Marx, *The German Ideology*, in *The Marx-Engels Reader*, ed. Robert C. Tucker, New York, 1978, p. 164; Michel Foucault, *The Order of Things*, New York, 1970, p. 387.

21. Ashley Montagu promoted a kind of Pelagian perfectionism against the Pauline-Augustinian notion of man's inevitable state of sin. Montagu believed that "instinct" (like "original sin") was an excuse humans used to relieve themselves of the guilt they *should* feel at their sins—particularly the sin of violence. Man has made himself, therefore he has the obligation to make himself free from aggression. Consider the "Seville Statement on Violence," with its great number of intellectual and organizational signatories from India and the West: "We conclude that biology does not condemn humanity to war, and that humanity can be freed from the bondage of biological pessimism....The same species who invented war is capable of inventing peace. The responsibility lies with each of us" (reprinted in *Aggression and War: Their Biological and Social Bases*, ed. Jo Groebel and Robert A. Hinde, Cambridge, 1989, p. xv).

view of "human nature" set in motion a great maelstrom of possibilities, of hopes and desires (including the desire to be free of all restraining, imprisoning instincts), which, in turn, engendered feelings of impotence. To return to Geertz: "One of the most significant facts about us may finally be that we all begin with the natural equipment to live a thousand kinds of life but end having lived only one."[22]

As an instinct-free creature, one feels impotent precisely because one feels that everything is possible and that therefore one's limitations, one's inability to be and have everything, are a failing and a result of inadequacy. It is not very surprising that late-twentieth-century "cultural constructionism" is a radical relativism that nevertheless often leads also to a type of determinism, the individual and his or her experience of the world being shackled by his or her culture's existing chains of signification.[23]

In this impossible freedom, humans become their own ventriloquists' dummies: there can be no authentic voices that yet speak. The only really (really, really) authentic, genuine, and original voice is the silenced, obliterated, "erased" one. Sincerity, authenticity, originality are simultaneously both unrealizable and sorely lamented, their "loss"—or, better, "theft"—deeply resented. Paradoxically, in a philosophy designed to free humans from biological determinism and so enhance their dignity, there can be, finally, no will, no being, no honor.

22. "The Impact of the Concept of Culture," p. 45.

23. I can give here only a tiny sampling of similarly expressed ideas. Rom Harré declares: "We can do only what our linguistic resources and repertoire of social practices permit or enable us to do" ("An Outline of the Social Constructionist Viewpoint," *The Social Construction of Emotions*, ed. Rom Harré, Oxford, 1986, p. 4). Humans are limited to "the repertoire of language games available in a culture" (ibid., p. 13). For Edward Sapir, "Language . . . becomes elaborated into a self-contained conceptual system which previsages all possible experience. . . . [Meanings] are not so much discovered in experience as imposed upon it, because of the tyrannical hold that linguistic form has upon our orientation to the world" ("Conceptual Categories in Primitive Language," *Science* 74 [1931]: 578). "Human beings . . . are very much at the mercy of the particular language which has become the medium of expression for their society. . . . We see and hear and otherwise experience very largely as we do because the language habits of our community predispose certain choices of interpretation" ("The Status of Linguistics as a Science," in *Selected Writings of Edward Sapir in Language, Culture, and Personality*, ed. David G. Mandelbaum, Berkeley, 1949, p. 162). For Pierre Bourdieu, the "habitus," "an acquired system of generative schemes objectively adjusted to the particular conditions in which it is constituted, . . . engenders all the thoughts, all the perceptions, and all the actions consistent with those conditions and no others" (*Outline of a Theory of Practice*, trans. Richard Nice, Cambridge, 1979, p. 95; cf. pp. 81–83, 86). For Michelle Rosaldo, "What individuals can think and feel is overwhelmingly a product of socially organized modes of action and talk" ("Towards an Anthropology of Self and Feeling," in *Culture Theory: Essays on Mind, Self and Emotion*, ed. Richard A. Shweder and Robert A. LeVine, Cambridge, 1984, p. 147). This determinism often embraces the inarticulate as well as the articulate aspects of a culture. To give just a few examples: Claude Lévi-Strauss has a cultural unconscious that he would fill up with the "real" universal logical structures and categories of the mind; Noam Chomsky has the rules of grammar inscribed in neurophysiological mechanisms; Pierre Bourdieu has the *habitus*, the cultural "programming," created by the objective structures in which the young child matures.

Those who (for whatever reason) long for genuine and authentic voice are often deeply disappointed once a Roman woman—like the poetess Sulpicia—starts to speak, or once the slave—like the litter-bearer Iucundus—advertises his virtues in stone. They are already, it is so clear, implicated, compromised, shackled, like Livy's Brutus. But, I would suggest, to understand Roman emotional life one must abandon one's nostalgia for the original or the unmediated. Brutus's spirit, his *ingenium*, was expressed through, even while hidden in, his rod of cornel wood.

HISTORIAN OF THE ABSURD

His thoughts wandered again.
Almost unconsciously he traced with his fingers in the dust of the table: 2 + 2 = 5.
GEORGE ORWELL[24]

If I am anything philosophically, it is a radical skeptic. But there are two types of radical skeptics. There are the "Academic" skeptics who can take a stand and say, "Everything is open to doubt—*except* this statement." And then there are those slippery eels, the "Pyrrhonian" skeptics, who say, "Everything is open to doubt—*including* this statement." According to Richard Popkin, "Unlike Academic Scepticism, which came to a negative dogmatic conclusion from its doubts, Pyrrhonian scepticism…is a purge that eliminates everything including itself."[25] Cicero explains: "Whereas Socrates had said, 'I only know one thing, which is that I know nothing,' Arcesilaus [the founder of the New Academy, who gave it a "Pyrrhonian" turn] added: 'And I don't even know that'" (*Academica* 1.12.45). Being a skeptic, I am inevitably drawn to a highly relativistic view of the world (which is a kind of "Academic" or "dogmatic" skepticism)—and so to the relativism of "social constructionism."[26] But it is the *radical* or Pyrrhonian skeptic in me that dares me to assert both the capriciousness of my will and my fellow-feeling for other creatures against a vision of the world in which I, unlike the other creatures, am totally free (or totally determined). I *want* to be, I *choose* to be with the other contingent beings of the world, the nameless accidental things that creep and crawl, the spiders and sea urchins, the lunatics and the dead, the wild child of Aveyron and the blind and deaf Helen Keller. I want to share my world with the lion as well as with Androcles, with the nameless beast turning the mill as well as with the emperor Marcus Aurelius.

If I am willing to let go of the lever by which I can overturn the world, if I am willing to be catapulted from the center of the universe, perhaps I can make the weightlessness of my position into a methodology, a methodology of the untenable position. The alternative to complete control would be (as it was for Ovid or Petronius or Apuleius) endless metamorphosis, endless transformation, endless revision.

---

24. *Nineteen Eighty-Four: Text, Sources, Criticism*, Irving Howe, ed., New York, 1963, p. 128.
25. *The History of Scepticism from Erasmus to Spinoza*, Berkeley, 1979, p. xv.
26. On the dogmatism of ancient Academic skepticism, see Cicero, *Academica* 2.29.

BIBLIOGRAPHY OF MODERN WORKS
CITED IN THE TEXT

Abu-Lughod, Lila, *Veiled Sentiments: Honor and Poetry in a Bedouin Society*, Berkeley, 1986.

Adams, J. N., *The Latin Sexual Vocabulary*, Baltimore, 1982.

Adcock, Frank, "The Character of the Romans in Their History and Their Literature," *Essays on Roman Culture: The Todd Memorial Lectures*, ed. A.J. Dunston, Toronto, 1976, 95–117.

————, *Roman Political Ideas and Practice*, Ann Arbor, 1959.

Africa, Thomas, "The Mask of an Assassin: A Psychohistorical Study of M. Junius Brutus," *Journal of Interdisciplinary History* 8 (1978): 599–626.

Alföldi, Andreas, *Der Vater des Vaterlandes im römishen Denken*, Darmstadt, 1971.

Allen, Frederic D., "On 'os columnatum' (Plautus *M.G.* 211) and Ancient Instruments of Confinement," *Harvard Studies in Classical Philology* 7 (1896): 37–64.

Allman, F., *The Stone Age Present*, New York, 1994.

André, Jean-Marie, *L'otium dans la vie morale et intellectuelle Romaine*, Paris, 1966.

Asch, Solomon, "Studies of Independence and Conformity: A Minority of One against a Unanimous Majority," *Psychological Monographs* 70 (1956): 1–70.

Astin, A. E., *Cato the Censor*, Oxford, 1978.

————, *Scipio Aemilianus*, Oxford, 1967.

Ausubel, David, "The Relationship between Shame and Guilt in the Socializing Process," *Psychological Review* 62 (1955): 378–390.

Ayers, Edward, *Vengeance and Justice: Crime and Punishment in the Nineteenth-Century American South*, Oxford, 1984.

Babbitt, Irving, "Lights and Shades of Spanish Character," in *Spanish Character and Other Essays*, Boston, 1940, 1–20.

Babcock, Barbara, "Liberty's a Whore: Inversions, Marginalia and Picaresque Narrative," in *The Reversible World*, ed. Barbara Babcock, Ithaca, 1978, 95–116.

Badian, Ernst, *Foreign Clientelae 264–70 B.C.*, Oxford, 1958.

Bakan, David, *Disease, Pain and Sacrifice: Toward a Psychology of Suffering*, Chicago, 1968.

Bakhtin, Mikhail, *The Dialogic Imagination*, Austin, [1975] 1981.

————, *Rabelais and His World*, trans. Helene Iswolsky, Cambridge, Mass., [1929] 1968.

Balsdon, J. P. V. D., "*Auctoritas, Dignitas, Otium*," *Classical Quarterly* n.s. 10 (1960): 43–50.

Baratte, François, *Le trésor d'orfèvrerie romaine de Boscoreale*, Paris, 1986.

Barrow, R. H., *Slavery in the Roman Empire*, New York, 1928.

Bartch, Shadi, *Actors in the Audience: Theatricality and Doublespeak from Nero to Hadrian*, Cambridge, Mass., 1994.

Barthes, Roland, *Empire of Signs*, trans. Richard Howard, New York, [1970] 1982.

Barton, Carlin, "Savage Miracles: The Redemption of Lost Honor in Roman Society and the Sacrament of the Gladiator and the Martyr," *Representations* 45 (winter 1994): 41–71.

———, *The Sorrows of the Ancient Romans*, Princeton, 1993.

———, "*Vis Mortua:* Irreconcilable Patterns of Thought in the Literature of the Neronian Period," Ph.D. diss., Berkeley, 1985.

Bataille, Georges, *Erotism*, trans. Mary Dalwood, San Francisco, [1957] 1986.

Bateson, Gregory, *Naven*, Stanford, 1958.

———, *Steps to an Ecology of Mind*, New York, 1972.

Bateson, Gregory, and Margaret Mead, *Balinese Character: A Photographic Analysis*, New York, 1942.

Bauman, Richard, "Performance and Honor in Thirteenth-Century Iceland," *Journal of American Folklore* 99 (1986): 131–150.

Baumgartner, M. P., "Social Control from Below," in *Towards a General Theory of Social Control*, ed. Donald Black, vol. 1, Orlando, 1984, 303–345.

Beard, Mary, "Ancient Literacy and the Function of the Written Word in Roman Religion," in *Literacy in the Roman World, Journal of Roman Archaeology*, Supplementary Series no. 3, ed. J. H. Humphrey, Ann Arbor, 1991, 35–58.

———, "The Sexual Status of Vestal Vergins," *Journal of Roman Studies* 70 (1980): 12–27.

———, "Writing and Ritual: A Study of Diversity and Expansion in the Arval Acta," *Papers of the British School at Rome* 53 (1985): 114–166.

Benedict, Ruth, *The Chrysanthemum and the Sword*, New York, 1946.

———, *Patterns of Culture*, New York, 1934.

Bennassar, Bartolomé, *The Spanish Character: Attitudes and Mentalities from the Sixteenth to the Nineteenth Century*, Berkeley, 1979.

Benveniste, Émile, *Le vocabulaire des institutions indo-europeénnes*, 2 vols., Paris, 1969.

Béranger, Jean, *Recherches sur l'aspect idéologique du Principat*, Basel, 1953.

Berger, Adolf, *Encyclopedic Dictionary of Roman Law*, Philadelphia, 1953.

Berger, Peter, "On the Obsolescence of the Concept of Honor," in *The Homeless Mind*, New York, 1973, 83–96.

Berger, Peter, and Thomas Luckmann, *The Social Construction of Reality*, Garden City, N.Y., 1966.

Bergmann, Bettina, "The Pregnant Moment: Tragic Wives in the Roman Interior," in *Sexuality in Ancient Art: Near East, Egypt, Greece and Italy*, ed. Natalie Boymel Kampen et al., Cambridge, 1995, 199–218.

———, "The Roman House a Memory Theatre: The House of the Tragic Muse," *The Art Bulletin* 76 (1994): 225–256.

Beseler, Gerhard von, "Bindung und Lösung," *Zeitschrift der Savigny-Stiftung für Rechtsgeschichte: Romanistische Abteilung* 49 (1929): 404–460.

———, "*Fides*," *Atti del congresso internazionale di diritto romano* 1 (1934): 135–167.

Bettelheim, Bruno, "Individual and Mass Behavior in Extreme Situations," *Journal of Abnormal and Social Psychology* 38 (1943): 417–452.

Bieber, Margarete, *The History of the Greek and Roman Theatre*, Princeton, 1961.

Blacking, John, "Towards an Anthropology of the Body," in *The Anthropology of the Body*, ed. John Blacking, London, 1977, 1–28.

Black-Michaud, Jacob, *Cohesive Force: Feud in the Mediterranean and the Middle East*, Oxford, 1975.

Blok, Anton, "Rams and Billy-Goats: A Key to the Mediterranean Code of Honour," *Man* n.s. 16 (1981): 427–440.

Blümlein, Carl, "Zum Wortspiele *onus-honor*," *Archiv für lateinische Lexikographie*, vol. 8, Leipzig, 1893.

Bolchazy, L., *Hospitality in Early Rome*, Chicago, 1977.

Bonfante, Larisa, "Nudity as a Costume in Classical Art," *American Journal of Archaeology* 93 (1989): 543–570.

Bonner, Stanley F., *Education in Ancient Rome*, Berkeley, 1977.

Bonte, Pierre, " 'To Increase Cows, God Created the King': The Function of Cattle in Intralacustrine Societies," in *Herders, Warriors and Traders*, ed. P. Bonte and John G. Galaty, Boulder, Colorado, 1991, 62–86.

Bourdieu, Pierre, "The Historical Genesis of the Pure Aesthetic," in *Analytic Aesthetics*, ed. R. Shusterman, Oxford, 1989.

———, *Outline of a Theory of Practice*, trans. Richard Nice, Cambridge, 1979.

———, "The Sense of Honor," in *Algeria 1960*, trans. Richard Nice, Cambridge, 1979, 95–132.

———, "The Sentiment of Honour in Kabyle Society," in *Honour and Shame*, ed. J. G. Peristiany, Chicago, [1966] 1974, 193–241.

Bowman, Alan K., "Literacy in the Roman Empire: Mass and Mode," in *Literacy in the Roman World, Journal of Roman Archaeology*, Supplementary Series no. 3, ed. J. H. Humphrey, Ann Arbor, 1991, 119–132.

Boyancé, Pierre, *Études sur la religion romaine*, Rome, 1972.

———, "Fides et le serment," *Hommages à Albert Grenier, Collection Latomus* 58, vol. 1, Brussels, 1962, 329–341.

Boyarin, Daniel, *Unheroic Conduct: The Rise of Heterosexuality and the Invention of the Jewish Man*, Berkeley, 1997.

Boyle, Anthony J., "Introduction: The Roman Song," in *Roman Epic*, ed. A. J. Boyle, London, 1993, 1–18.

Bradley, F. H., "On Pleasure, Pain, Desire and Volition," *Mind* 49 (1988): 1–36.

Braithwaite, John, *Crime, Shame, and Reintegration*, Cambridge, 1989.

Brelich, Angelo, *Die geheime Schutzgottheit von Rom*, Zürich, 1949.

Bremmer, J. N., and N. M. Horsfall, eds., *Roman Myth and Mythography*, London, 1987.

Bresson, Robert, director, *Un condamné à mort s'est échappé*, 1956.

Briggs, Jean, "Living Dangerously: The Contradictory Foundations of Value in Canadian Inuit Society," in *Politics and History in Band Societies*, ed. Eleanor Leacock and Richard Lee, Cambridge, 1982, 109–131.

———, *Never in Anger*, Cambridge, Mass., 1970.

———, "Out of the Garden of Eden: Morality Play in the Life of a Canadian Inuit Three-Year-Old," unpublished paper.

Brilliant, Richard, *Gesture and Rank in Roman Art*, New Haven, 1963.

Briquel, Dominique, "Formes de mise à mort dans la Rome primitive: Quelques remarques sur une approche comparative du problème," in *Du châtiment dans la Cité: Supplices corporels et peine de mort dans le monde antique, collection de l'École Française de Rome* 79 (Rome, 1984): 225–240.

Brisson, Jean-Paul, "Les mutations de la Seconde Guerre Punique," *Problèmes de la Guerre à Rome,* Paris, 1969, 33–59.

Brunt, P. A., "Reflections on British and Roman Imperialism," *Comparative Studies in Society and History* 7 (1965): 267–288.

Büchner, Karl, "Altrömische und Horazische *virtus,*" in *Römische Wertbegriffe,* ed. Hans Oppermann, Darmstadt, 1967, 376–401.

Burck, Erich, "Drei Grundwerte der römischen Lebensordnung *(labor, moderatio, pietas),*" *Gymnasium* 58 (1951): 161–183.

Burgess, Thomas, *The Physiology or Mechanism of Blushing,* London, 1828.

Burkert, Walter, *The Creation of the Sacred,* Cambridge, Mass., 1996.

Butterfield, Fox, *All God's Children: The Bosket Family and the American Tradition of Violence,* New York, 1995.

Bux, Ernst, "*Clementia Romana:* Ihr Wesen und ihre Bedeutung für die Politik des römischen Reiches," *Würzburger Jahrbücher für die Altertumswissenschaft* 3 (1948): 201–230.

Cantarella, Eva, "Adulterio, omicidio leggitimo e causa d'onore in diritto Romano," *Studi in onore di Gaetano Scherillo,* Milan, 1972, 243–274.

Castelfranchi, Cristiano, and Isabella Poggi, "Blushing as Discourse: Was Darwin Wrong?" in *Shyness and Embarrassment: Perspectives from Social Psychology,* ed. W. Ray Crozier, Cambridge, 1990, 230–251.

Cattaneo, Peter, director, *The Full Monty,* 1997.

Chodoff, Paul, "Effects of Extreme Coercive and Oppressive Forces: Brainwashing and Concentration Camps," in *American Handbook of Psychiatry,* ed. Silvano Arieti, vol. 3, New York, 1966, 384–405.

Cioran, E. M., *Drawn and Quartered,* trans. Richard Howard, New York, [1971] 1983.

Clarke, John, "Hypersexual Black Men in Augustan Baths: Ideal Somatypes and Apotropaic Magic," in *Sexuality in Ancient Art,* ed. Natalie Kampen et al., Cambridge, 1996, 184–198.

———, "Look Who's Laughing at Sex: Men and Women Viewers in the Apodyterium of the Surburban Baths at Pompeii," in *The Roman Gaze: Vision, Power and the Body in Roman Society,* ed. David Fredrick, Baltimore, 2001.

Clendinnen, Inga, *Aztecs: An Interpretation,* Cambridge, 1991.

———, "The Cost of Courage in Aztec Society," *Past and Present* 107 (1985): 44–89.

Cole, Thomas, "In Response to Nevio Zorzetti, 'Poetry and the Ancient City: The Case of Rome,'" *Classical Journal* 86 (1991): 377–382.

Coleman, K., "Fatal Charades: Roman Executions Staged as Mythological Enactments," *Journal of Roman Studies* 80 (1990): 44–73.

Commager, Steele, *The Odes of Horace,* Bloomington, Indiana, 1962.

Confucius, *Analects,* trans. D. C. Lau, Harmondsworth, 1979.

Conrad, Joseph, *Heart of Darkness,* New York, [1899] 1963.

Corbeill, Anthony, *Controlling Laughter: Political Humor in the Late Republic,* Princeton, 1996.

Corbier, Mireille, "L'écriture en quête de lecteurs," in *Literacy in the Roman World, Journal of Roman Archaeology,* Supplementary Series no. 3, ed. J. H. Humphrey, Ann Arbor, 1991, 99–118.

Cornell, Tim, "The Tyranny of the Evidence: A Discussion of Possible Uses of Literacy in Etruria and Latium in the Achaic Age," in *Literacy in the Roman World, Journal of Roman Archaeology,* Supplementary Series no. 3, ed. J. H. Humphrey, Ann Arbor, 1991, 7–34.

Crook, J. A., *Law and Life of Rome, 90 B.C.–A.D. 212*, Ithaca, 1967.
———, "*Patria Potestas*," *Classical Quarterly* n.s. 17 (1967): 113–122.
———, "*Sponsione Provocare:* Its Place in Roman Litigation," *Journal of Roman Studies* 66 (1976): 132–138.
Csikszentmihalyi, Mihaly, and Isabella Selega Csikszentmihalyi, eds., *Optimal Experience: Psychological Studies of Flow in Consciousness*, Cambridge, 1988.
Curtiz, Michael, director, *Angels with Dirty Faces*, 1938.
Darwin, Charles, *The Expression of the Emotions in Man and Animals*, Chicago, [1872] 1965.
Daube, David, *Roman Law: Linguistic, Social and Philosophical Aspects*, Edinburgh, 1969.
———, "The Self-Understood in Legal History," *Juridical Review*, n.s. 18 (1973): 126–134.
———, " 'Suffrage' and 'Precedent,' 'Mercy' and 'Grace,' " *Tijdschrift voor Rechtsgechiedenis* 47 (1979): 235–246.
David, Jean-Michel, "La faute et l'abandon: Théories et pratiques judiciaires à Rome à la fin de la République" in *L'aveu: Antiquité et Moyen Age*, Rome, 1986, 69-87.
Demos, John, "Shame and Guilt in Early New England," in *Emotion and Social Change*, ed. Carol Z. Stearns and Peter Stearns, New York, 1988, 69–85.
Des Pres, Terrence, *The Survivor: An Anatomy of Life in the Death Camps*, Oxford, 1976.
Dickinson, Emily, *The Complete Poems*, Boston, 1890.
Dickison, Sheila K., "Claudius: *Saturnalicius Princeps*," *Latomus* 36 (1977): 634–647.
Doi, Takeo, *The Anatomy of Dependence*, trans. John Bester, Tokyo, 1973 (= *Amae no kozo*, 1971).
Dostoevsky, Feodor, *Notes from Underground*, trans. Richard E. Matlow, New York, 1960.
Douglas, Mary, *Natural Symbols*, New York, 1970.
Douglass, Frederick, *Narrative of the Life of Frederick Douglass, An American Slave, Written by Himself*, Boston, 1845.
Drexler, Hans, "*Gloria*," *Helikon* 2 (1962): 4–36.
———, "*Honos*," in *Römische Wertbegriffe*, ed. Hans Oppermann, Darmstadt, 1967, 446–467.
duBois, Page, *Torture and Truth*, New York, 1991.
Ducos, Michèle, "La crainte de l'infamie et l'obéissance a la loi," *Revue des Études Latines* 57 (1979): 146–165.
Dumézil, Georges, *Horace et les Curiaces*, Paris, [1942] 1978.
———, *Idées romaines*, Paris, 1969.
———, "*Maiestas et Gravitas:* De quelques différences entre les romains et les austronésiens," *Revue de philologie* 3e s. 25 (1951): 7–21.
———, *Mitra-Varuna*, trans. Derek Coltman, New York, [1948] 1980.
———, *La religion romaine archaïque*, Paris, 1974.
Dumont, Louis, *Homo Hierarchicus: The Caste System and Its Implications*, Chicago, [1966] 1980.
———, "A Modified View of Our Origins: The Christian Beginnings of Modern Individualism," in *The Category of the Person*, ed. Michael Carrithers, Steven Collins, and Steven Lukes, Cambridge, 1985, 93–122.
Dunbabin, Katherine M. D., "*Baiarum grata voluptas:* Pleasures and Dangers of the Baths," *Papers of the British School at Rome* 57 (1989): 6–46.
Dupont, Florence, "L'aveu dans la tragédie romaine," in *L'aveu: Antiquité et Moyen Age*, Rome, 1986, 119–132.
———, *Daily Life in Ancient Rome*, Oxford, 1993 [= *La vie quotidienne du citoyen romain sous la République*, 1989].

Durkheim, Émile, "The Determination of Moral Facts," *Sociology and Philosophy*, trans. D. F. Pocock, Glencoe, Ill., 1953.

Earl, Donald, *The Moral and Political Tradition of Rome*, London, 1967.

———, "Political Terminology in Plautus," *Historia* 9 (1960): 235–243.

———, *The Political Thought of Sallust*, Cambridge, 1961.

Edelstein, Ludwig, "Horace, *Odes* II.7.9–10," *American Journal of Philology* 62 (1941): 441–451.

Edwards, Catherine, *The Politics of Immorality in Ancient Rome*, Cambridge, 1993.

Eibl-Eibesfeldt, Irenäus, *Ethology: The Biology of Behavior*, New York, 1970.

———, *Love and Hate*, New York, 1971.

———, "The Myth of the Aggression-Free Hunter and Gatherer Society," in *Primate Aggression, Territoriality, and Xenophobia*, ed. Ralph B. Holloway, New York, 1974, 452–454.

———, "Ritual and Ritualization From a Biological Perspective," in *Human Ethology: Claims and Limits of a New Discipline*, ed. M. von Cranach, K. Foppa, W. Lepenies, and D. Ploog, Cambridge, 1979, 3–55.

Eisenhut, Werner, *Virtus Romana: Ihre Stellung im römischen Wertsystem*, Munich, 1973.

Ekman, Paul, "Biological and Cultural Contributions to Body and Facial Movement," in *The Anthropology of the Body*, ed. John Blacking, London, 1977, 39–84.

Eliot, T. S., *The Complete Poems and Plays*, 1952.

Elliott, Robert C., *The Literary Persona*, Chicago, 1982.

Ellison, Ralph, *Invisible Man*, New York, 1947.

Erikson, Erik H., "Childhood and Tradition in Two American Indian Tribes," *The Psychoanalytic Study of the Child* 1 (1945): 315–350.

———, *Identity, Youth, and Crisis*, New York, 1968.

Ernout, A., and A. Meillet, *Dictionnaire étymologique de la langue latine*, Paris, [1932] 1985.

Eyben, Emiel, "Fathers and Sons," in *Marriage, Divorce, and Children in Ancient Rome*, ed. Beryl Rawson, Oxford, 1991, 114–143.

———, *Restless Youth in Ancient Rome*, trans. Patrick Daly, London, 1993.

Falk, Pasi, "Corporeality and its Fates in History," *Acta Sociologica* 28 (1985): 115–136.

Farès, Bishr, *L'honneur chez les arabes avant l'Islam*, Paris, 1932.

Fears, J. Rufus, "The Cult of Virtues and Roman Imperial Ideology," *Aufstieg und Niedergang der römischen Welt*, vol. 2.17.2, Berlin, 1981, 827–948.

———, "The Theology of Victory at Rome: Approaches and Problems," *Aufstieg und Niedergang der römischen Welt*, vol. 2.17.2, Berlin, 1981, 736–826.

Feeney, D. C., "*Si licet et fas est:* Ovid's *Fasti* and the Problem of Free Speech under the Principate," in *Roman Poetry and Propaganda in the Age of Augustus*, ed. Anton Powell, London, 1992, 1–25.

Feldman, Sandor, "Blushing, Fear of Blushing, and Shame," *Journal of the American Psychoanalytic Association* 10 (1962): 368–385.

Ferenczi, Sandor, "Embarrassed Hands," in *Further Contributions to the Theory and Technique of Psychoanalysis*, New York, [1926] 1953.

Ferguson, John, *Moral Values in the Ancient World*, London 1958.

Fingarette, Herbert, *Confucius: The Secular as Sacred*, New York, 1972.

Finley, Moses I., "Debt-Bondage and the Problem of Slavery," *Economy and Society in Ancient Greece*, Middlesex, 1981, 150–166.

Fisher, Seymour, *Body Consciousness*, New York, 1974.

Fitzgerald, William, "Power and Impotence in Horace's *Epodes*," *Ramus* 17 (1988): 176–191.

Foucault, Michel, *Discipline and Punish*, trans. Alan Sheridan, New York, 1977.

————, *The History of Sexuality*, trans. Robert Hurley, New York, 1978.

————, *The Order of Things*, trans. Robert Hurley, New York, 1970.

————, "Technologies of the Self," in *Technologies of the Self*, ed. Luther H. Martin, Huck Gutman, and Patrick H. Hutton, Amherst, 1988, 17–49.

Fowler, W. Warde, "Passing under the Yoke," *Classical Review* 27 (1913): 48–51.

Fraenkel, Eduard, "Two Poems of Catullus," *Journal of Roman Studies* 51 (1961): 46–53.

————, "Zur Geschichte des Wortes *Fides*," *Rheinisches Museum für Philologie* 71 (1916): 187–199.

Franklin, James L,. Jr., "Literacy and the Parietal Inscriptions of Pompeii," in *Literacy in the Roman World*, *Journal of Roman Archaeology*, Supplementary Series no. 3, ed. J. H. Humphrey, Ann Arbor, 1991, 77–98.

Fraschetti, Augusto, "Roman Youth," in *A History of Young People in the West*, ed. Giovanni Levi and Jean-Claude Schmitt, trans. Camille Naish, Cambridge, Mass., 1997, 51–82.

Frazer, James, *Balder the Beautiful*, vol. 2, New York, 1935.

Freud, Sigmund, *Beyond the Pleasure Principle*, trans. James Strachey, New York, [1920] 1961.

————, "Taboo and the Ambivalence of Emotions," in *Totem and Taboo*, trans. A. A. Brill, 1918, 26–97.

————, *Wit and Its Relation to the Unconscious*, in *The Basic Writings of Sigmund Freud*, ed. and trans. A. A. Brill, New York, [1905] 1938.

Freyburger, G., *Fides*, Paris, 1986.

————, "Supplication grecque et supplication romaine," *Latomus* 47 (1988): 501–528.

Friedl, Ernestine, *Vasilika: A Village in Modern Greece*, New York, 1962.

Friedrich, Paul, "Sanity and the Myth of Honor," *Ethos* 5 (1977): 281–305.

Fuchs, H., "Der Friede als Gefahr," *Harvard Studies in Classical Philology* 63 (1958): 363–385.

Gagé, Jean, "La théologie de la Victoire impériale," *Revue historique* 171 (1933): 1–43.

Garfinkel, Harold, "Conditions of Successful Degradation Ceremonies," *American Journal of Sociology* 61 (1956): 420–424.

Garnsey, Peter, *Social Status and Legal Privilege in the Roman Empire*, Oxford, 1970.

————, "Why Penalties Became Harsher: The Roman Case, Late Republic to Fourth Century Empire," *Natural Law Forum* 13 (1968): 141–162.

Geertz, Clifford, "From the Native's Point of View: On the Nature of Anthropological Understanding," in *Culture Theory: Essays on Mind, Self, and Emotion*, ed. Richard A. Schweder and Robert A. LeVine, Cambridge, 1984, 123–136.

————, "The Impact of the Concept of Culture on the Concept of Man," *The Interpretation of Cultures*, New York, 1973, 33–54.

Gellner, Ernest, *Plough, Sword, and Book: The Structure of Human History*, Chicago, 1988.

Gelzer, Matthias, *Caesar: Politician and Statesman*, trans. Peter Needham, Oxford, 1968.

————, "Römische Politik bei Fabius Pictor," *Hermes* 68 (1933): 129–166.

Gill, Christopher, "Personhood and Personality. The Four-*Personae* Theory of Cicero, *De Officiis* I," *Oxford Studies in Ancient Philosophy* 6 (1988): 169–199.

Gilligan, James, "Beyond Morality: Psychoanalytic Reflections on Shame, Guilt, and Love," in *Moral Development and Behavior*, ed. Thomas Likona, New York, 1976, 144–158.

————, *Violence: Reflections on a National Epidemic*, New York, 1997.

Gilmore, David, *Manhood in the Making: Cultural Concepts of Masculinity*, New Haven, Conn., 1990.

Gleason, Maud W., *Making Men: Sophists and Self-Presentation in Ancient Rome*, Princeton, 1994.

————, "Truth Contests and Talking Corpses," in *Construcions of the Classical Body*, ed. James I. Porter, Ann Arbor, 1999, 287–313.

Gluckman, Max, "Gossip and Scandal," *Current Anthropology* 4 (1963): 307–315.

Goetz, G., *Thesaurus glossarum emendatarum* (*Corpus Glossariorum Latinorum*, vol. 6), Amsterdam, 1965.

Goffman, Erving, "Embarrassment and Social Organization," *American Journal of Sociology* 62 (1956): 264–271.

————, *Interaction Ritual: Essays on Face-to-Face Behavior*, New York, 1967.

————, *Stigma: Notes on the Management of Spoiled Identity*, New York, 1963.

Gold, Barbara, "But Ariadne Was Never There in the First Place: Finding the Female in Roman Poetry," in *Feminist Theory and the Classics*, ed. Nancy Sorkin Rabinowitz and Amy Richlin, 1993, 75–101.

Goode, William J., *The Celebration of Heroes: Prestige as a Control System*, Berkeley, 1978.

Goody, Jack, *The Domestication of the Savage Mind*, Cambridge, 1977.

Goody, Jack, and Ian Watt, "The Consequences of Literacy," *Comparative Studies in Society and History* 5 (1963): 303–345.

Gordon, R., "The Real and the Imaginary Production and Religion in the Graeco-Roman World," *Art History* 2 (1979): 5–34.

Gore, Robert, *The Legend of Cato Uticensis from the First c. B.C. to the Fifth c. A.D.*, Brussels, 1987.

Gorn, Elliott J., " 'Gouge and Bite, Pull Hair and Scratch': The Social Significance of Fighting in the Southern Backcountry," *American Historical Review* 90 (1985): 18–43.

Gouldner, Alvin, *Enter Plato*, New York, 1965.

Graf, Fritz, "Gestures and Conventions: The Gestures of Roman Actors and Orators," in *A Cultural History of Gesture*, ed. Jan Bremmer and Herman Roodenburg, Ithaca, 1991, 36–58.

Greenberg, Kenneth, "The Nose, the Lie, and the Duel in the Antebellum South," *American Historical Review* 95 (1990): 57–74.

Greenidge, A. H. J., *Infamia: Its Place in Roman Public and Private Law*, Oxford [1894] 1977.

Griffin, Jasper, "Augustus and the Poets: *Caesar qui Cogere Posset*," in *Caesar Augustus: Seven Aspects*, ed. Fergus Millar and Erich Segal, Oxford, 1984, 189–218.

————, "Propertius and Antony," *Journal of Roman Studies* 67 (1977): 17–21.

Griffin, Miriam, "Cynicism and the Romans: Attraction and Repulsion," in *The Cynics*, ed. R. Bracht-Branham and Marie-Odile Goulet-Cazé, Berkeley, 1996, 190–204.

Griffiths, J. Gwyn, *Apuleius of Madauros: The Isis Book* (*Metamorphoses Book 11*), Leiden, 1975.

Grisé, Roland, *Le suicide dans la Rome antique*, Paris, 1982.

Groebel, Jo, and Robert A. Hinde, *Aggression and War: Their Biological and Social Bases*, Cambridge, 1989.

Gruen, Erich, "The Exercise of Power in the Roman Republic," in *City-States in Classical Antiquity and Medieval Italy: Athens and Rome, Florence and Venice*, ed. Anthony Molhe, Kurt Raaflaub, and Julia Emlin, Stuttgart, 1991, 251–267.

————, *The Hellenistic World and the Coming of Rome*, Berkeley, 1984.

————, *The Last Generation of the Roman Republic*, Berkeley, 1974.

————, *Studies in Greek Culture and Roman Policy*, Leiden, 1990.

————, "The Theatre and National Identity in Republican Rome," in *Culture and National Identity in Republican Rome*, Ithaca, 1992, 183–223.

Gusdorf, Georges, *L'expérience humaine du sacrifice*, Paris, 1948.

Gustafson, Mark, " '*Inscripta in fronte*': Penal Tattooing in Late Antiquity," *Classical Antiquity* 16 (1997): 79–105.

Guyer, J., "The Multiplication of Labor: Gender and Agricultural Change in Modern Africa," *Current Anthropology* 29 (1988): 247–272.

Habinek, Thomas, *The Politics of Latin Literature,* Princeton, 1998.

———, "Towards a History of Friendly Advice: The Politics of Candor in Cicero's *De Amicitia*," in *The Poetics of Therapy,* ed. R. C. Nussbaum, *Apeiron* 23 (1990): 165–185.

Hadas, Moses, "*Gravitas quousque,*" *Classical Journal* 31 (1935): 17–24.

———, "Livy as Scripture," *American Journal of Philology* 61 (1940): 445–457.

Hall, Edward, *The Silent Language,* New York, 1959.

Hallett, Judith, "Perusinae Glandes and the Changing Image of Augustus," *American Journal of Ancient History* 2 (1977): 151–171.

———, "Women as 'Same' and 'Other' in Classical Roman Elite," *Helios* 16 (1989): 59–78.

Hampl, Franz, "Römische Politik in republikanischer Zeit und das Problem des Sittenverfalls," in *Das Staatsdenken der Römer,* ed. Richard Klein, Darmstadt, 1966, 144–177.

———, "'Stoische Staatsethik' und frühes Rom," in *Das Staatsdenken der Römer,* ed. Richard Klein, Darmstadt, 1966, 116–142.

Harré, Rom, "An Outline of the Social Constructionist Viewpoint," in *The Social Construction of the Emotions,* ed. Rom Harré, Oxford, 1986, 2–14.

Harris, William V., *Ancient Literacy,* Cambridge, Mass., 1989.

———, "The Roman Father's Power of Life and Death," *Studies in Roman Law in Memory of A. Arthur Schiller,* ed. Roger S. Bagnall and William V. Harris, Leiden, 1986, 81–95.

———, *War and Imperialism in Republican Rome 327–70 B.C.,* Oxford, 1979.

Harrison, E., "Horace's Tribute to His Father," *Classical Philology* 60 (1965).

Harrison, Jane Ellen, *Themis: A Study of the Social Origins of Greek Religion,* Cleveland, [1912] 1962.

Hatch, Elvin, "Theories of Social Honor," *American Anthropologist* 91 (1989): 341–353.

Hawthorne, Nathaniel, *The Scarlet Letter,* Boston, 1850.

Heesterman, Jan C., *The Broken World of Sacrifice: An Essay on Ancient Indian Ritual,* Chicago, 1993.

Heinze, Richard, "*Fides,*" *Hermes* 64 (1929): 140–166.

———, "*Supplicium,*" in *Vom Geist des Römertums: Ausgewählte Aufsätze,* ed. Erick Burck, Darmstadt, 1960, 28–41.

Hellegouarc'h, J., *Le vocabulaire latin des relations et des partis politiques sous la République,* Paris, 1963.

Hemingway, Ernest, *Death in the Afternoon,* New York, 1932.

Hendrickson, G. L., "Verbal Injury, Magis or Erotic Comus? (*Occentare ostium* and Its Greek Counterpart)," *Classical Philology* 20 (1925): 289–308.

Henry, Jules, *Jungle People,* New York, 1964.

Herington, C. J., "Senecan Tragedy," *Arion* 5 (1966): 422–471.

Hershkowitz, Debra, "*Dissimulare etiam sperasti?* The Poetics of Dissimulation," unpublished manuscript.

———, "Sexuality and Madness in Statius," *Materiali e discussioni per l'analisi dei testi classici* 33 (1994): 123–147.

Herzog, Werner, director, *Aguirre: The Wrath of God,* 1972.

Hess, Henner, *Mafia and Mafiosi: The Structure of Power,* trans. Ewald Osers, New York, 1970.

Highet, Gilbert, "*Libertino patre natus,*" *American Journal of Philology* 94 (1973): 268–281.

Hillesum, Etty, *An Interrupted Life: The Diaries of Etty Hillesum, 1941–43,* New York, 1981.

Hiltbrunner, Otto, "*Vir gravis,*" *Sprachgeschichte und Wortbedeutung: Festschrift Albert Debrunner,* Bern, 1954, 195–207.

Hinard, François, "La male mort: Exécutions et statut du corps au moment de la première proscription," *Du châtiment dans la Cité: Supplices corporels et peine de mort dans le monde antique,* collection de l'École Française de Rome 79 (Rome, 1984): 295–311.

Hirschfeld, Otto, "Augustus und sein *mimus vitae,*" *Wiener Studien* 6 (1884): 116–119.

Hirzel, Rudolf, *Der Eid,* New York, [1902] 1979.

Hopkins, Keith, and Graham Burton, "Ambition and Withdrawal: The Senatorial Aristocracy under the Emperors," in *Death and Renewal: Sociological Studies in Roman History,* vol. 2, Cambridge, 1983, 120–200.

Hopkins, Keith, and Melinda Letts, "Death in Rome," in *Death and Renewal: Sociological Studies in Roman History,* vol. 2, Cambridge, 1983, 201–256.

Horsfall, N.M., "Statistics or States of Mind?" in *Literacy in the Roman World, Journal of Roman Archaeology,* Supplementary Series no. 3, ed. J.H. Humphrey, Ann Arbor, 1991, 59–76.

———, "Virgil, History and the Roman Tradition," *Prudentia* 8 (1976): 73–89.

Huizinga, Johan, *Homo Ludens: A Study of the Play Element in Culture,* Boston, [1944] 1950.

Hunter, Tim, director, *The River's Edge,* 1986.

Huvelin, P., "Magie et droit individuel," *L'année sociologique* 10 (1905–1906): 1–47.

Ikegami, Eiko, *The Taming of the Samurai: Honorific Individualism and the Making of Modern Japan,* Cambridge, Mass., 1995.

Imbert, Jacques, "'*Fides*' et '*Nexum*'," *Studi in onore di Vincenzo Arangio-Ruiz,* vol. 1, Naples, 1952, 339–363.

Ingold, Tim, ed., *Key Debates in Anthropology,* New York, 1966.

James, William, *The Varieties of Religious Experience,* Glasgow, [1902] 1960.

Jhering, Rudolf van, *Geist des römischen Rechts,* 2 vols., Darmstadt, [1894] 1968.

Johnson, Samuel, "The Nature and Remedies of Bashfulness," *The Rambler* no 159 (Tuesday, September 24, 1751), in *The Works of Samuel Johnson,* vol. 3, Troy, N.Y., 1903, 290–294.

Jones, C.P., "Stigma: Tattooing and Branding in Graeco-Roman Antiquity," *Journal of Roman Studies* 77 (1987): 139–155.

Joshel, Sandra R., "Female Desire and the Discourse of Empire: Tacitus's Messalina," *Signs* 21 (1995): 50–82.

———, *Work, Identity, and Legal Status at Rome: A Study of the Occupational Inscriptions,* Norman, Okla., 1992.

Kaster, Robert A., "The Shame of the Romans," *Transactions and Proceedings of the American Philological Association* 127 (1997): 1–19.

Katz, Richard, *Boiling Energy: Communal Healing among the Kalahari Kung,* Cambridge, 1982.

Keene, Donald, *Chushingura: The Treasury of Loyal Retainers,* New York, 1971.

Keitel, Elizabeth, "Principate and Civil War in the *Annals* of Tacitus," *American Journal of Philology* 105 (1984): 306–325.

Keller, Helen, *The Story of My Life,* New York, [1902] 1961.

Kellum, Barbara, "The Phallus as Signifier: The Forum of Augustus and Rituals of Masculinity," in *Sexuality in Ancient Art,* ed. Natalie Boymel Kampen, Cambridge, 1996, 170–183.

———, "The Play of Meaning: The Visual Culture of Ancient Roman Freedmen and Freedwomen" (forthcoming).

———, "Sculptural Programs and Propaganda in Augustan Rome: The Temple of Apollo on the Palatine," in *The Age of Augustus,* ed. R. Winkes, Providence, 1985, 169–176.

————, "What We See and Don't See: Narrative Structure and the *Ara Pacis Augustae*," *Art History* 17 (1994): 26–45.

Kelly, J. M., "'Loss of Face' as a Factor Inhibiting Litigation," *Studies in the Civil Judicature of the Roman Republic*, Oxford, 1976, 93–111.

————, *Roman Litigation*, Oxford, 1966.

Kermode, Frank, *The Sense of an Ending*, Oxford, 1966.

Kinston, Warren, "A Theoretical Context for Shame," *International Journal of Psychoanalysis* 64 (1983): 213–216.

Kipp, "*Confessio*," *Paulys Realencyclopädie der classischen Altertumswissenschaft*, vol. 4.1, Stuttgart, 1900, cols. 864–870.

Klingner, Friedrich, "Virgil und die Idee des Friedens," in *Römische Geisteswelt: Essays zur lateinischen Literatur*, Stuttgart, [1965] 1979, 614–644.

Klose, Friedrich, *Die Bedeutung von honos und honestas*, Breslau, 1933.

Kluckhohn, Clyde, "The Moral Order in the Expanding Society," in *The City Invincible*, ed. Carl H. Kraeling and Robert M. Adams, Chicago, 1960, 391–404.

Knoche, Ulriche, "Der Beginn des römischen Sittenverfalls," in *Vom Selbstverständnis der Römer*, Heidelberg, 1962, 99–123.

————, "Der römische Ruhmesgedanke," in *Römische Wertbegriffe*, ed. Hans Oppermann, Darmstadt, 1967, 420–445.

Kohlberg, Lawrence, "Moral Stages and Moralizations," in *Moral Development and Behavior: Theory, Research and Social Issues*, ed. Thomas Likona, New York, 1976, 31–53.

Kohut, Heinz, "On Courage," in *Self-Psychology and the Humanities: Reflections on a New Psychoanalytic Approach*, ed. Charles B. Stozier, New York, 1985, 5–50.

Konik, Eugeniusz, "*Clementia Caesaris* als System der Unterwerfung der Beseigten," in *Forms of Control and Subordination in Antiquity*, ed. Toru Yuge and Masaoki Doi, Leiden, 1988, 226–238.

Kroll, Wilhelm, *Die Kultur der ciceronischen Zeit*, Leipzig, 1933.

Lacey, W. K., "*Patria Potestas*," in *The Family in Ancient Rome*, ed. Beryl Rawson, Ithaca, 1986, 121–144.

Laing, R. D., *The Divided Self*, Harmondsworth, 1965.

Lanata, Guiliana, "Confessione o professione? Il dossier degli Atti dei Martiri," in *L'aveu: Antiquité et Moyen Age*, Rome, 1986, 133–140.

Laqueur, R., "Über das Wesen des römischen Triumphs," *Hermes* 44 (1909): 215–236.

Latte, Kurt, "Über eine Eigentümlichkeit der italishen Gottesvorstellung," *Archiv für Religionswissenschaft* 24 (1926): 244–258.

Lau, Dieter, *Der lateinische Begriff labor*, Munich, 1975.

Lea, Henry Charles, *A History of Auricular Confession and Indulgences in the Latin Church*, vol. 1, Philadelphia, 1896.

Leach, Eleanor W., "Horace's *Pater Optimus* and Terence's Demeas," *American Journal of Philology* 92 (1971): 616–632.

Leary, Mark R., and Sarah Meadows, "Predictors, Elicitors, and Concomitants of Social Blushing," *Journal of Personality and Social Psychology* 60 (1961): 254–262.

Lebra, Takie Sugiyama, *Japanese Patterns of Behavior*, Honolulu, 1976.

————, "The Social Mechanisms of Guilt and Shame: The Japanese Case," *Anthropological Quarterly* 44 (1971): 241–255.

Leighton, Dorothea, and Clyde Kluckhohn, *Children of the People: The Navaho Individual and His Development*, New York, [1947] 1969.

Lemosse, Maxime, "L'aspect primitif de la *fides*," *Studi in onore di Pietro de Francisci*, Milan, 1956, 41–52.

Lendon, John, *Empire of Honour*, Oxford, 1997.

Levi, A. C., *Barbarians on Roman Imperial Coins and Sculpture*, New York, 1952.

Levi, Primo, *Survival in Auschwitz*, New York, 1961 [= *Se questo è un uomo*, Torino, 1947].

Lévi-Strauss, Claude, *Totemism*, trans. Rodney Needham, Boston, 1962.

Lévy-Bruhl, Henri, "The Act *per aes et libram*," trans. F. de Zulueta, *Law Quarterly Review* 60 (1944): 50–62.

———, *Recherches sur les actions de la loi*, Paris, 1960.

Lewis, Bradford, "The Rape of Troy: Infantile Perspective in Book II of the Aeneid," *Arethusa* 7 (1974): 103–113.

Lewis, Helen Block, "Shame and the Narcissistic Personality," in *The Many Faces of Shame*, ed. Donald L. Nathanson, New York, 1987, 93–132.

Lewis, Mark Edward, *Sanctioned Violence in Early China*, Albany, 1990.

Lienhardt, Godfrey, "Self: Public, Private. Some African Representations," in *The Category of the Person*, ed. Michael Carrithers, Steven Collins, and Steven Lukes, Cambridge, 1985, 141–155.

Lifton, Robert Jay, *The Nazi Doctors: Medical Killing and the Psychology of Genocide*, New York, 1986.

Lind, Levi Robert, "The Tradition of Roman Moral Conservatism," *Studies in Latin Literature and Roman History*, vol. 1, Brussels, 1979, 7–58.

Linton, Ralph, *The Cultural Background of Personality*, New York, 1945.

———, *The Study of Man*, New York, 1936.

Lintott, A. W., "The Tradition of Violence in the Annals of the Early Roman Republic," *Historia* 19 (1970): 12–29.

———, *Violence in Republican Rome*, Oxford, 1968.

Litchfield, Henry Weatland, "National *Exempla Virtutis* in Roman Literature," *Harvard Studies in Classical Philology* 25 (1914): 1–71.

Löfstedt, Einar, "Taboo, Euphemism, and Primitive Conceptions in Language," in *Late Latin*, Oslo, 1959, 181–194.

Long, Anthony A., "Cicero's Politics in *De Officiis*," in *Justice and Generosity: Studies in Hellenistic Social and Political Philosophy*, ed. André Laks and Malcolm Schofield, Cambridge, 1994, 213–240.

Lutsch, Otto, "Die *Urbanitas* nach Cicero," *Festgabe für Wilhelm Crecelius*, Elberfeld, 1881, 80–89.

Lynd, Helen Merrell, *On Shame and the Search for Identity*, New York, 1956.

Lyne, R. O. A. M., "Lavinia's Blush: Vergil, *Aeneid* 12.64–70," *Greece and Rome* 30 (1983): 55–64.

MacMullen, Ramsay, *Changes in the Roman Empire*, Princeton, 1990.

———, *Roman Social Relations, 50 B.C. to A.D. 184*, New Haven, 1974.

———, "Romans in Tears," *Classical Philology* 75 (1980): 254–255.

Majors, Richard, and Janet Mancini Billson, *Cool Pose: The Dilemmas of Black Manhood in America*, New York, 1992.

Malherbe, Abraham, ed., *The Cynic Epistles*, Missoula, Mont., 1977.

Malina, Bruce J., *New Testament World: Insights from Cultural Anthropology*, Atlanta, Georgia, 1981.

Maltby, Robert, *A Lexicon of Ancient Latin Etymologies*, Leeds, 1991.

Martin, R. H. and A. J. Woodman, *Tacitus, Annals, Book IV*, Cambridge, 1989.

Marx, Karl, *The Marx-Engels Reader*, ed. Robert C. Tucker, New York, 1978, 16–36.

Maslakov, G., "Valerius Maximus and Roman Historiography: A Study of the *exempla* Tradition," *Aufstieg und Niedergang der römischen Welt*, vol. 11.32.1, Berlin, 1984, 437–496.

Masson, Jeffrey, and Susan McCarthy, *When Elephants Weep: The Emotional Lives of Animals*, New York, 1995.

Mastronarde, Donald, "Seneca's Oedipus: The Drama in the Word," *Transactions and Proceedings of the American Philological Society* 101 (1970): 291–315.

Mattern, Susan, *Rome and the Enemy: Imperial Strategy in the Principate*, Berkeley, 1999.

Matthiessen, Peter, *Under the Mountain Wall*, New York, 1962.

Mauss, Marcel, "L'âme, le nom, et la personne," in *Oeuvres*, vol. 2, Paris, 1969, 131–135.

———, "A Category of the Human Mind: The Notion of Person, the Notion of 'Self,'" in *Sociology and Psychology: Essays*, trans. Ben Brewster, London, 1979.

———, *The Gift: Forms and Functions of Exchange in Archaic Societies*, trans. Ian Cunnison, New York, [1925] 1967.

———, "L'Histoire de la Confession," in *Oeuvres*, vol. 2, Paris, 1969, 640–642.

Mayor, J. B., *Thirteen Satires of Juvenal*, London, 1872.

McCall, Nathan, *Makes Me Wanna Holler*, New York, 1994.

McCartney, Michael, "Democracy and the Dangerous Man," Ph.D. diss., University of Massachusetts, 1997.

McCrone, John, *The Ape That Spoke: Language and the Evolution of the Human Mind*, New York, 1991.

Merton, Thomas, *The Way of Chuang Tzu*, San Francisco, 1969.

Miles, Gary B., "The First Roman Marriage and the Theft of the Sabine Women," *Innovations of Antiquity*, ed. Ralph Hexter and Daniel Selden, New York, 1992, 161–196.

Millar, Fergus, "The World of the Golden Ass," *Journal of Roman Studies* 71 (1981): 63–75.

Miller, Patricia Cox, "In Praise of Nonsense," in *Classical Mediterranean Spirituality*, ed. A. H. Armstrong, New York, 1986, 481–505.

Miller, Susan, *The Shame Experience*, Hillsdale, N.J., 1985.

Milton, John, *Samson Agonistes*, London, 1896.

Momigliano, A., "Marcel Mauss and the Quest for the Person in Greek Biography and Autobiography," in *The Category of the Person*, ed. Michael Carrithers, Steven Collins, and Steven Lukes, Cambridge, 1985, 83–92.

———, review of Laura Robinson, *Freedom of Speech in the Roman Republic*, *Journal of Roman Studies* 32 (1942): 120–124.

Mommsen, Theodor, *Römisches Strafrecht*, Leipzig, 1899.

———, "Sui modi usati dei Romani nel conservare e publicare le leggi ed i senatusconsulti," *Gesammelte Schriften*, vol. 3, Berlin, 1965, 290–318.

Montagu, A. F. Ashley, *The Human Revolution*, New York, 1965.

———, *Man and Aggression*, London, 1968.

Montague, Holly, "Advocacy and Politics: The Paradox of Cicero's *Pro Ligario*," *American Journal of Philology* 113 (1992): 559–574.

Montaigne, Michel de, *Complete Essays*, trans. Donald M. Frame, Stanford, 1958.

Moore, Marianne, *The Complete Poems*, New York, 1967.

Moore, Timothy J., *Artistry and Ideology: Livy's Vocabulary of Virtue*, Frankfurt am Main, 1989.

Morisaki, Seiichi, and William B. Gudykunst, "Face in Japan and the United States," in *The Challenge of Facework*, ed. Stella Ting-Toomey, Albany, 1994, 47–93.

Morris, Ron, *Wallenda: A Biography of Karl Wallenda,* Chatham, New York, 1976.

Morrison, Andrew P., "Shame and the Psychology of the Self," in *Kohut's Legacy: Contributions to Self Psychology,* ed. Paul E. Stepansky and Arnold Goldberg, Hillsdale, N.J., 1984, 71–90.

Morrison, Toni, *Beloved,* New York, 1987.

Most, Glenn W., *"Disiecti membra poetae:* The Rhetoric of Dismemberment in Neronian Poetry," in *Innovations of Antiquity,* ed. Ralph Hexter and Daniel Selden, New York, 1992, 391–419.

Muller, F. Max, *Biographies of Words,* London, 1888.

Nagler, Michael N., "Towards a Generative View of the Oral Formula," *Transactions and Proceedings of the American Philological Association* 98 (1967): 269–311.

Nathanson, Donald L., "A Timetable for Shame," in *The Many Faces of Shame,* ed. Donald L. Nathanson, New York, 1987, 1–63.

Nietzsche, Friedrich, *Beyond Good and Evil,* trans. R.J. Hollingdale, Harmondsworth, 1972.

———, *Daybreak,* trans. R.J. Hollingdale, Cambridge, 1997.

———, *The Genealogy of Morals,* trans. Francis Goffing, Garden City, N.Y., 1956.

———, *Human, All Too Human,* trans. Marion Faber, Lincoln, Neb., 1984.

Nippel, Wilfried, "Policing Rome," *Journal of Roman Studies* 74 (1984): 20–29.

———, *Public Order in Ancient Rome,* Cambridge, 1995.

Noailles, Pierre, *Du droit sacré au droit civil,* Paris, 1949.

Oliensis, Ellen, "Canidia, Canicula, and the Decorum of Horace's *Epodes,*" *Arethusa* 24 (1991): 107–138.

Ong, Walter, *Fighting for Life: Contest, Sexuality, and Consciousness,* Amherst, 1981.

Onians, Richard B., *The Origins of European Thought about the Body, the Mind, the Soul, the World, Time and Fate,* Cambridge, 1954.

O'Rahilly, Cecile, ed. and trans., *Táin Bó Cuailnge,* Dublin, 1976.

Orwell, George, *Nineteen Eighty-Four: Text, Sources, Criticism,* ed. Irving Howe, New York, 1963.

Oshima, Nagisa, director, *Merry Christmas, Mr. Lawrence,* 1983.

Otto, Walter, *"Fides,"* *Paulys Realencyclopädie der classischen Altertumswissenschaft,* vol. 6.2, Stuttgart, 1909, cols. 2281ff.

———, *"Religio* und *Superstitio,"* *Archiv für Religionswissenschaft* 12 (1909): 533–554.

Paradisi, Bruno, *"Deditio in Fidem,"* *Studi di storia e diritto in onore di Arrigo Solmi,* Milan, 1941.

Partner, Nancy F., "No Sex, No Gender," *Speculum* 68 (1993): 419–443.

Paterson, Jeremy, "Politics in the Late Republic," in *Roman Political Life, 90 B.C.–A.D. 69,* Exeter, 1985, 21–43.

Patterson, Orlando, *Slavery and Social Death,* Cambridge, Mass., 1982.

Perniola, Mario, "Decorum and Ceremony," trans. Barbara Spackman, in *Recoding Metaphysics: The New Italian Philosophy,* ed. Giovanna Borradori, Evanston, Ill., 1988, 105–116.

Peters, Edward, *Torture,* New York, 1985.

Pétré, H., *"Misericordia:* Histoire du mot et de l'idée du paganisme au Christianisme," *Revue des études latines* 12 (1934): 376–389.

Pheterson, Gail, "The Whore Stigma: Female Dishonor and Male Unworthiness," *Social Text* 37 (1993): 39–64.

Philipps, C. Robert, III, "Poetry Before the Ancient City: Zorzetti and the Case of Rome," *Classical Journal* 86 (1991): 382–387.

Pierrugues, P., *Glossarium Eroticum Linguae Latinae,* Berlin, 1908.

Piganiol, André, *Recherches sur les jeux romains: Notes d'archéologie et d'histoire,* Strasbourg, 1923.

———, *"Venire in Fidem," Revue internationale des droits de l'antiquité* 5 (1950): 339–347.

Pinguet, Maurice, *Voluntary Death in Japan,* trans. Rosemarry Morris, Cambridge, 1993.

Pitt-Rivers, Julian, "Honour and Social Status," in *Honour and Shame: The Values of Mediterranean Society,* ed. J. G. Peristiany, Chicago, 1966, 21–77.

Plass, Paul, *The Game of Death in Ancient Rome,* Madison, 1995.

———, *Wit and the Writing of History,* Madison, 1986.

Polanyi, Karl, *Primitive, Archaic and Modern Economies: Essays of Karl Polanyi,* ed. George Dalton, Garden City, N.J., 1968.

Polanyi, Karl, et al., eds., *Trade and Market in the Early Empires,* Glencoe, Ill., 1957.

Pommeray, Léon, *Études sur l'infamie en droit romain,* Paris, 1937.

Popkin, Richard H., *The History of Scepticism from Erasmus to Spinoza,* Berkeley, 1979.

Radcliffe-Brown, A. R., "Taboo," in *Structure and Function in Primitive Society,* New York, [1952] 1965.

Ramage, Edwin, *Urbanitas: Ancient Sophistication and Refinement,* Norman, Okla., 1973.

Rangell, Leo, "The Psychology of Poise," *International Journal of Psycho-Analysis* 35 (1954): 313–332.

Rankin, H. D., *Celts and the Classical World,* London, 1987.

Raschke, Wendy J., "The Virtue of Lucilius," *Latomus* 49 (1990): 352–369.

Rawson, Beryl, "Adult-Child Relations in Roman Society," in *Marriage, Divorce and Children in Ancient Rome,* ed. Beryl Rawson, Oxford, 1991, 7–30.

Redfield, Robert, *The Primitive World and Its Transformations,* Harmondsworth, [1953] 1968.

Rheinfelder, Hans, *Das Wort 'Persona': Geschichte seiner Bedeutungen mit besonderer Berücksichtigung des französischen und italienischen Mittelalters,* Halle, 1928.

Rich, John, "Fear, Greed, and Glory: The Causes of Roman War-Making in the Middle Republic," in *War and Society in the Roman World,* ed. John Rich and Graham Shipley, New York, 1993.

Richlin, Amy, "Carrying Water in a Sieve: Class and the Body in Roman Women's Religion," in *Women and Goddess Traditions in Antiquity and Today,* ed. Karen L. King, Minneapolis, 1997, 330–374.

———, "Cicero's Head," in *Constructions of the Classical Body,* ed. James I. Porter, Ann Arbor, 1999, 190–211.

———, "The Ethnographer's Dilemma and the Dream of a Lost Golden Age," in *Feminist Theory and the Classics,* ed. Nancy Sorkin Rabinowitz and Amy Richlin, New York, 1993, 272–303.

———, *The Garden of Priapus: Sexuality and Aggression in Roman Humor,* New Haven, 1992.

———, "Towards a History of Body History," in *Inventing Ancient Culture: Historicism, Periodization, and the Ancient World,* ed. Mark Golden and Peter Toohey, New York, 1997, 16–36.

Riezler, Kurt, "Comment on the Social Psychology of Shame," *American Journal of Sociology* 48 (1942–1943): 457–465.

Robbins, Tim, director, *Dead Man Walking,* 1995.

Roberts, C. M., *A Treatise on the History of Confession until It Developed into Auricular Confession, A.D. 1215,* London, 1901.

Rosaldo, Michelle, *Knowledge and Passion: Ilongot Notions of Self and Social Life,* Cambridge, 1980.

————, "The Shame of Headhunters and the Autonomy of Self," *Ethos* 11 (1983): 135–151.

————, "Toward an Anthropology of Self and Feeling," in *Culture Theory: Essays on Mind, Self and Emotion,* ed. Richard A. Shweder and Robert A. LeVine, Cambridge, 1984, 137–157.

Rosenstein, Nathan, *Imperatores Victi: Military Defeat and Aristocratic Competition in the Middle and Late Republic,* Berkeley, 1990.

Rostand, Edmund, *Cyrano de Bergerac,* trans. Brian Hooker, New York, 1923.

Rouselle, Aline, "Parole et inspiration: Le travail de la voix dans le monde Romain," *History and Philosophy in the Life Sciences* 5 (1983): 129–157.

————, "Personal Status and Sexual Practice in the Roman Empire," in *Fragments for a History of the Human Body, Part Three,* ed. Michel Feher, Ramona Naddaff and Nadia Tazi, New York, 1989, 301–333.

Rowell, Thelma, "The Concept of Social Dominance," *Behavioral Biology* 11 (1974): 131–154.

Ruggiero, Guido, *Binding Passions: Tales of Magic, Marriage, and Power at the End of the Renaissance,* Oxford, 1993.

Rykwert, Joseph, *The Idea of a Town: The Anthropology of Urban Form in Rome, Italy, and the Ancient World,* Princeton, 1976.

Sachers, E., "*Potestas patria,*" *Paulys Realencyclopädie der classischen Altertumswissenschaft,* vol. 22.1, Stuttgart, 1953, cols. 1046–1175.

Saller, Richard, "Corporal Punishment, Authority, and Obedience in the Roman Household," in *Marriage, Divorce, and Children in Ancient Rome,* ed. Beryl Rawson, Oxford, 1991.

————, *Patriarchy, Property, and Death in the Roman Family,* Cambridge, 1994.

————, "Poverty, Honor, and Obligation in Imperial Rome," unpublished lecture, Princeton, 1993.

Salvan, Jacques, *To Be and Not To Be: An Analysis of Jean-Paul Sartre's Ontology,* Detroit, 1962.

Sandoz, Mari, *Crazy Horse, The Strange Man of the Oglalas: A Biography,* Lincoln, Neb., [1942] 1969.

Santoro l'Hoir, Francesca, "Heroic Epithets and Recurrent Themes in *Ab Urbe Condita,*" *Transactions and Proceedings of the American Philological Association* 120 (1990): 221–241.

Sapir, Edward, "The Status of Linguistics as a Science," in *Selected Writings of Edward Sapir in Language, Culture and Personality,* ed. David G. Mandelbaum, Berkeley, 1949, 160–166.

Sarsila, Juhani, "Some Notes on *Virtus* in Sallust and Cicero," *Arctos* 12 (1978): 135–143.

Sartre, Jean-Paul, *La nausée,* Paris, 1938.

————, *Situations,* trans. Benita Eisler, London, 1965.

Scapini, Nevio, *La confessione nel diritto romano,* vol. 1, Turin, 1973.

Scheff, Thomas J., "Shame and Conformity," in *Microsociology: Discourse, Emotion and Social Structure,* Chicago, 1990, 71–95.

————, "The Shame-Rage Spiral: Case Study of an Interminable Quarrel," in *The Role of Shame in Symptom Formation,* H. Lewis, Hillsdale, N.J., 1987, 109–149.

Scheid, John, "La Spartizione à Roma," *Studi Storici* 4 (1984): 945–956, esp. 951–953 [= "La Spartizione sacrificiale à Roma," in *Sacrificio e Società nel mundo antico,* C. Grottanelli Parise, Rome, 1988, 267–292].

Scheler, Max, "Der 'Ort' des Schamgefühls und die Existenzweise des Menschen," *Gesammelte Werke,* vol. 10, Bern, 1957, 67–154.

Schmeling, Gareth, "*Confessor Gloriosus:* A Role of Encolpius in the *Satyrica,*" *Würzburger Jahrbücher für die Altertumswissenschaft* 20 (1994/1995): 207–224.

Schork, R.J., "The Final Simile in the *Aeneid:* Roman and Rutilian Ramparts," *American Journal of Philology* 107 (1982): 260–271.

Schulten, *"Dediticii,"* *Paulys Realencyclopädie der classischen Altertumswissenschaft,* vol. 4.2, Stuttgart, 1901, cols. 2359–2363.

Schulz, Fritz, *Principles of Roman Law,* Oxford, [1936] 1956 (= *Prinzipien des römischen Rechts,* 1934).

Schunck, Peter, "Römische Sterben," Ph.D. diss., Heidelberg, 1955.

———, "Studien zur Darstellung des Endes von Galba, Otho und Vitellius in den Historien des Tacitus," *Symbolae Osloenses* 39 (1964): 38–82.

Scott, James C., *Domination and the Arts of Resistance,* New Haven, 1990.

Seager, Robin, *"Populares* in Livy and the Livian Tradition," *Classical Quarterly* n.s. 27 (1977): 377–390.

Sedgwick, Eve Kosofsky, "Queer Performativity: Henry James' *The Art of the Novel,"* *GLQ* 1 (1993): 1–16.

Segal, Charles, "Boundary Violation and the Landscape of the Self in Senecan Tragedy," *Antike und Abendland* 24 (1983): 172–187.

———, "Ovid's Metamorphic Bodies: Art, Gender, and Violence in the *Metamorphoses" Arion* 5 (1998): 10–41.

Segal, Erich, *Roman Laughter: The Comedy of Plautus,* New York, 1968.

Seidman, Steven, *Contested Knowledge: Social Theory in the Postmodern Era,* Oxford, 1994.

Shackleton Bailey, D. R., *Cicero,* London, 1971.

Shaw, Brent, "Body/Power/Identity: Passions of the Martyrs," *Journal of Early Christian Studies* 4 (1996): 269–312.

———, "The Passion of Perpetua," *Past and Present* 139 (1993): 3–45.

Sherk, Robert, *Roman Documents from the Greek East,* Baltimore, 1960.

Shostak, Marjorie, *Nisa: The Life and Words of a !Kung Woman,* Cambridge, Mass., 1981.

Simmel, Georg, *Conflict,* trans. Kurt H. Wolff, in *Conflict and the Web of Group Affiliations,* Glencoe, Ill., 1955, 13–123.

———, *The Sociology of Georg Simmel,* ed. and trans. Kurt H. Wolff, New York, 1950.

Skultans, Vieda, "Bodily Madness and the Spread of the Blush," in *The Anthropology of the Body,* ed. John Blacking, London, 1977, 145–160.

Smith, Huston, "Western and Comparative Perspectives on Truth," *Philosophy East and West* 30 (1980): 425–437.

Smith, R. E., "The Aristocratic Epoch in Latin Literature," *Essays on Roman Culture: The Todd Memorial Lectures,* ed. A. J. Dunston, Toronto, 1976, 139–157.

Sperling, Samuel, "On the Psychodynamics of Teasing," *Journal of the American Psychoanalytical Association* 1 (1953): 458–483.

Spiegel, John, and Pavel Machotka, *Messages of the Body,* New York, 1974.

Spielberg, Steven, director, *Schindler's List,* 1993.

Strassburger, Hermann, "Poseidonius on Problems of the Roman Empire," *Journal of Roman Studies* 55 (1965): 40–53.

Strathern, Andrew, "Why Is Shame on the Skin?" in *The Anthropology of the Body,* ed. John Blacking, London, 1977, 99–110.

Sullivan, Francis, A., "Cicero and *Gloria,"* *Transactions and Proceedings of the American Philological Society* 72 (1941): 382–391.

Sutherland, C. H. V., *Roman Coins,* New York, 1974.

Suzuki, Daisetz, "The Role of Nature in Zen Buddhism," in *Zen Buddhism: Selected Writings of D. T. Suzuki,* Garden City, N.J., 1956.

———, *Zen and Japanese Culture,* Princeton, 1959.

Swift, Johnathan, *The Writings of Johnathan Swift*, ed. Robert A. Greenberg and William B. Piper, New York, 1973.

Sykes, Gresham, *The Society of Captives: A Study of a Maximum Security Prison*, Princeton, 1958.

Syme, Ronald, "A Roman Post-Mortem: An Inquest on the Fall of the Roman Republic," *Essays on Roman Culture: The Todd Memorial Lectures*, ed. A.J. Dunston, Toronto, 1976, 139–157.

———, *Tacitus*, Oxford, 1958.

Täubler, Eugen, *Imperium Romanum: Studien zur Entwicklungsgeschichte des römischen Reichs*, Leipzig, 1913.

Taylor, Lily Ross, *Party Politics in the Age of Caesar*, Berkeley, 1949.

———, *Roman Voting Assemblies from the Hannibalic War to the Dictatorship of Caesar*, Ann Arbor, 1966.

Thébert, Yvon, "Public Life and Domestic Architecture in Roman Africa," in *A History of Private Life*, ed. Philippe Ariès and Georges Duby, vol. 1, Cambridge, Mass., 1987.

Thomas, Elizabeth Marshall, *The Harmless People*, New York, [1958] 1989.

Thomas, Rosalind, *Literacy and Orality in Ancient Greece*, Cambridge, 1992.

Thomas, Yan, "*Confessus pro iudicato:* L'aveu civil et l'aveu pénal à Rome," in *L'aveu: Antiquité et Moyen Age*, Rome, 1986, 89–117.

———, "*Vitae necisque potestas*," in *Du châtiment dans la Cité: Supplice corporels et peine de mort dans le monde antique, collection de l'École française de Rome*, no. 79, Rome, 1984, 499–548.

Tomkins, Silvan S., *Affect, Imagery, Consciousness*, vol. 1, New York, 1962.

———, "Shame," in *The Many Faces of Shame*, ed. Donald L. Nathanson, New York, 1987, 131–161.

Tomkins, Silvan, and C. E. Izard, *Affect, Cognition, and Personality*, London, 1965.

Trendelenburg, Adolf, "A Contribution to the History of the Word Person," trans. Carl H. Haessler, *The Monist* 20 (1910): 336–363.

Trigger, Bruce G., *The Children of Aataentsic: A History of the Huron People to 1600*, Montreal, 1976.

Trowbridge, Mary Luella, *Philological Studies in Ancient Glass*, Urbana, Ill., 1930.

Tucker, T. O., *Etymological Dictionary of Latin*, Chicago, 1985.

Turner, Victor, "Variations on a Theme of Liminality," in *Secular Ritual*, ed. Sally F. Moore and Barbara G. Meyerhoff, Amsterdam, 1977, 36–52.

Usener, Hermann, "Italische Volksjustiz," *Kleine Schriften*, vol. 4, Osnabrück, 1965, 356–382 (= *Rheinisches Museum* 56 [1906]: 1–28).

van der Post, Laurens, *The Lost World of the Kalahari*, New York, 1958.

Van Gennep, Arnold, *Rites of Passage*, trans. Minika B. Vizedom and Gabrielle L. Caffee, Chicago, 1960.

Van Sickle, John, "The Elogia of the Cornelii Scipiones and the Origin of Epigram at Rome," *American Journal of Philology* 108 (1987): 41–55.

Vansina, John, *Oral Tradition as History*, Madison, 1985.

Vasaly, Ann, "Personality and Power: Livy's Depiction of the Appii Claudii in the First Pentad," *Transactions and Proceedings of the American Philological Association* 117 (1987): 203–226.

Verhoeven, Paul, director, *Basic Instinct*, 1992.

Versnel, H. S., *Triumphus: An Inquiry into the Origin, Development and Meaning of the Roman Triumph*, Leiden, 1970.

Vessey, D. W. T. C., "Thoughts on Tacitus' Portrayal of Claudius," *American Journal of Philology* 92 (1971): 385–409.

Veyne, Paul, "Le Folklore à Rome et les droits de la conscience publique sur la conduite individuelle," *Latomus* 42 (1983): 3–30.

———, *Le pain et le cirque: Sociologie historique d'un pluralisme politique,* Paris, 1976.

Ville, Georges, *La gladiature en Occident des origines à la mort de Domitien,* Rome, 1981.

Waal, Frans de, *Peace-Making Among Primates,* Cambridge, Mass., 1989.

Wagenvoort, Henri, "*Fas sit vidisse,*" *Studies in Roman Literature, Culture and Religion,* London, 1956, 184–192.

———, "*Gravitas et Maiestas,*" *Mnemosyne* 5 (1952): 287–306.

———, *Roman Dynamism,* Westport, Conn., [1947] 1976.

Walbank, F. W., *Commentary on Polybius,* vol. 1, Oxford, 1967.

Waley, Arthur, *The Analects of Confucius,* New York, 1938.

Walker, B., review of Giancotti, *Octavia, Classical Philology* 52 (1957): 163–173.

Wallace, Anthony F. C., *The Death and Rebirth of the Seneca,* New York, 1972.

———, "Handsome Lake and the Great Revival in the West," *American Quarterly* (summer 1952): 149–165.

Wallace-Hadrill, Andrew, "*Civilis Princeps:* Between Citizen and King," *Journal of Roman Studies* 72 (1982): 32–48.

———, "The Emperor and His Virtues," *Historia* 30 (1981): 298–323.

———, *Houses and Society in Pompeii and Herculaneum,* Princeton, 1994.

Walsh, P. G., "Livy and Stoicism," *American Journal of Philology* 79 (1958): 355–375.

Walters, Johnathan, "Invading the Roman Body: Manliness and Impenetrability in Roman Thought," in *Roman Sexualities,* ed. Judith P. Hallet and Marilyn B. Skinner, Princeton, 1997, 29–43.

Watson, Alan, *Roman Slave Law,* Baltimore, 1987.

———, *Rome of the Twelve Tables,* Princeton, 1975, 125–133.

Watt, William Montgomery, *Muslim-Christian Encounters,* London, 1991.

Wegehaupt, Helmut, "Die Bedeutung und Anwendung von *dignitas* in den Schriften der republikanischen Zeit," Ph.D. diss., Breslau, 1932.

Weinstock, Stefan, *Divus Iulius,* Oxford, 1971.

———, review of Brelich, *Der Geheime Shutzgottheit von Rom,* in *Journal of Roman Studies* 40 (1950): 149–150.

———, "*Victor* and *Invictus,*" *Harvard Theological Review* 50 (1957): 211–247.

Welsford, Enid, *The Fool: His Social and Literary History,* Garden City, N.Y., 1935.

Wiedemann, Thomas, *Adults and Children in the Roman Empire,* New Haven, 1989.

Wikan, Unni, "Shame and Honour: A Contestable Pair," *Man* n.s. 19 (1984): 635–652.

Wilamowitz-Moellendorff, Ulrich von, "*Res Gestae Divi Augusti,*" *Hermes* 21 (1886): 626–627.

Wilde, Oscar, *De Profundis,* in *De Profundis and Other Writings,* London, 1949, 183–184.

Williams, Donna, *Nobody Nowhere,* New York, 1992.

Wilson, Emmett, Jr., "Shame and the Other: Reflections of the Theme of Shame in French Psychoanalysis," in *The Many Faces of Shame,* ed. Donald L. Nathanson, New York, 1987, 162–193.

Wilson, Peter, *The Domestication of the Human Species,* New Haven, 1988.

Wirszubski, Chaim, "*Audaces:* A Study in Political Phraseology," *Journal of Roman Studies* 51 (1961): 12–22.

———, "Cicero's *cum dignitate otium:* A Reconsideration," *Journal of Roman Studies* 44 (1954): 1–13.

————, *Libertas as a Political Idea at Rome During the Late Republic and Early Principate*, Cambridge, 1960.

Wiseman, T. P., *Catullus and His World*, Cambridge, 1985.

————, "Competition and Co-operation," in *Roman Political Life 90 B.C.–A.D. 69*, Exeter, 1985, 3–19.

————, "*Conspicui postes tectaque digna deo:* The Public Image of the Aristocratic and Imperial Houses in the Late Republic and Early Empire," in *L'urbs: Espace urbain et histoire (1er siècle av. J.-C.–3e siècle ap. J.-C.)*, Rome, 1987, 393–413.

Wurmser, Leon, *The Mask of Shame*, Baltimore, 1981.

Wyatt-Brown, Bertram, *Honor and Violence in the Old South*, Oxford, 1986.

————, "The Mask of Obedience: Male Slave Psychology in the Old South," *American Historical Review* 93 (1988): 1228–1252.

Wyden, Peter, *Stella*, New York, 1992.

Yaron, R., "*Vitae necisque potestas,*" *Tijdschrift voor Rechtsgeshiedenis* 30 (1962): 243–251.

Yavetz, Zvi, "*Existimatio and Fama,*" appendix to *Julius Caesar and His Public Image*, London, 1983 (originally published Düsseldorf, 1979).

————, *Plebs and Princeps*, Oxford, 1969.

————, "The Urban Plebs in the Days of the Flavians, Nerva and Trajan," in *Opposition et résistance à l'empire d'Auguste à Trajan*, ed. Adalberto Giovannini, Geneva, 1986, 135–181.

Zanker, Paul, *The Power of Images in the Age of Augustus*, trans. Alan Shapiro, Ann Arbor, 1988.

Zeitlin, Froma, "Petronius as Paradox: Anarchy and Artistic Integrity," *Transactions and Proceedings of the American Philological Society* 102 (1971): 631–684.

Ziolkowski, Adam, "*Urbs direpta,* or How the Romans Sacked Cities," in *War and Society in the Roman World*, ed. John Rich and Graham Shipley, New York, 1993, 69–91.

Zorzetti, Nevio, "Poetry in an Ancient City: The Case of Rome," *Classical Journal* 86 (1991): 377–382.

Zulueta, F. de, "The Recent Controversy about *Nexum,*" *Law Quarterly Review* 114 (1912): 137–153.

INDEX

Text:	10/12 Baskerville
Display:	Baskerville
Composition:	Impressions Book & Journal Services
Printing and binding:	Thomson-Shore, Inc.

CPSIA information can be obtained
at www.ICGtesting.com
Printed in the USA
BVOW03*0724231217
503289BV00009B/7/P